Northwest Vista College
Learning Resource Center
3535 North Ellison Drive
San Antonio, Texas 78251

PUTTING

❊ HISTORY ❊

TO THE

QUESTION

PUTTING  HISTORY TO THE QUESTION

POWER, POLITICS, AND SOCIETY
IN ENGLISH RENAISSANCE DRAMA

Michael Neill

COLUMBIA UNIVERSITY PRESS ❋ NEW YORK

Columbia University Press
Publishers Since 1893
New York   Chichester, West Sussex

Library of Congress Cataloging-in-Publication Data
Neill, Michael.
Putting history to the question : power, politics,
and society in English Renaissance drama / Michael Neill.
p. cm
Includes bibliographical references and index.
ISBN 0–231–11332–3 (alk. paper)
1. English drama—Early modern and Elizabethan. 1500–1600—History and criticism.   2. Politics and literature—Great Britain—History—16th century.
3. Politics and literature—Great Britain—History—17th century.   4. Literature and society—England—History—16th century.   5. Literature and society—England—History—17th century.   6. English drama—17th century—History and criticism.   7. Political plays, English—History and criticism.   8. Literature and history—Great Britain—History.   9. Power (Social sciences) in literature.
10. Renaissance—England.   I. Title.
PR658.P65N45   2000
822'.309358—dc21   99–29886

Printed in the United States of America

c 10 9 8 7 6 5 4 3 2 1

For my children,

Anna, Tuataroa, and Te Ao Huri

Contents

❉

List of Illustrations, *ix*

Acknowledgments, *xi*

A Note on Texts, *xiii*

Introduction, *1*

PART I ❀ THE STAGE AND SOCIAL ORDER

1. Servant Obedience and Master Sins: Shakespeare and the Bonds of Service, *13*

2. "This Gentle Gentleman": Social Change and the Language of Status in *Arden of Faversham*, *49*

3. Massinger's Patriarchy: The Social Vision of *A New Way to Pay Old Debts*, *73*

4. "The Tongues of Angels": Charity and the Social Order in *The City Madam*, *99*

5. "In Everything Illegitimate": Imagining the Bastard in English Renaissance Drama, *127*

6. Bastardy, Counterfeiting, and Misogyny in *The Revenger's Tragedy*, *149*

7. "Amphitheaters in the Body": Playing with Hands on the Shakespearean Stage, *167*

PART 2 ❀ RACE, NATION, EMPIRE

8. Changing Places in *Othello*, *207*

9. "Unproper Beds": Race, Adultery, and the Hideous in *Othello*, *237*

10. "Mulattos," "Blacks," and "Indian Moors": *Othello* and Early
Modern Constructions of Human Difference, *269*

11. Putting History to the Question: An Episode of Torture at Bantam
in Java, 1604, *285*

12. "Material Flames": Romance, Empire, and Mercantile Fantasy in
John Fletcher's *Island Princess*, *311*

13. Broken English and Broken Irish: Nation, Language, and the Optic
of Power in Shakespeare's Histories, *339*

14. "The Exact Map or Discovery of Human Affairs": Shakespeare
and the Plotting of History, *373*

15. The World Beyond: Shakespeare and the Tropes
of Translation, *399*

Notes, *419*

Index, *509*

Illustrations

1. Vesalius demonstrating the anatomy of the hand, *171*

2. Examples of manual rhetoric from Bulwer's *Chirologia*, *176*

3. Examples of manual rhetoric from Bulwer's *Chirologia*, *177*

4. The transparent eloquence of the hand, *179*

5. The orators Demosthenes and Cicero taking instruction from the actors Andronicus and Roscius, *187*

6. Spaniards amputating the hands of Amerindians, *196*

7. Spaniards amputating the hands of Amerindians, *197*

8. The bedchamber scene in *Othello* (1709), *239*

9. The bedchamber scene in *Othello* (1785), *241*

10. The bedchamber scene in *Othello* (1789), *242*

11. The bedchamber scene in *Othello* (1800), *243*

12. The bedchamber scene in *Othello* (1799), *244*

13. *Tregear's* Black Jokes, *No. 9*, *246*

14. The torture of John Clarke at Amboyna, *307*

15. Frontispiece to Samuel Purchas, *Hakluytus Posthumus or Purchas His Pilgrimes* (1625), *317*

16. *Sphaera Civitatis*, *345*

17. Rory Og O More in a wood, *365*

18. *The Rainbow Portrait* of Queen Elizabeth I, *369*

19. Frontispiece to Richard Brathwait, *A Survey of History* (1638), *377*

20. Frontispiece to John Speed, *The Theatre of the Empire of Great Britaine* (1611), *381*

21. Map of Cumberland (1611), *382*

22. Map of Northumberland (1611), *383*

23. Map of Wiltshire (1611), *384*

24. Map of Herefordshire (1611), *385*

25. Map of Leicestershire (1611), *386*

26. Frontispiece to John Weever, *Ancient Fvnerall Monvments* (1631), *387*

27. Portrait of John Weever, *388*

28. Frontispiece to Sir Walter Raleigh, *The History of the World* (1614), *389*

29. Ribaut's marker-column from de Bry's *America* (1591), *390*

30. "Monaghan Fort" by Richard Bartlett, *394*

31. "Dungannon and Tullaghogue" by Richard Bartlett, *395*

Acknowledgments

❀

Versions of the essays in this book have appeared in a number of journals and collections. I am grateful to the publishers of *Renaissance Drama* for permission to reprint material in chapters 3 and 12; to the publishers of *Shakespeare Quarterly* for permission to reprint material in chapters 9, 10 and 13; to the publishers of *Shakespeare Survey* for permission to reprint material in chapters 7 and 8; to the publishers of *Studies in English Literature* for permission to reprint material in chapter 6; to the publishers of *Medieval and Renaissance Drama in English* for permission to reprint material in chapter 2; to the publishers of *English Literary Renaissance* for permission to reprint material in chapter 11; to the publishers of the *Yearbook of English Studies* for permission to reprint material in chapter 5; to Cambridge University Press for permission to reprint material in chapter 4; to Associated University Presses for permission to reprint material in chapter 15; and to the British Academy for permission to publish material in chapter 1.

The debts I have incurred to colleagues, friends, and institutions over the twenty years to which this collection belongs are by now far too numerous to list with any completeness, but I owe particular thanks to Jim Shapiro, without whose enthusiastic support the book would never have seen the light of day, as well as to my editor, Jennifer Crewe, and the admirable staff at Columbia University Press. The Folger Shakespeare Library in Washington, D.C., has been extraordinarily generous, supporting my work with fellowships in 1988–9 and 1997–8, as well as inviting me to conduct a seminar series on Shakespeare and the designs of empire in 1993; the Newberry Library helped with a short-term fellowship in 1993; the British Academy invited me to deliver their annual Shakespeare Lecture (which provided the basis for chapter 1) in 1998; the University of Auckland has assisted with several research grants and regular sabbatical leave. Staff at the Folger and Auckland University Libraries have been unfailingly patient and helpful. Loata Vuetibau cheerfully retyped large portions of the manuscript. Among colleagues in adjacent disciplines, Leonard Andaya, Judith Binney, Hiram

Morgan, Linda Levy Peck, John Pocock, and Andrew Sharp have at various times done their best to put me right about early modern history; while in literary matters David Bevington, Sebastian Black, Al Braunmuller, Tony Dawson, Andy Gurr, Jocelyn Harris, Margo Hendricks, Jean Howard, Mac Jackson, John Kerrigan, Jonathan Lamb, Naomi Liebler, Mercedes Maroto Camino, Barbara Mowat, Roger Nicholson, Brian Parker, Patricia Parker, Gail Paster, Jyotsna Singh, Don Smith, Susan Snyder, and Michael Wright have been as generous in ideas as in friendship. As always, I owe much to the kindness and encouragement of Anne Barton. It goes without saying that none of these people is in any way responsible for the numerous shortcomings of what follows.

A Note on Texts

Except where otherwise indicated quotations from Shakespeare are taken from G. Blakemore Evans, ed., *The Riverside Shakespeare* (Boston: Houghton Mifflin, 1974), while those from other Renaissance plays are from Russell A. Fraser and Norman Rabkin, eds., *Drama of the English Renaissance*, 2 vols. (New York: Macmillan, 1976). In quotations from old-spelling texts, orthography and punctuation have been silently modernized, but for bibliographic reasons I have chosen to leave titles unaltered.

PUTTING

HISTORY

TO THE

QUESTION

Introduction

Distinction: *Lord, you have forgot Ambiguity, shall he not be rack'd?*
I would fain be his Procrustes.
—Richard Zouche, *The Sophister*

The business of historicist criticism, it has become fashionable to say, is to "interrogate" the literature of the past. The metaphor has a certain uneasy appropriateness, since the artifacts of other cultures seldom yield up their meaning without the application of a certain amount of judicious intellectual force, and the risk must always be that in the process the objects of such interrogation will be wrenched and mangled beyond recognition. This danger is especially acute in the case of texts that, like so many plays of the early modern period, cover their more contentious meanings with a veil of equivocation. It is true that Protestant culture habitually protested its horror of equivocal language. In Shakespeare's *Macbeth*, to take a well-known example, ambiguity or "equivocation" is stigmatized as the dialect of evil, a rhetoric of doubleness by which the instruments of darkness ensnare their victims. But *Macbeth* itself equivocated with its audience through its elaborate pattern of oblique contemporary allusions—thereby illustrating the way in which ambiguity (as Richard Zouche's neomorality drama reminds us) was actually an indispensable theatrical resource in a society where the inherently controversial nature of public performance made it necessary for playwrights to devise elaborate strategies of occlusion whenever their writing touched on vexatious issues. Dramatists learned of necessity, Paul Yachnin has argued, to wear the mask of Janus: "The production of a two-faced political meaning remained a central feature of Elizabethan and Jacobean drama, the means by which playwrights both put into practice the ideology of the separateness of poetic discourse and maintained the powerlessness of their theatre."[1] The effect of this self-protective stratagem was to create a dialectic of suspicious reading in which ostensibly innocent texts were always liable to be scanned for hidden intentions, rather as scripture was habitually "racked" by radical interpreters in ways that the authorities sought desperately to contain. "Application," Ben Jonson complained in the dedicatory epistle to *Volpone*, "is now grown a trade with many; and there are [those] that profess to have a key for the deciphering of everything: but let wise and noble persons take heed how they be too credulous, or give leave to these invading interpreters to be over familiar with their fames, who cunningly utter their virulent malice under other men's simplest meanings." Through protestation of this sort Jonson and his fellow writers sought (in Yachnin's words) to "transfer . . . the production of potentially offensive topical meaning from their own texts to the 'malicious' imaginings of their audience." Yet of course the satire of *Volpone* is itself partly dependent on its ability to compel such application—not least by forcing the audience to recognize in the ludicrous interpretative fetches and "discoveries" of Sir Politic Would-be a mirror for their own "malicious imaginings."[2]

The paradoxes of this strategic duplicity have significant implications for anyone attempting a historicizing approach to early modern drama, especially since—as the deployment of *Richard II* by the Essex plotters or Hamlet's equivocal manipulation of "The Murder of Gonzago" demonstrate—topical meanings were typically unstable and often audience-specific. As I argue in chapter 12, contemporary responses to a play such as Fletcher's *Island Princess*, for example, must have been significantly shaped by its setting in the fiercely contested Spice Islands, where a prolonged struggle for commercial supremacy between the English and Dutch East India Companies was coming to a head at the time of the play's first performance in 1621. But the importance of that context will have varied according to the composition of the audience, and the play's political implications will almost certainly have been more resonant at court, where pro- and anti-Dutch factions jostled for influence, than in the less highly charged atmosphere of the Blackfriars, let alone at the socially heterogeneous Globe; while in a performance away from the mercantile interests of London, the dramatist's choice of setting might have registered as little more than a glamorous exoticism. The danger of "local reading," as one of its subtlest practitioners, Leah Marcus, has recognized, is that "the very discursivity required by our efforts to familiarize ourselves with a distant culture creates an overlay of order and predictability . . . [that] radically alters the spotty, intermittent, multilayered ways in which topical meaning was likely to be registered by contemporaries." Ambiguity is handed over to the ruthless questioning of Distinction.[3]

It is partly for this reason—and not because I consider such local meanings uninteresting or unimportant—that most of the essays in this collection are committed to the recovery of a different sort of historical content. The local is by its very nature elusive and evanescent, and in the case of early modern dramatic texts, the conditions of its production render it indeterminate and often irrecoverable.[4] But these texts are dense with other kinds of information about the society and culture to which they belonged—information that may sometimes be directly related to conscious authorial intention but that often found its way more or less unconsciously into the work because it was integral to the world the writers inhabited, inscribed in the very language by which they knew it. It is this that makes literary texts (despite the skepticism of many professional historians) among the richest historical repositories that we possess—not because they often have much to tell us about the "facts" of history but because they are unfailingly sensitive registers of social attitudes and assumptions, fears and desires. A study of the theatrical representation of bastards, for example, will cast little or no light on the actual incidence of illegitimate births in the early modern period, nor is it even likely to be of much use in reconstructing the legal provisions and definitions that formally defined the condition of illegitimacy. But as I try to show in chapters 5 and 6, it can offer extraordinary insight into the functioning of bastardy in the psychic economy of early modern society. Similarly, plays like *King Lear* and *The Changeling* may be relatively uninformative about the precise material conditions of domestic labor in the early seventeenth century, but they are remarkably illuminating about the ideology and experience of service in a society that imagined itself as a hierarchy of servants and masters, in which only the anomalous category of "masterless men" was exempt from servant obligation (see chap. 1). And while historians may argue about the actual degree of social mobility in early modern England, no one who reads a domestic tragedy like *Arden of Faversham* or the comedies of Philip Massinger with any attentiveness can doubt that anxiety about the instability and disorder attendant on social ambition and the transgression of status boundaries was one of the abiding preoccupations of this society (see chaps. 2–4). In some ways it may actually be more important to understand what people *thought* was happening to their world than to gauge the accuracy of these beliefs, since what people believe to be true is typically what determines the way they act.

As the earlier essays in this collection show, my interest in this dimension of Renaissance literature was originally shaped by the older historicism of critics like L. C. Knights, E. M. W. Tillyard, and M. C. Bradbrook—as well as by the new social history developed by Peter Laslett and the Cambridge school. But the more recent essays are inevitably influenced by the new modes of historical reading associated with British Cultural Materialism and American New Historicism, which have pioneered ways of decoding the political unconscious of texts from the past. In this respect, like anyone working in this field, I owe a particular debt to the brilliantly innovatory work of Stephen Greenblatt, whose application of anthropological techniques to the interpretation of literary texts taught us to respect the intractable otherness of Tudor and Stuart culture. An essay like "Amphitheaters in the Body" (chap. 7), with its attempt to unpack some theatrical consequences of inhabiting and interacting with bodies that were swathed in meanings quite different from those our own culture teaches us to regard as "natural," would have been impossible without the work of Greenblatt—not to mention the ingenious physiological exegeses of Gail Paster and Peter Stallybrass. It has been Greenblatt, too, who has contributed more than any other critic to tracing the complex entanglement of early modern literature with the emergent ideologies of nation and empire, and the essays that make up the second part of this collection are greatly indebted to this aspect of his writing—as they are to the work of critics such as John Gillies, Richard Helgerson, Peter Hulme, and Louis Montrose, who have supplemented his work in important ways. It will be apparent, however, especially from the essay that gives this collection its title (chap. 11), that I have some reservations about Greenblatt's anthropologizing, since (ironically enough for a critic who habitually identifies with Caliban) it often seems to claim a Prospero-like power over the objects of historical enquiry, which are supposed not to know their own meaning until the critic endows their brutish gabble with words that make them known. Recognizing the otherness of the past can involve a proper humility before the text, a willingness to accept its resistances, its refusal to be co-opted to our own purposes, but it can just as well provoke a determination to violate that silence, to break open the body of the text and ransack it for significance— something uncannily like the drive to compel meaning that seized Edmund Scott and his fellow-interrogators when faced by the stubbornly unspeaking body of the alleged arsonist, Hinting, in a text that Greenblatt himself invokes when exemplifying his own methodology.[5]

One of the underlying assumptions of this book is that the past can be as eloquent in its troubling familiarity as it is taciturn in alterity—and that the business of historical criticism is to trade as tactfully as possible between these contraries. This need not be as difficult as it sounds, however—especially if we assume that the Foucauldian insistence that history proceeds by pardigmatic leaps and bounds, rather than by comprehensible (if unevenly paced) processes of evolution, constitutes (like many of Foucault's arguments) a rhetorically useful paradox, a necessary corrective to the complacencies of Whig history, rather than an irreducible truth. My skepticism about the ingenious stratagems of much poststructuralist criticism springs from a related conviction that, in its fascination with the decoding of arcana and its seeming determination to replace the worship of authorial genius with a priesthood of critics, it is always in danger of falling into the Faustian error mocked by the poet Rochester that first "frames deep mysteries, then finds 'em out."[6] Not only are the denizens of the past sometimes disconcertingly (or reassuringly) like ourselves, but even at their most seemingly alien, their ideas and emotions are recognizably ancestral to our own. More than this, they have become (especially in the case of cultural institutions like Shakespeare) constitutive of our ways of understanding the world—of the very language that we speak. One consequence of this is that a properly equipped historicism must make full use of the practices of close reading from which current practice has too often seemed to distance itself. The witty and dazzlingly inventive work of Patricia Parker is a constant reminder of the ways in which the skills associated with new critical aestheticism can be put to the service of theoretically informed historical analysis; and indeed the persuasiveness of Greenblatt's best work is inseparable from the fact that he is, among other things, a wonderfully deft close reader.

To recognize the ways in which the kind of history I am interested in exploring may be inscribed in the minutest detail of dramatic texts is, of course, to recognize the final inseparability of the aesthetic from the social and political in literary works. To say this is not, I think, to edge toward a recuperation of the universal but to acknowledge that aesthetic values themselves are historically and culturally inflected. To read *King Lear*, for example, is to encounter a tragedy whose extraordinary power (though one might hesitate to call it universal) still seems mysteriously unconfined by the intensely local, historically specific circumstances that produced it. Yet I insist that its grandeur is in no way separable from what is local about it, and it is possible, I think, to get a glimpse of how this is so by looking at one very small (and seemingly trivial) linguistic detail from near the end of the play. This involves Shakespeare's delicate manipulation of personal pronouns—something that, since it depended on deeply ingrained social assumptions and habits of expression, almost certainly operated below the level of conscious artistry, but that nevertheless reveals an intensely imagined emotional life such as only the greatest artists can produce.

In early seventeenth-century English the singular and plural forms of the second-person pronoun still carried much the same valencies as they do in modern French or German: "thou" could be used to express intimacy, condescension, or even aggressive contempt, while "you" indicated distance, polite neutrality, or respect. Thus in the opening scene of *Lear*, only the outraged Kent, of all Lear's courtiers, dares to *tutoyer* the king, thereby symbolically stripping him of his royalty ("What wouldst *thou* do, old man?" 1.1.146; emphasis added). Even between the princely equals, Lear, France, and Burgundy, the restrained courtesy of the plural form is maintained until France's distress at Cordelia's plight produces a violent change of register:

❀

FRANCE:
Thy *dowerless daughter, King, thrown to my chance,*
Is queen of us, *of* ours, *and* our *fair France.* . . .
LEAR:
Thou *hast her, France; let her be* thine, *for* we
Have no such daughter, nor shall ever see
That face of hers again. Therefore begone,
Without our *grace,* our *love,* our *benison!*
 1.1.256–65; EMPHASIS ADDED

❀

Within the family circle, the old man may address his daughters with a "thou" that expresses both parental authority and affection, but they must respond to him with a deferential "you." Thus there is even a sense in which the language of the heart that Lear longs to hear from his youngest daughter (and that she in turn yearns to speak to him) cannot be uttered—at least in this public context, where what necessarily takes its place is the hyperbolic rhetoric of love prepared by Goneril and Regan. It is not until the end of act

4, in the intimacy of a "restoration scene" that constitutes the first of the play's painfully deceptive false endings, that Cordelia can begin to articulate this inward language of love, and one can hear it properly only if one is attuned to the nuances of pronominal usage. Her fierce tenderness toward her father is beautifully registered in the singular pronouns with which she soothes his unconscious body:

> O my dear father! Restoration hang
> *Thy* medicine on my lips; and let this kiss
> Repair those violent harms that my two sisters
> Have in *thy* reverence made. . . .
> And wast *thou* fain, poor father,
> To hovel *thee* with swine and rogues forlorn
> In short and musty straw? Alack, alack!
> 'Tis wonder that *thy* life and wits at once
> Had not concluded all.
> 4.1.26–42; EMPHASIS ADDED

Only at one point does she employ the plural form, when remembering the paternal authority violated by Goneril and Regan ("Had *you* not been their father," l. 30). The moment Lear wakes, however, she must revert to the deferential "you" of the opening scene ("How does my royal lord. . . . Sir, do *you* know me?" ll. 44–8; emphasis added) in a gesture that underlines her attempt to restore his pillaged majesty (symbolized in the king's "fresh garments" and regal chair), even as it seeks to acknowledge his paternal role through the family ritual of blessing:

> O look upon me, sir,
> And hold *your* hand in benediction o'er me.
> *[Lear falls to his knees]*
> No, sir, *you* must not kneel.
> LL. 57–9; EMPHASIS ADDED

Lear himself, on the other hand, as he hesitantly pieces together the shards of his identity, can no longer command the condescending "thou" of their first encounter, and the same confusion of roles that is expressed in his mute appeal for his own daughter's blessing is marked by his constantly addressing her as "you"—a sign of anxious estrangement that persists even when full recognition dawns upon him:

❈

LEAR:

Do not laugh at me,
For, as I am a man, I think this lady
To be my child Cordelia.

CORDELIA:

And so I am, I am.

LEAR:

Be your tears wet? Yes, faith! I pray, weep not.
If you *have poison for me, I will drink it.*
I know you *do not love me, for* your *sisters*
Have, as I do remember, done me wrong.
You have some cause; they have not.

LL. 68–75; EMPHASIS ADDED

❈

Only at one point does he *tutoyer* Cordelia, when he resentfully mistakes her for a "soul in bliss" come to mock his torments (l. 46). By the time they next appear, however, the painful distance preserved in these plural forms has dissolved. In theatrical terms the moment of dissolution is marked in the simple dumb show at the beginning of act 5, scene 2, announced in the quarto's wonderfully moving stage-direction, "Enter Cordelia, with her father in her hand." This, significantly, is the brief scene in which Edgar, for the first time, is able to speak to his father in the accent of intimacy, with his repeated "Give me *thy* hand" (5.2.5, 7; emphasis added); and it is immediately followed by the reentry of the captive Lear and Cordelia, both of whom can now speak (as if the stage were empty of all but themselves) in that same intensely private idiom:

❈

CORDELIA:

For thee, *oppressed King, I am cast down.* . . .

LEAR:

We two alone will sing like birds i' th' cage;
When thou *dost ask me blessing I'll kneel down*
And ask of thee *forgiveness.* . . .

Upon such sacrifices, my Cordelia,
The gods themselves throw incense. Have I caught thee?
5.3.4–21; EMPHASIS ADDED

❉

Reading historically, one might argue that the embrace performed here, in this drama of family crisis, signals something like the birth of the modern affective family whose slow emergence in the seventeenth century has been documented by Laurence Stone, and part of the scene's continuing emotional power no doubt depends on our recognition of this socially charged moment. But for the moment to develop its full theatrical potential it will be necessary for the actors to sense with what intense difficulty Lear and Cordelia have made this crossing into new emotional territory—a crossing for which the pronouns I have discussed serve as precarious stepping stones.[7]

Of course such nuances are unlikely to make any direct impression upon a modern audience, but they are part of the finespun emotional fabric of Shakespeare's writing that actors ignore at their peril. Their significance is something that can now be recovered only by an effort of historical imagination—one that involves the sympathetic reimagining of a society whose local assumptions about rank, gender, and family structure we might utterly repudiate but whose structures of feeling we can nevertheless recognize. We can do so not because they are any longer quite our own but because, as surely as the genetic histories imprinted in every cell of our bodies, they helped (in ways that this play helps us to understand) to make us what we are. To understand them is, for all of us who have been shaped by the past—and by the language—to which *King Lear* belongs, an essential question of location. History, they remind us, is always about the present, about ourselves.

The essays in this volume span two decades of engagement with the drama of the Elizabethan and Stuart periods. Inevitably, therefore, some of them contain ideas and formulations with which I am no longer satisfied. But I have resisted the temptation to subject them to significant revision since this would have involved changing them beyond recognition or perhaps discarding them altogether. I have thought it best instead to let them bear the marks of their own histories, however local or even parochial these may now seem. They belong after all to a process of questioning in which the answers are invariably time-bound, provisional, and subject to endless reinterrogation.

PART I

The Stage
and Social Order

Servant Obedience and Master Sins: Shakespeare and the Bonds of Service

Masters are as well bound to duties as servants. God's law requireth as much. . . . So also doth the law of nature which hath tied master and servant together by mutual and reciprocal bond.
—William Gouge, *Of Domesticall Duties*

As for slaves and bondmen, we have none; nay, such is the privilege of our country by the especial grace of God and bounty of our princes, that if any come hither from other realms, so soon as they set foot on land they become so free of condition as their masters, whereby all note of servile bondage is removed from them.
—William Harrison, *The Description of England*

ROGUES, PLAYERS, AND SERVANTS

Being your slave, what should I do but tend
Upon the hours and times of your desire?
I have no precious time at all to spend
Not services to do till you require.
Being your vassal bound to stay your leisure,
O let me suffer, being at your beck,
Th' imprisoned absence of your liberty. . . .
I am to wait, though waiting be so hell,
Not blame your pleasure, be it ill or well.
—Shakespeare, *Sonnets 57, 58*

Slave, vassal, bondman, attendant, servant, waiting-man. These are the terms in which the speaker of this linked pair of sonnets construes his emotional dependency on the friend to whom they are addressed. On one level this extended conceit can be understood as no more than an elegant complimentary flourish—a homosocial (or homoerotic) reworking of a conventional trope from the repertory of courtly love, but such a display of erotic self-abasement itself made sense only in the context of a particular construction of master-servant relationships. So, however circumspectly one chooses to interpret the witty autobiographical performance of Shakespeare's sonnet-sequence, this language of subordination is an unavoidable reminder of the extent to which the experience of service was an immediate and sometimes humiliating fact of the dramatist's life. Despite his purchased coat-of-arms and the honorific "Master" that adorns his name on the folio title page, William Shakespeare was, after all, a professional writer dependent for social and material success not simply on the commercial fortunes of the company in which he was an actor-shareholder, but on the favor of aristocratic patrons, one of whom the sonnets project as the ambiguous "master-mistress" of his duty and love (Sonnet 20). Under these circumstances it is perhaps hardly surprising that his plays should return so often to the institution of service. In this, however, they are hardly exceptional; indeed a concern with the politics of master-servant relations is so pervasive in the drama of the period that it is paradoxically easy to overlook the phenomenon altogether—very much as the politics of gender were overlooked for so long—as if such matters were an unproblematic given of the preindustrial world. Yet the layered ambivalence that characterizes Shakespeare's evocation of service in the lines I have quoted should be enough to check such complacency. His, after all, was a world in which, as Lisa Jardine has suggested, "dependency [was] a social category more symbolically compelling than gender." And there were good historical reasons—some of them specific to the theatrical profession itself—why dramatists should have been interested in probing the ideology of service, exposing its contradictions and corruptions, and exploring its recurrent mortifications; for they were responding to shifts in the ideology and material conditions of service that were of some importance in the early modern transformation of the social order.[1]

In order to understand a little better what was involved in the idea of "service" and the players' relation to it, it may be helpful to begin not with Shakespeare himself but with some passages from the life of one of his earliest recorded admirers—the Jacobean highwayman Gamaliell Ratsey. Ratsey is chiefly famous these days (thanks to Andrew Gurr) for the incidental light that is cast on theater history by one of his escapades. This was the elaborate practical joke performed upon a company of strolling players, in the course of which, having persuaded the leader of the troupe to provide a taste of his quality, Ratsey commended him as a potential contender for the part of Hamlet. The story is told near the beginning of a cony-catching pamphlet entitled *Ratseis Ghost*—the second of two tracts devoted to the highwayman's "mad pranks and robberies" that were published shortly after his execution in March 1605. The pamphleteer's chief interest in the story, however, lay a long way from the triumphs of Richard Burbage. What justified giving this "pretty prank" pride of place in his narrative is signaled by the chapter title's description of these players as men who impiously "denied their own lord and master, and used another nobleman's name"—they were types, in other words, of the False Servant, whose humiliation at the hands of the highwayman is presented as their properly ironic nemesis. The sweetest part of the joke, to anyone familiar with Ratsey's career, was that he, after all, was not only a man out of service but one whose criminal success depended on his ability to usurp the role of master in a series of performances that were as wittily subversive as they were lucrative.[2]

Ratsey was in many ways a classically marginal figure: a discarded soldier whose origins in the small gentry of Lincolnshire had not prevented him from joining those predatory outcasts who haunted the imagination of early modern England—the crew of "masterless men" whose numbers were swollen, according to William Harrison by "our great swarms of idle serving-men," who "having not wherewith of their own to maintain their excesses, do search in highways, budgets [pouches], coffers, mails [bags], and stables which way to supply their wants." At the beginning of *The Life and Death of Gamaliell Ratsey* (the tract to which *Ratseis Ghost* is the sequel) this "famous thief" is introduced as the son of an eminently respectable father, "Richard Ratsey, a Gentleman, and *belonging to some honorable personage* of this land, whom he followed a long time in great favour and estimation." The formula that defines the elder Ratsey's worth and locates his social "place" is precisely that which the well-known "Act for the punishment of vagabonds" (1572) deployed against those "common players in interludes . . . not *belonging to any . . . honourable personage*" who were to be treated as "rogues, vagabonds, and sturdy beggars." The rebellious Ratsey junior became a *vagabond* in this quite literal sense—one who wandered outside the constraining bonds of the master-servant relation that the act conceives as fundamental to the social order. Feeling himself "disparaged by living at home" the adolescent Gamaliell "grew less duteous and more desirous to range abroad." Abandoning "the life and exercises of a scholar" in which he had shown such promise, he resolved to "betake himself to the fortunes and profession of a soldier," engaging to serve in a company that formed part of Essex's expedition to Ireland (A2v). Here he briefly prospered, rising to the rank of sergeant; with the defeat of Tyrone, however, Ratsey was discharged to join the ranks of cast soldiery whose bitter sense of displacement made them an especially dangerous faction among the masterless. Rather than return to what he saw as his shamefully subordinate condition at home, he embarked upon the career whose assaults on property exploited a self-consciously ironic mimicry of the very proprieties to which his father had given such devoted allegiance.[3]

According to *The Life and Death*, Ratsey launched his life of crime with a pair of "mad pranks" or "conceits" that involved "gull[ing] the servant . . . [to] deceive . . . the master"(A3v). The first failed, and Ratsey narrowly escaped hanging, but the second succeeded, thanks to his crafty seduction of a serving-man, whom he persuaded "to lie at my inn . . . and be to me as my man . . . and continue my credit' (B2v). Thus armed with the countenance of a gentleman, he used his "credit" to possess himself of two geldings belonging to the man's master—the better of which he sold for the considerable sum of nineteen pounds, before riding away on the other. The success of this confidence trick is a reminder of the extent to which rank was a *visible* quality in this period—legible not only in the sartorial codes of the "vestimentary system" but in the deferential theater of master-servant relations.[4] In early modern society the mere presence of liveried followers was at least as important as any practical functions they might serve; indeed the status of a gentleman was actually marked, as William Harrison and others observed, by his extravagant capacity to maintain a retinue of "idle servants," and Ratsey was soon able to give a more permanent gloss to his gentlemanly port by the acquisition of two "servant" accomplices, George Snell and Henry Shorthose (*Life and Death*, B3–4), as well as a page "very richly [attired] in green velvet" (*Ghost*, C4). In a style reminiscent of Falstaff, these "servants to the *moon*" (*Ghost*, C4) impressed potential victims by waiting on Ratsey "as dutifully, as if they had had a master of better condition" (*Life and Death*, C4).[5]

Snell, in particular, seems to have made a specialty of servant roles, effecting many of his most distinguished villainies through what he liked to call "his conceit of blue-coats." Hearing of any banquets or revels "where noble men or gentlemen had cause to use their retainers forth of the country," Snell would insert himself into the company by assuming stolen livery and "either buy[ing] or hir[ing] the badge or cognisance of any man that should fit his purpose." He would then "be as forward and diligent as the best" in pressing his services upon "such as were of the best rank," and at last, even as he "held the basin and ewer to a nobleman to wash his hands," he would contrive to make off with these costly items, together with such "velvet cloaks, plate . . . silver and gilt rapiers, and daggers . . . embroidered girdles, and hangers, or any thing of worth as it lay in his way" (*Ghost*, C1-C1v).

The pamphleteer's attitude toward the implicit subversiveness of these "pranks and sleights" (*Ghost*, C1v) is revealingly equivocal. Admiring Ratsey's generosity to the poor, even as he ostentatiously deplores his knavery to the rich, he exhibits a pleasure in the wit of the highwayman's impositions that invites us to read his life as a kind of practical satire on master-servant relations; yet he crowns the *Life and Death* with a set of autobiographical verses entitled *Ratseys repentance*, ostensibly written while the highwayman was awaiting execution, in which, self-consciously casting himself in the role of Prodigal Son, Ratsey looks back nostalgically to "my *service* in my country's good" (E3; emphasis added) and, proclaiming that "my God to *serve* shall now be all my care," assumes the godly livery of penitence: "My colour'd suits I now exchange for black" (F3; emphasis added). These "colour'd suits" are the protean garments he shares with his fellow-highwaymen, whose course of life Ratsey presents as a travesty of vestimentary decorum:

> And like chameleons must your suits be strange,
> Who doth by kind change colours every day,
> Without respect, forgetting what you be,
> Masking in sin, as if God could not see.
> 4v

The antitheatrical language of this stanza exactly anticipates the pamphleteer's denunciation of the players in *Ratseis Ghost*, when he describes how, on their second encounter with Ratsey, they presented themselves "not in the name of the former nobleman's servants, for like chameleons they had changed that colour" (A4). It is as if their habit of false service were a natural adjunct of their protean trade—a trade that ironically links them with their persecutor, who "every day had new inventions to obtain his purposes

. . . studying as much how to compass a poor man's purse, as players do, to win a full audience" (A4). But the affinity between their performance and his does not end there. Just as Ratsey's deceptions rely upon the gentlemanly countenance conferred by the attentiveness of his pretended servants, so the success of this troupe of impostors is dependent on their ability to usurp the "countenance" of the various lords whose "servants" they claim to be as they move about the country (A4–A4v). The serving-man's bluecoat livery, whose unvarying appearance was meant to proclaim the unchanging stability of the social order, becomes just another item in the actor's wardrobe of "strange suites." Unfortunately for these players, however, by "denying their own lord and master" (A3v), they invite his wrath. And sure enough, we are told that "when he heard of their abuse, he discharged them, and took away his warrant," thereby reducing them to a masterless condition very much like Ratsey's own (A4). The players' risky impertinence wins no favor from Ratsey, however, who, after enjoying a taste of their quality, robs them upon the high road. Warning them that he is "not to be played upon by players," the highwayman exhibits a wry pleasure in presenting himself as a spokesman for the proprieties of servant relations, even as he relieves his victims of their material goods. Sententiously inviting them to see the robbery as a providential chastisement for their iniquity—"hereafter be not counterfeits, abuse not honorable personages, in using their names and countenance without their consent and privity"—he then mockingly consoles them with the offer of his own patronage: "because you are now destitute of a master, I will give you leave to play under my protection" (B1). Wittily satirizing the social ambitions of a profession whose leading practitioners "buy . . . some place or Lordship in the Country" and "are grown so wealthy, that they have expected to be knighted, or at least be conjunct in authority . . . with men of great worship" (A4), Ratsey at last dubs the leader "one of my knights, and the first knight that ever was player in England" (B1v).

More than a sense of shared proteanism, it should be clear, informs Ratsey's ambivalent identification with the players. For this quality itself seems consequential upon another attribute of their trade—namely their dangerously marginal position as men whose livelihood conformed only in a very tenuous way to the medieval model of service inscribed in the names of their companies. It was no accident that official hostility to players so often focused on a mode of life that threatened to evade the normal bounds of social authority. In their errant habits the members of acting companies bore a significant resemblance to men like Ratsey whose restlessness made them desirous to "range abroad." Though players took the livery of the nobleman whose "servants" they nominally were, and to whom (like the players in *The Taming of the Shrew*) they might offer performances as a mode of "service" (*Shrew*, induction, 1.77–8), for most practical purposes the relationship seems to have been a rather distant one.[6] Whether, like the senior members of Shakespeare's company, they were shareholders in the joint-stock system characteristic of early modern capitalism or whether they were the hirelings of entrepreneurs like Henslowe or Beeston, in the material conditions of their trade, actors belonged more to the fluid world of urban commerce than to the ostensibly unchanging domain of feudal retainers. Yet, just as their liveried presence might be important to their patron on certain public occasions, so the fiction of "service" could be vital whenever they required protection from hostile authorities, and their real vulnerability was illustrated by the way in which companies often disintegrated or faced radical restructuring upon the death of their nominal "masters."[7]

They were thus uneasily poised between the traditional ideal in which the social identity of a servant was in some sense subsumed in that of his master (whose "creature" he might quite properly be called) and the subversive liberty claimed by masterless men whose histrionic "self-fashioning," unconstrained by social propriety, could choose any shape whose "countenance" it was capable of sustaining. It is hardly surprising that the drama produced by these companies should reflect their familiarity with the intertwined consolations and humiliations of service on the one hand and the mingled intoxication and abjection of the masterless condition on the other. But this restless probing of the ideology and material realities of master-servant relations also spoke to the lived contradictions of a larger society in which service was simultaneously idealized as a virtually universal state—a defining condition of social order—and recognized as a particular social institution subject to disconcerting local and historical pressures.

— ✤ —

UNIVERSAL SERVICE AND
MASTERLESS MEN

This title (servants) is a general title . . . applied to all such as by any outward civil bond, or right, owe their service to another . . . of what kind soever their servitude is: whether more servile or liberal.
—William Gouge, *Of Domesticall Duties*

As the elaborate organization of royal courts into a hierarchy of often menial-sounding domestic offices reminds us, the early modern world was one in which power itself, no matter how exalted, could only be imagined as the ability to command service.[8] In Marlowe's *Doctor Faustus*, for example, the protagonist construes omnipotence as an apotheosis of desire in which "The God thou *servest* is thine own appetite" (2.1.11), and the action turns on the profoundly equivocal significance of that reflexive service, which may be read either as supreme mastery or abject enslavement. Moreover, the play is actually structured as a kind of household drama in which the continuing "duty" and "service" tendered to his master by the loyal servant Wagner (5.1.58–9, 1) is set against the treachery of Mephistophilis and the other "servile spirits" whom Faustus pretends to command (1.1.98). Mephistophilis introduces himself as "servant to great Lucifer" (1.3.42) but ostensibly repudiates his allegiance to this infernal "master" (1.3.102) through the bond of indenture that makes him Faustus's *"servant, [to] be by him commanded"* (2.1.97–8). This charade of diabolic service is maintained right up to the last act, where Faustus continues to address Mephistophilis as his "good servant" (5.1.99), even as the demon arraigns him for *"disobedience* to my sovereign lord" (l. 84; emphasis added). The B text ushers in the ending with a stage direction for Faustus's Last Supper in which his appetite for power is parodically realized through a parade of "Devils with covered dishes"—a strikingly domestic demonstration of Valdes's promise to make the spirits "always serviceable" to the magician's will (1.1.124). And the play ends with a show of self-consuming appetite, in which the B text's scholars identify "Master Doctor's" reward for the abject servitude he confused with mastery: "The devils whom Faustus *served* have torn him thus" (5.1.339). "Witches and conjurers," as George Gifford proclaimed, "are seduced and become *vassals* of Satan: they be his *servants*, and not he theirs."[9]

If the fantasy of omnipotence for which Faustus gambles his soul can only be conceived as a version of the most familiar kind of household relationship, something very similar is apparent in *The Tempest*, Shakespeare's oblique revisiting of the Faust story. Here Prospero's relationship with the restive spirit he calls his "industrious servant" (4.1.32) forms part of an elaborate set of variations on the theme of mastery and service that begins with that type of embattled authority, the ship's master, and comes to include virtually every character in the play—from the rebellious slave Caliban and his patient log-bearing rival Ferdinand, to the ambitious menials Stephano and Trinculo, and Antonio, the grand usurper of "[his] brother's servants," formerly his "fellows," now his "men"(2.1.268–9). Even what we are now accustomed to reading as an allegory of colonial rebellion can be figured only as the domestic treason of a servant-monster ("has a new master; get a new man," 2.2.185); for, as the dutiful Gonzalo's utopian fantasy of a commonwealth without "the use of service" (2.1.152) reminds us, there is literally *no place* outside the defining bonds of master and servant. To be "free," in the way that both Prospero and Ariel, master and servant, yearn to be, is to be outside the play—so much so that Prospero can envision it for himself only in the nonspace of the epilogue.

One of the hardest things to reimagine about what Peter Laslett called "the world we have lost" is the extensiveness of its notion of "service." Not only did it provide the model by which all relationships involving power and authority were understood but—as the use of the term "masterless" to define a reprobate condition of social exile indicates—it was almost impossible to conceive of a properly human existence outside the hierarchy of masters and servants that made up the "society of orders." From this point of view, indeed, the very notion of a "masterless man" constituted something of an oxymoron, since service was presented as a condition so universal that properly to be a man was to be somebody's "man." "To be no part of any body, is to be nothing," wrote John Donne, in a letter lamenting the failure of his ambitions in the "service" to which he had "submitted [him]self." Beyond the world of service lies only antisocial chaos of a Tempest that seems to undo all "authority" or the asocial wilderness that *Lear* calls the heath. "Servant," according to the Puritan divine William Gouge, was "a general title." Not only did a period of household service form part of the normal experience of most English adolescents but the social "place" of every individual was to some degree determined by his servant dependence upon a more powerful master. In this construction society consisted of an unbroken chain of service that stretched from the humblest peasant to the monarch who owed service only to God.[10]

Even those privileged males who were titular masters of their own households lived out their lives (at least nominally) as someone else's "man"; thus the wealth and prestige of a rising landowner like Master Arden in *Arden of Faversham* are evidently dependent on his being (like his confidant Franklin) "my lord protector's man." Minor gentry and the younger sons of more prominent families typically filled the higher domestic offices in the households of wealthy gentlemen and nobles.[11] Even men of loftier social standing—members of Parliament or justices of the peace—might commonly be enrolled as upper servants in the households of great noblemen like the Earl of Derby or of statesmen like Lord Burghley.[12] On the eve of the Restoration, William Cavendish, Marquis of Newcastle, looked regretfully back to a time when he had witnessed "Sir George Booth, a Cheshire knight of six or seven thousand pounds a year, wearing my Lord of Shrewsbury's blue coat on . . . St George's day, as did Sir Vincent Corbett, whose brother had twenty thousand pounds a year and who after the death of his brother, had four or five thousand pounds a year." In their turn, even the most powerful lords were themselves subjected to their own form of service since (as the North Country squire and man of letters, Richard Brathwait, insisted) "Men in great place . . . are thrice servants; servants of the sovereign, or state; servants of fame; and servants of business. So as they have no freedom, neither in their persons, nor in their actions, nor in their times."[13]

Although no individual could be considered "his own master" in any absolute sense, however, the claim to be "master of one's own" was not a trivial one since in the world of service, admission to full social membership depended on a man's role as "master" of a household whose subordinate members possessed no identity properly independent of his.[14] For servants below a certain rung in the ladder of dependency, at least, this had significant material consequences, especially in the case of adult males. For whereas women and children were thought to be consigned by nature to a condition of obedient dependency (being "Bound to obey and serve," as Jane Seymour's motto proclaimed), male domestic servants *voluntarily* surrendered any claim they might have to authority over their own lives. "While the term of their service lasteth," wrote William Gouge, "they are not their own. . . . Both their persons and their actions are their master's."[15]

So literally was this the case that, while a master could not legally dispose of the person of his servant, he could certainly sell his labor, which must often have felt like the same thing.[16] Servants, insisted Gouge,

> so properly belong to a master for the time of their service, as he may not only keep them himself for his own service, but also pass them over, and give or sell them to another. By God's law not only strangers, but Jews also might be sold for servants. The customs and statutes of our land do also permit masters to make over their servants from one to one: and on their death-beds to bequeath them to whom they will, even as their goods and possessions.[17]

In effect (as Steffano Guazzo put it) a well-trained and loyal servant became simply a "part of his master," obeying him, in Dod and Cleaver's simile, "not as a water-spaniel, but as the hand is stirred to obey the mind." In this organic figure we can begin to glimpse the symbolic meaning of "livery" (a word that significantly links clothing and food). The liveried man was not merely clothed in his master's identity but absorbed into his social body, to be fed as his own body was fed. But the master's apparent fullness of identity was limited in turn by his obligations to a higher master. Thus when Gonzalo salutes his rescue from an outcast condition in which "no man was his own," we can understand that claim to self-ownership only in the contingent sense that depends on the restoration of a proper hierarchy of service—one that has been disturbed by the expulsion of Duke Prospero and by the manifest contradictions of Gonzalo's own too-serviceable role as "master of that design" (1.2.163).[18]

Ultimately, of course, the authority of masters was both authorized and constrained by their relation to God. Caliban's acknowledgment of the authority in which Prospero is now visibly dressed ("How *fine* my *master* is," 5.1.262; emphasis added) is functionally inseparable from his desire for "grace" (l. 295), just as Kent's last profession of allegiance to Lear ("My master calls me, I must not say no," 5.3.324) deliberately mimics the language of religious vocation. In Massinger's *City Madam*, Luke Frugal's ambitious rebellion against the "servile office" to which he is consigned in his brother's household is enough to damn him as a "Revengeful , avaricious atheist" (1.1.141; 5.3.135).[19] And the same religious language is deployed against the outcasts of the companion play *A New Way to Pay Old Debts*. Here the treacherous Marrall abjectly acknowledges his brutal dismissal as "the *heaven*

/ False servants still arrive at" (5.1.349–50; emphasis added), while his tyrannous master, the "atheist" Overreach, who has plotted to reduce the entire
aristocracy to slavish servitude, is consigned to the torments of a living hell
(5.1.365–81). Massinger's comedies, though they lay great stress on "fitting
differences" between masters and the various ranks of servants who populate
their households, hark back nostalgically to a world in which service was supposedly governed by bonds of friendship and mutual obligation rather than
the economic bondage that is the source of Overreach's authority. The idealized households of Lord Lovell and Lady Allworth conform to Gouge's own
authority for this conception of God as the universal master, which lay in
orthodox Anglican doctrine, represented by those well-known homilies that
ransacked the Gospels for text and parables to demonstrate that "obedience .
. . [is] the principal virtue of all virtues, and indeed the very root of all virtues,
and the cause of all felicity," urging servants to obey their masters as an
expression of their Christian duty of glad submission to a Lord "whose service is perfect freedom."[20]

This is the paradox that underlies Ferdinand's offering of "service" to
Miranda "with a heart as willing / As bondage e'er of freedom" (*Tempest*,
3.1.65, 88–9), in an episode that nicely illustrates how even the potential subversiveness of romantic love could be contained by the chivalric conventions
that rewrote its affront to authority as a licensed inversion of hierarchy. The
courtly lover played out the role of "servant" to his "mistress" in a self-consciously extravagant mimesis of social subservience that (in comedy at least)
would be ended by marriage—a convention neatly upended in *Twelfth Night*
when Orsino presents his betrothal to Viola as an act of manumission "for
your service done him": "And since you called me master for so long. . . . You
shall from this time be / Your master's mistress" (5.1.324–6).[21]

No play better represents the all-encompassing ideals I have described
than *King Lear* (1604–5), a tragedy whose preoccupation with the true nature
of "bonds" and "service" was first explored by Jonas Barish and Marshall
Waingrow in 1958.[22] From the servile pliability of the "super-serviceable"
Oswald and Edmund's parade of false-service, through Lear's struggle for
rhetorical mastery of the "servile ministers" who batter him in the storm, to
the loyal non serviam of Cornwall's servant who reneges at the blinding of
Gloucester, the play keeps returning to this theme, constructing a vision of
human society as an order of services whose only alternative is the wilderness where "humanity must perforce prey on itself / Like monsters of the
deep" (4.2.49–50). It is no accident that Edgar should present "Poor Tom"—

the "unaccommodated" creature outside that order, whose chaotic babble renders him as languageless as the "monster" Caliban before his enslavement—as a fallen "serving-man," an ambitious upstart "false of heart, light of ear, and bloody of hand" who, like Edmund, "served the lust of [his] mistress' heart" and was destroyed by his corruption (3.4.85–90). The physical nakedness that figures Edgar's masterless condition mirrors the political undressing of the king, for whom authority is indeed a kind of dress (4.6.157–65) and whose waning mastery is figured in the stripping away of his hundred followers—a "train" fittingly imagined as an extension of his royal livery ("nature needs not what thou gorgeous wear'st," 2.4.269).[23]

Lear survives his exposure to the bare heath only because of the fidelity of Kent, the man who, refusing to be "better suited" than his livery will allow, molds his life into a parable of true service—one that is physically enacted through his stubborn "following" of his royal master in his frantic wanderings across the kingdom. For Kent the idea of "service" is so comprehensive as to constitute (in another of the play's key terms) a kind of second "nature," whereas (at the other extreme) for Edmund the "nature" to whose law his "services are bound" (1.2.1–2) is precisely that force which evacuates the meaning of such "services" as he pretends to offer Kent in the opening moments of the play: "My services to your lordship . . . I shall study deserving" (1.1.28–30). At the end of the play, liberated from his self-chosen disguise as the rustic retainer Caius, Kent identifies himself to his king in words whose characteristic bareness belies their extraordinary resonance: "Are you not Kent?" the king hesitatingly inquires. "The same / Your *servant* Kent," he replies. "Where is your *servant* Caius?" And then, answering himself, he declares "I am the very *man*" (5.3.282–7; emphasis added), thereby reasserting his identity with a kind of riddle that plays across the distance between two seemingly very different kinds of "service" and manhood: the obedience and courtly deference owed by a feudal magnate to his king and the humble toil performed by a household serving-man for his master. Edgar has spoken of that drudgery, in accents at once admiring and deprecating as "service / Improper for a slave" (ll. 221-2). But of course the whole point of Kent's performance has been to demonstrate the inadequacy of such a notion of propriety—to insist that these two kinds of service are essentially "the same."[24]

The language of this crucial exchange looks back to the beginning of the play, where the nature of true service was first opened to question—to act 1, scene 1, where Kent allegorized himself as Duty contending with Flattery for the favor of regal Power, and especially to act 1, scene 4, where the newly disguised earl first announced his riddle of identity to the uncomprehending king. There, faced with Lear's peremptory "What art thou?" and "What wouldst thou?" Kent in effect answered both questions with the single word that for him defines the very bonds of humanity—a word that in this play can seem almost as comprehensive as "love," with which indeed it is often synonymous—"service."[25] It is a term that, properly understood, defines both "what" he is ("who" would not matter to him) and what he desires (anything he could possibly wish for). Thus Kent's servile guise is ultimately no disguise at all, for in contrast to the "serviceable" persona of the time-serving Oswald or the glozing manners of the play's other seemers, it is a livery in which he is absolutely vested, a personation so perfectly expressive of "that within which passes show" that it binds him to follow Lear to the grave itself: "My master calls me; I must not say no" (5.3.322).

At the opposite extreme from the "honest-hearted" Kent's self-investment in the idea of service (one so entire that it renders his guise impenetrable even to his own master), stands the equally theatrical performance of another ostentatiously "honest" exponent of servant obedience, Iago. Iago, we might say, has learned the politics of service expounded in Marlowe's *Edward II* by Spencer Junior and Baldock. For these ambitious royal followers, the role of servant, depending as it does not on ancient sanctities of allegiance but on the arbitrary "favor" of patronage and the mutual calculation of advantage, is a matter of manipulating the "formal toys" of deferential behavior while always standing ready to "stab, as occasion serves" (2.1.31–53).[26] Iago, the consummate improviser, is nothing if not a master of "occasion," but in him the cheerful cynicism of Baldock has turned to an embittered contempt for all the signs of "obsequious bondage"—"forms and visages of duty," "shows of service," and "complement extern"—with which underlings like himself, who "keep their hearts *attending* on themselves" to "do themselves homage" (*Othello*, 1.1.41–65; emphasis added), are forced to mask their real allegiance. In the envious tirade with which he opens his play, Iago justifies his bile by reference to what he calls "the curse of service" (1.1.35). In Venice, he maintains, the very ground of service has been undermined, as the ancient proprieties of loyalty and reward ("the old gradation") have given way to the arbitrary interventions of patronage and influence ("letter and affection"). In such a world, he insists, the bond between master and servant—the imagined sympathy of love and service— is pure ideology, a phantom of false-consciousness:

Now, sir, be judge yourself
Whether I in any just term am assigned
To love the Moor. . . .
I *follow* him to *serve* my turn upon him:
We cannot all be *masters*, nor all *masters*
Cannot be truly *followed*. . . .
In *following* him, I *follow* but myself.
          1.1.38–59; EMPHASIS ADDED

In his valuable study of masters and servants in the drama and culture of this period, Mark Burnett speaks of Iago's speech as founded on an "analogy" that makes "striking" use of "a master and servant paradigm." But this, I think, is to misunderstand something essential about early modern ideas of service and hence to misapprehend the significance of Iago's challenge to social convention. Military "place" was not imagined as something *analogous* to domestic "office" but rather (as the use of the term "officer" in both domestic and military contexts suggests) as another aspect of precisely the same system. Thus Vallentine, in *The English Courtier*, conceives of a single "profession of service," dependent on "either arms or learning" and advises "him that affecteth the war, [to] apply himself to *serve* or *follow* some nobleman, or expert captain, that is either in continual service martially, or that is likely to be used at occasion." In the absence of a fully professional army organized by the state, military enlistment was necessarily thought of in quasi-feudal terms as a form of "service" founded on a mutual arrangement of duties and reward, something given (in the first instance at least) to a particular individual—the commander of a company, who in turn served the "captain" or "general" above him. So at the end of Massinger's *New Way to Pay Old Debts*, the reformed Wellborne's promise of "service / To my king and country" can only be realized through submission to the immediate "command" of Lord Lovell (5.1.395–9).[27]

In *Antony and Cleopatra*, a play that explores the disintegration of such a system of allegiance, the petty kings and generals who progressively fall away from Antony are defined as his "followers" or servants ("In his *livery* / Walked crowns and crownets," 5.2.90–1; emphasis added), creatures who, as the "master-leaver" Enobarbus discovers to his cost, cannot exist except as aspects of his "presence" or "countenance." And though battles here are increasingly won, as Ventidius reminds us, by the mercenary exertions of "well-paid ranks" (3.1.32), Antony's entourage is bound to him, in the style of an old-fashioned aristocratic household, by the casual magnificence of "bounty": "realms and islands were / As plates dropped from his pocket" (5.2.91–2). Similarly in *Othello*, Iago and Cassio are as much a part of the general's military "household" as courtiers like Kent and Gloucester are members of the royal household in *Lear*. *Othello* is often described as a "domestic tragedy," on the grounds that its concern with romantic love confines it, like *Romeo and Juliet*, to an essentially "private" world, but the common preoccupation of *Lear* and *Othello* with ideas of service is a pointer to how limiting and distortive such a notion of the domestic can be—especially when applied to literature from an era without a well-defined distinction between "public" and "private" spheres. In this culture all tragedy, one is tempted to say, is domestic.

"THE CURSE OF SERVICE"

England is the paradise of women, the purgatory of servants, and the hell of horses.
—French proverb, cited in Camden, *Remains Concerning Britain* (1605)

Service in the essentially feudal sense espoused by Kent and Enobarbus must sometimes have seemed like a condition of being. Yet it is clear—not least from the texts that most vociferously assert its persistence—that the idea of universal service was subjected to significant strains in this period. These were felt not only in enterprises whose socially marginal and mercenary character made them resistant to subsumption within familiar models of service but also within the household, at the very heart of the institution. Exacerbated by the economic crisis of the 1590s, the strain seems to have resulted, at least in part, from social and organizational changes that highlighted the mercenary or commercial character of certain forms of labor, making it difficult to reconcile them with traditional ideals of service. An important factor in these changes, in the minds of conservative social critics, was the decay of "housekeeping." Ushered in by the Tudor effort to reduce the large numbers of liveried retainers kept by noblemen and gentry, it was further accelerated by changing styles of household management, which led to a steep drop in the demand for domestic labor. Between 1590 and 1620 the numbers of servants in aristocratic households fell from an average of a hundred to between a half and a third of that number.[28]

The pressures leading to that decline are already apparent in an anonymous pamphlet of 1586, entitled *The English Courtier, and the Countrey Gentleman,* which is structured as a debate on the merits of old-fashioned housekeeping between Vallentine, a courtier schooled in the arts of Castiglione, and Vincent, a conservative country gentleman. When Vallentine criticizes the rural practice of supporting large numbers of "sturdy fellows and needless servants" in idleness, Vincent sarcastically demands to know whether it "were . . . for the worship of a gentleman, having good land and revenues to keep no more servants, than (as they do in cities) those that for their necessary uses they must needs employ? . . . If he walk in the city without servants attending on him, no man will put off his cap to him or do him reverence: how can then such a man be honorable?"[29] The whole point of such servants (like Lear's idle retinue of one hundred knights) is that they should be visibly underemployed as a sign of their master's liberality and magnificence. Their function is essentially that of actors in an elaborate theater of deference. Thus in *The Taming of the Shrew* the tasks that are detailed as essential to persuading Christopher Sly that he is a lord belong first and foremost to the spectacle of rank (*"Look* how thy servants do attend on thee," Induction, 2.33; emphasis added), to be valued in inverse proportion to their actual usefulness:

> if he chance to speak, be ready straight
> And with a low submissive reverence
> Say, "What is it your honour will command?"
> Let one attend him with a silver basin
> Full of rose-water and bestrew'd with flowers,
> Another bear the ewer, the third a diaper,
> And say, "Will't please your lordship cool your hands?"
> Some one be ready with a costly suit,
> And ask him what apparel he will wear.
> INDUCTION, 1.52–60

The role of servants, as Vincent explains, is simply to attend upon our table, and follow us in the streets, when we be at London, or any other great town, and furnish our halls at home. . . . Neither is it the manner to offer them any labor or drudgery, for thereof would they take great scorn, being comely personages." Instead they must exhibit those polite accomplishments best calculated to enhance their master's gentlemanly port and countenance: they must be "expert in sundry seemly, and necessary knowledges, without which

they cannot (as they do) serve a noble man, or gentleman. . . . Besides that
they all . . . can well and decently wear their garments, and chiefly their livery coats, their swords and bucklers, they can also carve very comely at your
table. . . . Some of them also can wrestle, leap well, run and dance. There are
also of those, that can shoot in long bows, crossbows, or handgun. Yea there
wanteth not some that are both so wise, and of so good audacity, as they can,
and do . . . entertain their master with table talk . . . be it either of pleasure or
profit, these good fellows know somewhat in all." For Vallentine on the other
hand (as for Lear's daughters), servants are simply a commodity, to be valued
according to economic "need" or "necessity": unprofitable servants should
be cut down like barren apple trees.[30]

However rational such views might seem, their effect, from the stand-
point of commentators like "I.M.," the author of *A Health to the Gentlemanly
profession of Seruingmen: or, The Seruingmans Comfort* (1598), was to undermine the pieties of mutual obligation, of "hospitality" and "liberality," that
had governed relations in the traditional household, tying servants with an
"undissoluable bond of assured friendship" to their masters. In Marston's
Histrio-mastix (1599) the devaluation of traditional service is seen as a consequence of urban consumerism. The young lords Mavortius and Philarchus
strip their servants of their liveries and discharge them on the grounds that
these "drowsy drones" are "chargeable . . . to feed" and threaten to "break
our backs"; no, reply the victims of this "savage recompense," it is the toys
of conspicuous consumption, "rich-laced suits . . . straight-laced mutton . . .
[and] rascal boys, / Who Ape-like jet in guarded coats," that are undoing
them—an accusation soon confirmed by Mavortius's gleeful admission that
he alone will save "A thousand pound a year . . . For revelling, and banquet-
ing and plays" (3:271).[31]

Explicit anxiety about the nature and conditions of service in the new dispensation is a marked feature of many of the tracts, conduct books, and manuals that offer advice on the conduct of domestic government. "What doth a
gentleman care nowadays for his man than to serve his present turn?" asks
"I.M.," in a passage that recalls the plight of Old Adam in *As You Like It*:

No, no more for him than he doth for his dog or his horse, who, while
they can do him service, he is content to allow them meat and other nec-
essaries. But when the horse falls blind or lame, knock him in the head;
when the dog grows so old as he can do nothing but lie by the fire, cut
his throat; and the serving-man, when the summer of his years are

spent, and that crooked old age hath summoned him to make her many courtesies, with bended knees . . . then off go his shoes and he is turned into the common. . . . What estate, degree, or calling, can then be more miserable than that of a serving-man? Here today and gone tomorrow. In good credit with his master at noon, and Jack-out-of-office before night.[32]

The neglect railed at by the likes of Marston and "I.M." must have been partly an effect of the economic difficulties faced by many households during the crisis of the 1590s, but in the judgment of the conduct-book writer Richard Brathwait, things were no better thirty years later: "Of all other vices incident to *masters*," he writes in *The English Gentleman*, "there is none more hateful in the sight of God and man, than the unthankfulness or disrespect of *masters* towards their *servants*, when they have spent their strength, and wasted them in their service. . . . But, alas, do we not see how nothing is more contemptible than an old serving-man. . . . There is no man that will know him, since his blue-coat knew no cognizance." The "hatefulness" of such ingratitude lay precisely in the way that it threatened to expose the increasingly threadbare fiction of "assured friendship" that was so crucial to the ideology of service.[33] And Iago's power to compel the sympathy of his audience must have lain partly in his ability to articulate the discontents that such commentators were so anxious to dispel:

> You shall mark
> Many a duteous and knee-crooking knave,
> That doting on his own obsequious bondage,
> Wears out his time much like his master's ass,
> For naught but provender, and when he's old, cashier'd.
> 1.1.44–48

The brutal effectiveness of Iago's analysis lies partly in the ferocity with which "cashiered"—a newly coined term-of-art imported by soldiers returning from the Low Countries in 1585—exposes the pecuniary realities concealed by the chivalric rhetoric of military "service."[34] Not to achieve promotion is already to feel the violence of cashierment, to know its constant possibility as a degrading condition of "soldiership." Properly understood, Iago insists, military "service" is not (as presupposed by "the old gradation") a relationship determined by natural ties of "love" and "duty" but a species of commercial contract, a system of calibrated rewards for services rendered, governed by legally enforceable "just term[s]" (ll. 37–40). To imagine otherwise is to deliver yourself to the disparagement of an "obsequious bondage" in which livery is reduced to stables "provender"—a bondage that mockingly disguises itself in the naturalized language of "bonds" and "following." Thus it is not any diabolically unmotivated Machiavellism that compels Iago to trim himself in the "forms and visages of duty" (l. 50); rather his "shows of service" (l. 52) themselves constitute (or so he would like Roderigo and the audience to believe) a *demonstration* of the necessary hypocrisies to which any honest servant must be driven if he is not to fall victim to the ideological cheat by which his profession is controlled. The sneering force of "cashiered" is enhanced, of course, by the quibble that links it to Iago's denunciation of the Cassio ("Cashio")—whose name itself appears to derive from the Italian, *casso* = "cashiered." Iago has presented this alleged "counter-caster" as an epitome of the mercenary world of "debitor and creditor" where cash is the key to all relationships—the world whose cynical values he must patiently explain to Roderigo ("Put money in thy purse"). But of course it is actually Iago himself who is the perfect denizen of that world, and it is the essentially mercenary nature of the service he professes that has led some modern producers to interpret his role in anachronistic class terms, typing him as a disgruntled NCO.

The conflicting attitudes toward service exemplified by Iago and Cassio are mirrored in their close kinsmen Antonio and Bosola, the true and false servants of John Webster's *Duchess of Malfi* (1613–14). As Master of the Household and Provisor of the Horse, these men are senior court officers, but their lofty titles count for little in a world that allows scant room for the exercise of honorable service, and the action of the play repeatedly collapses the difference between them. For to be a servant of any kind in Webster's corrupted palaces is to expose oneself to insufferable degradation since "places in the court" as Bosola insists, "are but like beds in the hospital where this man's head lies at that man's foot, and so lower and lower" (1.1.68–70). Antonio's sense of himself as a gentleman who has "long served virtue, / And ne'er ta'en wages of her" (1.1.443–4) is no defense against Ferdinand's contemptuous dismissal of him as a venal drudge, "A slave, that only smelled of ink and counters, / And never in's life looked like a gentleman, / But in the audit time" (3.3.71–3). And what Antonio calls "the inconstant / And rotten ground of service" (3.2.198–9) is amply illustrated in Bosola's humiliating quest for the "reward" and "pension" he considers due to one who has placed obedience above integrity and "rather sought / To appear a true servant than an honest man" (4.2.292, 310, 330–1). For this disappointed scholar, service offers only a succession of humiliations, the reward for his faithfulness to the cardinal being seven years in the galleys and a place whose lofty title is merely a euphemism for "the base quality / Of intelligencer" (3.2.326–7). "You may see, gentlemen," says Antonio in his playlet of the just steward falsely accused, "what 'tis to serve / A prince with body and soul," (3.2.207–8), and his motto reflects the play's deep and pervasive skepticism about the very nature of service.

Such skepticism is perhaps unsurprising in a dramatist whose first tragedy had satirically anatomized the systematic corruption of "courtly reward / And punishment" (*White Devil*, 1.1.3–4), and one whose sturdily independent dedicatory epistle, with its measured offer of "duty and *observance*," is so careful to repudiate any suggestion of servility toward his intended patron.[35] Indeed Webster's stance can be explained, at least in part, as that of city dramatist instinctively suspicious of court culture. But his indignation at the venality of master-servant relations brings him close to conservative social commentators like "I.M." for whom it was precisely the reinscription of service as a purely monetary connection that threatened to unstitch the proper bond between master and servant. In an analysis that anticipates Marx's description of how the bourgeoisie annihilated "the motley feudal ties that bound man to his *natural superiors*, [leaving] no other nexus between man and man than naked self-interest, than callous *cash-payment*," the pamphleteer describes how a purely material relationship, in which masters "reward only with bare wages," is taking the place of the old "kind usage and friendly familiarity." No wonder, then, that for servants money has become "the mark whereat they all shoot, the master whom they all obey . . . and the man to whom they all do reverence." Of course household relations continued to be governed to some degree by the traditional notion of servants as inferior members of the master's family, dependent more upon his bounty than upon the mechanical regulation of "bare wages"; yet by the early 1620s William Gouge appeared to take it for granted that service was to be treated as a marketable commodity when, in a significant turn of phrase, he reminded masters that "wages is due for labor, *as money for wares*."[36]

In this world of progressively demystified relationships, most household service was coming to seem like a form of wage-slavery, more and more difficult to reconcile—whatever Kent would have us think—with honor or gentility.[37] Even in mercantile Venice, Tommaso Garzoni regarded such employment as vile because the servant, abandoning his "dear liberty," must "surrender himself to his master in exchange for money." As a result, those like "I.M." who were anxious to uphold the dignity of their "gentlemanly" profession were at pains to establish a qualitative difference between the honorable calling of "serving-men" and the base "droyling drudgery" or "servile servitude" of those dismissed as mere "servants." But such distinctions—as Antonio's prickly insistence that his virtuous service is something for which he has "ne'er ta'en wages" indicates—were hard to draw. The status of upper servants and "officers" had always been an ambiguous one, uneasily poised between family intimacy and dependence, and there is evidence that by the latter end of Elizabeth's reign "the services of well-born retainers" were increasingly "neither sought nor offered" as "more and more men came to feel that household service imposed too many burdens for too little reward." Moreover, at least in "I.M.'s" view, the boundaries between "serving-men" and mere "servants" were liable to constant blurring by the ambitions of an upstart group that was busily inserting itself into the ranks of his own profession, thereby "compounding . . . this pure and refined metal (whereof serving-men were first framed) with untried dregs and dross of less esteem."[38]

The pamphleteer's indignation echoes the defensive snobbery of the protagonist in *Arden of Faversham* when he denounces the erstwhile "velvet drudge" Mosby as a "base peasant" who has "Crept into service of a nobleman, / And by his servile flattery and fawning / Is now become the steward of his house, / And bravely jets it in his silken gown" (i.322–3, 27–30). Whatever the objective truth behind such claims, it is clear that, in the minds of some gentlemen at least, household service of any kind had become a source of disparagement. "When this mixture of mingle-mangle began," wrote "I.M." "and that [the gentlemanly] serving-man saw himself consorted with a crew of such clusterfists, he began to wax weary of his profession, even loathing to live in fellowship with such unserviceable people, and disdaining the degree of a servile drudge" (p. 134).[39] Indeed such abject employment could appear incompatible not merely with gentle birth but with the increasingly powerful idea of the "free-born Englishman"—that fortunate inhabitant of a country from which (in William Harrison's phrase) "all note of servile bondage is removed."[40] The Swiss traveler Thomas Platter described England as "a servant's prison, because their masters and mistresses are very severe"—a view that would have been understood by Thomas Whythorne, the musician and autobiographer. Whythorne was so convinced that his profession entitled him to be considered "mine own man, and therewith a master" that when he was approached by a wealthy widow to become "both her servant and also her schoolmaster" he was outraged: "I said that to be a schoolmaster I did not mislike, but to be a serving-creature or serving-man, it was so like the life of a water-spaniel, that must be at commandment to fetch or bring here, or carry there, with all kind of drudgery, that I could not like of that life." So much for Dod and Cleaver's instinctive union of hand and mind! For all his proud speeches, however, Whythorne enrolled himself in the widow's household and, fearful of losing her good will, made himself "very serviceable to please her."[41]

Whythorne's rhetorical non serviam reflects his conviction that to be a "serving-creature" was incompatible not merely with the gentle status proudly announced on the title page of his autobiography or with the dignity of his calling as a musician but in some fundamental way with what it meant to "be one's own man." Whythorne's language prizes open the gap between Harrison's "servile bondage" and the "undissoluble bonds" of service celebrated by "I.M." And in his determination "to be free and not bound . . . [or] slave-like" he looks forward to the defiant proclamation of the leveler Richard Overton in *An Arrow against All Tyrants and Tyrany* (1646) that "to every individual in nature is given an individual property by nature. . . . By natural birth all men are equally and alike born to like propriety, liberty and freedom."[42] That ideas of this kind were already widespread in the 1620s is indicated by the seventh treatise of Gouge's *Domesticall Dvties*, which prefaces its account of the duties of servants with a lengthy demonstration "of the lawfulness of a master's place and power," including a point-by-point rebuttal "of the Anabaptists' arguments against the authority of masters, and subjection of servants." Among the objections that Gouge professes to demolish, by his insistence that true liberty is an inward condition, unaffected by the outward constraints necessary to our fallen condition, are the following:

> "It is against nature for one to be a servant, especially a bond-servant to another."

> "It is the prerogative of Christians to be *all one*: but subjection of servants to masters is against that prerogative."

> "This subjection is against the liberty that Christ hath purchased for us, and wherewith he hath made us free."

"We are expressly forbidden to be *servants of men* (1 Corinthians 7.23)."[43]

Gouge's domestic world is full of servants who, failing to understand that they are "the Lord's freemen," just as their masters are "the Lord's servants" (p. 691), think "their master's house a prison to them, muttering and murmuring against their strait keeping in, as they deem it" (p. 611). This vicious insubordination has become especially prevalent, he maintains, among the very servants "born of gentlemen, and men of good degree" in whom "I.M." vested the dignity of his "gentlemanly profession":

> The reason is, because their birth and parentage maketh them forget their present place and condition; or else (which is worse) maketh them wilfully presume above it. . . . Muttering and murmuring . . . [daring] unseasonable interruption . . . answering their master at their own leisure . . . flapping their master in the mouth with a lie . . . [and using] evil language . . . behind his back.[44]

Reading such passages one is likely to be reminded of the fuming resentments of Massinger's Luke Frugal in *The City Madam* or of De Flores in Middleton and Rowley's *Changeling*. Reduced to the condition of a "slave" by his own nieces who "find employment for him / Fitting an under-prentice, or a footman" (1.1.102, 42–3), Luke sees himself as "the family's drudge, design'd / To all the sordid offices their pride / Imposes on me" (3.2.5–7), and he dreams only of usurping "The reverence, respect, the crouches, cringes" that his brother can command (2.1.83)—a fantasy that achieves temporary fulfillment in his enslavement of Lady Frugal and her tyrannical daughters.[45] De Flores's even more savage indignation at the degrading nature of household service is first expressed in the course of a prolonged meditation on his unlucky physiognomy, where, in a sudden indignant swerve, he appeals to a sense of what is owing to him by virtue of his birth: "Though my hard fate has thrust me out to servitude, / I tumbled into th' world a gentleman" (2.1.48–9). Like Bosola or Antonio, De Flores appears to be an upper servant, some sort of steward or seneschal, a man entrusted with keys to Vermandero's whole castle; yet the text is curiously nonspecific about his precise place, and his life is measured out in trivial "errands" (2.1.30, 59) in a way that makes it (as Whythorne would say) "no better than a water-spaniel's." His master can order him to retrieve a fallen glove as though he were a mere lackey (1.1.226). Moreover even this humiliating kind of employment, we are made to see, hangs on the whim of Vermandero's spoiled daughter—"The next good mood I find my father in, / I'll get him quite discarded" (2.1.92–3). De Flores's sexual obsession with Beatrice-Joanna is shown as inseparable from the deep sense of social displacement that results. When she engages him to get rid of her inconvenient fiancé, he masks the role of hired killer with a half-satiric, half-sentimental appeal to worn-out conventions, dressing himself in the rhetoric of chivalry, as though he were some medieval knight offering "service" to his chatelaine in exchange for a grant of "mercy" (2.1.64): "I would but wish the *honour of a service* / So happy as this mounts to. . . . It's a *service* that I kneel for to you" (2.1.96–6; emphasis added). De Flores's model here (as in so much else) is Iago, whose mock-betrothal to Othello is similarly sealed by a ritual kneeling and an offer of a bloody but eroticized "service" : "Witness that here Iago doth give up, / The execution of his wit, hand, heart / To wronged Othello's *service*" (*Othello*, 3.3.465–7). For her part Beatrice—though we know that she means only to "*serve* [her] turn upon him" (2.2.68; emphasis added)—almost seems ready to gratify De Flores's fantasy: "Hardness becomes the visage of a man well, / It argues *service*, resolution, manhood. . . . There's horror in my *service*, blood and danger. . . . I throw all my fears upon thy *service*" (2.2.92–3, 119, 140; emphasis added).[46] De Flores's courtly flourishes may be undercut by his acknowledged appetite for the grosser form of "service" inscribed in his name ("That were much / For one of my *performance*, and so *warm* / Yet in my *service*," 3.4.55–7; emphasis added), but his sense of social outrage when Beatrice discloses the mercenary nature of his "employment" is none the less genuine for that:

> What, *salary?* Now you move me. . . .
> Do you place me in the *rank* of *verminous fellows*
> To destroy things for *wages?* Offer *gold*. . . .
> I could ha' *hir'd*
> A *journeyman* in murder at this rate,
> And mine own conscience might have slept at ease,
> And have had the work brought home.
> 3.4.63–71; EMPHASIS ADDED

"Salary," "wages," "hire"—to soil oneself with such considerations is to be reduced from the stately rank of gentleman to the rank state of a louse-ridden peasant, a mercenary mechanical.

At the end of Middleton and Rowley's tragedy, the baffled Alsemero begins a chorus of moralization on the seeming metamorphoses that have turned his world upside down. As he contemplates his bride's murderous adultery with De Flores, it seems to him not only that beauty (which his naive Platonism equated with virtue) has "turned to ugly whoredom" but also that "*servant* obedience" has unmade itself in the performance of "a *master*-sin, *imperious* murder" (5.3.197–9; emphasis added). Technically, as Frances Dolan and others have shown, De Flores and Beatrice-Joanna's crimes are alike, since each (according to the statutes that legally defined the patriarchal order of things) is guilty of petty treason. But there the resemblance ends. For in sharp contrast to that earlier tragedy of domestic usurpation *Arden of Faversham*—where the discontented wife, just as much as the ambitious subordinate, is drawn into murder by a desire to "rule herself," to be her own master—*The Changeling* attributes no conscious politics to Beatrice-Joanna's crime. It appears to issue simply from the caprice of an overindulged child. In De Flores, by contrast, the dramatists uncover a murderous resentment that springs less from mistaken ambition than from the rankling sense of displacement produced by his servile condition, and his "master-sin," with its violent usurpation of authority, is shown as driven by desires that are inseparable (indeed almost indistinguishable) from his social resentments. For De Flores's desire for Beatrice is also a desire to level her with himself and thereby render her his "equal" (3.4.133)—a desire to literalize the fantasy of disparagement inscribed in the codes of courtly "service." The measure of his triumph lies in the way he compels Beatrice to accept their liaison in his own pseudochivalric terms ("The east is not more beauteous than his *service*," 5.1.72; emphasis added), even as he himself sardonically describes it in the language of peasant debauch ("I coupled with your mate / At barley-brake" 5.3.163).

William Gouge saw refractory servants as impious social revolutionaries, declaring that "they who are contrary minded, who are rebellious, and disdain to be under the authority of another, and are ready to say of their master, *We will not have this man to reign over us*, are fitter to live among Anabaptists, then orthodoxal Christians."[47] And from Alsmero's appalled perspective, De Flores's crime is tantamount to such a domestic revolution. But it is "revolution" in a peculiarly seventeenth-century sense, one that seeks to reassert old values rather than to install new ones. Like the savage melancholy of the satyr-satirists who scourged the corrupt courts of earlier

Jacobean drama or the protestations of those political dissidents who sought to reaffirm the pieties of an "ancient constitution," De Flores's bitterness is fueled more by nostalgia than by any desire of radical innovation. In that sense he is as much the kinsman of Kent as he is the offspring of Iago.[48]

DOMESTIC ENEMIES AND THE
HISTRIONICS OF SERVICE

*The natural tendency of slavery is to convert the master into a tyrant, and the slave into the
cringing, treacherous, false, and thieving victim of tyranny.*
—Father Josiah Henson, *Father Henson's Story of His Own Life* (1849)

When Vermandero is at last forced to recognize the true nature of the man everyone thinks of as "honest De Flores," he does so in words that fasten on the public significance of what has been exposed: "An host of *enemies* entered my citadel / Could not amaze like this" (5.3.147–8; emphasis added). What amazes him, turning his secure fortress into the menacing "labyrinth" of Beatrice's imagination (3.4.71), is his discovery that the real enemy lies within, concealed, as it were, in those secret spaces to which De Flores's keys and his intimate mastery of domestic topography give him privileged access.[49] The way in which Middleton and Rowley capitalize on traditional allegory, to associate control of the castle with possession of the aristocratic body, perfects this nightmare of intimate betrayal—a nightmare that corresponds to a significant change in the attitude of masters toward servants and their place in the family. Dod and Cleaver warn masters against the kind of abuse that can make a servant feel "hated like a dog . . . [so that] after he becometh desperate like an horse which turneth upon the striker." In the seventeenth century such enmity was increasingly seen as structural to the master-servant relationship. Dod and Cleaver's servant is supposed "to love [his master and mistress], and to be affectioned towards them, as a dutiful child is to his father." But servants are more likely to be characterized as "enemies to their masters, to their friends, and to themselves."[50] So William Wentworth, in his *Advice to His Son* (1604), warns him against the duplicitous flattery of serving-men, insisting that "almost all treacheries have been wrought by ser-

vants, [because] the final end of their service is gain and advancement."
Advising him of "the small love that servants commonly bear to their masters,"he insists that only "trembling fear" will keep such creatures under control. After all, as William Gouge acknowledged in a significant repudiation
of patriarchal sentiment, "there are not those motives to stir up love in servants to their masters, as in children to their parents. Except, therefore,
through awe and dread they be kept in compass, they will exceedingly trans-
gress."[51]

The same fears seem to have haunted sixteenth-century Venetian house-
holders who, according to Dennis Romano, "projected onto servants their
fears of murder and mayhem." "One has as many enemies as one has servants," declared Fabio Glissenti, dismissing them all as "rogues, parasites and
sluggards," while Tommaso Garzoni denounced haughty and disloyal
domestics (in language that resonates interestingly with *Othello*) as "vile
kings of trickery . . . unfaithful like the Moors, thieves like Gypsies, assassins
like the Arabs, traitors like the Parthians—people who were 'created from
nothing' and deserve nothing but discipline and labor." "The image that
emerges," writes Romano, "is of duplicitous rogues and rascals who feign
loyalty and obedience but in the end disobey and rob their masters. They turn
the world upside down and become masters of the situation themselves." So
too in ancien régime France, Cissie Fairchilds demonstrates a growing tendency for servants to be regarded less as members of the family than as mercenary and "self-interested stranger[s]" who might at any moment "rise up
and murder them in their beds."[52] "He is my domestic enemy," says the master of his thirteen-year-old valet in Marana's *L'espion dans les cours des princes*,
while a contemporary police ordinance remarks on the "general belief that
those whom necessity subjects to servanthood consider their masters as so
many enemies."[53] Among English commentators, "I.M." compares mercenary servants to "Judas, that false traitor, [who] even for the covetous desire
of coin, betray[ed] his own master, Christ" (p. 148). Gouge similarly
denounces neglectful servants as "enemies to their masters, to themselves, to
the city and country where they live, and to their friends and parents"—not
merely because they neglect their duties but because they often act "even as
treacherous spies, the most dangerous enemies that may be" or are "so possessed with a devil, as they will seek all the revenge they can, if they be cor-
rected[, and] secretly endeavour to take away the life of their masters" (pp.
609, 629, 614).[54] Nor is such malice confined to those who are seen to act upon
it, since "many that have not the opportunity to practice such villainies, do

notwithstanding in their hearts wish their masters' destruction, and make most fearful imprecations against them; whereby they make themselves guilty of blood before God" (p. 614). Any servant, apparently, no matter how honest and obliging he seems, may nourish rebellion in his heart.

No wonder, then, that so many dramatic texts focus on the figure of "the ambitious frustrated servant" locating his duplicitous subjectivity, as Frances Dolan notes, "in anger and violence." Like the routine violence meted out to stage servants, such emotions have been too easily explained away by appeal to theatrical conventions deriving from Greek and Roman comedy (as though convention operated in a social vacuum). The work of Dolan, Burnett, and Frank Whigham has gone some way toward correcting such misconceptions, but because contemporary historicism has generally been more interested in gender than in class, rebellious servants have attracted less attention, even from historically minded critics, than the refractory women with whom they are often associated.[55] Part of the problem may be that, as social historians have taught us, it is not strictly "class" that is at issue but rather less familiar discriminations of status in what Laslett described as a "one-class society."[56] This is why the disaffections of service typically appear not as the anger of an oppressed underclass, but as the envy or resentment of marginal men—figures whose claims to gentility are felt as increasingly compromised by anything that smacks of a servile dependency. In *Twelfth Night* (1601) the vicious baiting of a steward by a confederacy involving his mistress's impoverished kinsman, the waiting-woman he is destined to marry, and a compliant household gentleman has everything to do with the precariousness of rank and the uncertain nature of "alliance" and "rule" at the ambiguous social margin they all inhabit. And Toby's challenge to Malvolio, "Art any more than a steward?" (2.3.114), serves only to illustrate the instability of the status-boundary it means to declare. Employing the embittered Feste against Malvolio to "make a fool of him . . . and . . . a *common* recreation" (115, 121; emphasis added) is their way of shoring up their own place by reducing the ambitious steward to a position inferior even to that of the mercenary clown who (for all his "allowance") is among the lowest members of Olivia's household.[57]

It is probably no accident that the seventeenth century's two most powerful dramatizations of servile resentment and domestic subversion should have been the work of marginal gentlemen whose fathers had both been stewards in great houses—Philip Massinger and William Congreve. The same "anger and violence" that *Twelfth Night* reveals as the ground (or even the source) of Malvolio's ingratiating desire provides one of the central motifs in Massinger's deeply reactionary comedy of social climbing, *A New Way to Pay Old Debts* (1621–5). As the title indicates, Massinger's satire is aimed at an upstart "money-get" world in which riches have been transformed (in Lady Allworth's words) from a "useful servant" to a "bad master" (4.1.188–9) and in which the ideal of liberality, exemplified in the households of Lord Lovell and Lady Allworth, is travestied in the generous lines of credit that the usurer Sir Giles Overreach winds around the victims he means to enslave. The play ostensibly celebrates a vision of domestic reciprocity and grateful obedience in which master and servant are indeed joined by "I.M.'s" "undissoluable bond of assured friendship," epitomized in the affectionate offers of mutual "service" (2.2.13–4) between Young Allworth and his mother's domestic staff. But all Massinger's imaginative energy is invested in the nightmares of servile enmity generated by the primitive capitalism of Overreach with his aggressive desire to "have all men sellers, / And I the only buyer" (2.1.32–3). The play begins with a scene in which the prodigal Wellborne attempts a brutal reassertion of authority over his former under-butler, Tapwell, who takes a sneering pleasure in the prospect of changing places with his déclassé master: "I may allow you thirteen pence a quarter, / And you shall thank my worship" (1.1.70–1); and its denouement is precipitated by the fulfillment of the abject Marrall's fantasies of revenge against his own master, Overreach. Accused of being a "rebel," the parasitical lawyer hurls Sir Giles's overweening insults back in his teeth :

> The "idiot," the "patch," the "slave," the "booby,"
> The property fit only to be beaten
> For your morning exercise, your "football" or
> "The unprofitable lump of flesh," your "drudge,"
> Can now anatomize you, and lay open
> All your black plots, and level with the earth
> Your hill of pride, and, with these gabions guarded,
> Unload my great artillery and shake,
> Nay, pulverize the walls you think defend you.
> 5.1.215–24

The irony that the play means us to relish is that this leveling language is aimed at a tyrant whose "strange antipathy" to "the true gentry" has made him a leveler in his own right, one whose most powerful desire is to annihilate those "fitting difference[s]" by which Lord Lovell's world is ordered (3.1.27) and to humble his aristocratic enemies by forcing "their issue . . . [to] kneel to mine as bondslaves" (2.1.82–3). We are asked to recognize that the rebel Marrall, like the vindictive Tapwell, is merely an Overreach writ small, so that all three insurgents rightly suffer the same fate of expulsion from the social order they have sought to undo. In this sense the play seems the proper testament of a dramatist whose epistle dedicatory subscribes him "true servant" to the Earl of Caernarvon, and boasts of his having been born "a devoted servant to the thrice noble family of your incomparable lady." But Sir Henry Moody's encomiastic verses on *A New Way*, in their playful vision of an audience helplessly indebted to the poet's wit, toy with a different Massinger, whose mirror-figure in the play is not the dutiful steward, Order, but Overreach himself:

> whilst you teach to pay, you lend. . . .
> All are grown indebted more,
> And when they look for freedom run in score.
> It was a cruel courtesy to call
> In hope of liberty, and then enthrall,
> The nobles are your bondmen, gentry and . . .
> I am your debtor, too, but to my shame
> Repay you nothing back, but your own fame.
> LL. 3–18

It is not just the retrospective knowledge of Moody's death as an undischarged bankrupt in Restoration Virginia that gives his mercenary conceits their edge, since they speak to material psychological realities masked by the deferential gallantry of Massinger's address to his hoped-for patron. Nowhere is such masking more brilliantly exposed than in the ambiguous antihero of Congreve's comedy of domestic revolution, *The Double Dealer*. A man poised uneasily between the roles of upper servant and family confidant, the treacherous Maskwell is Marrall's lineal descendant. And in the mastery of domestic topography that facilitates his erotic ambition, he is the heir of De Flores too. His name, however, draws attention to another aspect of his servile lineage, recalling, for example, Mosca's self-delighting hymn to the profession of parasite—a "fine elegant rascal that can . . . change a *visor* swifter than a thought" (*Volpone*, 3.1.29; emphasis added)—and Iago's egotistical homily on those "fellows [with] some soul" who "trimmed in forms and *visages* of duty, / Keep yet their hearts attending on themselves" (1.1.50–1; emphasis added). It is not enough to say that the histrionic parasite, like the witty insubordinate or the boneheaded drudge whose master must cuff him into reason, is a stock figure deriving from Plautus and Terence. The convention takes on new life in this period precisely because it speaks to the very anxieties about domestic enmity that I have traced. Thus the enigmatic "I am not what I am" in which Iago defines his "native act" and "show of service" might almost be a deliberate paraphrase of the deceitful servant in Glissenti's *Discorsi* who reveals that "in the presence of the master I'm on guard and this rather pleases me, for he doesn't really come to know me, and in his presence *I put on a show of being that which I am not*" (p. 193; emphasis added). Cissie Fairchilds's description of how servants in the ancien régime became "of necessity skilled actors and actresses, constantly engaged in and extremely adept at hiding their true feelings from their masters" would scarcely have surprised William Gouge. For Gouge, even virtuous service is histrionic in character, since "rule and subjection are matters of outward policy," but this is even more the case with that deceitful subservience that, following Saint Paul, he calls "eye-service" (Eph. 6.6). As the vicious "contrary to sincere service," eye-service takes two forms: "parasitical service" and "hypocritical service." The first of these is a subtle form of disobedience like that practiced by Ratsey's actors: "such servants are they who will be very diligent and faithful in doing such things as their masters see . . . but otherwise behind their master's back, and in things which they hope shall never come to his knowledge, they will be as negligent, and unfaithful as if they were no servants. Yet to satisfy their masters, and to soothe them, they will do anything though never so unlawful."[58]

The second is much more menacing: "*hypocritical* service" is described in language uncannily reminiscent of Iago's self-homage as that "which is done merely in show: when that is pretended to be done which indeed is not done . . . when servants have *a heart*, and a heart—making show of one heart outwardly, and have another, even a clean contrary heart within them. . . . Such an one was *Judas*." But such a one also was Thomas Whythorne, the recalcitrant music master. On discovering that the "service" required by his employer was erotic as well as domestic, Whythorne feared that the widow meant only to increase her power over him by bringing him "in such doting love towards her, whereby I should suffer her to ride and deride me as she list." Concluding "that to dissemble with a dissembler was no dissimulation," he therefore resolved to preserve his "self-propriety" through a strategy of outward compliance, "playing with her as the hunter doth who hunteth a hare" and preserving "her good will" by making himself "very serviceable to please her"—a Machiavellian proceeding that he justified in language startlingly reminiscent of Iago: "and as she so intended but to make me *serve her turn*, so in the meanwhile I intended to make the most of her that I could to *serve my turn* . . . [and thus] well feathered my nest."[59]

In the figure of the hypocritical servant, the man with "a heart, and a heart," who is not what he is and who claims a kind of liberty-in-servitude through his mastery of performance, we are confronted by the baser and more calculating equivalent of Hamlet's claim to have "that within which passes show." And in Whythorne's confession or Iago's soliloquies it is possible to witness the production of a recognizably modern subjectivity—the style of selfhood that will achieve its apotheosis in Diderot's *Rameau's Nephew*.[60] To place the perfectly veiled egotism of an Iago or a De Flores beside the resolute self-abnegation of a Kent, the servant who can realize himself only in the enactment of absolute fidelity, is to sense a sharp historical divide. On one side of it lies the "society of orders" described by social historians—a society that still imagines itself as an organically connected hierarchy bound by reciprocal duties and obligations, insisting that to be a man at all is to be another's "man"; on the other lies a world of competitive individuals, organized by the ruthless and alienating power of money into something that is beginning to resemble a society of classes. *King Lear* maintains that the bonds between master and servant are as irrefragable as those between parent and child: Lear may banish Kent, but it is a form of discharge paradoxically sustainable only through Kent's continuing loyalty ("on thine *allegiance* hear me"), and since, in terms of the moral allegory he spells out to the king, Kent's dismissal is based on a misconception of the proper relation between "power" and "duty," he is duty bound to repudiate it and to reassert the proprieties of the master-servant bond by reappearing—a return of the feudal repressed—in the guise of "servant Caius." Hence Kent's refusal, even after Cordelia's restoration of the king, to "be better suited" expresses an insistence upon the symbolic power of livery to express the proper relation between him and his royal master: "Where is your servant Caius? . . . I am the very man" (5.3.284–7). De Flores, by contrast, already inhabits a world of temporary engagements where the merest whim can "get him quite discarded" (2.1.93). There is no heath in *The Changeling*, only a madhouse whose seething, barely governable appetites make it the secret double of the aristocratic castle, the offstage cries of its lunatics "within" announcing that the space of the other, of alienation from the bonds of service is not outside but within.

In a provocative essay on *Othello*, Camille Slights has argued that for early modern culture, slavery and autonomous subjectivity were analogous (and quite readily interchangeable) states, forms of alienation from the body of humankind that amounted to "social death."[61] It is Othello's "unhoused free condition" that renders him liable to enslavement by Iago, just as it is Iago's contempt for what Donne called "just relation" that finally renders him in Venetian eyes no better than a slave. Given the play's explicit concerns, however—the way in which it circles from Iago's repudiation of servile "follow[ing]" back to Othello's claim to "have done the state some service"—these arguments might be strengthened and complicated by placing slavery inside the larger matrix of changing attitudes toward service. In this chapter I have sketched part of the process by which the notion of what it meant to be a "servant" was progressively narrowed and specialized until it came to refer almost exclusively to a form of domestic wage-labor, a potentially degrading occupation fundamentally distinct from other forms of "service." Of course the process was neither as uniform nor as rapid as I have made it appear: like most historical processes, it was piecemeal and fraught with contradictions. With hindsight, it would be easy to mistake the gap between the idealization of service in *King Lear* and the cynical realism of *The Changeling* as representing a chronologically definable shift toward the modern. But the real significance of this opposition lies in what it reveals about the tense coexistence of such fiercely conflicting attitudes. That said, it is clear that De Flores's ability to articulate the humiliations of servitude marks a symbolically important moment.

Ghosts of the old idea of universal service would linger for a long time—whether in trivial forms like the epistolary subscription "your humble servant" or more substantially in the ideology attached to concepts like that of the "civil servant" and of national or military "service." For at least another two centuries, moreover, small gentry would continue to be employed in superior household offices, but these functions were increasingly set apart from those of the liveried caste (or class) now properly described as "servants," a growing number of whom (significantly enough) were now women. By the end of the seventeenth century "Celia Fiennes could find it incongruous that Lord Paget could still summon local gentlemen to wait on him on solemn feast days," and her sense of the incompatibility of servitude with gentility is reflected in the company's tactful obfuscation of

Maskwell's domestic role in *The Double Dealer*: is he servant or friend? He cannot easily be both, for "servants" are no longer automatically defined as part of the "family."[62]

By the time we reach Farquahar's *Beaux' Stratagem* (1706), though it contemplates a dangerously fluid society where "there is no scandal like rags, nor any crime so shameful as poverty" and where yesterday's handsome foot-man "rides in the coach, that he formerly used to ride behind" (1.1.127–8, 138–9), there is no longer any real intermediate space to be exploited between the downstairs world of Scrub the butler and the upstairs world of Lady Bountiful. Struggling to demonstrate their "intrinsic value," the decayed gentlemen-of-fashion Aimwell and Archer are able to maintain the counte-nance necessary to their amorous "knight-errantry" (1.1.155, 180) only by the Ratsey-like device of alternating as each other's menservants. But their stratagem is a fragile one. Not only does their landlord suspect that the "mas-ter . . . is so much a gentleman in every manner of way, that he must be a high-wayman" (2.2.58–9), but the real highwayman, Captain Gibbet, dreams of "buy[ing him]self some pretty employment in the [royal] household," where he will "be as snug and honest as any courtier of them all" (4.2.145–7). Even Cherry, the innkeeper's daughter and chambermaid, recognizes in Archer's degrading guise a tacit capitulation to the leveling world of monetary reward that will license her to purchase him as a husband:

O sweet sir, I'm *your humble servant;* you're fairly caught. Would you persuade me that any gentleman who could bear *the scandal of wearing a livery* would refuse two thousand pound, let the condition be what it would. No, no, no, sir. —But I hope you'll pardon the freedom I have taken, since it was only to inform myself of the respect I ought to *pay* you.

2.2.215–20; EMPHASIS ADDED

Like *The Tempest, The Beaux' Stratagem* is a comedy of manumission. The deus ex machina who resolves its plot is called Sir Charles Freeman, and the play's closing couplet cheerfully insists that "Consent is law enough to set you free." But the ambitious Cherry's reward is to be returned to the natal "servitude" she so hated (2.2.190): "and for the daughter" (Archer asks the now wealthy Aimwell), "persuade your bride to take her into service" (5.4.162–3). What the play unequivocally shows is that "freedom" is contin-gent less upon consent than upon cash. And for those like Cherry who cannot keep their hands on it, the happiest ending is to submit to the chains of class and wages, and to accept—as one of Farquahar's own penurious daughters had soon to do—the "scandal of wearing a livery." Cherry's perception of that "scandal" marks the precise distance at which her society stands from the world nostalgically celebrated by the Marquis of Newcastle—the world of universal service in which even "a knight of six or seven thousand pounds a year" might think it no scandal to "wear . . . my Lord of Shrewsbury's blue coat on . . . St George's day."

This paper was originally written as the 1998 British Academy Annual Shakespeare Lecture. I record my gratitude to the participants in Susan Zimmerman's 1997–8 Folger Colloquium, to the members of the 1998 Columbia Shakespeare Seminar, and to Linda Levy Peck and Mark Thornton Burnett for their helpful comments and advice on earlier versions.

2

"This Gentle Gentleman": Social Change and the Language of Status in Arden of Faversham

In a now-classic essay that has set the terms for most subsequent discussion of the play, Catherine Belsey located *Arden of Faversham* inside a series of re-presentations of "Alice Arden's Crime," in which the murder of a husband was figured as an event that troubled both the politics of the state and the politics of gender. Through the various tellings of the story, beginning with the Wardmote Book of Faversham and Holinshed's *Chronicle*, it was possible to trace the outlines on the one hand of "a discursive struggle for the meaning of resistance to absolutism," and on the other of "a discursive contest between distinct meanings of marriage [and the family]."[1]

While there is no doubt that the elaborate recontextualization begun by Belsey has transformed our understanding of *Arden*, it is, I think, arguable that the theatrical life of the play and its quality as a dramatic artifact have been somewhat obscured in the process. It has generally been a weakness of contemporary historicist criticism, with its temperamental suspicion of the New Critical fetishization of well-wrought urns, that it has devoted more space to the identification and description of discursive contexts than to the detailed analysis of texts themselves. The consequences, I argue, are not simply aesthetic, for a fully informed historicism cannot afford to overlook the way in which historical meaning is embedded in every aspect of a dramatic text down to the level of its most intricate verbal details.

Taking their cue from Holinshed or from the catchpenny title page of the 1592 quarto with its didactic emphasis on the treachery of Arden's "disloyal and wanton wife . . . Wherein is shewed the great malice and dissimulation of a wicked woman," most recent historicist readings of *Arden of Faversham* have concentrated either upon its reinforcement of patriarchal ideology or upon its essentially bourgeois interest in the acquisition and control of property. A case in point is Lena Cowen Orlin's treatment of the play in her formidably learned *Private Matters and Public Culture in Post-Reformation England.* Orlin treats *Arden* as a control text for examining the system of analogies between political and household "government" that gave stories of domestic revolt and husband-killing their exemplary importance in Elizabethan culture. Building on Belsey's work, she argues that it was these analogies that warranted the seemingly anomalous inclusion of Thomas Ardern's murder in Holinshed's *Chronicles*, raising his wife's crime to "notional parity with the opening of trade with Muscovy, the defeat of the Spanish Armada, and, most especially, the assassination of an anointed king." Construed under Elizabethan law as an act of "petty treason," husband-murder was seen to constitute such a fundamental assault on the patriarchal order of society that a bourgeois domestic scandal could be justified as a fitting subject for tragedy—albeit (as the dramatist ruefully acknowledged) a "naked" one, bereft of the "filed points" of stylistic ornament normally thought proper to the decorum of this elevated genre (epilogue, l. 14–18).[2]

One advantage of Orlin's approach is that it helps account for what might otherwise seem a peculiar narrowing of focus in a tragedy supposedly concerned with large social issues. Virtually ignoring the charges of greed and corruption leveled against the historical Thomas Ardern, the dramatist turned away from the controversial public life in order to concentrate upon the pathos of Arden's domestic role and the tragic consequences of his "disastrous . . . misrule" (p. 97). But Orlin is able to show that this seeming paradox rests upon an anachronistic dichotomizing of "public" and "private" spheres. In selecting his material as he did, the dramatist was merely contributing to the process by which successive commentators "purg[ed] the story of its extradomestic elements" in order to stress the true significance of the murder as a paradigm of impious assaults upon sovereign authority (p. 64). In tracing how the play locates its claim to public significance precisely in what we might think of as the "private" world, Orlin rightly draws attention to the politically charged language in which Mosby and Alice are made to articulate their challenge to Arden's domestic authority: "And then I am *sole ruler of mine own*"; "what hath he to do with thee, my love / Or *govern me* that am to *rule myself?*"; "Poor wench abused by thy *misgovernment*" (viii.36; x.89–90; xiii.113; emphasis added). Moreover her meticulous interest in the material arrangements of Elizabethan households enables Orlin to point up the semiotics of usurpation involved in details like Mosby's appropriation of Arden's chair (xiv.287)—a concrete symbol of prestige and authority that identifies the murder as a species of domestic regicide.[3] For all its substantial virtues, however, her account remains so indifferent to the play's literary and theatrical dimensions that it is in danger of reducing the tragedy to a two-dimensional fable of patriarchal orthodoxy.

Garrett Sullivan's essay on the play, though it usefully enlarges our sense of *Arden*'s social dimension by stressing the importance of the protagonist's role as estate manager, exhibits a similar unconcern for the dramatic. Sullivan shows how *Arden* addresses the anxieties aroused by the progressive shift from a "conception of property as social office" toward an agrarian capitalism in which land was increasingly regarded as another form of commodity, displacing "the feudal idea of the beneficent, fatherly landlord" in favor of "a more unabashedly economic relationship between lord and tenant." What is at stake in the play, he argues, is not simply the distribution of authority but the control of property. In this context Alice is to be seen both as a contested possession in herself and (even more importantly) as a crucial instrument in Mosby's struggle to possess himself of Arden's wealth. Thus "Arden's relationship to the land is [so] intertwined with his relationship with his wife" that "Alice's love for Mosby cannot be separated from the potential mismanagement of her husband's affairs." Indeed "[her] lack of love for Arden takes the material form of undermining the stability of his estate" through her careless pledges of reward to Greene, Michael, and Clarke, as well as through the threat to proper inheritance posed by her adultery.[4]

However, Sullivan's lack of interest in the verbal structures that sustain the play's dramatic life leads him to overlook what is arguably the most important function of land in the *Arden* world—its paradoxical role as both an index of rank and a fungible commodity, the very things that render it such a crucial instrument in the struggles over status that consume all the characters of the play. In the medieval world (as the social, political, and economic meanings of "estate" remind us) the possession of landed property had been inseparable from notions of feudal hierarchy, and although sixteenth-century England witnessed an increasing commodification of land, this did not simply convert it into a highly visible form of material possession; rather it made it a key *mechanism* by which mere pelf could be transformed into social prestige, conferring an aura of legitimacy upon upward mobility. For it was still the ownership of landed estates that served, better than anything else, to mark the most important of all divisions in early modern society: that between the nobility and gentry on the one hand and the commonality on the other—between those who (by and large) owned the land and those who worked it. In this connection it is of obvious importance that the land at issue in *Arden* should have been acquired from the dissolved Abbey of Faversham, since the extraordinary disruption of tenure produced by the crown-sponsored break-up and redistribution of monastic estates at once accelerated the general commodification of land and rendered disturbingly conspicuous the social mobility attendant upon it. The Lord Protector's grant to Arden of "All the lands of the Abbey of Faversham" is the first thing we hear about in the play, taking precedence even over the disclosure of Alice's adulterous liaison with Mosby. And while Sullivan's analysis helps to explain the importance of this land not merely to Arden but to the rival claimants, Greene, Mosby, and Reede, it offers no account of how the abbey lands figure in the ferocious jostling for status that occupies so much of the dramatic action.

This deficiency had been addressed in an important book by Frank Whigham that explores the crucial significance of the Henrician redistribution of monastic estates for an understanding of the play's social vision. For Whigham, *Arden* is nothing less than "a direct dramatic study of the fruits of the Dissolution," a cataclysm he recognizes as having "unleashed a deluge of social flux deriving from the suddenly movable status of hitherto rock-solid land, once the uncirculating sign of the aristocracy, now increasingly a commodity." It is Whigham's alertness to the extraordinary fluidity of status in the *Arden* world that helps to account for the great virtue of his approach—a willingness to use the techniques of close reading to reveal the sheer linguistic density of the play's dramatization of conflicts over rank and status. In its exploration of the fiercely nuanced languages of compliment, deference, and social insult in the play, this chapter is in many ways a supplement to Whigham's work. We do, however, disagree about the handling of a number of salient dramatic details. Not the least of these involves the dramatist's treatment of Arden's murder.[5]

❀ ❀ ❀

The epilogue to *Arden of Faversham* makes much of the coincidence that "Arden lay murdered on that plot of ground / Which he by force and violence held from Reede" (ll. 10–11), thus foregrounding the importance of land in the social competition that contributes to Arden's death; yet it is not, significantly enough, the possession of land that preoccupies the murderers in the climactic scene of butchery at Master Arden's table. As they plunge their weapons into Arden's body, Mosby, Shakebag, and Alice account for their actions in a brief but telling litany:

❧

MOSBY:
There's for the pressing iron you told me of.
SHAKEBAG:
And there's for the ten pound in my sleeve.
ALICE:
What, groans thou? Nay then, give me the weapon.
Take this for hind'ring Mosby's love and mine.
XIV.241–4

❧

Belsey's approach, with its stress on the ideological transgressiveness of Alice Arden's crime, would encourage a reader of the scene to focus on Alice's usurpation of the masculine prerogative of violence ("give me the weapon") as an assertion of her role as desiring subject. But the stark juxtaposition of Alice's frustrated desire with Mosby's wounded pride and Black Will's mercenary greed reflects the play's keen sense of the close interrelationship of all three motives, and we should not, I think, overlook the precedence given in this arrangement to Mosby's social resentment, highlighted as it is by the brilliant detail of the pressing iron.

This implement is imported, of course, from Holinshed's original account of Thomas Ardern's death, where it is specified as one of the murder weapons. Mosby, we are told, "having at his girdle a pressing-iron of fourteen pounds weight, struck [Arden] on the head with the same, so that he fell down and gave a great groan, insomuch that they thought he had been killed."[6] And the New Mermaid editor, Martin White, conjecturing that the dramatist too "intended that Mosby should kill Arden with an iron" (p. 91), even inserts a stage direction to this effect. He is supported in this assumption by Whigham, who further proposes that Alice in turn should "take the iron from Mosby and use it."[7] But this, surely, is to miss the whole point of the transformation through which Holinshed's purely sensational detail is con-

verted into a socially and emotionally charged symbol. In the play the pressing iron is given no physical presence; it exists instead only as an instrument
of lacerating fantasy—but a fantasy that lurches into vicious life at the
moment of the killing, reactivating an episode of invented stage business
from the opening scene, where Arden publicly humiliated his rival with a
sneering reminder of Mosby's former trade as a botching tailor:

> So, sirrah, you may not wear a sword.
> The statute makes against artificers,
> I warrant that I do. Now use your bodkin,
> Your Spanish needle, and your pressing iron,
> For this shall go with me.
> 1.310–14

In accordance with the play's recognition of the bond between status and
sexual power, a double insult is involved here; for the sword is not merely (as
Arden's citation of statute insists) the most publicly visible sign of the
wearer's claim to gentility but a symbol of his masculinity and phallic aggres-
siveness, while bodkin, needle, and iron are at once the mechanic instruments
of a "base artificer" and domestic artifacts compromisingly associated with
the female domain. If the sword stands for all that Mosby desires to be, then
the iron stands for all that has made him what he is and (by the same token)
for everything that constantly threatens to undo him—just as, on the level of
theatrical convention, the clash between pressing iron and sword foregrounds the play's anomalous nature as "domestic tragedy" and its deliberately embarrassing tendency to collapse into the idiom of low comedy.[8]

It is difficult to overemphasize the brilliance of the intuitive stroke by
which the playwright discovered in the casual detail of the pressing iron a
clue to the social and psychological significance of a story that Holinshed had
presented as a simple, though rather confused, moral fable. Conscious that
Arden's murder might "seem to be but a private matter, and therefore . . .
impertinent to this history," Holinshed justified its inclusion in his chronicle
"for the horribleness thereof," presenting it both as an exemplary demonstration of the horrors of domestic rebellion and as a warning against the
greed and oppression of landlords. But beyond the providential piety that
makes the murderers into scourging instruments of God's "vengeance"
against an Arden who is seen as "a covetous man and a preferer of his private
profit before common gain," Holinshed sees no connection between these
potentially contradictory moralizations. For the dramatist, by contrast, the

two are indissolubly linked by the issues of rank and status on which almost every detail of the action is seen to turn, and it is the pressing iron that becomes the primary symbol of that connection.[9]

In Holinshed, Mosby is described as "a tailor by occupation, a black swart man, servant to Lord North," but neither his humble past profession nor his present status is accorded any particular significance.[10] The dramatist, by contrast, makes the adulterer's social standing the key to his whole relationship with Arden. Indeed the base origin of his rival seems to cause Arden as much pain as the adultery itself, exposing him as it does to degrading scorn in the "common table-talk" of "all the knights and gentlemen of Kent" (i.343–4): "Ay, but to dote on such a one as he / Is monstrous, Franklin, and intolerable" (i.22–3).[11] Described in Arden's wounding oxymoron as "a velvet drudge," the upstart steward has become the epitome of disruptive social aspiration, tricked out in the rich stuffs that the sumptuary laws reserved for the nobility: "A cheating steward, and base-minded peasant" who "bravely jets it in his silken gown" (i. 322–3, 30). For his own part, Mosby is presented as a self-conscious overreacher, a man who at times feels giddy at the dangerous ambition that has driven him "to [climb] the top bough of the tree / And . . . build my nest among the clouds" (viii.15–16). His desire for Alice Arden is shown as functionally inseparable from his sense of her superior rank: "Make love to you? Why 'tis unpardonable; / We *beggars* must not breathe where *gentles* are" (viii.138–9; emphasis added). Not only do such wounded sarcasms expose a vulnerability that mirrors Arden's own, they also prepare us for a revenge that will expressly serve to cancel out his rival's slights and reassert a claim to gentility that (with a neatly exacting irony) Mosby means to bolster by possessing himself of Arden's estate. When *this* Mosby strikes at Arden, it will surely be with a sword—for that is the only instrument with which he can fitly reclaim his genteel status in a triumphant usurpation of Arden's rank, property, and domestic office. By the same token, the symbolic cancellation of the pressing iron marks the point at which "this naked tragedy" discards those "common errors of our lives" that Sidney had defined as the proper stuff of comedy and decisively asserts its own upstart claim to "bravely jet it" on the stage of tragedy.[12]

❋ ❋ ❋

I concentrate on the details of pressing iron and sword because they epitomize the mastery of theatrical and verbal nuance through which the dramatist played on the social consciousness of his audience. Considered by itself,

Arden's overwhelming concern with issues of status and with the dangerous fluidity of rank in what Ben Jonson called "the money-get, mechanic age" simply associates it with the most well-worn clichés of its era—a time in which (or so its moralists repeatedly alleged) "Prince, Subject, Father, Son, [were] things forgot." "Was there ever less obedience," demanded Philip Stubbes, "in youth of all sorts, both menkind and womenkind, towards their superiors, parents, masters, and governors." From the dramatist's perspective, Alice's treason, Arden's avarice, and Black Will's anarchic greed are all symptoms of this larger malaise—one that is perfectly emblematized in the fantasy of Mosby's pressing iron. What makes the play something more than another rehearsal of the moral commonplaces of its age, however, is the sure theatrical instinct with which the playwright *dramatizes* these anxieties, producing in the process, the first play about that perennial English preoccupation that would come to be called "class."[13]

To recognize just how intensely the social anxieties of the age are woven into the play's dramatic texture, it is necessary to subject it to the kind of close verbal analysis to which current practice is typically averse; for it is above all through the characters' minutely inflected language of deference and abuse that issues of rank are negotiated and a ferocious competition for status played out. A properly historicized reading needs to be as alert to this social weaponry in *Arden of Faversham* as it would be in the classic theater of social competition known as "comedy of manners." Yet it is difficult for modern readers to remain alert to the nuances of this battle—not just because its key terms ("gentleman," "master," "peasant," "knave," "villain" and "churl") were long ago stripped of real social reference but because the play itself (in a way that can make it sound deceptively modern) actually traces the beginnings of that very process. When Arden protests to Franklin that he is "by birth a gentleman of blood" (i.36), or when Franklin, in another overanxious tautology calls him "this gentle gentleman" (iv.42), they have something quite particular in mind. "Gentleman" is by now one of the most vacuous words in the entire English lexicon, barely preserving even the loose snobbish connotations it still had a few decades ago. To Arden and his contemporaries, however, the right to call yourself a "gentleman" was a matter of solid material significance, as Peter Laslett explains:

> the word *gentleman* meant something tangible . . . if uncertain in precise definition. . . . [It] marked the exact point at which the traditional social system divided up the population into two extremely unequal sections.

About a twenty-fifth . . . of all the people living in the England of the Tudors and Stuarts . . . belonged to the gentry and to those above them in the social hierarchy. This tiny minority owned most of the wealth, wielded the power and made all the decisions, political, economic and social for the national whole.

If you were not a gentleman, if you were not ordinarily called *"Master"* by the commoner folk, or *"Your Worship"*; if you, like nearly all the rest, had a Christian and a surname and nothing more; then you counted for little in the world outside your own household, and for almost nothing outside your small village community and its neighbourhood.

You would remain, that is to say, effectually *nameless*, your history excluded from the honourable roll-call that in *Henry V* ends with "Davy Gam Esquire," merely gesturing at the obscure heap of "other men" with a dismissive "None else of name" (*Henry V*, 4.8.104–5). To exercise power, then, to be free of the society of England, to count at all in the record we call historical, you had to be a gentleman. When you came to die you had to hold one of those exceptional names in a parish register which bore a prefix or a suffix.[14]

It is always at such imprecise but fiercely contested boundaries, as Laslett notes, that the strains of social mobility are most acutely felt. No wonder then that the proper deployment of honorifics was something over which men would fight and even kill—as we can see from Massinger's *New Way to Pay Old Debts*, where the bankrupt gentleman Welborne is driven to savage violence against his former underbutler, Tapwell, when the latter sardonically reduces him from "Master Francis" to plain "Welborne," looking forward to a future in which "I may allow you thirteen pence a quarter, / And you shall thank *my worship*."[15]

A similar sensitivity is everywhere apparent in *Arden*. So in the first scene, when Alice confides to Mosby about her burgeoning conspiracy with "Master Greene—Dick Greene, I mean," the change of appellation is less an attempt to distinguish her coplotter from any other Greene, than a maneuver designed to flatter her lover by socially reducing the acquaintance to whom she will refer with measured irony later in the speech as "the gentleman" (l. 563). In contrast to *A New Way*, however, where the traditional aristocracy have learned to shore up their position by the cynical application of Machiavellian stratagem, *Arden of Faversham* presents a world of ambitious bourgeois, upstart serving-men, and masterless swaggerers, in which

Laslett's crucial boundary between the gentle and the common appears dangerously porous. Though the terminology of social difference is obsessively used, the various terms of respect are given or withheld simply according to an individual's power to exact or refuse them, and status, as a result, is shown to be a largely contingent thing.

Nothing, ironically, illustrates this better than the career of the protagonist, "Master Arden" himself—though Lena Orlin, rather puzzlingly, treats his claim to genteel status as a matter of fact. Orlin argues that the dramatist deliberately effaced the aggressive "new man" of his sources to create a tragic protagonist "nobler" in both character and lineage than the historical Thomas Ardern. Arden, she insists (quoting his own words) is "an established 'gentleman of blood.' " But this is to make the error of taking the character at his own estimate. In fact the dramatist provided a significant clue to Arden's origins through the very man who is most supportive of his social amour propre. "Franklin" is a name powerfully suggestive of Arden's liminal position in Kentish society, since it links him by association with that group of prosperous yeomen-farmers whose substantial estates frequently rivaled those of the small gentry—men whose wealth, in other words, placed them precisely on Laslett's uneasy dividing line "between the minority which ruled and the mass which did not rule." "Master Franklin," as Arden solicitously calls him, seems close enough to achieving gentle status; yet, as the Ferryman's jesting with Franklin slyly suggests, such "bold yeomanry" may in the end be little different from "flat knavery" (xi.31–3).[16]

By a neat irony, moreover, the very land on which this aspiring "gentleman" sets so much store serves only to make his position more uncertain; for if the Duke of Somerset's generosity to Arden and his heirs seems to promise the establishment of a landed dynasty, the disputed commercial transaction by which Arden claims to have bought Reede's land symbolically ensures that this will never come to be. It is as if the prizing away of land from its "true" possessors functioned as the social equivalent of original sin, threatening to unstitch the entire fabric of society. For once land is recognized as a commodity, possession (and the status it entails) are laid open to the ruthless vagaries of competition. Thus, in a fashion that points up the contradiction in his ambitious designs, Arden's estate is at once the proof of his claim to gentility and the very thing that exposes the vulnerability of this claim. By a telling extension of this irony, Arden's dependence on the patronage of Lord Protector Somerset immediately associates him with his principal rival for possession of the abbey land, the upstart Mosby, who enjoys the favor of another nobleman, Lord Clifford (i. 27–32). Mosby himself will claim to have been "offered" the lands by a third claimant, Greene—another of the play's emulous pretenders to gentility, whose own status is in turn dependent on his client relationship to an apparently less powerful patron, Sir Antony Ager. All three rivals, we are meant to see, are men whose ability to preserve the "countenance" of a gentleman is critically dependent (as Franklin reminds us) on their being "countenance[d]" by a nobleman (i.31). Furthermore, Arden's uneasy resemblance to the very man whose degraded origins render Alice's adultery so insufferable to his pride (i.22–43) is enhanced by his engagement in business activities (i.81–90, 220–3) that are functionally no different from the "base brokage" to which he himself attributes Mosby's advancement (i.26).

In this context, Arden's extreme sensitivity about rank is bound to seem more like the overanxious prickliness of an arriviste than the wounded amour propre of a true "gentleman of blood." If he is repeatedly addressed as "Master Arden" and accorded other terms of respect that appear to fix his position in the hierarchical "society of orders," this is done almost exclusively by his friends, members of his household, or those with reasons to fear him. Alice, it is true, promotes him to Mosby as "a *gentleman* / Whose *servant* thou mayst be" (i.203–4; emphasis added), but she does so only in order to humiliate her ambitious lover for his sudden coolness toward her. Moreover, if Arden is presented by his sympathizers as a linchpin of the social hierarchy, a "gentle gentleman," whose "*gentle* life," in Michael's telling phrase, "is *leveled* at" by the domestic revolutionaries Mosby and Alice (iii.201; emphasis added), he is just as often stigmatized by his enemies with the same disdainful epithets that—in an effort to assert his own superior status—he habitually applies to them.

Thus Arden jeers at Mosby as a "base-minded peasant" (i.323) and a "ribald knave" (xiii.78), using the same term he applies to his servant, Michael (iii.16), whom he rebukes for his interest in that "base . . . trull" Mosby's sister (iii.30), while he dismisses the indignant Reede as a "knave" and "villain"—that is to say a *villein*, one of "vile" or low-born status (xiii.54–5). But his social assumptions are called in question when these same insults are turned back on him by his enemies. Both Greene and Reede, for example, repeatedly slight him as a "churl" or "carl" (i.488, 509, 513; xiii.9, 50)—a term whose modern sense of "rustic, or boor" had yet to be differentiated from its more precise feudal meaning of "villein," "serf" or "peasant." And this slur is picked up by Arden's own wife (i.520, 567), whose much-flaunted aristocratic origins suggest the principal motive behind his marriage (i.489–91). Alice despises her "saving husband" as a niggardly bourgeois who "hoards up bags of gold / To make our children rich" (i.220), and Greene affects to share her contempt for Arden's acquisitive miserliness ("Desire of wealth is endless in his mind, / And he is greedy-gaping still for gain" i. 474–5).[17] Just as Alice's disdain is framed by resentful pride in her own noble family (i.202), so Greene sharpens his indignation by implying that he too is Arden's natural superior: "Nor cares he though young *gentlemen* do beg, / So *he* may scrape and hoard up in his pouch" (i.474–7; emphasis added). He goes on to flatter Alice by contrasting Arden's allegedly humble status with her own aristocratic origins:

> Why, Mistress Arden, can the *crabbed churl*,
> Use you *unkindly?* Respects he not *your birth*,
> Your *honourable* friends, or what you brought
> Why all Kent knows *your parentage* and what you are.[18]
> 　　I.488–91; EMPHASIS ADDED

Alice responds in kind, larding Greene with respect ("Alas, poor *gentleman*, I pity you . . . *Master* Greene," ll. 483–87; emphasis added), echoing his contemptuous description of Arden ("Endanger not yourself for such a *churl*," i.520; emphasis added) and gleefully reiterating the insult in the account she gives to Mosby of their interview:

> I told him all, whereat he stormed amain
> And swore he would cry quittance with the *churl*. . . .
> I whetted on the *gentleman* with words,
> And to conclude, Mosby, at last we grew
> To composition for my husband's death.
> I gave him ten pound to hire *knaves*
> By some device to make away the *churl*.
> 　　I.558–67; EMPHASIS ADDED

" 'Twere cheerful news," Mosby confesses in reply, relishing her contemptuous epithet, "to hear the *churl* were dead" (i.574; emphasis added).

The real significance of such traded insults, with their collapsing of social differences, is not so much to cancel one another out as to suggest how much any claim to status is dependent on the claimant's power to enforce it.

This is made chillingly clear in the scenes involving the two most socially degraded characters in the play, the masterless former soldiers Black Will and Shakebag. The moment Black Will receives his cash advance on Arden's murder from Greene, he perceives his victim as a man given into his power and stripped of any claim to status by that very fact: "My fingers itches to be at the *peasant*"—an attitude Greene is careful to nourish when the two cut-throats show signs of reneging: "Remember how devoutly thou hast sworn to kill the *villain*" (ii.110; iii.90–1; emphasis added). From Black Will's and Shakebag's perspective, Arden's helplessness reduces him to the level of his cowardly servant, Michael, the "milksop *slave*" (v.37; vii.4) who grovels to "Master Shakebag" (iii.133) and whom they repeatedly abuse as a "coistrel" (v.41,59), "hind" (v.44) "villain" (vii.1) and "peasant" (iii.136; v.38). As Whigham notes, Black Will's amour propre is offended by the upstart pre-tension he detects in Michael's daring to undertake an oath of murder: "How comes it then that such a *knave* as you / Dare swear a matter of such conse-quence" (iii.153–4). And in a marvelous touch of psychological realism, it is Will's social insults that haunt Michael's nightmares, when he imagines "piti-less Black Will" crying "Stab the *slave*! / The *peasant* will detect the tragedy!" (iv.80–1). What Michael's terror reveals, with desperate clarity, is that in the last analysis the application of such language is simply a function of the ruthless capacity for violence exercised by the brutes whom he is com-ically careful to address as "gentlemen" (iii.166) and "sirs" (vii.4).

Cynical as their abuse of such language may be, however, it is important to recognize that Black Will and Shakebag are far from being indifferent to the feverish competition for status in which the other characters are embroiled. Black Will's readiness to murder Arden is entangled with fantasies of the humiliating power it will enable him to exercise over Mosby and Alice:

> Say thou seest Mosby kneeling at my knees,
> Offering me *service* for my high attempt;
> And sweet Alice Arden, with a lap of crowns,
> Comes with a *lowly curtsey* to the earth,
> Saying, "Take this but for thy quarterage;
> Such yearly *tribute* will I answer thee."
> III.95–100; EMPHASIS ADDED

Moreover Will's relations with his past and present companions are themselves defined by a persistent barging and jostling for status. Thus a good deal of the action in his first scene is taken up with the edgy by-play in which the cutpurse asserts his superiority to the prosperous goldsmith, Bradshaw. Bradshaw is a former companion in arms, and in close conversation with the man he respectfully hails as "Master Greene" (ii.1,7,72,77), the goldsmith has identified Shakebag as "a knave" simply for bearing Black Will company, "for such a *slave*, so *vile* a rogue as he / Lives not again upon the earth" (ll. 3–6; emphasis added). When, however, Bradshaw appears anxious to repudiate the familiarity implied in the rogue's greeting of him as "fellow Bradshaw," Will is quick to remind him of their shared past as soldiers in France,

> where I was a corporal and thou but a *base mercenary groom?* "No fellows now" because you are a goldsmith and have a little plate in your shop? You were glad once to call me "fellow Will" and, with a curtsey to the earth, "one snatch, good corporal," when I stole the half ox from John the victualler, and *domineered* with it amongst good fellows in one night. . . . [Those days be not past with me], for I keep that *honourable* mind still. Good *neighbour* Bradshaw, you are too proud to be my fellow, but were it not that I see company coming down the hill, I would be fellows with you once more, and share crowns with you too.
>
> LL. 19–31; EMPHASIS ADDED

Later in the play, as his confidence swells, Black Will will strike a similarly aggressive stance toward the man by whom he was first hired, addressing him insultingly as "Sirrah Greene" and boasting that "I have cracked as many blades as thou has done nuts" (xiv.1, 10). Moreover Will's constant prickliness about status is what fires his quarrel with his companion Shakebag when they begin to argue about their relative prowess in taking purses—

> You were best swear me on the interrogatories
> How many pistols I have took in hand,
> Or whether I love the smell of gunpowder
> Or dare abide the noise the dag will make,
> Or will not wink at flashing of the fire.
> I pray *thee*, Shakebag, let this answer *thee*,
> That I have took more purses in this Down
> Than e'er *thou* handlest pistols in *thy* life.
>
> IX.6–14; EMPHASIS ADDED

And when Shakebag defies him, Will once again appeals to his "honourable" record as a soldier:

> It is not for mine honour to bear this.
> Why, Shakebag, I did serve the king at Boulogne,
> And *thou* canst brag of nothing *thou* hast done.
>
> LL. 23–5; EMPHASIS ADDED

The tone of Will's remonstrations, which makes a brawl between these two inevitable, is established by another linguistic detail to which modern ears are unattuned—the contempt implicit in his aggressive deployment of the second-person singular pronoun. In late sixteenth-century English the use of "thou" and "you" continued to be governed (as in a number of modern European languages) by a carefully modulated semantics of power and solidarity. "Thou" was the pronoun of intimacy, but it also replaced the more distant and respectful "you" to express condescension toward children, servants, and other social inferiors. In the latter usage it could, of course, be highly provocative if directed, in breach of semantic protocol, at social equals or superiors—as, for example, when Sir Toby Belch advises Sir Andrew Aguecheek to stir up his imagined rival, "the Count's youth," with an insultingly phrased challenge: "Taunt him with the license of ink. If thou thou'st him some thrice, it shall not be amiss" (*Twelfth Night*, 3.2.42–4).[19] The emotional temperature of almost every scene in *Arden* can be monitored through the characters' management of such niceties of address. Thus in his confrontation with Arden in scene xiii, Reede begins (despite his expressed resentment against "the carl") by addressing him in a mollifying language of respect: "*Master* Arden . . . my coming to *you* was about the plot of ground / Which wrongfully *you* detain from me" (ll. 11–13; emphasis added). But Arden derisively responds to him as "fellow" (l. 18) and "sirrah" (l. 21), and then belabors him with six condescending singular pronouns in as many lines:

> If with *thy* clamorous impeaching tongue
> *Thou* rail on me as I have heard *thou* dost,
> I'll lay *thee* up so close a twelve month's day
> As *thou* shalt neither see the sun nor moon.
> Look to it; for, as surely as I live,
> I'll banish pity if *thou* use me thus.
>
> LL. 22–7; EMPHASIS ADDED

Reede responds in kind, thou-ing Arden remorselessly, contemptuously
stripping him of his honorific ("What, wilt *thou* do me wrong and threat me
too? / Nay then, I'll tempt *thee, Arden;* do *thy* worst," ll. 28–9), and at last collapsing all distance between them in the murderous intimacy of his departing
curse "And thus I go, but leave my curse with *thee*" (l. 53).

Returning to the first explosive confrontation between Arden and
Mosby, we can trace the rising tension of the encounter through the characters' careful fencing with honorifics and pronouns. Alice attempts to set the
tone for the scene by audibly addressing her lover as "Master Mosby" (i.291),
using the term of respect hitherto accorded him only by the exaggeratedly
deferential Clarke (l. 259). She does this not only to deceive her husband by
suggesting a properly courteous distance between herself and their visitor
but (more subversively) to imply an equality of status between lover and husband.[20] Mosby immediately capitalizes on her tactic, hailing his rival as
"Master Arden" even as he is careful to deny the term to "Greene," whom he
rhetorically consigns to the dependent role of "one of Sir Anthony Ager's
men [servants]"—thus implying a parity between himself and Arden that
equivocates dangerously between flattery and challenge:

> *Master* Arden, being at London yesternight,
> The Abbey lands whereof you are now possessed
> Were offered me on some occasion
> By *Greene*, one of Sir Antony Ager's men.
>   I.292–5; EMPHASIS ADDED

Arden's cutting riposte dismisses Mosby's pretensions by depriving him of
the prefix Alice has ostentatiously awarded him, while peremptorily asserting
authority over his wife:

> *Mosby*, that question we'll decide anon.
> Alice, make ready my breakfast; I must hence.
> As for the lands, *Mosby*, they are mine.

Finally he breaks into open insult, shifting from the courteously distant
"you" to a contemptuous "thou" as he stigmatizes Mosby with his low-born
origins:

> But I must have a mandate for my wife;
> They say you seek to rob me of her love.

Villain, what makes *thou* in her company?
She's no companion for *so base a groom*.
    1.298–305; EMPHASIS ADDED

Only when Mosby has publicly repudiated his designs on Alice and confessed the distance between them by acknowledging that his own sister is her
waiting-maid (l. 334) will Arden condescend to dignify him as "Master
Mosby," tactfully separating him from his would-be brother-in-law, the servant whom he dismisses as "Sirrah Michael" (l. 363). He will repeat this con-
ciliatory gesture in scene xiv, after their second public quarrel, in which a
brawl has been precipitated by Arden's baldly insulting greeting "Mosby . . .
thou ribald knave" (xiii.77–8). Throughout their parade of reconciliation
Arden and Mosby lard one another with the disputed honorific in a display of
competitive homosocial courtesy that climaxes in Mosby's sardonically triumphant signal to his fellow-murderers: "Ah, Master Arden, 'Now I can take
you' " (l. 232).
    "Master" here is effectively in ironic quotation marks. Far from fixing his
place in any "historical record," Arden's titular mastership turns out to mark
the site of a murderous struggle for position. Indeed it is the linguistic equivalent of that domestic throne that Mosby has dreamed of possessing (viii.31)
and at which Alice gestures in one of the play's most tellingly contradictory
moments:

I'll have my will.
Master Mosby, sit you in my husband's seat.
    XIV.286–7

This is the point at which the whole patriarchal order threatens to
unravel, in a fashion wickedly underlined by the sexual pun on "seat"; for if
the woman is indeed to have her "will," then the usurper's mastership (as
Mosby fears) is itself in danger of usurpation.[21] No wonder that the servant
Michael, in a provocative aside, now suggests that he and the serving-woman
he once flatteringly wooed as "Mistress Susan" (iii.3) should themselves sit
down and repudiate their servile roles. In the confusion that surrounds
Arden's murder, the panicky Alice (as if unconsciously registering the way in
which her destabilization of the social order will leave her more exposed than
ever to the power of competing males) not only dignifies Michael with the
epithet "gentle" (xiv.30, 40) and salutes Shakebag, Black Will, and Greene as
"gentlemen" (xiv.50) but indiscriminately flatters Mosby, Franklin, the

Mayor, and even Greene and the lowly Bradshaw with the title of "master" (xiv.278, 281, 285, 287, 349, 362, 369, 374, 408). In this way the very language that is designed to assert and reinforce the differences of rank and status serves only to confuse them, constantly reminding us that, just as there are no true "peasants" in the play, so there are no certain "gentlemen" either. The only exception is Lord Cheiny, whose sudden appearance in scene 9 miraculously delivers Arden from the ambush on Rainham Down, prompting Black Will's sardonic reflection on his role as deus ex machina:

✿

GREENE:
The Lord of Heaven hath preserved him.
BLACK WILL:
The Lord of Heaven a fig! The Lord Cheiny hath preserved him.
    IX.142–3

✿

In Cheiny's presence, Arden (whom he is condescending enough to greet as "*Master* Arden") and Franklin (whom he more brusquely identifies as "My Lord Protector's *man*") compete in expressions of carefully inflected deference. Arden expresses himself *"Your honour's* always! *Bound* to do you *service,"* while Franklin, acknowledging his place as servant to the Lord Protector, also declares himself "highly *bound* to you"(ll. 101, 106; emphasis added). Even Black Will gives way to uncharacteristically abject wheedling:

God save *your honour.*
I am your *beadsman, bound* to pray for you.
    LL. 119–20; EMPHASIS ADDED

Yet the moment rescuer and intended victim have left the stage, Will's suppressed loathing and contempt bursts out in a fury of indignation, in which the coin that Cheiny has disdainfully given him is transformed into a violent revolutionary metaphor:

The Devil break your necks at four miles' end!
Zounds, I could kill myself for very anger! . . .
I would his crown were molten down his throat. . . .
If all the Cheinies in the world say no,

I'll have a bullet in [Arden's] breast tomorrow.
  LL. 128–32, 146–7

In the end lordship matters here no more than mastership, and it is perhaps significant that Cheiny has no part to play in the tragedy's ambiguous denouement, where the imperfect restoration of order is entrusted to the eminently bourgeois and anonymous figure of the mayor.

  The inevitable result of such destabilization of traditional hierarchies, *Arden* suggests, is the unfettered play of individual desire, a Hobbesian contest of wills in which even the most intimate of bonds of loyalty and kinship cease to count for anything. What is foreshadowed is nothing less than the absolute social disintegration where everything includes itself in power, will, and appetite that is imagined by Shakespeare's Ulysses—though the vision is uncomplicated by the nihilistic irony that compromises every moral posture in *Troilus and Cressida*. If the social climbing of Arden, Mosby, and Greene is echoed in the subversive desire of Arden's wife to "rule herself," it is also reflected in his servant Michael's plan to secure his marriage into Mosby's rising family by usurping his elder brother's estate:

> I'll make her more worth than twenty painters can,
> For I will rid mine elder brother away,
> And then the farm of Bolton is mine own.
> Who would not venture for a house and land,
> When he may have it for a right-down blow?
>   I.171–5

The logical end of such rampant individualism is represented in the cheerful self-advertisement of Black Will and Shakebag:

🏵

BLACK WILL:
How? Twenty angels? Give my fellow George Shakebag and me twenty angels, and if thou't have thy own father slain that thou mayest inherit his land we'll kill him.

SHAKEBAG:
Ay, thy mother, thy sister, thy brother, or all thy kin.
  II.87–90

❋ ❋ ❋

Readings of *Arden of Faversham* that concentrate on the sexual intrigue between Alice and Mosby, pitching her "bourgeois Clytemnestra" against his "low-pressure Macbeth," habitually overlook the imbrication of erotic desire (and indeed of affective relations generally) with the appetite for property and status that is everywhere apparent in the play.[22] Michael's expressed willingness to "kill my master, / Or anything that you will have me do" (i.162–3) is not simply a *response* to Alice's promise to reward him with Susan Mosby's hand, any more than his preparedness to "rid mine elder brother away" is the *result* of a wish to gratify his bride; these things are shown as inseparable corollaries of one another. It is no accident that Alice should reinforce her promise of Susan's hand to Clarke with the asseveration "as I am a gentlewoman" (i.286), for a kind of gentility by association is what the marriage promises the painter—as Mosby in effect acknowledges by dressing plain "Clarke" with the title of "Master" at the very point where he declares "I am content my sister shall be yours" (i.607). Just as the painter Clarke's "love" for Susan is the expression of his ambition to claim as "brother" (i.262) the man he salutes as "Master Mosby" (l. 259) and flatters for his "noble mind" (l. 269), so Michael's "love" is indivisible from his ambitious rivalry with Clarke ("I'll make her more worth than twenty painters can"). Clarke cuts short his Ovidian protestations with the tellingly abrupt demand, "Then tell me, Master Mosby, shall I *have* her" (l. 259), just as Michael's inept love letter is interlarded with abject expressions of duty and respect for "Mistress Susan" (iii.3–15). The final confrontation between these two rivals turns not on the degree of their love for their "mistress" but on their mutually inflamed sense of social superiority—Clarke sneering at Michael as "a serving-creature" (x.61) and Michael responding to Clarke's threat of beating with a variation on Arden's contemptuous flourish with the pressing iron, "What, with a dagger made of pencil?" (l. 70).

Nowhere, of course, is the entanglement of sexuality and status more apparent than in the adulterous triangle at the center of the play. It is entirely fitting that Alice should define her relationship with husband and lover in terms of Mosby's superior "title" to her heart (i.102), since "title" is a word that expresses the traditional relation between property and status. "Mosby," she tells him, in response to his insinuating request to be allowed "to play your husband's part" (i.637), "you know who's master of my heart; / He well may be the master of the house" (638–9). Sexual and social "part," wife's body and husband's estate become at this point absolutely interchangeable.[23] Alice's disputed body resembles the disputed abbey land in that both are vehicles of status. Arden's resentment at her degrading affair with the "servile" Mosby is in exact proportion to the pride in her aristocratic connections implicit in his habitually ingratiating forms of address, "gentle Alice" (i.87, 91) and "gentle Mistress Alice" (i.380; xiv.206). Mosby's soliloquy on ambition at the beginning of scene eight frankly acknowledges that Alice is merely the instrument by which he means to supplant Arden and to become "sole ruler of mine own" (viii.36), and their scenes together make the social basis of their infatuation painfully apparent. When, at their first encounter in the play, Mosby shows signs of cooling, Alice immediately taunts him with his debased origins:

> *Base peasant*, get thee gone,
> And boast not of thy conquest over me,
> Gotten by witchcraft and mere sorcery,
> For what hast *thou* to countenance my love,
> Being *descended of a noble house*
> And matched already with a *gentleman*
> Whose *servant thou* may'st be.
>   I.198–204; EMPHASIS ADDED

Wounded by her slurs, Mosby's only recourse is to strip Alice herself of the very terms of respect that mark her desirability and her power over him: so he denounces her as "Ungentle and unkind" (i.205)—as exhibiting, that is to say, behavior improper to one of her supposedly genteel "kind" *(genus, gens)* and thus betraying her essential baseness.

The gesture is at this point only an expression of pique, but when they fall to quarrelling again in scene eight, after he has resolved on the need to "cleanly rid [his] hands of her" once he has secured Arden's estate, Mosby is ready to demolish the basis of Alice's power. Alice at first seems ready to repent their liaison and return to her role as "honest Arden's wife," and she once again berates Mosby for the baseness that has made her "sland'rous to all my kin":

> Even in my forehead is *thy* name engraven,
> A *mean artificer*, that *low-born name*.
>   VIII.76–7; EMPHASIS ADDED

But Mosby now feels strong enough to reply in kind, arguing that her very liaison with him has emptied her claim to rank and made him her superior, elevating his claim to bourgeois "credit" above her hollow appeal to aristocratic honor:

> if you stand so nicely at your fame,
> Let me repent the credit I have lost.
> I have neglected matters of import
> That would have stated me above thy state. . . .
> Ay, Fortune's right hand Mosby hath forsook
> To take a wanton giglot by the left.
> I left the marriage of an honest maid
> Whose dowry would have weighed down all *thy* wealth. . . .
> *Thou* art not *kind*, till now I knew *thee* not
> And now the rain hath beaten off *thy* gilt
> Thy *worthless copper* shows *thee counterfeit*. . . .
> Go, get *thee* gone, a copesmate for *thy hinds*!
> I am too good to be *thy* favourite.
>   VIII.82–106; EMPHASIS ADDED

Finally, by harping sarcastically on her view of him as a "base artificer"—"Make love to *you?* Why 'tis unpardonable; / *We beggars* must not breathe where *gentles* are" (viii.135–9; emphasis added)—he forces from her the confession that amounts to an absolute abdication of her inherited power over him:

> Sweet Mosby is as gentle as a king,
> And I too blind to judge him other wise.
> Flowers do sometimes spring in fallow lands,
> Weeds in gardens, roses grown on thorns;
> So whatso'er my Mosby's father was,
> Himself is valued *gentle* by his worth,
>   LL. 140–5; EMPHASIS ADDED

The edge of cruelty in this relationship makes it tempting to read the play as a Strindbergian investigation of the sexual excitements of class. But that would, I think, be to fall into an anachronism, because it would imply the *priority* of sexual desire, whereas in *Arden* even Alice's desire for Mosby is largely a function of her desire to live, as she puts it, "without control" (i.273), to throw off the government of her husband and "to rule myself" (x.90). The irony of her situation, of course, is that (Caliban-like) she can, in the last resort, conceive no way of doing this other than by substituting a new (and worse) master for the old. It goes without saying, however, that this does not in any way diminish the transgressiveness of her actions—quite the reverse.[24]

As with Cleopatra or with Beatrice Joanna in *The Changeling* it is rank that appears to be the primary source of Alice's sexual attractiveness, and for that reason she experiences sexuality itself as a legitimate mode of power—one that enables her to exploit the patriarchal hierarchy of social relations even as she helps to destabilize it. This is the power we see Alice shamelessly exercising over Black Will, as though instinct had taught her to respond to his sexually charged fantasy of "Sweet Alice Arden with a lap of crowns."[25]

> For every drop of his detested blood
> I would have crammed in angels in thy fist,
> And kissed thee, too, and hugged thee in my arms. . . .
> Come, Black Will, that in mine eyes art fair.
> Next unto Mosby do I honor thee.
> Instead of fair words and large promises
> My hands shall play you golden harmony.
> XIV.74–6, 117–20

In Alice's "golden harmony," or the "crowns" that Black Will's imagination heaps in her lap, the play's ruthlessly materialist conflation of honor, wealth, status, power, and sexual attractiveness becomes as explicit as it could possibly be. What *Arden* suggests is that sexuality provides the only medium through which women can enjoy the power that attaches to status, the only means by which they can pretend to act "without control" and exercise a claim to "rule" or "government." Yet the exercise of this power, whether in the domination of their natural domestic "masters" or in the seduction of their social inferiors must inevitably (like male ambition) undermine the very order on which its gratification depends. In this context Alice's flirtation with Black Will acquires a kind of emblematic status: his ferocious egoism, like his name, providing a kind of answer to the old riddle about what it is that women most desire. Women are dangerous not, as the Ferryman suggests, because they are "governed by the moon" (xi.17)—that is, by their sexual organs, or "wills"—but rather because they themselves have a will to govern. "Friend," inquires Franklin of the Ferryman, "what is thy opinion of this mist." The Ferryman replies with what seems at first sight a puzzling analogy: "I think 'tis like to a curst wife in a little house, that never leaves her husband till she have driven him out of doors with a wet pair of eyes" (xi.11–13). But *Arden of Faversham* contemplates a world that is indeed "in a mist" (to use the phrase with which Webster's Bosola evokes a rather different vision of social disorder), its boundaries and systems of difference fatally blurred.

The account of *Arden* I offer by no means seeks to replace the approaches of Belsey, Orlin, and others. Instead I seek to demonstrate that historical criticism ought to mean more than simply assimilating dramatic texts to dominant discourses, however rich and compelling the contextual fabric in which these are evoked. A fully historicized reading, as Whigham's work reminds us, needs to be a literary reading too—one that is responsive to the distinctive ways in which the texts traditionally privileged as "literature" can illuminate the past. Any summary account of the social vision of *Arden of Faversham* will show it as both conventional and conservative. What makes the play historically fascinating as well as theatrically compelling is the way it is able to bring that vision alive, to dramatize it by exploiting the very fractures and tensions that the discourse of rank was produced to disguise. To read *Arden* (or any literary work) in this way is discover a point at which the aesthetic and the historical become effectively indivisible.

Massinger's Patriarchy: The Social Vision of A New Way to Pay Old Debts

An household is as it were a little commonwealth, by the good government whereof God's glory may be advanced, and the commonwealth which standeth of several families benefitted.
—John Dod and Robert Cleaver, *A Godly Forme of Household Gouernment*

Strangely, since it is one of Massinger's few acknowledged successes and the most frequently performed of his plays, *A New Way to Pay Old Debts* has received scant critical attention. The play's continuing popularity evidently depends on the powerful characterization of Sir Giles Overreach, but the scale of this villain-hero and the violence of his end have led to uneasiness about the "melodramatic" quality of the action, and about the moralization that accompanies it.[1] Moreover the tendency to read the play simply as Jonsonian satire of an extortionate arriviste—an outsize burlesque of Sir Giles Mompesson—can make the love plot of Margaret Overreach and Alworth seem an irrelevant exercise in Fletcherian pathos, and the graver courtship of Lord Lovell and Lady Alworth a concession to the courtly preciosity of the Phoenix audience.[2] Seen like this, *A New Way* may appear not only structurally confused but morally objectionable—especially in its vindication of Welborne, whose only obvious "right" to restoration of the fortune he has wantonly squandered is that indicated by his name: the birthright he shares with the idealized "true gentry" of the play. Coolly regarded, Welborne's "new way" is no more than a usurpation of the Machiavellian stratagems of the new man Overreach himself, and it is justifiable only by a kind of indulgent snobbery little better than the time-serving deference of characters like Marrall and Tapwell.

> When he was rogue Welborne, no man would believe him
> And then his information could not hurt us.
> But now he is right worshipful again,
> Who dares but doubt his testimony? . . .
> He has found out such a new way
> To pay his old debts, as 'tis very likely
> He shall be chronicl'd for't.
> 4.2.13–29

The lines are those of Tapwell, who respects no other chronicle than his alehouse register "in chalk" (1.1.25–6), but there can be no doubt that from Massinger's point of view the Welborne who offers his service to "king and country" at the end of the play, is already reenrolled in the chronicles of honor. "True gentry, " it would seem, for all its fine rhetoric of "honour," "report," and "chronicle," can survive only through the unscrupulous improvisation of the entrepreneur. To be "worshipful," to be "worthy" in this world is to be "worth" enough to pay your debts—to be a "good man" in Shylock's sense of the term. And if that is truly the case, then the whole elaborately created world of manners, of polite decorum and nice social discriminations, by which the dramatist sets so much store, becomes a dishonest decoration on the surface of reality.[3]

However, it appears to me that *A New Way* is at once more coherent in its dramatic structure and more consistent in its social vision than this reading would imply—even if there remain lurking contradictions that Massinger's comic catastrophe never satisfactorily resolves. Like *The Merchant of Venice*, with which it is often compared, *A New Way* is about the pangs of transition to a capitalistic, cash-nexus society, and like Shakespeare, Massinger takes a fundamentally conservative attitude toward that process, asserting the primacy of communal bonds over legal bondage, of social obligation over commercial debt, and of love over the law.[4] *The Merchant*, however, founds its critique of bourgeois values upon a familiar Christian mythos—the opposition of the Old Law and the New—and in a reassuring comic paradox neutralizes its new man, the Machiavellian capitalist, by making him a representative of the Old Law, rendered obsolete by the sacrifice of Christ. The Jew-Devil Shylock "stands for" Law, Portia for Sacrifice.[5] Though Sir Giles Overreach is sometimes made to appear like yet another diabolic incarnation from the Moralities, and though Massinger invokes scriptural analogues for his judgment of prodigal Welborne and the false servant Marrall, *A New Way* has no such thorough mythic foundation.[6] Instead it appeals to a whole set of normative social assumptions that, although they were customarily justified by the scriptures, were in fact peculiar to Massinger's own epoch. Because they belong, in Peter Laslett's phrase, to "the world we have lost," they can make *A New Way* seem a less universal comedy than its predecessor, but they also make it considerably more vivid as a document of historical attitudes. Massinger brings alive, as perhaps none of his contemporaries can, the ingrained social beliefs that were to make Sir Robert Filmer's writings the handbook of a generation of Royalist gentry.[7]

In the last big speech of the play, Welborne reminds us of the double nature of the "debts" that must be paid before the social order can be reestablished:

> There is something else
> Beside the repossession of my land,
> And payment of my debts, that I must practise.
> I had a reputation, but 'twas lost
> In my loose courses; and till I redeem it
> Some noble way, I am but half made up.
>   5.1.390–5

The "making up" of his "worshipful" self is dependent on the "making up" of a moral obligation more powerful than any merely financial debt. The method of redemption he proposes is that of "service"—service to his king, fittingly discharged through the medium of his immediate social superior, Lord Lovell (5.1.396–400). The idea of service is a crucial one in the play, one that is pointedly taken up in the epilogue, where Massinger playfully sees himself as the servant of the audience, seeking his freedom by the "manumission" of their applause (epilogue, ll. 403–4). He elaborates the conceit in his dedicatory epistle, by way of graceful compliment to the Earl of Caernarvon, whose protection he seeks to earn by "my service," recalling that "I was born a devoted servant, to the thrice noble family of your incomparable Lady," and then hopefully subscribing himself "Your Honour's true servant." Massinger, though he came of minor gentry, was born into service in the sense that his father was steward to the household of Henry Herbert, Earl of Pembroke, and the dedication invites us to read *A New Way* as a tribute to the ideals he imbibed at Wilton—as itself a new way to pay a personal debt of honor.[8]

Even the element of topical satire in the play can be seen to accord with this complementary purpose, since, as Patricia Thomson has pointed out, Mompesson, as Buckingham's protégé, was a natural enemy of the Herberts. But Overreach's villainy, of course, touches only tangentially on Mompesson's malpractice. Mompesson is important to the dramatist's imagination less as a venal monopolist than as the hideous type of an alarming social tendency. A contemporary comment on Mompesson, cited by L. C. Knights, may help to make this point clearer:

> Sir Giles Mompesson had fortune enough in the country to make him happy, if that sphere could have contained him, but the vulgar and universal error of satiety with present enjoyments made him too big for a rustical condition, and when he came at court he was too little for that, so that some novelty must be taken up to set him in *aequilibrio* to the place he was in, no matter what it was, let it be never so pestilent and mischievous to others, he cared not, so he found benefit by it.[9]

Mompesson's crime amounted to a double violation of that principle of service on which the order of society was founded: he had betrayed the obligations of that office in which the king had placed him, and he had attempted to rise above that position in society to which God had called him. Overreach is an incarnation of the anarchic impulse that seemed to fuel Mompesson's corrupt ambition. In his brutal assault on the bonds of a society felt to subsist on an intricate hierarchical network of communal service and mutual obligation, he is the nightmare projection of emergent capitalism, the monstrous herald of that new social order whose perfection Marx was to describe:

> The bourgeoisie, wherever it has got the upper hand, has put an end to all feudal, patriarchal, idyllic relations. It has pitilessly torn asunder the motley feudal ties that bound man to his *natural superiors*, and has left remaining no other nexus between man and man than naked self-interest, than callous *cash-payment*. . . . The bourgeoisie has stripped of its

halo every occupation hitherto honoured and looked up to. . . . It has converted the physician, the lawyer, the priest, the poet, the man of science, into its paid wage-labourers. The bourgeoisie has torn away from the family its sentimental veil, and has reduced the family relation to a mere money-relation.[10]

Overreach's household includes Marrall, Will-do, and Greedy—lawyer, priest, and justice—among its paid wage-laborers. And "family" for him— as his relations with his nephew, and ultimately with his daughter too, illustrate—simply denotes a nexus of money relationships: when Welborne has lost his money, Overreach will no longer acknowledge their kinship.

In contrast to the vast and ruthlessly impersonal machine conceived by Marx, the social order imagined by most of Massinger's contemporaries was that of a large family ruled by a father-sovereign. Each family was itself a commonwealth (a paternal monarchy), and the state a family of such petty commonwealths. The relationship was not merely one of analogy, for it was from the first family that the state itself had grown.[11] The hierarchic order of society was thus a natural part of the divinely ordained scheme of things. Whatever the philosophic limitations of such patriarchalist thought, it took immense strength, as Gordon Schochet has shown, from its close correspondence to the practical socialization of the vast majority of seventeenth-century Englishmen, for whom the family, or household, was the focus of most activity: "some form of paternal authority was the only kind of status relationship with which most of these people were familiar. . . . Childhood was not something which was eventually outgrown; rather it was enlarged to include the whole of one's life."[12]

Sir Robert Filmer's *Patriarcha*, written in the 1640s, is only the best known of a series of works that adumbrated the patriarchal model of society. With his *Observations upon Aristotle's Politiques* (1652) it constitutes the latest and most systematic attempt to work out a set of ideas that were already among the commonplaces of social thought in Massinger's time. When King James wrote in *Basilikon Doron* that a prince should act toward his people "as their natural father and kindly Master," he appealed implicitly to a whole context of commentary that made of the Fifth Commandment a scriptural justification for all authority.[13] Prominent contributions to this pious tradition include Bartholomew Batty's *Christian Mans Closet*, translated by William Lowth in 1581, and two immensely popular books by John Dod and Robert Cleaver, *A Godly Forme of Household Gouernment* (1598) and *A Plaine and*

Familiar Exposition of the Ten Commandements (1604).[14] Society, from the perspective of these patriarchalists, consists of a community of priestlike fathers and their families, natural autocracies modified only by a carefully ordained set of mutual duties and obligations. "Parents are God's vicars in earth," writes Batty, in laying out "The Duty of Children towards their Parents," and "all are understood by the name parents, under whose government we live," including "Magistrates, Elders, Preachers, Masters, Teachers, Tutors and such like." Dod and Cleaver similarly warn children "that whatsoever they do to their fathers and mothers . . . they do it to God," and in the word *father* "are contained all superiors in what place soever set above us." Thus the servant, too, is to remember that his master "stands in the place to Christ unto thee, being of his family."[15] The principal duty of the paterfamilias is to ensure the fit ordering of his household, to enforce the proprieties of place: "There are two sorts in every perfect family: 1. The Governors. 2. Those that must be ruled." If this sounds like a formula for domestic tyranny, Dod and Cleaver insist that "these two sorts have special duties belonging to them, the one towards the other" and that fathers must not act "as tyrants" but treat children and servants alike "lovingly and Christianly." In laying out this "godly form of household government," Dod and Cleaver are not simply elaborating a metaphor, for in their estimation "it is impossible for a man to understand how to govern the commonwealth, that doth not rule his own house." The connection must have seemed a natural one in a society where, as Schochet emphasizes, political identity was effectively itself a function of familial headship.[16]

For the lesser members of the domestic commonwealth "social identity was altogether vicarious. The family was represented to the larger community by its head . . . and those whom he commanded were 'subsumed' in his social life."[17] Constrictive as such a family looks from our point of view, it provided its members with a sense of secure identity and gave to society at large a comfortably human scale whose threatened loss was understandably painful.[18] Massinger's play is in some sense about this threat, and the horror it evokes in the dramatist helps to explain the titanic stature of Overreach. If Sir Giles's colossal ambition seems somehow too large for the world of social comedy, that is because, in Massinger's imagination, he represents those forces whose insurgence menaces the very possibility of such a world, of an order that is in any familiar sense "social" at all.[19] In the imagery of religious outrage with which this usurper is condemned, Massinger is appealing, like Dod and Cleaver before him, to the hallowed sanctions of patriarchalist ideology.

The very popularity of such treatises as Dod and Cleaver's in a period when traditional organic models of political organizations were subject to an increasingly critical scrutiny is a testimony to the social insecurities that Massinger's play attempts to soothe. But patriarchalist writing itself reflects the pressures of Puritan dissent and the contractual theories with which such dissent was frequently associated. Michael Walzer has argued that the domestic commonwealth imagined by the Puritans Dod and Cleaver already has many features in common with the conjugal family that was to replace the traditional patriarchy. Their conception of the father's role is to some extent a legalistic one, which emphasizes "office" and "duties" at the expense of the natural bonds of affection. Thus it tends to downgrade the historical bonding of kinship, and for the mutual obligations of parent and child, master and servant, to substitute the absolute authority of a father confirmed in office by a divinely ordained contract. In this autocratic commonwealth the nice distinctions of hierarchy that are native to the true patriarchal family are at a discount; where a household can be so simply divided into "The Governors" and "Those that must be ruled," even the basic distinction between children and servants is blurred.[20] Overreach's autocratic tyranny, in which daughter and servants alike are treated as legally indentured agents of the master's will and where the bonds of legal debt take the place of kinship as the principal links in the social chain, is as much an embodiment of a familial as of a commercial "new way." Though the connection may be one that the dramatist himself has not fully grasped, *A New Way to Pay Old Debts* is in some sense a play about religion and the rise of capitalism, and it is a reflection of Massinger's bitter conservatism that an atheistic iconoclast should come to epitomize the Puritan household governor.

In accord with his social menace, Sir Giles Overreach is presented as no common, petty miser—which even Shylock finally is—but a figure of heroic stature. He is a commercial and domestic Tamburlaine, whose *virtu* invites the admiration of Lady Alworth's servants even as they denounce him for his griping extortion:

❁

FURNACE:
To have a usurer that starves himself,
And wears a cloak of one-and-twenty years
On a suit of fourteen groats, bought of the hangman,
To grow rich, and then purchase, is too common:

But this Sir Giles feeds high, keeps many servants,
Who must at his command do any outrage;
Rich in his habit; vast in his expenses;
Yet he to admiration still increases
In wealth, and lordships.
        2.2.106–14

The glamour of his conspicuous consumption links him with Jonsonian antiheroes like Volpone, whose energetic delight in stratagem he explicitly echoes:

I enjoy more true delight
In my arrival to my wealth, these dark
And crooked ways, than you shall e'er take pleasure
In spending what my industry hath compasss'd.
        4.1.135–8[21]

But he is something larger and more terrifying than Jonson's vulpine magnifico: both "a lion, and a fox" (5.1.25), as Lady Alworth sees him—a figure who embodies the martial aspect of the Machiavellian tyrant as well as his politic cunning. It is in heroic terms that we are repeatedly asked to see his diabolic prowess—by Order, for instance:

His frights men out of their estates,
And breaks through all law-nets, made to curb ill men,
As they were cobwebs. No man dares reprove him.
Such a spirit to dare, and power to do, were never
Lodg'd so unluckily.
        2.2.114–8

by Lord Lovell:

I, that have liv'd soldier,
And stood the enemy's violent charge undaunted
To hear this blasphemous beast am bath'd all over
In a cold sweat: yet like a mountain he,
Confirm'd in atheistical assertions,
Is no more shaken, than Olympus is

When angry Boreas loads his double head
With sudden drifts of snow.
    4.1.150–7

And not least in his own vaunting hyperbole:

❀

LOVELL:
Are you not frighted with the imprecations,
And curses, of whole families made wretched
By your sinister practices?
OVERREACH:
Yes, as rocks are
When foamy billows split themselves against
Their flinty ribs; or as the moon is mov'd,
When wolves with hunger pin'd, howl at her brightness.
I am of a solid temper, and like these
Steer on a constant course: with mine own sword
If call'd into the field, I can make that right,
Which fearful enemies murmur'd at as wrong. . . .
Nay, when my ears are pierc'd with widows' cries,
And undone orphans wash with tears my threshold;
I only think what 'tis to have my daughter
Right honourable.
    4.1.111–29

❀

"To have my daughter / Right honourable": the reiterated phrase becomes a kind of transformed bathos, like Tamburlaine's "sweet fruition of an earthly crown," Overreach's equivalent of riding in triumph through Persepolis. While at one extreme such language may link him with the mock-heroic bombast of Greedy, that "monarch . . . of the boil'd, the roast, the bak'd" (3.2.20–1) and pillager of Furnace's pastry fortifications (1.2.25–47), at the other it invites comparison with Lovell's heroic enterprise in the Low Countries. And the power struggle in which Sir Giles is engaged is, the play suggests, of equal moment to that undertaken by his noble adversary. For Overreach is a "blasphemous beast" not merely by virtue of those "atheistical assertions" that horrify Lovell, but through his titanic struggle to subvert an order of society decreed by God himself.

Massinger builds his social argument on the contrasted arrangement of four households or families. Temporarily excluded from this society is the déclassé Welborne, once a "lord of acres," who has prodigally squandered his estates and thus forfeited those titles ("Master Welborne," "your worship") that defined his proper place in the social order. The principal intrigue in the play is devoted to the restoration of this outcast to the power and privileges that belong to his gentlemanly rank and more specifically to his designated position as master of a great household. To fully understand the parameters of his situation and to sympathize with the melancholy rage it inspires in Welborne, one must be sensitive to the nuances of social address by which the play sets so much store. Peter Laslett emphasizes the critical importance of the terminology of rank in this society:

> The term gentleman marked the exact point at which the traditional social system divided up the population into two extremely unequal sections. About a twenty-fifth . . . belonged to the gentry and to those above them in the social hierarchy. This tiny minority owned most of the wealth, wielded the power and made all the decisions. . . . If you were not a gentleman, if you were not ordinarily called *"Master"* by the commoner folk, or *"Your Worship"*; if you, like nearly all the rest, had a Christian and a surname and nothing more; then you counted for little in the world outside your own household. . . . The labourers and husbandmen, the tailors, millers, drovers, watermen, masons, could become constables, parish clerks, churchwardens, ale-conners, even overseers of the poor. . . . [But] they brought no personal weight to the modest offices which they could hold. As individuals they had no instituted, recognised power over other individuals, always excepting . . . those subsumed within their families. Directly they acquired such power, whether by the making or the inheriting of wealth, or by the painful acquisition of a little learning, then they became *worshipful* by that very fact. . . . To exercise power, then, to be free of the society of England, to count at all as an active agent in the record we call historical, you had to be a gentleman. . . . You had to hold one of those exceptional names in a parish register which bore a prefix or a suffix. . . . The commonest addition to a name . . . is *Mr*, for the word "Master," and *Mrs*, for the word "Mistress." . . . *Gent.* and *Esq.* are rare . . . as is the word *Dame*, . . . and *Knight* and *Baronet* are, of course, much rarer still. The reader with the whole population in his mind . . . will, of course, occasionally come across the titles *Lord* or

Lady, and the ceremonious phrase "The right Honourable the . . ." which was often used to introduce them.[22]

Plain Timothy Tapwell and Froth, his wife, belong to that overwhelming majority who are not "free of the society of England," who have no natural powers beyond the compass of their own household. From Welborne's point of view, Tapwell, as his former underbutler, is still a "slave," a "drudge," a servant still bound to his master by the patronage Welborne has given him (1.1.17, 28). Tapwell, on the other hand, sees himself very differently. Having acquired "a little stock" and "a small cottage" through frugal opportunism, he has duly "humbled" himself to marry Froth and set up as an alehouse keeper, his own man (1.1.59–61). From this base he has risen to the point where he is "thought worthy to be scavenger," and from the humble post of parish rubbish-collector he confidently expects to climb to even more exalted office

> to be overseer of the poor,
> Which if I do, on your petition Welborne,
> I may allow you thirteen pence a quarter,
> And you shall thank *my worship*.
> 1.1.68–71; EMPHASIS ADDED

Tapwell, in fact, is a kind of low-life Overreach, his desire to become "worshipful" echoing Sir Giles's passion to have his daughter made "right honourable." He will have Welborne his petitioner as Sir Giles will have Margaret attended by whole trains of "errant knights" and Lady Downefalnes. For both men, "office" denotes not the large Ciceronian concept but a narrow, functionally determined accession of personal power and prestige. Like Sir Giles, too, Tapwell professes a view of society that denies all traditional sanctions; it acknowledges no past, only a pragmatically organized present and a future of untrammelled aspiration.[23] Welborne's appeals to ancient right and to the debts imposed by past generosity are equally vacuous to a man like Tapwell—there is no chronicle of honor or register of benefits in his commonwealth:

❀

WELBORNE:
Is not thy house, and all thou hast my gift?

TAPWELL:
I find it not in chalk, and Timothy Tapwell
Does keep no other register. . . .
What I was *sir, it skills not;*
What you are *is apparent.*
1.1.24–30; EMPHASIS ADDED

❖

His chalk register of debt is the equivalent of Sir Giles's parchment deeds, and both are presented, like Shylock's bond, as the emblems of a social vision that seeks to make the narrow scruple of commercial law the sole principle of human organization. For Tapwell, his fellow office-man the constable is the great prince of this legalistic realm:

There dwells, and within call, if it please your worship,
A potent monarch, call'd the constable,
That does command a citadel, call'd the stocks;
Whose guards are certain files of rusty billmen.
1.1.12–15

This sarcastic degradation of heroic language anticipates, in its heavy way, the cynical wit of the pun with which Sir Giles will deflate the pretensions of "errant" knighthood (2.1.79).

Tapwell can detail the story of that "man of worship, / Old Sir John Welborne, justice of peace, and *quorum*" and even recall the magnanimity of his housekeeping, but the whole report is swept away in a single contemptuous phrase: "but he dying" (1.1.30–7). Sir Giles (who has the current JP, a jumped-up tailor's son, in his pocket) roundly confesses to Lovell, "I do contemn report myself, / As a mere sound" (4.1.91–2). He is equally contemptuous of the obligations of friendship and the duties of office:

'tis enough I keep
Greedy at my devotion: so he serve
My purposes, let him hang, or damn, I care not.
Friendship is but a word.
2.1.19–22

"Words," he insists, "are no substances" (3.2.128)—they are empty ceremonious "forms" that disguise the fact that society is merely an arrangement of
services rendered for cash. Given Overreach's philosophy, his desire to
"Have all men sellers, / And I the only purchaser" (2.1.32–3) is nothing less
than a longing for absolute tyranny. Dod and Cleaver's prescription for wise
domestic government includes a warning against borrowing and usury:
"Salomon saith, The borrower is servant to the lender: that is, beholding to
him, and in his danger." The chain of debt created by Overrreach's lending
is one that seeks to override the traditional obligations of society and to
replace the patriarchal hierarchy with a vicious commercial autarchy governed by himself, the unfettered master of an antifamily of slaves. His own
household, where officers of church and state are already thrown together in
indiscriminate bondage with children and servants, is the model for this new
tyranny, where the issue of his inveterate opponents, the "true gentry," will
be forced "To kneel to mine, as bond-slaves (2.1.81–9).[24]

Set against the conspicuous consumption and cash-nexus relationships of
Sir Giles's household is the ideal of liberal housekeeping embodied in the
households of Welborne's dead father, of Lord Lovell, and most immediately of Lady Alworth. If the anarchic individualism and all-engrossing
ambitions of Sir Giles are emblematized in the names of Marrall and Greedy,
the values of traditional society are suggested by those of the Alworth servants, Order and Watchall. Order, in particular, seldom misses an opportunity for sententious observation on the morality of true service and the hierarchical decorum for which he stands.

> Sir, it is her will,
> Which we that are her servants ought to serve it,
> And not dispute.
>   1.3.4–6[25]

> Set all things right, or as my name is Order,
> And by this staff of office that commands you;
> This chain, and double ruff, symbols of power;
> Whoever misses in his function,
> For one whole week makes forfeiture of his breakfast,
> And privilege in the wine-cellar.
>   1.2.1–6

The sturdy sense of place that informs Order's humor in this last speech contrasts with the ludicrously exaggerated deference of Marrall who addresses even Lady Alworth's waiting-man as "your worship" (2.2.132) and whose groveling before the reborn prodigal shows Massinger's gift for satiric farce at its best:

❋

MARRALL:
Then in my judgement sir, my simple judgement,
(Still with your worship's favour) I could wish you
A better habit, for this cannot be
But much distasteful to the noble lady
(I say no more) that loves you, for this morning
To me (and I am but a swine to her)
Before th' assurance of her wealth perfum'd you,
You savour'd not of amber.

WELBORNE:
I do now then?

MARRALL:
This your batoon hath got a touch of it.
/Kisses the end of his cudgel/
       2.3.20–8

❋

The caricature of courtly style with its self-deprecating parentheses and tactful circumlocutions culminates in a perfect frenzy of servility. Marrall explicitly seeks a "place" in return for his vassalage, "the lease of glebe land [fittingly] called Knave's-Acre." But for him service is merely enslavement, place merely hire and salary. Like Greedy, devastated by the prospect of losing "my dumpling . . . And butter'd toasts, and woodcocks" (3.2.307–8), Marrall finds his "worship" only too readily dispensable.

True service on the other hand, because of its function in a system of mutual obligation, implies self-respect, a solid conviction of one's own worth. Spelled out in this way the opposition may seem too pat, but it is given dramatic life in the easy condescensions and unforced kindness that characterizes relationships in the Alworth household—in the indulgence with which the mistress treats the choleric outbursts of her cook, Furnace, for example—the dignity of his office wounded by her failure to eat (1.2) and in the comically touching affection between the servants and "Our late young master," Alworth (1.2 and 2.2). The language in which young Alworth acknowledges their "service"—"Your courtesies overwhelm me; I much grieve / To part from such true friends, and yet find comfort" (2.2.27–8)— gracefully echoes the terms of his conversation with his own master, Lord Lovell, and with his stepmother, so placing the relations of the domestic "family" in living continuum with the more intimate connections of kinship.[26]

If Alworth is "young master" to his family servants, he himself owes "service" to Lady Alworth and to Lord Lovell—to his stepmother as the explicit incarnation of his father's patriarchal authority (1.2.85–94) and to Lovell as both ruler of his household and as a benevolent patriarch who has been "more like a father to me than a master" (3.1.30). To Lovell is given the crucial speech that defines the difference between the generous housekeeping of "true gentry" and the domestic tyranny of the ambitious arriviste:

> Nor am I of that harsh, and rugged temper
> As some great men are tax'd with, who imagine
> They part from the respect due to their honours,
> If they use not all such as follow 'em,
> Without distinction of their births, like slaves.
> I am not so condition'd; I can make
> A fitting difference between my foot-boy,
> And a gentleman, by want compell'd to serve me.
>   3.1.21–8

Though Alworth is technically a "stipendiary," in the language of Welborne's prickly vanity (1.1.173), his relations with Lovell are governed by a firm sense of mutual obligation—so that if Alworth's duty as a servant requires that he yield his rights in Margaret to his master (3.1), Lovell in turn must prove his paternal care by contriving their elopement from the tyranny of Sir Giles.

Overreach, by contrast, with his leveling disdain for "difference" and "distinction," governs by treating even his own family as stipendiary slaves.[27] Since the only bonds he acknowledges are those of financial debt, he contemptuously denies his bankrupt nephew's kinship—"Thou art no blood of mine. Avaunt thou beggar!" (1.3.40). By the same token, once he recognizes new prospects of indebtedness, he seeks Welborne's friendship with disarming candor, hailing him as "nephew" once again:

> We worldly men, when we see friends, and kinsmen,
> Past hope sunk in their fortunes, lend no hand
> To lift 'em up, but rather set our feet
> Upon their heads, to press 'em to the bottom,
> And I must yield, with you I practis'd it.
> But now I see you in a way to rise,
> I can and will assist you.
>   3.3.50–6

He proposes to redeem Welborne's debts and send him "a *free man* to the wealthy lady" (1.68; emphasis added). But the manumission is one that, as Welborne notes with urbane irony, only "Binds me still your servant" (l. 70). The courtesies of speech are those of the traditional society, their meanings wantonly perverted:

> My *deeds* nephew
> Shall speak my love, what men report, I weigh not.
>   3.2.75–6; EMPHASIS ADDED

For honorable "deeds," the conventional subject of "report," Sir Giles in fact proposes to substitute the parchment deeds that will encompass the final downfall of true gentry. Significantly, this exchange is immediately juxtaposed with a genuine manumission—Lovell's "discharge" of Alworth "from further service" (4.1.1–3), which ends in the acknowledgment of a very different kind of debt, one that admits the primacy of honorable report:

> Let after-times report, and to you honour,
> How much I stand engag'd, for I want language
> To speak my debt.
>   4.1.5–7

It is the opposition we have met before, between Timothy Tapwell's register of chalk and the chronicles of ancient right and historic obligation—between the new morality of contract and the traditional morality of "benefits."

Sir Giles's relation with his daughter, significantly called to account as

"The blest child of my industry, and wealth" (3.2.53), is not qualitatively different from that with his nephew. For it is once again conceived in master/slave terms. Margaret owes him an absolute and peremptory duty (even to the point of prostituting herself to Lovell) and he owes her nothing in return except the promise of those honorable titles that serve to cocker up his own vanity. Shylock's wish to have his revolted daughter dead at his feet can still be read as the outrage of a distorted love; Overreach's attempt to kill Margaret is merely the calling-in of a debt—"thus I take the life / Which wretched I gave to thee" (5.1.292–3).[28] Shylock at least can suffer the pain of lost affection through the ring "I had . . . of Leah when I was a bachelor" (*Merchant of Venice*, 3.1.120); Sir Giles's ring bonds him to no one but becomes the ironic instrument of his daughter's loss to Alworth. His corruption of family relationship to bond-slavery includes his courtship of Lady Alworth—as it must have included the courtship of Mistress Welborne, Margaret's mother. It is finally a matter of indifference to Sir Giles whether the lady marries Welborne or himself: either match will put her fortune in his power. Set against the business contract of the two marriages Overreach attempts to contrive is the "solemn contract" (5.1.66) undertaken by the ideal couples of the play—a contract hedged about by nicely balanced mutual obligations of "honour," "service," and "duty" (4.1, 4.3, and 5.1).

The ending of the play vindicates, as it is bound to do, the traditional bonds of service, housekeeping, and the patriarchal family. Marriage unites the ideal households of the true gentry and establishes young Alworth as master of his own, while Welborne, his financial and moral debts discharged, sets out to redeem his honor under Lord Lovell in "service" to the supreme patriarchy, "my king, and country" (5.1.398–9). The subverters of patriarchal order, on the other hand, are made to feel the hopeless isolation of their position. Marrall, the epitome of perverted service and false friendship, is somewhat smugly dismissed by Welborne to take his own place, stripped of office, among the masterless outcasts of this society:

> You are a rascal, he that dares be false
> To a master, though unjust, will ne'er be true
> To any other: look not for reward,
> Or favour from me. . . .
> I will take order
> Your practice shall be silenc'd.
>
> 5.1.338–44

If "This is the haven / False servants still arrive at" (ll. 349–50), the fate of false masters is even more desperate. Overreach, who hurls from the stage seeking "servants / And friends to second me" (ll. 312–3), finds only revolted slaves. Forced to confront the ironic truth of his own aphorism, "Friendship is but a word," he is left to the maniacal self-assertion of despair:

> Why, is not the whole world
> Included in my self? to what use then
> Are friends, and servants? say there were a squadron
> Of pikes, lin'd through with shot, when I am mounted,
> Upon my injuries, shall I fear to charge 'em? . . .
> No, spite of fate,
> I will be forc'd to hell like to myself.
>   5.1.355–71

If this speech seems to recall *Richard III*, the echo is fitting and perhaps deliberate, since Overreach has come to embody that same anarchic principle of self-love that Shakespeare incarnates in Richard of Gloucester. The forms and bonds of communal society, which for Overreach were vacuous nothings, prove immutably solid, while his own omnipotent bond becomes literally "nothing," "void" (ll. 289, 323), showing (through Marrall's ingenuity) "neither wax, nor words" (l. 186).[29] By the same token the chronicles of honor, which in Overreach's eyes were so much historical dust, prove indestructible, while his own "deed" turns to dust before his eyes:

> What prodigy is this, what subtle devil
> Hath raz'd out the inscription, the wax
> Turn'd into dust! The rest of my deeds whole,
> As when they were deliver'd! and this only
> Made nothing.
>   5.1.190–4

Like Shylock, Sir Giles appeals to law, threatening the power of "statute" and "a hempen circle"—but the whole episode is like a parable of Dod and Cleaver's "justice," a "virtue, that yieldeth to every man his own"; "the riches gotten by ill means, have a heavy destiny uttered against them: The gathering of riches by a deceitful tongue is vanity, tossed to and fro of them that seek death." And Sir Giles's fate is an ample illustration of the doom reserved for the merciless man: "He that stoppeth his ear at the crying of the poor, he shall also cry, and not be heard."[30] Overreach's repudiation of society leaves him to the punishment of his own consuming egotism, "myself alone," without servants, friends, or even kin—a man without a family.[31]

The last irony of his situation, of course, is that his whole enterprise has been designed to build a family, to establish himself as the founding patriarch of a dynasty of "right honorable" descendants. Despite his bitter scorn for the "forms" of the hereditary order, for the hollowness of "word," "name," and "title," Sir Giles is nevertheless mesmerized by these ceremonial tokens. The obsession renders him incapable of living consistently by his ruthlessly economic analysis of society. The unrecognized paradox of his desire to have his daughter made "right honorable" is what finally blinds him to Lovell's stratagem and lures him into a pit of his own digging. He is ultimately destroyed by the same monstrous fury of self-contradiction that drives him to threaten honorable revenge against the man he hopes his daughter will seduce:

> Do I wear a sword for fashion? Or is this arm
> Shrunk up? Or wither'd? does there live a man
> Of that large list I have encounter'd with,
> Can truly say I e'er gave inch of ground,
> Not purchas'd with his blood, that did oppose me?
> Forsake thee when the thing is done? He dares not.
> Give me but proof he has enjoy'd thy person,
> Though all his captains, echoes to his will,
> Stood arm'd by his side to justify the wrong,
> And he himself in the head of his bold troop,
> Spite of his lordship, and his colonelship,
> Or the judge's favour, I will make him render
> A bloody and a strict accompt, and force him
> By marrying thee, to cure thy wounded honor.
>
> 3.2.140–53

Marrall's intervention ("Sir, the man of honor's come," l. 154) points up the absurd irony. The gestures, the rhetoric are those of the very code he is seeking to subvert; they acknowledge debts and accounts of a kind he professes not to countenance, and they are echoed with savage pathos in the berserk frenzy of his final speech:

I'll through the battalia, and that routed,
I'll fall to execution.
[*Flourishing his sword unsheathed*]
Ha! I am feeble:
Some undone widow sits upon mine arm,
And takes away the use of 't; and my sword
Glu'd to my scabbard, with wrong'd orphans' tears,
Will not be drawn.
     5.1.360–5

The disproportion between the ranting heroics of Overreach's defiance and the domestic ordinariness of the situations that provoke it is not an arbitrary comic device: it is the expression of that fatal confusion of purpose on which his life is wrecked. Sir Giles is an instinctive revolutionary whose vision is fatally constricted by the values of the society against which he is in revolt.[32]

But the confusion is not his alone: it also infects his maker. For all the consistency with which Massinger attempts to construct his patriarchal arguments, ambiguities remain in his own stance. Some of these appear in the characterization of his villain. The sense of unbalance that has worried critics of the play has much to do with the overplus of energy and dramatic life in Sir Giles—as though a part of Massinger identified with his violent iconoclasm. And something of the same subversive impulse may be felt in the treatment of Marrall. The psychological penetration with which Massinger uncovers the source of his peculiarly vicious symbiosis of envy and subservience surely springs from the dramatist's own early experience among the upper servants of a great household. The hysterical fury with which Marrall announces his own revolt reveals a sense of deep violation that helps to account for the other revolutionary currents in the play:

❀

OVERREACH:
Mine own varlet
Rebel against me?
MARRALL:
Yes, and uncase you too.
The idiot; the patch; the slave; the booby;
The property fit only to be beaten

For your morning exercise; your football, or
Th' unprofitable lump of flesh; your drudge
Can now anatomize you, and lay open
All your black plots; and level with the earth
Your hill of pride; and with these gabions guarded,
Unloaded my great artillery, and shake,
Nay pulverize the walls you think defend you.
    5.1.213–23 [33]

❦

Yet the levelers of the play can make no common cause. Marrall's revolt
is merely against Sir Giles, and both are simply individualist anarchs. It was
not until Congreve brought the two together in the character of the Double-
Dealer, Maskwell, who combines something of Overreach's iconoclastic
energy with Marrall's humiliated bitterness, that the English stage could produce a genuinely revolutionary comedy. Congreve, significantly, came from
a social background very similar to Massinger's, but he wrote with two revo-
lutions behind him—and even Maskwell is treated as a monster who must be
destroyed in the end.

A further uneasy ambiguity involves the problem of Overreach's own
patriarchal authority, and this may be partly a function of Massinger's
attempt to combine Jonsonian satire with a romantic comedy more immediately appealing to the Phoenix audience. The conventions of satire require
that Marrall be thoroughly punished for his revolt; the conventions of comic
romance insist that Margaret be rewarded for hers. Massinger the conservative satirist is forced to argue that even the worst masters deserve to be
obeyed, even while Massinger the romancer is vindicating the overthrow of
tyrannical fathers. A sincere patriarchalist can hardly have it both ways, since
the authority of fathers and masters is one and indivisible. But both ways are
the way Massinger likes to have it. In *The Roman Actor*, for instance, a similar dilemma is resolved by a pious, but fundamentally evasive, appeal to legitimacy. The First Tribune acknowledges that Domitian was a tyrant who
deserved his end, but warns his assassins that

he was our prince,
However wicked; and, in you, 'tis murder,
Which whosoe'er succeeds him will revenge.
    5.2.77–9

Moralists like Dod and Cleaver had insisted on the limits to patriarchal authority, especially in the matter of forced marriages:

> This is a most unnatural and cruel part, for parents to sell their children for gain and lucre, and to marry them when they list, without the good liking of their children, and so bring them into bondage. . . . Especially in this matter of greatest moment and value of all other worldly things whatsoever, let them . . . beware they turn not their fatherly jurisdiction and government into a tyrannical sourness and waywardness, letting their will go for a law. . . . The rule of parents over their children, ought to resemble the government of good princes toward their subjects: that is to say, it must be mild, gentle, and easy to be borne.[34]

But children are granted no right of revolt against parental bondage— "whatsoever they doe to their fathers and mothers . . . thy do it to God"— and those who marry without their parents' consent incur "the curse of God." Batty similarly insists that even foolish and crabbed parents must be obeyed, and inveighs against the impiety of "private spousages and secret contracts . . . enterprised and taken in hand without the consent of parents."[35] Most patriarchal writing, however, admits an escape clause, and it is one that Massinger gratefully seizes upon. The child's final duty, after all, is to his Father in Heaven, and thus resistance becomes possible to parents or magistrates who command "wicked and ungodly things." "We must obey God rather than man," says Batty: "Honor thou thy father, so that he doth not separate thee from thy true father."[36] From the moment Sir Giles orders Margaret to prostitute herself to Lovell and she identifies the projected match as founded on "devilish doctrine" (3.2.122), from the moment, too, at which Lovell, in confirmation, castigates the blasphemer's "atheistical assertions" (4.1.154), we are meant to see that Overreach's government undermines the very foundations of patriarchal authority. No longer to be regarded as a natural father, he has become simply what Alworth called him, "Mammon in Sir Giles Overreach" (3.1.83).

The invocation of this Morality abstraction exactly anticipates the device by which Massinger seeks to bolster the uncertain ordering of his conclusion. That stroke of divine vengeance that suddenly paralyzes Overreach's sword arm—reminiscent of the astonishing coup by which

D'Amville is made to dash out his own brains in the denouement of *The Atheist's Tragedy*—invites us to review the whole action in theological terms:

> Here is a precedent to teach wicked men
> That when they leave religion, and turn atheists
> Their own abilities leave them.
>   5.1.379–81

In the light of this comfortable moralization a quasi-allegorical scheme begins to emerge by which the whole conclusion is seen to hang on three familiar parables. Most obviously Welborne's redemption from his life of prodigal abandon recalls the forgiveness accorded to another repentant prodigal in Christ's parable. Hungry and in rags in the opening scene, Welborne is the very image of the starving prodigal in Luke. Lady Alworth kills the fatted calf in the feasting that marks his readmission to the patriarchal order, while Sir Giles, that "scourge of prodigals," is ironically cozened into sharing the biblical father's role:

> But the father said to his servants, Bring forth the best robe, and put it on him; and put a ring on his hand, and shoes on his feet.
>   LUKE 15.22

Overreach similarly commands Marrall

> go to my nephew;
> See all his debts discharg'd, and help his worship
> To fit on his rich suit.
>   4.1.33–5

"This my son was dead, and is alive again; he was lost and is found" declares the father of the parable (Luke 15.24). And Overreach, however hypocritically, acknowledges a similar resurrection of the nephew whose kinship he once denied. At the same time the envy and astonishment of the elder brother at the restoration of his wastrel sibling is echoed in the baffled indignation of both Marrall and Overreach at Welborne's sudden elevation. Finally, Welborne's offer of "service" to Lovell and his king at the end of the play is a transposition of the prodigal's penitence:

I will arise and go to my father, and will say unto him, Father, I have
sinned against heaven, and before thee,
And am no more worthy to be called thy son: make me as one of thy
hired servants.

    LUKE 15.18–19

The identification of "Mammon in Sir Giles Overreach" links the fable
in turn to the parable that immediately follows the Prodigal Son in Luke—
the Unjust Steward, a fable about the payment of debts and the morality of
true service that precisely anticipates the play's judgment of Marrall:

If therefore ye have not been faithful in the unrighteous mammon, who
will commit to your trust the true riches?
And if ye have not been faithful in that which is another man's, who
shall give you that which is your own?
No servant can serve two masters: for either he will hate the one, and
love the other; or else he will hold to the one, and despise the other. Ye
cannot serve God and mammon.

    LUKE 16.11–13

"I must grant," Lady Alworth has reflected, as though with this passage
in mind, "Riches well got to be a useful servant, / But a bad master"
(4.1.187–9). Sir Giles's own fate more loosely paraphrases the last of the
parables in this series, that of Dives and Lazarus. The Overreach described
by Furnace who "feeds high, keeps many servants . . . [is] rich in his habit;
vast in his expenses" (2.2.110–2) recalls that "rich man, which was clothed in
purple and fine linen, and fared sumptuously every day" (Luke 16.19); he
spurns the beggar Welborne as Dives spurns the beggar Lazarus, and his desperate fate at the end of the play is equally suggestive. As Sir Giles is carried
off to "some dark room" in Bedlam, his daughter reaches out to him—"O
my dear father!" (5.1.378)—but between them, as between Dives and
Lazarus, "there is a great gulf fixed." Overreach tormented by "furies, with
steel whips / To scourge my ulcerous soul" (ll. 368–9) is already in hell.

In the end this invocation of a theological scheme is a kind of cheat
designed to silence the awkward questions the play has raised. Who, finally,
are the real innovators in this social upheaval: the old gentry who contrive a
deceitful "new way" to pay their "old debts" or Overreach, the proponent of
contract and statute law? In *The Merchant of Venice* such questions are pre-

empted by the triumphant appeal from Old Law to New that is implicit in the play's whole mythic structure. The Jonsonian realism of Massinger's satire forbids so neatly consistent a solution. Furthermore, the play's very conservatism has a revolutionary potential: Overreach, in many ways, is less an usurper than a legitimate patriarch who has tyrannically abused his powers and who accordingly is deposed. In the light of this we may remember that Coleridge thought Massinger "a decided whig," and that some dozen years after *A New Way* the dramatist's views on Charles's personal rule were to attract the indignation and censorship of the king himself. Overreach's deposition, though carried out in the name of the old hierarchic order, has awkward contractual implications—implications of a kind that would be spelled out in the trial and execution of the royal patriarch, Charles I.[37]

Outwardly, however, the social vision of the play remains impeccably conservative. Once again the rigid and indiscriminate operation of law—the new way—is mitigated by the equity of communal obligation—the old debts. The patriarchal hierarchy is conceived not simply as a ladder of authority but also as a family circle—a circle bound by Seneca's decorum of giving, receiving, and returning. The symbol for that bonding, here as in *The Merchant*, is the ring. The ring with which Overreach unwittingly secures his daughter's marriage to young Alworth completes with benign irony a Senecan circle of obligation, by returning to Alworth the lands unjustly taken from his father. Another such circle, broken by the ingratitude of Tapwell and the unkindness of Overreach, is knit up in the restoration of Welborne—a restoration brought about through Lady Alworth's acknowledgment of obligations and determination to "redeem" what's past (1.3.118–9). In the last analysis the play's "new way" (for all its witty duplicity) is an old way, the way of a vanishing society—new only by virtue of its unsatisfactory appeal to New Testament values against the Old (ironically epitomized in the "new man" Overreach). However harmonious the circles contrived in this old new way, they cannot, even in comic fantasy, contain those turbulent spirits whose rise would break the circle forever. Whatever was restored in 1660, it did not include an intact patriarchal ideology. The literature of the Restoration from *Aureng-Zebe* to *Abasalom and Achitophel*, from *Venice Preserved* to *Love for Love*, is full of failing patriarchs, enfeebled, corrupt, and ridiculous by turns. It contemplates a world where, in Otway's words, "the foundation's lost of common good" and that "dissolves all former bonds of service."[38]

"The Tongues of Angels": Charity and the Social Order in The City Madam

"Though you spake with the tongues of angels to me, / I am not to be alter'd." When Luke Frugal dismisses the appeals of his desperate creditors for "patience" and "charity" in this sardonic parody of Saint Paul, he signals what has become the ruling theme of Massinger's comedy of City manners— "though I speak with the tongues of men and of angels, and have not charity, I am become as sounding brass, or a tinkling cymbal" (1 Cor. 13.1)[1] The episode, like many others in the play, is contrived as a formal tableau, illustrating with comic patness Luke's profession of his new faith in the preceding scene:

> Religion, conscience, charity, farewell.
> To me you are words only, and no more,
> All human happiness consists in store.
>   4.2.131–3[2]

In charity, Massinger suggests, is the proof of religion and conscience, and the very words in which Luke rejects it—"like the adder [I] stop mine ears" (4.3.45)—mark him as one of the Psalmist's "ungodly" who are "as venomous as the poison of a serpent: even like the deaf adder that stoppeth her ears."[3] The refusal of charity is more than a mere sin of omission; it becomes, as these perversions of scripture wittily suggest, a sign of diabolic inspiration, for Luke is the apostle of an idolatrous Pentecost, filled with the powerful language of the only "angels" this world recognizes—gold coins.[4] These are not casual touches but characteristic devices of a comedy whose argument, like that of Massinger's earlier *New Way to Pay Old Debts*, hangs upon an elaboration of familiar scriptural texts.[5] Underlying the entire action is Saint Matthew's parable of the Unjust Debtor (Matt. 18.21–35). A certain servant owed a vast debt, to meet which "his lord commanded him to be sold, and his wife, and children, and all that he had"; upon the servant's prostrate appeal for patience, the master, "moved with compassion," forgave him the debt. The servant, however, responded to this gesture by dunning one of his fellows for a trifling sum, denying his appeal for patience and throwing him into prison, whereupon the master, learning of this ingratitude, "delivered him to the tormentors, till he should pay all that was due unto him."

The parable answers a question about the nature of charity—"how oft shall my brother sin against me, and I forgive him?"—in terms of a financial fable directly applicable to Massinger's world of City merchants; and the play repeats its pattern in Sir John Frugal's redemption of his younger brother from the bonds of debt, in Luke's merciless treatment of Fortune, Penurie, and Hoyst, and in the ingrate's condemnation to the final torment of exile in the "desert" of Virginia until he repents. Visually the parable is further echoed in a series of striking tableaux of appeal, culminating in the mute eloquence of the "magic" spectacle that follows the Masque of Orpheus in act 5, scene 3 ("They all kneel to Luke, heaving up their hands for mercy" l. 59 SD), and in the penitent prostration of Sir John's household at the end of the same scene (ll. 81–125).[6] Combined with the Unjust Debtor is a second parable, Saint Luke's Waiting Servants, in which a lord, having made his "faithful and wise steward . . . ruler over his household to give them their portion of meat in due season" (Luke 12.42), returns to find him abusing his authority:

> If that servant say in his heart, My lord delayeth his coming; and shall begin to beat the menservants and maidens, and to eat and drink, and to be drunken;
> The lord of that servant will come in a day when he looketh not for him, and at an hour when he is not aware . . . and will appoint him his portion with the unbelievers.
>
> LUKE 12.45–6

In similar fashion, Sir John, having ostensibly retired into a monastery and given his brother power over his household as a "faithful steward to his wife and daughters" (3.3.67), returns when least expected to uncover Luke's iniquitous mistreatment of his family and to "appoint him his portion" among the pagan unbelievers of Virginia. This latter parable belongs to a passage in which Christ sets the sin of covetousness against the charity of alms-giving:

> But God said unto him, Thou fool, this night thy soul shall be required of thee: then whose shall those things be, which thou has provided?
> So is he that layeth up treasure for himself, and is not rich toward God.
> . . .
> Sell that ye have, and give alms; provide yourselves bags which wax not old, a treasure in the heavens that faileth not, where no thief approacheth, neither moth corrupteth.
> For where your treasure is, there will your heart be also.
>   LUKE 12.20–1, 33–4

Massinger echoes the language of this sermon in the tableau of Luke emerging from his counting house, a "sacred room" (3.3.19) that he sees as "Heaven's abstract, or epitome" (l. 31), the treasury of his own "heart" (l. 17) that his fevered imagination makes the helpless prey of "thieves" (l. 45).

Properly speaking, of course, charity (caritas) is by no means confined to alms-giving. Indeed, though alms may be a fit expression of Christian love, the one does not necessarily imply the other, as Saint Paul insisted: "Though I bestow all my goods to feed the poor . . . and have not charity, it profiteth me nothing" (1 Cor. 13.3). In the seventeenth century, however, one can detect an appreciable narrowing of the word's meaning; increasingly it tends to refer to expressions of material generosity—and, more than that, to those forms of institutionalized benevolence that the word principally describes in our own day. The late sixteenth and early seventeenth centuries were marked, as the historian of philanthropy W. K. Jordan has shown, by "an immense outpouring of charitable wealth," a phenomenon that had significant political and social, as well as religious implications. On the one hand it reflected the ideology of the Elizabethan Poor Law, the "almost obsessive preoccupation of [the Tudor] rulers with the question of public order"—an order that seemed to them dangerously threatened by the growing masses of vagrant poor; on the other hand, financed as it principally was by the new class of wealthy City merchants, it answered both to this group's enhanced sense of social prestige and to its broadly Puritan commitment to the doctrine of the stewardship of wealth.[7]

While Calvinists repudiated the Catholic belief in justification by works, they acknowledged that good works remained a fruit of grace demanded by God of his saints. Wealth, though it might be a sign of divine favor, was lent rather than given. The rich were accountable to God for its use, and the obligation of mercy required that they distribute their surplus to the poor. "The rich man," declared one preacher, "is no more than God's steward and the poor man's treasurer," so that (in the words of Henry Smith) the wealthy must reckon "the overplus of their riches none of theirs, but the poor's, whom they slay and murder, as much as in them lieth, when they detain it."[8] Charity, the Puritan divines insisted, "is the badge or cognisance of Christ, and the very character of a Christian. . . . He is no Christian man therefore, he is scarce a man, that hath no compassion of other men's miseries. . . . It argueth a want of love to Christ, when men have no commiseration of the members of Christ, being in want or misery, in distress, danger or extremity." But what was a sign of faith might also be good business, as William Perkins, in a characteristically blunt paraphrase of Saint Luke, reminded his readers: Alms-giving is "the best kind of thrift or husbandry" because it is a kind of pious usury, "lending . . . to the Lord, who in his good time will return the gift with increase."[9] Charity, moreover, is clearly recognized as an indispensable adjunct of the social order; extremes of wealth and poverty are created by God specifically in order to provide an occasion for expressions of charitable mercy.[10] And true charity must never be confused with that leveling impulse that seeks to remove social divisions and disturb the proper ordering of the members of Christ's mystical body; rather the exercise of charity serves, by alleviating the wretchedness of the poor, as a necessary plaster to social discontents.[11]

There is of course a good scriptural basis for such a broad social reading of charity. Saint Paul, in that same passage of 1 Corinthians from which Massinger's Luke draws his mock text, sees patience, humility, and self-restraint as aspects of true charity: "Charity suffereth long, and is kind; charity envieth not; charity vaunteth not itself, is not puffed up, / Doth not behave itself unseemly" (1 Cor. 13.4–5). And in Colossians he presents charity as a social bond whose effectiveness depends on each person's recognition of his allotted place in the social order:

Put on charity, which is the bond of perfectness. . . .
Wives, submit yourselves unto your own husbands. . . .
Children, obey your parents in all things. . . .
Servants, obey in all things your masters according to the flesh. . . .
Knowing that of the Lord ye shall receive the reward of the
    inheritance. . . .
Masters, give unto your servants that which is just and equal.
    COLO. 3.14–24, 4.1

An important part of Saint Paul's idea of charity is the belief, widely argued in the seventeenth century, that this virtue involves not merely certain positive obligations toward the needy but also significant restraints on the activities of the affluent—on the sharpness of their business practice, the extravagance of their lifestyle, and the reach of their social ambitions. Thus Thomas Adams's tract *The White Devil* (1613) inveighs against the pretence that alms-giving can atone for commercial overreaching: "It is not seasonable, nor reasonable charity, to undo whole towns by your usuries, enclosings, oppressions, impropriations; and for a kind of expiation, to give three or four the yearly pension of twenty marks; an almshouse is not so big as a village."[12]

Equally reprehensible is that "monstrous pride" that turns the charitable duty of "hospitality into a dumb show" of conspicuous consumption, so that "that which fed the belly of hunger, now feeds the eye of lust." "Where lies the wealth of England?" asks Adams; "in three places, on citizens' tables, in usurers' coffers, and upon courtiers' backs." Charles Richardson's *Sermons against Oppression* links hunger for status with prodigal expenditure as another expression of that covetousness that robs the poor to feed the rich: "Men, having gotten a deal of wealth together, give many hundred pounds to buy one degree of honor after another, to make themselves great in the world, and I know not how many thousand pounds to advance their daughters in marriage, to make them ladies or great personages."[13]

This was a mode of ambition that Massinger had attacked in his first comedy, *A New Way to Pay Old Debts*, where the titanic greed of Sir Giles Overreach is equally manifested in the extravagant style of his housekeeping

To grow rich, and then purchase, is too common:
But this Sir *Giles* feeds high, keeps many servants. . . .

> Rich in his habit; vast in his expenses.
>
>   2.2.109–12[14]

and in his consuming social drive to have his daughter, at whatever cost, made "right honourable." Sir Giles is a City parvenu, a usurer-villain who has married into the gentry and turned his eyes on landed wealth, but *A New Way* is not strictly a City play. Its country setting is of a piece with its commitment to the aristocratic values of the patron to whom Massinger offered it; accordingly its ideas of charity do not go beyond the old-fashioned conception of noble "housekeeping" in which the dramatist found the idealized model of a benevolent patriarchal society. *The City Madam*, though it often remembers the earlier play, takes a new direction.[15]

As the sardonic oxymoron of his title suggests, Massinger's London is a society, like the Nottinghamshire of *A New Way*, engaged in a furious competition for wealth and status.[16] The model for this society is once again that "little commonwealth," the family—here converted to a "house of pride" (2.2.187). Sir John Frugal's patriarchy has been turned upside down by the ambitious revolt of those "wise viragos" his wife and daughters (2.2.166). The dramatized prologue, framed by the commentary of the prentices Tradewell and Goldwire, introduces us to a family whose natural "shape and proportion" (1.1.20) is already distorted by an ambition that "swells my young mistresses, and their madam mother, / With hopes above their birth, and scale" (ll. 16–17). Not content with reducing her prodigal brother-in-law, Luke, to a condition of humiliating slavery in which the slightest murmur is construed as "rebellious" (ll. 36–48, 103), Lady Frugal extends her attack on the masculine hierarchy by challenging her own husband's sovereignty. Her consciousness of the implications of this challenge is registered in her openly political language—the making up of marriages, she claims, belongs to the realm of female prerogative:

> And I by special privilege may challenge
> A casting voice. . . .
> In these affairs I govern. . . .
> You may consult of something else, this province
> Is wholly mine.
>
>   2.2.15–20

Sir John, like some reluctant constitutional monarch, still claims "the power to do" (l. 23), while effectively abandoning governance to his wife, and the full extent of the female insurrection is exposed in the marriage treaty the Frugal women seek to impose on the suitors Plenty and Sir Maurice Lacie in a brutal anticipation of the Restoration "proviso scene."[17] Encouraged by Stargaze's prophecy of "rule, preeminence, and absolute sovereignty in women" (ll. 84–5), Anne and Mary insist on "articles" and "conditions" of the most draconian character, "obedient husband[s]" and "the country's sovereignty" (ll. 127, 179). Nothing short of complete surrender will serve.

Since Massinger conceives of social hierarchies in terms of a seamless web of duty and obedience, it is entirely fitting that this domestic revolt should be linked with even more extravagant social ambitions. Like Sir Giles Overreach, Lady Frugal is a rebel commander who imagines victory in terms of usurpation rather than revolutionary overthrow; accordingly her ambition turns her City household into "a little court in bravery" (1.1.24)—not merely in "variety of fashions" and other forms of conspicuous consumption, but in its ridiculous obsession with the "addition[s]" of court life, titles, marks of distinction, and nicely graded honorifics" (ll. 9–11). She has taught her daughters to dream of becoming "countesses" (1.1.18); they long for "princely husbands" (3.2.197) and dismiss Lord Lacie with the contemptuous observation that he is "but a Lord"—their thoughts 'soar higher" (3.2.188–9); her very waiting woman nourishes fantasies of precedence that recall Overreach's schemes for humiliating the "true gentry":[18]

> I hope to see
> A country knight's son and heir walk bare before you
> When you are a countess, as you may be one
> When my master dies, or leaves trading; and I continuing
> Your principal woman, take the upper-hand
> Of a squire's wife, though a justice.
>
> 1.1.72–7

When Sir John's bogus will announces his "jubilee of joy," Luke continues to cocker up the women's vanity by promising that they will triumphally revive "the pomp . . . Of the Roman matrons, who kept captive queens / To be their handmaids" (3.2.161–3). He answers Lord Lacie's strictures on the "decorum" by which "the Court [should be] / Distinguished from the City" (ll. 152–3) with a vision of a sumptuous masquing world in which Lady Frugal will appear "Like Juno in full majesty, and my nieces / Like Iris, Hebe, or what deities else / Old poets fancy" (ll. 164–6). And even after Luke has scourged their vanity through his wryly chosen role of "new satirist" in act 4, scene 4, Lady Frugal's pride is still sufficiently fantastic to be lured by his preposterous offer to make them all "queens in another climate" (5.1.99); indeed she is deterred only by the revelation that their proposed "seat of majesty" is to be none other than the dreaded Virginia—a place they wisely reckon fit only for the transportation of "strumpets and bawds" (ll. 104, 108).

Actually the intended punishment is by no means arbitrary. In the abortive proviso scene the infuriated Sir Maurice sneeringly suggested that the most fitting husband for their minxships would be "The general pimp to a brothel" (2.2.194), and Massinger means to suggest that their determination to trade their portions and persons for status is no better than a kind of whoredom. It is Dingem, pimp-general to Shavem, who cynically reminds Young Goldwire that in "marriage, and the other thing too, / The commodity is the same" (3.1.80–1). And Shavem's term-driving relationship with her clients merely repeats in a lower key the Frugal girls' relationship with their suitors. The hectors, Ramble and Scuffle, come swaggering and roaring to her door in act 3, scene 1 as Plenty and young Lacie brawled before Frugal's in act 1, scene 2. With the assistance of the disguised Goldwire and Dingem, they are humbled and forced to kneel to "Mistress *Shavem*," and "Mistress *Secret*" for mercy, as the suitors were meant to prostrate themselves before "Mistress *Anne* and *Mary*." Shavem, that "brave virago" (l. 67), relishes her conquest with all the tyrannical extravagance of a Lady Frugal: "I am their sovereign, and they my vassals, / For homage kiss my shoe-sole rogues, and vanish" (ll. 65—6). Not surprisingly Shavem's imagination plays on her own dreams of conspicuous consumption—coaches, muskmelons, asparagus, mutton, and wine (ll. 12–22), and though she hyperbolically affects to prefer prentices to "Lords . . . Commanders, / And country heirs" (ll. 86–8), she too is susceptible to the seductions of status and display:

❧

YOUNG GOLDWIRE:
Thou shalt have thy proper and bald-headed coachman;
Thy tailor and embroiderer shall kneel
To thee their idol. Cheapside and the Exchange
Shall court thy custom, and thou shalt forget
There ever was a St. Martin's. Thy procurer

Shall be sheath'd in velvet, and a reverend vail
Pass her for a grave matron.
    4.2.23–9

❧

The moral of all this seems clear enough: the successive peripeteias of acts 4 and 5 reduce first Shavem's gang and then the Frugal battalion to "penitent tears" and pleas for mercy. Each gets, in Luke's phrase, "what is fitting" (4.2.72): those who offer rebellion against the patriarchal hierarchy or seek to rise above their ordained place in society are compelled to recognize the iron necessities of decorum.

❧

SIR JOHN:
Make you good
Your promis'd reformation and instruct
Our City dames, whom wealth makes proud, to move
In their own spheres, and willingly to confess
In their habits, manners, and their highest port
A distance 'twixt the City, and the Court.
    5.2.1 50–5

❧

Frugal's conclusion, echoing as it does Lord Lacie's reflection on that fit decorum that divides court from City, seems to fix Massinger's social ideal decisively enough—it is simply an urban version of the triumphantly restored patriarchy of *A New Way to Pay Old Debts*.

In fact, however, as befits the dramatist's departure from the country, with its fiction of unchanging hierarchies, to the conspicuously mobile world of City commerce, the social ideology of *The City Madam* is a good deal more flexible than this comfortable restoration would imply.[19] A clue to the degree of adjustment involved is given by the clash between Plenty and Sir Maurice Lacie in act 1, scene 2. It is an image of the conflict between old landed wealth and new money enacted in a whole series of plays from *Arden of Faversham* to *A New Way* itself, and Plenty indeed might be a scion of that dynasty which the upwardly mobile Tapwell hoped to found in Massinger's earlier comedy.[20] Lacie taunts Plenty with his humble origins:

Thy great grandfather was a butcher,
And his son a grazier, thy sire constable
Of the hundred, and thou the first of your dunghill,
Created gentleman.
          1.2.67–70

In the eyes of Lacie and his page, Plenty's transformation into "a gallant of the last edition" (l. 3), his rich display and pretension to the genteel code of honor, learned "At the academy of valour, / Newly erected for the institution / Of elder brothers" (ll. 22—4), mark him as a type of upstart vanity and ambition. Yet Plenty emerges from their flyting with more dignity than his aristocratic antagonist. There is an impressive restraint about his pride in fulfilling the offices of "plain Gentleman" (l. 49) and in his commitment to an ideal of generous housekeeping that avoids both courtly extravagance and City ostentation (ll. 38—60). Where Tapwell was scorned and humiliated for his designs, Plenty, his arriviste successor, is endorsed to the point of earning the friendship of young Lacie as well as the respect of Frugal. Lady Frugal's own upward progress, as her brother-in-law outlines it, is granted a similar acceptance, so long as it remains within the bounds of decorum:

Your father was
An honest country farmer, Goodman Humble,
By his neighbours ne'er call'd "master." Did your pride
Descend from him? But let that pass: your fortune,
Or rather your husband's industry, advanc'd you
To the rank of a merchant's wife. He made a knight,
And, your sweet mistress-ship ladyfied, you wore
Satin on solemn days, a chain of gold. . . .
Thus far
You were privileg'd, and no man envied it;
It being for the City's honor, that
There should be a distinction between
The wife of a patrician and plebian.
          4.4.67–81

The decorum insisted on, clearly, is one determined not by inherited rank, but simply by the contingencies of acquired status—it depends, that is to say, solely on the individual's immediate relationship to the social order. In this new scheme the orders of society are imagined as having an immutable and almost abstract existence, quite independent of the arbitrary placing of individuals within them. Lady Frugal's privilege is entirely contingent on her husband's rise, but his trappings of rank in turn are seen as proper not so much to his personal industry as to the dignity of the "patrician" order within the City hierarchy. Status, like wealth, then, can be conceived as something lent rather than given, an object of stewardship, another counter in the elaborate system of debt and obligation that makes up the bonds of society. Thus Lord Lacie rebukes Lady Frugal's "pride . . . and stubborn disobedience" as another form of debt-reneging—"wilfully forgetting that your all / Was *borrowed* from him" (3.2.60–5; emphasis added).

In such a scheme, downward mobility, though it may invite pity and charity, must be as acceptable as upward. The entire plot of *A New Way* is devoted to rescuing the prodigal Welborne from his fallen condition—the individual's loss of status, however much he may have brought it on himself, is felt to undermine the time-hallowed social order quite as dangerously as the rise of his unscrupulous opponents. No such automatic rescue is extended to the debtors of *The City Madam*, however—whether they are collapsed gentlemen like the prodigal Hoyst, marginal men like the pauper Penurie, or broken merchants like Fortune, whose career so precisely mirrors Frugal's own:

> You were the glorious trader,
> Embrac'd all bargains; the main venturer
> In every ship that launch'd forth; kept your wife
> As a lady: she had her coach, her choice
> Of summer-houses, built with other men's moneys
> Took up at interest—the certain road
> To Ludgate in a citizen
>
> 1.3.22–8

The view of society implied is barely distinguishable from that implied by Timothy Tapwell's register in chalk—"What I *was*, sir, it skills not, / What you *are* is apparent" (*A New Way*, 1.1.29—30, emphasis added):

> 'Tis but justice,
> That I should live the family's drudge, design'd
> To all the sordid offices their pride

Imposes on me. . . .
'Tis not fit
I should look upward, much less hope for mercy.
    3.2.4–7, 16–17

In his world a man is only what fortune and his own enterprise make him.

    Given such a view of society, it is not surprising that social identity in *The City Madam* should be understood not in terms of preordained "place" but rather as a matter of arbitrarily assumed roles. Metamorphosis, consequently, becomes one of Massinger's ruling motifs. It is initiated by that first extraordinary tableau of the Frugal ladies, their extravagant attire transforming them, as the choric prentices point out, from their proper selves:

❈

GOLDWIRE:
Look these
Like a citizen's wife and daughters?
TRADEWELL:
In their habits
They appear other things; but what are the motives
Of this strange preparation?
    1.1.49–52

❈

    The true answer to Tradewell's question is really indicated by the narcissistic self-absorption of their "several postures, with looking-glasses at their girdles" (1.1.48 SD)—a self-absorption marvelously exaggerated in Lady Frugal's primping before the mirror of Milliscent's flattery that preposterously re-creates her as "a virgin of fifteen" (l. 83). What Luke will later call their "monstrous metamorphosis" (4.4.92) is paralleled in Plenty, who, in the skeptical eyes of the page, is similarly "transform'd [to] a gallant of the last edition" (1.2.2–3). At the other extreme is Luke, the erstwhile "companion / For the nobility," new-clothed in the humble garments of service, whom only the courtesy of Lord Lacie now grants even the bare title of gentility:

Your hand *Master* Luke, the world's much chang'd with you
Within these few months; then you were the gallant.
    1.2.111–2

Luke himself—it is one reason for his successful imposition on the
world—has a sharp ear for those niceties of address that mark the gradations
of status; "your honor" for Lord Lacie, "noble" for Sir Maurice, "worshipful
master" for Plenty, "master" for Hoyst (1.2.110, 78—9, 108). But for him
they are signs merely of the deference owed to the "prerogatives" of
money—"since all the titles, honours, long descents / Borrow their gloss
from wealth" (3.2.157—8), and his meticulousness in the matter only gives
decorous expression to that peculiar "ravishing lechery" with which he
excites the prentices in act 2, scene 1—his desire for

> the reverence, respect, the crouches, cringes,
> The musical chime of gold in your cramm'd pockets
> Commands from the attendants and poor porters.
>   2.1.83–5

Money for this revolutionary is the leveler of all social pretensions—

> My lord no sooner shall rise out of his chair—
> The gaming lord I mean—but you may boldly
> By the privilege of a gamester fill his room,
> For in play you are all fellows.
>   2.1.93–6

just as it is the only passport to status and power, the quasi-magical agent of
a perfect metamorphosis: "Have money and good clothes, / And you may
pass invisible" (2.1.100–1). A man's proper claim to the "gallant tincture /
Of gentry," he argues, with a passion born of utter conviction, is the ungoverned
instinct of acquisition, to "take boldly, / And no way be discover'd" (ll.
51–6). Luke's precepts about clothes and status receive comic confirmation
through Young Goldwire's theatrical "device" in act 3, scene 1, when he
appears in the role of a justice of the peace, with Dingem and the Musicians
as constable and watch, but his philosophy receives its fullest illustration
through the disguise-plot contrived by Lord Lacie and Sir John.[21] Hardly is
Luke presented as his brother's heir than Dingem and Gettall come to
announce, as though in fulfillment of his advice to the prentices, the deferential tributes of the gallant world to this City Croesus:

> The news hath reach'd
> The ordinaries, and all the gamesters are

Ambitious to shake the golden golls
Of worshipful *Master Luke*.
    4.1.20–3

So complete is his metamorphosis that Luke can soliloquize about what seems, even to himself, an "entrance to / My alter'd nature" (4.2.117–8). The "wondrous brave . . . habit [which speaks him] a merchant royal" (5.2.16–17) emblematically takes the place of "the shape / I wore of goodness" (5.3.25–6), and his transformation is matched by that of the Frugal women who, finding themselves in an upside-down world where "The scene's chang'd, / And he that was your slave, by fate appointed / Your governor" (3.2.92–4), are subject to a second, equally emblematic metamorphosis, through the penitential "coarse habit" that prefigures their ultimate penitence. "What witch hath transform'd you?" asks the astonished Milliscent, confronted by this travesty of the "glorious shape" promised by Luke (4.4.23). "The world" as the grimly satisfied steward, Holdfast, observes "[is] well alter'd" (4.4.21).

But the metamorphoses are not yet complete. In the last act all are restored to their proper shapes, and the vehicle of their restoration is one of the most elaborate transformation scenes outside Shakespeare's late romances. What's involved, as at the end of *The Winter's Tale* or *The Tempest*, is a kind of magic—not one effected by supernatural powers but one that expresses the mysterious influence of human love. It begins with the Masque of Orpheus, in which a group of dancers mime the story of Orpheus's passage through the underworld; the point of the fable is to illustrate the transformative power of harmony (that characteristic expression of the principle of love) to "Alter in fiends their nature" (5.3.45). The incredulous disdain with which Luke responds to this sublime fiction ("in my self I find / What I have once decreed, shall know no change," ll. 46–7) is immediately confirmed in the "magic" tableau of "spirits" called up by Sir John in his guise as Indian shaman:

Sad music. Enter GOLDWIRE *and* TRADEWELL, *as from prison;* FORTUNE, HOYST, PENURIE *following after them;* SHAVEM *in a blue gown;* SECRET, DINGEM, OLD TRADEWELL, *and* OLD GOLDWIRE *with* Sergeants *as arrested. They all kneel to* LUKE *heaving up their hands for mercy.*
    5.3.59 SD

The effect of this conjuring is to produce a kind of moral metamorphosis—
though it is of the opposite kind to that demonstrated in the Orpheus mime:

> This move me to compassion? Or raise
> One sign of seeming pity in my face?
> You are deceiv'd: it rather renders me
> More flinty and obdurate. A south wind
> Shall sooner soften marble.
>
>   5.3.60–4

It is as though Luke were turned to stone, as hard, cold and inflexible as
a marble statue. The image echoes Lord Lacie's description of the Frugal
women, "charm'd" by Luke's promises of future greatness—"Are we all
turn'd statues?" (3.2.178)—as well as recalling the strange postures in which
they were frozen by vanity in act 1, scene 1. By contrast, the scene's final
transformation will show the supposed statues of Plenty and Sir Maurice
"magically" brought to life as though in response to the love and penitent
prostration of Lady Frugal and her daughters. Luke is made to point the
moral with didactic insistence:

❀

SIR JOHN:
Does not this move you?

LUKE:
Yes, as they do the statues, and her sorrow
My absent brother. If by your magic art
You can give life to these, or bring him hither
To witness her repentance, I may have
Perchance some feeling of it.

     5.3.97–102

❀

The absent are made present, the lifeless brought to life by love. As in *The
Winter's Tale* or *The Tempest*, it is as if the act of repentance had the trans-
formatory power to redeem time past.[22]

Compared with its Shakespearean models, of course, this scene has
something schematic about it. It is conspicuously without the numinous sug-

gestion surrounding the restoration of Hermione or even the tableau of restored children with which Prospero concludes his play. The effect may even be close to burlesque, but that is not entirely inappropriate since in the end this last transformation is merely part of the elaborate hocus-pocus of "wonders" (3.3.120) associated with the "Indians"—another comic sign of the blinkered vision produced by greed and ambition. Its "magic" extends no further than the simple didactic metaphors of Sir John's enacted parable. But the device seems right, partly because so much of the play's action has been built upon metaphors of false magic, devil-worship, and idolatry. Closely connected with these is an important vein of religious parody—and here the point of reference is Jonsonian rather than Shakespearean.[23]

The life of luxury evoked by Luke in his catechizing of the prentices is "enchanting" (2.1.108); the "charm" of his seductive promises to the Frugal ladies is presented as a kind of base Hermetic conjuring:

> Only hold me
> Your vigilant Hermes with aerial wings,
> My caduceus my strong zeal to serve you,
> Press'd to fetch in all rarities may delight you,
> And I am made immortal.
>   3.2.168–72

The real source of immortality, in Luke's fevered imagination, is of course that "great elixir," gold, or rather, not so much gold, as the power it confers, symbolized by the key to Sir John's treasure—the metamorphic agency to which he addresses the great mock encomium of the ensuing scene:

> Thou dumb magician that without a charm
> Didst make my entrance easy, to possess
> What wise men wish and toil for: Hermes' moly,
> Sybilla's golden bough, the great elixir
> Imagin'd only by the alchemist
> Compar'd with thee are shadows; thou the substance
> And guardian of felicity. . . .
> I am sublim'd! Gross earth
> Supports me not: I walk on air!
>   3.3.9–15, 43–4

Paralleling his "magic" are the equally gold-centered "sorceries" of the prostitute Shavem (4.2.20) who offers "Medea's drugs, restoratives" to the withered youth of Luke (4.1.51), and the similarly fraudulent practices of that bombastic "oracle" Stargaze (2.2.70), who has his own "Hermes moly" in "the aphorisms of the old Chaldeans, Zoroastes, the first and greatest magician, Mercurius Trismegistus, the later Ptolemy, and the everlasting prognosticator, old Erra Pater" (2.2.87–90).

Fittingly enough, it is as the hierophant of diabolic arcana that Sir John, in his Indian guise, presents himself to Luke:

❧

THE DEVIL:
Why start you at his name? if you
Desire to wallow in wealth and worldly honours,
You must make haste to be familiar with him.
This Devil, whose priest I am and by him made
A deep magician (for I can do wonders),
Appear'd to me in Virginia.
　　5.1.26–31

❧

This Virginian devil, who seemingly has a taste for wordplay as well as human sacrifice, demands the blood of "Christian Virgins" in exchange for pelf.

Extravagant and melodramatic as this idolatry may seem, it does no more than give a horridly literal cast to the proceedings by which Massinger's City world is governed. Young Goldwire, for instance, envisages Shavem's stipendiaries "kneel[ing] / To thee their idol" (4.2.24–5), just as Luke recalls the groveling of beggars before the wealth of the Frugal women as a species of "idolatry":

And going
To church not for devotion, but to show
Your pomp, you were tickl'd when the beggars cried
"Heaven save your honor!"
　　4.4.115–8

In this context the successive tableaux of kneeling, with their desperate appeals for mercy, take on a tricky ambiguity. Looked at from one point of view they are emblematic illustrations of the harshness of the rich and of the need for charity; viewed in a slightly different way they become enactments of the idolatry of wealth, the deification of status and money-power—like the ludicrous kneeling of the Frugal women to "give thanks" for the prophecies of Stargaze (2.2.68).[24] This is evident, for example, when Sir John Frugal dismisses Penury as an "infidel . . . in not providing better" for his wife and family (1.3.19–20); for though he is consciously invoking a text from Saint Paul ("if any provide not for his own, and specially for those of his own house, he hath denied the faith, and is worse than an infidel," 1 Tim. 5.8), it is ultimately Penury's neglect of the pieties of commerce that damns him in the merchant's eyes. Massinger's London, in fact, is repeatedly shown as an idolatrous society, whose mores are not fundamentally different from those of flesh-trading "pagans" such as Shavem and Secret.[25] Its true mirror is the colonial dystopia conjured up by Sir John Frugal and his fellow Indians— Virginia, the destination of "strumpets and bawds, / For the abomination of their life / Spewed out of their own country" (5.1.108–10), where the City madams will purportedly be "ador'd . . . / As goddesses" (5.1.117–8); Virginia, whose supposed emissaries, though they at first seem "infidels" to their unwilling benefactor (3.3.78), prove to be the priests of "sacred principles" (l. 126) that are those of London itself, a city where indeed "All deities serve Plutus," the god of riches (l. 108).

Act 3, scene 3, where Luke first encounters the Indians, is a conversion scene, and conversion in Massinger's metaphoric structure is the last form of metamorphosis, the ultimate magical transformation. Each act of the comedy, in fact, has its conversion scene, beginning with Luke's preaching the virtues of charity and compassion to his brother in a sermon whose eloquence, according to Lord Lacie, "Our divines" cannot match (1.3.96). "It will damn him," remarks the expectant Hoyst, "if he be not converted" (ll. 80–1), and Sir John's ensuing change of heart toward his creditors together with the repudiation of his "atheist" behavior toward Luke (l. 126) is presented as just such a conversion. This scene is juxtaposed with Luke's counter-sermon to the prentices, Tradewell and Goldwire, in act 2, scene 1, persuading them of the pleasures of peculation and prodigality, which produces the rapt Tradewell's declaration of his new faith, neatly linking the religious and profane senses of conversion:

I am converted.
A Barbican broker will furnish me with outside,
And then a crash at the ordinary.
    2.1.131–3

The "religious, good, and honest" Luke (1.3.152), as befits his pious
front, is named for one of the Evangelists, the reputed author of that saga of
conversion, the Acts of the Apostles, but his appearance with the great key to
Frugal's treasury at the beginning of act 3, scene 3 more immediately recalls
the iconography of another apostle, Saint Peter, who bears the key to the
Heavenly Jerusalem; for Luke, the key grants access to a material paradise, a
"sacred room" (l. 19), a place of "perpetual day," (l. 24) "heaven's abstract,
or epitome" (l. 31).[26] The supposed Indians appear almost as though magically summoned by his act of idolatrous worship. They have been sent, Luke
is to believe, as a charitable testimony by his brother—himself now converted to a life of monastic devotion. Luke is to be responsible "for their conversion" (3.3.98) but fears that language may be an obstacle to this holy purpose. Lacie, however, is able to reassure him, with a heavy double entendre,
"They have liv'd long / In the English colony, and speak our language / As
their own dialect" (ll. 99–101). There follows a neat illustration of their linguistic competence. Lacie departs urging Luke to "Continue . . . a pious /
And honest man" (ll. 102—4), a description he offers to translate into the
"heathen language" of his own City mores: "That is, interpreted, / A slave
and beggar" (ll. 104–5); it is a dialect the Indians, hitherto confined to fustian
gobbledygook, instantly understand:

✤

SIR JOHN:
You conceive it right,
There being no religion, nor virtue
But in abundance, and no vice but want.
    3.3.105–7

✤

The "worldly wisdom" announced by this "oracle" (l. 108), in his parodic inversion of Luke's earlier sermonizing on charity, is identifiably of the
same order as that offered by the play's other "oracle," Stargaze (2.2.70). It is

of course richly ironic that Indians should be made the spokesmen for the play's frankest statement of corrupted commercial values, since nearly all commentators agreed that a characteristic of Indian peoples (no matter how brutish, barbarous, or savagely idolatrous they were alleged to be) was their indifference to wealth and ignorance of the value of gold.[27] The "dialect" of Massinger's Indians, by contrast, is merely the dumb language of gold rendered articulate, the true language of the City:

> Temples rais'd to ourselves in the increase
> Of wealth, and reputation, speak a wise man. . . .
> All knowledge else is folly.
>   3.3.109–14

They profess Luke's own faith with a directness that turns his world upside down, persuading him that "You are learn'd Europeans, and we worse / Than ignorant Americans" (ll. 127–8). The pretended missionary is himself converted—and the agent of his conversion is that same "Angels' language" that "ravish'd" Lady Frugal in Stargaze's prophecies (2.2.63) and that Gettall will hear jingling in Luke's promise of reward ("There spake an angel," 4.1.44):

> Be confident your better angel is
> Enter'd your house.
>   3.3.115–6

Sir Maurice's assurance points directly at the play's favorite pun and creates Luke's conversion as a kind of blasphemous Pentecost, marking his possession by the unholy spirit of gold and its "tongues of angels."

Luke's public conversion to the diabolical service of Plutus is a metamorphosis that reveals his true nature—not least to the once-credulous Lord Lacie, who has been persuaded by the "cunning shape" of "this devil" to think him "a saint" (5.2.3, 5). Yet ironically enough, this damnable lapse also serves to bring about the genuine redemption of the Frugal ladies. Though Luke's inquisition in act 4, scene 4 is carried out for the pure pleasure of revenge, his posture of satyr-"satyrist," scourging "a general vice" (4.4.61–2), brings the City madams to a repentant acknowledgment of their faults of pride and disobedience (ll. 149–54), a penitence that prepares the way for the final conversion of the Indians to their former Christian selves in act 5, scene 3. In his chastisement of the women, then, Luke is made to fulfil the calling of his Evangelist namesake, becoming, in Lady Frugal's words, "a rough physician" to their moral sickness. With his harsh purgatives he takes the place of the false "parcel Physician," Stargaze, whose flattering prescriptions taught his mistress to diet upon pride (2.2.33–4), and the unintended success of his devilish ministrations gives a kind of ironic confirmation to the opinion of the suitors that "what's bred in the bone / Admits no hope of cure. . . . Though saints and angels / Were their physicians" (2.3.36–8). Where even saints might fail, the pretended saint, with his demonic angel's tongue, paradoxically triumphs.

The effect of his triumph is to restore the Frugal household and its dependents to a state of charity, from whose orphic harmony Luke's "sounding brass" alone is excluded. But more than a restoration, this is a conversion, for the idea of charity with which the play began has, by its end, been significantly transformed. The virtue trumpeted by Lady Frugal in the opening scene is above all a mode of power, a purchase on gratitude and servility:

> Dar'st thou in a look
> Repine, or grumble? Thou unthankful wretch,
> Did our charity redeem thee out of prison,
> Thy patrimony spent, ragged and lousy,
> When the sheriff's basket and his broken meat
> Were your festival exceedings; and is this
> So soon forgotten?
> 1.1.110–16

Lord Lacie, indeed, contrasts Luke's enforced slavery with what he sees as the true "charity to your debtors" exercised by Sir John Frugal under Luke's persuasions (1.3.123). This scene, the first of the play's tableaux of charity, appears to establish a firm contrast between the City mores of the elder brother ("He is a Citizen, / And would increase his heap, and will not lose / What the law gives him," 1.2.140–2), and the Christian idealism of the younger. Massinger is trading here not only on the conventionally sympathetic role of the younger brother but also on expectations set up by his own earlier comedy. For the two Frugals seem initially to occupy the positions of Overreach and his kinsman Welborne. Sir John shares with Sir Giles an appetite for country manors (1.1.6) and a seemingly merciless attitude toward debt slavery:

I have heard
In the acquisition of his wealth, he weighs not
Whose ruins he builds upon.
     1.1.137–9

I know no obligation lies upon me
With my honey to feed drones.
     1.3.12ˉ13

His commercial code merely translates into a loftier language the "Ka me, ka thee" ethics of young Goldwire (2.1.127). Luke, on the other hand, seems to be the champion of a social vision that stresses the bonds of human community over the bondage of debt—bonds honored in the traditional generosities of patriarchal housekeeping:

Not as a brother, sir, but with such duty
As I should use unto my father (since
Your charity is my parent), give me leave
To speak my thoughts. . . .
You have many equals: such a man's possessions
Extend as far as yours; a second hath
His bags as full; a third in credit flies
As high in the popular voice; but the distinction
And noble difference by which you are
Divided from 'em, is that you are styl'd
Gentle in your abundance, good in plenty,
And that you feel compassion in your bowels
Of others miseries (I have found it, sir,
Heaven keep me thankful for't) while they are curs'd
As rigid and inexorable.
     1.1.41–4, 52–62

While the idea of true status (gentility) as being determined by the fulfillment of social obligation is one the play will confirm, a closer inspection of Luke's charitable doctrine reveals that it too is compromised by the perception of good works as an agent of power. To spare his debtors, he argues, will do Sir John himself "a benefit":

By making these your beadsmen. When they eat,
Their thanks next heaven will be paid to your mercy.
When your ships are at sea, their prayers will swell
The sails with prosperous winds, and guide 'em from
Tempests and pirates, keep your warehouses
From fire, or quench 'em with their tears. . . .
Write you a good man in the people's hearts,
Follow you everywhere.
     1.3.101–8

Charity here becomes at once a kind of thrift or prudence and another mode of ambitious self-advertisement, distinguished from conspicuous consumption only by the accident of its effect. To be a charitable beadsman, as the "beadsman-brother" Luke best knows (3.2.1), is merely to wear an enforced livery. In this sense, his first response to his inheritance in act 3 is not necessarily to be seen as an entire hypocrisy. In his vision of debtors become devoted beadsmen, Luke is savoring the first delights of power:[28]

And now methinks I see
Before my face the jubilee of joy,
When it is assur'd my brother lives in me,
His debtors in full cups crown'd to my health
With paeans to my praise will celebrate
The forfeiture of a bond.
     3.2.130–6

And it is precisely to this corrupted ideal of alms-giving that the trio of debtors appeal in their flattering prophecies of Luke's exalted future as a lord mayor, outdoing his famously lavish predecessor Gresham in munificence: "Hospitals, / And a third Burse erected by his honour. . . . We his poor beadsmen feasting / Our neighbours on his bounty" (4.1.72–8). At least part of his objection to Sir John's scheme for conversion of the Indians must be that it is presented as "testimony" of his brother's "religious charity" rather than his own. All that the Indians do is to instruct Luke in the logic of his self-absorption. The charitable dispensation of wealth may be an exhibition of power, but money is the thing itself: "All human happiness consists in store" (4.2.133). Insofar as he continues to speak the language of charity ("What's mine is theirs," 4.1.38), it is only for the pleasure of luring his victims into a confidence that renders them even more pathetically vulnerable to his power. To the prentices and their suburban hangers-on he seems to show himself "a second Anthony" in "magnificent bounties" (4.2.40–1) the more to enjoy their despair when he throws them into Bridewell; to the debtors he offers "charity" and "patience" purely to enhance the pleasure of consigning them to his old debt-hole, the Counter, where the only benefactions will be the sheriff's basket "and a coal-sack for a winding-sheet" (4.3.60). And having reduced the Frugal women to his own condition at the beginning of the play, dressing them in coarse cloth and forcing them to "serve one another" (4.4.136), he crowns his masterpiece of ironic revenge by offering them up to sacrifice in a deal that the Indians present as a black parody of charitable alms-giving:

❧

LACIE:
Know you no distressed widow, or poor maids,
Whose want of dower, though well born, makes 'em weary
Of their own country?
5.1.47–9

❧

If Lady Frugal and her daughters are forced to take Luke's old place, he himself begins to talk the language of Sir John. Where the elder brother dismissed the debtors as "drones" undeserving of his "honey," the younger expels Milliscent and Stargaze as "useless drones" (4.4.138); where Sir John feared that his mercy to the debtors would be laughed at as a "foolish pity / Which money men hate deadly" (1.3.115–6), Luke rejects the appeals of Old Goldwire and Old Tradewell with the reflection,

Should I part
With what the law gives me, I should suffer mainly
In my reputation. For it would convince me
Of indiscretion. . . .
They cannot look for't, and preserve in me
A thriving citizen's credit.
5.2.38–44

"Conscience" and "wealth," he declares, as though passing his own comment on the play's ruling parable, "are not always neighbours" (ll. 37–8). The City world of which Luke has come to be the spokesman is in fact a world without neighbourhood, where "hospitality" to poor neighbours is "a virtue / Grown obsolete, and useless" (5.1.144–5); it is a world of appetitive individuals, each of which "lives wisely to himself" (5.3.13), bound to those around him only by the links of commercial obligation and legal contract:

> If there be law in London your father's bonds
> Shall answer for what you are out.
>   4.2.90–1

> Your bonds lie
> For your sons truth, and they shall answer all. . . .
> I have your bonds, look to't.
>   4.2.44–51

Even Luke's old patron, Lord Lacie, finds the very estate from which his title comes a forfeit to remorseless law. The peak of Luke's ecstasy in the counting-house scene was his discovery of "A manor bound fast in a skin of parchment, / The wax continuing hard, the acres melting" (3.3.36–7), and now the bond proves to be Lacie's:

> And it please your good lordship, you are a noble man
> Pray you pay in my moneys. . . .
> Look you to your bonds.
>   5.2.67–78

The tone is distinctly Shylockian, but the bitter humor is infused with Massinger's characteristic sensitivity to the accents of caste hatred. The heavy stress on "good" suggests an equivoque that sarcastically undercuts the carefully chosen honorific offered by a ruthless materialist for whom nobles (gold coins) are the only proper tokens of nobility.

The banquet with which Luke ends his reign is constructed as a pageant of anticharity. Traditionally the banquet is a symbolic celebration of human community, an exhibition of that hospitality by which the wealthy acknowl-

edge their stewardship of wealth and their charitable duty toward all their
neighbors. Luke's, by contrast, is only for himself:

> I will sit
> Alone, and surfeit in my store, while others
> With envy pine at it. My genius pamper'd
> With the thought of what I am, and what they suffer
> I have mark'd out to misery.
>> 5.1.145–9

As he sits at his feast he reflects mockingly on his beadsman-brother's charity:

> Let my brother number
> His beads devoutly, and believe his alms
> To beggars, his compassion to his debtors,
> Will wing his better part, disrob'd of flesh,
> To soar above the firmament.
>> 5.3.26–30

He revels, Overreach-like, in the benefits of his own uncharitable rigor:

> And so I surfeit here in all abundance;
> Though styl'd a cormorant, a cut-throat, Jew,
> And prosecuted with the fatal curses
> Of widows, undone orphans, and what else.
>> 5.3.31–4

The tableau of pleading beggars conjured up by the Indian magus to challenge his compassionate instincts merely gratifies Luke's triumphant self-
esteem:

> This move me to compassion? Or raise
> One sign of seeming pity in my face? . . .
> 'Tis my glory
> That they are wretched, and by me made so,

It sets my happiness off. I could not triumph
If these were not my captives.
    5.3.60–70

This is Luke's most magniloquent speech, and it marks the moment at which he most closely approaches the grandiose villainy of Sir Giles. But it is his most ridiculous moment too. The "magic" banquet and the pantomimes of "spirits" that accompany it, are reaches of Sir John's supposed Indian "art" that parodically recall the "wonders " of Prospero's brave new world, just as the animated statues of Plenty and Young Lacie imitate the mysteriously enlivened image of Hermione in Leontes's Sicily. But the magic here is of a kind that would deceive only those blinded by the self-absorption of pride and greed. The hard-headed commercial realism that animated Luke from the moment of his conversion proves to be as fertile a source of fantastical self-delusion as the ladies' preposterous vanity; the gulling hypocrite, the great disguiser is gulled by the most transparent disguise of all—gulled, indeed, to the point where he is made to be his own judge and pass his own irrevocable sentence ("may I ne'er find pity" 5.3.58). To be denied pity is to be denied compassion, fellow-feeling—to be cast out, in effect, from the charitable community of humankind. Behind the tableau of beggars at the feast lies the last of Massinger's controlling parables, Dives and Lazarus:

There was a certain rich man, which was clothed in purple and fine linen, and fared sumptuously everyday:
And there was a certain beggar named Lazarus, which was laid at his gate full of sores,
And desiring to be fed with the crumbs which fell from the rich man's table.
LUKE 16.19–21

And over the figure of the departing Luke (as over the demented Sir Giles) hangs the shadow of the damned and outcast Dives cut off by a great gulf of despair even from the proffered mercy of those he has wronged: "I care not where I go, what's done, with words / Cannot be undone" (5.3.146–7).

"In Everything Illegitimate": Imagining the Bastard in English Renaissance Drama

In Conan Doyle's story "The Adventure of the Priory School," Holdernesse Hall, the country seat of that stately patriarch the Duke of Holdernesse, is threatened by a peculiar revenant. Mr. James Wilder is to all appearances a modern young man who occupies the mundane post of secretary to the duke, but he is actually a sinister intruder from the past, whose family tree reaches back, through nineteenth-century melodrama and Gothic fiction, to the bastard-figures of Jacobean tragedy. An illegitimate son of the duke, Wilder is a vindictive misfit, bent, like Edmund in *King Lear* or Spurio in *The Revenger's Tragedy*, on the displacement of the half brother whose legitimacy he so bitterly resents. By comparison with his seventeenth-century kin he may appear somewhat colorless. Unlike Spurio he does not actually seek to cuckold his father but is content to sow a fatal discord in his marriage. His conspiracy against the legitimate sibling is limited to kidnapping and blackmail, and the story's only murder is an almost accidental consequence of his accomplice's attempt to avoid pursuit. Nevertheless, this bastard's identity as a dangerous social outsider, an incarnation of the disruptive antisocial energies associated with his begetting, is signified by his name, Wilder. It marks him, evidently, as the symbolic denizen of that realm of unredeemed nature, the moor on which Holmes and Watson follow the tracks of his crime. Their task is made more difficult by the fact that Wilder has shod the horses of his kidnap vehicle with shoes "shaped below with a cloven foot of iron"—sup-posed relics of the "marauding Barons of Holdernesse in the middle ages." As well as equipping the villain with suitably Gothic credentials and stamp-ing him with the cloven-footed mark of the diabolic, these shoes, which are designed to "counterfeit . . . the tracks of cows" reveal in him the passion for fraudulent substitution that sixteenth- and seventeenth-century dramatists identified as natural to his spurious kind. Their mysterious tracks, indeed, are nothing less than the spoor of Wilder's ancestry.[1]

The reappearance of an identifiable theatrical type in so unexpected a context is a testimony to the imaginative power and persistence of the bastard figure as Renaissance dramatists created him. Yet the genealogy of the liter-ary bastard remains curiously obscure. Some years ago Peter Laslett lamented the lack of a proper cultural history of bastardy including its liter-ary manifestations. Despite a small flurry of recent interest in Elizabethan and Jacobean literary bastards, that history remains to be written—the pres-ent chapter may be read as a preliminary essay toward such a history.[2]

"Why bastard, wherefore base. . . . Why brand they us with baseness, bastardy, base, base?" What exactly *did* it mean to be branded a bastard in Edmund's world? A useful way to begin answering his question might be with the outrage of a legitimate son. Returning from Paris, as Hamlet had returned from Wittenberg, on the news of his father's death, the enraged Laertes bursts into the court seeking revenge from Claudius; Gertrude, exactly as she has done with Hamlet in the first court scene, restrains him with an appeal for calm. Laertes's answering assertion of his natural right to grief is cast in language so hyperbolic that it would seem a mere extravagance if it did not exactly echo the terms of Hamlet's anguish:

> That drop of blood that's calm proclaims me bastard,
> Cries cuckold to my father, brands the harlot
> Even here between the chaste unsmirchèd brow
> Of my true mother.
>   4.5.117–20

These words, with their striking paraphrase of the closet scene, might be Hamlet's own.[3] Indeed they serve as a reminder of the shocking possibility that lies, only half-articulated, beneath Hamlet's reaction to Claudius's mag-nanimous assumption of paternity: "a little more than kin, and less than kind" (1.2.65). For if his aunt-mother is the whore that her precipitate marriage seems to make her, what guarantee remains of Hamlet's "true" paternity?[4] It was, of course, the painful lot of that "uncertain man" the bastard to be "a little more than kin"—yet less than kind since he typically expressed the unnaturalness of his begetting by the monstrous unkindness of his nature. "Wise men know well enough what monsters you make of them," Hamlet tells Ophelia (3.1.140–1), and the corollary of that horned monster, the cuckold, is that anomaly in nature, the mixed thing called a bastard.

Detached from legitimate sequence and symbolically bastardized by an uncle-father whose illegitimate rule requires him to repudiate all the duties that "nature" demands on behalf of his "true" father, Hamlet (far more absolutely than Laertes) makes revenge a matter of legitimation—of proving himself Old Hamlet's "true" and "natural" son. Yet it is a proof that (as Freudian critics, approaching the matter from a slightly different angle, have observed) involves him in the profoundly unnatural act of killing the man who substitutes for (and might even be) his actual father. Hamlet's way of coping with this paradox is suitably paradoxical. Like Prince Hal, another royal heir to regicide, coping with the perplexities of "legitimate" inheritance in a usurper's court, he chooses, in effect, to play the part of "a bastard son of the King's" (2 Henry IV, 2.4.286), liberating himself from the constraints of legitimacy by embracing the indecorous license proper to the child of sexual misrule.[5] Playing the bastard is what enables Hamlet to express the contradictions of his position. Through it he at once mimes the illegitimacy of the heir-apparent role in which Claudius has cast him and mocks the powerlessness that seems to compromise the "truth" of his legitimate inheritance. It is a performance that, more than anything, is responsible for converting The Tragedy of Hamlet, Prince of Denmark into one of those tragical-comical hybrids that so perplex Polonius's taxonomic skills, and it establishes him in unexpected kinship with Thersites, the bastard chorus of that masterpiece of dramatic illegitimacy that closely succeeded Hamlet—Troilus and Cressida.

The bastard, as I aim to show, is habitually figured as a creature who reveals the "unnaturalness" of his begetting by the monstrous unkindness of his nature. An "out of joint" member of a hybrid genus, he is defined as neither one thing or the other. To play the bastard, as Hamlet does, is to place oneself doubly outside the order of the "natural," to become at once a counterfeit and a self-conscious anomaly. It is to break "the mould of form," to become a creature of the uncertain margin—an "antic" in both the theatrical and the grotesque senses of that slippery word and a creature whose mixed nature is expressed in an idiom that systematically subverts the "natural"

decorums of kind. Energetic, witty, iconoclastic, and profoundly resentful of
the legitimate order, the bastard, as John Danby put it, "is the Elizabethan
equivalent of 'outsider.' . . . He is outside Society, he is outside Nature, he is
outside Reason," so that he functions, in Kingsley Davis's words, as "a living
symbol of social irregularity."[6]

Thus when Spurio in *The Revenger's Tragedy* proclaims that "adultery is
my nature" he appeals to a whole set of cultural assumptions that made of the
bastard a distinct subspecies among the swarm of attractive villains who populate late Elizabethan and Jacobean drama. Yet the reasons why the bastard
should have acquired such archetypal presence as a transgressive bogeyman
in the period are by no means obvious. In its origins "bastard" had been a relatively neutral descriptive term. Apparently deriving from Old French *bast*
(packsaddle), it distinguished the placeless packsaddle child from the established offspring of the marriage bed. Social historians are generally agreed
that, while the medieval period saw a gradual hardening of such distinctions,
with the bastard being formally defined as *filius nullius* by the end of the
twelfth century, the definition carried no particular stigma; rather it served,
within the patriarchal system of primogeniture, simply to mark off the children who were entitled to inherit from those who were not. The *filius nullius*
(as the rules of heraldic cadency imply) was not so much the son of nobody,
as the *heir* of nobody.[7] Even in the later Middle Ages, when church attitudes
were becoming more censorious, an allegation of bastardy was primarily a
weapon in struggles over inheritance, rather than a slur on character and reputation. Historians generally argue that the condition of illegitimacy began
to incur a significant degree of publicly articulated moral opprobrium only
toward the end of the sixteenth century, when it attracted the attention of
Puritan reformers on the one hand and of Poor Law administrators, keen to
protect the parish from the charge of unwanted infants, on the other. The zeal
of reformers and officials alike was evidently exacerbated by what seems to
have been a rapidly rising rate of illegitimate births from the middle of the
sixteenth century, reaching a peak in the years 1600 to 1620.[8]

However, while these social and demographic circumstances cast an
interesting sidelight on such plays as *A Chaste Maid in Cheapside, The Witch
of Edmonton*, and *Love's Sacrifice*, where unlicensed pregnancies and packsaddle infants play an important part in the plotting, they can have only an
oblique connection with the emergence of the adult bastard as a type of subversive irregularity.[9] For theatrical bastards, after all, typically belong to the
princely and aristocratic orders of society, among whom illegitimacy rates

apparently underwent "a sharp fall" in the first half of the seventeenth century—and who, in any case, accorded bastardy a large degree of practical toleration.[10] Nor did the conniving ambition of bastard princes, which was to become a seriously destabilizing factor in the later seventeenth century, significantly impinge on Elizabethan and Jacobean politics. Among contemporary royal bastards, Philip II's half brother, the bastard Don John of Austria—a possible inspiration for the turbulent Don John in Shakespeare's *Much Ado about Nothing*—had reputedly had designs on Mary Queen of Scots and the English throne, but the danger was not taken particularly seriously in England. It is of course possible that heightened public concern over the moral and social aspects of bastardy, issuing in acts of Parliament in 1576 and 1610, may have exacerbated the embarrassments surrounding the uncertain legitimacy of Elizabeth and even of her successor, James.[11] Still, while such awkwardnesses may have given particular piquancy to the dramatization of bastard ambition, they are hardly sufficient in themselves to account for the disruptive power of the bastard figure in the drama. To fully understand his transgressive potential, I think we need to look beyond the more or less rational realms of politics, moral judgment, and social regulation into regions of more obscure anxiety.

THE DIRTY BASTARD

In the drama, bastards are typically presented as a special class of transgressive male. Female bastard figures are exceptionally rare, the only significant example being Joan La Pucelle in *1 Henry VI*. While in practice at least 50 percent of illegitimate children must have been female, this asymmetry is not necessarily surprising—legal bastardy being so much a category of disinheritance that, within a system of patriarchal primogeniture (where women could be, at best, only equivocally legitimate inheritors), it was almost automatically imagined as a male condition. From this point of view La Pucelle's self-proclaimed bastardy is merely an extreme manifestation of her transsexual monstrosity. She usurps, as it were, the role of male usurper. At the same time bastard figures seem to have been typed as male because they embodied a certain kind of disruptive energy that was supposed to derive from the unfettered "vehemence" of their begetting, a sexual drive imagined as essentially male ("some stirring dish / Was my first father," *Revenger's Tragedy*, 1.2.180–1). Bastardy, like cuckoldry, involved a transaction *between men*, in which the mother's role (as exemplified by Lady Faulconbridge in *King John*) was confined to that of witness and mediator—a vehicle of pollution in the male line of descent.[12]

The factor of pollution is crucial. In popular superstition the bastard was an oddly ambiguous figure. Credited with exceptionally passionate energies, a "composition and fierce quality" derived from the "lusty stealth" of his begetting, he was also imagined as indelibly stained by the viciousness of this origin (*King Lear*, 1.2.11–12). Thus Donne's Problem 9, in explaining "why have bastards best fortune?" invokes "the old natural reason . . . that these meetings in stolen love are most vehement, and so contribute more spirit then the easy and lawful," together with "the old moral reason . . . that bastards inherit wickedness from their parents."[13]

The belief that "bastards . . . have better wits and abilities" no doubt contributed to a paradoxical tradition of virtuous bastardy, which cited Hercules, Romulus and Remus, Alexander the Great, King Arthur, and William the Conqueror among its heroes.[14] But the force of the paradox naturally depended on its running counter to the received view of the bastard's inherent viciousness.[15] According to Thomas Fuller's *Worthies*, popular etymology "deduced bastard from the Dutch words *boes* and *art*, that is an abject nature," while the jurist Sir John Fortescue justified the statutory disinheritance of illegitimate children by their inherently corrupt condition. Citing a passage in Judges 9 to show how there might be "more wickedness in one bastard child, than in seventy-nine lawful sons," he asserted that "if a bastard be good it cometh to him by chance . . . by special grace, but if he be evil that cometh to him by nature." Drawing "a certain corruption and stain from the sin of his parents," a bastard was not merely "the child of sinners" but the "child of sin" itself. And nature accordingly "mark[ed] the natural or bastard children as it were with a certain privy mark in their souls." Thus "the stain of bastardy" described by one seventeenth-century diarist was no mere heraldic metaphor but a literal brand of infamy.[16]

There were in fact good scriptural grounds for such ideas, insofar as Old Testament law regarded the bastard as polluted by the very circumstances of his begetting, so that he was forbidden entry "into the congregation of the Lord: even to his tenth generation shall he not enter" (Deut.23.2). Canon law followed this proscription by denying illegitimates ordination to the priesthood, as Fortescue observed, and there are reasons for thinking that such superstitious fears of the bastard as a potential source of pollution may have been even more widely diffused. The social historian Alan Macfarlane, for example, finds in Thomas Becon's citation of this law (*Workes*, 1560) hints of "a widespread view that bastards should not be christened." Why should mere illegitimacy have invited such symbolically charged ostracism? Part of the answer may be suggested by a sermon, preached by Dr. Ralph Shaw at Paul's Cross on 22 June 1483, on the text "Bastard slips shall not take root," which prepared the way for the bastardization of Edward IV's children and the accession of Richard III.[17] In the Geneva Bible the relevant passage reads:

> the bastard plants shall take no deep root, nor lay any fast
>   foundation. . . .
> For the unperfect branches shall be broken, and their fruit shall be
>   unprofitable and sour to eat, and meet for nothing.
> For the children that are born of the wicked bed, shall be witness of the
>   wickedness against their parents when they be asked.
>   (WISD. OF SOL. 4.3–6)

The implication here is that there is something inherently tainted about bastard stock—that their begetting constitutes an act of polluting mixture that renders the offspring in some sense unnatural or unclean. So indeed it seems to Shakespeare's Lucrece as she justifies her suicide with a paraphrase of the same text: "This bastard graff shall never come to growth. / He shall not boast who did thy stock pollute" (*Lucrece*, 1062–3). The ultimate scriptural foundation for such views is to be found in the rules of separation laid out in Leviticus: "Thou shalt not let thy cattle gender with a diverse kind: thou shalt not sow thy field with mingled seed" (Lev. 19.19). Commenting on this elaborate regime of differentiation in her chapter "The Abominations of Leviticus," Mary Douglas concludes that "holiness is exemplified by completeness. Holiness requires that individuals shall conform to the class to which they belong. And holiness requires that different classes of things shall not be confused. . . . Holiness means keeping distinct the categories of creation. It therefore involves correct definition, discrimination and order. Under this head all the rules of sexual morality exemplify the holy." While not necessarily discounting the function of such sexual rules in the preservation of property rights and inheritance, Douglas insists that their primary function is to preserve the natural (divinely ordained) proprieties of separation: "Incest and adultery are against holiness, in the simple sense of right order. . . . Holiness is more a matter of separating that which should be separate than of protecting the rights of husbands and brothers."[18]

If bastards were forbidden the priesthood or banished from the congregation of the Lord, it was because they were unholy, and they were unholy because their adulterous procreation constituted an act of forbidden mixture that rendered them unwhole. Scriptural texts, significantly, do not always distinguish clearly between marital infidelity and simple fornication. Either can be described as "adultery," since each involves sexual mingling unlicensed by the fiction of nuptial union. Bastards are unwhole because they are the offspring not of "one flesh" but of two bodies—there is an inherent and sinister doubleness about their begetting (one may think of Iago's "beast with two backs") that renders them neither one thing nor the other, at once indeterminate and duplicitous. A bastard, as Spurio puts it in *The Revenger's Tragedy*, is "an uncertain man," consigned by his very begetting to be a denizen of the unstable margin (1.2.133). He is thus the human equivalent of dirt, as Mary Douglas defines it—matter in the wrong place, belonging to "a residual category, rejected from our normal scheme of classifications," a source of fundamental pollution.[19]

This is the belief that underlies Talbot's speech in *1 Henry VI*, for example, when he scornfully offers to avenge his son's "*pure* blood" upon the "*Contaminated*, base / And misbegotten blood" of the Bastard of Orleans (4.6.21–4; emphasis added). And it is expressed with peculiar intensity in Ford's *Broken Heart*, where Penthea's conviction that her forced marriage to Bassanes is irremediably adulterous leaves her a prey to suicidal self-loathing, grounded in the belief that her blood is now tainted by "mixtures of pollution" (4.2.150).[20] Apart from its relation to Judaic rules of separation, this way of thinking about adultery is embedded in the etymology of the word itself. In Latin *adultero* meant not only "to commit adultery" but also "to pollute or defile," a pollution that once again seems to have been understood as the consequence of inadmissible mixture, since *adulterium* (adultery) also referred, for example, to the grafting together of different varieties of plant. That is the meaning that underlies the supposititious bastard Perdita's aversion to botanical hybrids as "nature's bastards" (*Winter's Tale*, 4.4.83).[21]

This way of thinking extended not only to plants and to the animal kingdom but to the developing notions of racial difference and "purity" that served to underpin the emergent ideology of empire. Thus in *1 Henry VI*, as Phyllis Rackin has shown, Talbot's pride of blood is inseparable from a strategy that impugns the legitimacy of the French cause by stigmatizing it with bastardy. If the French are led by a self-indicted bastard, Joan La Pucelle, under the patronage of another, the Bastard of Orleans, it is, by implication, because they are a "bastard" nation. "What ish my nation?" asks *Henry V*'s furious Captain Macmorris in his bastard English. "Ish a villain and a bastard and a knave and a rascal" (3.2.125). He has no doubt been reading Spenser's *View of the Present State of Ireland*, where the barbaric nature of the Irish is associated with their claim to Spanish antecedents: "Of all nations under heaven . . . the Spaniard is the most mingled, most uncertain and most bastardly."[22] It can hardly be accidental that the type of such adulterate mingling should be Caliban, the rebellious slave of Prospero's "new world" empire, in Shakespeare's profoundly ambivalent drama of colonization, *The Tempest*. The bastard nature of the island's only "native" is what symbolically disinherits him of a kingdom that he claims in the right of "Sycorax, my mother" (1.2.333) and makes him naturally subject to Prospero's imperial authority.[23]

Stigmatized by his master as a "demi-devil . . . a bastard one" (5.1.272–3), Caliban is supposedly the offspring of his witch mother's unnatural commerce with "the devil himself," as a result of which he is "not honour'd with / A human shape" (1.2.283–4). His monstrous form is the sign of an inner deformity that renders him fundamentally recalcitrant to that "print of goodness" that is the badge of submission to Prospero's civil order, and his adulterate origin is expressed in the desire to violate the honor of Miranda and to people the island with his own bastard kind. But that very ambition serves as a reminder that Caliban's monstrousness is not simply to be understood as marking his status as subhuman Other, a creature of unregenerate nature awaiting the civilizing discipline of empire. For Caliban too is a colonist, cast away on the island with his mother in uncanny prefiguration of Prospero's and Miranda's arrival.

Of course his adulterate desire for Miranda anticipates the colonial fantasies of the black rapist with which so many commentators have associated it. But it is also, as Prospero's reluctant acceptance of his paternal foster-role ("This thing of darkness I / Acknowledge mine," 5.1.275–6) implies, a kind of incest. If, from one perspective, the identification of Caliban-as-colonist anticipates the familiar colonialist mystification by which indigenous peoples are revealed as being no more than settlers themselves, from another perspective, he represents the enduring fear of "degeneration," which might turn the colonizers into a "bastard" people, such as the "Old English" were supposed to have become in Ireland. According to Spenser's *View of the Present State of Ireland*, for example, these former settlers, as a result of the

"Contagion [of] licentious conversing with the Irish, or marrying, or fostering with them," had become "now much more lawless and licentious then the
very wild Irish. . . . grown to be as very Patchcockes as [them] . . . barbarous
and bastard like," exhibiting their "degenerate" condition by a "devilish dislike of their own natural country, as that they would . . . bite of the dug from
which they sucked life."[24] So it is that Caliban, notorious biter of the feeding
hand, can be presented as the rival and degenerate double of Ferdinand, a figuration of all those adulterate desires (for both sexual conquest and political
usurpation) that the young prince is required to suppress before he is licensed
to inherit.[25]

THE CHEATING BASTARD

The bastard, as the action of *The Tempest* with its pattern of usurpation, disinheritance, and illegitimate substitution suggests, is not merely the vehicle of
polluting mixture but an epitome of the counterfeit.[26] Perhaps because the
unnaturalness of adulterous mingling must necessarily be reflected in false,
impure issue, the Latin *adulter* came to mean not just an adulterer (or in
Vulgate Latin the offspring of adultery—a bastard) but also (usually in the
form *adulter solidorum*) "a counterfeiter or adulterator of coin," while *adultero* similarly acquired the sense "to falsify, adulterate, or counterfeit." The
same extended meaning is present in Medieval English *adulter* ("corrupt" or
"debase") and is everywhere apparent in the expanded sixteenth- and seventeenth-century terminology of adultery.[27] Thus the Countess of Salisbury, in
the anonymous *Edward III* (1592–5), wards off the king's advances by urging
that the act of adultery would "stamp [God's] image in forbidden metal"
(2.1.259). Themselves counterfeit, since they are not the "true" sons of their
fathers and carry the taint of their "double" origin, stage bastards are habitually stigmatized as counterfeits or associated with counterfeiting practice.[28]
     In *The Troublesome Raigne of King John* (1588), for example, the illegit-
imate Faulconbridge is somewhat ambivalently identified as the "lively counterfeit / Of *Richard Cordelion*" (*1 Troublesome Raigne*, ll. 192–3); while in
Edmond Ironside (1595) the "degenerate bastard" Edricus boasts of the
"counterfeiting guile" and "dissimulation" with which he advances his
usurping ambitions (1.1.166, 3.6.1238, 4.1.1426).[29] In *Troilus and Cressida* the

bastard's counterfeiting becomes an agent of subversive mockery, as Thersites's imagination "coins slanders like a mint / To match [his legitimate superiors] in comparisons with dirt" (*Troilus and Cressida*, 1.3.193–4). Thersites's satiric coining, like that of Patroclus, the rival whom he denounces as a "gilt counterfeit" (2.3.25), itself frequently takes of the form of degrading theatrical imitation—a form of counterfeiting that links him with that bastard-getting magnifico Volpone. In Jonson's vicious comedy of unnatural fatherhood, the protagonist is an heirless patriarch who is nevertheless "the true father of his family"; and Volpone's profligate coining of bastards is ironically matched by the fertile theatrical counterfeiting and getting of false heirs that enables him to "coin [his victims] into profit" (1.1.86)—as he himself will ultimately be "coined" by that spurious inheritor Mosca (2.2.23).[30]

Nowhere, perhaps, is the notion of bastard counterfeiting more elaborately developed than in *The Revenger's Tragedy*, where the villainous Spurio, a bastard "true-begot in evil," carries a name that means both "bastard" and "counterfeit." For Spurio the possession of his stepmother's body is an act of adulterous usurpation that prefigures his usurpation of the body politic—as the bawdy double entendre of "a bastard scorns to be out" reminds us (5.1.168).[31] It is at once a confirmation of his adulterate nature and a revenge for it. By substituting himself in the old duke's bed Spurio symbolically reverses the act of his own "false" begetting, inscribing his father's wife with the mark of his own adulteration ("The pen of his bastard writes him cuckold," 1.2.109), and thereby legitimates himself in the eyes of the duchess ("His bastard son, but my love's true-begot," 1.2.210). The satisfaction of this adulterine revenge is compounded in the bastard's scheme to displace his legitimate rival, Lussurioso, by surprising him in the adulterous act of fornication, thus wittily disinheriting him "in as short a time / As I was when I was begot in haste" (2.2.125–6). In this way Spurio becomes a dramatized embodiment not only of the literal adultery that he claims as his birthright ("Adultery is my nature," 1.2.177) but also of the usurping desire for illegitimate substitution that drives the politics of this whole corrupt court. More than this, his counterfeit presence constitutes a kind of rebus for all those fraudulent politic stratagems of which the play's villain-hero, Vindice, is both the scourge and principal exponent. If the surreptitious vice of the court, in Vindice's hallucinated imagination, itself amounts to a species of counterfeiting ("Now cuckolds are a-coining," 2.2.43), ironically it can be combatted only with counterfeiting of his own, as he adopts the role of that "base-coined pander" described by Hippolito (1.1.80) and connives in the adulterous seduction of his mother and sister ("We must cóin. / Women are apt you know to take false money," 1.1.102–3).

If Vindice (whose own parentage will be placed under question by the discovery of his mother's viciousness [2.1.162–4]) has to coin new identities to become so "far . . . from [himself]" that it is "as if another man had been sent whole into the world" (1.3.1–2), his need for histrionic counterfeiting merely mirrors the bastard's aboriginal condition as one who is, in effect, born far from himself. This is the "curse of the womb" that renders Spurio "the thief of nature" (1.2.159), as if self-robbed of his "true" or "natural" self—which is to say his proper social identity—in the very act of coming to be. Stamped with a name that signals only his inauthenticity, Spurio epitomizes the radical anonymity with which the child consigned to "nameless bastardy" (*Lucrece*, l. 522) has to contend.[32] In *King John* the bastard Faulconbridge may "come one way of the Plantagenets" (5.6.11), but (as his rebaptism in act 1, scene 1 and the uncertain shifting of his stage name in the folio text both remind us) the "counterfeit" *way* he comes does not even endow him with a "real" name.[33] In *King Lear* Edmund is equivocally "acknowledged" by Gloucester, but only as a whore's son, fathered it seems more by the "good sport at his making" than by any deliberate act of paternity. "I cannot wish the sport undone," Kent laughs, "the issue of it being so proper" (1.1.17–18). But his banter turns on a cruel pun, since to be a "proper" person in seventeenth-century England (as James Calderwood has pointed out) is "to be propertied . . . to possess," while Edmund's alienation from what Lear calls "Propinquity and property of blood" (1.1.114) renders him an "unpossessing bastard" (2.1.67)—fundamentally improper. Coming "saucily into the world" before his time, like his close kin the "rudely stamped" Richard of Gloucester (around whose monstrous birth and physical deformity hang metaphoric suggestions of the very bastardy with which he stigmatizes his own nephews), the bastard too feels "scarce half made up" (*Richard III*, 1.1.21). As a result he is compelled to shape himself in the mirror of his own wit. Stripped of paternal authorization (like Spurio, sardonically convinced that "some stirring dish was my first father" or that he was "stolen" [counterfeited] by the obscene union of "Damnation [with] the sin of feasts, drunken Adultery") he has no option but to become his own maker.[34]

Spurio's sour jokes play on a post-Reformation distortion of the doctrine of *filius nullius*, as a result of which the bastard "became indeed the son of no-one, isolated in law from all his natural relatives."[35] The effect was to turn him into a kind of living embodiment of that unnatural paradox "the portrait of nobody." For the *filius nullius* became author of himself by desperate necessity, a kind of self-animated fiction—"Caesar o nullo" as the celebrated motto of Caesar Borgia in *The Divils Charter* (1607) has it. The "unpossessing bastard" of the drama, displaced from the narrative of history by the circumstances of his begetting, is cast loose to locate and possess himself by whatever invention he can contrive, discovering in his illegitimate condition something of the outlaw's paradoxical freedom. He becomes a perfect figure for that spirit of ambivalent individualism, at once restlessly ambitious and full of the bitterness of displacement, that Thomas Hyde evokes in his study of the best known of all literary bastards, Giovanni Boccaccio. Hyde observes how the Italian writer turned his own illegitimacy "into an image for the new age he helped to inaugurate. An illegitimate and upstart age, cast loose from historical succession . . . wishing for legitimacy but unwilling to accept its imaginative restraints, struggling greedily and guiltily to inherit."[36]

From the defiance of the bastard Faulconbridge's "mounting spirit" ("I am I, howe'er I was begot," *King John*, 1.1.175) to Don John's dyspeptic bile ("I cannot hide what I am. . . . Let me be that I am and seek not to alter me" *Much Ado about Nothing*, 1.3.13–37) and Edgar's sardonic wit ("Fut! I should have been that I am had the maidenliest star in the firmament twinkled on my bastardizing" *Lear*, 1.2.131–33), the stage bastard repeatedly insists on his own self-begotten sufficiency in overreaching language that insolently travesties the divine "I am," confounding his own essential formlessness and namelessness with the name of originary form itself. That such blasphemy is often echoed in the language of other Elizabethan overreachers merely serves to illustrate the representative character of the bastard. If the bastard was, in Danby's formulation, "the Elizabethan equivalent of [an] 'outsider,' " he was also a sinister insider—a surreptitious insertion into the body of the family. An alien graft who had struck root in the family tree, he could stand for all those obscure forces that threatened to corrupt and subvert society from within.[37]

THE MONSTROUS BASTARD

Every bastard, then, in the scheme I outline, is like the "filthy rogue" Thersites (*Troilus and Cressida*, 5.4.29) or the "filth" Caliban (*The Tempest*,

3.2.346), a figure of dirt (matter in the wrong place) and pollution (illegitimate mixture), whose very existence violates the natural order of things. But
at the same time, by his counterfeiting he also exemplifies a sinister sophisti-
cation or falsification of the "true" or the "natural." When Spurio declares
that "Adultery is my nature" he is simultaneously quibbling on the idea of
himself as a "natural son" and elaborating a vicious paradox, according to
which—by virtue of the "nature" given him by his adulterate birth
(natura)—he is naturally unnatural, essentially counterfeit, and purely adulterous: the proper fruit of a society where "fruit fields are turned into bastards" (1.3.51) and the irregular epitome of a state whose officers of law have
become "authority's bastards" (3.4.73). In *King Lear* a similar series of quibbling associations underlies the counterfeiting Edmund's paean to the tutelary of bastards: "Thou, Nature art my goddess" (*Lear*, 1.2.1). If Spurio
expresses his adulterate nature by embracing the incestuous desires of his
stepmother ("For indeed a bastard by nature should make cuckolds / Because
he is the son of a cuckold maker," *Revenger's Tragedy*, 1.2.201–2), Edmund
equally displays his by contracting adulterous liaisons with Goneril and
Regan. Together, these two characters reveal how, through one of those
strange linguistic contradictions that expose cultural double-think, the bastard could be at once "spurious" ("unnatural") and yet a "natural child"—
just as the term "natural child" itself, in sixteenth- and early seventeenth-century usage, could be used to distinguish *either* legitimate or illegitimate offspring—an ambiguity nicely caught in Gloucester's embrace of Edmund as
"Loyal and natural boy" (2.1.84). The naturally unnatural character of the
bastard makes him into a living exemplar of those ironic mechanisms by
which nature revenges itself on the perpetrators of vicious and unnatural
acts. Adultery begets its own proper punishment—as Gloucester (like the
dying duke in *The Revenger's Tragedy*, his eyes forced open to witness himself made cuckold by his own bastard) painfully discovers: "The dark and
vicious place where thee he got / Cost him his eyes" (*Lear*, 5.3.173–4).[38] So
too, in *The Misfortunes of Arthur* (1588) King Arthur traces his downfall to
the adultery and incest that shaped both his own and Mordred's bastard
natures:

> Well: 'tis my plague for life so lewdly led,
> The price of guilt is still a heavier guilt.
> For were it light, that ev'n by birth my self
> Was bad, I made my sister bad: nay were

That also light, I have begot as bad.
Yea worse, an heir assigned to all our sins.
    3.4.18–23[39]

The paradox of the bastard's unnatural kind is close to the heart of *King Lear*, where notions of "nature" and "kind" are extensively problematized and where the oppositions between the "true" and the "bastard" the "natural" and the "unnatural" are alternately supported and confounded by the behavior of Lear's and Gloucester's children. In a desperate endeavor to maintain the "natural" boundaries between the legitimate and illegitimate, the two fathers rhetorically bastardize their legitimate children—making of Cordelia a *filia nullius*, denouncing Edgar as an "unnatural . . . monster" (1.2.76–94), and repudiating Goneril as "degenerate bastard . . . More hideous . . . Than the sea-monster" (1.4.254–61).[40] But for Lear the conviction that "Gloucester's bastard son / Was kinder to his father than my daughters / Got 'tween the lawful sheets" (4.6.114–17) begins to collapse all such distinctions into a misogynist vision of universal adultery, where all are bastardized and bemonstered by the very circumstances of their begetting between the centaur thighs of their mothers.[41] In the context of such a vision, Edmund comes to seem less exceptional than representative—his bastardy, like Spurio's, an outward sign of the inner deformity afflicting a whole society where the "unnatural" has become obscenely naturalized and "Humanity [preys] on itself / Like Monsters of the deep" (4.2.49–50).

This association of the bastard with the monstrous is by no means peculiar to *Lear*, of course. By the sixteenth century the word *bastard* itself had acquired a range of meanings closely comparable to those of "adultery" and its derivatives, referring not only to the "spurious" or "counterfeit" but also to the "mongrel" or "hybrid"—in effect, the monstrous.[42] The anomalous condition of the *filius nullius* was an expression of "the irregular intercourse of which he was the fruit," defining him as monstrous because he represented the offspring of an unnatural union, one that adulterated what were proposed as among the most essential ("natural") of all boundaries.[43] So in Ford's *'Tis Pity She's a Whore*, for example, Hippolita's curse on her partner-in-adultery, Soranzo, for what she regards as his doubly adulterous marriage to Annabella, equates bastardy and monstrosity: "mayst thou live / To father bastards, may her womb bring forth / Monsters" (4.1.99–101). And her curse seems to have been granted a kind of ironic fulfillment when Soranzo discovers the existence of the "gallimaufry" that is already "stuffed in

[Annabella's] corrupted bastard-bearing womb" (4.3.13–14). The "monstrous" nature of bastards is further exemplified in Volpone's anomalous brood (dwarf, eunuch, and hermaphrodite) and punningly invoked in Fletcher's *Woman's Prize* when Petronius denounces his rebellious daughters: "When I got these two wenches . . . I was drunk with bastard, / Whose nature is to form things like itself, / Heady and monstrous" (2.1.11–14).[44]

Being unholy, the bastard can never be "whole": thus bastards are expressly linked with "Deformed persons, and eunuchs" in Francis Bacon's "Of Envy" as creatures whose "natural wants" may render them vicious, and the same connection is suggested by the deformity of the heteroclite brood—dwarf, eunuch, and hermaphrodite—which Volpone has supposedly begotten through adulterate commerce with "Gypsies, Jews, and black-moors" (*Volpone*, 1.1.506–7).[45] Thus when the Watch in *Much Ado about Nothing* uncover (with a telling Freudian malapropism) "the most dangerous piece of *lechery* that ever was known in the commonwealth" and promise to expose the villains' accomplice, "one *Deformed*," they speak wiser than the audience may suppose, since "Deformed" is actually none other than that moral monster Don John the Bastard (3.3.161–7; emphasis added). Nowhere, perhaps, is the deformed nature of the bastard more apparent than in that literal "monster," the "salvage and deformed slave" Caliban, who combines the physical malformation of Volpone's offspring with the misshapen psychology of a Don John, an Edmund, or a Spurio.[46]

This sense of the bastard's inherent deformity may attach itself even to those like Faulconbridge in *King John* whose character is in many respects attractive, even admirable. An invention of Shakespeare's principal source, *The Troublesome Raigne*, the bastard had already established himself as the effective hero of that play, but there his bastardy figured merely as a factor in the dramatized debate as to who should properly inherit the patriotic mantle (or lion skin) of Richard Coeur-de-lion. Shakespeare's adaptation, however, makes the issue of his illegitimacy symbolically central to a play in which (in Phyllis Rackin's words) "every source of authority fails and legitimacy is reduced to a legal fiction" and where, as a result, "All form is formless, order orderless" (3.1.253).[47] In *King John* the legitimacy of all claimants to the throne is under challenge. Not only is bastardy polemically alleged against both Prince Arthur and his father in act 2, scene 1 (ll. 121–31), but the king himself is denounced in the opening exchange for the illegitimate usurpation of his "borrowed majesty"—usurpation that the French king figures as an act of violent adultery by which John has "Cut off the sequence of posterity, / Outfaced infant state, and done a rape / Upon the maiden virtue of the crown" (2.1.96–8). As "the presiding spirit" of this play, "the human embodiment of every kind of illegitimacy," the Bastard incarnates the deformity in the body politic that is the consequence of John's adulterous usurpation of the crown and that Salisbury insists Prince Henry is born to reform: "for you are born / To set a form upon that indigest / Which he hath left so shapeless and so rude" (5.7.25–7).[48] The expressive vehicles of this deformity are the "rude" speech (1.1.64) and "wild council" (2.1.395) with which he persistently subverts the shaping authority of official language—as, for example, in the confrontation between the rival kings at Angers, where his subversive asides disrupt the very meter and syntax of the royal argument:

❋

KING JOHN:
I bring you witnesses,
Twice fifteen thousand hearts of England's breed—

BASTARD:
(aside) *Bastards and else.*

KING JOHN:
To verify our title with their lives.

KING PHILIP:
As many and as well-born bloods as those—

BASTARD:
(aside) *Some bastards too.*

KING PHILIP:
Stand in his face to contradict his claim.
    2.1.275–81

❋

From the Bastard's perspective, however, the authorized language of chivalric heroism is merely another version of the rhetoric of patriarchal reproof that first pronounced his own illegitimacy:

Here's a large mouth indeed. . . .
What cannoneer begot this lusty blood?
He speaks plain cannon. . . .

> Zounds, I was never so bethumped with words,
> Since I first called my brother's father Dad.
>   2.1.457–68

It is this iconoclastic license that, in a world tainted with illegitimacy, makes Faulconbridge, as Joseph Candido observes, "a sort of moral oxymoron . . . a true bastard to the time," endowing him with a paradoxical quality of "authenticity." Significantly Faulconbridge must surrender this dialect of liberty before he can offer his "true subjection" to the "lineal state" of King Henry and become the choric spokesman of the legitimate and the "true" (5.7.101–5). For as long as it is sustained, however, it makes him the most energetic presence in the play, and this disruptive idiom is one he conspicuously shares not only with the likes of Spurio ("Old dad dead?" *Revenger's Tragedy*, 5.1.111) and Edmund ("Fine word 'legitimate,' " *King Lear*, 1.2.18) but above all with the most linguistically progenitive as well as the most degenerate of all his bastard kin, Thersites.[49]

Homer's Thersites was "the ugliest man that had come to Ilium" and became proverbial for his deformity of body and mind.[50] But only in Shakespeare does he identify himself as a bastard. And in *Troilus and Cressida* his bastardy operates as a sign of the work's own generic illegitimacy. His function as the play's deformed chorus serves as a reminder that when the Renaissance thought of literary "kind" it was not so much speaking metaphorically as imagining the laws that governed a second order of nature. At every point, in its recurrent imagery of the monstrous *Troilus and Cressida* seems aware of its affront to the "natural" laws of composition. Spurning what Agamemnon would call the "surmised shape" and "promised largeness" of its epic design, it grows deliberately "bias and thwart." A piece of "ridiculous and awkward action," a "counterfeit" more shameless than any of Patroclus's or Thersites's strutting imitations, *Troilus* revels in its own illegitimacy. This play is bastard work par excellence, delighting in the humiliations it visits upon the head of Homer, the patriarchal begetter, whose frustrated yet defiant heir it seems to be.

With Thersites, more comprehensively than with any of his rivals, the deformity of the bastard infects his whole world, utterly subverting the generic integrity of a play whose monstrous design comes to mirror his own adulterate and irregular nature. *Troilus* is by common consent the most bafflingly mixed of Shakespeare's performances—a hybrid creation that from the very beginning has seemed to confound the taxonomy of kinds. First published as a "history," in a quarto whose second state included a preface that identified it as a "comedy" (and one that rivaled the best work of Terence and Plautus), it was nevertheless offered to readers of the folio as *The Tragedy of Troilus and Cressida*—while twentieth-century rediscoverers of the play have variously labeled it as a romantic tragedy, an abortive heroic tragedy, a comical satire, a mock-heroic burlesque, and a deliberate exercise in the grotesque. To Heinrich Heine it was a play in which the tragic muse chose to "act the clown"—"it is as though we should see Melpomene dancing the *cancan* at a ball of *grisettes*, with shameless laughter on her pallid lips, and with death in her heart." Swinburne hailed it as a marvelous artificial monster— "this hybrid and hundred-faced and hydra-headed prodigy." In the end *Troilus* is perhaps best described in the self-referential flourish that Swinburne unconsciously paraphrased—as a literary creature that, like that "blended knight" the "mongrel" Ajax (2.1.13; 4.5.86) "hath robbed many beasts of their particular additions. . . . [Its] valour crushed into folly, [its] folly sauced with discretion. . . . [Having] the joints of everything, but everything so out of joint that [it] is a gouty Briareus, many hands and no use, or purblind Argus, all eyes and no sight" (1.2.19–30). Less extravagantly, we might see it as a mocking exemplum of Sidney's "mongrel tragicomedy" or as a marvelous reductio ad absurdum of Guarini's paradoxical defense of the tragicomic hybrid—a genre in which the very mixtures that conventionally identify "an unseemly and monstrous story" become the marks of "a good and legitimate poem" because it imitates a world where contraries are naturally linked in all kinds of "illegitimate" conjunction.[51]

It is entirely in accord with this indecorous decorum that a professing illegitimate should emerge as the moving spirit of a play that, like him, is "bastard begot, bastard instructed, bastard in mind, bastard in valour, in everything illegitimate" (5.7.17–18). What more proper chorus than a bastard, after all, for a play that improperly corrupts the whole epic "matter of Troy" into a battle for "contaminated carrion" (4.1.72), a fable of adultery in which "all the argument is a whore and cuckold" (2.3.72–3)? The reductiveness of this parody of a Jonsonian *argumentum fabulae* is absolutely characteristic. For if Sidney objected to mongrel plays in which degree was violated by "mingling kings and clowns," *Troilus* is a play that annihilates degree by rendering them systematically indistinguishable—so that Ajax, for example, takes the clownish Thersites for King Agamemnon himself (3.3.260–1). Helplessly nostalgic for an order of "distinction" and "authentic place" in which "what hath mass or matter by itself / Lies rich in virtue and *unmingled*" (1.3.27–30, 108), where the singleness of truth is expressed in sublime tautology ("as true as truth's simplicity," 3.2.167), its denizens inhabit a world of degenerate and confused mixture where the very opposites of "right and wrong" appear to "lose their names" (1.3.116–8), and where truth becomes a false or bastard thing, since "to say the truth" is to say "true and not true" (1.2.98).

Symbolically speaking, Thersites is the polluted source of this plague of indistinction, the leveling satire that renders "the cur Ajax" indistinguishable from "that dog of as bad a kind . . . the cur Achilles," or "that same dog-fox Ulysses" (5.5.11–15), or ultimately from that *whoreson indistinguishable* cur" Thersites himself (5.1.27–8; emphasis added).[52] It is the touch of Thersites's bastard nature that makes this whole world indistinguishably kin (but distinctly less than kind). Saluted by Achilles as "crusty botch of nature"—at once a source of pustular infection and a clumsily botched copy of humankind—Thersites is the monstrous "core of envy" from which flows the stream of poisonous comparison that reduces Agamemnon himself to a "botchy core" (5.1.4–5; 2.1.6).

In Thersites's disintegrative vision of what Faulconbridge calls the "undetermined differences of Kings" (*King John*, 2.1.355), each particular warrior becomes merely a *"general"* symptom of the "plague of Greece," "the *common* curse of mankind, folly and ignorance" (2.1.12, 2.3.27–8; emphasis added). This is a play where kings and clowns are not merely thrust together by the head and shoulders but where each becomes a simulacrum of the other, and both are mirrored in one supremely reductive image of debased mixture—Hector's last conquest of a warrior whose sumptuous armor is stripped to display a "putrefied core" of filthy indistinction, the image of his own undistinguished death.[53]

Offering itself, in a characteristic oxymoron, as a pageant of "monumental mockery," *Troilus and Cressida*, far from defying the depredations of time, monstrously collaborates in the oblivious work of that "great-siz'd monster of ingratitudes" (3.3.147, 153) through its systematic debasement of heroic memory.[54] Its self-canceling frenzy is perfectly expressed in its spurious chorus, whose final appearance brings Thersites into confrontation with his fellow-bastard Margarelon. Although Thersites may refuse this combat with a mirror-self as unnatural ("one bear will not bite another, and wherefore should one bastard?" 5.7.18–20), the confrontation nicely epitomizes the self-devouring tendency of his satire. For Thersites is by his own confession "lost in the labyrinth of [his] own fury"—at once minotaur and victim, consumed in a satirical plague of his own generation. In this he is the true scion of a work whose bastardizing vision so levels distinction that language itself seems to fail, rendering it, for all its storms of rhetoric, once again like Ajax, "a very landfish, languageless, a monster" (3.3.263).

Nestor describes him as "A slave whose gall coins slanders like a mint, / To match us in comparisons with dirt" (1.3.193–4), and his rhetoric perfectly embodies the undifferentiating tendency of dirt, as Mary Douglas describes it: "In [the] final stage of total disintegration, dirt is utterly undifferentiated. . . . Dirt was created by the differentiating activity of mind, it was a by-product of the creation of order. So it started from a state of non-differentiation; all through the process of differentiating its role was to threaten the distinctions made; finally it returns to its true indeterminable character [of] formlessness."[55]

The bastard, I suggest, is indeed the human equivalent of dirt—a category of being "created by the differentiating activity of mind" as a by-product of the attempt to define and preserve a certain kind of social order. But his role, *by definition*, is also to challenge that order, "to threaten the distinctions made." And in *Troilus and Cressida* it is the bastard's adulterate vision that seems to reduce his world (and the whole fabulous "matter of Troy") to the condition of pure dirt, of matter in "its true indeterminable character of formlessness" imagined in Ulysses's nightmare of indistinction when "The primogenity and due of birth" loses its "authentic place" and "Each thing melts / In mere oppugnancy":

> the bounded waters
> Should lift their bosoms higher than the shores,
> And make a sop of all this solid globe;
> Strength should be lord of imbecility,
> And the rude son should strike his father dead;
> Force should be right—or rather, right and wrong
> (Between whose endless jar justice resides),
> Should lose their names, and so should justice too!
> Then everything includes itself in power,
> Power into will, will into appetite,
> And appetite, an universal wolf
> (So doubly seconded with will and power),
> Must make perforce an universal prey,
> And last eat up himself.
>
> 1.3.111–24

Bastardy, Counterfeiting, and Misogyny *in* The Revenger's Tragedy

We must coin.
Women are apt you know to take false money.
—*The Revenger's Tragedy, 1.1.102–3*

We are all bastards. . . . Some coiner with his tools
Made me a counterfeit.
—*Cymbeline, 2.5.2–6*

As the sign and currency of exchange, the invaded woman's body bears the full burden of
pollution. . . . If marriage uses the woman's body as good money and unequivocal speech,
rape transforms her into counterfeit coin, a contradictory word that threatens the whole system.
—Patricia Kleindienst Joplin, *"The Voice of the Shuttle Is Ours"*

The Revenger's Tragedy is a play under false colors. By a weird irony, given its preoccupations, circumstances have conspired to visit a kind of disinheritance upon it. Not only has it been robbed of its true paternity, it appears even to have been cheated of its proper name. For more than three hundred years it has been credited to an author who almost certainly did not write it, Cyril Tourneur, and it has gone under a title that was in all likelihood not chosen by the man who probably did, Thomas Middleton—for there are good indications that this is the same play that Middleton submitted to Robert Keysar of the Queen's Revels company in May 1606 under the name of *The Viper and Her Brood*. In some ways the uncertainty regarding the play's nomenclature is just as significant as that regarding its authorship. The existing title makes revenge the nominal subject of the play, and it is of course true that the comic extravagance of this play's intricate revenge plotting accounts for much of the pleasure of its action. But revenge is scarcely dramatized as a *problem* here in the way that it is in *The Spanish Tragedy*, say, or even *Hamlet*. In fact Vindice's description of vengeance as "murder's quit-rent . . . tenant to tragedy" (1.1.39–40) nicely suggests its purely conventional role in Middleton's scheme. By contrast *The Viper and Her Brood* foregrounds the importance of the gender-coded issues of inheritance and usurpation, which are given exceptional prominence in the play's satiric design. The serpent carelessly nourished in the bosom of Middleton's state is the duchess, and her brood is a hatch of apparently fatherless sons, together with the duke's bastard whose vindictive desires she stimulates and who shares their usurping ambitions.[1]

As their place among the "four excellent characters" of Vindice's opening chorus suggests, the two most important figures in this group are the illegitimate son and the transgressive mother. In the previous chapter, I argued that Spurio is given a symbolically central role in the social economy of his play. In this chapter I attempt a fuller exploration of that role. Looking at the bastard as a kind of living emblem for the usurping appetite that dominates Middleton's world of courtly counterfeits, I examine ways in which the taint of his condition is metaphorically extended to other characters—notably to the villain-hero, Vindice, who is at once the scourge of courtly counterfeiting and yet himself the play's principal "coiner." In the process I aim to modify my earlier overstressing of the extent to which "bastardy (like cuckoldry) involved an affair *between men*, in which the mother's role . . . was confined to that of witness and mediator—a vehicle of pollution in the male line of descent."[2] For clearly the very definition of a bastard as "whore's son" implies that the anxieties surrounding bastardy had a great deal to do with its disruption of the proper line of paternity through the creation of a male child who could only be defined as his mother's son. Such an offspring by his very existence constituted a challenge to the patriarchal order and its fictions of legitimate descent. Any full understanding of Spurio's role must consider how the trope of illegitimacy helps to shape both the misogynistic social vision of Middleton's tragic hybrid and its bitterly satiric response to the dynastic politics of early seventeenth-century England.[3]

When Spurio proclaims that "Adultery is my nature" (1.2.177), he does more than simply justify incest with his stepmother as a wittily symmetrical revenge against his adulterous father. His self-description concentrates, in its bitter oxymoron, a whole history of cultural stigmatization, and in the process it foregrounds the symbolic significance of the bastard in Middleton's tragical satire. I have already discussed the construction of illegitimate children as "a special class of transgressive male" whose subversive energy and vicious disposition were seen as resulting from the peculiar circumstances of their birth.[4] Bastards were credited with an unusually passionate and vigorous nature—the "composition, and fierce quality" claimed for his kind by Edmund in *King Lear*—which derived, according to contemporary humoral doctrine, from the "lusty stealth" of adulterous conception (*King Lear*, 1.2.11–12). But a bastard also carried the inevitable moral taint of this illegitimate origin. Drawing "a certain corruption and stain from the sin of his parents" (in the words of the jurist Sir John Fortescue), he was identified not merely as "the child of sinners" but as the "child of sin" itself, and nature accordingly "mark[ed] the natural or bastard children as it were with a certain privy mark in their souls."[5] Thus "to live a bastard," in the words of Middleton's duchess, was to be branded as

> The curse o'the womb, the thief of nature,
> Begot against the seventh commandment,
> Half damned in the conception by the justice
> Of that unbribed everlasting law.
> REVENGER'S TRAGEDY, 1.2.158–62

Intensifying the moral opprobrium that attached to illegitimacy were deep-laid social anxieties, warranted by scriptural laws of separation.[6] Bastardy constituted a form of adulteration because it was the fruit of forbidden mixture, polluting the "pure" blood of legitimate descent, and it was interpreted as a form of genealogical counterfeiting because it threatened to displace the "true" heir with a "false" and debased substitute. Moreover, as Spurio's oxymoron suggests, to have one's very nature stamped with adultery was to be entangled in vicious paradox, since as the offspring of improper mingling, a bastard was unnatural by nature, a corrupt hybrid, or species of monster. These things made the bastard, in his numerous theatrical manifestations, the natural tutelary of a drama that delightedly flaunted its own "mongrel" quality through open defiance of the prescriptions that were thought to shape "a good and legitimate poem." Plays such as *The Revenger's Tragedy, Troilus and Cressida*, and *King John*, in which elements of tragedy, satire, and history are violently and sometimes confusingly yoked together, constitute a kind of literary bastard-work whose generic deformity renders it "in everything illegitimate." Moreover, as the case of Thersites, the bastard chorus of *Troilus and Cressida*, abundantly illustrates, the homology between these violations of literary and biological "kind" stood for a connection that was felt as essential rather than metaphorical. The plague of undifferentiating mixture that Thersites discovers in the collapsing hierarchies of Shakespeare's Trojan War and that he himself exemplifies is mirrored in the self-canceling formal confusions of a play that Swinburne aptly described as a "hundred-faced and hydra-headed prodigy." Thersites is himself presented as a kind of satiric dramatist whose practice deliberately confounds the order of the Greek leadership, for as Ulysses complains, he "coins slanders like a mint, / To match us in comparisons with dirt" (*Troilus and Cressida*, 1.3.193–4), and there could be no more fitting satirist of Ulysses's discredited ladder of degree than one whose own birth constitutes an illegitimate insertion into what *King John* calls the due "sequence of posterity" (2.1.96). As an adulterator of the "true" patriarchal line of inheritance, the bastard was marked as inherently "false"—a kind of usurping substitute or (in the telling metaphors that identified the womb as a mint in which was stamped the genealogical coinage of the patriarchal economy) a "counterfeit."

COUNTERFEIT COIN

The extensive interchangeability of the vocabulary of currency and (especially adulterous) procreation is a cultural phenomenon that deserves more attention than it has received. The origins of this association evidently lie deep in European culture. In Latin *adulter* came to mean not just an adulterer (or, in Vulgate Latin, the offspring of adultery—a bastard) but (usually in the form *adulter solidorum*) "a counterfeiter or adulterator of coin," while *adul-*

tero similarly acquired the sense "to falsify, adulterate, or counterfeit"—an extended meaning that is also present in Medieval English *adulter* ("corrupt" or "debase"). By the same token, silver or gold coin was said to be "debased" when its composition was adulterated with admixtures of so-called base metals. Indeed for the late seventeenth-century monetary theorist Rice Vaughan, the process of debasement "wherein silver is incorporated with other baser metals, not only for alloy *but to the extinction of the denomination of silver*" even seems to threaten something like a genealogical eradication of precious metal. If coin could be adulterated or bastardized, the adulterous getting of bastards could equally be figured as a species of counterfeiting or coining. Thus when the Countess of Salisbury, in the anonymous *Edward III* (1592–5), wards off the king's advances by reminding him that the act of adultery would "stamp his image in forbidden metal" (2.1.258), the wit of her defiance depends upon the idea that a bastard bears the improper "stamp" of his father precisely as counterfeit coin bears the unlicensed figure of the monarch. Illegitimate birth, in other words, amounted to the debasement of a sacred patriarchal image exactly comparable to "The Dishonour that accompanies *base Moneys*" as described by Vaughan: "What can be more dishonourable than to have the image of the Prince impressed upon false and counterfeited stuff: according to the saying of an Emperor, *Quid enim erit tutum si in nostra peccetur effigie?*"[7]

The notion that the counterfeiting or debasement of specie disgraced the monarch whose effigy it bore depended ultimately on ancient magical beliefs about the essential relatedness of persons and their images (reflected in the meanings of *imago* as both "representation" and "ghost" or "spirit"). To assault the image is to inflict damage upon the original, as the tribunes Murellus and Flavius discover to their cost in *Julius Caesar* when they are "put to silence" for "pulling scarfs from Caesar's images" (1.2.285–6). Impressed upon a coin, the image of a monarch authenticates and protects the integrity of the coinage while simultaneously expressing its intrinsic value. The coin is stamped with the king's authority as the son is stamped with the authenticating features of his father. Thus offenses such as clipping, gilding, restamping, and counterfeiting were capital matters not merely because they constituted a form of theft but because they amounted to iconoclastic degradation of the royal image and a bastardizing usurpation of royal authority. The excessive anxiety that attaches to such activities in the early modern period, however, reflects the beginnings of a major shift from an intrinsic to a representational notion of money-value, which significantly destabilized what had been felt as a fixed and essential relationship between the royal image and the value of the currency on which it was displayed. There could be no more eloquent symbol of the paradoxes produced by this destabilization than Elizabeth's desperate alteration of her half brother Edward's image in order to distinguish true from base and counterfeit coin.[8]

Just as *Julius Caesar* describes the transition between the old world of magically potent images, epitomized by the ancestral statue in which Brutus invests his sense of destiny, and a new world of synthetic image-making, represented by the "images" of Caesar that Antony manipulates to such effect, so plays like *Troilus and Cressida, Volpone*, and *The Revenger's Tragedy* respond to a society where value, because it no longer seems inherent in its signifiers, is in danger of becoming a fluid and manipulable function of "particular will" (*Troilus and Cressida*, 2.2.53), a creature of appetite subject to infinite metamorphoses. Thus in *Volpone*—to choose an example where these matters are made unusually explicit—the protagonist's opening hymn to his gold pretends to define an intrinsic relation between treasure and its proprietor. Volpone's gold is described as being at once his "soul" (1.1.3) and his "substance" (l. 74); hailed as "the son of Sol," it is the offspring of the royal Sun itself. Yet this last patriarchal hyperbole is revealed—through the complex wordplay on "son/sun" and on "Sol" as both the alchemical name for gold and a denomination of gold coinage—to be merely an inflated tautology. And when Volpone goes on to identify gold with "virtue, fame, / Honor, and all things else" (ll. 25–6) he unwittingly expresses the arbitrary, attributive nature of its value. Gold in this play is less the imagined *object* of desire, than its *symbol;* less the repository of absolute unchanging value than a fungible agent of bizarre alchemical transformations. It is exactly this instrumental power that Volpone celebrates when he professes to "glory / More in the cunning purchase of [his] wealth / Than in the glad possession" (ll. 30–2). Gold is the "elixir" that not only promises to "recover" the apparently moribund Volpone (ll. 372–6) but also converts the decayed patriarch Corbaccio to an ambitious heir. And it is that which serves, in the most ruthless metamorphosis of all, to coin people (including ultimately Volpone himself) into profit. Gold is thus the instrument and epitome of unnatural relationship; it is what, in the corrupted patriarchy of Jonson's Venice, effectually replaces the bonds of natural kinship. Through its agency true children are bastardized, as in Corbaccio's disinheritance of Bonario (4.2), while the counterfeit patriarch Volpone is legitimated as "the true father of his family"—a doubly bastard brood begotten (according to Mosca) upon outsiders and aliens, "beggars, / Gypsies . . . Jews, and black-moors" (1.1.505–10). *Volpone* imagines a society where the very terms of familial authority, succession, and inheritance—father, son, and heir—have become mere coinages, a freely manipulable (and counterfeitable) currency of relationship that defines no intrinsic bond whatsoever. So that Volpone's pseudopatriarchal role is demonstrated precisely by the arbitrary power to create heirs and disinherit them at will that he shares with the other true (i.e., false) fathers of the play, Corvino and the Fourth Avocatore.

What results is a radical instability to which even the principal coiner himself falls victim. When Volpone, as he invests Mosca with the treasury keys that are the badge of his heir-apparency, salutes the parasite as "my better angel" (2.2.21) the high-sounding language of Morality drama is inevitably adulterated by the sly pun on "angel," which identifies Mosca from Volpone's point of view as merely another of those whom he coins into profit. But the pun recoils on the punster through the careless irony of his following lines, anticipating the process by which the magnifico will be restamped as the issue of Mosca's own counterfeiting:

> Gold, plate, and jewels, all's at thy devotion.
> Employ them how thou wilt, nay, *coin* me too,
> So thou in this but *crown* my longings, Mosca.
> *Volpone*, 2.2.22–4; EMPHASIS ADDED

In the process, patron and knave change places, the presumptive heir usurping the role of the patriarch, while Volpone finds he has "lost [him]self" (5.6.22) in the maze of his counterfeit impositions.

An even more extravagant irony of self-loss is thematized in *The Revenger's Tragedy*, which seems to have been written within a few months of *Volpone*. In this play Hippolito's nervous warning "Brother, we lose ourselves" (4.4.201) achieves a bizarrely literal fulfillment when Vindice is hired to murder his counterfeit self, Piato, in the form of the old duke's disguised corpse: "Brother that's I: that sits for me: do you mark it. And I must stand ready here to make away myself yonder; I must sit to be killed, and stand to kill myself" (5.1.5–7).[9] There could of course be no wittier illustration of the governing principle of revenge drama, whereby the revenger is transformed into the simulacrum of the criminal he seeks to punish. But the episode has also to be read as an illustration of the destabilization of identity characteristic of a world of bastard coining.

If Jonson characteristically imagines his own era as a base travesty of the classical golden age, "the Money-get, Mechanic Age" that he sardonically types the "Age of Gold," Middleton locates his court, where everything goes "in silk and silver" (1.1.52) in a degraded silver age, mockingly emblematized by the "silver years" of the duke (1.2.11) and the silver hairs of his morally dubious successor, Antonio (5.3.86).[10] Just as the action of the play displays a progressive debasement of the currency of dukedom, climaxing in the farcical substitutions of act 5 where five dukes rise and fall in quick succession, so it serves to strip away the plated surface of the court exterior and expose the base metal beneath—precisely as Vindice's rhetoric strips away the "costly three-piled flesh" of courtly "fat folks" to expose the terror of "death's vizard."

Vindice satirizes the court as a place of monstrous sexual forgery where "cuckolds [together with the bastards foisted upon them] are a-coining, apace, apace, apace" (2.2.142); yet in his theatrical self-multiplication he ironically proves himself to be the most prolific and successful of all the play's counterfeiters. From the moment that he agrees to become "the child o' the court" (1.3.4) and to "put on" the role of "base-coined pander" proposed to him by Hippolito (1.1.92, 80), Vindice acknowledges a surreptitious kinship with the base-coined Spurio. The very name he chooses for this "strange composed fellow" (l. 95), "Piato" (plated) identifies him with that form of spurious currency known as "blanched" coin (base metal plated over with silver to improve its appearance), thereby associating him with the deceptive glitter of the whole court.[11] And in a last turn of the satiric whirligig, the completion of his revenge is punningly imagined as yet another spurious adulteration of currency: "And if we list *we could have nobles clipped* / And go for less than beggars" (5.3.122–3; emphasis added).

If men are coiners, it is women, according to Vindice, who are most "apt . . . to take false money" (1.1.103). But women not only *take* money (and help to fake it) they *become* it. In the grotesque economy of the sexual mint, where cuckolds and bastards are coined together, pander and whore too are struck from the same metal, so that if Piato is blanched coin, Gratiana and Castiza are liable to be "changed / Into white money" by his labors (2.2.26–7). As Vindice/Piato urges Gratiana to put Castiza in "use" with Lussurioso (2.2.98), his sister's flesh is metamorphosed into a form of material wealth: "I would count / My yearly maintenance upon her cheeks, / Take coach upon her lip, and all her parts / Should keep men after men" (2.1.96–9). "Common usury" thus becomes, in Castiza's bitter phrase, a synonym for prostitution

(4.4.104)—the vice whose principal patron is the duke himself, in his role as "usuring father."[12] In traditional doctrine, usury, with its unnatural "breeding" of money, was denounced as a travesty of biological generation. The language of Middleton's play reverses this equation by turning fornication, with its prolific coining of bastards and cuckolds, into a monstrous form of usury.

— ❦ —

"TREASON ON THE LAWFUL BED"

For Spurio to declare that "Adultery is my nature," then, is to identify himself as counterfeit coin, and in his scheme to displace Lussurioso in the line of ducal succession he wittily seeks to pay his father back in his own spurious currency. This act of "treason on the lawful bed," as well as ironically linking him with his legitimate rival (4.1.22), points toward the significance of his name. In ways that I partially explored in chapter 5, "Spurio" serves as an important index to the bastard's function. In the brief cratyllic catalog that supplies an allegoric key to the play's moral scheme, "Spurio" appears at first sight slightly anomalous. Most of the major characters—Vindice, Lussurioso, Ambitioso, Supervacuo, Gratiana, and Castiza—are typed, Morality-fashion, with names that identify them with particular vices and virtues. But "Spurio," glossed in John Florio's Italian dictionary as "a bastard, a baseborne," looks like a purely factual label, comparable with "duke," or with "Junior" for the duchess's youngest son—indeed he is at one point actually referred to by Vindice as "*the* Spurio" (2.2.114), as though Middleton were merely substituting the Italian word for "bastard." Even considered purely as a label, however, the name is not without allegoric force, since in early modern thinking bastardy was as much a moral as a genealogical category, so that Florio's further gloss on *spurio*—"Also adulterate or counterfeit"—does not really involve a significant metaphoric extension of the term.[13] By virtue of the constant stress on his illegitimate state, moreover, the application of Spurio's name is highlighted in a way that is otherwise true only of Vindice's. Apart from this general suggestiveness, "Spurio" has an even more particular referentiality that points toward the function of bastardy in the misogynist gender politics of the play, for the name derives from the Latin term *spurius*, which denoted, according to Isidore of Seville, not just any illegitimate offspring but one born from a noble but spouseless mother to an unknown or plebeian father. Such children, who could not take the paternal name, were called *spurius* because they sprang in effect from the mother alone—the word itself deriving, Isidore explained (following Plutarch), from *spurium*, an ancient term for the female genitalia. Thus as Thomas Laqueur puts it, "while the legitimate child is from the froth of the father, the illegitimate child is from the seed of the mother's genitals, *as if the father did not exist.*"[14]

To be "the son of a cuckold-maker" (1.2.202) then is, in effect, to be one's mother's son, and the spurious child constitutes a living affront to the patriarchal order, seeming by his "stolen" existence (1.2.187) to cancel the father out, implicitly denying the exclusive function of the womb as patriarchal mint. This is one of the things that makes Middleton's bastard "the thief of nature" (1.2.159). Though he is reputedly the duke's child, Spurio remains "his son but falsely . . . an uncertain man / Of more uncertain woman" (1.2.131–4). And his satiric conjectures as to his own paternity—"may be his groom / O'the stable begot me. . . . I'd a hot-backed devil to my father" (1.2.134–5, 163)—conclude in a sardonic burlesque of the very notion of patrilineal descent: "Faith, if the truth were known I was begot / After some gluttonous dinner—some stirring dish / Was my first father" (1.2.178–9). If the freak of the bastard's conception means that he is "By one false minute disinherited" (l. 166), his status as *filius nullius*—as it were the son of nobody—implicitly puts in question the whole charade of "legitimate" inheritance, serving as a reminder that, for all the dubious benefit of "report," his supposedly legitimate brother may very well be "as falsely sown" as himself, since "Women must not be trusted with their own" (1.2.195–8).[15]

Spurio's misogynist gibe foregrounds patriarchal anxieties concerning the problematic relation between property and women's bodies that lie close to the heart of Middleton's play, helping to explain the prominence of the bastard's role. The laws of primogenitive inheritance were designed to regulate the passage of property between generations, which is to say the handing down of wealth from father to son. Properly speaking, women had no role in such transactions, except as vehicles of transmission; and if property was never truly their own, their bodies, as the vehicles of its transmission, necessarily became another species of masculine property with whose disposition they were not to be trusted. "Virginity," as Gratiana is made to say, "is paradise, locked up. . . . And 'twas decreed that man should keep the key"

(2.1.153–5). Man has been granted this authority in order to secure the "true," unpolluted transmission of the line of inheritance, and female sexuality needs to be secured and contained by vigilant policing because women are, in the phrase that Gail Paster has made famous, "leaky vessels" whose incontinent "disease o'the mother" constantly threatens the "close" discipline of the patriarchal order. "Tell but some woman a secret over night," Vindice declares, "[and] Your doctor may find it in the urinal i'the morning" (1.3.83–4).[16]

Just as female porousness is always prone to release what should be contained, so it is liable to admit what should be excluded. Vindice's graphically imagined catalog of the sins that crowd the sunset hour characteristically focuses on women exposed in acts of surreptitious opening:

> This woman in immodest thin apparel
> Lets in her friend by water, here a dame
> Cunning nails leather hinges to a door
> To avoid proclamation.
>   2.2.139–42

In this vision the very water on which the adulterous lover arrives operates as a powerful signifier of the leaky, fluid, and "uncertain" nature of womankind. The female body, once it surrenders the "close" condition of virginity (1.3.137), constitutes a dangerous kind of opening in the otherwise impermeable edifice of patriarchal power and property-holding, a conduit of pollution, debasement, and usurpation that requires constant regulation.[17] For as the fates of Gloriana and Antonio's wife reveal, ultimately only death can preserve the closeness of virginity against the voracious "moths" that "lust to eat / Into [the proprietor's] wearing" (1.4.33–4). Where men are conceived as being "made close" (1.3.81) by their very gender, rendering them, ideally at least, self-contained and impenetrable, for women such impenetrability would amount to a violation of their very nature: "That woman is all *male* whom none can enter" as Vindice's contemptuous pun expresses it (2.1.112; emphasis added).

Understood as the product of improper penetration, a spurious and destabilizing insertion into the body of patriarchy, the bastard constitutes a living sign of the dangerously porous boundary produced by the incorporation of the female into the dominant order. This is the source of the bastard's peculiar bitterness, for it robs him of any possibility of becoming "a proper man," of standing for himself. In the patriarchal order, where the "proper" self is, in the last analysis, defined by the possession of property, to be identified as a son is always to stand for someone else—as a potential substitute for the father, but even younger sons may hope one day to achieve that substitution, to inherit the paternal office and at last to stand for themselves as full members of the body politic. The "unpossessing bastard," by contrast, is forever excluded from that possibility. Legally defined as *filius nullius* (no man's son or heir) and in the vernacular as a "whoreson" (whore's son), he stands not for his father but for his mother—or more precisely, for her disgrace, her shameful openness. Thus, for example, the bastard "demi-devil" Caliban in *The Tempest*, though supposedly sired by the devil, is habitually defined by his relation to his "dam," Sycorax. He is his mother's child, as surely as his virtuous opposites, Ferdinand and Miranda, are their father's children, and it is for this reason that the island inheritance he claims "by Sycorax my mother" can be discounted and violently taken from him.

For most theatrical bastards the psychological effect of their radical displacement from the patrilineal order of inheritance is to force them to become defiant authors of themselves. The bastard contrives a desperately self-animated fiction of masculine identity, discovering in his own illegitimacy something of an outlaw's paradoxical freedom.[18] But for all his swaggering parade of masculinity, he is nevertheless consigned to a curiously anomalous position in the economy of gender relations—one from which he can never wholly escape since it is part of his unnatural nature. For all his supposedly "unnatural" qualities, the bastard was traditionally described as a "natural child" because, conceived without benefit of matrimony, his origins lay outside the order of culture (imagined as masculine) in the (typically feminine) domain of nature.

Thus since the bastard, whether fathered by "some stirring dish" or begotten by "Damnation [upon] the sin of feasts, drunken Adultery" (1.2.179, 187–8), is anything but his father's son, he embodies the subversive challenge posed by the "outlaw feminine" to patrilineal proprieties. Accordingly, the prominence of Spurio in the play's opening procession points not toward the inversion of moral values implicit in Vindice's ironic oxymoron "thou his *bastard true-begot* in evil" (1.1.3; emphasis added) but to a disturbance of gender roles that makes the play's patterns of usurpation especially unsettling. The duchess's sexual alliance with her bastard stepson—which she imagines as constituting an impertinent legitimation of his dubious lineage ("His bastard son, but my love's true-begot," 1.2.110)—has a double appropriateness in this context. Not only does her seduction tutor Spurio in an adultery that replicates the circumstances of his own begetting, teaching him how to realize "the vengeance that [his] birth was wrapped in" (1.2.167), but in the act of cuckolding her husband the duchess mounts a symbolic assault on the patriarchal order of inheritance. To "arm [his] brow with *woman's heraldry*" (1.2.175; emphasis added) is to substitute the badges of female fecundity and "uncertainty," for the immemorial signs of masculine "sequence and succession." Where men's heraldry constitutes an emblematic picturing of the closed boundaries of lineage, "woman's heraldry" blazons a reminder of the scandalous biological openness concealed by such devices, and in the duchess's case it highlights her role as a conduit for the illegitimate ambitions of her own conspicuously fatherless sons.[19]

The bastard's witty sarcasms concerning the culinary origins of his own paternity draw attention to his symbolic centrality in a work preoccupied with patrimony and inheritance. Even more than *Hamlet*, the play to which it is so self-consciously indebted, *The Revenger's Tragedy*, with its gathering frenzy of illegitimate substitutions both sexual and political, is obsessed with issues of paternity and succession in which virtually all its characters are entangled. The result is an elaborate structure of parallels and resemblances in which the protagonist is once again ironically implicated. The opening scenes establish a curious symmetry between Spurio, the counterfeit diamond of the ducal house (1.2.148–9), and Vindice in his role as Piato, the "base-coined pander" (1.1.80) of Lussurioso's household.[20] If Spurio has been rendered fatherless and "disinherited" by the "one false minute" of his disgraceful conception, Vindice too finds himself effectually stripped of his patrimony by his father's disgrace and impoverished death (1.1.118–26). And in the character of the "displaced" malcontent Piato, the bastardized "child o'the court" (1.3.4), he appears like an exemplum of his own satiric vision of universal disinheritance:

> I have seen patrimonies washed a-pieces,
> Fruit fields turned into bastards,
> And in a world of acres
> Not so much dust due to the heir 'twas left to
> As would well gravel a petition.
>   1.3.50–54

If Vindice's vengeful bitterness is fueled by the loss of his patrimony, Spurio too conceives his planned murder of Lussurioso as a symbolic reenactment and reversal of the sin that ensured his disinheritance:

> Well, have at the fairest mark—So said the Duke when he begot me—
> And if I miss his heart or near about
> Then have at any—a bastard scorns to be out.
>   5.1.167–70

Moreover just as the bastard's revenge against his father includes a plot to "disinherit [his legitimate brother] in as short a time / As I was when I was begot in haste" (2.2.125–6), so Vindice's revenge includes a scheme to "disheir" the duke through the murder of his son Lussurioso (1.3.175).

Of course the disruption of inheritance and dissolution of patrimony are by no means confined to these two revenge plots. Middleton's court is merely the mirror of an entire commonwealth where, since "farmers' sons agreed, and met again, / To wash their hands and come up gentlemen" (2.1.217–8) place is governed by ambition rather than the proprieties of due succession. Vindice's opening soliloquy introduces us to a world of perversely disrupted succession where just as "marrowless age" contrives to "riot it *like a son and heir*" (1.1.11; emphasis added), so inheritance is only the occasion for prodigal waste:

> Oh, she was able to ha' made a usurer's son
> Melt all his patrimony in a kiss,
> And what his father fifty years told
> To have consumed.
>   1.1.26–7

The image of the usurer's prodigal heir will be given grotesque life in the central murder scene (3.5), where the juxtaposition of the duke's self-consuming lechery with Spurio's incestuous embrace of the duchess forms the basis for Vindice's sardonic emblem of violated patrimony: "A usuring father to be boiling in hell, and his son and heir with a whore dancing over him" (4.2.87–8). If the duke himself riots it "like a son and heir," he finds his actual son guilty of trying to duke it like a father:

This boy that should be myself after me
Would be myself before me. . . .
Intending to depose me in my bed.
    2.3.19–22

Similarly Spurio's and Vindice's plots to dis-heir the duke are matched by the efforts of the duchess's sons to disinherit their half brother ("He's the next heir; yet this true reason gathers; / None can possess that dispossess their fathers," 2.3.87–8) and the attempts of each to proclaim himself "heir—duke in a minute" (3.1.13), climaxing in the knockabout farce of false succession and disinheritance that is triggered by the murder of Lussurioso:

SUPERVACUO:
Then I proclaim myself. Now I am duke.
Ambitioso. Thou duke! brother thou liest.
[Stabs SUPERVACUO.]
SPURIO:
Slave! So dost thou.
[Stabs AMBITIOSO.]
NOBLE:
Base villain, hast thou slain my lord and master?
[Stabs SPURIO.]
    5.3.53–5

As mother's sons, Ambitioso, Supervacuo, and Junior, although not formally typed as bastards, are allotted a structural position closely parallel to that of Spurio in the undermining of patriarchal inheritance and possession. And just as Spurio's usurping designs upon the dukedom are symbolically enacted in the doubly adulterous usurpation of his father's bed when he makes "horn royal" (2.2.165) with the duchess, so Junior's "double adultery" (1.2.44) with Antonio's wife not only "eats into [the husband's] wearing" but announces an implicit affront to the stepfather's potency: "Oh, what it is," complains the duchess, contrasting her son's sexual aggression with her husband's judicial passivity "to have an old-cool duke / To be as slack in tongue as in performance" (1.2.74–5).[21]

Nor does the complicated chain of resemblances end there. It is an indication of the deeply ambiguous role played by Vindice and Hippolito that by the end of the play their own position has developed an uneasy similarity to that of Ambitioso and Supervacuo. The parallel is made most apparent at the end of act 4 in a sequence of three scenes where the rival sets of brothers swear to punish their mothers for polluting their family honor. Vindice's vow to "conjure that *base* devil out of our mother" is immediately followed by the outrage of the duchess's sons at the shame to which they have been exposed: "The nobler she is, the *baser* she is grown" (4.2.229; 4.3.10; emphasis added). In the same way Vindice's claim to have tried Gratiana on behalf of "the duke's son" and to have found her "base metal" echoes Supervacuo's disgust at a mother debased by "the duke's bastard" (4.4.31–2; 4.3.15). Both pairs of brothers feel themselves to be, in effect, bastardized by the openness of a mother whose behavior implicitly calls in question their claims to be their fathers' sons. "It is a wise child now," reflects the sage Castiza, wittily extending an old proverb about the uncertainty of patrilineal descent, "that knows her mother" (2.1.163). "Most right," choruses Vindice, for whom the discovery of his mother's openness entails an unstitching of proper identity that will lead him to "doubt / Whether I'm myself or no" (4.4.24–5). There is a curious sense in which Vindice's gradual submergence in the role of "Piato" seems to act out this sense of self-loss, to the point where, in the character of "Vindice," the second false persona assumed for the benefit of Lussurioso, he becomes in effect his own counterfeit, a spurious version of himself.

❖ ❖ ❖

With its bitterly satiric view of courtly vice and nauseated sense of fleshly corruptibility, *The Revenger's Tragedy* has long been typed as a classic expression of the so-called Jacobean disillusionment. While contemporary historicist criticism is rightly cautious about such impressionistic periodization, I believe the patterns I have traced, which foreground the dramatist's preoccupation with spurious substitution and false inheritance, give a certain substance to the traditional view.

The processional tableau with which *The Revenger's Tragedy* begins is constructed, as all such courtly ceremonials are, as an image of "due sequence and succession": the incumbent royal couple are followed by a line of royal sons, in order of heritability (the heir, his half brothers, the bastard) and a "train" of courtiers.[22] This conventional picture of patrilineal legitimacy is ironized, however, by Vindice's characterization of the duke as "gray-haired adultery" and his metaphoric promotion of the bastard son as the "royal lecher's" proper heir ("true-begot in evil"). Against the adulterous passion and unnatural vigor of the "parched and juiceless luxur" whose "hollow bones" are filled with a "marrow" of unnatural desire, Vindice sets an ironic emblem of purity and chastity, his mistress's skull. From one point of view his obsession with the skull only highlights the confusedness of Vindice's motives. Is he, as the bereaved and impoverished son of an unfairly disgraced father (1.1.118–26), primarily a Hamlet-like agent of true inheritance, or is he (as the diseased eroticism that characterizes his recollections of the dead mistress might suggest) merely the passion-driven agent of a treasonable private vendetta? If the action of the play tends to favor the latter reading, we should notice that the dead woman will later be given a name whose powerful resonance associates the skull itself with the motif of improper or debased inheritance. " 'tis the skull / Of Gloriana whom thou poisonedst last" announces Vindice as the duke recoils from the envenomed kiss of the counterfeit "country lady" (3.5.148–9, 132). As critics have observed, the dressing of a skull in Elizabeth's best-known sobriquet less than four years after the queen's death can hardly have been innocent gesture—especially in the light of Elizabeth's self-promotion as the type of unassailable, "close" virginity and of James's controversial right of succession. When it is remembered, moreover, that this succession was secured through the maternal line, and most immediately through a female whose notorious openness called his own legitimacy into question, one reason why *The Revenger's Tragedy* has often seemed such a quintessentially "Jacobean" work becomes strikingly apparent.[23]

Of course this is not to say the duke is in any simple way a figure for James—indeed it might be conjectured that the dynastic layout of this court was deliberately designed to confuse the possibility of any such dangerous "application." Rather the play draws on (and exploits) widely diffused anxieties about questions of legitimacy and succession, which *Hamlet* had already begun to articulate at the end of Elizabeth's reign—questions that left the new Stuart dynasty in an uncomfortably exposed position. Nor should the identification of the idealized "Gloriana" with the dead queen encourage a reading of the play as a piece of straightforward Elizabethan nostalgia; for not only can the "bony lady" in her velvet tires be construed as an uncomfortably burlesque reminder of the cosmetic grotesqueries of the old queen's last years, but the disguised skull has, after all, become the very instrument of Vindice's ambiguous involvement with courtly counterfeiting and corruption in his role as "base-coined pander."

"Amphitheaters in the Body": Playing with Hands on the Shakespearean Stage

> *In more than one respect, man's hands have been his destiny.*
> —Elias Canetti, *Crowds and Power*
>
> *The hand is a peculiar thing.*
> —Martin Heidegger

"Hath not a Jew hands?" What exactly does Shylock mean when he makes the hand a defining mark of humanity? The gesture called for by his rhetorical demand is likely to make us feel that something more than the mere possession of opposable thumbs is involved, but we might be hard pressed to say precisely what. The question can be answered in a somewhat oblique way by invoking a powerful piece of ritual from Frank McGuinness's *Observe the Sons of Ulster Marching towards the Somme*, a play whose action displays an almost fetishistic fascination with the human hand—gesturing, reaching, clasping, crafting, drumming, striking, "seeing," and bleeding. At the climax of the second act, the protagonist, Kenneth Pyper, signs his reluctant allegiance to the atavism of Protestant tribal history by slashing his left hand: "Red hand," goes the chant, "Red sky. Ulster." In the London production the significance of this gesture was underlined by the backdrop against which the entire action was performed—a huge Ulster flag with the blood-red hand at its center.[1]

Although the Red Hand was originally a native Irish device (the clan badge of the Northern O'Neill) and served as a Republican emblem in 1916 (as the Irish Labor Movement's "Red Hand of Liberty"), it is by now exclusively associated in most minds with the intransigent politics of Orange Unionism. Simplified to a political traffic sign, an Ulster *no passaran*, what it says is No Surrender! McGuinness's ritual, however, complicates this message by reactivating the emblem's origins in the Ulster foundation myth, where the soil of Ireland was successfully claimed by one of two Milesian brothers who severed his own hand and hurled it ashore before his rival could touch land. What results is an odd kind of alienation effect that bathes all the hands of the play in an unfamiliar light, investing them with a density of semiotic suggestiveness that the modern hand has lost. In this way, McGuinness's hands belong (like so much else in Northern Ireland) to an archaic, seventeenth-century world.

The political effectiveness of the foundation myth embodied in the Red Hand clearly depends on its ability to concentrate the symbolism of possession and sacrifice into a single extraordinary gesture. Yet at some level its darkly suggestive power refuses to be contained by the allegory, and it resonates, in ways that help to explain why Freud should have considered severed hands among the most potent signs of the uncanny, with other episodes of mutilation whose surface meanings are very different—the terrifying story of an American slave about to be sold away from her family who cut off her hand and flung it in her master's face or (to choose a literary example that may seem closer to my business here) the grotesque episode in Shakespeare's *Titus Andronicus* where the protagonist lops off his hand and sends it to the emperor by way of ransom for his sons. For the Ulster hero the hand is the instrument of seizure and appropriation; for the slave woman it is the tool of labor, the determinant of her market-value; for Titus it is the shield-hand, the sign of his achievements as Rome's defender ("Tell him it was a hand that warded him / From thousand dangers," 3.1.194–5). Yet in each case the amputated member seems charged with an overplus of obscure significance that threatens to rupture the semiotic boundaries of the gesture, rendering it as impossibly full (or empty) of meaning as a scream.[2]

For Freud, predictably enough, the feeling of uncanniness aroused by such images "springs from [their] proximity to the castration complex," and the mutilated hands that uncannily linked the two 1993 prizewinners at the Cannes Film Festival—Jane Campion's *Piano* and Chen Kaige's *Farewell My Concubine*—reflect the explanatory force of his conjecture. Yet the vagueness of Freud's "proximity" seems to hint that he was less than fully satisfied with his own explanation, and the three very differently inflected mutilations I cite are perhaps enough to indicate that the persistence of the hand as a suggestive motif in human culture has less to do with any single universal significance than with its extraordinary symbolic adaptability.[3]

Of course the mysterious stenciled handprints in Neolithic rock paintings are a recognizable reminder that the hand has an ancient metonymic pedigree as a mark of human presence. As the instrument of making and acting it is a widely recognizable symbol of power—like the "hand of God" in which scripture imagines the absolute authority of Jehovah, or the hand of Fatima, which in North African Muslim belief serves as a potent talisman for warding off the evil eye. The meaning of hands seems also to have been shaped by the peculiar relation to the bicameral brain, which has made them a crucial element in the deep structure out of which human beings shape their understanding of the world—the dualistic oppositions of right and left that are so densely inscribed in the language and practices of every culture.[4]

But as the checkered history of the Red Hand reminds us, such universals are invariably overlaid with a superstructure of historically and locally specific meanings—meanings that are inseparable from those of the culturally articulated body to which the hand belongs. For bodies, as recent work in cultural history has made us aware, are artifacts of culture as much as nature: infants come naked into the world, but they are swaddled in meanings almost as quickly as they are swathed in clothes. And those meanings are constitutive of the "body" recognized by culture. We have gradually begun to understand how profoundly unlike, in its (only too legible) physiological operations, its thresholds of shame, its peculiar modes of interiority, was the early modern body to our own. Variously allegorized as a complex heraldic device, a castle, a landscape, a model of the state, a *mappa mundi*, or a microcosm of God's creation, this was a body that invited decipherment, blazoning, mapping, and discovery. Through its humoral relation to the material world on the one hand and its sympathetic relation to the astrological universe on the other, it was seen as indelibly marked with the signs of its own nature and with the signatures of its fate, while in social terms it was understood as a carefully fashioned semiotic structure organized according to elaborate rules of gender and rank, whose meanings became thicker the higher its position in the societal pyramid. The minutely ordered codes of the "vestimentary system" ensured that the very clothes that covered it did not so much adorn as complete this body, enclosing it in a membrane of metaphor that was felt to constitute an inalienable part of the "person."[5]

The hand had a peculiar role in the hierarchy of this construction that is not easily recaptured. Something of its symbolic prominence is indicated by the way in which early modern anatomists from Vesalius and Giulio Casserio to Rembrandt's Doctor Tulp often chose to have themselves represented while engaged in the dissection of the hand (see fig. 1). More was involved here than a mere self-referential play upon the idea of anatomy as a manual art; for the hand, in the words of Vesalius's disciple Columbus, was *organum organorum*, "the organ of organs," and had been cited by such diverse authorities as Aristotle and Galen as the most characteristically human part of the whole body. To anatomize such an organ was to demonstrate anatomy's claim to fulfil the ancient philosophical goal of self-knowledge *(nosce teipsum)*: to know the hand was to know the self.[6]

The hand was also privileged by this culture as an expressive instrument. In contemporary Anglo-Saxon culture, the hand is most characteristically experienced, perhaps, as a site of embarrassment, something we don't quite know what to do with. It may still have access to a diminished range of symbolic gestures but they are generally deployed in an unconscious and incoherent way, and its full expressive power is glimpsed only in very specialized contexts—in certain forms of dance, for example, or in the dazzling manual choreography of the deaf. For Shakespeare and his contemporaries, by contrast, it was not only a primary site of meaning but the conduit of extraordinary energies. Thus for example—as the delicate gestural ballet of *Romeo and Juliet* act 1, scene 5 seems designed to remind us—the simple ritual of handfasting was still considered sufficient to establish the mystical bond of marriage between man and wife without intervention by the church—a bond traditionally emblematized in the clasped hands of *fede*, or wedding rings.[7] In certain highly charged circumstances, moreover, the hand (infused, as it were, with the spiritual current that passes between the hands of God and Adam on the Sistine ceiling) might become a surrogate for the divine hand itself. This was the source of the power that in early modern belief informed not merely the sanctified hands of priests and kings but those of ordinary parents in the daily rites of family blessing. Such details are enough to remind us that, like the rest of the human body, the hand is not what it was and that it must once have occupied a quite different place in the psychic topography of the human body.[8]

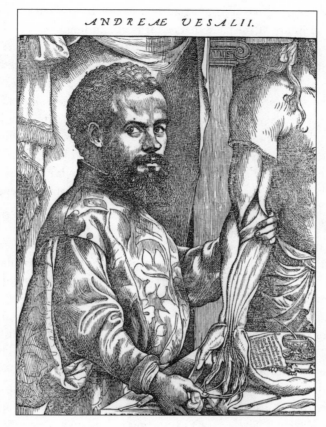

1. Vesalius demonstrating the anatomy of the hand. Frontispiece to Andreas Vesalius, De Humanis Corporis Fabrica *(1543), reprinted by permission of the Folger Shakespeare Library.*

SIGNATURES OF THE HAND

If the early modern body was a densely textualized site, no part of it was more prominently inscribed than the hand. When the Soothsayer of *Antony*

and Cleopatra offers to read from "nature's infinite book of secrecy" (1.2.10)
it is to the scripture of the palm that he turns. According to seventeenth-century chiromantic theory there was a *"Secret Concordance, and Harmony"*
between the stars and the human hand, whose lines were reckoned to be produced "from the *Imagination* [of the soul] of the Greater *World* . . . in the
Generation of *Man*." This power, "otherwise called *Predestination, Science,*
Fate," performed "its Authority and Office by the *Stars*," which engraved the
"Signatures" of fate on the infant's palm.[9] Such signatures, according to Sir
Thomas Browne, were made by "the Finger of God [which] hath left an
Inscription upon all His works"—one that, if we learn how to read it, contains the Adamic name in which is expressed the true nature of every creature. In human beings, the inscription is jointly composed of "Characters in
our Faces" and of "certain mystical figures in our Hands, which I dare not
call mere dashes, strokes *a la vollee*, or at random, because delineated by a
Pencil that never works in vain; and hereof I take more particular notice,
because I carry that in mine own hand which I could never read of nor discover in another."[10]

The potent signatures of identity and destiny borne by the hand help to
account for the occult power ascribed to it in rituals of witchcraft—such as
those the Duchess of Malfi fearfully associates with the amputated hand sent
by her brother, or those the witches perform with "pilot's thumb" and "finger of birth-strangled babe" in *Macbeth* (1.3.27; 4.1.30). But they also seem to
contribute to the talismanic authority invested in the written signature and
the writer's "hand." The very act of writing indeed may seem to involve an
uncanny mimesis, for if scripture routinely represents "the hand of God" as
the instrument of divine power, it also expresses destiny as a kind of script—
like the fatal handwriting of Belshazzar's feast (Dan. 5.5, 24–8). According to
the chiromancer Johann Rothmann, the hand was chosen to bear its potent
signs of difference precisely as a result of qualities that gave it a kind of natural sympathy with the inscribing hand of destiny—its powers not merely of
"action" but of signification: "if you desire to know wherefore these
Signatures are found in the *Hand*, and perhaps not in any other *Part* of the
Body, you must conceive, that our *Hands* are the most *Noble Members* in perfecting of all manner of *Actions;* they are the executors of our *Primary*
Conceptions. . . . therefore our *Fate* for the most part, and our *Power* are very
much reposed in our *Hands*."[11]

On a more mundane level the hand was invested with the social authority of handwriting, whose enhanced prestige, reflected in the pedagogic prac-

tice of Tudor grammar schools, has been amply documented by Jonathan Goldberg.[12] The hand here had a double role: it was both that which made possible full participation in the new print culture and that which served as a symbolic guarantor of individual difference, privacy, and possession against the mechanical usurpations of print. The quasi-magical authority of hand-writing was most evident in the power invested in the signature as a sign of individual presence and consent. The symbolic equivalence between the appending of a signature and the giving of a hand is neatly registered in Middleton and Rowley's *Changeling*, where Alsemero's "confirmation by the hand royal" punningly equates the act of signing with the ritual of handfast-ing (1.1.80–1). But the written "hand" was also more generally understood as a mark of authenticity. Thus one could speak metaphorically of the presence of a writer's "hand" in a printed work, meaning that it bore the authentic marks of his peculiar genius.[13]

The 1623 folio of Shakespeare's plays is famously prefaced by Droeshout's portrait engraving, a "Figure" whose illuminated head is designed, as Ben Jonson's accompanying verses suggest, to advertise the con-tents as the distinctive product of the poet's "wit." In their address "To the great Variety of Readers," however, the actor-editors Heminge and Condell place as much emphasis upon the creative function of the poet's *hand*. They offer the plays as the work of one "Who, as he was a happy imitator of Nature, was a most gentle expresser of it. His mind and hand went together: and what he thought, he uttered with that easiness, that we have scarce received from him a blot in his papers." Just as Hamlet's "character" is pun-ningly made vivid in his "hand" (*Hamlet*, 4.7.51–2) or as Edgar's allegedly unfilial "character" is exposed in the vicious "hand" of the conspiratorial let-ter flourished by Edmund (*King Lear*, 1.2.56–68), so it is as if the poet is most present to his colleagues' imagination through the manuscript signatures of his genius—the unblotted "papers" they received from him in the playhouse, the "True Original[s]" from which the folio itself has supposedly been pro-duced.[14]

Thus the very existence of the folio becomes a powerful testimony to the growing power and prestige of the writer's hand, and it is a sense of the unbroken chain linking the printed text, the manuscript, the writing hand, and the author's individual genius that shapes the controlling conceit of Hugh Holland's encomiastic sonnet "Upon the Lines and Life of the Famous Scenic Poet, Master William Shakespeare." Summoning the audience to wring their own generous hands in mourning (as they once brought them together in applause), Holland finds in the dead playwright's printed verses a testimony to the immortality of his "hand": "For though his line of life went soon about, / The life of his lines shall never out." Holland was no doubt remembering that in the sonnets Shakespeare had registered his own sense of the peculiar metonymic authority of the writer's hand: in 65 the "swift foot" of time is challenged by the "strong hand" whose presence is miraculously preserved in the black ink of the text (ll. 12–14); in 49, the poet's hand is playfully "uprear[ed]" against himself (l. 11) as if it were a kind of malign double—rather as Benedick and Beatrice discover in their written professions of love "our own hands against our hearts" (*Much Ado About Nothing*, 5.4.91–2).[15]

Such conceits, in which the hand develops an uncanny life of its own— as though it were a kind of second or alternative self mediating between the writer and his book, and capable of standing for either (or both)—are by no means exceptional. The feminist pamphleteer "Constantia Munda," for example, dedicates a tract to her mother, reaffirming the filial "bond" with an extraordinary metonymic flourish—"I here present you with my writing hand"—in which the printed text stands in for the manuscript, which in turn stands for the hand now vicariously offered as a pledge and token of her essential self. But perhaps the most elaborate examples of such play occur in a text exclusively devoted to the expressive power of the human hand, John Bulwer's two-part treatise on "manual rhetoric," *Chirologia/Chironomia*. For Bulwer's encomiasts, the author's hand is consubstantial with the text, in which "each line's a line of life." Bulwer himself, playfully maintaining that his "Fancy" is ruled by his "*Hand's* Genius," attributes the book's very authorship to the invention of "my Soul's inspired *Hand*," making it a work of "autography" in which "the *Hand*. . . . hath . . . proved its own Biographer." In writing itself the hand writes the self.[16]

THE SIGNIFYING HAND

But if the hand writes the self, it also speaks it, and this, for Bulwer, is its greatest glory. It is, he notes, an ancient "symbol of action," but it specially excels in rhetorical *actio*—the repertory of bodily signals with which orators and actors amplified and intensified their verbal performances—through which it is able to "translate a thought into discoursing signs . . . while the articulated Fingers supply the office of a voice."[17] For Bulwer, gesture is not a mere ornament of speech but a vehicle of communication in its own right, a "language" with its own rules (see figs. 2 and 3). Thus he can describe the hand as "the *Spokesman* of the body" and second only to the tongue, whose "*Substitute* and *Vicegerent*" it is. He calls it "the Tongue of *hearty goodwill*," "the Engineer of invention, and wit's true *Palladium* . . . cousin german to the Fancy," and the "relative" of the heart.[18] Often, indeed, this "famous *companion of Reason*" begins to sound superior to the tongue, which it is able "to over-match . . . in speaking labours, and the significant variety of important motions."[19] In the dedication to *Chirologia*, the hand's expressive capacity is conveyed by a remarkable theatrical conceit. Bulwer imagines the body as a piece of biological architecture whose most arresting features are "Two Amphitheaters," upon whose stages are displayed "the voluntary motions of the Mind"; these structures, are identified as "the *Hand* and the *Head*," and of the two it turns out to be the hand that, by virtue of its expressive immediacy, is capable of the greatest eloquence.[20] "An *active Wit*," as one of his encomiasts puts it, "employs a *speaking Hand*," because the hand is privileged to express the motions of the mind with a directness denied to any other organ.[21]

Like the head, of course, the hand stands in need of education through *The Art of Manuall Rhetorique* outlined in *Chironomia*, but (also like the head) it is endowed with natural gifts that are among the defining characteristics of humankind. "In regard of the Rhetorical properties of the *Hand*," writes Bulwer, "*Man may well be called Chirosophus, id est Manu sapiens*, Hand-wise." And such, he insists, are its "force and estimation among all Nations," that anyone who fails to master its techniques of "*benevolent insinuation*" will seem "to be disarmed of all humanity."[22]

Far from representing the eccentric enthusiasm of a self-styled "chirosopher," such views (as Bulwer was at pains to remind his reader) were grounded in the authority of a number of classical philosophers—notably Aristotle, who argued (*De Anima*, 2, 9, 421a) that humans were "far more intelligent than [other animals]" precisely because they had "a far more accurate sense of touch," and Anaxagoras, who maintained that man was "the wisest of all creatures, because he had *Hands*."[23] This perception of a deep causal link between human intelligence and the unique capacities of the human hand anticipates the conclusions of those modern anthropologists who argue that it was in the hand, rather than its symbolic double the head,

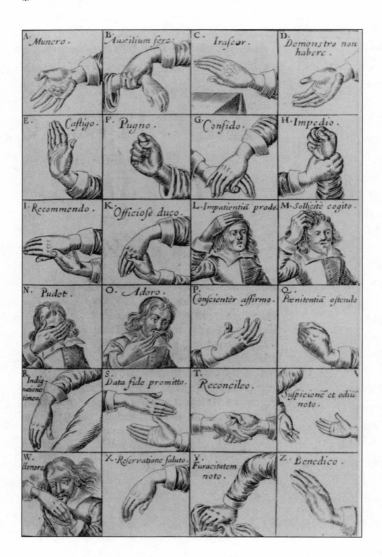

2. Examples of manual rhetoric from John Bulwer, Chirologia *(1644), reprinted by permission of the Folger Shakespeare Library.*

that the crucial developments occurred that separated human beings from other primates. Indeed, if Elias Canetti is right, it is to the activities of the hand that we must look for the origins of language itself.[24]

Renaissance theorists of communication like Bulwer, similarly con-

3. *Examples of manual rhetoric from John Bulwer,* Chirologia *(1644), reprinted by permission of the Folger Shakespeare Library.*

vinced that "the *Hand* and meaning ever are allied," further justified their claims by appealing to scripture.[25] Bulwer claimed that gesture "hath since been sanctified and made a holy language by the expressions of our Saviour's *Hands;* whose gestures have given a sacred allowance to natural significations of ours. And God speaks to us by the signs of his *Hand* (as *Bernard* observes) when he works wonders which are the proper signs of his *Hand*. . . . And as God speaks to us with his *Hand*, by a supernatural way: so we naturally speak to Him, as well as unto men, by the *appeal* of our *Hands* in *admiration*, *attestation*, and *prayer*." Moreover, as "the only speech that is natural to Man," gesture seemed to preserve the universal transparency of prelapsarian speech. Identifying in it the traces of an Adamic eloquence that had "had the happiness to escape the curse at the confusion of Babel," Bulwer acclaimed it as "the *Tongue and general language of Human Nature*, which, without teaching, men in all regions of the habitable world do at the first sight most easily understand."[26]

Such views were in fact widespread among early modern theorists of language. Thus Montaigne, for example, could describe gesture as constituting "a language common and public to all . . . [which] must be . . . deemed the proper and peculiar speech of human nature," whereas the Italian apostle of manual rhetoric Giovanni Bonifacio devoted his *L'arte de'cenni* (1616) to the task of restoring the "universal language" that humankind had foolishly abandoned "in favour of so many different artificial ways of speaking, that one region cannot understand or agree with another."[27] The anxiety that such texts display about the problems of cultural exchange is a useful reminder that while their notions of gestural universality were solidly grounded in manuals of classical rhetoric, they had a direct application, as Dilwyn Knox has observed, to the "exploring, converting and plundering [of] the New World and elsewhere."[28]

From one point of view, indeed, a work such as Bulwer's *Chirologia* deserves to be placed alongside Hakluyt's *Voyages* and Purchas's *Pilgrimes*, as a primary text of English imperialism. For Bulwer, along with his encomiasts, makes it abundantly clear that the burgeoning interest in the science of universal languages was a direct product of early voyaging enterprise and of the desire for trade that was the principal driving force of English expansionism.[29] Already, Bulwer assured his readers, the language of hands had enabled English merchants to open "commerce with those salvage nations . . . of the West. . . . driving a rich and silent Trade, by signs, whereby many a dumb bargain without the crafty Brokage of the tongue is advantageously made."[30] Properly mastered, according to one of his encomiasts, this "grand, / And express Pantotype of speech," would "redeem [humankind] . . . from *Babel's* doom" by establishing a "universal Idiom" in which "All Tribes shall now each other understand / Which (though not of one lip) are of one Hand." In the ensuing golden age of communication, commerce would flourish even with "those rational Brutes" of Africa, "the dumb *Guinea Drills*."[31] As though in fulfillment of Bulwer's dream, the frontispiece to Cave Beck's *Universall Caracter* (1657) features an Englishman in converse with a turbanned Hindu, an African, and a Brazilian Indian who raises his hand in a gesture of silent eloquence (see fig. 4).

4. *The transparent eloquence of the hand. Frontispiece to Cave Beck*, The Universall Caracter *(1657), reprinted by permission of the Folger Shakespeare Library Chapter.*

— ❉ —

THE ACTOR'S HAND

Shakespeare appears to mock such touching faith in the capacity of gesture to transcend the culture-bound limits of ordinary speech in *The Comedy of Errors*, where the luckless Dromio of Ephesus is baffled by the forceful manual rhetoric of the Syracusan stranger whom he takes for his own master: "He told his mind upon my ear. / Beshrew his hand, I scarce could understand it. . . . He strook so plainly, I could too well feel his blows, and withal so doubtfully, that I scarce could understand them" (2.1.48–54). And in *The Tempest*, it is typically the sentimental Gonzalo who celebrates the perfect transparency of the "excellent dumb discourse" employed by the monstrous "people of the island" (3.3.30, 39). It is, of course, part of Shakespeare's irony that the creatures of Ariel's antimasque should not be true "islanders" at all but "actors," spirit-performers in a "living drollery," reminding us that the theater had its own particular reasons for nourishing an interest in the communicative efficacy of bodily "action." Indeed the very term "acting" referred originally only to the player's art of gesture and did not acquire its expanded meaning until the early seventeenth century.[32]

The frontispiece that Bulwer commissioned for *Chironomia* acknowledges the role of theater as an ancient nursery of manual rhetoric—even if the author is anxious to distinguish between the more restrained style of gesture proper to the orator and that which "is scenical, and belongs more to the theater, than the forum." In the engraving, the stage players Andronicus and Roscius are shown tutoring the orators Demosthenes and Cicero. Andronicus holds up a mirror to his pupil, inscribed with the word *actio*, and Bulwer explains that his task was to reform "the defect that was before in [Demosthenes'] Orations for want of Action." It is *actio*, the language of the hand, more than anything, that endows rhetoric with the active power of eloquence.[33]

B. L. Joseph long ago recognized the relevance of Bulwer's treatises for an understanding of sixteenth-and seventeenth-century theatrical convention. The chirosopher's elaborate codification of oratorical practice identifies appropriate "actions" for practically every imaginable affective context—and some of these, as Joseph was able to demonstrate, have an obvious application to particular theatrical moments in Shakespeare. For example,

Bulwer's account of *Gestus 58 Injurias remitto* ("TO PRESS HARD AND WRING ANOTHER'S HAND . . . a natural *insinuation of love, duty, remembrance, supplication, peace, and of forgiveness of all injuries*") actually cites the same passage in Plutarch from which Shakespeare derived the famous stage direction for Coriolanus's reconciliation with his mother, "holds her by the hand, silent" (*Coriolanus* 5.3.182). Yet it is also clear, as Andrew Gurr has shown, that by the end of the sixteenth century, gestural pedantry of the kind favored by Bulwer was regarded in theatrical circles as somewhat old-fashioned. More important than the details of Bulwer's system, I would argue, is what it implies about the extraordinary *visibility* of hands in Elizabethan society generally and on Shakespeare's stage in particular.[34]

An emphasis on the power of *actio* is understandable in a theater whose rhetorical inheritance and playing conditions combined to give particular prominence to the actor's body in all its corporeal fullness of presence. But it also reflected the practical necessities of an industry that was engaged in its own form of mercantile expansionism. In the first half of the seventeenth century, English touring companies found a significant market for their talents in continental Europe, where (as the pantomimic arts of *Hamlet*'s "Tragedians of the City" arguably remind us) cultivation of the language of gesture became especially important.[35] Indeed when Fynes Moryson witnessed the performance of a rather down-at-heel English company at Frankfurt in 1592, he observed that, despite the actors' want of decent scripts and "any good apparel [or] ornament of the stage . . . the Germans, not understanding a word they said . . . flocked wonderfully *to see their gesture and action*." It was, evidently, their hands that spoke.[36]

SPEAKING HANDS

"Speak hands for me!" When, in *Julius Caesar* (3.1.76), Casca thrusts his envious dagger into Caesar's body, he might seem, at first sight, to be simply renouncing language in favor of action: "where words prevail not," as Kyd's Lorenzo has it, "violence prevails" (*Spanish Tragedy*, 2.1.108).[37] Certainly Casca's *actio* puts into practice his earlier insistence that "every bondman in his own hand bears / The power to cancel his captivity" (1.3.101–2)—at the same time consciously reversing Brutus's kiss of feigned submission to the power of Caesar's hand (3.1.52). But his apostrophe is energized by a viciously witty play upon the idea of the hand as "the *Spokesman* of the body" in Bulwer's phrase. This will be speech that kills, killing that speaks— a gesture that collapses the distinctions between speech, *actio*, and action, just as it cancels out the distance between the literal and the metaphorical.[38]

As Shakespeare stages the assassination scene, however, the unmediated directness of utterance to which Casca lays claim will be complicated and confused by an obsessive focus upon hands—gesticulating, clasping, and smeared with blood.

❋

BRUTUS:

Stoop, Romans, stoop
And let us bathe our hands *in Caesar's blood*
Up to the elbows, and besmear our swords. . . .
And waving our red weapons o'er our heads,
Let's all cry, "Peace, freedom, and liberty!"

ANTONY:

I do beseech you, if you bear me hard,
Now whilst your purpled hands *do reek and smoke,*
Fulfil your pleasure. . . .

BRUTUS:

Though now we must appear bloody and cruel,
As by our hands *and this our present act*
You see we do, yet see you but our hands,
And this the bleeding business they have done.
Our hearts you see not; they are pitiful.

3.3.103–9, 157–9, 165–9; EMPHASIS ADDED[39]

❋

The symbolic fulcrum of the scene is Brutus's hand-washing ritual, with its uncanny fulfillment of Calphurnia's dream, in which "many lusty Romans . . . did bathe their hands" in the blood fountaining from Caesar's statue (2.2.78–9), and it is significant that both details appear to have been entirely of Shakespeare's invention.[40] The hand washing is a *gestus* whose power to shock depends partly on its travesty of one of the most familiar of all manual signs—one that plays a key role in the action of at least two other

Shakespeare plays, *Richard II* and *Macbeth*—the Pilate-like gesture called by Bulwer "Innocentiam ostendo," and used, he says "by those who would *profess their innocency* and declare *they have no Hand in that foul business, not so much as by their manual assent.* . . . A gesture very significant, for the *Hands* naturally imply, as it were in Hieroglyphic, men's acts and operations; and that cleansing motion denotes the *cleanness of their actions.* As this expression is heightened by the addition of water, 'tis made by the Egyptians the Hieroglyphic of innocency."[41]

Ironically designed as a symbolic "profession of innocency"—demonstrating Brutus's claim that the murder is the work of priestly "sacrificers [and] not butchers" (2.1.166)—the ritual becomes a "hieroglyphic" of guilt, whose meaning is brought home to the audience by Antony's ambiguous counter-ritual of hand-clasping. As a vicious replay of the rite of bonding to which Brutus invited the conspirators in act 2, scene 1, "Give me your hands all over, one by one" (l. 112), Antony's gestures shockingly invert the elaborate symbolism of truce-making, faith-pledging, reconciliation, and "forgiveness of all injuries" discovered by Bulwer in the act of shaking and pressing another's hand:[42]

❀

ANTONY:
Let each man render me his bloody hand
First, Marcus Brutus, will I shake with you;
Next, Caius Cassius, do I take your hand;
Now, Decius Brutus, yours; now yours, Metellus;
Yours Cinna, and my valiant Casca, yours;
Though last, not least in love, yours, good Trebonius.
    3.1.184–89

❀

Antony's falsification of "manual faith" coincides with the transfer of blood from the conspirators' hand to his own. The hand that in this way vicariously imbrues itself in the victim's blood is, the action compels us to notice, the same hand that two scenes later licenses a new round of murder ("look, with a spot I damn him," 4.1.6). A modern audience will respond immediately to the theatrical cruelty of this moment through the tactile immediacy of those hands, sticky with blood, but may have difficulty reimagining the original force of the handclasping itself or in recognizing its important symmetry with the gesture that closes the scene, when Antony reaches out to Octavius's servant: "Lend me your hand" (3.1.297). While the celebrated Arafat-Rabin handshake of 1993 is evidence that in certain highly charged circumstances such gestures can regain something of their old emblematic power, it remains true (as one historian of gesture has recently argued) that the meanings of the early modern handshake were richer and more intense than those that are preserved in the commonplace courtesy of today.[43] The reason for this, not surprisingly, lay not so much in the gesture as in the instrument; for the hand, as Bulwer explained, possessed occult properties that made it not merely a passive vehicle but an active agent in such affective transactions. "There is," he writes, "some Pythagorical mystery in this authentic guise of the *Hand* in *warrantizing faithful dealings*," a mystery that, "flows from a secret and religious reverence to that comprehensive number *Ten* . . . since meeting in their formal close they seem to greet one another in that number." He further observes that "Physicians the subtle and diligent observers of nature, think that there is in the *Hand* a certain secret and hidden virtue, and a convenient force or philtre to procure *affection*," so that the holding of hands does not merely represent but actually *produces* the "*knitting* together of *hearts*." There is, moreover, an inherent "sympathy between the will and the *Hand*: for, the will affectionately inclined and moved to stretch forth her self, the *Hand*, that is moved by the same spirit, willing to go out and set a gloss upon the inward motion, casts itself into a form extending to a semblance of the inward appetite."[44] Thus Bulwer argues,

> nature . . . seems to have ordained the *Hand* to be the general instrument of the mind. Therefore when the mind would disclose the virtue, strength, and forcible operation of her *favor* and *good-will*, out of the abundance of her *love he puts forth the hand*, and in that as it were the *heart* itself, with *affectionate love;* and receives them again by a natural bill of exchange in the *Hand of another; which is verily a sign of mutual agreement*, and of a *perfect conjunction;* for which cause *Pindarus a Poet* of an aspiring wit, placed the heart and *Hand* as relatives under one and the same parallel.[45]

What Bulwer describes is a "conjunction" that is as much literal as it is symbolic, and it is just such a "conjunction" that visibly binds the "inward souls" of the French and English kings in act 3, scene 1 of *King John*:[46]

> This royal hand and mine are newly knit,
> And the conjunction of our inward souls
> Married in league, coupled, and link'd together
> With all religious strength of holy vows. . . .
> And shall these hands, so lately purg'd of blood,
> So newly join'd in love, so strong in both,
> Unyoke this seizure and this kind regreet?
> Play fast and loose with faith? so jest with heaven?
> Make such unconstant children of ourselves,
> As now again to snatch our palm from palm,
> Unswear faith sworn.
>   3.1.226–45

The theatrical power of Philip's repudiation ("England, I will fall from thee," l. 320) can thus be fully realized only through the implied direction to drop John's hand—a gesture that does not merely *stand for*, but vividly *embodies* their spiritual rupture.[47]

It is, more than anything, this intense intimacy with mind, will, and heart that makes the hand (as it is again for Brutus in *Julius Caesar*, 2.1.58) into a metonymic extension of the self, so that it is with no sense of exaggeration or paradox that Bulwer can assert that anyone who "forfeits the Recognizance of his *Hand* . . . by falsifying his manual faith proves a kind of renegado to himself."[48] No wonder, then, that Othello should scan Desdemona's "liberal hand" with such ferocious intensity for the signs of her "liberal [libertine] heart"—only to be convinced of the unnatural divorce of hand and heart emblazoned in "our new heraldry" (*Othello*, 3.4.36–47); no wonder either, perhaps, that the token of his faith and her supposed betrayal should be a *hand*-kerchief that has been promiscuously passed from hand to hand, a handkerchief fittingly "dy'd in mummy. . . . Conserv'd of maidens' hearts" (3.4.74–5).

THE SEVERED HAND

Julius Caesar's simultaneous association of hands with blood and rhetoric suggests that just behind the action of the murder scene lie recollections of one of the most notorious atrocities that followed in the wake of Caesar's assassination—the killing and mutilation of Cicero, whose philippics against Julius Caesar had incurred the enmity of Mark Antony. Antony had the orator's body dismembered, commanding that "his head and his hands should straight be set up over the pulpit for orations, in the place called Rostra." This display not only drew sarcastic attention to the dead man's hands as (silenced) instruments of eloquence, but also (according to Plutarch's "Life of Marcus Antonius") gave special prominence to the right hand "with the which he had written the invective orations (called *Philippides*) against Caesar." The meaning of this vindictive display was abundantly clear to the populace who in this "fearful and horrible sight . . . thought they saw not Cicero's face, but an image of Antonius' life and disposition." According to Bulwer "the malice of *Antony* forced tears and lamentations into the eyes of the Romans, when they saw *Cicero's* Right Hand, instrument of his divine Eloquence, with which he penned and pronounced the Philippics, nailed fast unto his head, and set upon the . . . Pulpit of Common Pleas in the *Forum*."[49]

If *Julius Caesar* displaces the sanguinary symbolism of Antony's revenge onto the bloodstained hands of the conspirators, it is relished and elaborated in the barbaric spectacles of Shakespeare's first Roman tragedy, *Titus Andronicus* (1589). The play's notorious parade of mangled limbs bodies forth the dismemberment of the body politic itself, and partly because the injured Titus *is* himself the hand that wards the royal head from danger (just as Coriolanus is imagined "the arm our soldier," 1.1.116), severed hands are especially conspicuous here. Even the play's title seems designed to alert the audience to the metonymic importance of such images; for while "Andronicus," like the other characters of Shakespeare's tragedy, is entirely fictional, his name recalls those of three historical characters: the Byzantine Emperor Andronicus Commenus (1183–5) whose right hand was cut off by the mob who butchered him; the Andronicus of 2 Maccabees 4.34, who entrapped his enemy by the fraudulent offer of his hand; and (most pertinently of all) the Greek actor whose figure adorns the title page of Bulwer's *Chironomia* as an embodiment of the communicative power of theatrical *actio*—that too in a context that directly associates him with the fatally eloquent hand of Cicero (see fig. 5). In Shakespeare, as in Plutarch, the severed hand is identified as an emblem of silenced eloquence—a sign, like Lavinia's severed tongue, of speech cut off at the very root.[50]

But while educated playgoers would have been reminded of the Roman orator's fate by the spectacle of mutilated tongues, heads, and hands that

5. *The orators Demosthenes and Cicero taking instruction from the actors Andronicus and Roscius. Frontispiece to John Bulwer,* Chironomia *(1644), reprinted by permission of the Folger Shakespeare Library.*

expresses the tragedy's preoccupation with the breakdown of language and the disintegration of the body politic that follows from it, more hands than Cicero's are being remembered here. Titus's willing surrender of his own hand also seems calculated to recall one of the most celebrated demonstrations of Roman *virtus*—the sacrifice of his right hand by the captured warrior Gaius Mucius Scaevola—an episode spectacularly dramatized in Heywood's *Rape of Lucrece* (1607).[51] Heywood's Scevola thrusts his "base hand" into the fire to punish it for his own failure to assassinate the Etruscan king, Lars Porsena (ll. 2739–45).[52] Just as Scevola mutilates his right hand as an expression of contempt for Rome's royal enemy, so Titus sacrifices his left as a defiant offering to his own tyrannical emperor, Saturninus. If *Titus Andronicus* played off such recollections, it was able to do so partly because these classical anecdotes, in turn, resonated so powerfully with much more recent events. Mutilated hands figure prominently in several Protestant martyrologies—most famously in Foxe's account of Cranmer's burning (1556), where the archbishop punishes the hand that has written his recantation, thrusting it into the flames in a gesture that rewrites Gaius Mucius's heroism in the language of Christian bodily discipline: "And if thy hand offend thee, cut it off" (Mark 9.43).[53] Just ten years before the staging of *Titus*, moreover, England had been scandalized by the punishments inflicted upon the Protestant polemicist John Stubbs and his publisher William Page for a pamphlet attacking Elizabeth's prospective marriage to the Duke of Alençon. Page and the unluckily named Stubbs were prosecuted under a statute of Mary's that prescribed amputation of the right hand for "the authors and sowers of seditious writings," and when Titus offered his ambivalent proof of allegiance to the emperor, many in the audience might have recalled the pamphleteer's stubborn display of loyalty to Elizabeth: "notwithstanding the bitter pain and doleful loss of my hand immediately before chopped off, I was able, by God's mercy, to say with heart and tongue, before I left the block, these words, 'God save the Queen!'"[54]

Characteristic of all these narratives, as of Shakespeare's play, is the apparently disproportionate sense of outrage and revulsion that attaches to mutilation of the hands. In both his accounts of Cicero's death, Plutarch emphasizes the special "cruelty" of Antony's proceeding, and his indignation is further highlighted by North's marginal commentary. Yet compared with the treatment of Philologus, forced to broil and eat "little morsels" of his own flesh—a punishment whose "goodness" Plutarch commends by way of contrast—the "wicked" treatment of Cicero's corpse seems relatively mild.

By the same token, many worse torments were inflicted upon the long-suffering bodies of Elizabeth's subjects than those experienced by Stubbs and Page, yet their case seems to have been regarded as especially shocking—and it is probably significant that the Marian statute under which they were condemned, though fully consistent with a language of punishment that habitually marked the criminal body with the signs of its crime, was very rarely invoked.[55] According to the Spanish ambassador, the penalty appalled even Alençon himself, who averred that "he was very sorry they had cut off the hands of the men concerned with the book, and he would indeed be glad if he could remedy it, even at the cost of two fingers of his own hand."[56]

Such reactions make sense, it seems to me, only in terms of the extraordinary symbolic value invested in the hand—a value that the circumstances of early modern culture had, if anything, enhanced. It was no accident the bodies of early modern suicides should have been symbolically punished for their self-canceling crime by amputation of the right hand.[57] When Thomas Beard wanted to demonstrate the exemplary meaning of Marlowe's inadvertent suicide (to take a notorious example), he gloatingly stressed the way in which, through a murderous frenzy of self-division, "the very hand that had writ those blasphemies" became the chosen instrument of divine vengeance against the poet's equally blasphemous head. Nor was such symbolism only a tool of oppression, since the victims were often as anxious as their tormentors to exploit the symbolic potential of their hands. Just as the captured Roman warrior disdainfully sacrificed his defeated sword hand, so the Henrician cleric resolved to punish his writing hand for signing things "contrary to my heart."[58] And Stubbs, as if remembering Cranmer's example, declared upon the scaffold, "I will not have a guiltless heart and an infamous hand," before offering his arm to the executioner's axe. His publisher held up a bleeding stump as the signature of his violated loyalty to the queen: "I have left there a true Englishman's hand."[59]

The force of such gestures depends on the way in which the hand is figured as the locus of a kind of second self—one that can be distanced, and if necessary separated, from the true self.[60] Thus it can be made to suffer as a scapegoat, drawing punishment away from those symbolic loci of identity with which it is so often paired—the head and the heart. Stubbs is at pains to admit that his writing has "offend[ed] the laws" but "without an evil meaning" (p. xxxv). Thus his hand can be "infamous" and deserving of punishment, even as his heart remains "guiltless." And just as Gaius Mucius's actions rehabilitated the normally "sinister" left hand (to the point where he

was henceforth proud to be known by the ill-omened name of Scaevola—
"left-handed"), so the errant pamphlet writer is at pains to demonstrate the
continuing loyalty of his left hand: "Stubbs, having his right hand cut off, put
off his hat with his left, and said with a loud voice, 'God save the queen' " (p.
xxxvi)—thus reestablishing, as he later insisted, an essential consonance of
inner and outer self, of heart and tongue. Using the same codes to rather different effect, Shakespeare's Titus offers his sinister hand to the emperor as a
(deliberately ambivalent) sign of loyalty and integrity—while his right hand
is used to deal out symbolic discipline to his refractory heart:

> This poor right hand of mine
> Is left to tyrannize upon my breast,
> Who, when my heart, all mad with misery,
> Beats in this hollow prison of my flesh,
> Then thus I thump it down.
>
> 3.2.7-11

This readiness of victims to turn the symbolic power of the hand against
their oppressors helps to illustrate how the very things that made the hand
such a potent token in the language of punishment also made it a dangerous
and volatile instrument. For what finally seems to have rendered the treatment
of a Stubbs or a Cicero so objectionable was not any simple excess of cruelty,
much less the vicious symmetry between offense and retribution, but a sense
that violence inflicted upon the hand broke an important taboo, making its
exemplary implication in the process of punishment somehow unbearable.
What is at issue, I suggest, is a threat to the body's power to mean—a threat,
that is, to its very humanity. *Titus Andronicus* can help us see how this is so.

In *Titus* the visual prominence accorded to hands is more than matched
by a compulsive rhetorical elaboration that drives the deranged Titus to his
infamous quibble "O, handle not the theme to talk of hands" (3.2.29). This
rebuke has a brutally comic redundancy that serves only to emphasize the
"theme" it pretends to suppress, drawing attention to the way the play can't
stop handling hands. The troping of hands begins in the opening scene,
where the hand of paternal blessing to which Lavinia appeals ("O, bless me
here with thy victorious hand," 1.1.163) is transformed to the bloody hand of
murder ("Lord Titus here . . . With his own hand did slay his youngest son,"
1.1.415–8). Then from the reaching and clasping hands that seal the fates of
Martius and Quintus in the pit (2.3.237–45) and the fatal handwriting that

supposedly confirms their guilt, through the successive amputations of Lavinia's (2.4) and Titus's hands (3.1.191), and on to the final clasping of Marcus's and Lucius's hands (5.3.132–9), which signifies the knitting up of Rome's "broken limbs . . . into one body" (5.3.72), both action and language compulsively highlight the physical presence, the vulnerability and violence, as well as the expressive power of hands.

Most striking of all is the weird procession contrived by Titus at the end of act 3, scene 1, in which the handless Lavinia is required to carry her father's severed hand in her own tongueless mouth. If this, by once again forcing together the two mutilated organs of expression, seems to mimic Antony's vindictive emblem, the connection is appropriate because of *Titus Andronicus*'s persistent association of hands with writing and speech. Titus sees his hands first as the instruments of martial action ("For hands to do Rome service is but vain," 3.1.80), to the point where his heroic identity becomes embodied in his severed hand ("give his majesty my hand. / Tell him it was a hand that warded him / From thousand dangers, bid him bury it," 3.1.193–5)—just as Lavinia's feminine identity was invested in the "lily hands" described by Marcus that "could have better sew'd than Philomel" and "Tremble[d], like aspen leaves upon a lute" (2.4.43–5).[61] But once severed from the body their hands cease to bear the print of gender and are almost exclusively imagined as the instruments of rhetorical *actio*, tools of signification. Lavinia's hands are amputated not only to prevent her from writing ("See how with signs and tokens she can scrowl," 2.4.5) but to deny her the eloquence of gesture. Deprived of hands as well as tongue, she becomes in a double sense a "Speechless complainant"—forced to the painful foot-and-mouth calligraphy of act 4, scene 1. Her very "signs" are "martyr'd," her very "action" rendered "dumb" (3.2.36–40). If language, as Aristotle had maintained, defines the human *polis*, then the Rome for which Lavinia stands is close to becoming an absolute wilderness, shorn, by the "barbarous, beastly" trimming (5.1.97) of Goth and Moor, even of the universal language to which the most barbarous peoples had access.

Titus symbolically participates in his daughter's dumbness when he consents to the amputation of his own left hand:

> Thy niece and I, poor creatures, want our hands,
> And cannot passionate our ten-fold grief
> With folded arms.
>
> 3.2.5–7

No, not a word, how can I grace my talk,
Wanting a hand to give it action.[62]
>   5.2.17–18

Thereafter he must painstakingly attempt to reassemble his disintegrated
world, "perfecting" himself in a "dumb action" that wants even the assistance
of hands. Finally, as if returning to the very origins of language, Titus finds
a way to make his remaining hand speak for him, as he repeats the founding
act of the Roman hero Virginius by slaying "his daughter with his own right
hand" (5.3.37).[63] Like the political order from which it is ultimately inseparable, speech, the play suggests, begins in the violence of the hand that kills, just
as it ends in the violence of the mouth that eats.[64]

At the same time, it is as if any assault upon the hand, as a crucial, even
originary site of meaning, can be interpreted as an assault on meaning itself.
Thus "the stern, ungentle hands" that have stripped Lavinia's trunk "Of her
two branches" have (in Marcus's quibbling conceit) cut the "mean" from
her—not merely the means of expression, but the ability to "mean" at all
(2.4.16–18, 40), leaving her father to reinvent language, as it were, from
scratch:

That shalt not sigh, nor hold thy stumps to heaven,
Nor wink, nor nod, nor kneel, nor make a sign,
But I, of these, will wrest an alphabet,
And still by practice, learn to know thy meaning.
>   3.2.42–5

These verbal and gestural quibbles on "mean" and "meaning" themselves belong to an elaborate scheme of wordplay associated with hands—a
scheme that is often regarded simply as a function of the play's conceited
Ovidian rhetoric or of its archaic "moral heraldry"—but that serves to
advertise the polysemous identity of hands.[65] It is as if, over and above their
much-emphasized connection with writing, gesture, and the language of
signs, hands are invested with a semantic surplus that overflows in sequences
of spontaneous wordplay:

Speak, Lavinia, what accursed *hand*
Hath made thee *handless* in thy father's sight? . . . .
'Tis well, Lavinia, that thou hast no *hands*,

For *hands* to do Rome service is but vain.
  3.1.66–7, 79–80; EMPHASIS ADDED

Lend me thy *hand*, and I will give thee mine . . .
Good Aaron, give his majesty my *hand* . . .
  3.1.187, 193; EMPHASIS ADDED

What violent *hands* can she lay on her life?
Ah, wherefore dost thou urge the name of *hands*. . . .
O, *handle* not the theme, to talk of *hands*
Lest we remember still that we have none.
Fie, fie, how frantically I square my talk,
As if we should forget we had no *hands*,
If Marcus did not name the word of *hands*!
  3.2.25–33; EMPHASIS ADDED

As sure a card as ever won the set. . . .
I play'd the cheater for thy father's hand.
  5.1.100, 111; EMPHASIS ADDED

❧

TITUS:
O sweet Revenge, now do I come to thee,
And if one arm's *embracement will content thee,*
I will embrace thee in it by and by.

TAMORA:
This closing with him fits his lunacy. . . .
I'll find some cunning practice out of hand,
To scatter and disperse the giddy Goths,
Or, at the least, make them his enemies.
  5.2.67–79; EMPHASIS ADDED

❧

  Nor are such bouts of manual quibbling peculiar, as is often supposed, to the black humor of a play in which severed hands are self-consciously "cut off and made a merry jest" (5.2.174). To the contrary they can be matched in a number of contemporary texts where the semiotic importance of the hand is foregrounded. Porsenna, overcome by the heroism of the "handless" Scevola, protests "And were we not so much *engaged* to Tarquin, / We would not *lift a hand* against that nation that breeds / Such noble spirits" (ll. 2756–8; emphasis added). Even Stubbs on the scaffold cannot resist punning: "The hand ready on the block to be stricken off, he said often to the people, 'Pray for me, now my calamity is at hand.' "[66] His appeals from prison are studded with references to the queen's "merciful hands" and to the plight of one who "hath no longer his own hand to declare his own grievous plight" or to demonstrate the loyalty of his "unfeigned heart."[67] Stubbs's wordplay asserts an essential connection not merely between the hand that writes, the hand that gestures, and the hand that pledges but also between these hands and the hands of power (shadowed in the violent hands of the executioner) to which his missing hand makes its pathetic appeal.

The prefatory material that introduces Bulwer's treatises on "manual rhetoric," is full of such play on the practical and symbolic functions of the hand. Bulwer dedicates *Chirologia* to Edward Goldsmith, with the reflection that "However this *Chirosophy* or first Fruits of my *Hand* be accepted abroad, having put forth my *Right Hand* in sign of amity to you, and for performance of promise: there remains nothing (most noble *Chirophilus*) but that you take it between Yours in token of warranty and protection." And the text is prefaced with a clutch of commendatory verses praising "the Very Pure and Beloved Hand of John Bulwer" in elaborately quibbling language—most notably those by "F. W.":

> I feel my Hand, deep struck in friendship's vein,
> With rich invention flowing out amain.
> And where such force the *Pen's* engagement draws,
> There an unskillful *Hand* may give applause.
> Were I *Bellona's* Darling, I would fight:
> But at that Spirit's rate that Thou dar'st write;
> Mercurial valour in Thy conquering Pen
> Equals the Hand of War in ord'ring men.
> I find Thee (Friend) well armed to repel
> Th' affronts of any scoffing Ishmael;
> Whose carping Hand 'gainst every man is bent,
> And each man's Hand 'gainst his Hand's cross intent.
> Thou may'st such blows without a Gauntlet ward. . . .
> But if a Viper through the glove invade
> Thy harmless *Hand;* shak't off, and to thy aide

Raise thy own new Militia, thy Hands,
Nature's best squadron, and Art's Trained Bands.[68]

In the case of *Titus*, however, the wordplay is given particular signifi-cance by its association with spectacles of barbaric violence and dismember-ment, culminating in an extraordinary cannibal fantasy—a conjunction that makes sense once it is recognized that *Titus* plays out, in a displaced form, one of the recurrent nightmares of early modern culture—the encounter with the barbaric threat of unmeaning on the beaches of the New World. It is no acci-dent, I think, that among the most powerful images of atrocity that accom-pany the "Black Legend" of Spanish imperialist desecration are the de Bry engravings in which the "civilized" conquerors hack the hands from their "savage" victims, stripping them of the very instruments of "natural lan-guage" in which the universal kinship of humankind was embodied, symbol-ically amputating them from the body of meaning itself (see figs. 6 and 7).

— ❄ —

THE BLOODY HAND

The severed hand effectively disappears from Shakespeare after *Titus*.[69] But the bloodstained hand remains as a recurrent symbol—not merely of guilt, but of the necessary intimacy of violence and power—from *Richard III* to *Macbeth*. *Richard II*, for example, systematically opposes the sacred dialect of Richard's hands to the Machiavellian idiom of Bolingbroke's. The sacra-mental gesturing that marks Richard's return to England shows how the imagined power of his "royal hands" is expressed in their ability to confer blessing on the earth, to "salute" and "do . . . favours" to a soil that is allegedly rendered "gentle" by his touch (3.2.6–11). Bolingbroke's hand, by contrast, is defined as "royal" simply by its acts of "possession" (4.1.110). Bolingbroke's is identified with the naked force of "the hand of death" (3.1.30); Richard's, with the invisible puissance of "the hand of god" (3.3.77), from which its sanctity is vicariously derived ("For well we know no hand of blood and bone / Can gripe the sacred handle of our sceptre, / Unless he do profane, steal, or usurp," ll. 79–81). In the deposition scene the contest between the rival ideas of monarchy for which their hands stand is perfectly expressed in the gestural emblem that Richard devises: "here

6. Spaniards amputating the hands of Amerindians. Engravings by J. T. de Bry and J. L. de Bry, from Bartolomé de Las Casas, Narratio Regionum Indicarum *(1614), reprinted by permission of the Folger Shakespeare Library.*

cousin, seize the crown . . . On this side my hand, and on that side thine" (4.1.181–3), just as the self-undoing paradoxes of Richard's surrender are expressed in the gestures with which he gives up the trappings of royalty: "Now mark me how I will undo myself: / I give this heavy weight from off my head, / And this unwieldy scepter from my hand. . . . With mine own hands I give away my crown, / With mine own tongue deny my sacred state" (ll. 203–9).

   Cleansed by the blandly self-exculpatory gestures with which he washes away all guilt for the execution of Richard's favorites (3.1.5–6), Bolingbroke's is the coldly efficient hand of policy; yet it remains tainted, even in the imagination of the trimmer York, by its association with "the rude misgoverned hands" that throw "dust and rubbish" on Richard's "sacred head" (5.2.5–6, 30). It is even more damningly marked by its identification with the "fierce hand" of Exton, whose murderous blows "stain the king's

7. *Spaniards amputating the hands of Amerindians. Engravings by J. T. de Bry and J. L. de Bry, from Bartolomé de Las Casas,* Narratio Regionum Indicarum *(1614), reprinted by permission of the Folger Shakespeare Library.*

own land" in an impious reversal of Richard's sanctifying favors (5.5.109–10). It is not only Richard who identifies his oppressors with Pilate ("Though some of you, with Pilate, wash your hands . . . yet . . . Water cannot wash away your sin," 4.1.239–42); Bolingbroke himself is haunted by the image of his own guilt, as he stares aghast at Exton's "fatal hand": "I'll make a voyage to the holy land, / To wash this blood off from my guilty hand" (5.6.35, 49–50).

The same opposition between the bloodstained "unlineal hand" (*Macbeth*, 3.1.62) of *de facto* power and the sanctified hand of divinely ordained monarchy underlies the action of the tragedy in which Shakespeare's language of hands is at once most eloquent and most brutally limited. The central symbol of *Macbeth* is, of course, the hand that cannot be cleansed:

What hands are here? . . .
Will all great Neptune's ocean wash this blood
Clean from my hand? No, this my hand will rather
The multitudinous seas incarnadine,
Making the green one red.
    2.2.56–60

Here's the smell of the blood still. All the perfumes of Arabia will not
sweeten this little hand.
    5.1.50–1

And such is the imaginative force of the horror with which Shakespeare
invests this symbol of pollution that the play's first recorded viewer, the
physician and magus Simon Foreman, was convinced that he had actually
seen the Macbeths vainly scouring the blood from their hands "by which
means they became . . . much amazed and affronted." The overwhelming
power of the image is not, however, simply a local effect of the poetry that
bodies forth the killers' inflamed imaginations, but grows out of the play's
obsessive preoccupation with sanctified and unsanctified hands. The very
infection that devours the body politic of Scotland is spread by Macbeth's
"hand accursed" (3.6.49), while the miraculous power of "Gracious
England" to cure "the evil" is attributed to the special "sanctity" that "heaven
[hath] given his hand" (4.3.144). Indeed Lennox's prayer for English aid to
redeem Scotland from its sufferings expressly equates the war against
Macbeth with the gesture of "blessing" by which "the King's Evil" was supposedly cured.

Yet if the idea of sacred monarchy is treated less equivocally in this play
than in *Richard II*, that is perhaps only because its mystical aura, though
posthumously attached to the "sainted" Duncan (4.3.109), is primarily
invested in the shadowy offstage figure of the saintly English King Edward
the Confessor. The blessed hand of ideal kingship is given an emblematic
presence as the instrument of life-giving fertility and wisdom in act 4's
apparitions of "A Child crowned, with a tree in its hand" and "the last king
with a glass in his hand," but otherwise the only hands that are granted a significant physical presence in the play are the blood-soaked hands of the
Macbeths and the withered claws of the witches. Moreover it is impossible to
ignore how the healing touch of England's hand is achieved only through an
action that (as critics have often observed) uncannily replicates Macbeth's

first action in the play, the decapitation of Macdonwald: "Enter Macduff with Macbeth's head." Banquo conceived of a world where each one stood "In the great hand of God" (2.3.130). But when the "hands uplifted in [Malcolm's] right" (4.3.42) merely seem to repeat the murderous gestures of Macbeth's "heavy hand" (3.1.89), then the "even-handed justice" that haunted the protagonist's imagination (1.7.10) becomes difficult to distinguish from the blind handy-dandy logic of revenge. And the spectacle of Macduff with the "dead butcher['s]" head in his hand can seem to exhibit the same cruel and absurd reflexiveness as Lady Macbeth's taking of her own life "by self and violent hands" (5.9.35–6).

No longer the instruments of bonding, but violent cancelers of humane bonds (3.2.48–9), hands in this play become so exclusively the violent "symbol of action" that even such familiar gestures of affection and fellowship as the handclasp are admitted only by way of grotesque irony, as in the description of Macbeth's encounter with Macdonwald:

> Which nev'r *shook hands*, nor bad farewell to him,
> Till he unseam'd him from the nave to th' chops,
> And fix'd his head upon our battlements.
> 1.2.21–3; EMPHASIS ADDED

—or in the widdershins dance of the weird sisters with its travesty of the Three Graces' circle of giving, receiving, and returning:

> The weird sisters, *hand in hand* . . .
> Thus do go, about, about;
> Thrice to thine, and thrice to mine,
> And thrice again to make up nine,
> 1.3.31–5; EMPHASIS ADDED

When the Sisters make their first appearance, their gestures seem to Banquo to speak the same universal language that offered travelers access to the world of the Other: "You seem to understand me, / By each at once her choppy finger laying / Upon her skinny lips" (1.3.43–5). This might be the *gestus* Bulwer calls *Inventione laboro*, indicating that they are momentarily at a loss for words to answer his questions; it is more likely, however, to be the familiar *Silentium indico*, a gesture that, in the wider context of the play, might be read as a refusal of meaning—a forbidding of interpretation, in

Banquo's terms. For the witches, with all the sinister gobbledygook of their doggerel incantations and the self-canceling doubleness of their prophetic utterances ("Lost and won," "Fair is foul, foul is fair," "lesser and . . . greater" "Not so happy, yet much happier"), inhabit the very world of meaningless "sound and fury" into which they lure Macbeth—a world of desperate contingency whose only watchword is "I'll do, and I'll do, and I'll do" (1.3.10). In such a world the only thing to be done is "a deed without a name" (4.1.49). Bloody hands are the sign of that doing—the symbol of a kind of action that, because it turns out to be related only to itself, must in the end turn on itself.

"Strange things I have in head, that will to hand, / Which must be acted ere they may be scann'd" (3.4.138–9). The "strange things" of which Macbeth speaks at the end of the banquet scene are precisely deeds that cannot be named, because to name them would be to "scan" them, exposing them to the intolerable "speculation" that has manifested itself in the "glare" of Banquo's ghost. The contradiction in Macbeth's figure—it speaks deeds that in Lady Macbeth's phrase "must not be thought" (2.2.30)—is entirely characteristic of their willed self-division: "To know my deed, 'twere best not know myself" (2.2.70). Although the hand nominally translates into action the ideas of the head (3.4.138) or the impulses of the heart ("The very firstlings of my heart shall be / The firstlings of my hand," 4.1.147–8), the murderous compulsiveness of doing is such that thought can seem the unlucky consequence of action, rather than its necessary precursor. In terms of the play's dominant figurative scheme, it is once again as if the hand had a life of its own separate from the head, as if acting were detached from seeing, the hand severed from the eye: "This deed I'll do before this purpose cool. / But no more sights!" (4.1.154–5).

Not only should the eye guide the hand, it is also bound to it by the language of the gesture, which, as the play's patron, James I, had once remarked, "speaketh to the eye"; without the eye, guiding and interpreting, the hand cannot "make sense," it is capable of signifying nothing.[70] But *Macbeth* presents a world in which eye and hand, seeing and doing, are set in unnatural opposition to one another:

Let not light see my black and deep desires;
The eye wink at the hand; yet let that be
Which the eye fears, when it is done, to see.
   1.4.51–3

In Macbeth's vision of the dagger with its handle temptingly "toward my hand," eye and hand seem briefly to collude, until that vision discloses itself as one of impotence ("I have thee not and yet I see thee still," 2.1.35) and guilt ("And on thy blade and dudgeon gouts of blood," l. 46). The more Macbeth is tormented by the "filthy witness" of his "hangman's hands" (2.2.25, 44), the more violently his hands seem to turn against his eyes, in an impossible rage for self-cancellation: "What hands are here? Ha! they pluck out mine eyes!" (2.2.59). As the eye functions only in the daylight world from which Macbeth recoils, so his imagination consigns the hand to the occult world of "night's black agents," where it operates less as the blind man's tactile substitute for sight than as a literal "instrument of darkness." So intense, indeed, does this identification become that night itself comes to be figured as a "bloody and invisible hand" blindfolding "the tender eye of pitiful day" (3.2.47–8).[71]

Because that "tender eye" inevitably recalls the fearful and compassionate "eye of childhood" whose "sorry sight" Lady Macbeth sought to suppress in act 2, scene 2, and Macbeth's own terrified glimpse of "Pity, like a naked new-born babe . . . blow[ing] the horrid deed in every eye" (1.7.21–4), it inevitably becomes proleptic of the actual infanticide in act 4, scene 2, identifying it as a kind of self-murder. And there is a sense, of course, in which all those "secret murders sticking on his hands" belong to a chain of self-destructive doing in which Macbeth repeatedly attempts to destroy his own double (Macdonwald, Cawdor, Duncan, Banquo, Macduff—a line stretching potentially to the crack of doom). All that the tyrant succeeds in doing, however, is to "murder sleep"—as it were to tear the very eyelids from his eyes so that nothing can occlude their fascinated stare. And even as he is about to hurl himself into the dark, the repressed returns (how else?) in the sleepwalking figure of the repressor, her uncannily open eyes fixed in horror upon the very hands that she once offered to cleanse with "a little water"—"What, will these hands ne'er be clean?" (5.1.43). The sleepwalking scene ends with a gesture that recalls Macbeth's vain grasping at the air-drawn dagger, as Lady Macbeth reaches out for her husband's hand, to find inscribed upon its phantasmagoric palm the implacable signature of their fate: "Come, come, come, come, give me your hand. What's done cannot be undone" (ll. 67–8)—the lines of a narrative "signifying nothing."

— ❋ —

THE BARE HAND

The "nothing" of *Macbeth* is an effect of canceled human bonds, imagined as writings torn by the "bloody and invisible hand" of power (3.2.48)—bonds for which, ironically enough, the human hand itself should properly stand. The last play I consider, *King Lear*, is also haunted by the self-annihilating violence of the "bloody hand"—a phrase that echoes through the play (3.2.53; 3.4.92; 4.6.160) and is brought to hallucinatory life in the "robbers' hands" that tear out Gloucester's eyes (3.7.40). *Lear* begins with a scene that initiates a progressive unstitching of the social fabric through the king's formal undoing of the bond that ties him to his daughter. The repudiation of Cordelia is expressed in a powerfully gestural language that formally reverses the rite of parental blessing ("So be my grave my peace as here I give / Her father's heart from her," 1.1.125–6)—the very rite Cordelia vainly tries to reinvoke in the restoration scene: "O, look upon me, sir, / And hold your hand in benediction o'er me" (4.7.57–8). In the last of many reversals around which this prodigal father fable is plotted, Lear responds by kneeling in the posture of the suppliant child—a gesture that by the final scene has come to express for him the essence of their new relationship ("When thou dost ask me blessing I'll kneel down / And ask of thee forgiveness," 5.3.10–11). But Cordelia's hand is extended only to raise him to his feet ("sir, you must not kneel," 4.7.58); neither's hand is now invested with magical power.[72] For one of the things that this play has witnessed, in its remorseless stripping away of all those meanings in which the Renaissance body was clothed, is something like the discovery of a modern hand—the desanctified hand that Gloucester must not kiss because it "smells of mortality" (4.6.133), a hand that is no longer a magic vehicle of eloquence or power but offers itself as an inarticulate token of mere animal presence, an instrument of bare sensation:

> I know not what to say.
> I will not swear these are my hands. Let's see,
> I feel this pin-prick.
> 4.7.53–5

This is the unadorned "friendly hand" that Edgar repeatedly offers to his blind father (4.6.25, 223, 230, 284; 5.2.5, 7), the hand that is foregrounded in the extraordinarily moving quarto stage direction that opens act 5, scene 2: "Enter the powers of France over the stage, Cordelia with her father in her hand." It is a hand that has learned to "see . . . feelingly" (4.6.149) perhaps—"Be your tears wet? Yes, faith!" (4.7.70)—but one whose only eloquence is touching. This hand has forgotten how to speak. It is a hand that lays claim to what the novelist J. M. Coetzee calls "the innocence of hands," a hand that, like the "scrubbed and sour humble hands" of Dylan Thomas's Ann Jones, seems to mean no more (or less) than what it does: "Pray you undo this button" (5.3.310). It is (to return to the text with which I began this chapter), the hand Frank McGuinness's play sets up against the overinscribed dead hand of mythic history: "When I touched your hand, I smelt bread of it. I smelt life."[73]

PART II

Race, Nation, Empire

Changing Places in Othello

But when you come to love, there the soil alters;
Y'are in another country.
—Thomas Middleton, *Women Beware Women*

In nature things move violently to their place, and calmly in their place.
—Francis Bacon, "Of Great Place"

Othello is a tragedy of displacement, a drama of jealousy and resentment that traces the destructive symbiosis of two men, each of whom is tormented by a sense of intolerable usurpation. As its very subtitle *(The Moor of Venice)* suggests, it is concerned with belonging and estrangement, with occupation and dispossession, and it explores the psychological connection between the various ideas of "place" with which its symbiotic rivals are obsessed. Of course there is a sense in which "place," in its physical sense, is important in all Shakespeare's tragedies—to the point where the character of each play can seem to be registered in its particular idea of place. The cold prison of Elsinore with its waiting graveyard, Macbeth's hell-castle, the imperial panorama of *Antony and Cleopatra*—each substantially defines the imaginative world of its play. Place may be employed in a loosely suggestive, symbolic fashion as it is in *King Lear*, or it may be realized with the densely social particularity of *Romeo and Juliet*, but it is always closely bound up with the metaphoric structure of the work.

Othello is no exception: an essentially domestic tragedy is elevated to heroic dignity partly by the boldness of its geographic scale. Like *Antony and Cleopatra* it straddles the Mediterranean, but there the resemblance ends. The action of the latter play is characterized by a continual advance and retreat, which matches the psychological vacillation of its masculine protagonist, the flux of his political fortunes, and the corresponding ebb and flow of the audience's sympathies. The movement of *Othello*, by contrast, is as remorselessly one-way as the current of that Pontic Sea to which the hero compares his driving passion of revenge. There is, accordingly, only a single significant change of place—the voyage from Venice to Cyprus at the end of act 1. This contrast in part reflects the different power-relationships prevailing in the political worlds of the two plays: Rome and Egypt are rival constellations, Cyprus a mere satellite of Venice. Armies and orders issue from Venice; Cyprus receives them. The metropolis is a source of power; the colony a passive object of competing powers. Where in *Antony and Cleopatra* the movement from Egypt to Rome or from Rome to Egypt always contains the potential for enlargement of the self—or at least for liberation of those aspects of the self that one or other of the play's antithetical worlds suppresses—in *Othello* the translation from Venice to Cyprus leads to self-estrangement and a kind of diminution. It is (as a number of recent directors, taking their cue from John Barton's 1971 Stratford-upon-Avon production, have emphasized) a movement to a narrower, more enclosed world, a place of colonial exile—a movement from city to garrison town. Its finality is marked by the storm that intervenes between the first and second acts, dividing the two worlds of this play as absolutely as the tempest that concludes the first movement of *The Winter's Tale*; but here there will be no lucky peripety, no countermovement of redemption. The "foul and violent tempest" that parts the ships of Cassio and the Moor (2.1.34) clearly anticipates the storm of passion that will part their friendship forever. The voyage itself parts Desdemona and Othello before their marriage can be consummated, and here too the tempest symbolically announces a division that will be resolved only in the perverted consummation of act 5. As so often in Shakespeare, the sea voyage amounts to a rite of passage: it is as though some fatal boundary had been crossed—from this bourn no traveler returns.[1]

Venice is the city of the play, its metropolitan center and repository of civil values, but the civilization it represents proves, on closer inspection, to be no more ideal than that of its counterpart in *The Merchant of Venice*. Iago's racial slurs and Brabantio's answering outrage make it plain from the beginning that, beneath its ceremonious courtesies, Shakespeare's Venice is a soci-

ety capable of treating any stranger, any ethnic outsider with the same calculating cruelty it meted out to Shylock. "There's many a beast then in a populous city,/And many a civil monster," Iago tells Othello in a characteristically veiled sarcasm (4.1.63–4). The remark is doubly Janus-faced,
for beyond its glance at the supposed horning of Othello by the urbane monsters Cassio and Desdemona, it means to point at the Venetian Moor himself
as a kind of tamed Caliban, a civilized barbarian, while by a further reach of
irony Iago identifies himself as the true beast of his populous city, the
"Spartan dog" of Lodovico's final denunciation (5.2.360), a barbarous monster beneath his civil guise of honesty. The fetches of Iago's policy are
designed to expose the essential savagery of his "stranger" general, but what
they produce is an Othello remade in Iago's own monstrous image.[2]

Like the Venice of *The Merchant of Venice*, too, this is a city whose most
humane values can seem compromised by its mercantile ethics: its language
of love, typically, is tainted by metaphors of trade, purchase, and possession.
Here women are to men rather as Cyprus is to Venice and Turkey—objects
of competition, ownership, and "occupation." Indeed Brabantio's reply to
the duke's sententious consolation on the loss of his daughter—"The
robbed that smiles steals something from the thief"—makes precisely that
equation:

> So let the Turk of Cyprus us beguile,
> We lose it not so long as we can smile.
>   1.3.206, 208–9

It is natural in this world that Iago and Brabantio should concur in seeing
Desdemona's abduction as, like Jessica's, the theft of a father's rightful property; it is perhaps more disturbing to notice that even Othello's language, for
all its rhetorical magnificence, pictures love as a fabulous treasure, an object
of erotic commerce:

> The purchase made, the fruits are to ensue:
> The profit's yet to come 'tween me and you.
>   2.3.9–10

However gracefully bantering its expression, the metaphor here is close
to that crass possessiveness that lies at the root of all jealousy—as we may
quickly feel in the more obviously corrupted language of the temptation
scene:

❀

OTHELLO:
What sense had I of her stolen hours of lust? ...
He that is robbed, not wanting what is stolen,
Let him not know't, and he's not robbed at all.
        3.3.335, 339–40

❀

Cruelly enough, the attitude persists even through Othello's finest agonies of
remorse, where his imagination seems tormented by the sense of the prize he
has lost (to the virtual exclusion of the living woman he has destroyed):[3]

> If heaven would make me such another world
> Of one entire and perfect chrysolite,
> I'd not have sold her for it.
>   5.2.143–5

> one whose hand
> Like the base Indian threw a pearl away
> Richer than all his tribe.
>   5.2.342–4

Even Othello, then, has partly absorbed the values of a Venice that, for
all its civilized and heroic airs, is less remote than might appear from the
metropolis of greed in Jonson's *Volpone* or the Adriatic Whore of Otway's
Venice Preserved. If Venice was acknowledged as a model of republican civility, generations of travelers had also fixed it in the English imagination as the
capital of European prostitution. Indeed it is precisely upon this sense of the
city as a community of "customers" that Iago, that busy merchant-factor, is
able to capitalize in presenting Desdemona to her husband as "that cunning
whore of Venice / That married with Othello" (4.2.88–9):

> I know our country disposition well:
> In Venice they do let God see the pranks
> They dare not show their husbands; their best conscience
> Is not to leave't undone, but keep't unknown.
>   3.3.199–202

Yet with all its deficiencies and occasional ugliness, for all the hidden savagery of its "civil monsters," Venice remains a true *polis*, a civilizing and ordered place where the calm and rational interventions of ducal authority are an effective check against the storms of a Brabantio's wrath or an Iago's envy. No such effective sanctions govern Cyprus: it is another country.

Shakespeare's audience knew Cyprus as a former Venetian colony that had enjoyed a brief respite from Turkish conquest after the triumphant Battle of Lepanto in 1571, so that, as Emrys Jones has demonstrated, the action of *Othello* is tied to a fairly precise historical as well as geographical location.[4] It capitalizes, however, on much older associations. Cyprus, the audience might also have remembered, was sacred to foam-born Venus as the place where the goddess renewed her virginity after her adulterous liaison with Mars. This was the island of erotic myth where John Ford would locate his *Lover's Melancholy* (ca. 1629), and the Cyprus to which we are introduced at the beginning of Shakespeare's second act seems at first to be infused with something of that ancient grace. The miraculous tempest that providentially scatters and destroys the Turkish fleet is evoked in exuberant and sprightly verse, whose tone contrasts as sharply as possible with the brooding ratiocination of Iago's soliloquy at the end of act 1. Retrospectively, we may see the storm as prefiguring the emotional turbulence of the later acts, but in its immediate context it has the effect of a welcome release to the pent-up emotional energies of act 1—a feeling emphasized by the lively excitement and bustle of Montano and his comparisons. It is as though the air were suddenly cleared of that murk of slander and intrigue that fouled the atmosphere of Venice; and the marvelous gaiety of the Venetians' arrival helps to confirm the impression that they have indeed been translated to the traditional domain of Love. Cassio is at his most spiritedly cavalier; Desdemona full of high, nervous anticipation; and even Iago, playing with disarming insouciance the role of urbane jester in a lady's court, appears for a short time (however misleadingly) liberated from his claustrophobic hutch of resentment. As for Othello, he speaks with the relaxed and affectionate confidence of one who has come home:

> How does my old acquaintance of this isle?
> Honey, you shall be well desired in Cyprus:
> I have found great love amongst them.
> 2.1.197–9

In fact, of course, as their departure for the citadel quickly reminds us, this is an island prepared not for love but for war, and these voyagers have come to the shut-in society of a garrison town, the sort of place that feeds on rumor and festers with suspicion. Amply fulfilling the sinister confusions of black and white suggested in Iago's teasing riddles at the harbor (2.1.128–32), this is a world whose whispering can transform the marriage bed itself to the centerpiece of some luxurious Venetian brothel and make the "fair Desdemona" seem indistinguishable from the prostituted Bianca (whose own name, ironically enough, means "white" or "fair"). It is a place where no one is truly at home and where (significantly) the only native Cypriot we meet appears to be this jealous camp follower—though Bianca too may have come from Venice. The oppressive sense of enclosure that results is crucial to the mood of the play. "Jealousy in itself," Northrop Frye remarks, "tends to create an enclosed prison-world," and this Cyprus is its perfect physical correlative.[5] Far from providing a refuge from urban corruption, it is a colonial outpost of civilization where the worst Venetian values can flourish unchecked by any normative social order. Desdemona above all is a stranger to it. Cut off from her family, effectively removed from those "Of her own clime, complexion and degree," a woman almost alone in a conspicuously masculine realm, she is as isolated and potentially vulnerable as Othello was in the subtle world of Venice. To the extent that the Cyprus wars have returned the martial Othello to the military environment he knows best, husband and wife may seem at first to have changed places. But the activity of the civil monster Iago ensures that this impression is short-lived. Desdemona has merely come to share the Moor's continuing isolation; each is a stranger whose only secure "place" is in the other's heart. In the first act Othello speaks of his marriage to Desdemona in terms of a willing exchange of freedom:

> But that I love the gentle Desdemona,
> I would not my unhousèd free condition
> Put into circumscription and confine
> For the seas' worth.
>   1.2.25–8

The claustrophobic constriction of the island will give an ugly new meaning to that careless metaphor as the action of the play moves from the relative freedom of the city to the cramping confines of a besieged citadel. The siege that seems to be lifted at the opening of act 2 has, in reality, only just begun.

Desdemona's virtue is its imagined object; Othello's consciousness, its true battleground—for that is the fortified "place" that Iago will methodically reduce and occupy. Indeed the whole action of the play might be read in terms of sinister distortions and displacements of the old metaphor of erotic siege.

But "place" has another, even more potent significance in *Othello*—one that provides the key to Iago's consuming passion of resentment. The importance of Venice as the metropolitan center of the play world is that it supplies, or offers to supply, each individual with a clearly defined and secure position within an established social order. Indeed it is precisely the city's idea of "place" (a term that includes "office" and "rank" as well as "status") that distinguishes it from the barbarous world beyond—that vaguely imagined wilderness to which Iago consigns his "stranger" general. It is solely by virtue of the "place" they bring with them, above all their rank in the state's military hierarchy, that the dislocated Venetians of the Cypriot garrison are able to place themselves. In such circumstances "place" is liable to become an object of unusually ferocious competition, but of course it was already an issue before the departure from Venice. The magnifico, Brabantio, woken by the "malicious bravery" of Iago and Roderigo, instinctively rebukes them with an appeal to "My spirit and my place" (1.1.104)—the same lofty "place" upon whose potency he relies in arraigning Othello before his fellow senators (1.3.53). To be thus confident of one's place is to feel at home in a very important sense: it is to have a particularly firm idea of the rights and dignities attaching to one's function in society. Neither Iago nor Othello is at home in quite this way; that is the basis of their fatally shared insecurity.

Iago presents himself as a man whose personal worth is guaranteed not merely by his innate qualities and the "proof" of his services but on his implicit claim (despite his conspicuously Spanish name) to be a native of the place called Venice. This, in his estimate, properly raises him above such outsiders as Othello and Cassio. From Iago's point of view (as to Brabantio's and Roderigo's prejudiced eyes) Othello is a man without any true place, "an extravagant and wheeling stranger / Of here and everywhere" (1.1.137–8), a foreigner whose undeserved office can be tossed aside with that dismissive mock honorific "his Moorship" (1.1.22). He discovers a special bitterness, therefore, in the fact that it should be this contemptible alien who has conspired to keep him from his own rightful place—and that in favor of yet another stranger, "One Michael Cassio, a Florentine" (1.1.20). The heavy metrical stress on the first syllable of "Florentine" exactly catches the force

of Iago's scorn, the curl of his lip. In his own estimate he is a man doubly displaced, and this is the theme of his tirades in the opening scene:

> Three great ones of the city,
> In personal suit to make me his lieutenant,
> Off-capped to him: and by the faith of man,
> I know my price, I am worth no worse a place.
>   1.1.8–11

Iago's sense of self, as this speech already suggests, is founded upon the
treacherous relativities of comparison. For such a man to be bilked of the
place that answers to his conviction of his own market price is to be cheated
of identity, since the very center of his being is to be found in that obsessive
concern for what is "wholesome to my place" (1.1.146).

Iago is possessed by comparison. It is hardly too much to say that he has
become comparison. For him nothing (and no one) has a value in and of itself
but only as a measure or object of comparison—hence his overriding faith in
money, that supremely reductive instrument of comparison that offers to
place everything within a comprehensive taxonomy of price. Such a construction of the world invokes its own nemesis, for it commits one to a
devouring torment of self-comparison that has, in principle, no end. In act 1
Iago offers himself to Roderigo as a model of rational self-love (1.3.311), one
of those who know how to "Do themselves homage" (1.1.54); he is thus a free
man, liberated from those bonds of service, affection, and duty that, by putting a man comprehensively in his place, serve as constant provocations of
unwelcome comparison, stinging reminders of the price that others put upon
oneself. Yet ironically enough the very speeches in which this claim is most
fiercely advanced are full of nagging self-comparison—both with those
whose servitude he despises and those whose superior authority he resents:

> We cannot all be masters, nor all masters
> Cannot be truly followed. You shall mark
> Many a duteous and knee-crooking knave
> That, doting on his own obsequious bondage,
> Wears out his time, much like his master's ass,
> For naught but provender, and when he's old—cashiered!
> Whip me such honest knaves. Others there are
> Who, trimmed in forms and visages of duty,

Keep yet their hearts attending on themselves. . . .
It is as sure as you are Roderigo,
Were I the Moor, I would not be Iago:
In following him, I follow but myself.
    I.1.43–59

Iago dreams of a world without comparison, a bureaucratic utopia in which place is determined by the "old gradation, where each second / Stood heir to th' first" (1.1.37–8); yet this ideal of egalitarian succession is contradicted by his wounded sense of superiority to both the braggart Moor, with his "bombast circumstance / Horribly stuffed with epithets of war" and to the desk-soldier Cassio, that "counter-caster" with his "bookish theoric." The true accountant, endlessly poring over his ledger of "debitor and creditor," is, needless to say, Iago himself (1.1.13, 31). For Iago is a kind of moral mercantilist. There is only a certain stock of virtue in the world, and by that rule one man's credit must necessarily be another's debit:

If Cassio do remain
He hath a daily beauty in his life
That makes me ugly.
    5.1.18–20

Cassio's charm, Desdemona's goodness, Othello's nobility—none of these can be granted an intrinsic worth or independent significance; each is comprehensible only as an implicit criticism of Iago's life. Intolerable objects of comparison whose very existence challenges his place in the order of things, they must be eliminated.

The villain's preoccupation with displacement is, interestingly enough, one of Shakespeare's principal additions to the story. In Giraldi Cinthio's *Hecatommithi*, Iago's equivalent, the Ensign, is motivated not by thwarted ambition but by lust; it is not his rival's rank the Ensign covets but his favor with Disdemona. It is worth asking why Shakespeare, who seems to have worked with a version of this text beside him and who seldom departs from his sources without good reason, should have chosen to make "place" the point at issue in this way.[6] Kenneth Muir's explanation (representative of most critics who have troubled to pose the question) is that it is merely a device to complicate the villain's motives.[7] The loss of promotion is one of three stings of envy that have lodged in Iago. It combines with "pathological

jealousy of his wife" and "a jealous love of Desdemona" to arouse his hatred
of the Moor, but in Muir's estimate it is the least important of the three
because it "is not directly mentioned after the start of the play, except once."[8]
I argue that the sheer dramatic prominence given to the lost lieutenancy by
the opening dialogue establishes it as so much an essential *donnée* of the
action that it scarcely needs reiteration—particularly since Iago's nagging
consciousness of the slight is registered in a self-lacerating punctilio over
Cassio's title of rank. He uses the world "lieutenant" more often than all the
other characters of the play together: fifteen of its twenty-five occurrences
are from his mouth, where it increasingly sounds like a kind of sarcastic
caress. Just as tellingly it is Othello's "Now art thou my lieutenant"
(3.3.475)—perhaps the weightiest half line in the tragedy—that announces
Iago's moment of supreme triumph.

Far from being a mere aggravation of the villain's envious disposition,
then, the question of place lies at the very heart of the play. Properly understood it is the only begetter of that "monstrous birth" that issues from the fertile womb of Iago's resentment, and a crucial pointer to its significance is
contained in the title of lieutenant itself, which becomes the focus of obsessive wordplay. Of course, as soon as Shakespeare decided to make Cassio's
promotion the trigger for Iago's plot, he was compelled to alter Giraldi's military hierarchy. In the Italian story the Iago-figure is described as the Moor's
alfiero (standard-bearer), which corresponds exactly to Shakespeare's
"ancient" or ensign. But Cassio's counterpart is merely *un Capo di Squadra*—
a title translated by some modern editors as "captain" but glossed in a contemporary Italian-English dictionary as "corporal" and evidently denoting a
rank inferior to that of *alfiero*. In the play, by contrast, Cassio's position is
clearly that of Othello's second-in-command, "lieutenant" here being a
rough equivalent to the modern "lieutenant-general." The choice of designation is clearly a considered one. Elsewhere in Shakespeare's work, where
"captain" (a loose term that could designate almost any kind of military officer) is common, "lieutenant" is relatively rare. It occurs only nine times in the
rest of the canon. In six instances it appears to denote a junior grade of officer (a "lieutenant-captain"), more or less equivalent to the modern rank, but
in the others it carries its older, more general sense of "deputy" or "substitute." Clearly, then, the word had not yet stabilized to its modern meaning
and still carried a good deal of its original French sense "one holding
[another's] place" *(lieu tenant)*, and in the mouth of Iago, consumed as he is
with a burning sense of displacement, it inevitably develops the force of a bit-

ter pun, a tormenting reminder of his conviction that Cassio is not merely the man appointed to deputize in the general's place but the one who is standing in his own.[9]

While Cassio is in the ascendant, Iago probes the word as one might an aching tooth, goading the pain of his own deprivation, and then, as his rival's star begins to wane, "lieutenant" becomes a term of contempt, a covert sarcasm anticipating their change of places. Thus the high point of Iago's vindictive pleasure in the drinking scene is reached with Cassio's stumbling recognition that he is behaving in a fashion "unworthy of his place" (2.3.96). Iago's triumph is registered in his softly crowing response. "It's true, good Lieutenant (l. 100), and confirmed by Montano's sober expression of disappointment:

'tis great pity that the noble Moor
Should hazard such a *place* as his own second
With one of an ingraft infirmity.
        2.3.138–40; EMPHASIS ADDED

When Othello enters to check the ensuing brawl, Iago is ready with a rebuke that uses the terms of rank to hint successfully at cashierment while maintaining an air of honest and properly deferential concern: "Hold, ho, lieutenant, sir. . . . Have you forgot all sense of place and duty" (ll. 165–7). Once the cashierment is achieved, Cassio's place must surely follow "the old gradation" and fall to Iago, and Othello's promise at the end of the temptation scene, "Now art thou my lieutenant," sounds almost like a formal commissioning. Iago, characteristically, registers his richly ironic satisfaction at this change of places by continuing to dignify his rival with his lost rank, a joke that develops a special relish in his last veiled jeer at the wounded Cassio (as the first quarto prints it): "*O my lieutenant*, what villains have done this?" (5.1.56; emphasis added). The plot to kill Cassio, after all, has stemmed not (as is commonly assumed) from the desire to get rid of an inconvenient potential witness ("the Moor / May unfold me to him," 5.1.20–1) but from Iago's bitter spite at the discovery that "there is especial commission come from Venice to depute Cassio in Othello's place" (4.2.219–20). This is lieutenantry with a vengeance! By a kind of cheating pun, it mockingly fulfills the very libel he has put on Cassio, while robbing Iago of the coveted place he has just obtained with so much labor. With that final "my lieutenant" Iago means to say good night to one who has never done more than hold his own rightful place, but is now about to surrender it forever.

Since Coleridge first accused him of "motiveless malignity," there has been much debate over the allegedly confused and contradictory nature of Iago's motives. But the problem exists only if one makes the doubtful assumption that, to be psychologically plausible, motivation need be coherent, systematic, and rational. What is significant about Iago's various self-explanations is not so much their apparent factual inconsistencies as their deadly consistency of tone and attitude. It hardly matters that the alleged reasons for his behavior are changeable or even mutually incompatible, since they are, in the last analysis, only stimuli to the expression of that underlying resentment that is the principal defining trait of his personality. They are all, to this degree, rationalizations for an attitude toward the world whose real origins lie much deeper, within the impregnable fortress of silence into which Iago withdraws at the end of the play. Indeed I take it to be profoundly true of emotions like resentment, envy, and jealousy that they are in some sense *their own motive*. As Emilia puts it, in response to Desdemona's baffled reaching for a "cause," the jealous

> are not ever jealous for the cause,
> But jealous for they're jealous. It is a monster
> Begot upon itself, born on itself.
>   3.4.160–2[10]

Resentment dreams of usurpation as jealousy dreams of cuckoldry, but is itself the cuckoo of displacement: "*it* is the cause"—at once motive, justification, and purpose in a system as hermetically closed as the enigmatic syntax of Othello's great soliloquy.

Psychologically speaking then, there is no conflict between Iago's professional envy and his sexual jealousy. One follows naturally from the other, since both are symptomatic expressions of his core of resentment, the cancer of comparison at the heart of his being. *Dis*placement from one office can seem almost tantamount to *re*placement in the other; the only doubt concerns the question of who is to be held responsible—the man who has put him out of his place or the one who has taken it? To begin with it is Othello who is the single object of a suspicion that seems to grow spontaneously from those fantasies of sexual athleticism that Iago concocts for Brabantio:

> Your heart is burst, you have lost half your soul.

Even now, now, very now, an old black ram
Is tupping your white ewe.
    1.1.88–90

The striking thing about this speech is that it presents the abduction of a daughter as though it were an act of adultery—an adultery conceived (as Othello will subsequently imagine Desdemona's) in terms of both physical and psychological displacement. The elopement is said to rob Brabantio of half his own soul. It is almost, as the quibble promoted by the relentless hammered stresses on "your white *ewe*" suggests, as though the rape were on Brabantio's own person. The imaginative intensity of Iago's vision far exceeds what is required by the mere theater of the occasion. In the "old black ram," the "Barbary horse," and the heaving "beast with two backs," are projected Iago's own loathing and fear of Othello as sexual rival. Yet the imposture works upon Brabantio as effectively as it does only because of the degree of Iago's own emotional engagement with the scene he invents. By the same token, it is only through the weird excitement of his invention that Iago discovers his own sexual insecurity and with it the new torment of comparison to which his soliloquy in scene 3 gives voice:

I hate the Moor,
And it is thought abroad that 'twixt my sheets
He's done *my office*.
    1.3.380–2; EMPHASIS ADDED

The point of promoting Cassio to Othello as a rival for Desdemona is not merely to "get his place" but to turn the tables on the cuckold-maker by exposing him to the shame of cuckoldry. The wounding comparison to which Iago has been subjected by Othello's sexual prowess will be canceled by subjecting the Moor to a similar denigration. Ironically, however, the logic of Iago's temperament ensures that his leering recollection of Cassio's "person . . . framed to make women false" (ll. 391–2) plants a further seed of resentment and suspicion that matures in the following scene. By now he has convinced himself that the adultery is a matter of simple fact:

That Cassio loves her, I do well believe 't:
That she loves him, 'tis apt and of great credit.
    2.1.286–7

Resentment typically tends to reduce everything to its own level, and the fantasy is flattering because, by putting Cassio in Othello's place, it puts Othello in Iago's own.[11] Beyond that, it appeals to the perverse eroticism that is a paradoxical constituent of all jealousy.[12] And it is this that produces the parallel fantasy in which Iago imagines himself taking Cassio's place in Desdemona's bed:

> Now, I do love her too;
> Not out of absolute lust—though peradventure
> I stand accountant for as great a sin—
> But partly led to diet my revenge
> For that I do suspect the lusty Moor
> Hath leaped into my seat, the thought whereof
> Doth, like a poisonous mineral, gnaw my inwards,
> And nothing can, or shall, content my soul
> Till I am evened with him, wife for wife.
>   2.1.291–99

The shocking way in which the metaphors of eating here ("diet . . . gnaw") confuse sexual appetite with the devouring emotions of jealousy and revenge emphasizes the dangerously volatile interrelation of these apparently opposite desires, but Iago is able to protect himself against the frenzy into which a similar welter of feelings will drive Othello by retreating into the reassuringly objective language of moral accounting ("evened with him, wife for wife").[13] This calculus, however, leads to its own disturbance, for insofar as Cassio seems a likely usurper of Othello's seat, he may just as well have pilfered Iago's cap of matrimonial office: "I fear Cassio with my night-cap too" (1. 298). It is a suspicion that, at a casual glance, may seem to disappear as suddenly and arbitrarily as it grips him, but in fact it is another of those extraordinary flashes that fitfully illuminate the dark night of Iago's inner self, making him seem a figure of infinitely greater complexity than the stage devil or vice he is sometimes mistaken for. It is possible to trace his painfully self-wounding fascination with Cassio's sexual potency through the elaborate dream-fantasy of the temptation scene. Just as his sexual envy of the Moor was first apparent in the bestial pornography of the "black ram" speech, so here his jealous hatred of the lieutenant surfaces through the ambiguous sexual excitements of his concocted night with Cassio:

In sleep I heard him say: "Sweet Desdemona,
Let us be wary, let us hide our loves":
And then, sir, would he gripe and wring my hand,
Cry "O sweet creature!" and then kiss me hard,
As if he plucked up kisses by the roots,
That grew upon my lips; then laid his leg
Over my thigh, and sighed and kissed, and then
Cried "Cursèd fate that gave thee to the Moor!"
  3.3.419–26

As in the earlier episode with Brabantio, the calumny can lodge its sting so effectually only because of Iago's intense identification with the sexual humiliation he describes. In this context it is tempting to see his attempt on Cassio's life, his determination to make him "uncapable of Othello's place" (4.2.228), as constituting in part an act of sexual revenge. The political murder he envisages, as the sardonic pun on "uncapable" suggests and as that mysteriously emphasized wound "in the leg" tends to confirm, is also a physical emasculation, a final and absolute displacement of the hated usurper.[14]

It should be clear, then, that from the very opening of the play Iago's imagination feeds upon (as it is eaten by) fantasies of displacement—public, domestic, and sexual. Such is the self-devouring nature of that "green-eyed monster" whose habit he understands so well. But there is another side to his scheming, revealed in the glee with which he contemplates the ingenious symmetries of his vengeful design. In act 1, scene 3 the inculpation of Cassio holds out the prospect of a "double knavery" (1. 338). Setting out "To get [Cassio's] place" (1. 337), he will achieve it by making Cassio appear to have taken Othello's. Cassio's crime against Iago will be matched by the lieutenant's imagined crime against his general—the usurpation of one rightful place being balanced against the usurpation of another, and the effect will be to link Cassio and Desdemona in Othello's mind as disloyal seconds who have proved unworthy of their office. The growing conviction that both Othello and Cassio have usurped his own place with Emilia gives a further ironic aptness to this scheme by making Othello his own surrogate as both cuckold-victim and revenger. For a time he even dreams of crowning his elaborately witty contrivance by himself taking the Moor's place with Desdemona, but that is perhaps too commonplace a solution for him. His last and most perfect usurpation will be to take Desdemona's place with Othello. Such refinements help one to remember how much Iago owes to the earlier villain-heroes of the Elizabethan stage such as Barabas and Richard III. Like them he is a conscious and self-delighting artist in evil (much more than the detached Baconian scientist of Auden's famous essay), and his pleasure in the aesthetic cunning of his creations is matched by a delight in verbal ingenuity, in puns, double entendres, and ironic equivoques.[15] Like Richard's tutor-Vice, Iniquity, he has learned to "moralise two meanings in one word," and he weaves his net for Cassio, Othello, and Desdemona from the threads of ambiguous hint and ambivalent suggestion. But this verbal duplicity also operates at a deeper and more vicious emotional level. When, for instance, the mechanism of Iago's revenge first begins to move in the drinking scene, his satisfaction at the smoothness of its functioning finds play in a passage of intensely private innuendo. He steers the lieutenant toward Desdemona in a speech whose apparently innocent language is full of gloating sexual suggestiveness:

> Confess yourself freely to her; importune her help to *put you in your place* again. She is so *free*, so *kind*, so *apt*, so blessed a disposition, that she holds it a vice in her goodness not to *do* more than she is requested.
> 2.3.309–12; EMPHASIS ADDED

"Place" here (though Cassio cannot hear it) has begun to carry that obscene sense that Iago will deploy to such deadly effect in the temptation scene:

> Although 'tis fit that Cassio have his *place*,
> For sure he *fills it up* with great *ability*,
> Yet, if you please to hold him off awhile,
> You shall by that perceive him and his means;
> Note if your lady *strain* his *entertainment*
> With any strong or vehement importunity—
> Much will be seen in that.
> 3.3.244–50; EMPHASIS ADDED[16]

Even the concluding appeal to "hold her *free*" (1. 255; emphasis added) seems to involve, beneath its frank concession of Desdemona's probable innocence, a dark suggestion of licentiousness. That these double entendres have found their mark is suggested by Othello's tight-lipped response, "Fear not my government" (1.256), tersely asserting his claim not merely to stoical self-control but to domestic and sexual rule.[17] Othello has always felt his political "government" to be in some sense dependent on the private office of his love; now he is being lured into the demented conflation of the two that first appeared in Iago's diseased imagination.

By its wanton insistence on arbitrary associations, punning is a perfect instrument of emotions such as jealousy and resentment, which thrive on paranoid connection. It is characteristic of jealousy, with its obsessional reaching after certainties, which it at once needs yet cannot bear to face, that it should track the paths of suspicion with the doubtful clues of pun and equivoque, and it is no accident that wordplay should be of special significance both in *Othello* and in Shakespeare's other study of sexual jealousy, *The Winter's Tale*. In each case the action can be seen to hang upon the fatal doubleness of certain words, the ambiguity of certain signs. There is a kind of awful decorum about this, that jealousy with its compulsive dreams of adulterous substitution should discover a self-lacerating pleasure in what is essentially a form of semantic displacement, in which one meaning surreptitiously, adulterously even, takes the place of another. The pun is a kind of verbal bedtrick—as essential to the process of inner displacement by which an Othello or a Leontes collaborates in his own destruction as Iago's sleight-of-hand. The very triviality of the device (which Shakespeare seems reflexively to acknowledge in Leontes's murderous teasing-out of meaning from the innocence of "play") corresponds to that ultimate triviality of motive so characteristic of jealousy.[18] It is what carries the drama of jealous passion uncomfortably close to the border of black comedy (which *The Winter's Tale* often crosses), and what helps make the action of *Othello* the most meanly degrading—in some respects, therefore, the cruelest—of all the tragedies.

This, of course, was the aspect of *Othello* that excited Thomas Rymer's notorious indignation. The particular focus of his scorn was the mechanism on which the entire plot turns: the handkerchief that provides Othello with the certainty he both craves and fears. This is the pivot of the tragic design, and yet, as Rymer saw, there is a kind of desperate frivolity about it.[19] The whole embroidery that Iago weaves about this patch of cloth, culminating in the carefully mounted "ocular proof" of act 4, scene 1 with Cassio's contemptuous account of "the bauble's" infatuation with him, amounts to nothing more than a piece of perspective juggling, a theatrical *trompe l'oeil*, an elaborate double entendre or enacted pun. What is perhaps less obvious is the way in which the handkerchief develops its grip on Othello's jealous mind through a chain of verbal associations that convert it to a material substitute for the love between Desdemona and himself. The Moor's first encounter with his wife after the temptation scene finds its emotional course through a series of feverish quibbles. "Give me your hand" he demands (3.4.36), as if seeking reassurance in the familiar gesture of affection, but hardly is her hand in his than it becomes an object of furious scrutiny, as though the simple flesh itself concealed some treacherous meaning: "This hand is moist. . . . This argues fruitfulness and liberal heart. . . . This hand of yours requires / A sequester from liberty. . . . 'Tis a good hand, / A frank one. . . . A liberal hand! The hearts of old gave hands; / But our new heraldry is hands, not hearts" (3.4.36–47). If the hand will not give up its secret, the words do: "hand" leads by habitual association to "heart," and the condition of the heart in turn is disclosed by the maddening sexual quibbles on "liberal," "liberty," and "frank." At the same time, by a curious semantic alchemy, hand and heart combine to remind him of that "*hand*kerchief . . . dyed in mummy . . . Conserv'd of maidens' *hearts*" (11. 55–75; emphasis added).[20] Thus the hand-kerchief becomes for Othello both heart and hand together; it does not merely stand for but, imaginatively speaking, *is* all that he has ever given Desdemona, all that she owes to him:

> *That handkerchief which I so loved* and gave thee,
> Thou gav'st to Cassio. . . .
> By heaven I saw my *handkerchief* in's *hand!*
> O perjured woman! Thou dost stone my *heart*. . . .
> I saw the *handkerchief.*
> 5.2.48–66; EMPHASIS ADDED

Once Othello has been injected with the poison of suspicion, language becomes for him a fabric of mocking duplicities, as the world seems a tissue of deceiving appearances, so that by act 4, scene 1, when Iago's medicine has already thoroughly done its work, the most innocent remark can inspire a frenzy of jealous rage. He is like Wycherley's Pinchwife surrounded by that "power of brave signs," each one of which carries its secret message of cuck-oldom.[21] Desdemona's harmless reference to "the love I bear to Cassio" (1. 231) is heard as an outrageously public declaration of infidelity, provoking his enraged "Fire and brimstone!" And her pleasure in Lodovico's ill-timed announcement of the order "Deputing Cassio in his government" (1. 237) only seems to redouble the public insult. To Othello's ear the order itself sounds as a covert taunt, gratuitous and cruel, and on the sexual double enten-dre lurking in "government" depends the equally wounding ambivalence of

Lodovico's soothing praise of Desdemona as "an obedient lady" (l. 248), a compliment Othello instantly converts to the mocking description of a compliant whore:

> Sir, she can turn, and turn, and yet go on,
> And turn again. And she can weep, sir, weep.
> And she's obedient; as you say, obedient,
> Very obedient.
>   4.1.255–8

Othello here is close to breakdown; he arrests the collapse briefly by turning away from this seeming travesty of domestic duty to the larger world of political obligation ("I obey the mandate," l. 261) only to confront once again the grotesque confusion of the two. Language now begins to break upon the rack of equivocation:

> Cassio shall have my place. And, sir, tonight
> I do entreat that we may sup together.
> You are welcome, sir, to Cyprus. Goats and monkeys!
>   4.1.263–5

Just beneath the surface of this speech there is a thread of frightful association ("Cassio . . . my place . . . Tonight . . . Sup together . . . welcome . . . to Cyprus") that runs like a subterranean fuse toward the explosion of disgust and rage in "Goats and monkeys!" It is as Iago has warned: Cassio has usurped his function, and by that fact Othello now seems to occupy precisely Iago's position at the beginning of the play, forced to surrender his military place to one he suspects of having stolen his domestic office. To the baffled Lodovico it is as though the Moor's very self had been displaced: "Is this the nature / Whom passion could not shake?" (ll. 267–8). He is not altogether mistaken; the deliberately muddy ambiguity of Iago's reaction exposes for the audience his satisfaction at the ironic perfection of Othello's metamorphosis: "He's that he is. . . . If what he might he is not / I would to heaven he were" (2.272–4). The riddling patter takes us back to the beginning of the play and to Iago's "I am not what I am"; now it is Othello who is not what he might be. As the Moor's sudden collapse into Iago's characteristic language of bestiality confirms, the two have changed places.

Othello, it must be said, is peculiarly vulnerable to such displacement. If

Iago suffers from the devouring resentment of a man cheated of his place, Othello is threatened from the beginning with the even more radical insecurity of placelessness. He has, it is true, a strongly developed sense of the dignity of his rank. Preparing to answer the libels of Brabantio he invokes the pride of his inheritance "From men of royal siege" (1.2.22), and in requesting "fit disposition" for Desdemona during his absence at the wars he relies as much upon what is fitting to one of his status ("Due reference of place") as upon the proprieties demanded by "her breeding" (1.3.234–7).[22] But in Venice Othello's place must always be, to some degree, that of a stranger dependent on the favor of others for "The trust, the office I do hold of you" (1.3.118); it is given warrant only by appeal to "My services, which I have done the signory" (1.2.18). This appeal opens Othello's first significant speech in the play, an aria of self-affirmation that is echoed at the end in a splendidly defiant reassertion of the theme: "I have done the state some service and they know't" (5.2.335). Just as the first act of the tragedy climaxes in Othello's investiture as general commander against the Turk, so its last concludes with his formal repudiation of that command—a final self-canceling exhibition of service by a Venetian officer whose very name, with its teasing suggestion of "Othoman" (as Ottoman was often spelled) has an oddly Turkish ring to it:

> And say, besides that in Aleppo once
> Where a malignant and a turbaned Turk
> Beat a Venetian and traduced the state,
> I took by th' throat the circumcised dog
> And smote him thus.
>   5.2.348–52

Othello's strangely triumphant demonstration of the contradictions inherent in his designation as a "Moor of Venice" is the last of the play's enacted puns.[23] It makes of him a kind of anamorphic beast with two backs, both Venetian and Turk; it invokes the claims of his military "place" to declare his ultimate placelessness. What once promised to resolve these contradictions, what seemed to render his place something more than a mere mercenary rank, what properly located him within the order of the *polis*, was the love of a Venetian woman—the very thing he has now destroyed. Othello's Venetian self is to a large extent the creation of Desdemona's love—a love that is the more overwhelming because it was awakened by her romantic response to his history of placeless wandering:

> Wherein of antres vast and deserts idle,
> Rough quarries, rocks, and hills whose heads touch heaven
> It was my hint to speak—such was the process:
> And of the Cannibals that each other eat,
> The Anthropophagi, and men whose heads
> Do grow beneath their shoulders. . . .
> She swore, in faith 'twas strange, 'twas passing strange,
> 'Twas pitiful, 'twas wondrous pitiful. . . .
> She loved me for the dangers I had passed,
> And I loved her, that she did pity them.
> 1.3.139–67

It is above all his strangeness and extravagance (the very sources of Iago's resentful scorn) that excite Desdemona's wonder, pity, and love—emotions that, in their turn, waken Othello's sense of heroic selfhood. The wilderness landscapes, the human barbarities he recalls are touched with sublimity because he is seeing them, and by extension himself, through her beglamoured eyes. She is, in this sense, the very foundation of his conscious self, the "place" or citadel of his vulnerable identity. Not for nothing does Cassio speak of Desdemona as "our great Captain's Captain" (2.1.74) or Iago sardonically declare that "Our General's wife is now the General" (2.3.305–6), for it is as though only the self-esteem generated by the love of his "fair warrior" (2.1.176) can validate the public esteem he is granted, can smother self-doubt of this displaced stranger and enable him to fill his place in the Venetian state with the supreme confidence he at first displays. This is what makes him a man to be reckoned with—one who, outsider though he is, can bear comparison with any man in Venice. But it is this too that opens him so fatally to Iago's attack, for it means that his very being is invested beyond himself, where it can seem peculiarly exposed to the frailty or malice of others.

Othello's passion for Desdemona is, in a radical sense, selfish. This is not to call in question its sincerity or to denigrate its intensity, but it does indicate an essential qualitative difference from Desdemona's love for him. For both of them marriage is conceived as a form of "office," involving for Othello a willing "circumscription" of his "free condition" (1.2.24–8) and for Desdemona a voluntary submission to her "duty" (1.3.178–87).[24] But for her this implies a complete abdication of the will, an unqualified surrender of the self to the beloved other of which Othello is incapable ("My heart's subdued / Even to the very quality of my lord," 1.3.247–8). So absolute is this surrender that at the very point of death Desdemona can reassert herself only through an act of quiet self-denial; questioned by Emilia as to who is responsible for her death, she quite simply offers herself in Othello's place: "Nobody—I myself—farewell" (5.2.125). To embrace this paradox is indeed to make herself "nobody." In its humility it is as far from the histrionic display of Othello's self-canceling suicide as one could imagine. Yet there is no doubt which of the two has more thoroughly lost himself, for Othello has never been more than what his love and "occupation" have made him, and from these he has cut himself adrift.

The connection Othello makes between private and public roles is amply illustrated in his apologia to the senate:

If you do find me foul in her report,
The trust, the office I do hold of you
Not only take away, but let your sentence
Even fall upon my life.
1.3.117–20

The public trust is felt as naturally contingent upon his private faith; his political function, upon his domestic office. It is inevitable, then, that any betrayal of his love for Desdemona should strike him as a double displacement, an expulsion from that place where both his public and his private identity have been located. This is what is so agonizingly glimpsed in the notorious pun that concludes his litany of loss in the temptation scene, "Othello's occupation's gone" (3.3.354). The "occupation" at issue at once includes his governorship of Cyprus, his larger military calling, his command over the fortress of Desdemona's affection, and linked to this last (as John Bayley has rightly insisted), his claim to erotic possession. It is unnecessary to argue, as Bayley does, that the sexual double entendre is unconscious on Othello's part, since the various senses of the wordplay mark the point at which, with a shock of terrible insight, the Moor recognizes the consequences of that equation of public and private roles upon which he has built his life. He is, from that moment, a man utterly out of his place.[25]

Henceforth it is characteristically in terms of a lost or violated place that he imagines Desdemona's betrayal:

But *there where* I have garnered up my heart,
Where either I must live, or bear no life,
The fountain from the which my current runs,
Or else dries up—to be discarded *thence*
Or keep it as a cistern for foul toads
To knot and gender in! Turn thy complexion *there*,
Patience, thou young and rose-lipped cherubin,
Ay *there* look grim as hell!
    4.2.56–65; EMPHASIS ADDED

In the condensed language of this speech the obsessively indicated "there" is both the marriage bed (that locus of domestic office) and the beloved's breast (that lodging of Petrarchan hearts). But as the imagery of the speech gathers emotional force, it becomes something else, the equivalent of *Lear*'s "forfended place," the "dark and vicious place" of begetting—the female wellspring of life itself, obscenely imagined as a reptilian mating pond. The toad pool grows out of that earlier image of monstrous usurpation:

I had rather be a toad
And live upon the vapour of a dungeon
Than keep a corner in the thing I love
For others' uses.
    3.3.270–3

Desdemona is for him not merely the precious "thing," the stolen treasure of love's corrupted commerce, but herself the lost place of love, a violated paradise, transformed to an imprisoning hell—the very place that, in the brothel scene, he imagines guarded by that lieutenant of Satan, Emilia:

You, mistress,
That have the office opposite to Saint Peter
And keep the gate of hell!
    4.2.89–91

This hell-gate, surely, opens on the same torture chamber whose fires the maddened Lear imagines raging between a woman's legs—"There's hell, there's darkness, there is the sulphurous pit— / Burning, scalding, stench, consumption" (*King Lear*, 4.6.129–30).[26]

The ingenious symmetries of the revenge toward which Iago guides his victim are perfectly designed to exploit the latter's sense of cruel displacement. In the murderous consummation of his passion, the place of love itself must become the place of punishment: "Do it not with poison; strangle her in her bed, even the bed she hath contaminated" (4.1.206–7). For Iago this is perhaps no more than the counter-casting of resentment, but for Othello the precise ironic "justice" of the suggestion "pleases" because it converts the act of murder into a species of abstract ritual. It is not so much the annihilation of a living woman as the ceremonial cleansing of a polluted place ("Thy bed, lust-stained, shall with lust's blood be spotted," 5.1.36)—hence the curiously impersonal grammar of his soliloquy over the sleeping Desdemona, "this sorrow's heavenly— / It strikes where it doth love" (5.2.21–2). Not "whom" but "where." Desdemona is merely his place—the place Cassio has taken.[27]

To Othello's ear it is the mocking ambiguity of his orders from Venice ("Cassio shall have my place," 4.1.263) that puts the seal of public knowledge upon the double displacement that occurred when his own lieutenant ("mine officer!" 4.1.201) usurped him in the office of Desdemona's bed. The audience, however, will recognize that Othello's real displacement is achieved elsewhere, in the great temptation scene, and to their ear it is confirmed in the hideously resonant exchange with which that scene concludes:

❦

OTHELLO:
Now art thou my lieutenant.

IAGO:
I am your own for ever.

3.3.475–6

❦

Superficially, Othello merely offers to confirm Iago in the promotion he has for so long coveted. But Iago's reply, picking up the suggestion of diabolic symbiosis in the Moor's earlier "I am bound to thee for ever" (l.211), points to his occupation of a very different office—that of second to Othello's jealous passion, the monstrous other-self of Iago's own creation to which the general has surrendered his self-command. Iago has already hinted at its real nature in the mock reluctance of his engagement to prove Desdemona's treachery ("I do not like the office," l. 410), and the "service" he offers to Othello at lines 465–9 is that of a Mephistophillis whose unholy office is to dispossess his master of his soul, to drive him from the occupation of his own self. If Desdemona is in Othello's mind a usurped place, Othello himself by the end of this scene has become occupied territory. The worst of torments he might otherwise imagine, he will declare to Desdemona, would leave "in some place of my soul / A drop of patience" (4.2.51–2), but in the dungeon of his self no such place remains—patience has been dispossessed by the spirit of jealousy. Indeed the effect of the temptation is to make real the metaphor of diabolic possession with which Cassio lightheartedly toyed in the drinking scene ("It hath pleased the devil drunkenness to give place to the devil wrath," 2.3.287–8). Iago, evidently, is as much the informing spirit of Othello's revenge as he was that of Cassio's wrath.

The temptation scene, then, is about the sealing of a diabolical bond. It is the psychological equivalent of that episode in Marlowe's tragedy where Faustus signs away his soul to the devil, and Shakespeare constructs it as an elaborate reworking of the old morality triangle he himself had used in his sonnet of jealous passion (Sonnet 144) with Desdemona as the good angel "fired out" by the bad angel, Iago. What makes it so painful and shocking to witness is that (as the sonnet parallel suggests) it is also a love scene. Iago's design has grown far beyond the purely mechanical purpose he first announced—to destroy Cassio and punish Othello with the libel of Desdemona's adultery. The full obscenity of his stratagem consists in its methodical attempt to destroy the very bases on which a love such as Desdemona's and Othello's rests. The subject of the scene becomes the expulsion of one kind of love in favor of its corrupted travesty: Iago seeks not only to violate the bond between man and wife but to put another in its place.

The love espoused by Desdemona and Othello is an affront to Iago's construction of the world. The "freedom" (generosity, spontaneity, openness) he discerns in both their characters ("The Moor is of a free and open nature," 1.3.393; "She's framed as fruitful / As the free elements," 2.3.331–2), which is most fully expressed in their love for one another, is by its very bounty a rebuke to him, a source of wounding comparison. For Iago freedom consists only in the untrammeled exercise of the independent will, so that the self-abandonment of love can only seem an insupportable tax on the integrity of the self: "This, that you call love . . . is merely a lust of the blood and a permission of the will. Come, be a man. Drown thyself? Drown cats and blind puppies" (1.3.328–33). Love is simply a blind biological craving that reduces one to the helpless condition of a sightless puppy: that is his contemptuous redaction of the mythology of blind Cupid. Though "free" and "love" are characteristically among his favorite words, nothing for Iago is freely given—love least of all, for it can only be understood as a form of humiliating enslavement:

> His soul is so *enfettered* to her love,
> That she may make, unmake, do what she list,
> Even as her appetite shall play the god
> With his weak function.
>   2.3.345–8; EMPHASIS ADDED

If he seeks to make of Desdemona's loving nature the Hephaestus's "net / That shall enmesh them all" (ll. 361–2), such entanglement, he believes, is no more than they have already wished on themselves.

One way of reading the temptation scene is as a methodical demonstration of Iago's degraded idea of love. His method is to displace Desdemona as the captain of Othello's will—there can be no slavery more wretched than one subject to so easy and arbitrary a change of masters. At the same time, of course, there are perverse satisfactions to be tasted in the usurping of Desdemona's place. This is the last and most ingenious refinement of revenge; through it Iago accrues to himself not only the "price" of which he was bilked by Cassio's promotion, but the supreme price Othello has put upon the jewel of his love, Desdemona. The temptation is also a wooing, an act of erotic possession, punctuated by protestations of love:

> My lord, you know I love you.
>   3.3.116

> now I shall have reason
> To show the love and duty that I bear you
> With franker spirit.
>   LL. 191–3

> But I am much to blame,
> I humbly do beseech you of your pardon
> For too much loving you.
>   LL. 209–11

I hope you will consider what is spoke
Comes from my love.
    LL. 216–7

God bu'y you: take mine office. O wretched fool,
That lov'st to make thine honesty a vice! . . .
I thank you for this profit, and from hence
I'll love no friend, sith love breeds such offence.
    LL. 372–7

I do not like the office.
But sith I am entered in this cause so far—
Pricked to't by foolish honesty and love—
I will go on.
    LL. 407–10

The attitude struck, with Iago's gift of vicious mimicry, is a surreptitious burlesque of Desdemona's own long-suffering devotion, and by the destructive logic of comparison it is precisely this show of love that most inflames Othello's jealousy—Iago's fidelity rendering doubly intolerable Desdemona's apparent infidelity and Cassio's betrayal of trust. The scene reaches its climax with the Moor's formal repudiation of the bonds of matrimony:

All my fond love thus do I blow to heaven:
'Tis gone.
Arise, black vengeance, from thy hollow cell!
Yield up, O love, thy crown and hearted throne
To tyrannous hate!
    3.3.442–6

The spirit of revenge is here imagined as the usurper of love's royal seat, and the metaphor exactly corresponds to the displacement of the loving Desdemona by the vindictive Iago realized in the stage action that follows. The kneeling exchange of vows is presented as a blasphemous troth-plighting:

✸

OTHELLO:

Now, by yond marble heaven,
In the due reverence of a sacred vow
I here engage my words.
/He kneels/

IAGO:

Do not rise yet.
/He kneels/
Witness you ever-burning lights above,
You elements that clip us round about,
Witness that here Iago doth give up
The execution of his wit, hands, heart,
To wronged Othello's service! Let him command,
And to obey shall be in me remorse,
What bloody business ever.
/They rise/

OTHELLO:

I greet thy love,
Not with vain thanks, but with acceptance bounteous. . . .
Now art thou my lieutenant.

IAGO:

I am your own for ever.

3.3.457–76

✸

If there is any act of adultery in the play, this surely is it.[28]

"Lieutenant" here encompasses not merely Cassio's office but the role of
domestic deputy, which patriarchal theory gave to every wife. Through his
lurid fantasy of sharing Cassio's bed, Iago has already cast himself, in a
black-comic version of the bed-trick, as Desdemona's substitute. The intense
emotional identification of tempter and tempted reached by that point in the
scene ("I am bound to thee for ever." l. 211) made virtually interchangeable
figures of Othello and Iago in the fantasy, so that for Othello merely to listen
to the speech was to put himself imaginatively in Iago's place and, in effect,
to experience Cassio's adultery with Desdemona (as Brabantio was made to

experience her seduction by Othello) as a sexual assault upon his own person. The ending of the scene merely confirms in literal terms the psychological lieutenancy appropriated by means of Iago's ugly fiction. Iago has successfully usurped both Cassio's and Desdemona's places, and in that dank corner of the emotional prison that the two men share, Othello and he are bound to one another forever: they have become in an appalling sense, one flesh—this is hell, nor are they out of it.[29]

The Othello of the last two acts is a man without a place. The height of his agony of remorse is reached with the recognition of his utter dislocation and estrangement, the understanding that by the act of murder he has encompassed the very displacement he sought to avenge, expulsion from the anchoring haven of Desdemona's love. Before his eyes there burns a vision of future damnation, but what he describes is a state of present torment:

> when we shall meet at compt,
> This look of thine will hurl my soul from heaven,
> And fiends will snatch at it. . . .
> O cursèd, cursèd slave! Whip me, ye devils,
> From the possession of this heavenly sight!
> Blow me about in winds! Roast me in sulphur!
> Wash me in steep-down gulfs of liquid fire!
>   5.2.273–80

Othello knows his price: here is a final accounting more absolute and unforgiving than anything in Iago's meanly resentful balance sheet. The hallucinated landscape of this eternal exile ("steep-down gulfs of liquid fire") is the terrible counterpart of that romantically evoked wilderness ("antres vast and deserts idle, / Rough quarries, rocks, and hills whose heads touch heaven") through which the Moor first won his way to Desdemona's heart. It is as though she had cast him back into that savage and unredeemed world. Yet there remains a curious ambiguity. Like the earlier speech, this one is infused with the full power of Othello's enthralled imagination; and, like Faustus's great aria of damnation, it rises to a near rapture of despair—as if the prospect of punishment were charged with a kind of ecstasy. What Othello can no longer bear is "the *possession* of this heavenly sight," because to possess it is to be possessed *by* it, as one might be by a tormenting spirit. His ill angel has fired the good one out. Displaced, dispossessed, his occupation gone, Othello offers himself almost gratefully to a punishment that makes him once again "an extravagant and wheeling stranger of here and everywhere"—blown in the winds, washed to and fro in seas of fire, adrift, released. By comparison with this vision of magnificent desolation, the heroic self-regard of his last speech is likely to appear as emptily rhetorical as Leavis charged, but the comparison is one upon which Shakespeare himself, with all the unflinching clarity of his tragic vision, insists.[30]

"Unproper Beds:" Race, Adultery, and the Hideous in Othello

There is a glass of ink wherein you see
How to make ready black-faced tragedy.
—George Chapman, *Bussy D'Ambois*

The ending of *Othello* is perhaps the most shocking in Shakespearean tragedy. "I am glad that I have ended my revisal of this dreadful scene," wrote Doctor Johnson; "it is not to be endured."[1] His disturbed response is one the play conspicuously courts; indeed Johnson does no more than paraphrase the reaction of the scandalized Venetians, whose sense of the unendurable nature of what is before them produces the most violently abrupt of all Shakespearean endings. Though its catastrophe is marked by a conventional welter of stabbing and slaughter, *Othello* is noticeably shorn of the funeral dignities that usually serve to put a form of order upon such spectacles of ruin. In the absence of any witness sympathetic enough to tell the hero's story, the disgraced Othello has in effect to speak his own funeral oration—and it is one whose lofty rhetoric is arrested in midline by the "bloody period" of his own suicide (5.2.353). "All that's spoke is marred," observes Gratiano, but no memorializing tributes ensue. Even Cassio's "he was great of heart" (l. 357) may amount to nothing more than a faint plea in mitigation for one whose heart was swollen to bursting with intolerable emotion.[2] And in place of the reassuring processional exeunt announced by the usual command to take up the tragic bodies, we get only Lodovico's curt order to close up the scene of butchery: "The object poisons sight: / Let it be hid" (ll. 360–1). The tableau on the bed announces a kind of plague, one that taints the sight as the deadly effluvia of pestilence poison the nostrils.[3]

The congruence between Dr Johnson's desperately averted gaze and Lodovico's fear of contamination is striking, but it is only Johnson's agitated frankness that makes it seem exceptional. It renders articulate the anxiety evident almost everywhere in the play's history—a sense of scandal that informs the textual strategies of editors and theatrical producers as much as it does the disturbed reactions of audiences and critics. Contemplating the "unutterable agony" of the conclusion, the Variorum editor, Furness, came to wish that the tragedy had never been written, and his choice of the word "unutterable" is a telling one, for this ending, as its stern gestures of erasure demonstrate, has everything to do with what cannot be uttered and must not be seen.[4]

The sensational effect of the scene upon its earliest audiences is apparent both from the imitations it spawned and from the mesmerized gaze of Henry Jackson, who left the first surviving account of *Othello* in performance. He saw *Othello* acted by the King's Men at Oxford in 1610 and wrote how "the celebrated Desdemona, *slain in our presence by her husband*, although she pleaded her case very effectively throughout, yet moved us more after she was dead, when, lying in her bed, she entreated the pity of the spectators by her very countenance." More than any other scene, it was this show of a wife murdered by her husband that gripped Jackson's imagination, but even more distressing than the killing itself seems to have been the sight of the dead woman "lying in her bed"—a phrase that echoes Emilia's outrage: "My mistress here lies murdered in her bed" (5.2.184). For Jackson, the *place* seems to matter almost as much as the *fact* of wife-murder—just as it did to the nineteenth-century Desdemona, Fanny Kemble, when she confessed to "feel[ing] horribly at the idea of being murdered *in my bed*."[5]

The same anxious fascination is reflected in the first attempts to represent the play pictorially. It was the spectacle of the violated marriage bed that Nicholas Rowe selected to epitomize the tragedy in the engraving for his 1709 edition, and his choice was followed by the actors David Garrick and Sarah Siddons wanting memorials of their own performances.[6] In the great period of Shakespeare illustration from the 1780s to the 1920s, the bedchamber scene was overwhelmingly preferred by publishers and artists, whose images com-

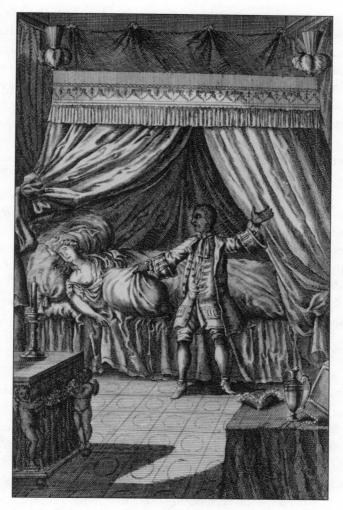

8. *The bedchamber scene in* Othello. *Francois Boitard (?),
from Tonson's 1709 edition of Shakespeare, reprinted by permission of the Folger Shakespeare Library.*

bined to grant it the same representative significance as the graveyard in
Hamlet or the monument in *Antony and Cleopatra*—as if announcing in this
display of death-in-marriage a gestic account of the play's key meanings (see
figs. 8–12).[7] Both graveyard and monument, however, in their different ways
help to clothe the tragic ending in traditional forms of rhetoric and ceremony

that mitigate its terrors, shackling death within a frame of decorum. What makes the ending of *Othello* so unaccountably troubling and so threatening to its spectators is precisely the brutal violation of decorum that is registered in the quasi-pornographic explicitness of the graphic tradition. The illustrators' voyeuristic manipulation of the parted curtains and their invariable focus upon the unconscious invitation of Desdemona's gracefully exposed body serve to foreground not merely the perverse eroticism of the scene but its aspect of forbidden disclosure.

Even more striking is the fact that these images were often designed to draw readers into texts whose bowdlerizing maneuvers aimed, as far as possible, to conceal everything that their frontispieces offer to reveal. While they could scarcely contrive to remove the scandalous property itself, late eighteenth- and nineteenth-century editors sought to restrict the curiosity that the final scene gratifies and to obscure its most threatening meanings by progressively excising from the text every explicit reference to the bed.[8]

Predictably enough, an even more anxious censorship operated in the theater itself, where, however, its consequences were much more difficult to predict. In the most striking of many effacements, it became the practice for nineteenth-century Othellos to screen the murder from the audience by closing the curtains upon the bed. This move was ostensibly consistent with a general attempt at desensationalizing the tragedy, an attempt whose most obvious manifestation was the restrained "Oriental" Moor developed by Macready and others. But the actual effect of the practice was apparently quite opposite, raising to a sometimes unbearable intensity the audience's scandalized fascination with the now-invisible scene. Years later Westland Marston could still recall the "thrilling" sensation as Macready thrust "his dark despairing face, through the curtains," its "contrast with the drapery" producing "a marvellous piece of colour," and so shocking was this moment, according to John Forster, that in his presence a woman "hysterically fainted" at it.[9]

The reasons for so extreme a reaction can be glimpsed in the offended tone of the Melbourne *Argus* critic, attacking an 1855 production that had flouted this well-established convention: "[The] consummation," he indignantly insisted, "should take place behind the curtain and out of sight."[10] The revealing word "consummation," when set beside the "hysterical" reaction to Macready's "marvellous piece of colour," suggests that the bed was so intensely identified with the anxieties about race and sex stirred up by the play that it needed, as far as possible, to be removed from the public gaze.[11] Yet the effect of such erasure was only to give freer play to the fantasy it was

OTHELLO.

Oth_____ *Yet I'll not shed her blood;*
Nor scar that whiter skin of hers than snow.
Act V. Scene II.

9. The bedchamber scene in Othello. *Philippe Jacques de Loutherbourg (1785), reprinted by permission of the Folger Shakespeare Library.*

designed to check, so that the violent chiaroscuro of Macready's blackened face thrust between the virgin-white curtains was experienced as a shocking sado-erotic climax. It was, of course, a stage picture that significantly repeated an offstage action twice imagined in the first half of the play, when Othello, first in Venice (1.2) and then in Cyprus (2.3), is unceremoniously

10. The bedchamber scene in Othello. *Conrad Metz (1789),*
reprinted by permission of the Folger Shakespeare Library.

roused from his nuptial bed. The unconscious repetition must have had the
effect of underlining the perverse eroticism of the murder just at the point
where the parting of the bed-curtains and the display of Desdemona's corpse
was about to grant final satisfaction to the audience's terrible curiosity about
the absent scene that dominates so much of the play's action.

For all their ostentatious pudency, then, the Victorian attempts at containing the danger of the play's ending reveal a reading unsettlingly consistent with the most sensational productions of more recent times, such as Bernard Miles's 1971 Mermaid *Othello* or Ronald Eyre's at the National in 1979, with their extraordinary emphasis on the significance and visibility of a bed.[12] It is a reading in which the folio stage direction at the beginning of

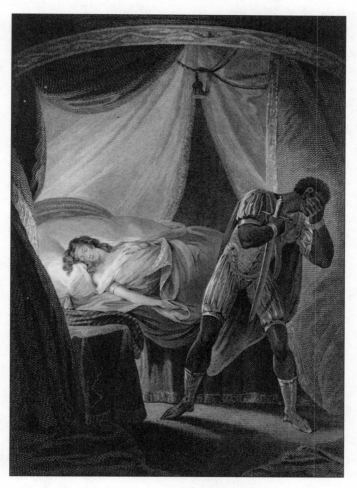

11. The bedchamber scene in Othello. *Engraving by George Noble, from a painting by Josiah Boydell for the Boydell Gallery (1800), reprinted by permission of the Folger Shakespeare Library.*

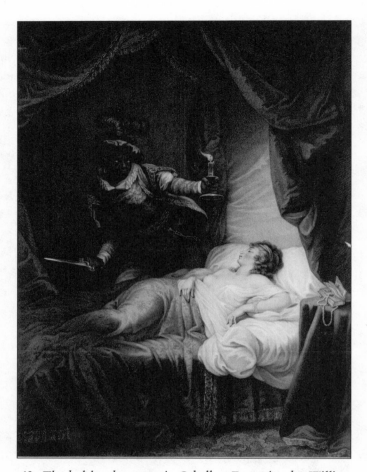

12. The bedchamber scene in Othello. *Engraving by William Leney from a painting by J. Graham for the Boydell Gallery (1799), reprinted by permission of the Folger Shakespeare Library.*

act 5, scene 2, "Enter . . . Desdemona in her bed," announces ocular proof of all that the audience have most desired and feared to look upon, exposing to cruel light the obscure erotic fantasies that the play not only explores but disturbingly excites. Forster's story of the woman who fainted at the sight of Macready's "dark despairing face" records a moment when (despite more than half a century of bleaching, "civilizing," and bowdlerizing) a subterranean image erupted to confirm the deep fears of racial/sexual otherness on which *Othello* trades—fears that are made quite embarrassingly explicit in the feverish self-betrayals of a nineteenth-century Russian literary lady reacting to Ira Aldridge's performance of the part. In her account the play exhibits nothing less than the symbolic rape of the European "spirit" by the "savage, wild flesh" of black otherness:

> A full-blooded Negro, incarnating the profoundest creations of Shakespearean art, giving *flesh and blood* for the aesthetic judgement of educated European society . . . how much nearer can one get to truth, to the very source of the highest aesthetic satisfaction? But *what is truth . . . ?* As the spirit is not the body, so the truth of art is not this profoundly raw flesh which we can take hold of, and call by name and, if you please, feel, pinch with our unbelieving, all-feeling hand. . . . Not the Moscow Maly Theater, but the African jungle should have been filled and resounded with . . . the cries of this black, powerful, howling flesh. But by the very fact that that flesh is so powerful—that it is genuinely black, so naturally *un-white* does it howl—that savage flesh did its fleshly work. It murdered and crushed the spirit . . . one's spirit cannot accept it—and in place of the highest enjoyment, this blatant flesh introduced into art, this *natural* black Othello, pardon me, causes only . . . revulsion.[13]

It is as if in Macready's coup the strange mixture of thrilled agitation, horror, and shame voiced here became focused with an unbearable intensity upon the occupation of the bed, where the transgression of racial boundaries was displayed as an offense punishable by death.

❆ ❆ ❆

The racial fear and revulsion lurking beneath the ambiguous excitements of the theatrical and pictorial traditions are made crudely explicit in an early nineteenth-century caricature, apparently of Ira Aldridge's Othello, published as number 9 in the series *Tregear's Black Jokes* (see fig. 13). The caricaturist sublimates his anxiety at the scene's sexual threat through the burlesque device of transforming Desdemona into an obese black woman, her snoring mouth grotesquely agape. The racialism paraded here for the amusement of early nineteenth-century Londoners is rarely so openly exhibited, but it has tainted even the most respectable *Othello* criticism until well into the present century. A sense of racial scandal is a consistent thread in commen-

13. Tregear's Black Jokes, *No. 9, reprinted by permission of the Folger Shakespeare Library.*

tary on the play, from Rymer's notorious effusions against the indecorum of a "Blackmoor" hero, to Coleridge's assertion that Othello was never really intended to be black, and F. R. Leavis's triumphant demonstration that the Moor was never intended for a hero.[14] It is as apparent in A. C. Bradley's nervously footnoted anxiety about how "the aversion of our blood" might respond to the sight of a black Othello as it is in Charles Lamb's frank discovery of "something extremely revolting in the courtship and wedded caresses of Othello and Desdemona." "To imagine is one thing," Bradley protests, "and to see is another," making painfully explicit his reaction against what Edward Snow describes as the play's insistence upon "bringing to consciousness things known in the flesh but 'too hideous to be shown.' " For the neo-Freudian Snow, however, these forbidden things are the male psyche's repressed fears of female otherness, which the accident of Othello's race "merely forces him to live out with psychotic intensity." It is clear, however, that for Bradley it was precisely Othello's blackness that made the play's sexual preoccupations so upsetting.[15]

For Coleridge the idea of a black hero was unacceptable because blackness was equivalent to savagery and the notion of savage heroism an intolerable oxymoron. His application of critical skin-lightener began a tradition of sterile and seemingly endless debate about the exact degree and significance of Othello's racial difference, on which critics dissipated their energies until well into the present century—M. R. Ridley's only lately displaced Arden edition (1958), with its ludicrous attempt to substitute "contour" for "colour" as the principle of discrimination, is merely the most disgraceful (because most prestigious) recent example. Since Coleridge, arguments about race in *Othello* have almost invariably been entangled, more or less explicitly, with arguments about culture, in which gradations of color stand for gradations of "barbarity," "animality," and "primitive emotion." If the dominant nineteenth-century tradition sought to domesticate the play by removing the embarrassment of savagery, the most common twentieth-century strategy has been to anthropologize it as the study of an assimilated savage who relapses into primitivism under stress. This was essentially Leavis's solution, and one can still hear it echoed in the new Cambridge editor's admiration for the weird mimicry of Laurence Olivier's "West African"/"West Indian" Othello, which he describes as a "virtuoso . . . portrait of a *primitive* man, at odds with the sophisticated society into which he has forced himself, *relapsing into barbarism* as a result of hideous misjudgement."[16]

At the other extreme stand revisionist readings like Martin Orkin's, which have sought to rehabilitate the tragedy by co-opting it to the antiracist cause, insisting that "in its rejection of human pigmentation as a means of identifying worth, the play, as it always has done, continues to oppose racism." Orkin's is an admirably motivated attempt to expose the racialist ideology underlying various critical and theatrical interpretations of the tragedy, but Shakespeare would surely have been puzzled to understand the claim that this play "opposes racism," cast as it is in a language peculiar to the politics of our own century. It would no more have been possible for Shakespeare to "oppose racism" in 1604, one might argue, than for Marlowe to "oppose anti-Semitism" in 1590: the argument simply could not be constituted in those terms. Julie Hankey, indeed, contemplating the pitfalls presented by Shakespeare's treatment of racial matters, concludes that his construction of racial difference is virtually beyond recovery, having become after four hundred years hopelessly obscured by a "patina of apparent topicality."[17]

Hankey's position has at least the merit of historicist scruple but seems in the end evasive, not unlike those liberal critiques that rob the play of its danger by treating Othello's color simply as a convenient badge of his estrangement from Venetian society—in effect a distraction to be cleared out of the way in order to expose the real core of the drama, its tragedy of jealousy.[18] But the history that Hankey herself traces is a testimony to the stubborn fact that *Othello* is a play full of racial feeling—perhaps the first work in English to explore the roots of such feeling—and it can hardly be accidental that it belongs to the very period in English history in which something we can now identify as a racialist ideology was beginning to evolve under the pressure of nascent imperialism.[19] In this context it is all the more curious, as Hankey notices, that Henry Jackson in 1610 seemed utterly to ignore this aspect of the tragedy, presenting it simply as a drama of wife-murder whose culprit is described in the most neutral language as "her husband." We cannot now tell whether Jackson was blind to the racial dimension of the action, or thought it of no interest, or merely too obvious to require mention. But his attention to the bed suggests a way around the dilemma posed by this odd silence; to explain why the bed should have caught his eye is to begin to understand theatrical strategies for thinking about racial otherness that are specific to the work's own cultural context. If Jackson elected to say nothing about these matters, it may have been because there was for him no real way of voicing them, in that they were still in some deep sense *unutterable*. But they were there on the bed for all to see.

What is displayed on the bed is something, in Othello's own profoundly resonant phrase, "too hideous to be shown" (3.3.107). The wordplay here (unusual, in this drama of treacherously conflicting meanings) amounts to a kind of desperate iteration: what is *hideous* is what should be kept *hidden*, out of sight.[20] "Hideous" in this sense is virtually an Anglo-Saxon equivalent for the Latinate "obscene" referring to that which is profoundly improper, not merely indecent but tainted (in the original sense) or unclean and that which, also according to Shakespeare's own folk-etymology, should be kept unseen, *offstage*, hidden.[21] The play begins with Iago's evocation of just such an obscenity; it ends by seeking to return it to its proper darkness, closing the curtains that Iago himself first metaphorically plucked aside. Edward Snow, in his perceptive study of sexual anxiety in *Othello*, observes that the play's "final gesture is on the side of repression," and he goes on to stress how necessarily that gesture is directed at the bed: "It is not just any object that is to be hidden but the 'tragic lodging' of the wedding-bed—the place of sexuality itself." But Snow's own strategy expressly requires that he himself suppress the anxiety that attaches to the bed as the site of racial transgression—the anxiety on which depends so much of the play's continuing power to disturb.[22]

✳ ✳ ✳

One of the terrifying things about *Othello* is that its racial poisons seem so casually concocted, as if racism were just something that Iago, drawing in his improvisational way on a gallimaufry of quite unsystematic prejudices and superstitions, made up as he went along. The characteristic pleasure he takes in his own felicitous invention only makes the effect more shocking. Iago lets horrible things loose and delights in watching them run, and the play seems to share that narcissistic fascination—or better, perhaps, Iago is the voice of its own fascinated self-regard. The play thinks abomination into being and then taunts the audience with the knowledge that it can never be *unthought:* "What you know, you know." It is a technique that works close to the unstable ground of consciousness itself, for it would be almost as difficult to say whether its racial anxieties are ones that the play discovers or implants in its (implicitly white) audience, as to say whether jealousy is something Iago discovers or implants in its black hero. Yet discovery, in the most literal theatrical sense, is what the last scene cruelly insists on. Like no other drama, *Othello* establishes an equivalency between psychological event (what happens "inside") and offstage action (what happens "within"); thus it can flourish its disclosure of the horror on the bed like a psychoanalytic revelation.

The power of the offstage scene over the audience's prying imagination is immediately suggested by the irritable speculation of Thomas Rymer, the play's first systematic critic. Rymer spends several pages of his critique exposing what he regards as ludicrous inconsistencies between what the play tells the audience and what verisimilitude requires them to believe about the occupation of "the Matrimonial Bed." The time scheme, he insists, permits Othello and his bride to sleep together only once, on the first night in Cyprus, but "*once* will not do the poet's business: the *audience* must suppose a great many bouts, to make the plot operate. They must deny their senses, to reconcile it to common sense."[23]

Rymer's method is taken to extraordinary extremes in an article by T. G. A. Nelson and Charles Haines, who set out to demonstrate, with a mass of circumstantial detail, that the marriage of Othello and Desdemona was never consummated at all. In this previously unsuspected embarrassment is to be found an explanation for the extreme suggestibility of the hero and thus the hidden spring of the entire tragic action. Their essay is remarkable not for the ingenuity of its finally unsustainable argument about the sequential "facts" of a plot whose time-scheme is so notoriously undependable but for what it unconsciously reveals about the effect of *Othello* upon its audiences. Their entire procedure mirrors with disturbing fidelity the habit of obsessive spec- ulation about concealed offstage action into which the play entraps the viewer as it entraps its characters. Nelson and Haines become victims, like the hero himself, of the scopophile economy of this tragedy and prey to its voyeuris- tic excitements.[24]

Norman Nathan has attempted a point-by-point rebuttal of Nelson and Haines, the ironic effect of which is to entrap him in the very conjecture he wishes to cut short. "If a lack of consummation is so important to this play, why isn't the audience so informed?" he somewhat testily inquires.[25] An answer might be—to make them ask the question. *Othello* persistently goads its audience into speculation about what is happening behind the scenes. This preoccupation with offstage action is unique in Shakespeare. Elsewhere, whenever offstage action is of any importance, it is almost always carefully described, usually by an eyewitness whose account is not open to question, so that nothing of critical importance is left to the audience's imagination. But in *Othello* the real imaginative focus of the action is always the hidden mar- riage bed, an inalienably private location, shielded until the very last scene from every gaze.[26] This disquietingly absent presence creates the margin within which Iago can operate as a uniquely deceitful version of the *nuntius*—one whose vivid imaginary descriptions taint the vision of the audi- ence even as they colonize the minds of Brabantio and Othello:

❀

IAGO:
Even now, now, very now, an old black ram
Is tupping your white ewe. . . .
You'll have your daughter covered with a Barbary horse. . . . Your daughter
and the Moor are now making the beast with two backs.
     1.1.89–90, 111–12, 116–18

❀

It is important that this fantasy, in which all the participants of this scene (Iago, Roderigo, and Brabantio) indulge, should have the characteristic anonymity of pornography—it trades only in perverted erotic stereotypes ("fair daughter" and "lascivious Moor," ll. 123, 127). Since the audience is exposed to these obscenities before it is allowed to encounter either Othello or Desdemona in person, they serve to plant the suggestion, which perseveres like an itch throughout the action, that the attractive public face of this marriage is only the mask for something unspeakably adulterate. The scenes that follow contrive to keep alive the ugly curiosity that Iago has aroused, even while the action concentrates on Othello's public magnificence, on Desdemona's courageous resistance to patriarchal authority, and upon idealized affirmations of the love between them.

Act 1, scene 2 opens with the entry of Othello and Iago "with torches," the flaming brands (a traditional property of both Hymen and Eros) serving as a reminder of the hero's sudden arousal from his marriage bed, so that Iago's probing "are you fast married?" (l. 11) is implicitly a question about consummation. With Iago's bawdy innuendo to Cassio, "he tonight hath boarded a land carack" (1.50), it continues the fitful illumination of that offstage scene. This lurid vision of the bed, kindled again in Brabantio's jealous outrage, may contaminate even the idealizing language of Othello—the high rhetoric that contrasts "My thrice-driven bed of down" with "the flinty and steel couch of war" (ll. 228–9)—and it invites a prying curiosity about the "rites" of love acknowledged in Desdemona's touching erotic frankness.[27]

> If I be left behind
> A moth of peace, and he go to the war,
> The rites for which I love him are bereft me.
>   1.3.252–4

But it is not until the soliloquy after Roderigo's exit that Iago's diseased preoccupation with Othello's bed begins to reveal a fascination deeper and more brooding than mere stratagem requires:

> I hate the Moor,
> And it is thought abroad that *'twixt my sheets*
> He's done my *office*.
>   1.3.380–2; EMPHASIS ADDED

This "office" between the sheets is Iago's characteristically debased version of Desdemona's "rites for which I love him"; with its reduction of lovemaking to the right and duty of a patriarchal place-holder, it equates adultery with Cassio's usurpation of Iago's place as Othello's "officer," seeing in both a kind of illicit substitution or counterfeiting for which the deceits of his own "double knavery" are merely a just requital.

Retrospectively regarded, act 1, built as it is around the boisterous and threatening disruption of a wedding night, has something of the character of one of those satiric rituals (rough musics, charivari, and skimmingtons) by which society expressed its disapprobation of transgressive marriages and adulterous liaisons.[28] And the storm that ensues, with its ominous division of the bride and groom, might be read as confirming its threats, mimicking the erotic violence always latent in the dangerous translations of a wedding night and liable to be released by an unsanctioned match. The happy reunion on Cyprus, however, makes it seem as if a particularly testing rite of passage has been successfully negotiated, a suggestion supported by the elated sensuality of the language in which Cassio imagines it

> Great Jove, Othello guard,
> And swell his sail with thine own powerful breath,
> That he may bless this bay with his tall ship,
> Make love's quick pants in Desdemona's arms.
> 2.1.77–80

—and seemingly confirmed in Othello's joyous eroticization of his arrival:

> If after every tempest come such calms,
> May the winds blow till they have wakened death,
> And let the labouring bark climb hills of seas,
> Olympus-high and duck again as low
> As hell's from heaven. If it were now to die,
> 'Twere now to be most happy. . . .
> 2.1.179–84

But the exhilarated poetry of the scene is undercut by the sardonic presence of Iago, who greets his general's arrival with a typically reductive pun ("The Moor! I know *his trumpet*," l. 174; emphasis added) and who remains after the general exeunt to focus attention on the hidden scene of marital celebration:

> When the blood is made dull with the act of sport, there should be, again to inflame it and to give satiety a fresh appetite, loveliness in favour, sympathy in years, manners and beauties—all which the Moor

is defective in. Now for want of these required conveniences, her delicate tenderness will find itself abused, begin to heave the gorge, disrelish and abhor the Moor; very nature will instruct her in it and compel her to some second choice. . . . Lechery, by this hand. . . . When these mutualities so marshal the way, hard at hand comes the master and main exercise, th' incorporate conclusion.

    2.1.226–63

With its concentration on the imputed grotesquerie of racial mésalliance, this speech is almost an exact repetition of Iago's first scene with Roderigo, and like that scene it ends in a soliloquy, with Iago brooding on the adulterous violation of his own sheets: "I do suspect the lusty Moor / Hath leapt into my seat. . . . / I fear Cassio with my night-cap too" (ll. 295–307).

    Thus when act 2, scene 3 opens with Othello and his bride preparing once again for bed

> Come, my dear love,
> The purchase made, the fruits are to ensue:
> That profit's yet to come 'tween me and you
>   LL. 8–10

the suggestion of a new beginning is already bitterly ironized. Their departure is at once the occasion for Iago's prurient commentary:

> He hath not yet made wanton the night with her; and she is sport for Jove. . . .
> And, I'll warrant her, full of game. . . .
> What an eye she has! Methinks it sounds a parley to provocation. . . .
> And when she speaks, is it not an alarum to love? . . .
> Well, happiness to their sheets!
>   LL. 15–26

In terms of Iago's unfolding plot, this is largely superfluous. More important is its dramatic function—together with the carefully offhand suggestion of racial outrage in the "black Othello" (l. 29)—in concentrating the audiences' imagination once again upon the erotic act in the bedroom. In this way the speech helps to prepare us for the interruption of the second bedding by the rough music of a "dreadful bell," the "black sanctus" that accompa-

nies the second of Iago's charivari-like improvisations, with its weird travesty of nuptial disharmonies ("Friends all but now . . . like bride and groom
/ Devesting them for bed: and then . . . tilting one at others' breasts / In
opposition bloody" (ll. 173–8).[29]

Up to this point in the play, Iago's operation has been principally aimed
at converting the absent/present bed into a locus of imagined adultery by
producing Othello's abduction of Desdemona as an act of racial adulteration, violating the natural laws of kind. In this way the marriage is systematically confused with Othello's and Cassio's supposed adulterous couplings
with Emilia and with the vindictive counter-adultery that Iago briefly contemplates with Desdemona. More generally, it is projected as being of a piece
with the usurpation of "natural" rights in Cassio's appropriation of the lieutenancy owed to Iago. The audience can become deeply implicated in this
network of interlocking prejudices and suspicions just because it is Iago's
habit to work by implication and association. Feelings and attitudes that
would hardly survive inspection by the light of reason are enabled to persist
precisely because they work away in this subterranean fashion. The accomplishment of Iago's plan, though it means bringing "this monstrous birth to
the world's light" (substantially from act 3, scene 3, onward), never fully
allows the audience to escape this entanglement. To the extent that it takes the
form of a sinister parody of the ingenious symmetries of revenge tragedy
(the biter bit or the adulterer cuckolded), his plot allows the audience a certain ironic distance, a space in which the villain is subject to their judgment.
But to the extent that it actually continues the process of realizing Iago's fantasy of sexual adulteration, culminating in the hideous ocular proof of the
final scene, it traps them in a guilty involvement.

In the temptation scene (3.3) the "secrets" that Othello sees himself
patiently excavating from Iago's mind are already horribly present to the
audience—not just because they are party to the villain's plotting but because
these ugly conceits in some sense echo the secret and unscrutinized imaginings he has planted inside their heads. As the monster at the heart of the psychic labyrinth is brought to light, the confession of Iago's hidden thoughts
gradually slides into the revelation of Desdemona's hidden deeds:

In Venice they do let God see the pranks
They dare not show their husbands.
    3.3.200–1

From that hint of invisible vice, the tempter edges, with his technique of elaborate *occupatio*, rhetorically exhibiting what he repeatedly insists can never be shown, into the scopophile excitements of erotic encounters evoked in increasingly lurid visual detail. The tupping ram of act 1, scene 1 makes its reappearance in another promiscuously mixed gallery of copulating beasts:[30]

> Would you, the supervisor, grossly gape on?
> Behold her topped?
> It were a tedious difficulty, I think,
> To bring them to that prospect. Damn them then
> If ever mortal eyes do see them bolster
> More than their own. . . .
> It is impossible you should see this,
> Were they as prime as goats, as hot as monkeys,
> As salt as wolves in pride, and fools as gross
> As ignorance made drunk.
>   LL. 395–405

The still merely verbal but powerfully suggestive metonym "bolster" gives way to the ruthlessly detailed night-piece in which Iago claims to have become an unwilling partner in Cassio's dream of fornication. Once again nothing is shown—the love act is merely a sleeping fantasy; "Desdemona" is only "Iago." Yet this doubly fictive scene of adultery is made to seem doubly adulterate by the homoerotic displacement of the kisses that grow upon Iago's lips—kisses that themselves disturbingly mirror the one real adultery of the play, the seduction of Othello in which Iago is at this very moment engaged.[31] The revelation is given an extra stamp of authenticity by being presented as Cassio's unwitting self-betrayal in a moment of compulsive secrecy: "Sweet Desdemona, / Let us be wary, let us hide our loves" (3.3.416–17). Iago's invention seems to part the curtains to display not merely the hidden scene but hidden thoughts themselves.

It is not, however, until the second temptation scene (4.1) that Iago is ready to move to a direct evocation of Desdemona's adultery, and here, for the first time, the bed itself comes into full imaginative view, providing the climax of the brutally brief passage of stichomythia on which the scene opens:

❀

IAGO:
Will you think so?

OTHELLO:
Think so, Iago?

IAGO:
What?
To kiss in private?

OTHELLO:
An unauthorized kiss.

IAGO:
Or to be naked with her friend in bed
An hour or more, not meaning any harm?

OTHELLO:
Naked in bed, Iago, and not mean harm?

     4.1.1–5; EMPHASIS ADDED

❀

In the peculiarly concrete vividness with which those two naked bodies on the bed are made to flash out of the darkness of uncertainty onto the screen of Othello's fantasy, this becomes a moment of rhetorical discovery—a counterpart to the physical discovery of act 5, scene 2. It is what—together with the triumphantly reintroduced detail of the handkerchief, that visible sign of Desdemona's hidden self—provokes the crisis of the scene:[32]

OTHELLO:
Lie with her? lie on her? . . . Lie with her! Zounds, that's fulsome!
Handkerchief—confessions—handkerchief!

    4.1. 35–7

Imaginatively linked to the stained sheets of the wedding bed, as Lynda Boose and Edward Snow have shown, and connected with the exposure of secrets by its former owner's magical ability "almost [to] read / The thoughts of people" (3.4.57–8), the handkerchief stands for "an essence that's not seen" (4.1.16). As it renders the invisible visible and the private public, it proves the natural unnatural and property itself "unproper": "There's millions now alive / That nightly lie in those unproper beds / Which they dare swear peculiar" (ll. 67–9). Thus it confirms the grotesque propriety of the fate that Iago, relishing his fictive symmetries, decrees for Desdemona: "And did you see the handkerchief? . . . Do it not with poison; strangle her in her bed, even the bed she hath contaminated" (4.1.172, 206–7).[33]

From this point on, as Othello moves toward his murderous final exposure of those "villainous secrets" for which Emilia is "a closet lock and key" (4.2.21), the bed becomes more and more explicitly the "place" upon which the action is centered. Above all it provides the emotional focus of Desdemona's two scenes before the murder, where (as though in unconscious collusion with Othello's fantasies) she perfects a tableau of deathly consummation. Its hidden program is supplied by the fashion, increasingly popular among aristocratic women in the early seventeenth century, for having one's corpse wound in the sheets from the wedding night.[34]

> Prithee tonight
> Lay on my bed my wedding sheets—remember;
> And call thy husband hither.
>   4.2.104–6

❋

> DESDEMONA:
> *He hath commanded me to go to bed,*
> *And bade me to dismiss you. . . .*
> *Give me my nightly wearing, and adieu.*
> *We must not now displease him. . . .*
>
> EMILIA:
> *I have laid those sheets, you bade, me, on the bed. . . .*
> *In one of those same sheets.*
>   4.3.12–24

❋

There is something oddly somnambulant about Desdemona's preparation for her death, as there is about Othello's conduct of the murder. It emerges particularly through the repetition compulsion associated with the wedding sheets—equating sheets and shroud, marriage-bed and death-bed—that mirrors the murderous repetition of Othello's vow: "Thy bed, lust-stained, shall with lust's blood be spotted" (5.1.36). The suggestion of automatism can work as it does only because of the remorselessly cumulative effect of the play's gestures toward the absent presence of the bed. The scope of the action appears to narrow progressively, closing ineluctably through these later scenes upon the final disclosure: "Enter Othello, [with a light], and Desdemona in her bed."[35] The appearance of the bed from within the curtained alcove at the rear of the stage, envisaged in the folio stage direction, signals a moment of quite literal *discovery*, when the hidden object of the play's imaginative obsession at last stands revealed. The torch plays its part in this symbology of revelation. Like the torches that accompany Othello's first entrance from the marriage chamber in act 1, scene 2, it recalls the emblematic brands of Hymen and Eros.

In common with so many of the play's images of light and dark, however, its traditional symbolism is inverted or at least radically confused; for the bringing to light of the hidden scene of Othello's fantasy corresponds to the simultaneous and deliberate occlusion of his reason: "It is the cause, it is the cause, my soul: / Let me not name it to you." To name his motive would be to render it liable to scrutiny, but Othello cannot bear the thought of what he then might see: "put out the light"(5.2.1–2, 7). The scene is rhetorically framed by gestures of repression ("Let me not name it to you," "Let it be hid"), as the tableau at its center is physically framed by the curtains that finally close upon it.

It would labor the point to demonstrate in detail the centrality of the bed in the play's denouement. The pattern of alternating revelations and concealments in the final scene is enacted through (and largely organized around) the opening and closing of those bed-curtains that, like theatrical quotation marks, figure so conspicuously in representations of the ending (ll. 1, 105, 121, 361). In the murder on the bed, with its shocking literalization of Desdemona's conceit of wedding-sheets-as-shroud ("thou art on thy death-bed," l. 52), the nuptial consummation, which the play has kept as remorselessly in view as tormentingly out of sight, achieves its perverse (adulterate) performance. It is on the bed, moreover, that Othello (in the quarto stage direction) throws himself, as though in a symbolic reassertion of the husband's place, when he first begins to glimpse the depths of Iago's treachery (l. 197). His place is symbolically usurped in Emilia's request to "lay me by my mistress' side" (l. 235), and its loss is cruelly brought home in the despair of "Where should Othello go?" (l. 269). He can reclaim it finally only through a suicide that symmetrically repeats Desdemona's eroticized murder:

I kissed thee, ere I killed thee: no way but this,
Killing myself, to die upon a kiss.
    LL. 354–5

The action of the play has rescued Othello and Desdemona from the cal-culated anonymity of Iago's pornographic fantasies, only for the ending to strip them of their identities once more. For most of the final scene, Othello is once again named only as "the Moor," and it is as if killing Desdemona had annihilated his sense of self to the point where he must repudiate even his own name ("That's he that was 'Othello': here I am," l. 281). Lodovico's valedictory speech reduces the corpses to the condition of a single nameless "object"—"the tragic loading of this bed," "it"—something scarcely removed from the obscene impersonality of the image in which they were first displayed, "the beast with two backs" (ll. 117–18).[36] Like a man rubbing a dog's nose in its own excrement, Lodovico, as the voice of Venetian author-ity, forces Iago (and the audience with him) to look on what his fantasy has made ("This is thy work," 5.2.360). But Iago's gaze is one that confirms the abolition of the lovers' humanity, and it thereby helps to license Lodovico's revulsion: "Let it be hid." In that gesture of concealment, we may discern the official equivalent of Iago's retreat into obdurate silence: "Demand me noth-ing. What you know, you know: / From this time forth I never will speak word" (ll. 300–1). Iago will no more utter his "cause" than Othello can nom-inate his; what they choose not to speak, we might say, Lodovico elects not to see.

✸ ✸ ✸

In so far as Lodovico voices the reaction of the audience, he articulates a scandal that is as much generic as it is social. It was precisely their sense of the play's ostentatious violation of the laws of kind that led Victorian producers to mutilate its ending. From the late eighteenth century it became usual to fin-ish the play on the heroic note of Othello's suicide speech, tactfully remov-ing the Venetians' choric expressions of outrage and dismay, as if recogniz-ing how intolerably Lodovico's "Let it be hid" serves to focus attention on what it insists must not be attended to. By diverting the audience's gaze from this radical impropriety, the cut was meant to restore a semblance of tragic decorum to the catastrophe.[37] Other cuts sought to disguise as far as possible the erotic suggestiveness of the scene: in particular Othello's "To die upon a kiss" was almost invariably removed so as to ensure that at the curtain Desdemona's body would remain in chaste isolation upon a bed "unviolated by Othello's own bleeding corpse."[38] In this way the significance of the bed might be restricted to the proper monumental symbolism so solemnly emphasized in Charles Fechter's midcentury production, where it was made to appear "as portentous as a catafalque prepared for a great funeral pomp."[39]

Of course Shakespeare's ending does play on such iconic suggestions but much more ambiguously. When Othello's imagination transforms the sleeping Desdemona to "monumental alabaster" (5.2.5), his figure draws theatrical power from the resemblance between Elizabethan tester tombs and the beds of state on which they were modeled.[40] But his vain rhetorical effort to clothe the violence of murder in the stony proprieties of ritual is thoroughly subverted by other conventional meanings that reveal the bed as a site of forbidden mixture, a place of literary as well as social and racial adulteration.

If the first act of *Othello*, as Susan Snyder has shown, is structured as a miniature romantic comedy, then the last act returns to comic convention in the form of cruel travesty.[41] For the tragedy ends as it began with a bedding—the first clandestine and offstage, the second appallingly public; one callously interrupted, the other murderously consummated. A bedding, after all, is the desired end of every romantic plot, and Desdemona's "Will you come to bed, my lord" (5.2.24) sounds as a poignant echo of the erotic invitations that close up comedies like *A Midsummer Night's Dream:* "Lovers to bed" (5.1.364). But where comic decorum kept the bed itself offstage, consigning love's consummation to the illimitable end beyond the stage-ending, the bed in *Othello* is shamelessly displayed as the site of a blood-wedding that improperly appropriates the rites of comedy to a tragic conclusion.

The result, from the point of view of seventeenth-century orthodoxy, is a generic monster. Indeed, just such a sense of the monstrosity of the play, its promiscuous yoking of the comic with the tragic, lay at the heart of Rymer's objections to it. Jealousy and cuckoldry, after all, like the misalliance of age and youth, were themes proper to comedy, and the triviality of the handkerchief plot epitomized for Rymer the generic disproportion that must result from transposing them into a tragic design. The words "monster" and "monstrous" punctuate his attempts to catalog the oxymoronic mixtures of this "Bloody Farce," a play he thought would have been better entitled "the *Tragedy of the Handkerchief.*" Iago himself, as the inventor of this "burlesque" plot, was the very spirit of the play's monstrosity: "The *ordinary of*

Newgate never had like monster to pass under his examination." Much of the force of Rymer's invective stems from the way in which he was able to insinuate a direct connection between what he sensed as the generic monstrosity of the tragedy and the social and moral deformity he discovered in its action. The rhetorical energy that charges his use of "monster" and "monstrous" derives from the electric potency in the language of the play itself. It is clear, moreover, that for Rymer ideas of literary and biological kind were inseparable, so that the indecorum of the design was consequential upon the impropriety of choosing a hero whose racially defined inferiority must render him incapable of the lofty world of tragedy. "Never in the world had any pagan poet his brains turned at this monstrous rate," declared Rymer, and he went on to cite Iago's "foul disproportion, thoughts unnatural" as a kind of motto for the play: "The poet here is certainly in the right, and by consequence the foundation of the play must be concluded to be monstrous."[42]

Rymer's appropriation of Iago's language is scarcely coincidental. Indeed it is possible to feel an uncanny resemblance between the scornful excitement with which the critic prosecutes the unsuspected deformities of Shakespeare's design and the villain's bitter pleasure in exposing the "civil monsters" lurking beneath the ordered surface of the Venetian state. It is as if the same odd ventriloquy that bespeaks Iago's colonization of the hero's mind were at work in Rymer. It may be heard again in Coleridge's objection to the play's racial theme: "It would be something *monstrous* to conceive this beautiful Venetian girl falling in love with a veritable negro. It would argue a *disproportionateness*, a want of balance in Desdemona." Even G. K. Hunter, in what remains one of the best essays on race in *Othello*, echoes this revealing language when he insists that "we feel the *disproportion* and the difficulty of Othello's social life and of his marriage (as a social act)." For all Hunter's disconcerting honesty about the play's way of implicating the audience in the prejudice it explores, there is a disturbance here that the nervous parenthesis, "as a social act," seems half to acknowledge. The qualification admits, without satisfactorily neutralizing, his echo of Iago—for whom, after all, concepts of the social (or the "natural") serve exactly as useful devices for tagging sexual/racial transgression.[43]

"Foul disproportion, thoughts unnatural" (3.3.231) is only Iago's way of describing the feelings of strangeness and wonder in which Othello discerns the seeds of Desdemona's passion for him: "She swore, in faith 'twas strange, 'twas passing strange, / 'Twas pitiful, 'twas wondrous pitiful (1.3.159–60). Like *Romeo and Juliet*, the play knows from the beginning that such a sense of miraculous otherness, though it may be intensified by the transgression of social boundaries, is part of the ground of all sexual desire; what Iago enables the play to discover is that this is also the cause of desire's frantic instability. That is why the fountain from which Othello's current runs can become the very source out of which his jealousy flows.[44] Much of the play's power to disturb comes from its remorseless insistence upon the intimacy of jealousy and desire, its demonstration that jealousy is itself an extreme and corrupted (adulterate) form of sexual excitement—an incestuously self-begotten monster of appetite, born only to feed upon itself, a creature of disproportionate desire whose very existence constitutes its own (natural) punishment. The more Othello is made to feel his marriage as a violation of natural boundaries, the more estranged he and Desdemona become; the more estranged they become, the more he desires her. Only murder, it seems, with its violent rapture of possession, can break such a spiral, but it does so at the cost of seeming to demonstrate the truth of all that Iago has implied about the natural consequences of transgressive desire.

Iago's clinching demonstration of Desdemona's strangeness makes her a denizen of Lady Wouldbe's notorious metropolis of prostitution, the city that Otway in *Venice Preserved* was to type "the whore of the Adriatic": "In Venice they do let God see the pranks / They dare not show their husbands."[45] This produces in Othello a terrible kind of arousal, which finds its expression in the pornographic emotional violence of the brothel scene—"I took you for that cunning whore of Venice / That married with Othello" (4.2.88–9)—where it is as if Othello were compelled to make real the fantasy that possessed him in the course of Iago's temptation: "I had been happy if the general camp, / Pioneers and all, had tasted her sweet body" (3.3.342–3). It is an arousal that his imagination can satisfy only in the complex fantasy of a revenge that will be at once an act of mimetic purgation (blood for blood, a blot for a blot), a symbolic reassertion of his sexual rights (the spotted sheets as a parodic sign of nuptial consummation), and an ocular demonstration of Desdemona's guilt (the bloodstain upon the white linen as the visible sign of hidden pollution): "Thy bed, lust-stained, shall with lust's blood be spotted" (5.1.36). In this lurid metonymy for murder, Othello's mind locks onto the bed as the inevitable setting of that fatal end to which his whole being, as in some somnambulist nightmare, is now directed; and it is an ending that, through the long-deferred disclosure of the scene of sexual anxiety, can indeed seem to have been inscribed upon Othello's story from the very beginning.[46]

In order fully to understand the potency of this theatrical image, it is necessary to see how it forms the nexus of a whole set of ideas about adultery upon which Othello's tragedy depends—culturally embedded notions of adulteration and pollution that are closely related to the ideas of disproportion and monstrosity exploited by Iago. The fact that they are linked by a web of association that operates at a largely subliminal level—or perhaps, more accurately, at the level of ideology—makes them especially difficult to disentangle and resistant to rational analysis, and that is an essential aspect of the play's way of entrapping the audience in its own obsessions. It is above all for "disproportion"—a word for the radical kinds of indecorum that the play at once celebrates and abhors—that the bed, not only in Iago's mind but in that of the audience he so mesmerizes, comes to stand.[47]

✸ ✸ ✸

Contemplating the final spectacle of the play, G. M. Matthews produces an unwitting paradox: "All that Iago's poison has achieved is an object that 'poisons sight': a bed on which a black man and a white girl, although they are dead, are embracing. Human dignity, the play says, is indivisible."[48] But if what the bed displays is indeed such an icon of humanist transcendence, then this ending is nearer to those of romantic comedy—or to that of *Romeo and Juliet*—than most people's experience of it would suggest: why should such an assertion of human dignity "poison sight"? Part of the answer lies in the fact that Matthews, in his desire for humane reassurance, has falsified the body count. To be fair, it is quite usual to imagine two bodies stretched out side by side under a canopy—and this is how it is commonly played. But if Emilia's "lay me by my mistress' side" (5.2.235) is (as it surely must be) a dramatized stage direction, there should be three bodies.[49] The tableau of death will then recall a familiar tomb arrangement in which the figure of a man lies accompanied by two women, his first and second wives, and read in this fashion, the bed can look like a mocking reminder of the very suspicions that Iago voiced about Othello and Emilia early in the play—a memorialization of adultery. It would be absurd to suggest that this is how Lodovico or anyone else on the stage consciously sees it, but I think the covert suggestion of something adulterous in this alliance of the corpses, combined with the powerful imagery of erotic death surrounding it, helps to account for the peculiar intensity of Lodovico's sense of scandal. The scandal is exacerbated by the fact that one of the bodies is black.

Jealousy can work as it does in this tragedy partly because of its complex entanglement with the sense that Iago so carefully nurtures in Othello of his own marriage as an adulterous transgression—an improper mixture from which Desdemona's unnatural counterfeiting naturally follows. "It is the dark essence of Iago's whole enterprise," writes Stephen Greenblatt, "to play upon Othello's buried perception of his own sexual relations with Desdemona as adulterous." Despite his teasing glance at the play's moral rhetoric of color ("dark essence"), Greenblatt is really concerned only with notions of specifically sexual transgression according to which "an adulterer is he who is too ardent a lover of his wife." But this perception can be extended to another aspect of the relationship in which the ideas of adultery and disproportionate desire are specifically linked to the question of race.[50]

In the seventeenth century adultery was conceived (as the history of the two words reminds us) to be quite literally a kind of *adulteration*—the pollution or corruption of the divinely ordained bond of marriage and thus in the profoundest sense a violation of the natural order of things. Its unnaturalness was traditionally expressed in the monstrous qualities attributed to its illicit offspring, the anomalous creatures stigmatized as bastards.[51]

A bastard, as the moral deformity of characters like Spurio, Edmund, and Thersites, and the physical freakishness of Volpone's illegitimate offspring equally suggest, is of his very nature a kind of monster—monstrous because he represents the offspring of an unnatural union, one that violates what are proposed as among the most essential of all boundaries.[52]

It is Iago's special triumph to expose Othello's color as the apparent sign of just such monstrous impropriety. He can do this partly by playing on the same fears of racial and religious otherness that had led medieval theologians to define marriage with Jews, Mahometans, or pagans as "interpretative adultery."[53] More generally, any mixture of racial "kinds" seems to have been popularly thought of as in some sense adulterous—a prejudice that survives in the use of such expressions as "bastard race" to denote the "unnatural" offspring of miscegenation.[54] More specifically, Iago is able to capitalize on suggestions that cloud the exotic obscurity of Othello's origins in the world of Plinian monsters, "the Anthropophagi, and men whose heads / Do grow beneath their shoulders" (1.3.143–4); even the green-eyed monster that he conjures from beneath the general's "civil" veneer serves to mark Othello's resemblance to yet another Plinian race, the Horned Men (Gegetones or Cornuti).[55] In the Elizabethan popular imagination, of course, the association of African races with the monsters supposed to inhabit their continent made it easy for blackness to be imagined as a symptom of the monstrous—not least because the color itself could be derived from an adulterous history. According to a widely circulated explanation for the existence of black peoples (available in both Leo Africanus and Hakluyt), blackness was originally visited upon the offspring of Noah's son Cham (Ham) as a punishment for adulterate disobedience of his father.[56]

In such a context the elopement of Othello and Desdemona, in defiance of her father's wishes, might resemble a repetition of the ancestral crime, a confirmation of the adulterous history supposedly written upon the Moor's face.[57] Thus if he sees Desdemona as the fair page defaced by the adulterate slander of whoredom, Othello feels this defacement, at a deeper and more painful level, to be a taint contracted from him: "Her name that was as fresh / As Dian's visage is now begrimed and black / As mine own face" (3.3.383–5). Tragedy, in Chapman's metaphor, is always "black-fac'd," but Othello's dark countenance is like an inscription of his tragic destiny for more reasons than the traditional metaphoric associations of blackness with evil and death. Iago's genius is to articulate the loosely assorted prejudices and superstitions that make it so and to fashion from them the monster of racial animus and revulsion that devours everything of value in the play. Iago's trick is to make this piece of counterfeiting appear like a revelation, drawing into the light of day the hidden truths of his society. It is Iago who teaches Roderigo, Brabantio, and at last Othello himself to recognize in the union of Moor and Venetian an act of generic adulteration—something conceived, in Brabantio's words, "in spite of nature" (1.3.96): "For nature so preposterously to err, / Being not deficient, blind, or lame of sense, / Sans witchcraft could not" (1.3.62–4). Even more graphically, Iago locates their marriage in that zoo of adulterate couplings whose bastard issue (imaginatively at least) are the recurrent "monsters" of the play's imagery: "you'll have your daughter covered with a Barbary horse; you'll have your nephews neigh to you, you'll have coursers for cousins, and jennets for germans" (1.1.111–14). Wickedly affecting to misunderstand Othello's anxiety about how Desdemona might betray her own faithful disposition ("And yet how nature erring from itself"), Iago goes on to plant the same notion in his victim's mind:

> Ay, there's the point; as (to be bold with you)
> Not to affect many proposed matches
> Of her own clime, complexion, and degree,

> Whereto we see in all things *nature* tends—
> Foh, One may smell in such, a will most rank,
> Foul *disproportions, thoughts unnatural.*
>   3.3.228–33; EMPHASIS ADDED

If at one moment Iago can make infidelity appear as the inevitable expression of Desdemona's Venetian nature, as the denizen of an unnatural city of prostituted adulterers, at another he can make it seem as though it were actually Desdemona's marriage that constituted the adulterous lapse, from which a liaison with one of her own kind would amount to the exercise of "her better judgement" (l. 234)—a penitent reversion to her proper nature. The contradictions, as is always the way with an emotion like jealousy, are not self-canceling but mutually reinforcing.

In this way the relentless pressure of Iago's insinuation appears to reveal a particularly heinous assault on the natural order of things. Not only in its obvious challenge to patriarchal authority and in the subversion of gender roles implicit in its assertion of female desire, but also in its flagrant transgression of the alleged boundaries of kind itself, the love of Desdemona and Othello can be presented as a radical assault on the whole system of differences from which the Jacobean world was constructed.[58] The shocking iconic power of the bed in the play has everything to do with its being the site of that assault.[59]

In early modern culture the marriage bed had a peculiar topographic and symbolic significance. It was a space at once more private and more public than it is for us. More private because (with the exception of the study or cabinet) it was virtually the *only* place of privacy available to the denizens of sixteenth- and early seventeenth-century households; more public because as the locus of the most crucial of domestic offices—perpetuation of the lineage—it was the site of important public rituals of birth, wedding, and death.[60] In the great houses of France, this double public-private function was even symbolized by the existence of two beds: an "official bed, majestic but unoccupied," located in the *Chambre de parement,* and a private bed, screened from view in the more intimate domain of the bedchamber proper.[61] Everywhere the same double role was acknowledged in the division of the bridal ritual between the public bringing to bed of bride and groom by a crowd of relatives and friends, and the private rite of consummation that ensued after the formal drawing of the bed curtains.[62] Part of the scandal of *Othello* arises from its structural reversal of this solemn division: the offstage elopement in act 1 turning the public section of the bridal into a furtive and private thing; the parted curtains of act 5 exposing the private scene of the bed to a shockingly public gaze. The scene exposed, moreover, is one that confirms with exaggerated horror the always ambiguous nature of that "peninsular of privacy": "The bed heightened private pleasure. . . . But the bed could also be a symbol of guilt, a shadowy place [or a place of sub-terfuge], a scene of crime; the truth of what went on here could never be revealed."[63]

The principal cause of these anxieties, and hence of the fiercely defended privacy of the marriage bed, lay in the fact that it was a place of licensed sex-ual and social metamorphosis, where the boundaries of self and other, of family allegiance and of gender were miraculously abolished as man and wife became "one flesh."[64] Because it was a space that permitted a highly special-ized naturalization of what would otherwise constitute a wholly "unnatural" collapsing of differences, it must itself be protected by taboos of the most intense character. In the cruel system of paradoxy created by this play's ideas of race and adultery, Othello as both stranger and husband can be *both* the violator of these taboos and the seeming victim of their violation—adulterer and cuckold—as he is both black and "fair," Christian general and erring bar-barian, insider and outsider, the author of a "*monstrous* act" and Desdemona's "*kind* lord."[65] As the most intimate site of these contradictions, it was inevitable that the bed should become the imaginative center of the play— the focus of Iago's corrupt fantasy, of Othello's tormented speculation, and always of the audience's intensely voyeuristic compulsions.

At the beginning of the play, the monstrousness of Desdemona's passion is marked for Brabantio by its being fixed upon an object "naturally" unbear-able to sight: "To fall in love with what she feared to look on! / . . . Against all rules of nature" (1.3.98–101). At the end she has become, for Lodovico, part of the "object [that] poisons sight." The bed is the visible sign of *what has been improperly revealed* and must now be hidden from view again—the unnamed horror that Othello fatally glimpsed in the dark cave of Iago's imagination: "some monster in his thought / Too hideous to be shown" (3.3.106–7); it is the token of everything that must not be seen and cannot be spoken ("Let me not name it to you, you chaste stars," 5.2.2), everything that the second nature of culture seeks to efface or disguise as "unnatural"—all that should be banished to outer (or consigned to inner) darkness; a figure for unlicensed desire itself. That banishment of what must not be contemplated is what is embodied in Lodovico's gesture of stern erasure. But as Othello's quibble upon the Latin root of the word suggests, *a monster* is also what, by virtue of its very hideousness, demands to be *shown*. What makes the tragedy of *Othello* so shocking and painful is that it engages its audience in a conspiracy to lay naked the scene of forbidden desire, only to confirm that the penalty for such exposure is death and oblivion; in so doing, the play takes us into territory we recognize but would rather not see. It doesn't "oppose racism," but (much more disturbingly) illuminates the process by which such visceral superstitions were implanted in the very body of the culture that formed us. The object that "poisons sight" is nothing less than a mirror for the obscene desires and fears that *Othello* arouses in its audiences—monsters that the play at once invents and naturalizes, declaring them unproper, even as it implies that they were always "naturally" there.[66]

If the ending of this tragedy is unendurable, it is because it first tempts us with the redemptive vision of Desdemona's sacrificial self-abnegation and then insists, with all the power of its swelling rhetorical music, upon the hero's magnificence as he dismantles himself for death—only to capitulate to Iago's poisoned vision at the very moment when it has seemed poised to reaffirm the transcendent claims of their union: the claims of kind and kindness figured in the love between a black man and a white woman and the bed on which it was made.

"Mulattos," "Blacks," and "Indian Moors": Othello *and Early Modern Constructions of Human Difference*

—— ❖ ——

"I think this play is racist, and I think it is not."[1] Virginia Vaughan's perplexed response to *Othello* is symptomatic of the problems faced by late twentieth-century critics in approaching the "racial" dimension of Shakespeare's play. For if the work of recent scholars has taught us anything about early modern constructions of human difference, it is that any attempt to read back into the early modern period an idea of "race" based on post-Enlightenment taxonomy is doomed to failure.[2] To talk about "race" in *Othello* is to fall into anachronism; yet not to talk about it is to ignore something fundamental about a play that has rightly come to be identified as a foundational text in the emergence of modern European "racial" consciousness—a play that trades in constructions of human difference at once misleadingly *like* and confusingly *unlike* those twentieth-century notions to which they are nevertheless recognizably ancestral. In the latter part of this chapter I try to cast some light on Shakespeare's treatment of what came to be called "race" by exploring an experience of alterity in the East Indian archipelago, a theater of colonial encounter that may seem at first sight far away from the Mediterranean world of *Othello*. However, it may help to frame that discussion by briefly considering some of the ways in which this tragedy perplexes the notions of ethnic and national identity that its subtitle so carelessly invokes.

In an essay that provides a useful corrective to anachronistically "post-colonial" understandings of "race" in *Othello*, Emily Bartels has stressed the ideological "openness" of the play's treatment of human difference, arguing that (except in the eyes of Iago and those he manipulates) "Othello *is*, as the subtitle announces 'the Moor of Venice.' . . . Neither an alienated nor an assimilated subject, but a figure defined by two worlds, a figure (like Marlowe's Jew of Malta) whose ethnicity occupies one slot, professional interests another, compatibly"—the fortunate possessor, then, of "a dual rather than divided identity."[3] But the invocation of Barabas as a parallel type of comfortably hyphenated hybridity seems something of a giveaway here. One has only to think of the extreme anxieties surrounding the question of what it meant to belong to, say, the "Old English" of Ireland to recall how easily "dual identity" could be interpreted as sinister doubleness or self-contradiction. From the point of view of "New English" settlers like Spenser the adoption of Irish customs and speech by the Old English descendants of Norman conquerors could signal only a treacherous repudiation of their birthright.[4] The unease of hybridity (whether elective or enforced), in a world where the hybrid was always liable to be construed as "prodigious" or "monstrous," is apparent in the ambivalent ethnographic discourse of one of Shakespeare's principal sources for *Othello*—*A Geographical Historie of Africa*, written by the Granada-born Moor, John Leo Africanus.

In a somewhat poignant moment, this native informant and Christian *converso*, for whom African peoples are both "them" and "us," describes himself as an "amphibian," thereby acknowledging his contradictory position as a denizen of both Muslim and Christian worlds, both African and European, humanist scholar and "barbarian"—a position that can seem inscribed in an adopted Latin name equally suggestive of dedicated papal allegiance and an unreconstructed bestial ferocity.[5] In much the same way, Othello's Africa is at once the place that authenticates his birth "from men of royal siege" and a wilderness of Plinian monstrosities, of "Anthropophagi and men whose heads / Do grow beneath their shoulders" (1.3.145). One way of describing the action of his tragedy is in terms of the process by which Iago progressively prizes open the contradictions in the oxymoronic subtitle that marks the uneasy translation of "erring barbarian" into "civil monster" (1.3.356 and 4.1.64)—the process (to put it another way) by which he successfully essentializes or "racializes" Othello's difference.

When Roderigo, under Iago's tutelage, dismisses Othello as "an extravagant and wheeling stranger / Of here and everywhere" (1.1.134–5), he issues a fundamental challenge to the syntax of identity inscribed in the play's subtitle, *The Moor of Venice*.[6] To be a Moor, he insists, is to be a fundamentally dislocated creature, a wandering denizen of that un-place known as wilderness, heath, or *moor*—"an erring barbarian" in the punning phrase with which Iago assimilates Barbary to the notoriously vagrant condition of barbarism (1.3.356). From Roderigo's perspective, then, to be a "Moor of Venice" is to represent a principle of wild disorder lodged in the very heart of metropolitan civilization—to be, in another of Iago's violent oxymorons, a kind of "civil monster" (4.1.64), and the innocent-seeming preposition that yokes Moorish origin to Venetian identity is a site of violent contradiction.[7] Yet the "of" in "Moor of Venice" is easily passed over as a mere instrument of descriptive amplification, as unproblematic in its implications as the similarly deployed locatives in, say, *Timon of Athens, The Two Gentleman of Verona*—or, indeed, *The Merchant of Venice*, a play that is in some respects *Othello*'s counterpart in Shakespeare's comic canon. To remember *The Merchant of Venice* in this context, however, is to recall the tellingly ambiguous description of the play in the Stationers' Register, "a booke of the Marchaunte of Venyce, or otherwise called the Jew of Venyce," and hence to be confronted with the troubling implications of Portia's question, "Which is the Merchant here? and which the Jew?" (4.1.174)—a question that directs us toward a reading of that play in which issues of place and identity, of the "native" and the "stranger" become so vexed as to seriously destabilize the innocent-seeming "of" that ties both Shylock and Antonio to their native city.

The effect is to send us further back to Marlowe's satiric deconstruction of geographic identity in *The Jew of Malta*. As the alienated representative of "a scattered nation," Barabas is not so much *of* Malta as *in* it—just as his vaunted colleagues in international Jewry are located "in" Bairseth, Portugal, Italy, and France.[8] Scorning allegiance not only to "those of Malta" but even to his own professed "countrymen," the fellow-Jews who share his persecution (1.1.121, 143, 159), Barabas takes sardonic pleasure in representing himself as an archetypal cosmopolitan, whose politic schooling in Machiavelli's Florence has helped him to manipulate "the wars 'twixt France and Germany" as it now enables him to exploit the conflict between Turk and Christian (1.1.1–48, 2.3.23, 186). Yet the pseudocathartic action of his "tragedy" with its ludicrously repeated efforts to purge him from the costive body-politic suggest a more organic relationship between this outsider and "those of Malta" than either Barabas or his Christian persecutors would acknowledge.

Of course the particular fear that attaches to the demon-Jew in early modern European culture has to do with his insidious role as the hidden stranger, the alien whose otherness is the more threatening for its guise of semblance. This was a culture whose own expansionism, ironically enough, generated fears of a hungrily absorptive otherness that were expressed in complementary fantasies of dangerous miscegenation, "degeneration," and cannibalistic desire; in its fictions the Jew represents the deepest threat of all—that of a *secret* difference, masquerading as likeness, whose presence threatens the surreptitious erosion of identity from within. One reason why Shylock remains such a deeply troubling figure at the end of *The Merchant* is the unspoken possibility that his forcible conversion (like that of Jews in six-teenth-century Spain) will only institutionalize the very uncertainty it is designed to efface. Jessica's marriage to Lorenzo—albeit that marriage in some sense confers the husband's identity on the wife—contains the same latent threat; hence perhaps the uneasy silence that surrounds her in the con-cluding moments of the play.[9]

The great advantage of Moors over Jews—or so it might seem to early modern Europeans—was that they could not so easily disguise their differ-ence. Blackness (as Aaron boasts in *Titus Andronicus*) "scorns to wear another hue" (4.2.99), and the ultimately reassuring thing about George Best's famous story of the English mother who gave birth to a black baby is that the taint of alterity seems compelled by nature to discover itself—"the black Moor," as scripture and proverb insisted, "[cannot] change his skin [any more than] the leopard his spots" (Jer. 13.23), for it was impossible "to wash the Ethiop white."[10]

Yet, of course, Aaron's boast is undercut by his own scheme to substitute the impeccably white offspring of his "countryman" Muliteus for Tamora's black infant. And—as the parallel campaigns of persecution against con-verted Jews *(marranos)* and converted Moors *(moriscos)* were calculated to demonstrate—it turns out that Moorishness was almost as capable as Jewishness of concealing its aggressive Otherness within the body of the Same.[11] This was the case partly because of the notorious indeterminacy of the term "Moor" itself. Insofar as it was a term of "racial" description, it could refer quite specifically to the Berber-Arab people of the parts of North Africa then rather vaguely denominated as "Morocco," "Mauritania," or

"Barbary," or it could be used to embrace the inhabitants of the whole North African littoral, or it might be extended to refer to Africans generally (whether "white," "black," or "tawny" Moors), or by an even more promiscuous extension, it might be applied (like "Indian") to almost any darker-skinned peoples—even on occasion, those of the New World.[12] Consequently when Marlowe's Valdes refers to the supine obedience of "Indian *Moors*" to "their Spanish lords," it is usually assumed that the two terms are simply mutually intensifying synonyms and that the magician means something like "dusky New World natives."[13] But "Moor" could often be deployed (in a fashion perhaps inflected, even for the English, by memories of the Spanish *reconquista*) as a religious category—thus Muslims on the Indian subcontinent were habitually called "Moors," and the same term is used in East India Company literature to describe the Muslim inhabitants of Southeast Asia, whether they be Arab or Indian traders or indigenous Malays. So Valdes's "Indian Moors" could equally well be Muslims from the Spanish-controlled Portuguese East Indies. In such contexts it is simply impossible to be sure whether "Moor" is a description of color or of religion or some vague amalgam of the two, and in the intoxicated exoticism of Marlovian geography such discriminations hardly matter.

But in less fantastical contexts they could matter a great deal—as for example when renegade Europeans in the East Indies were said to "turn Moor"—just as in the Mediterranean they were more usually said to "turn Turk."[14] In travel literature these two expressions are sometimes interchangeable, "Turk" being used even in descriptions of the East Indies as a loosely generic description of the people otherwise called "Islams" or "Mahomettans." The Dutch voyager William Cornelison Schouten, for example, describes an encounter with the men of Tidore "some [of whom] had wreathes about their heads which they say were Turks or Moors in religion."[15] Turkishness or Moorishness here is a matter of religious allegiance, rendered visible (like the malignancy of Othello's "turbanned Turk") in details of costume. Thus when Othello, the Moor turned Christian, accuses his brawling Venetian followers of "turning Turk," his hyperbole has a disturbing irony that (as critics now routinely observe) resonates with a suicide that takes the form of a reenacted slaughter of the Turk in act 5. Moreover, because the religious and "racial" parameters of "Moorishness" were seldom entirely distinct, the exact implications of the metamorphoses whereby Christians "turned Moor" and Moors "turned Christian" were disturbingly blurred.

If a Christian turned Moor, did he in some sense "blacken" himself? If a Moor "turned Christian" did he thereby cease in some important sense to be a Moor? If he did not, would residual Moorishness turn out to be a matter of blood, color, or faith?[16] It is true that the purely religious connotations of "Christian" produce a significant asymmetry between "turning Christian" and "turning Turk (or Moor)," making it seem as though the "racial" component of identity can perhaps be transformed only in one direction. Yet these questions were difficult to answer with any assurance, so long as the language of difference remained as shifting and uncertain as it was before the emergence of the modern discourses of "race" and "color"; and the history of the simultaneous (and largely inseparable) campaigns for purity of blood (*limpieza de sangre*) and purity of religion in Spain are only extreme symptoms of a larger European difficulty that threatened to turn a phrase like "Moor of Venice" into a hopeless oxymoron.[17] That, indeed, is what Richard Broome clearly felt it to be when he dubbed his comedy of senile jealousy *The English Moore* (1637). Broome's plot turns upon the performance of a masque of Blackamoors (a self-conscious travesty of his old master Ben Jonson's *Masque of Blackness*) in the course of which it is prophesied that the Princess of Ethiopia will be blanched by marriage to an Englishman. But in the play proper, metamorphosis never amounts to anything more than the shedding of the heroine's blackface disguise, and just as (in the words of the inset masque) " 'tis no better then a prodigy / To have white children in a black country" (4.4.22–3), so it appears that there can be no such thing in nature as an "English Moor."

Of course the English (like other Europeans) brought some important cultural baggage to their encounters with foreign peoples: ideas about genealogy, about the biblical separation of humankind, and about the moral symbolism of color, all of which pushed them toward an essentialist reading of phenotypic difference. Yet as Karen Ordahl Kupperman has argued, because they were predisposed to think "in terms of socially or culturally created categories," treating most "differences between people [as] 'accidental' [consequences of] environment or experience," they had not yet learned to "divide humankind into broad fixed classifications demarcated by visible distinctions." As with the disdainful attitudes of the English toward the Irish—a people whose physical similarities to the English were conveniently obscured by their cultural differences—categories like "civil" and "barbarous," "naked" and "clothed" were often of far more significance in establishing the boundaries of otherness than the markers of mere biological diversity. In the later sixteenth century, however, the rapid expansion of national horizons through exploration and trade increasingly presented the English with foreign cultures whose sophisticated ways of life resisted assimilation into the ancient cultural categories by which the threat of alterity had traditionally been contained.[18]

In the early part of the period these foreign peoples were often approached with a certain ethnographic objectivity. Much of the travel literature collected by Hakluyt is quite assiduous in cataloging the various "distinction[s] of color, Nation, language . . . condition" that divide the peoples of the earth, and variations of dress, weapons, manners, custom, social organization, and (above all) religion figure at least as prominently as differences of skin and feature. But as we move into the seventeenth century, the pressure of encounter with so many unfamiliar peoples begins to shift definitions of alterity away from the dominant paradigm of culture, and (in another telling asymmetry) it is possible to see color emerging as the most important criterion for defining otherness, even as "nation" becomes the key term of *self*-definition.[19] The gradations of color appear to cause significant difficulties to the Dutch traveler Van Linschoten, for example, in his influential *Voyages* (translated and published with Hakluyt's endorsement in 1598), as he struggles (in sometimes contradictory language) to define the nature of the differences between the various Asian peoples he encountered. The people of Ormus are "white like the Persians," those of Bengal "somewhat whiter then the Chingalas," "The people of Aracan, Pegu, and Sian are much like those of Chin, only one difference they have, which is, that they are somewhat whiter than the Bengalon, and somewhat browner then the men of China." In China itself, "Those that dwell on the sea side . . . are a people of a *brownish* color, like the *white* Moors in Africa and Barbaria, and part of the Spaniards, but those that dwell within the land, *are for color like Netherlanders and high Dutches*," yet "there are many among them that are *clean black*"; while "in the land lying westward from China, they say there are white people, and the land called Cathaia, where (as it is thought) are many Christians."[20]

The East Indian archipelago posed particular problems of definition during the period since the islands were themselves undergoing a rapid cultural transformation, as a militant, expansionist Islam progressively displaced well-established Hindu, animist, and surviving Buddhist practices. The proliferation of religious, cultural, and ethnic differences must have been baffling to the English newcomers, subjecting their available definitions to peculiar strains. The various indigenous peoples and the rival groups of traders who clustered in their towns could of course be classified according to the geographical or political entities to which they belonged as "Javans, Chinese, Men of Pegu, Bandaneses," and so forth, or they might be categorized according to religion as "ethnics," "pagans," or "Moors," or they might be grouped, together with the inhabitants of the Indian subcontinent, as "Indians" or "East Indians" (in a regional designation that the uncertainties of post-Columbian geography had permanently confused with differences of complexion). What precisely this meant in terms of color was a little confused. George Best's *True Discourse of the Late Voyages of Discoverie* (1578), for example, described East Indians, along with American "Indians," as being "not black, but white," though this was altered in Hakluyt's version of the *True Discourse* to "tawny and white"—a distinction that other observers typically aligned with gender, remarking that (in the words of Thomas Candish) "although the men be of tawny color . . . yet their women be of fair complexion"—something they attributed to the effects of clothing and exposure to the sun.[21] In the familiar (and deeply ambiguous) trope routinely employed in both West and East Indian contexts, the hue of the natives is figured as "the sun's livery."[22] So we are told of Princess Quisara in Fletcher's *Island Princess* (1621) that:

> The very sun, I think, affects her sweetness,
> And dares not as he does to all else, dye it
> Into his tawny livery.
>   1.1.60–2[23]

The princess's whiteness is the sign of an inward "sweetness" that will be expressed in the conversion to Christianity that accompanies her betrothal to the Portuguese hero Armusia at the end of the play. The issue of color cannot be entirely erased, however, and the cynical Pyniero is allowed to suggest that there is something unnatural about the princess's "wear[ing] her complexion in a case," because if exposed to the sun's kisses it would so readily convert to a dusky hue: "let him but like it / A week or two, or three, she would look like a lion" (ll. 63–4). East Indian tawniness (whether actual or, like Quisara's, merely potential) may constitute an accident of culture and geography, but it is also a kind of servile "livery"—the badge of allegiance to the false religion to which the princess and her countrymen are in thrall.[24] And it resonates dangerously with those contemporary discourses that interpreted dark skin (in both African and West Indian contexts) as a sign of natural servitude.[25]

One way of dealing with the taxonomic complications exemplified in Linschoten and reflected in *The Island Princess* was to develop a notion of difference that would effectually obscure the confusing variations of hue that Linschoten acknowledges in both European and non-European populations by establishing a more absolute division between "them" and "us." And during the first three decades of the seventeenth century uncertainties about the nature of human difference are gradually flattened out in the literature of East Indian voyaging as the peoples of the region begin to be categorized, according to the crudest distinction of color, as "black"—a designation that serves solely to distinguish them from "white" Europeans.[26]

This idea of Europeanness as a form of group identity delimited by color seems itself to have been something new. In a probing analysis of racial discourse in early modern England, Lynda Boose has posed the question of whether English notions of Moorishness, for example, were shaped by anything resembling "the modern sense of some definitively *racial* shared 'Europeanness.' Or was the difference between a 'Moor' and someone we would call a 'European' conceptually organized around the religio-political geography of Christian vs. Muslim more than around a geography of skin color?" In this regard, it might seem significant that the *OED*'s earliest cited use of "European" to distinguish the inhabitants of Europe from "Indians" is in Massinger's *City Madam* (1632)—"You are learn'd Europeans, and we worse / Than ignorant Americans" (3.3.127–8); in this case the grounds of distinction are clearly cultural and religious rather than racial. Moreover the dictionary offers no example of the word as a generic term for "white people" before 1696. But in fact Samuel Purchas had used "European" to define a community of color as early as 1613, when, in describing the divided condition of postlapsarian humankind, he contrasted "the tawny Moor, black Negro, dusky Libyan, ash-coloured Indian, olive-coloured American . . . with the whiter European." In Purchas's taxonomy Europeans are united by a common whiteness, while other peoples are divided by differing degrees of color, even as those colors taken together associate them in a common non-Europeanness.[27]

It is important to recognize, I think, that this way of discriminating otherness—whatever its ultimate *effects* may have been—was not in itself motivated by an aggressive colonialism. To the contrary, as the section of *Hakluytus Posthumus or Purchas his Pilgrimes* (1625) devoted to East Indian voyaging suggests, it seems to have arisen from the profound sense of insecurity experienced by the increasingly embattled English trading community in the region—an insecurity felt as a disorientating challenge to their own identity. Included among Purchas's documents is Edmund Scott's *Exact Discourse of the Subtilties, Fashions, Religion and Ceremonies of the East Indians*—a narrative that offers a particularly revealing glimpse of the processes by which an acute anxiety about the sustainability of their enterprise and community helped to shape an ideology of color. In the *Exact Discourse*, a work almost exactly contemporary with *Othello*, the negotiation and demonstration of various kinds of difference—in rank, nation, and color—becomes crucial to the preservation of the identity of the vulnerable enclave that Scott calls "the English nation at Bantan." The *Exact Discourse* survives in two significantly different texts—the original pamphlet of 1606, and the abbreviated and annotated version (apparently based on a separate manuscript) published in *Hakluytus Posthumus*.[28]

At the heart of Scott's narrative, as I argue elsewhere, is an acute anxiety about the threat to English identity experienced by the mercantile representatives of "the English nation" in the newly established trading factory of the East India Company at Bantam in Java.[29] This threat was triggered initially by the perplexing discovery (referred to elsewhere in Purchas's documents) that their Dutch rivals had been passing themselves off as English: "The common people knew us not from the Hollanders, for both they and we were called by the name of Englishmen, by reason of their usurping our name at their first coming to trade."[30] The potential for violence in such a confusion of identities is registered in the quibbling chapter title that Purchas added to Scott's narrative: "*Differences* [i.e., quarrels] betwixt the Hollanders (styling themselves English), the Javans, and other things remarkable." The problem was an especially vexing one because the English self-image was partially dependent on their sense of affinity with the Dutch, of whom Scott writes that "though we were mortal enemies in our trade, in all other matters we were friends, and would have lived and died one for the other" (H3). But the merchants were able to overcome this difficulty through a display of self-fashioning pageantry, when they resolved to stage their "difference" from the Dutch through an improvised Accession Day triumph. Marching in elaborately sinuous patterns up and down their compound, clad in their best finery, with scarves and hatbands of red-and-white taffeta, the tiny company ("being but fourteen in number") waved their banners of Saint George, beat their drums and discharged volumes of shot into the air. This swaggering (if undermanned) performance of Englishness so impressed the natives, according to Scott, that he and his companions felt empowered to deliver a brief disquisition on the linguistic and political distinctions between Dutch and English, thereby ensuring that this unhappy confusion would never be repeated.[31]

But even as Scott's band succeeded in shoring up their sense of national distinctiveness on one front, they found it threatened with dissolution on another; for this crisis of identity with the Dutch was quickly followed by a second in which the terms of difference were much less easy to define and whose menace the English could only disarm by appealing to a rhetoric of color. This "tragedy" (as Scott calls it) concerned "a *Mulatto* of *Pegu*" (i.e., a part-European from Burma) who, as a result of his ambiguous role as a servant in the English trading-factory, was taken for an Englishman. The story begins with what we might now read as an explosion of racial resentment on the part of its protagonist. Having been drinking with a second mulatto, "one of his countrymen" who belonged to a visiting Flemish vessel, the "English" mulatto became enraged when the Flemish provost attacked his fellow-Peguan and beat him back onto the Flemish ship. "Seeing his countryman misused, and being somewhat tickled in the head with wine," the mulatto planned to "revenge his countryman's quarrel" (D1v-D2). A small orgy of killing ensued. The mulatto sought out and stabbed both the Fleming and the other mulatto (whom he allegedly feared as a potentially hostile witness); he then tried unsuccessfully to kill a Filipino slave who accompanied his victims. And finally, "being nuzzled in blood," as Scott puts it, and "meeting with a poor *Javan* . . . [he] stabbed him likewise" (D2). Unfortunately for the killer, however, the Fleming lived long enough to give some clues as to the identity of his assailant, and the mulatto, incriminated by inconsistencies in his own story as well as by the testimony of the slave, was at last brought to confess to all three murders.[32]

Scott, who was now the senior East India Company man in Bantam, found himself torn between a righteous desire to appease "the blood of those Christians that were murdered" (D3v) and a proprietorial insistence on his exclusive claim to administer justice to members of his own community. He resisted both what he saw as extravagant Javan demands for compensation and an arrogant Dutch insistence that he hand over the killer for a lingering death—they "saying he should have the bones of his legs and arms broken, and so he should lie and die, or else have his feet and hands cut off, and so lie and starve to death" (D4r). Treating the issue as one of both personal pride

("I answered that it lay not in them to put him to death, if I list to save him,"
D3v) and national prestige ("for an Englishman scorns to give place to
Hollanders in any foreign country," D3r), he roundly declared that the murderer "should die the ordinary death of the country, and no other" (D4r).
Hiring a local executioner, he made him promise to dispatch the mulatto as
swiftly and humanely as possible, even lending the "hangman" his own well-
sharpened kris, "which was very serviceable for such a purpose" (D4v). The
choice of this quintessentially Malay (though English-owned) weapon to be
the proxy instrument of judicial Englishness seems fraught with ironies at
least as complicated as those that attend Othello's flourishing of Spanish steel
to reassert his hybrid identity as "Moor of Venice" (5.2.251). But the choice
had a certain appropriateness to a situation in which the contradictions of
mixed identity became a source of significant unease—an unease strikingly
illustrated, I think, in Purchas's brutal abridgement of this section of Scott's
narrative. In Purchas all but the bare details of the killing and of the murderer's execution have been excised—reducing Scott's complex "tragedy," to
a simple monitory account of physical *Dangers by a Mulatto*."[33] There are
numerous other cuts in Purchas's version of the pamphlet, but this is the only
one for which he feels constrained to apologize, in a marginal note that disin-
genuously pleads the danger of prolixity.

No doubt Purchas's anxiety, like Scott's own, had everything to do with
the ambiguous status given to the killer by the contradictory identity that the
text ascribes to him—that of a man "*of* Pegu" who is at the same time "*our*
mulatto.*" Scott's possessive pronoun mediates as uneasily between ownership, community, and kinship as the deeply equivocal "mine" that announces
Prospero's final acknowledgment of Caliban. It is the same unstable pronoun
that both defines and masks the relationship of Shakespeare's mercenary
"stranger" to the Venetian state when "the Moor" is transformed into "*our*
noble and valiant general" (2.1.1–2). In Scott, the dangerous ambiguity of
the connection that his "our" at once declares and mystifies becomes apparent at the point where the dying provost is said to have claimed that "an
Englishman had slain him" (D2r). A deputation of Dutch went at once to the
English house to inform Scott that "one of *our men* had slain one of *theirs* . .
. [and] they thought it was *our Mulatto*" (D2r; emphasis added). The Dutch
rhetoric here is pointed. They contrive to taint the English by association
with the mulatto killer who is denounced as "one of *our* men," while holding
themselves aloof from their own murdered mulatto who is carefully excluded
from the opposite category, "one of *theirs.*" Subsequent events intensify this

unhappy confusion but also provide Scott with an opportunity to purge it and to realign his own people with their fellow Europeans, the offended Hollanders.

When the mulatto denies the Dutch accusation, he is dispatched, along with Scott's deputy, Gabriel Towerson, to question the mortally wounded Fleming: "When they came, they asked him who had hurt him, he said an English man. Master *Towerson* asked him whether it was a white man, or a black[—]because he named still an English man, we were in some doubt: the Fleming being also in drink said, a white man, then presently he said again, it was dark, he knew not well, and so gave up his life" (D2v). Resonating with the symbolism of Othello's "Put out the light" soliloquy, darkness temporarily effaces the markers of difference here. But what is really extraordinary about the passage is the almost casual way in which the English seem to accede to the mulatto's inclusion in the category "English man"—almost as if there could be a such a creature as a "Mulatto of England." This temporary recognition of kinship was perhaps partly enabled by the murderer's status as "Christian"—"though he was a *Pegu* born, yet he was a Christian, and brought up among the *Portingals*"—so that Scott was at charitable pains to have the murderer brought to repentance before his death. The chosen agent of religious instruction, fittingly enough, was another hybrid figure—a renegade Muslim, "an *Arabian* born [who] belonged to the *Dutch* ships, and spake the *Spanish* tongue marvelous well"; this go-between convinced the murderer of the power of God's son "to redeem us, and to wash away our sins were they never so bloody" (D4r). The inclusive "us" here brings Scott momentarily close to the pieties of Purchas's climactic vision in the *Pilgrimage*, which prophesies a redemptive reunification of the divided branches of humanity, "*their long robes made white in the blood of the Lamb* . . . without any more distinction of color, nation, language, sex, condition" (p. 546). But the efficacy of this emulsifying mystery belongs only to the extratemporal moment of penitence. It cannot affect the day-to-day management of difference in a situation where any loss of distinction threatens the elimination of "the English nation at Bantam." The narrative now goes on to detach the condemned man from the English camp and to link him, through the indelible mark of color, with the proper denizens of Bantam, East Indian and Chinese, whose vicious and guileful "subtilties" he finds so threatening to English interests.

By a convenient rhetorical sleight, the mulatto is first kinned with his own executioner. Scott records with some satisfaction the hangman's promise to serve this prisoner better than he had earlier served a counterfeiter whose punishment he grievously botched: "when he killed the coiner," the man protests, "he did not execute his own father" (D4V). Scott explains this as a reference to the custom whereby "when a Javan of any account is put to death . . . their nearest of kin doth execute [the common executioner's] office, and it is held the greatest favour they can do them" (D4v). The executioner, we can surmise, intends a compliment to Scott by identifying the humblest of the "Englishmen" as his own senior kinsman. But Scott's failure to spell out the meaning of the hyperbole has the effect of stressing the tie between the headsman and his victim, rhetorically severing the mulatto from the English camp and consigning him to the community of Others. But then, as the condemned man is led into the fields outside the town of Bantam to meet his death, a large crowd of townspeople, "both *Javans* and *Chinese*," comes "flocking amain," excited by the rumor "that there was an Englishman to be executed." They are disconcerted by the sight of the victim, however. "Many were blank, and we might hear them tell one another it was a black man." Scott and his men immediately seize the opportunity to deliver a second lesson on difference, which completes the alienation of "our mulatto": "we told them, he was just of their own color and condition and that an Englishman or white man would not do such a bloody deed" (D4v). At this moment a common "blackness" is announced as the defining condition of all who are not English or "white," regardless of whether they are part-European, Chinese, Javan, or men of Pegu (groups whose various gradations of color are elsewhere quite carefully cataloged). By the same token, the mulatto's crime becomes a proof of his "racial" difference, just as his "color" is the badge of his reprobate condition.

Something very similar, it seems to me, happens in *Othello*, through the systematic blackening of the Moor and the symbolic detachment from Venice that it involves. To begin with, Othello's "blackness" seems to be an almost casual effect of Iago's improvisatory malice and of Roderigo's and Brabantio's gullibility. It is at best an accident whose superficial significance could even be underpinned (in ways to which Dympna Callaghan has alerted us) by the audience's pleasurable consciousness that it is only a cosmetic illusion.[34] Shakespeare, after all, expected the actor playing "Othello" to be a white man, and so his appearance of blackness is something easily annulled by the duke's invocation of that essential whiteness that unites all Christians under the skin ("your son-in-law is far more fair than black"). Yet, by the end of the play, the Venetian world—and the audience too, if they are not careful—will have come to see it as the sign not only of his reprobate condition

but of the irreducible alterity that the language of racial abuse insists is inseparable from it: "blacker devil," "filthy bargain," "gull . . . as ignorant as dirt,"
"dull Moor" (5.2.129, 153, 160, 223).[35] In the reading of the Moor's body so
successfully propagated by Iago, none of Othello's efforts to reinstitute the
sustaining paradoxes of his mixed condition as an "honorable murderer,"
whose suicide triumphantly enacts and cancels out the contradictions that
have been exposed in the designation "Moor of Venice," is sufficient to overcome the suggestion that such a creature can only constitute a kind of "civil
monster."

Othello's reenacted killing of the "circumcisèd dog" is also a reenactment of his original apostasy by one whose contradictory position forces him
to "turn, and turn . . . and turn again" (4.1.255–6), but such desperate iteration is as hopeless as it is compulsive; for as the outcast condition of Scott's
mulatto implies, while a Moor may turn Christian he can never "turn
Venetian." Like the mulatto's thinly motivated stabbing of "his own countryman," Othello's overdetermined killing of the "turbanned Turk" is on one
level a demonstration of his own essential unkindness; on another, like the
executioner's hyperbolic killing of "his own father," it enacts a violent reab-
sorption into the domain of the Other—confirming the rhetorical estrangement by which the Venetians return "he that was Othello" to the condition of
anonymous "Moorishness" in which he was first brought into the play. It is
in this sense that we can speak of the play's progressive "racialization" of the
protagonist.

Yet Emily Bartels's insistence on *Othello*'s openness is not entirely mis-
placed, and Virginia Vaughan's perplexity ("I think this play is racist, and I
think it is not") remains understandable. Even Edmund Scott, after all, is only
partially successful in his attempt to purge the "English nation at Bantam" of
the confusions created by the hybridizing presence of "our Mulatto." As the
murderer's body lies "gasping on the ground" Scott cannot forbear offering
it to the Dutch as a reproof to their own vices—"I openly told the Hollanders
that that was the fruit of drunkenness, and bid them ever after beware of
it"—thus carelessly blurring the boundary between colors and conditions
that his lesson to the townspeople had established. And as he pauses to reflect
on the fatal sickness of yet another of his fellow-merchants, the chief factor's
anxiety at the fragile state of the English trading community seems to read-
mit the ghostly presence of his scapegoat to membership of a "we" that is
once again exposed as dangerously unstable: "*we* had lost in all, since the
departure of our ships eight men *besides the Mulatto that was executed*, and we

were now ten living and one boy" (E1r; emphasis added). The Mulatto of Pegu is once again one of "our men," a Mulatto of England. In *Othello* it is precisely the desperate haste with which the Venetians seek to efface the admonitory spectacle of slaughter ("This object poisons sight: / Let it be hid," 5.2.362) that calls into question the sustainability of the racial scapegoating that Iago has brought about, forcing us to pay attention to a very different narrative—the one that ends not in the self-alienating and murderous expulsion of a Moor turned Turk again, but in a kiss that self-consciously proclaims an act of union. The play, however—and this is why it continues to torment us—refuses to align itself with either narrative, retreating instead into the obliquity of the taunting pleonasm with which Iago at once challenges and disables judgment: "What you know, you know. / From this time forth I never will speak word" (5.2.300–1).

Putting History to the Question: An Episode of Torture at Bantam in Java, 1604

If the story seems stupid, that is only because it so doggedly holds its silence. The shadow whose lack you feel is there: it is the loss of Friday's tongue. . . . The story of Friday's tongue is a story unable to be told, or unable to be told by me. That is to say, many stories can be told of Friday's tongue, but the true story is buried within Friday, who is mute. The true story will not be heard till by art we have found a means of giving voice to Friday.

—J. M. Coetzee, *Foe*

The deployment of suggestive anecdote has become one of the hallmarks of New Historicism. Although it is a technique that owes something to the rhetoric of poststructuralist anthropology and the mode of "thick description" favored by Clifford Geertz, its popularity has less to do with any systematically articulated methodology or theoretical position (to which New Historicists have been generally resistant) than with the seductive practice of the school's most celebrated exponent, Stephen Greenblatt.[1] In his introduction to *Learning to Curse*, an essay couched in the disarmingly confessional idiom he reserves for such occasions, Greenblatt reflects on the etiology of his approach to the writing of cultural history, which he sees as reflecting "my will to tell stories, critical stories or stories told as a form of criticism."[2]

The compulsive lure of narrative he associates with its capacity for "estrangement": "the narrative impulse in my writing is yoked to the service of literary and cultural criticism; it pulls out and away from myself. . . . I am committed to the project of making strange what has become familiar, of demonstrating that what seems an untroubling and untroubled part of ourselves (for example, Shakespeare) is actually part of something else, something different" (p. 8).

Citing Joel Fineman's remarks on the role of anecdote in New Historicism's "conjunction of the literary and the referential," he seeks to substitute a more tactical mode of historical enquiry for the strategic approach of traditional history, with its "grand, integrated narrative[s] of beginning, middle and end." Anecdote serves to put history to the question. Its effect, à la Foucault, is to fracture the reassuring coherence of such teleological structures by "introduc[ing] an opening" into their otherwise impermeable surface.[3] For Greenblatt, as for Fineman, what is so compelling about anecdote is exactly its "insistence on contingency"—its power to create "the sense if not of a break then at least of a swerve in the ordinary and well-understood succession of events." In a fashion quite opposed to the methods of traditional historiography, anecdote "functions less as an explanatory illustration than as disturbance, that which requires explanation, contextualization, interpretation" (p. 5). In orthodox practice, by contrast, historical evidence is deployed precisely "to lay contingency and disturbance to rest," and in so doing it suppresses the very response that, to Greenblatt's way of thinking, ought to link the "reading" of historical events with the reading of literature: "Anecdotes are the equivalent in the register of the real of what drew me to the study of literature: the encounter with something I could not stand not understanding, that I could not quite finish with or finish off. . . . I do not want history to enable me to escape the effect of the literary but to deepen it by making it touch the effect of the real, a touch that would reciprocally deepen and complicate history" (p. 5).

The emotion being evoked here, with more than a touch of nostalgia, is what Greenblatt (anxious in spite of everything to stake out a space for the aesthetic) calls "wonder." And the "conjunction of the literary and the referential" at which he aims is one designed to reinvigorate with "wonder" everything that conventional history and criticism have conspired to render (misleadingly) familiar.

It would be perverse to deny the brilliant successes of this anecdotal approach in the best of Greenblatt's work—especially in the book that established his reputation, *Renaissance Self-Fashioning*. But the gathering insistence in his more recent writing upon the centrality of wonder and estrangement, while bespeaking a sympathetic humility before the sheer *otherness* of the past, marks an increasing divergence from mainstream historicist practice and is associated with the sometimes wayward approach to documentary evidence of which professional historians often complain.[4] For all the parade of humility, moreover, it is difficult not to notice that Greenblatt's method is particularly well adapted to displaying the interpretative power of the critic, since the greater the sense of wonder and estrangement produced by a given anecdote, the more dazzling his own explanatory performance must seem. This in turn can involve a somewhat condescending stance toward the subjects of historical investigation who, Caliban-like, are supposed not to know their own meaning until the New Historicist Prospero arrives to endow their brutish gabble with words that make them known. *Learning to Curse*, ironically enough, offers a particularly striking case in point.

A little later in his introduction Greenblatt produces an arresting example of his anecdotal repertory in the form of Edmund Scott's account of the interrogation and execution of a Chinese goldsmith by the English factors at Bantam in 1604.[5] Scott's narrative, with its unsettlingly matter-of-fact cataloging of horrors, its occasional heavy-handed irony, and extraordinary excess of violence, is presented as perfectly exemplifying the function of anecdote as a vehicle of "disturbance"; all that is required to respond to it apparently is "a hatred of cruelty and a sense of wonder" (p. 13). Yet the provocation to wonder in this case proves to be frustratingly unprofitable, since the "explanation [and] interpretation" it seems to invite (the very things upon which the heuristic function of anecdote might seem to depend) are toyed with only to be deliberately and teasingly withheld.

Greenblatt proceeds as though he were about to satisfy the hermeneutic appetites he has so carefully aroused, explaining that Scott's narrative needs to be understood primarily as a weapon in the dispute over remuneration that broke out after his return from Java—a dispute arising from his uncertain status as an unsalaried factor who had risen to become the East India Company's principal agent in Bantam only after the death of two superiors. Insofar as Scott's pamphlet was designed to advance his cause "every detail may well reflect his idea of what would most impress the Company's directors" (p. 14).[6] In that case, the extremity of the English reaction to what was, after all, only a "crime against property," "an attempt to rob them of their gold" (pp. 11, 13) would simply be meant to illustrate Scott's tireless pursuit of the company's material interests. Against this grossness of motivation and Scott's "complacent acceptance of his own acts" Greenblatt sets the imaginative force of the victim's silence, which becomes an ironic demonstration of "the torturer's inability to turn pain into a manifestation of his power" (p.14). But at the very point when he seems about to discover "meaning" in this dumb resistance, the interpreter suddenly, and rather bafflingly, abdicates: "This is not the place to tease out the implications of Scott's text; I have only wanted to indicate the kinds of questions that it raises, for they are questions that are implicit in most of the essays" (pp. 14–15).

What is one to make of this move? The abdication is the more puzzling because Greenblatt has just exposed his own retelling to a number of probing questions: "What are we to do with such a passage? What is history to make of it? . . . Is it vulgar or even lurid to rehearse Scott's text? Scott is by our lights a sadist, but is it also sadistic to quote him?" (pp. 12–13). Given his use of the metaphor of "opening," it is not, I think, accidental that a story of torture should be employed to illustrate the compelling power of narrative. Noting that "the Chinese victim was uncannily, unimaginably, perhaps heroically silent," Greenblatt wonders whether it is proper "after all this time, finally to compel him to speak" (p. 13). But these questions remain rhetorical, serving only to point up the admirable reticence implicit in Greenblatt's gesture of withdrawal—a gesture that serves at once to dissociate him from the prosaically motivated cruelty of the torturer (with whom his own interrogation of history might otherwise uncomfortably associate him) and to exhibit his decent liberal concern for the victim's right to silence. Yet the abdication, however it may be cast as a repudiation of power over the Other (in the name of a nescient wonder) also functions, paradoxically enough, as an assertion of power, serving to reinforce the critic's authority—not only over the text but also over readers who have been seduced into participation in his confessional "we." Like Hamlet's enigmatic "O, I could tell you," Greenblatt's teasing aposiopesis announces the possibility of extraordinary revelations only to refuse them, leaving readers haunted by a story whose only function now is to call in question both their own interpretative capacity and their good faith: "Is there not some hidden pleasure, some imaginative provocation, in this spectacle of torture?" (p. 13). Certainly, we are meant to feel, there must be—and Greenblatt could expose it if he chose.

The strategy becomes more disturbing when it is recognized that his essay significantly misrepresents the circumstances of the goldsmith's arrest and interrogation. Seen in the full context of Scott's *Exact Discourse*, both the horrific extremity of the torture and the narrator's chilling attitude toward it become much more straightforwardly explicable than Greenblatt pretends.[7] In fact the narrative's power to disturb arises less from any sense of wonder and estrangement than from its troubling familiarity. Although the gold-smith's silence certainly introduces an element of painful undecidability into the text, Scott's account of matters remains, in ways that are only too recognizable, both coherent and psychologically consistent. Indeed his story of isolation and paranoia is one that, in many of its essentials, might have been invented by a much later traveler in the archipelago, Joseph Conrad. And to invoke wonder and estrangement in this context, I suggest, is to risk the dubious mystification with which Conrad's Marlow tries to protect himself against his recognition of Mr. Kurtz. Scott's narrative is singularly revealing about the entanglement of violence, racial feeling, and national self-consciousness in early imperial enterprise, but it will yield those revelations only if careful attention is paid to Scott's own voice.

For Greenblatt, the torture and killing of the goldsmith belong so much to the category of the "unimaginable," that to confront the question of their historicity is to "risk a loss of moral bearings," while to explain them in (say) traditional Marxist terms is to run the danger of "losing the dark specificity of [Scott's] account . . . [thus] absorbing the unspeakable but spoken rupture of human relatedness into an abstract, pre-packaged schema" (p. 13). It is the extreme disparity between motive ("an attempt to rob them of their gold") and action (the systematic mutilation and dismemberment of a human body) that seems to push the torturers' behavior into the realm of the criminal sublime. Yet it is plain from Scott's narrative that the English frenzy had much less to do with the loss of material goods than with the intense panic induced by the would-be thieves' undermining and firing of the English trading factory. It is equally clear, moreover, that from the point of view of the English in Bantam, "considering the place, and extremity we were in" (A2v), firing and undermining had become symbolically charged actions to which no response, however brutal, could appear excessive. Furthermore, by the time Scott came to compose his pamphlet in 1606, his terror of secret treason, undermining, and blowing up must have suggested to many of his readers uncanny parallels with the notorious events of 5 November 1605—parallels to which indeed his narration may be consciously tailored.[8]

— ❧ —

"A STORY OF THEFT AND FIRE"

The difficulties faced by the new English factory at Bantam were compounded by the fact that it was established during a period of acute instability in Java. Its installation further complicated already violent rivalries between the Dutch and Portuguese trading empires, and at the local level between Chinese, Indian, and Javan merchants, while it also added to the tensions created by local power struggles, including ethnic, factional, and dynastic rivalries that the newcomers did not well understand. Barely had Captain James Lancaster's fleet arrived than a quarrel broke out with some Javans who, according to Scott, "sought all means they could, to be revenged: in so much, that presently after the departure of our pinnace, they began to practice the firing of our principal house with fiery darts and arrows in the night: And not content with that, in day time if we had brought out any quantity of goods to air, we should be sure to have the town fired to windward not far from us" (A3v). The terror of arson, first enunciated in this inauspicious beginning, becomes a compulsive theme of Scott's pamphlet. While Greenblatt's synopsis refers offhandedly to "years of commercial rivalry with the Dutch, fear of fire and theft, and growing hatred of both the Javanese and Chinese natives" (p. 11), nowhere does he register the true extremity of fear, amounting to pyrophobia, that the constant threat of fire produced in Scott and the other English.[9]

As Scott reconstructs it, 1604 seems to have been a particularly terrifying year: "My pen affords to speak of little else but murder, theft, wars, fire, and treason" (D1v). Fire was, of course, a general hazard in places like Bantam, the construction of local houses rendering them even more combustible than their European counterparts. The *Exact Discourse* mentions at least eighteen major conflagrations during Scott's two-and-a-half year residency—including no fewer than five burnings of the town on the east side of the river, opposite the factory, in a period of only three months (C2). On many of these occasions the merchants not only sustained loss of goods but found their lives and factory threatened as well—being saved, as they judged, only by their own watchfulness and that well-known instrument of God's special providence toward the English, the wind. Scott was convinced that many of these fires were deliberately lit, noting that in the same short period the Javans also

attempted "many times" to burn the town "on our side" (C2).[10] His belief
that the arson was often directed specifically against the English was sustained by "many shrewd attempts to have fired our house" (F4v) or adjacent
buildings (B2v). In September 1604 a major conflagration "consumed all the
upper work of our three houses to our exceeding great danger" (H2v).
Repeatedly exposed to threats of burning (F4V, G3, I2v) and "secret firework" (G1v)—not to mention throat-cutting and the attentions of head-
hunters (A3v, B3v)—the English became increasingly desperate: "looking
every hour when we should be assaulted, [we] durst take no rest at night"
(C1v). Such was the a condition of near-madness to which they were reduced
by endless nocturnal alarms that men in their beds would "bustle up, and in
their sleep wound one another" (C1v). Sometimes they lived "in such fear of
fire, that neither I, nor my men durst go out of doors" (H2), and Scott's own
anxiety grew so obsessive that the very word "fire" became anathema to him.
Merely to write it, even months after his return, was sufficient to reawaken
the old panic:

> Oh, this word Fire! had it been spoken near me either in *English*,
> *Malays*, *Javans*, or *China*, although I had been sound a sleep, yet I
> should have leaped out of my bed: the which I have done some times
> when our men in their watch have but whispered one to another of Fire,
> in so much that I was forced to warn them not to talk of Fire in the
> night, except they had great occasion: and not only myself, but my fel-
> lows, *Thomas Tudde* and *Gabriell Towerson*, who after our watches had
> been out, and we heavy asleep, our men many times have sounded a
> drum at our chamber doors, and we never heard them; yet presently
> after, they have but whispered to themselves of Fire, and we all have
> run out of our chambers. . . . And I protest before GOD, I would not
> sleep so many nights in fear again for the best ship's lading of pepper
> that ever came from thence.
>
> C1V- 2.[11]

Only in the light of this extreme pyrophobic anxiety does it become possible to account for the terrible savagery of the episode that Greenblatt
recounts—a climactic "story of theft and fire" in which Hinting, the Chinese
goldsmith, is cast as a principal villain.[12] Objectively speaking, the attack on
the English factory amounted to nothing more than a burglary that went dangerously awry, but it was not the mere threat to his material livelihood that so
enraged Scott:

A long time we lived in fear of fire, but now we felt the brunt and smart of it, and if God most miraculously had not preserved us, we had all perished both lives and goods, which came to passe by the villainy of a *Chinese* born, but now turned *Javan*: who was our next neighbour. . . . This offspring of the devil, and heir of hell . . . became an engineer, having got eight firebrands of hell more to him, only to set our house afire.

These nine deep workers dug a well . . . from the bottom of which . . . they brought a mine quite under the foundation of our house. . . . When they came up to the planks of our warehouse . . . they durst not cut them. . . . [But] one of this wicked consortship, being a goldsmith and brought up always to work in fire, told his fellows he would work out the planks with fire, so that we should never hear nor see him.

EIV-2

Unluckily Hinting's candle set fire to some bales of cloth in the warehouse above and a nearly fatal conflagration ensued:

I hearing this word fire, although I was fast asleep, yet it was no need to bid me rise: neither was I long slipping on my clothes, but presently ran down and opened the doors whereat came out such a strong funk and smoke that had almost strangled us. . . . And all that time we had two great jars of powder standing in the warehouse, which caused us greatly to fear blowing up. . . . But had we known then that the *Chinese* had done it, we should have sacrificed so many of them, that their blood should have helped to have quenched the fire.

(E2; 2V; 3V)

Acting on information from their Dutch rivals, the English discovered the mine and apprehended a number of Chinese in the adjoining compound. Having been licensed by the protector of the town to "do justice on those we had when we would" (F1), they applied hot irons to one of their prisoners, who incriminated several accomplices, including Hinting. The goldsmith was then discovered "hid in a privy," and himself put to the question.[13]

If a kind of ironic aptness is implied in the suggestively named Hinting's place of concealment, an even more brutal irony governed the details of his torment. While describing the goldsmith's application of fire to the warehouse floor, Scott sardonically observes "little did he think [though "brought up always to work in fire"], that we should ever come to work with fiery hot irons upon him" (E2). Now the torturer begins to savor his vicious conceit:

He would tell us nothing. Wherefore because of his sullenness, and that it was he that *fired* us, I thought I would *burn* him now a little, for we were now in the *heat of our anger*. First I caused him to be burned under the nails of his thumbs, fingers, and toes with sharp hot iron, and the nails to be torn off, and because he never blemished at that . . . we burned him in the arms, shoulders, and neck, but all was one with him: then we burned him quite through the hands, and with rasps of iron tore out the flesh and sinews. After that I caused them to knock the edges of his shin bones with hot searing irons.

F2V; EMPHASIS ADDED

In the context of the pyrophobia that infuses Scott's writing, his punning reference to "the heat of our anger" (which in Greenblatt's telling seems mere tasteless embroidery) becomes hideously pointed through its play on the proverbial capacity of fire to drive out fire.[14] Scott presents the application of hot irons as a kind of sympathetic purgation of the goldsmith's diabolic wickedness.[15] What else but fire, after all, should extinguish a "firebrand from hell"? One may even feel the narrative's obsessive iteration of "fire" as attempting a rhetorical duplication of the purge, as if to cast out the terrors evoked by the word.

At the same time Scott's emphasis on the ironic symmetries of crime and punishment, echoing the familiar trope of the biter bit, can be felt to indulge the same brutal wit that shapes the vindictive climaxes of Jacobean tragedy ("Those that did eat are eaten").[16] Yet for all his grim relish, Scott does not seek to justify Hinting's torture primarily as an act of revenge; to the contrary, he is careful to present it as an instrument of interrogation or "discovery"—at once assisting in the operation of a distinctively English mode of justice and serving to expose the hidden enmities that perpetually threaten to "consume" the entire English enterprise in Bantam. It is fire, that hungry element that gives a paradoxical kind of shape to the nothingness it produces, which more than anything embodies that threat of being consumed; and the systematic application of fire to the source of fire can be read as an attempt to neutralize this threat—an attempt that is carefully (though less than successfully) located within a particular discourse of Englishness.

— ❋ —

"FIRE AND TREASON"

Coming to his text for the first time one is likely to be struck by the unquestioning alacrity with which Scott and his companions resorted to torture. By what right did these intruders seize on the person of a foreign subject, mutilate, and kill him? Scott himself never appears greatly troubled about the legality of his proceedings, for he is careful to record that authority to execute summary justice in their own immediate affairs had been delegated to the English by the Javan authorities (B3, F1), and to insist upon the restraint and scrupulosity with which they exercised this power (D4, F1, F3v).[17] In fact "authority to execute [both] justice on their own men offending [and] against injuries from the natives" was among eight key conditions Lancaster apparently sought to negotiate from the states with whom the English desired to establish trading relations.[18] Nevertheless even under this dispensation, the use of torture seems at first sight surprising, since it was nominally excluded from English judicial proceedings. Given that the Dutch had made the use of judicial torture routine in their trading depots, one might suppose the behavior of the English merely reflected a rapid and unquestioning adaptation to established local custom—were it not that Englishmen customarily made so much of the fact that, though it formed a routine part of the Roman inquisitorial procedures employed elsewhere in Europe, torture had no such properly defined place in English law.[19]

But torture of course, as its not infrequent appearance in popular drama would suggest, was by no means so unusual in England as such complacent propaganda implied.[20] Indeed, thanks to the work of Elizabeth Hanson and others, it has become clear that despite its having effectively disappeared from formal legal procedures in the mid-twelfth century, torture enjoyed a significant de facto revival in the Tudor period, reaching "its English heyday" in the second half of Elizabeth's reign.[21] And Scott seems to have thought of his use of it as consistent with a distinctively English practice. The key difference in the English use of torture was that, where in Roman-based legal systems its justification lay in the evidential value of the confessions it was designed to extract, in England, where it was normally legitimated by warrant from the Privy Council, it served primarily as a tool of investigation—one substantially restricted, moreover, to major crimes against the state—such as witchcraft and treason.[22] In this context it is significant that not only does Scott identify Hinting's crime as a species of "treason" (D1v) and the work of an "offspring of the devil" (E1v), but he is also careful to establish that the uncovering of hidden co-conspirators was the principal aim of his interrogation. Thus it is of a piece with his narrative's conscious display of Englishness and (by virtue of the dialectical nature of such self-definition) with its indignant discovery of the not-English.

English writing about torture suggests that its special appropriateness to such crimes as treason and witchcraft was governed as much by symbolic as by practical considerations. What made these offenses seem especially heinous, apart from their obvious threat to authority and the good order of the commonweal, was their clandestine character—revealed in the case of treason by the devious secrecy of its undermining practice. Deemed to occur "in the very thought and cogitation" of the perpetrator, long before it was translated into action, treason was imagined (in Bacon's words) as "a secret thing hidden in the breast of man [that] cannot be known but by an open fact or deed."[23] The suitability of torture to the policing of such surreptitious villainy depended on its power to lay open, in a fashion at once metaphoric and brutally literal, the otherwise inaccessible closet of the inner self.[24] Torture, as Elaine Scarry points out, habitually "dramatize[s] the connection between two dreaded forms of exposure, open wounds and confession," as the victim's "melting body is turned inside out, revealing the most inward and secret parts of him." The goal of English torture, as the language of official warrants made clear, was not confession but "discovery," the "manifestation," or "bolting forth of the truth."[25] So the dramatist Thomas Kyd, himself under torture, hopes his betrayers will in turn be put to the question, their lives "examined and ripped up effectually" to "break open their lewd designs and see into the truth." It was a procedure designed to enact, in a spectacular and exemplary fashion, the uncovering of hidden truths imagined as "actually contained within the victim's body."[26] Thus it always involved *agon* as well as agony and was marked (as the very terminology of "putting to the question" implies) by a distinct "rhetorical structure which posit[ed] a victim in possession of a *hidden truth* that the interrogator must struggle to uncover." In this sense, as Hanson suggests, it was part and parcel of a larger "discourse of discovery" in which, whether by "the crossing of seas or the parting of flesh, the mask is stripped away, making knowledge and sight seem equivalent." There is thus a certain telling symmetry in the placing of an episode of torture at the center of a voyaging narrative that offers to describe and lay bare the treacherous "subtleties" of a distant nation.[27]

For Edmund Scott the undermining and firing of the English factory was the climax in a catalog of "murder, theft, wars, fire, and treason" (D1v) that marked the passage of the year 1604—an act of "treason" (however loosely defined) that bore all the marks of guile and secret treachery that characterized the English experience of *"that rude and dangerous region"* (A2). In his "Instructions Left at Bantam," Lancaster had warned the English: "Wheresoever you be come, trust none of the Indians, for their bodies and souls be wholly treason."[28] And Scott's own title foregrounds the "Subtilties" (cunning, wily stratagems) and "Pollicies" (crafty devices) of the East Indians, both Chinese and Javan, while his narrative constantly draws attention to their untrustworthy nature, expressed in a propensity for such underhand vices as "stealing" (N2), "poisoning" (G2), and nocturnal throat-cutting (I1).[29] Deceit and fraud are all around, tainting even the behavior of their fellow Europeans. Warned by the Dutch early in their stay that the protector himself is plotting against them, the English quickly interpret this official's reassurances as "dissimulation to borrow money of us," while crediting his insistence that the Dutch themselves are dissemblers: "Now whether the *protector* lied to us, in denying it; or that the *Hollanders* did dissemble with us, we cannot certainly tell; but he said plainly, the *Hollanders* lied: and to speak truth, I think they can dissemble, and the *protector* is a villain" (B2).

Yet though the Dutch are convicted of dissembling in this way, it is not interpreted as a sign of their essentially deceitful make-up or understood to compromise their natural kinship with the English; indeed, Scott declares, "though we were mortal enemies in our trade, in all other matters we were friends, and would have lived and died one for the other" (H3). "The *Javans and Chinese*," by contrast, are identified as being "from the highest to the lowest . . . all villainies, [who] have not one spark of grace in them" (F3v). "The *Chinese*" are especially denigrated as "very crafty people in trading, using all kinds of cozening and deceit which may be possible to be devised . . . [who] will steal, and do any kind of villainy, to get wealth" (N2, N3v). They are interlopers whose relation even to their (innately treacherous) Javan hosts constitutes a kind of subtle treason since they are said (in a fashion that disconcertingly mimics the ambitions of the English themselves) to "suck away the wealth of the land," living "like *Jews* . . . crouching under them, [only to] rob them of their wealth, and send it for *China*" (M4v, N2). Thus even when a group of neighboring Chinese are persuaded to assist the

English after the firing of the factory, Scott instinctively knows, as they haggle over payment, that these seeming friends covertly "wish[ed] our house had been consumed, although they spoke it not before us: for . . . such is their wicked mind" (E3v).

Hinting the goldsmith is presented as the perfect epitome of this greedy and perfidious people—a clipper and counterfeiter of coins (F2v), who works by undermining and secret firework. At the same time this inherent viciousness is compounded by the suspicion that he and his confederates are merely the frontmen for even more dangerous hidden enemies—either "some great men of the country, or the rich *Chinese*" (F1v-F2); indeed, as Scott explains, "we were in a jealousy, that the protector and some other of the principal of the land had an interest in this act" (F). The suggestion of such a hidden conspiracy reaching to the very highest levels in the kingdom explains the exceptional narrative prominence given to this episode and to the interrogation that followed. For what was at stake in the questioning of Hinting and his co-conspirators was nothing less than an absolute stripping away of the mask of dissimulation and a "bolting forth" of all the secret treasons of Bantam to reveal the enemy's "wicked mind." In one significant respect only did the interrogation differ from the practice of the Queen's Privy Council: hot irons, the agents of purgative fire, were substituted for the rack.

At the level of literal detection the interrogation yielded only equivocal results, but on the symbolic level Scott endeavors to present it as something of a triumph. For however they respond to English threats and torture, the prisoners are made to reveal their own bent for dissimulation, while the inhabitants of Bantam are offered a signal lesson in the operation of English justice—not least through a carefully graduated treatment of the three prisoners.

Alternately confessing and recanting as torture is applied and relaxed, the first prisoner inculpates three other Chinese—Hinting, Boyhie, and Unitie—but declines to identify any hidden hand behind their plot, saying "he would accuse no man that was not guilty, how much soever we did torment him" (F2). Dissatisfied with these limited revelations, Scott promises to spare his life "if he would tell me the truth," but since the man will do no more than repeat his original story, Scott sends him to execution as an incorrigible dissimulator.

The most cooperative of the three prisoners is Boyhie, the last to be interrogated, who is spared torture on the promise of a full disclosure. But although Boyhie is sufficiently believed to mitigate his sentence, the truth of his confession is subtly compromised by its very self-inculpation, so that his list of "all that were the doers of it" is plausible only *"if one may believe a villain"* (F3v; emphasis added). Thus even the fullest and least forced confession carries the stigma of dissimulation.

But the greatest mark of villainy is discovered in the obdurate refusal to confess at all. For if the first prisoner exposes his falsehood by telling the wrong sort of story and the third by telling the right sort, the second reveals the grossness of his treachery by declining to speak at all, retreating into a "sullenness" that seems stubbornly resistant to any increase of agony ("all was one with him"). In English terms, he refuses to plead, a repudiation of due process, which itself justified the torture of *peine forte et dure*. The climax of his dumb recalcitrance is reached when Hinting seeks to destroy the very organ of his own speech: "he never shed tear, no nor once turned his head aside, nor stirred hand or foot: but when he [was] demanded any question, he would put tongue between his teeth, and strike his chin upon his knees to byte it off " (F2v-F3).[30]

There are no means of knowing the reasons for Hinting's seeming obduracy (assuming he even properly understood the questions that were put to him), much less for this allegedly extreme expression of it. Indeed it is perfectly conceivable that what Scott interpreted as a gesture of ultimate defiance was no more than an involuntary motor reaction, or it may have been the man's attempt to distract himself from one unbearable pain by the self-infliction of another.[31] But to English eyes his gesture must have seemed all too familiar, for it uncannily imitated the notorious catastrophe of one of the most celebrated plays in English theater—a drama of secret murder, treason, and revenge that had been revived (with new additions by Ben Jonson) a little before Scott's departure for Java, *The Spanish Tragedy*.[32] In Kyd's play Hieronimo responds to the king's threat of torture and the demand to reveal the names of his confederates by biting out his own tongue:

❄

HIERONIMO:
But never shalt thou force me to reveal
The thing which I have vow'd inviolate:
And therefore, in despite of all thy threats,
Pleas'd with their deaths, and eas'd with their revenge,
First take my tongue, and afterwards my heart.
[He bites out his tongue]

KING:

O monstrous resolution of a wretch.
See, Viceroy, he hath bitten forth his tongue
Rather than to reveal what we requir'd. . . .
We will devise th' extremest kind of death
That ever was invented for a wretch.

4.1.187–98

✿

As though in some vicious travesty of Hieronimo's heroic spite, Hinting stands revealed as a man who will stop at nothing to keep inviolate his treasonable secret. And like Kyd's enraged Spanish king, the English resolve to destroy what they cannot penetrate: "Between our men and the *Hollanders*, they shot him almost all to pieces before they left him." It is as if the tormenting opacity of the human body produces a terrible spiral of violence in the torturers. The less the suffering body reveals, the more it is deemed to betray the hiddenness of its own malice; the more obstinately hidden that malice, the greater the force required to unlock it.

The torture and execution of Hinting and his conspirators, then, has a central place in Scott's discovery of the treacherous "subtleties" of the East Indians, but it also plays a part in his carefully mounted parade of Englishness. Set against the exemplary justice meted out to the first two conspirators is the clemency exhibited toward the third. Boyhie is spared torture and allowed an honorable death by the kris not merely as a reward for the fullness of his confession but also so that the natives may "see, that *Englishmen* [know] as well how to be merciful as to torture, if occasion serve[s]" (F3v). Thus torture and mercy alike contribute to a discourse of national identity, setting off the denizens of the factory both from their East Indian hosts and from their Dutch rivals, and the lesson first offered to the natives is rehearsed again for English readers as part of the specifically nationalist-mercantilist project of Scott's text.[33]

— ✿ —

"THE ENGLISH NATION AT BANTAN"

Far from being designed simply as a weapon in a struggle over personal remuneration, as Greenblatt implies, the *Discourse* is clearly intended to stir up nationalist feeling in the interest of an expanded East India trade. Indeed the circumstances of its publication by a man with such strong company connections as Walter Burre suggest that the *Exact Discourse* was primarily intended to advertise the cause of the company, which was busily preparing for a third voyage.[34] From the beginning the East India governors had faced considerable obstacles in raising funds for their ventures, and several of the subscribers to the first voyage had failed to meet their engagements, exacerbating the company's already severe level of debt. The slowness of returns on the first voyage made for problems in mustering sufficient investors for the second. And although the first and second voyages ultimately returned a combined profit of 95 percent, difficulties experienced in disposing of some of their goods, especially the very large quantities of pepper obtained, meant the accounts of the two voyages could not be wound up until 1609, eight years after Lancaster's departure.[35] Consequently in 1606, facing a skeptical investment market, the company had every reason to encourage the publication of material designed to arouse patriotic enthusiasm for their adventuring.

Anxious lest his pamphlet be misapplied by opponents of the enterprise, Scott is careful to reassure potential successors and investors that (thanks in part to his own efforts) they can now expect much less dangerous conditions, "for then we were strangers, and now we have many friends there, and the country is grown to much better civility" (C2). At the same time maintenance of the Bantam factory is presented as essential to "the fame of the English nation."[36] Abandoning it, he insists at the very end of his narrative, "will purchase more infamy to our nation in all those parts and in *China*, then ever we have hitherto to gain credit, for it will be thought of them all that either poverty is the cause, or that we dare not come there for fear of the *Hollanders*" (I3v; M2-M2v).

In the context of this nationalist concern, it is significant that Scott's title page should promise not only to reveal the underhand "Subtilties" and "Pollicies" of the East Indians but also to recount "what hath happened to the *English* Nation at *Bantan*." Scott is anxious to persuade his readers that the survival of the English factory is critical to the fame and fortunes of the English nation at large. Of course "nation" could sometimes carry the restricted sense of "a number of persons belonging to a given nation," but the text is so shot through with an insistence upon the *representative* nature of this small English merchant community that their experiences acquire an exemplary status. Surrounded by a sea of hostile foreigners, threatened with treasonable conspiracy and undermining stratagem, the factory resembles a microcosm of the English nation, sustained by the same siege-mentality that was so decisive in shaping the Elizabethan sense of national identity.[37]

Fittingly enough the merchants chose the anniversary of Elizabeth's coronation for an extraordinary public assertion of their defiant Englishness. For reasons that remain mysterious—since they had been established in Bantam for several years before the arrival of the English—the Dutch are alleged to have stolen the identity of the English: "The common people knew us not from the *Hollanders*, for both they and we were all called by the name of *English*-men, by reason of their usurping our name at their first coming hither to trade: and as we passed along the stree[t]s we might hear the people in the market railing and exclaiming on the *English*-men, although they meant the Hollanders" (C2v).[38]

Casting about for ways to rectify this unsettling and potentially dangerous confusion, the English resolved on a spectacular display of heraldic difference and seized on the queen's Accession Day as an occasion for it. The choice was a predictable one, given the way in which "the queen's holy day" had been promoted as a festival of "national cohesion and solidarity":[39]

> Now the 17 day of November drawing near, the which we held to be our coronation day, (for at that time, nor the year, we knew not other but that Queen *Elizabeth* was living) we all suited ourselves in new apparel of silk, and made us all scarves of white-and-red taffeta, being our country's colors. Also we made a flag with the red cross through the middle: and because we that were the merchants would be known from our men, we edged our scarves with a deep fringe of gold, and that was our difference.
>
> Our day being come, we set up our banner of *Saint George* upon the top of our house, and with our drum and shot we marched up and down within our own ground, being but fourteen in number, wherefore we could march but single one after another; plying our shot, and casting ourselves in rings and esses.
>
> The *Sabindar*, and divers of the chiefest of the land, hearing our pieces, came to see us, and to enquire the cause of our triumph. We told them, that day six and forty year our *Queen* was crowned, wherefore all *English*-men, in what country soever they were, did triumph on that day.
>
> He greatly commended us for having our *prince* in reverence in so far a country.
>
> Many others did ask us, Why the *English*-men at the other house did not so? We told them they were no *English*-men but *Hollanders*, and that they had no king, but their land was ruled by *governors*.

Some would reply again and say, They named themselves to be *English*-men at the first, and therefore they took them to be *English*-men: but we would tell them again, they were of another country near *England*, and spoke another language; and if they did talk with them now, they should hear they were of another nation.

(c2v)

A certain pathos attaches to the fragile jingoism of this sadly under-manned pageant—especially in the light of the queen's recent demise, and Scott himself is embarrassed by the thought that it may be "counted fantastical, when it should be known in *England*" (C3). Indeed as the small band of English march up and down their compound, with flags waving, drums beating, and muskets firing, they resemble nothing so much as a troupe of those actors whose "triumphs" pageanted forth the history of English arms in France—Henry V's "happy few" facing overwhelming odds at Agincourt or Talbot's heroic band "parked and bounded in a pale, / A little herd of England's timorous deer / Mazed with a yelping kennel of French curs" (*1 Henry VI*, 4.3.45–7). But what might appear fantastically theatrical at home becomes an essential technique of self-representation here at the extreme margin of English power, where the acuteness of the need to establish a sense of national difference is exactly proportionate to the constant threat of its erasure.

The English triumph in Bantam had a distinctly more martial cast than was usual in London celebrations of the accession—though these sometimes involved the staging of mock battles and the discharge of ordnance from the tower, in addition to the usual bell-ringing, processions, and displays of civic pageantry.[40] Evidently modeled on the drilling of the city train bands in St. George's Fields, Mile End, its effect was to emphasize the militant nationalistic defiance that always underlay Accession Day festivities—their implicit identification of Elizabeth's royal authority with a Protestant eschatological history of deliverance from the papal Antichrist and their mobilization of a mythology of siege in which "the forces of evil still [menacing] England both within and without . . . were only kept at bay while God's holy handmaiden ruled."[41] In Scott's pageant English resistance to Dutch usurpation and Javan indifference replayed the trope of Protestant self-definition as a colonialist figure of purely national separation. It did so, moreover, in a ceremonial context that firmly located the London mercantile caste at the very heart of national identity. Later they would mount a still more elaborate triumph, heralded by a trumpeter and ten musketeers, "all very well furnished with their country's colours" by way of an English contribution to the coronation shows for the new King of Bantam (L2-L3). And in the following year (1604), still unaware of the queen's death, they once again marked her accession with feasting and an extravagant display of musketry.

Scott is at pains to insist on the salutary impression of such demonstrations upon the natives. The first Accession Day triumph immediately sets them apart from the Dutch rivals:

> The multitude of people did admire to see so few of us deliver so much shot: for the *Javans* and *Chinese* are no good shot.
> In the afternoon I caused our men to walk abroad the town and market, whereby the people might take notice of them.
> Their red-and-white scarves and hatbands, made such a show, that the inhabitants of those parts had never seen the like: so that ever after that day, we were known from the *Hollanders;* and many times the children in the streets would run after us crying, *Oran Engrees bayck, oran Hollanda iahad:* which is, the *English*-men are good, the *Hollanders* are naught.[42]
> (c3)

Despite this apparently decisive success, however, a continuing need to exhibit their difference from the Dutch is expressed in the endless jockeying for position that results in disputes over precedence at the Protector's court— "for an Englishman scorns to give place to Hollanders in any foreign country" (D3)—issuing in several open brawls, the last of which breaks out on the very eve of their departure ("they . . . thi[n]king to be lords of all those parts whe[n] we are gone" M2v).[43] Aggressive anxiety about the Dutch is matched by an equal determination to establish their own superiority to the East Indians. The Javans have to be impressed with the moral supremacy of the English, with their power to secure justice for themselves, and, where necessary, to enforce a bargain. The protector is roundly informed by Scott "that *kings* must keep their words, or else they were no *kings*"—a lesson, he is reminded, that their sovereign has already impressed upon the King of Spain, to the cost of "many thousands of men's lives": "it was well known to all nations, that we did not only burn and spoil at home, but also came into those parts of the world, and took away his subjects' goods, the which himself could witness" (G4). If the English are distinguished from the Dutch as people who have kings rather than governors, they are equally distinct from the

Javans and the Spanish as a people whose monarchy is subject to the limitations of the law.

Difference is insisted on for both tactical reasons (as a mode of psychological self-protection in a condition of real vulnerability) and for strategic ones (as a way of impressing on the natives the advisability of accommodating English commercial ambitions at the expense of their rivals), and it is re-rehearsed in the text itself as a means of enlisting patriotic identification with a commercial enterprise—indeed of asserting the essential identity of national and city mercantile interests. But the effect of such insistence is seldom, if ever, contained by its immediate objects. For what texts of this sort simultaneously produce is an ideology of cultural and ultimately of racial difference that will become part of the enabling discourse not merely of mercantile expansion but of imperial conquest.

This ideology is perhaps most nakedly disclosed when Scott recounts the "tragedy" of a mulatto slave accused of multiple murder. As "our mulatto" the slave is defined as both inside and yet ultimately excluded from "the English nation at *Bantan*." Ironically enough, his crime itself seems to have been provoked by an explosion of something like racial resentment. Having been drinking with "one of his countryman" who belongs to a visiting Flemish ship, he is enraged when the provost of the vessel tries to beat his companion on board. "Tickled in the head with wine" he seeks out and kills both the Fleming, and the other mulatto (who he fears will inform upon him), as well as "a poor *Javan*" (D2). The case attracts local notoriety because of the rumor "that there was an Englishman to be executed"; large crowds turn up to witness the execution but are taken aback to discover the prisoner "a black man." At this point Scott seizes the opportunity to instruct the Javans as to the racial significance of mulatto criminality: "we told them he was just of their own colour and condition and that an Englishman or white man would not do such a bloody deed" (D4v).

What bloody deeds an Englishman or white man *could* do the Javans would be taught in the case of Hinting and his companions. But like the mulatto, after all, they too might be dismissed (in Scott's crude ethnology) as persons of the same "colour and condition" as the Javans.[44] And the violence visited upon their bodies was governed, as Scott conceived it, by superior English notions of justice. Indeed he seems to have convinced himself that the torture of Hinting was an essential part of those efforts by which the English impressed "the fame of the English nation" not merely upon the Javans but upon the "many nations [that resort to this town of *Bantan*]":

We were grown a common admiration amongst them all; that we being
so few, should carry such a port as we did, never putting up the least
wrong that was offered either by *Javans* or *Chinese*, but always did justice our own selves. . . . (And I have heard many strangers speak it, that
have been present, when we have beaten some *Javans*.) That they never
knew . . . any nation but we, that were liegers there, that durst once
strike a *Javan*, in *Bantan:* and it was a common talk among all strangers,
and others, how we stood at defiance with those that hated us for our
goods, never offering any the least wrong to the meanest in the town,
and receiving from the better sort a commendation before the
Hollanders or any other nation: and it will be a thing generally talked of,
in all parts of the world, when it is likely there will be no *English* there.
  (14)

Yet for all the rhetorical strategies that seek to contain the wild excess of
Hinting's torture within the forms of English civility (rather as the pageant is
designed to contain their excess of fear), nothing can altogether disguise the
frenzy that discloses it as a half-deranged reaction to the stress of isolation and
the terror of fire, exacerbated by the uninterpretable obduracy of the victim.
Between the nullity of the victim's silence and the annihilation of firing there
is, in the end, little to choose. Both result in a kind of frantic defiance.

"Standing at defiance," confined in their small and vulnerable factory,
seems to be the characteristic posture of "the English nation at *Bantan*." But
ironically the very posture appears to court the annihilation they fear. No
sooner do they erect a fence to keep the enemy at bay than "we looked every
hour when it should be burnt down" (H3). Less than twenty years after
Scott's departure, his nightmare of a time "when there will be no English
there" was to be fulfilled by the massacre of English merchants at
Amboyna—where the dead included Scott's "fellow" Gabriel Towerson.[45]
Neither the subtleties of the Chinese nor the policies of the Javans were to
blame, however, but the imperial rivalry of the Dutch, those ambiguous
bosom friends and alleged usurpers of English identity, who now
"unbounded with covetousness and ambition," according to Arthur Wilson,
"strove to hinder their neighbours and best friends the English . . . and began
to practice their utter extirpation: not by a massacre, for that had been a *merciful mischief*, but by torture." The charge, as in the Hinting case, was "treason," and the torture, though similarly intended "to make their *cruelty justice*," was conducted "in so horrid and savage a manner" that, from the
English perspective, it again threatened to collapse the difference between

"white men" and barbarous Others—"as if they had sucked their *rage* from *Indian tigers*."[46] With a bitterly exacting irony, the sufferings of the English and their alleged Japanese accomplices mimicked the fiery pangs of Hinting and his companions (see fig. 14):

> *Amboyna* was the bloody *stage* where they acted this black tragedy; and *fire*, and *water* were their *engines*. For, pretending the chief *agent* Captain *Gabriel Towerson* and the rest of the *English factory* had an intention by the assistance of some few poor *Japaneses* to possess themselves of the castle, and expel the Dutch out of the *island*, they seized upon them, and set their bloody *engines* [i.e., the rack] a-work. . . . And such whose sturdy innocence would not be compelled to accuse themselves, they burned the soles of their feet with candles *and with those burning instruments made such holes in their sides that they might see their entrails, yet would not see their innocence.*[47]

For the Dutch torturers (as for their English counterparts) we might suppose, the maddening opacity of the human body was interpreted as the expression of a guilty obstinacy that must be laid open at any cost. The exigencies of inquisitorial torture, however, demanded a less ambiguous narrative resolution: "So *exquisite* were they in their devilish cruelty, as will be ghastly to express, what was it there to suffer! Thus having tired the poor men with torture, and they being willing to die quickly, confessed whatsoever their cruel tormentors would have them say. The *Dutch* having in the *furnace* wrought them to accuse themselves, got their *confessions* under their hands, and so concluded their *barbarism*, with cutting off some of their heads."[48]

What lessons are to be drawn from Greenblatt's curious (mis)appropriation of the story of Hinting's torture? At one level, of course, he is perfectly correct to remind us (once again) that history has been, for the most part, written by its winners and that enforced silence has too often been added to suffering as the price of defeat: the biting of Hinting's tongue seems a cruelly exact emblem for this double victimization. At the same time, it is possible to feel a degree of respect for Greenblatt's reluctance to intrude upon the victim's silence. Nevertheless his stance seems to me, in the last analysis, both evasive and dangerous. It is not simply that his substantially decontextualized use of the anecdote carelessly obscures what the pamphlet has to reveal about the emergent discourses of race and nation at a critical point in early imperial development, but that his insistence on the primacy of "estrangement" and

14. The torture of John Clarke at Amboyna. From A True Relation of the Barbarous Proceedings Against the English *(1624), reprinted by permission of the Folger Shakespeare Library.*

"wonder" permits a larger disingenuousness about history and the historicist project to which he is committed.

No one has more subtly or more movingly explored the anxiety about the complicities of narrative, power, and violence that trouble Greenblatt than the white South African novelist J. M. Coetzee. In two extraordinary parables, *Waiting for the Barbarians* and *Foe*, Coetzee puts his own writerly relation with history to the question. In the first of them, the narrator-protagonist, a kindly old magistrate in some unplaced frontier town, rescues a barbarian girl from the state's torturers, only to discover in his own need to understand her—to force in her impervious surface an opening out of which a narrative might be drawn—a version of the torturer's obsession. In the second (a reworking of *Robinson Crusoe* from which this chapter's epigraph is drawn) the narrator-protagonist, Susan Barton, supposedly Cruso's and Friday's fellow castaway on the island, tries to persuade the writer Mr. Foe of the need to tell Friday's story. Her own narrative efforts founder on the fact that Friday, an African slave, has (like Scott's victim) lost his tongue—though whether at the hands of slavers (as Cruso insists), or those of Cruso himself, or by Friday's own act remains uncertain. But their discussions persuade Foe that "Till we have spoken the unspoken we have not come to the heart of the story. . . . For as long as [Friday] is as he is dumb we can . . . continue to use him as we wish."[49] The writer, however, cannot help disclosing the coercive violence implicit in this sympathetically aroused ambition: "We must *make* Friday's silence speak" (p. 142; emphasis added). And Coetzee's novel ends by insisting on Friday's ultimate inaccessibility to the compulsions of the colonizer's narrative: "This is not a place of words. . . . This is a place where bodies are their own signs. It is the home of Friday" (p. 157).

The ending of *Foe* can be read as a surrender to the power of something that resembles Greenblatt's "wonder": Friday's "mouth opens. From inside him comes a slow stream, without breath, without interruption. It flows up through his body and out upon me; it passes up through the cabin, through the wreck; washing the cliffs and shores of the island, it runs northward, and southward to the ends of the earth. Soft and cold, dark and unending, it beats against my eyelids, against the skin of my face" (p. 157).

Is Greenblatt justified, then, in his abdication, with its implication that there are certain stories better left untold because there is no way of telling them that does not involve some collusion with the violence of the oppressor? Clearly I do not think so, and I cite Coetzee partly because his own answer to the challenge of *Foe* was to turn back, in *Age of Iron*, to a very different interrogation of history, one that seemed to confront, more directly than he had hitherto been willing to do, the history of the colonizers' oppression. *Age of Iron* is a book that acknowledges the ultimate inaccessibility of the Other's history, which is by definition off-limits, while insisting on the necessity, however intractable it may seem, of articulating one's own relation to it.

I have tried to show that, when it is placed in context, Scott's account of Hinting's torture is actually a great deal more articulate than Greenblatt allows it to appear; that it makes sense as a part of a narrative that can include the comic pathos of the improvised Accession Day triumph at one extreme, and the ugly racial arrogance associated with the mulatto's execution at another—a narrative in which the heartfelt anxieties of acute cultural dislocation are disconcertingly manipulated into the service of chauvinism and mercantile ambition. Such a story responds to a literary reading precisely because it resists formulaic moralization, and my final objection to Greenblatt's handling is that all his subtlety only serves to render it down to a simple fable about the iniquity of European empire, thinly veiled by the mystifications of "wonder." At the same time, his strategy of estrangement serves to put a quite impermissible distance between himself and the torturer—one that no full and sympathetic reading of the narrative would allow. In this fashion he contrives to identify himself with the silence of the victim—into which, indeed, he symbolically withdraws. I do not mean to cheapen Greenblatt's much-meditated sense of kinship with the victims of history's long holocaust when I say that it can lead to wilful misreadings of history. Part of the imaginative value of reading Scott should be to remind us (once again, if such a thing were needed) that atrocities are by no means the work of unnatural Others or the preserve of monsters. They belong to a humanly comprehensible history in which we are all, in deeply conflicting ways, implicated. That, I am afraid, is part of what it means to be human—to have a history at all. To think otherwise, however comforting it may be, is to give oneself to a deception whose consequences litter the world from the Middle East to Ireland and to the slaughterhouse that was Yugoslavia.

"Material Flames": Romance, Empire, and Mercantile Fantasy in John Fletcher's Island Princess

And his opportunity sat veiled by his side like an Eastern bride waiting to be uncovered
by the hand of the master.
—Joseph Conrad, *Lord Jim*

"THE SCENE INDIA"

When the Lord Chamberlain's Men constructed, from the dismantled timbers of London's first permanent playhouse, the edifice that was to become the most celebrated of early modern theaters, they chose for it a name even more universal and absolute than that of its predecessor. "The Theatre" now became "the Globe" itself, in a transformation that wittily exemplified the motto supposedly emblazoned on the trade sign of the new house: "Totus mundus agit histrionem." More was involved in the choice of name, however, than a playful inversion of the ancient *theatrum mundi* trope. The term "globe," after all, was a recent borrowing from French, closely associated with the revolutionary achievements of Renaissance cartography; not found in English before the mid-sixteenth century, it was linked from the beginning with the revolutionary conceptualization of terrestrial space produced by Martin Behaim's construction of the first cartographic globe at Nuremberg in 1492.[1] Thus the icon of "Hercules and his load" (*Hamlet*, 2.2.345) hanging above the entrance to the Globe drew attention to the role of Shakespeare's theater as an engine for reimagining the world: a space where, as the Swiss traveler Thomas Platter observed, a people not much given to travel could vicariously experience the wonder of unfamiliar places —an arena, therefore, in which dreams of geographic mastery, of national consolidation and expansion, of discovery, conquest, and mercantile splendor, could be played out.[2]

In recent years work on plays as diverse as Marlowe's *Tamburlaine* and *The Jew of Malta*, Heywood's *Fair Maid of the West*, Shakespeare's Roman and English histories, *Othello, The Merchant of Venice, Cymbeline*, and above all *The Tempest*, has made us familiar with the ideological dimensions of the various geographic fantasies that inhabited the space of the stage.[3] In all this busy historicization, however, little attention has been paid to the writing of the most popular of all Jacobean playwrights, John Fletcher, Shakespeare's successor as principal dramatist to the King's Men. This is perhaps because Fletcher's reputation as an essentially frivolous theatrical opportunist, an "entertainer to the Jacobean gentry" whose espousal of courtly values helped to father the so-called Caroline decadence, has (despite the New Historicism's professed canonical skepticism) continued to deflect serious critical attention from his work. Yet it would be surprising if someone as close to the centers of London intellectual and political life as the well-connected Fletcher should have remained indifferent to the geographic excitements that infused the work of his contemporaries. And toward the end of his career Fletcher attempted his own imaginative penetration of the regions of mercantile and colonial adventure in two plays that were to enjoy significant popularity throughout the century. Evidently designed as companion pieces, the pair were written for the King's Men within a short time of one another— *The Island Princess* having its first recorded performance at court on 26 December 1621, while *The Sea-Voyage*, produced in collaboration with Fletcher's own successor, Philip Massinger, was licensed for the stage on 22 June 1622.

The respective settings of these plays link them to the two principal sites of early imperial enterprise in what Donne called the "Indias of spice and mine"—the worlds of American plantation and of East Indian commercial expansion. And they exhibit a common preoccupation with the ideal of temperance, that recurrent theme of early English imperial discourse.[4] Of the two, *The Sea-Voyage* has attracted slightly more attention—probably because of its relation to Shakespeare's *Tempest*, on which (as Dryden was the first to observe) it is openly parasitic.[5] Rather as Fletcher's early comedy *The Woman's Prize; or The Tamer Tamed* (ca. 1607–8[?]) appropriated the

central character of *The Taming of the Shrew* to make its own spirited contribution to the debate on gender, so this satirical romance revisits the exotic territory of *The Tempest* to engage in a witty critique of colonial propaganda. If
The Sea-Voyage, in its oblique, allusive fashion, offers itself as an anticolonial
document, *The Island Princess* complements that position by fostering the
vision of a purely mercantile empire, untainted by the greed and appropriative violence of plantation. Set in the Moluccan spice islands during the early
period of sixteenth-century Portuguese commercial domination, it makes no
direct reference to English enterprise in the region; yet it is a work that makes
complete sense only in the context of the long-running propagandist debate
associated with that enterprise. This was a debate in which concepts of
national identity were systematically attached to the pursuit of particular
commercial objectives, and it was a debate that had developed a particularly
fierce edge in the second decade of the seventeenth century as a result of the
deteriorating fortunes of the English East India Company in the increasingly
vicious struggle with their Dutch counterparts for control of the lucrative
spice trade. Performed in the ideologically charged atmosphere of the court,
where pro- and anti-Dutch factions competed for influence, while propo-
nents of Western planting vied with the advocates of Eastern commerce, and
supporters of mercantile expansion tilted with the champions of a closed
economy, *The Island Princess* can hardly have seemed as innocent a fantasy as
it is likely to appear to most modern readers. Even in its public performances
it must have capitalized on popular fascination with exotic marvels to turn the
stage into a space of glamorous transformation in which the crude and often
brutal realities of Oriental commerce were metamorphosed into a dream of
chivalric heroism and erotic conquest, vicariously transporting its audience
to a scene of projected national triumph. The play's romantic fable is only
superficially escapist, and it would be a great mistake to see either the
romance plot or the theatrical display that embellishes it as simple distractions
from the politics of trade. Instead, the courtship and conquest of the
Moluccan princess Quisara by the Portuguese hero Armusia can be read as
giving a distinctively mercantile twist to a familiar gendered trope of territorial penetration and possession; while the spectacular firings of the town of
Ternata in act 2 and of the fort and palace of Tidore in act 5 appropriate a
recurrent nightmare of East Indian voyaging to create a theatrical emblem of
the moral and technological superiority by means of which English mercantile enterprise proposed to stamp its authority on the world.

Work by Gordon McMullan and Shankar Raman has gone some way
toward resituating *The Island Princess* and *The Sea-Voyage* in the discursive

context of early imperial enterprise to which they belong.[6] In the course of a welcome attempt to rescue Fletcher's oeuvre from the depoliticized world of aristocratic fantasy to which it has traditionally been relegated, McMullan explores the dramatist's interest in the discourse of colonial plantation. His reading of the two plays is skewed, however, by the same Atlantic bias that characterizes a great deal of writing on the literature of early modern imperialism, for he insists upon reading both as contributions to the debate surrounding Virginia Company activities in the New World. This makes some sense in the case of *The Sea-Voyage* where the shipwrecked passengers include the merchant Lamure, who plans to lay out his usurious wealth "To buy new lands and lordships in new countries" (1.1.11) , and the foolish courtiers Morillat and Franville, who dream of colonial enrichment in those "most fertile islands, / Where we had constant promises of all things" (3.1.89–90).[7] These colonial fantasies are set against the unhappy fate of the castaways who inhabit the actual islands where the play is set, "industrious Portugals" who have been driven "From their plantations in the Happy Islands" (5.2.96—7) by the fathers of the play's pirate-heroes, Albert and Raymond. But even here there is actually very little in the play to warrant McMullan's confident assumption of a specifically "American" location; indeed Fletcher takes almost as much care as Shakespeare to divorce his "desert islands" from any identifiable New World setting.[8] Where Shakespeare's lone islander, Caliban, has at least an anagrammatic relation to the natives of the Caribbean, the Amazons of Fletcher's play prove to be no more than shipwrecked Portuguese ladies who have adopted the habit and customs of its reputed but long-vanished indigenes. This odd effacement of the native population might seem like a recognizable strategy of colonial mystification were it not for the fact that, at the end of the play, far from desiring plantation of this new territory, Fletcher's Portuguese and French alike are (like Prospero) eager to "return / To [their] several homes" leaving the islands quite unmarked by their passing (5.4.114–5).

There can be no equivalent here of Prospero's civilizing mission. The play's island is merely an exotic stage on which to play out domestic issues: if the colonial economy intrudes on this fantastic space it is only as the source of "cursed gold" (1.4.87), the "fatal muck" (5.2.140) that infects the denizens of the islands with the distempered greed that drives them to piracy, mutual betrayal, and ultimately to the brink of cannibalism. In this sense *The Sea-Voyage* belongs with the strain of anticolonial propaganda that includes Samuel Daniel's poem "To Prince Henrie," with its scornful attacks on the moral and economic corruptions of New World pelf and its appeal to

Christian conscience against the colonial "inheritance of violence."

By contrast with the deliberate geographic vagueness of *The Sea-Voyage*, *The Island Princess* is assigned to a quite specific East Indian location. If this play bears any of the "clear traces of the American experience" claimed for it by McMullan, it is only, I think, by way of negative reflection, and to discount its highly particularized setting is to dehistoricize it in an important way. It is easy to forget, in the light of subsequent Atlantic history, that the main thrust of English expansion in the sixteenth century had been toward the East, which still bulked more largely on the English imaginative horizon than the New World.[9] And there were good reasons why English audiences in the early 1620s should have felt a quite immediate interest in the world of East Indian merchanting. Shankar Raman's essay returns the play squarely to this historical setting, reading it in the light of Hakluyt's *Principal Navigations* (1589), with its account of Drake's triumphant progress through the East Indian archipelago. For Raman, the play is a meditation on Portuguese decline and English opportunity in which Fletcher "looks at his object, the (hi)story of the Portuguese conquest of the Moluccas, with the present knowledge of England's exclusion from the Indies . . . resurrect[ing], in the names of these known yet faraway places, England's past in the Moluccas."[10] But while nostalgia for Drake's successes is certainly a recurrent theme in accounts of English voyaging in the region, the English in 1621 hardly saw themselves as *excluded* from the East Indies, where the East India Company had operated a number of successful trading factories since 1603. The company was, it is true, approaching the climax of a prolonged struggle for commercial dominance with its Dutch counterpart, but although the Dutch had by this time established a clear strategic advantage, the likely outcome of this rivalry was by no means as clear as it would be only eighteen months later in the wake of the disastrous setback to English fortunes produced by the so-called Massacre of Amboyna in February 1623.

To understand the history of this confrontation—and thereby gain a better sense of what precisely was at stake in the performance of Fletcher's play—we need to turn not to the *Principal Navigations* itself but to Samuel Purchas's sequel, *Hakluytus Posthumus or Purchas his Pilgrimes*, a work that provides the most detailed contemporary commentary on the gathering East Indian crisis. Although *Hakluytus Posthumus* was not published until early 1625, substantial portions of it had already circulated in pamphlet form. And its author (apart from what he had inherited from Hakluyt) must have been collecting material for his monumental folio for some years. Indeed the main East Indian section (pt. 1, bks. 3–5) seems to have been assembled by 1622, within a few months of the court performance of *The Island Princess*.[11] Perhaps the most striking difference between *Hakluytus Posthumus* and its predecessor is the prominence it gives to this material, which is placed at the beginning, in the immediate wake of Purchas's philosophic introduction on the theological and moral justifications of voyaging and merchant enterprise.[12] There was a solid practical reason for this priority: Purchas was working under the direct patronage of the East India Company, which granted him the substantial sum of one hundred pounds for his work.[13] In consequence, for all its scholarly and philosophical pretensions, *Hakluytus Posthumus* has to be seen (at least in part) as a work of company propaganda.[14] Like Fletcher's play, moreover, it seems to have been aimed in the first instance at a court audience, being dedicated to Charles, Prince of Wales (soon to be Charles I), a substantial shareholder in the East India Company, who would have been among the audience for the court performance of *The Island Princess*.[15]

Of course the ambitions of Purchas's book, which presents itself as nothing less than "a History of the World in Sea Voyages and Lande Travels by Englishmen and others," extend well beyond any local propagandistic purpose. As the iconography of its frontispiece suggests, it enshrines a vision of the English nation as the Chosen People, the role of whose navigational prowess is to foster the spread of God's word, the unification of all peoples, and ultimately the accomplishment of the millennial destiny of humankind (see fig. 15). The elaborately engraved frontispiece displays a portrait of the author poised between representations of the Eastern and Western Hemispheres, balancing them as carefully as it balances the competing claims of conquest and trade with the motto "Tam Marte quam Mercurio: soldiers and merchants the world's two eyes to see itself." But the text makes it plain the compiler was more impressed by the benefits of merchanting than of colonization—a preference fully in accord with the prominence given to eastward voyaging over westward discovery and plantation. From a perspective that invites the reader to treat all voyages as allegorical or anagogic performances of holy pilgrimage, it is the merchant rather than the soldier or the colonist who emerges as the truest type of the Christian pilgrim, since peaceable commerce, in Purchas's vision, is best equipped to foster a harmonious and godly unification of humankind.[16] It can do so because its friendly material intercourse reconciles the conflicting claims of that "universal tenure in the universe" that is the God-given birthright of all humanity with the "propriety in . . . peculiar possessions" that sets the bounds of habitation and possession for nations and individuals alike.[17]

15. Frontispiece to Samuel Purchas, Hakluytus Posthumus or Purchas His Pilgrimes *(1625), reprinted by permission of the Folger Shakespeare Library*

Hakluytus Posthumus is framed by a lengthy opening chapter (occupying more than a third of book 1), entitled "A Large Treatise of King Salomons Navie," which uses the voyage to Ophir to vindicate English mercantile ambition. This story is carefully chosen. If Jason's search for the Golden Fleece was the legend most frequently invoked as the type of

New World adventure, then Solomon's quest for the fabulous wealth of Ophir was the foundational myth of eastward navigation. Thus later in *Hakluytus Posthumus* we find John Davis, who visited Sumatra in 1599 and again in 1604, identifying the wealthy kingdom of "Achen" (Aceh) with the goal of Solomon's fleet.[18] For Purchas, the Old Testament story serves to demonstrate that "Merchandising and Sea trade" (unlike the wars of colonial conquest eschewed by the wise Solomon) are "[ap]proved by God's law," because they have the capacity to make "the whole world as one body of mankind" united in faith and amity.[19] Merchant enterprise promises to link

> Solomon and Hiram together, and both with Ophir; the West with the East, and [joining] the remotest . . . parts of the world . . . in one common band of humanity (and why not also of Christianity?) Sidon and Sion, Jew and Gentile, Christian and Ethnic. . . . And this also we hope shall one day be the true Ophirian navigation, when Ophir shall come unto Jerusalem as Jerusalem then went unto Ophir. Meanwhile we see a harmony in this sea-trade, and as it were the consent of other creatures to this consent of the reasonable, united by navigation, howsoever by rites, languages, customs, and countries separated.[20]

If James liked to see himself as the second Solomon, the monarchs of East India unite in Purchas's imagination as the Hiram of this providential union.

"King Salomons Navie" ushers in a brief history of navigation from ancient times, concluding with the circumnavigations of Magellan, Drake, Cavendish, de Noort, Spilbergen, and Schouten.[21] This is followed by three books chronicling English voyages to the East Indies. Part of the importance of the Drake and Cavendish sections is that (along with the fabulous journeys of Bishop Sighelm and Sir John Mandeville) they help to provide a heroic genealogy for English activity in the Spice Islands, predating the monopolistic claims of the Dutch, whom Purchas clearly sees as the principal obstacle to the providential fulfillment of England's mercantile destiny. Even before the first decade of the seventeenth century was over, the Dutch had succeeded the Spanish and Portuguese as the principal European power in the East Indian archipelago, and in the second decade, as the Vereenigde Oostindische Compagnie sought to establish a complete monopoly of the lucrative spice and pepper trade, English ambition had been answered by growing Dutch ruthlessness, often issuing in open hostilities.[22]

Responding to this situation, Purchas edited his material with a conscious eye to the predicament of the East India Company in its conflict with these better-established European rivals. Sometimes going out of his way to secure versions that placed the Dutch in the most unflattering light possible, he annotated his documents with numerous marginalia, drawing attention to their overweening "pride," "spite," perfidy, and "cruelty," to their brutal treatment of the East Indians, and to the doubtful legality of their monopolistic practice, urging his readers to "note that the Hollanders can shew no right to the islands, but *ius in armis*."[23] So virulent were these aspersions that Purchas, no doubt mindful of vaunted Dutch influence at court and the legacy of popular sympathy for Holland, felt the need to preface his book with an apologetic "Note touching the Dutch," disclaiming any "hatred to that nation" as a whole and insisting that his shafts were aimed only at the abuses of individual "Dutch zealots."[24]

Dutch enmity was not the only cause of East India Company anxiety, however; at home its interests were challenged by the skeptical criticisms of influential opponents who believed the luxury trade in spice and pepper could only serve to diminish the store of national wealth—especially since the company had secured a controversial exemption from the law prohibiting the export of bullion.[25] Such were the arguments advanced by pamphleteers like Robert Kayll in *The Trades Increase* (1615)—its title playing sardonically on the name of Sir Henry Middleton's ill-fated flagship in the catastrophic voyage of 1611. Kayll's attack provoked fierce legal reprisals from the company and triggered a campaign by company apologists, notably Sir Dudley Digges who, in *The Defence of Trade* (1615), denounces Kayll's work as an ill-informed "invective . . . against the East-Indian Trade."[26] Digges's arguments demonstrating that the company's activities actually resulted in a substantial surplus of imported over exported bullion were taken up again and elaborated by Thomas Mun in a series of sophisticated pamphlets published in the 1620s, one of which, the combative *Discourse of Trade from England unto the East Indies; Answering to divers Objections which are usually made against the same* (1621), Purchas selected to conclude his section on voyaging in the East Indian archipelago.[27] His reason for placing it in this decisive position is clear enough: the debate had been rejoined in the 1620s precisely because things had gone so badly for the company in the years since Kayll's attack. Profits, which despite the disastrous outcome of some voyages, had averaged 155 percent in the period 1601–12, declined to 87 percent in the years 1613–23; and from 1615 onward they came under particularly acute threat as conflict with the Dutch escalated in the Spice Islands of Banda and the Moluccas. By mid-1621 things had come to such a pass that the company faced proposals for dissolution.[28]

In this context, Fletcher's decision to locate his new play in the Moluccas can hardly have been an innocent choice. From the time of its first voyage the company had cast envious eyes on the clove and nutmeg islands of Ternata and Tidore, whose historic rivalry (as Fletcher's play reminds us) competing European powers had long exploited to their own advantage. Here the English endeavored to capitalize on favorable local memories of Drake's visit, in the course of which the King of Ternata had allegedly made an offer to put his kingdom under Elizabeth's protection.[29] However, despite some early flickers of interest on the part of the present king, who was suspicious of Dutch designs, the company found it impossible to gain a foothold in the Moluccas and instead concentrated its efforts on the adjacent islands of the Banda group, notably Pooloway (Pulo Ai) and Poolaroon (Pula Run), which in 1616 formally surrendered sovereignty to the English crown. Here the English apparently succeeded in ingratiating themselves with the islanders by persuading them that "our Nation . . . desired not to usurp, and bring them in subjection, or bondage, as the Hollanders and other Nations [had] formerly." Banda, however, was to prove, in Purchas's words "almost the bane, and as it were the Trojan Horse to our Indian Ilium, whence an Iliad of miseries and mischiefs . . . issued to that Society whereby their wonted gains [were] suspended." For here too their position was fiercely disputed by the Dutch who claimed absolute rights both through the alleged suzerainty of the King of Ternata (by now their puppet) and also on the basis of a separate treaty concluded with the Bandanese themselves in 1609. Regular attacks on English shipping, destruction of goods and property, and the maltreatment and public humiliation of English prisoners ensued, leading to a state resembling open warfare by mid-1619 when the principal English factor at Pula Run wrote to his superiors in Bantam complaining of the "intolerable pride and tyranny, that the Hollander useth in these parts upon us both, in bodies, and name . . . [and] the great outrage and infamy they have offered us . . . both in disgraceful speeches to our king and nation, and in their barbarous tyranny they have used to our weak forces, being captivated by them."[30]

In July of that year, after extensive negotiations, the rival companies signed a treaty of alliance agreeing to a division of the spoils of trade. But although this treaty substantially favored the Dutch, their commanders generally ignored its provisions except to levy English assistance against the

Portuguese and recalcitrant indigenes. "They saw," as a company pamphleteer expressed it, "[that] they could not make their reckoning to any purpose unless they utterly drove the English out of the trade of those parts; thereby to have the whole and sole traffic of the commodities . . . and so to make the price at their pleasure, sufficient to maintain and promote their conquests."[31] Attacks on English shipping and factories therefore continued unabated. In February 1620 the Dutch captured and burned the town of Lantore (Lonthor), where "Master Randall and other two English standing by the company's goods were taken and stripped to their skins, bound, beaten, thrown over the town wall; and carried aboard the general, and put in chains."[32] Then in October 1620 a Dutch fleet overran the last Bandanese factory of the English company at Pula Run and commenced a genocidal slaughter of the Bandanese hosts. Throughout 1620 and 1621 merchants who had suffered losses at the hands of the Dutch since the signing of the treaty petitioned the king and Privy Council for redress. In late 1621 the company, "imploring the Privy Council to observe how the Dutch have broken the treaty," dispatched two commissioners, Sir Dudley Digges and its deputy governor, Morris Abbott, to treat with the authorities in the Hague.[33] These negotiations finally broke down in early February 1622, and within a year the company's enterprise in the Spice Islands would be effectually snuffed out by the brutal *coup de main* against the Amboyna factory— an outrage still unredressed at the time of the Second Dutch War when Dryden staged its atrocities as part of a new propaganda campaign against Holland.

Such, then, was the charged context in which Fletcher's Moluccan drama was played before King James—a context that no doubt helped to preserve its popularity into the Restoration, where it was among the more frequently performed and adapted of Fletcher's plays. At first sight, it is true, *The Island Princess* seems distinguished mainly by the care with which it appears to distance itself from current politics (in striking contrast to Middleton's nearly contemporary *Game at Chess*, for example). The plot, based (sometimes very closely but with a number of highly significant departures) upon Le Seigneur de Bellan's novella *L'Histoire de Ruis Dias, et de Quixaire, Princess des Moloques* (1615), derives ultimately from a history of early Portuguese enterprise in the archipelago, Bartolome Leonando de Argensola's *Conquista de las Islas Molucas* (1609), a work Fletcher may have known at first hand. Concerned primarily with the erotic rivalry of a pair of gallant Portuguese soldiers for the hand of the Tidorian princess Quisara, de Bellan's novella seems as unconcerned with national rivalries as it is indifferent to the material realities of the spice trade. Nevertheless, there are ways in which the piece is particularly well attuned to promoting court enthusiasm for East Indian adventure. While there were still intermittent hostilities between English and Portuguese in the East Indies, these were completely overshadowed by the fierce contest with the Dutch, and it is possible to detect a certain identificatory nostalgia for Portuguese adventure in *Hakluytus Posthumus*, in whose vision (as James Boon puts it) "if Portugal had been the Prophet of the arts of Navigation, Britain was to be the Savior." By locating his action in the era of Portuguese dominance, the dramatist could at once protect himself against the Dutch faction in court (whose hostility even Purchas would attempt to beg off) and offer a pattern for the triumph of English mercantile adventure.[34]

— ✤ —

"A RECOMPENSE SO RICH"

The plot of Fletcher's play centers on competition for the hand of Quisara, Princess of Tidore, among a group of Portuguese and East Indian suitors, including the neighboring rulers of Bakam, Siana, and Ternata, the Portuguese captain Ruy Dias, and their newly arrived countryman, the "noble and daring" Armusia. In a radical departure from de Bellan's novel, Armusia takes the place of the young Tidorian aristocrat, Salama, as the hero of the piece. In de Bellan it is Salama who rescues the captive King of Tidore, confounds his Portuguese rivals, wins the love of Quixaire, and shortly afterward succeeds to her brother's throne. In Fletcher these feats are transferred to Armusia, except that the narrative concludes not with the hero's assumption of the Tidorian throne but with the religious conversion of the royal house. Having previously sought to persuade her lover to "change your religion, / And be of one belief with me" (4.5.34–5), Quisara is so moved by the steadfastness of his faith in the face of torture and martyrdom that she elects to "embrace [his] faith . . . [and] fortune" (5.2.121). Her gesture in turn leaves her brother also "half persuaded . . . to be a Christian" (5.5.66), and the play ends with the king's proclaiming a "peace" that resembles a fulfillment of Purchas's millenarian vision: "No more guns now, nor hates, but joys and triumphs, / And universal gladness fly about us" (5.5.90–1).[35]

As McMullan observes, Fletcher's alteration of the plot, by displacing a native with a foreign husband, transforms the meaning of the story and gives a distinctively colonial twist to its sexual politics. Indeed McMullan reads the play's romantic ending with its "thoroughgoing sexual and familial infiltration of Moluccan culture by the Portuguese" as a conscious refashioning of the classic narrative of "colonial intermarriage" (p. 224) and "appropriation through 'legitimate' inheritance" (p. 230)—the wedding of the Algonquin Princess Pocahontas to the Virginia planter John Rolfe. But there is, I think, no necessary reason why contemporaries should have understood the Quisara plot in quite this way. The feminization of exotic territory, as Patricia Parker and Louis Montrose have taught us, was a recurrent feature of early modern colonialist discourse.[36] And one might argue that in its own time the power of the Pocahontas story itself was less that of an originary New World myth than of an exceptionally vivid literalization of a pervasive colonial trope—that of European voyager or colonist as predestined husband come to claim the feminized body of the land. This, though seemingly best fitted, by its underlying quibble on "husbandry," to the agricultural projects of Irish or Virginian plantation, was in practice just as readily mobilized in the service of Guianese gold-hunting or East Indian merchanting. *Connubium*, as James Boon points out, was the necessary complement of *commercium*, in a perpetuated alliance of kings such as Purchas dreamed of in the East Indies. For Boon "Purchas's symbology of East/West reciprocal relations remained incomplete and therefore transitory" precisely because of the absence of this connubial ideal: "The marriage of Thames and Ganges . . . was not even imagined."[37] In point of fact, however, the trope of marriage is widespread in *Hakluytus Posthumus*, where it is deployed not merely in reference to the "virgin" territory of Virginia but as a way of figuring mercantile desire in East India. Always implicit in this trope and part of its strategic attractiveness is the idea of the colonial "husband" as appointed guardian of his bride's honor, bound to defend it against the violent assaults of less temperate rivals. Thus, just as Purchas will justify the expropriation of American territory by claiming that "Virginia was violently ravished by her own ruder natives," so he represents the Dutch conquest of Banda as an assault upon "a rich and beautiful bride [who] was once envied to English arms, and seemeth by the cries on both sides, to have been lately ravished from her new husband, unwarned, unarmed, I know not whither by greater force or fraud."[38] Humphrey Fitzherbert similarly figures the loss of Pula Run as a species of rape, whose dishonor the East India Company is bound to restore: "Poolaroon (in imitation of her sisters, the other islands) is turned Dutch. There was in her neither pleasure nor profit, yet the ambitious King Coen hath made a conquest of her chastity. The civil law denieth a violent rape to be incontinency, because although the body be forced, the mind may yet be free. Recall her again and right this uncivil outrage by your wise and civil censure."[39]

Half a century later Dryden would make similar use of the trope in *Amboyna*, where the Dutch usurpation of English commercial privilege is figured in Young Harman's rape of Ysabinda, the newly acquired Amboynese bride of the heroic English factor Gabriel Towerson—whose marriage is fittingly described as his "golden day" (3.3. p. 47).[40]

In Fitzherbert, if the principal Dutch commander is cast as the usurping "King Coen," the island of Amboyna itself is represented as "queen" of the Spice Islands: "Amboyna sitteth as Queen between the isles of Banda and the Moluccas; she is beautified with the fruits of several Factories, and dearly beloved of the Dutch. . . . Neptune is her darling, and entertained in her very bosom." A passage such as this is sufficient to alert us to the subdued quibble in the very title of *The Island Princess;* where Fletcher's romance differs from *Hakluytus Posthumus*, however, is that it appears to render the trope literal in its identification of the rich territory of Tidore with the body of its princess, Quisara.[41]

From the beginning Fletcher's Portuguese imagine their national enterprise in erotically charged language that will have sounded wholly familiar to English ears. Pyniero celebrates his country's natural propensity to "bring . . . forth / Stirring unweary souls to seek adventures" (1.3.6–8), and the hint of sexual excitement in *stirring* is taken up in his fantasy of exotic territories that willingly open themselves to the exploitative embrace of their discoverers: "Where time is, and the sun gives light, brave countrymen, our names are known, new worlds *disclose* their *riches*, their *beauties*, and their *prides* to our *embraces*. And we the first of nations find these wonders" (1.3.9–11; emphasis added). The newly arrived Armusia evokes the landscape in a rapturous display of the rhetorical technique known as *enargeia* or *evidentia* that instinctively assimilates the "beauties" of Moluccan women with the "riches" of an earthly "Paradise," "where every wind that rises blows perfumes" (1.3.17–20).[42] Transformed by his autoptic vision, the stage becomes a *locus amoenus* whose seductive welcome recalls the sensual delights of Raleigh's Guiana:[43]

We are arrived among the Blessed Islands,
Where every wind that tides blows perfumes,
And every breath of air is like an incense:
The treasure of the sun dwells here; each tree,
As if it envied the old Paradise,
Strives to bring forth immortal fruit; the spices
Renewing nature. . . .
The very rivers as we float along
Throw up their pearls, curl their heads to court us;
The bowels of the earth swell with the births
Of thousand unknown gems, and thousand riches;
Nothing that bears a life, but brings a treasure.
 1.3.16–31

In the context of such images, the love-plot of *The Island Princess*—with its triangular contest between Quisara's native suitors, the established foreign commander (and "ruler" of the princess's affections) Ruy Dias, and the gallant newcomer, Armusia—asks to be read as a struggle for control of the islands's material resources.[44] Indeed Pyniero goads his uncle, Ruy Dias, by describing Armusia's successful courtship of Quisara precisely as if it were a mercantile success: Armusia "has ended his market before you be up . . . and tied the bargain, / Dealt like a man indeed, stood not demurring, / But clapped close to the cause" (2.6.63–6. The repeated stress on Armusia's tactical weakness as "a stranger," "a gentleman scarce landed, / Scarce eating of the air here, not acquainted" (2.6.64, 80, 70–1) emphasizes how this struggle mirrors the shifting and uneasy relationship between native East Indians, the established Dutch company, and their intrusive English rivals.[45]

The loose correspondence between English-Dutch rivalry and the erotic competition of Fletcher's Portuguese factions is complicated, however, by the displacement of some alleged Dutch characteristics onto the villainous Governor of Ternata—a displacement that reveals something of the deeply conflicted nature of English attitudes toward the Hollanders. In a significant departure from de Bellan, Fletcher expands the role given to the King of Tidore's traditional enemy, the King of Ternata, transforming him from rivalrous prince to Machiavellian villain and renaming him "Governor"—a title calculated to remind viewers of Ternata's current subservience to Dutch power, and so to suggest a congruence between his politic ambitions and the machinations of the Hollanders. Unlike the virtuous Armusia, who specifically declines to "force" the affections of Quisara (2.6.163), the Governor is presented as a would-be rapist whose capture of Quisara's brother puts him in a position to "take her" with "a compelled or forced affection" (1.1.80–1). And just as company propaganda denigrated the Dutch as ambitious "usurpers" of both English rights and East Indian authority, so the legitimacy of the Governor's power will be denounced by the King of Tidore at the end of the play: "His island we shall seize into our hands, / His father and himself have both *usurped* it" (5.5.78–9; emphasis added). At the same time the King's award of the Governor's town and castle to Pyniero comes near to legitimating another reading of a familiar colonial sort, according to which their "heathen policy" (5.1.50) exposes the recalcitrant natives as usurpers of their own territories, which they are thereby bound to surrender to the invader—this potentially awkward implication is however kept in check by the final installation of the King of Tidore as sovereign ruler of both islands.[46]

Fletcher's use of rival groups of Portuguese to reflect the competition of Dutch and English merchant interests is likely to confuse modern readers, but would have been readily licensed by the way in which the English (much as they may have resented the East Indian propensity to confuse the two nations) habitually conceived of their relation with the Dutch as a species of emulous brotherhood, founded in their long history of alliance against Catholic Spain.[47] Thus the Bantam factor Edmund Scott declared of the Hollanders that "though we were mortal enemies in our trade, in all other matters we were friends, and would have lived and died one for the other."[48] In *The Island Princess*, Armusia's courtship of Quisara provokes the mortal enmity of Ruy Dias who denounces him (in language that echoes Dutch resentment of English intruders) as "that new thing, that stranger, / That flag stuck up to rob me of mine honor" (3.1.43–4). Ruy Dias duly conspires with his nephew Pyniero to have his rival "taken off" (l. 62) and then provokes a duel that drives Armusia into wry reflection on their sibling rivalry: "Strange dearth of enemies, / When we seek foes among ourselves" (4.3.10–11). Yet like Scott's mercantile competitors, they prove ready enough to live and die for one another when the machinations of the governor unite the various Moluccan forces against the foreigners, and Armusia ends the play with a gracious acknowledgment of the "brave Ruy Dias" to whom he owes "my life, my wife and honor" (5.5.85–7).

If the rival Portuguese factions are joined by this common determination to resist the "villainies" of their East Indian enemies in their plot "to blow us with a vengeance out o' th' islands" (5.1.8–11), they are at the same time set apart by the very different attitudes that condition their relationships with the native population. Pyniero's opening speech urges his guards to keep "Their vigilant eyes fixed on these islanders. / They are a false and desperate people, when they find / The least occasion open to encouragement, / Cruel and crafty souls, believe me, gentlemen" (1.1.3–6). Armusia, by contrast, discovers in them a people "brave too, civil mannered, / Proportioned like the masters of great minds" (1.3.33–4). Much later, as he faces martyrdom for his refusal to change religion, Armusia will himself denounce the Moluccans as "base malicious people" (5.5.32), only to apologize a few lines later, "for I was once angry, / And out of that might utter some distemper" (5.5.72–3).

Pyniero's suspicion of East Indian craft and duplicity was, of course, by no means alien to English discourse about the region. Edmund Scott, for example, exhibits an almost paranoid obsession with the "subtleties," "villainies," "treasons," and habitual "dissembling" of the Javans. Nevertheless it became increasingly important to the self-justification of English ambitions that they should represent themselves as sympathetic friends to the natives, in contrast to the overweening Hollanders with their "intolerable pride and tyranny."[49] English sympathy and Dutch tyranny, as company propaganda had it, flowed naturally from the different designs of the two nations—the English desiring friendly commerce, where the Dutch sought conquest and control. Thus the 1624 East India Company pamphlet *A True Relation of the Vnivst, Crvell, and Barbarovs Proceedings against the English at Amboyna* boasts of "the different end and design of the English and Dutch Companies. . . . The English being subjects of a peaceable prince, that hath enough of his own, and is therewith content, without affecting of new acquests; have aimed at nothing in their East-India trade, but a lawful and competent gain by commerce and traffic with the people of those parts." Even when sovereignty was ceded by a local ruler to enable them to protect their trade, the company insisted, they would strive to respect and preserve local law, custom, and privilege, while "on the other side, the Netherlanders, from the beginning of their trade in the Indies, not contented with the ordinary course of a fair and free commerce, invaded divers islands, took some forts, built others, and laboured nothing more, than the conquests of countries, and the acquiring of new dominions."[50]

In this context it is significant that whereas Ruy Dias and his nephew Pyniero are represented as captains of the military garrison, Armusia's appears to be a civilian role—a contrast that is given considerable symbolic

weight when he and his companions achieve the feat of which their complacent soldier-rivals prove incapable and effect the rescue of the King of
Tidore by donning "habits like to merchants" in order to penetrate the
enemy's stronghold (1.3.242).

In act 2, scene 2 Armusia and his followers enter "like merchants, armed
underneath" to reflect on the success with which "policy" has prepared the
way for "manly force" (ll. 16–17): "Suspectless have I travelled all the town
through, and in this merchant's shape won much acquaintance, surveyed
each strength and place that may befriend us, viewed all his magazines, got
perfect knowledge of where the prison is, and what power guards it. . . . No
man suspecting what I am but merchant" (2.2.10–14, 44).

Then in the following scene the "merchants house," which they have
occupied, becomes the instrument for firing the governor's adjacent magazine and castle, enabling Armusia's successful raid upon the prison. One
way of reading this piece of action (which Fletcher embroidered upon
de Bellan's rather bare plot) is as a fable of mercantile chivalry, designed
(like the Belmont plot in Shakespeare's *Merchant of Venice*/Venus) to put
a gloss of nobility and romance upon the base world of commerce
and thereby to answer the play's own carefully posed question about the
limits of honorable behavior.[51] Act 1 opens with a discussion of East
Indian manners in which Pyniero and Christophero express puzzlement
at the King of Tidore's recreations, wondering how such "base pleasures, /
As tugging at an oar, or skill in steerage" can possibly "become princes"
(1.1.16–18):

❈

PYNIERO:
Base breedings love base pleasure;
They take as much delight in a baratto,
A little scurvy boat, to row her tightly,
And have the art to turn and wind her nimbly,
Think it as noble too, though it be slavish,
And a dull labor that declines a gentleman:
As we Portugals, or the Spaniards do in riding,
In managing a great horse which is princely,
The French in courtship, or the dancing English
In carrying a fair presence.
    1.1.18–27

In act 2, however, the king's "little scurvy boat" will have its counterpart in the vessel that ensures Armusia's "prosperous passage" to and from Ternata on the pretended merchant adventure whose "purchase" he claims in such strikingly materialist language:

There is reward above my action too by millions:
A recompense so rich and glorious,
I durst not dream it mine. . . .
It was her open promise to that man
That durst redeem ye; beauty set me on,
And fortune crowns me fair, if she receive me.
      2.6.141–57

"Well," confesses Pyniero, "he's a brave fellow, and . . . has deserved her *richly*" (l. 188; emphasis added). Thus Armusia's rescue of the king is figured as a piece of consciously commercial enterprise, but one that reveals the inherent honor and bravery of its chivalrous factor. This is a trade that ennobles rather than degrades—a trade moreover that is squarely identified with the honor of the nation that pursues it, as Pyniero makes clear when he summons his uncle to Armusia's aid: "Now to make those believe, that held you backward and an ill instrument, you are a gentleman, an honest man, and you dare love your nation, dare stick to virtue though she be oppressed . . . now redeem and vindicate your honor" 5.1.58–64.

In this way *The Island Princess* seems well calculated to serve the purposes of a company whose propaganda sought to identify its own mercantile interests with the honor and "fame of the English nation."[52] At the same time, however, the play runs the danger of disclosing the more aggressive designs that were typically entangled with mercantile voyaging. Indeed one might argue that Armusia's stratagem against the Ternatans rather awkwardly confirms the charges levied against the Portuguese by their governor. Assuming the mantle of a pagan prophet, he seeks to turn the King of Tidore against the intruders with a remarkable piece of anticolonial invective. They first arrived, he claims, as abject suitors to their island hosts: "These men came hither as my vision tells me. Poor, weatherbeaten, almost lost, starved, feebled; their vessels like themselves, most miserable; made a long suit for traffic, and for comfort, to vent their children's toys, cure their diseases."[53]

But once established, they used their commercial foothold to prosecute their imperial ambitions:

> They had their suit, they landed, and to th' rate
> Grew rich and powerful, sucked the fat and freedom
> Of this most blessed isle, taught her to tremble;
> Witness the castle here, the citadel,
> They have clapped upon the neck of your Tidore,
> This happy town, till that she knew these strangers.
> 4.1.44–54[54]

However, the governor's insistence that the Portuguese pursuit of "traffic" has simply served as a Trojan horse, concealing their hegemonic ambitions, is ironized by the fact that he is himself disguised at this point in the play, employing his priestly persona to penetrate the enemy's walls and to advance his own plot against Tidore.[55] Thus he masks his tyrannical designs in very much the way the Dutch were supposed to have masked theirs by libeling the English—presenting them, according to the King of Ternata, as usurpers who "came not as peaceable merchants, but to dispossess us of our kingdoms."[56] The play's comic catastrophe is precipitated by an act of emblematic "discovery" in which Pyniero strips off the false prophet's "beard and hair" to demonstrate the fraudulence of his "holy shape" (5.5.52–62). At the same time Fletcher abbreviates his source-narrative in a fashion that conveniently blurs the awkward issues of royal succession and territorial power attached to the marriage of Quisara. Since the king remains alive and firmly ensconced on the twin thrones of Ternata and Tidore, the princess's betrothal to Armusia need stand for nothing more than the amity and "universal gladness" promised by the propagandists of commerce.

"MORE TEMPERATE LESSONS"

In converting de Bellan's novella into a narrative of miscegenation, Fletcher established a convenient metaphor for the "bond of humanity" by which Purchas's "Ophirian Navigation" would unite the peoples of the earth in mercantile bliss. Inevitably he also raised the specter of "degeneration," which is a persistent theme in the colonial discourse of the period—a specter whose presence becomes especially threatening when, following their initial betrothal, Quisara urges Armusia to change religions. The pages of *Hakluytus Posthumus* are haunted by anxiety about Europeans who abandon their faith or "turn Moor"—the standard phrase suggesting that religious apostasy is actually imagined as a kind of "racial" transformation or degeneration.[57] Racial anxiety is a factor even in the source, where actual miscegenation is avoided. De Bellan takes pains to justify the infatuation of Quixaire's Portuguese suitors by reassuring his readers that they should not imagine the beauty of East Indian females as darkened by "une couleur basanee [sun-burnt, swarthy], ou tout à fait More-Couleur [Moor-colored]," since the women are careful to keep out of the sun and therefore remain (unlike their men) "extremement blanches" [extremely fair], while their hair (in a telling analogy) is "de la mesme couleur de l'or qu'on nous apporte de leurs contrees" [the same color as the gold that is brought to us from their lands].[58]

Early in *The Island Princess* Christophero is made to remark in similar terms on the princess's admirable fairness:

> The very sun, I think, affects her sweetness,
> And dares not as he does to all else, dye it
> Into his tawny livery.
>   1.1.60–2

Here, however, the issue is not so easily erased, and Pyniero cynically implies that there is something unnatural about the princess's "wear[ing] her complexion in a case," because if exposed to the sun's kisses it would so readily convert to a dusky hue: "let him but like it / A week or two, or three, she would look like a lion" (ll. 63–4). As it turns out, the crisis of act 4 will present Armusia with the illusion of just such a racialized metamorphosis: at the point when Quisara urges her lover to forsake his faith, her beauty is suddenly transformed in his eyes to a black ugliness that "looks like death itself" (4.5.104). The racial suggestiveness of this simile is confirmed in the following act, where a penitent Quisara recognizes in the fairness of Armusia's countenance a sign of the purity of his religion:

> your faith, and your religion must be like ye,
> They that can show you these, must be our mirrors;

When the streams flow clear and fair, what are the fountains?
5.1.118–20

A few lines later she will denounce her brother for what she describes as his "foul swart ingratitude" toward Armusia's "fair virtue"—a darkening of his moral self that has, she proclaims, "taken off thy sweetness . . . [and] turned thee devil" (5.2.46–51).[59]

Color, religion, and virtue, then, are imagined in Fletcher's play as virtually interchangeable markers of difference, and as we might expect from contemporary imperial and colonial discourse, "temperance" is the moral attribute that more than any other distinguishes the "manly" virtue of the hero. It raises him above the violent jealousy of Ruy Dias (4.3.28) and is prominent among the qualities that earn the love and admiration of Quisara and the king. It was, of course, by their superior temperance that Raleigh's English would distinguish themselves from their intemperate Spanish rivals and infallibly earn the admiration and allegiance of the natives of Guiana. "Navigation" itself, Purchas would argue, was inherently linked to this virtue as "a school of sobriety and temperance"—for though the sea's riches might sometimes "make men's minds sea-sick, wavering, inconstant, distempered and . . . subject to tempestuous temptations," yet the sea itself "holds them in good temper, and is a correction house to the most dissolute; but the land makes them forget the sea and temperance altogether."[60] Typically, of course, the "sun-burnt" peoples of the tropics were supposed to be deficient in this cool quality. In Shakespeare's tragedy of imperial degeneration, for example, the "tawny" Cleopatra is the very embodiment of Oriental intemperance— a woman who, according to her Roman detractors, causes the hero's heart to "renege . . . all temper" (*Antony and Cleopatra*, 1.1.8) and earns from him the bitter rebuke "Though you can guess what temperance should be, / You know not what it is" (3.13.122).

In *The Island Princess* Philo's opening denunciation of Antony's intemperate dotage has its equivalent in Pyniero's satiric incredulity at his uncle's passion for Quisara:

that he
That would drink nothing to depress the spirit,
But milk and water, eat nothing but thin air
To make his blood obedient, that this youth
In spite of all his temperance, should tickle

And have the love-mange on him.
1.1.103–8

At the same time he sneers sarcastically at the hot-tempered King of Siana, one of Ruy Dias's local rivals, as "he that's wise and temperate" (1.1.57). As it turns out, however, temperance in *The Island Princess*, though it certainly establishes a clear hierarchy of virtue, proves not to be an absolute marker of distinction between Eastern vice and Western virtue. To the contrary, it is precisely their admiration for temperate behavior that raises Quisara and her royal brother above the "fierce . . . unfaithful" governor, the intemperate East Indian princes, and the distempered populace of "barbarous slaves" (5.1.19). These are rulers fitted to belong to Purchas's imagined "panorama of legitimate monarchy . . . with James I (or . . . Charles I) at its apostolic center."[61] The king impresses even his Moorish captors by his capacity to "look . . . temperately. . . . No wildness, no distempered touch upon him" (2.1.38–40), while his sister actively seeks to temper the wild extravagances of her court. Quisara's first entry is to calm her brawling East Indian suitors. Urging them to "be tempered / Or . . . no more . . . my servants," she proclaims that any man who hopes to win her "Must put his hasty rage off, and put on / A well confirmed, a temperate, and true valour" (1.3.116–7, 127–8). Disapproving of Ruy Dias's jealous distemper (3.3.127), she is ultimately won by Armusia's demonstrations of temperance to embrace his religion and to share the martyrdom it seems about to earn him:

I have touched ye every way, tried ye most honest,
Perfect, and good, chaste, blushing-chaste, and temperate,
Valiant, without vainglory, modest, staid,
No rage, or light affection ruling in you:
Indeed the perfect school of worth I find ye,
The temple of true honor.
5.2.111–16

By the same token it is the violence and cruelty of the pretended "priest" that encourages Quisara's waiting-woman, Panura, to betray the disguised governor to Pyniero: "Sure he's a cruel man," she declares, "methinks religion / Should teach more temperate lessons" (5.4.27–8). If temperance is the quality that separates Christian from pagan worlds, it is nevertheless East Indian tractability to Western tempering that warrants Armusia's identification of these people as "civil mannered, / Proportioned like the masters of great minds" (1.3.32–3).

— ✿ —

"FLAMES SO IMPERIOUS"

Closely related to the play's idealization of cool temperance is its elaborate troping of fire, which has a complex and slightly paradoxical valency. The flames that visibly ravage Fletcher's East Indian landscape are at once material and immaterial: literal effects of European technological power and figurations of the destructive power of inflamed passion. Fire is, from one point of view, the symbolic opposite of temperance—a signature of the uncontrolled barbarity associated with the island world of pagan sun-worship; yet it can also be used to discipline that barbarity as the sympathetic instrument of temperance. It stands for a passion that may briefly "distemper" the agents of mercantile empire and their native allies, but it can also stand for the trials that will help to perfect their temper, as steel is tempered in the swordsmith's furnace.

There is a small hint for this in the source, where the fires of Salama's diversionary arson in Ternata seem to be mirrored in the description of Peynere's passion for the princess ("le feu secret qu'il nourrissoit dans son coeur" [the secret fire that he nourished in his heart).[62] But in *The Island Princess*, where Fletcher's plot elaborates de Bellan's cursory account of Salama's Ternata escapade into two climactic episodes of firing, flames both metaphoric and literal break out everywhere. The first of these episodes involves Armusia's raid on Ternata (2.2–5), and the second Ruy Dias's and Pyniero's assault on the town and palace of Tidore (5.1–5), as well as the fiery torture the governor intends to impose on Armusia ("Make the fires ready," 5.2.104). In the first, fire spreads through Ternata ("pox o' their paper-houses, how they . . . light like candles, how the roar still rises," 2.3.35–6), menacing the governor's powder magazine (ll. 37–8), spreading to his seat of power ("The castle now begins to flame" l. 42), sowing panic in the town (2.4–5), and threatening to consume its citizen's stock of "wealth" (2.3.60–1) with its "imperious" flames. In the second, the "fire-spitting" Portuguese bombardment of Tidore "push[es] down palaces, and toss[es] . . . little habitations like whelps" (5.3.2, 14–15), alternately enraging and terrifying the citizenry ("A vengeance fire 'em. . . . Come, let's do anything to appease this thunder," ll. 11, 33–4).[63]

Here the play seems to be responding to more immediate English experience of the East Indian world, for the danger of fire in the flimsily constructed towns of Java and the Spice Islands is a recurrent preoccupation in the East Indian sections of *Hakluytus Posthumus*—notably in Scott's *Exact Discourse* where it acquires nightmarish significance.[64] In the factor's anxious imagination, fire figures primarily as a native weapon, a characteristic instrument of those "subtleties," "policies," and "treasons" by which the enemies of the English sought to undermine and destroy their trade. In the most terrifying of these episodes, a group of Javan and Chinese thieves, whom Scott punningly describes as "eight *firebrands* of hell," undermined the English factory from a neighboring house and, as they endeavored to burn their way through the floor, inadvertently set fire to the building, destroying quantities of goods and nearly setting off some barrels of gunpowder.[65] Taking their revenge for this fright with gloating exactitude, the English merchants turned their persecutors' own weapon back upon them, torturing them with fire, as if determined to prove themselves masters of the very instrument with which their enemies had threatened to destroy them.[66]

It is possible, I think, to trace a recollection of this reversal in *The Island Princess*, where Armusia, working from the cellar of his "merchant's house next joining" (2.4.11), prepares for his raid on the king's prison cell by setting fire to the governor's storehouse, "Where all his treasure lies, his arms, his women" (2.2.28). The striking parallels with the attack on Scott's storehouse are emphasized by the citizens' outrage at this "treason" of a "neighbour." And in the bawdy dialogue of act 2, scene 4 there is a distinct implication that the Ternatans are burned with the fire of their own intemperance:

🏵

2 CITIZEN:
I have been burnt at both ends like a squib. . . . Give me whole tuns of drink, whole cisterns; for I have four dozen of fine firebrands in my belly, I have more smoke in my mouth, than would bloat a hundred herrings. Thy husband's happy, though he was roasted, and now he's basting of himself at all points; the clerk and he are cooling their pericraniums— Body o' me, neighbours! there's fire in my codpiece. . . . I fry like a burnt marrow-bone . . . run, wenches, run . . . run as the fire were in your tails.[67]

2.4.3–46

❀

This suggestion of vindictive symmetry is made even more apparent in the second episode where "the *fire-brand*" prophecy of the disguised governor, as it "fires" and fans the king's rage, seems to have literally ignited the flames now consuming the city (5.4.28). The efforts of the false prophet and his followers "blow [the strangers] with a vengeance out o' th' islands," and their attempt to sacrifice Armusia to "the fires" of torture are then met with the fiery counterblast of gunpowder, through which (as in the case of Scott's burning of the Chinese "firebrand" Hinting) the intruders use fire to cast out fire. Responding to the threat of Armusia's execution, Pyniero declares

> They dare as soon take fire and swallow it, take stakes and thrust into
> their tails for clysters. . . . I have physic in my hand for 'em shall give
> the goblins such a purge. . . .
> Let [the fort] but spit fire finely. . . .
> [we'll send 'em] fine potatoes
> Roasted in gunpowder, such a banquet sir
> We'll prepare their unmannerly stomachs.
>   5.1.40–6, 69–77

Again and again in the play these material flames are treated as though they were allegoric displays of the psychological states of those who produce them. Thus Ruy Dias, stung by jealousy at the "blaze" of Armusia's honor after his triumphant arson in Ternata (3.1.54), brags of the "fire" that burns in his own "brave thoughts" (4.3.31–4). In the last act his followers similarly boast that they are "all on fire" for their incendiary assault on the recalcitrant Ternatans (5.1.80), while Panura accuses the disguised governor of fanning the king's vindictive flames against Armusia and his compatriots: "he fires him on still, / And when he cools enrages him" (5.4.3–4). These are stock metaphors, of course, but they are given a special charge by the scenes that give such spectacular theatrical emphasis to the troping of fire.[68]

Flames do not simply express the firestorms of ungoverned passion, however. Just as fire is used on the literal level to overcome fire, so on the metaphoric level it is identified with emotional states to which, provided they are moderated by a temperate self-control, the romantic plot gives complete endorsement. Quisara, for example, blames Ruy Dias for his "cold" reluctance to "fly like fire" to her brother's rescue (1.3.158), while

Pyniero flatters the princess herself as "the eye . . . From which all hearts take fire" (3.1.241–3). And Quisara's conversion to Christianity is imaged in a figure that imagines the bonfire of martyrdom ignited by the tinder of erotic passion—

> I feel a sparkle here,
> A lively spark that kindles my affection,
> And tells me it will rise to flames of glory.
>   5.2.122–4

Even more strikingly, in a fashion reminiscent of the weird punning inspired by Scott's obsession with fire ("I thought I would burn him a little, for we were in the heat of our anger"), Armusia envisages his torching of the governor's town as though it were the literal expression of his fiery passion for the princess:[69]

> The fire I brought here with me shall do something
> Shall burst into material flames and bright ones,
> That all the island shall stand wond'ring at it,
> As if they had been stricken with a comet:
> Powder is ready, and enough to work it,
> The match is left a-fire; all, all hushed and locked close,
> No man suspecting what I am but merchant:
> An hour hence, my brave friends, look for the fury,
> The fire to light us to our honoured purpose.
>   2.3.38–47

The literal flame that razes the East Indian towns of *The Island Princess* is, in the end, an instrument of a European technology that controls and manages its violent effects precisely as temperance controls, manages, and directs the fiery tempests of inward passion. But in the marvelously telling metamorphosis of love's fire into the "material flames" of Ternata, Fletcher's language discloses the links between sexual desire, mercantile greed, and imperial violence, which the play's official ideology struggles in vain to suppress. More than one "discovery," then, will be made by what Armusia calls the "comely light" (2.3.54–5) of the burning towns. When "imperious" flames first "turn . . . to ashes" the objects of the governor's "worship" (2.2.48–50) and then threaten to consume the "palace" and "temples" of Tidore to make

way for Armusia's "monument" (5.5.38–9), they illuminate a scene of imperial desire.[70] It is the very scene on which is fixed the covetous gaze of what
Purchas calls "the world's two eyes to see itself "—the "soldiers and merchants" of his mercantilist vision. Like that vision it masks its violent appe-
tencies with talk of "peace" and "universal gladness" instituted in a wedding
that asserts the "common bond of humanity," and it can do this the more
effectively because of the mystifying effect of the historical displacements
that conceal its role as instrument of nationalist propaganda in the trade war
against the Dutch. In its celebration of heroic temperance as the providential
instrument of Christian empire, we can glimpse the beginnings of that
process by which the people whom Napoleon would dismiss as "a nation of
shopkeepers" learned to clothe mercantile interest in the romance of a civilizing mission.

This chapter was originally written for the Theatre and Nation Conference at
Waterloo in July 1997; it has since been revised in the light of Shankar Raman's
"Imaginary Islands: Staging the East" (see n. 6 this chap.).

13

Broken English and Broken Irish: Nation, Language, and the Optic of Power in Shakespeare's Histories

The English have always governed Ireland not as a conquered people by the sword and the conqueror's law, but as a province united upon marriage.
—Fynes Moryson, *"The Commonwealth of Ireland"*

So be there 'twixt your kingdoms such a spousal
That never may ill office or fell jealousy,
Which troubles oft the bed of blessed marriage,
Thrust in between the paction of these kingdoms
To make divorce of their incorporate league.
—Henry V, 5.2.362–6

The husbandman must first break the land, before it be made capable of good seed: and
when it is thoroughly broken and manured, if he do not forthwith cast good seed into it,
it will grow wild again, and bear nothing but weeds. So a barbarous country must first
be broken by a war, before it will be capable of good government.
—Sir John Davies, *A Discovery of the True Causes Why Ireland Was Never Entirely Subdued*

Things thus succeeding according to English desires so that none now remained able
to resist their power, nevertheless they did not cease to rage against . . . all the conquered
people, in such fierce and savage fashions as can scarce be heard or told without horror.
For in the towns, forts, and villages they seized many who had up to this survived, and . . .
drove all without distinction of age, sex, rank or deserts into old barns and setting them
on fire destroyed those shut up therein. But if any of the victims attempted to break out,

the surrounding enemy either drove them back into the fire or cut them off with
the sword. When they came across a few persons either wandering abroad or lying at home,
they at their pleasure shot them with muskets, or ran them through with swords. Some
they hung on trees by the wayside or on gallows, amongst whom was sometimes seen
the cruel spectacle of mothers hanging on crosses, the little ones still lying or crying
on their breasts, strangled in their hair and hanging from this new fashioned halter;
and other children wherever met or found it was an amusement and sport to toss in the air
with spears or lances, or to pin them to the ground, or dash them against the rocks,
with other atrocities of this sort, because if they were suffered to live they would
one day be rebelly papists.
—Peter Lombard, *The Irish War of Defense*

Were now the General of our gracious Empress,
As in good time he may, from Ireland coming,
Bringing rebellion broached on his sword,
How many would the peaceful city quit
To welcome him!
—Henry V, 5.chor., LL. 30–41

"No man or woman," writes the Kenyan novelist Ngũgĩ wa Thiong'o in an incautious moment, "can choose their biological nationality."[1] The phrase "biological nationality" sounds especially odd in the mouth of a professing Marxist. And now that even "race" has been deconstructed as an effect of ideology, it is not easy to see how "nationality" can be defended as "biological." For that very reason, however, Ngũgĩ's slip is all the more revealing, exposing the deep essentialism that infects our thinking about such matters. Nations, as Benedict Anderson has famously reminded us, are "Imagined Communities," things that get thought up; yet, in the teeth of reason and history, we persist in experiencing these fictions as "natural"—things to which we are native, like fish to the sea. And if nationality seems to be somehow "in the blood," nationhood has come to be imagined as equally essential—as much the ordained form of civil society as the *polis* was for the Greeks.

People may argue about the proper boundaries of the nation—about its geographical, political, cultural, linguistic, or racial constitution—but there is seldom any doubt in the minds of the disputants that such boundaries *really exist*, nor that (after due process of "ethnic cleansing") they can be established and placed beyond dispute. When, in the course of this century's first great anticolonialist revolution, Irish patriots sang of "a nation once again," they celebrated the "renaissance" of something that in the strict sense was being born for the first time—though the roots of their belief in Irish "nationhood" can be traced back to the sixteenth century and the earliest systematic attempt to absorb Ireland into the English body politic.[2]

In fact the idea of Irish nationhood (as Irish cultural historians have increasingly begun to recognize) was as much the product of English imperial ambition as any of the later anti-imperial nationalisms that succeeded it in Asia, Africa, the Americas, and elsewhere.[3] Moreover, since nationality can only be imagined as a dimension of difference—something that sets one apart from what one is not—it goes without saying that Ireland played an equally crucial part in the determination of "English" identity, functioning as the indispensable anvil upon which the notion of Englishness was violently hammered out. Indeed it might be argued that the struggle in Ireland, or its equivalent, was a prerequisite for the idea of an English national body politic in principle separable from the body of the monarch—the idea of the nation, that is, as a "commonwealth" with an essential and permanent existence distinct from the king's estate and determined by something other than the dynastic accidents that fixed the boundaries of feudal kingdoms—an idea of extraordinary consequence for the whole course of seventeenth-century history.[4] It was the Irish "wilderness" that bounded the English garden; Irish "barbarity" that defined English civility; Irish papistry and "superstition" that warranted English religion; it was Irish "lawlessness" that demonstrated the superiority of English law and Irish wandering that defined the settled and centered nature of English society.

Yet if the Irish were essential to the formation of English identity, they also threatened it. For in the English mind, Ireland constituted not merely a defining limit but a dangerously porous boundary, a potential conduit of papal subversion—which the tenaciously held Irish conviction of their Spanish origins did nothing to allay.[5] Thus while the ideology of national difference required that the Irish be kept at a distance and stigmatized as a barbaric Other, the practicalities of English policy more and more pressingly required that Ireland be absorbed within the boundaries of the nation state.

As the site of England's first true war of colonial conquest, Ireland became both a proving ground for methods of "plantation" that would later be applied in Virginia and elsewhere, and a forcing house for the enabling discourses of racial and cultural difference on which successful colonization would depend.[6] Yet justification of the conquest meant that Ireland had also to be redefined as a recalcitrant part of the nation, an errant province to be "subdued" rather than a foreign land to be subjugated. The effect of this peculiarly tense contradiction was to produce a significant shift in English attitudes toward Ireland in the course of the sixteenth century.

— ✦ —

METAMORPHOSIS, DEGENERATION, AND THE TROPES OF IRISH DIFFERENCE

Some aspects of this change have been described in an important article by Ann Jones and Peter Stallybrass who rightly stress the importance of the historical ethnography of Irish barbarism developed by sixteenth-century English polemicists in order to vindicate plantation as the imposition of English civility upon a savage people. More than that, Jones and Stallybrass believe, the new ethnography helped to produce a paradigmatic transformation in English policy toward the native Irish from one of gradual assimilation to one of conquest and terror. For them, this shift is exemplified by the contrast between the stance of the 1537 "Act for the English Order, Habit and Language," with its insistence that "the King's true subjects, inhabiting this land of Ireland" compose "wholly together one body," and the attitude of texts such as Spenser's *View of the Present State of Ireland* (1596) with its emphasis on "the absolute difference between English and Irish."[7]

I believe that the actual process was a little less straightforward than they make it appear, however, in that assimilationist rhetoric by no means disappeared in the 1590s. Indeed as late as 1594 Richard Beacon could approvingly quote the 1537 statute as an example of the measures by which the English had sought to eradicate the superficial "difference of laws, religion, habit, and language, which by the eye deceiveth the multitude, and persuadeth them that they be of sundry sorts, nations, and countries, when they be wholly together but one body." And Spenser himself, through his spokesman Irenius, wishes (even as he proposes the destruction of the barbarians by deliberate mass starvation) "to bring [the English colonists and the native Irish] to be one people, and to put away the dislikeful concept both of the one and the other." Moreover, Spenser's notion of "one people" was at least theoretically more comprehensive than the 1537 act's "one body," since the latter properly applied only to "the King's subjects within this land"—a term that did not then extend to that great majority of native Irish who declined formal allegiance to the English monarchy. It was not until four years later that these Irish, in a move that somewhat recalls the papal apportionment of New World natives to Spain and Portugal half a century before, were formally reclassified as subjects of the English crown. Under this act (Statute 33 of Henry VIII), passed by the Dublin parliament in 1541, the English monarch was transformed from "Lord" to "King" of Ireland, while the recalcitrant Celts outside the pale who had formerly been described as "the King's Irish enemies," foreigners with whom English colonists were forbidden to intermarry, were now to be included among "the King's Irish subjects" and summoned to obedience. It is difficult to overestimate the significance of this statute for the subsequent direction of Irish affairs, for it marks the point at which wholesale incorporation of the native Irish into the body politic defined by English settlement became, for the first time, legally enunciated policy. Under this new dispensation a systematic war of subjugation could be presented not as the aggressive conquest of an alien people, but as a defensive operation designed to secure the good order of the realm against rebels.[8]

Thus, far from the sixteenth century's witnessing a shift from a discourse of assimilation to one of absolute difference, it appears to have been the Tudors who, in a fashion characteristic of their centralizing ambitions, made assimilation a policy. Jones and Stallybrass are right, of course, to emphasize the increasingly venomous tone with which Elizabethan and Jacobean polemicists harped upon the barbarous otherness of the Irish. But it is at least arguable that such attitudes represented a reaction to the policies of assimilation and incorporation rather than a move away from them. Indeed the more writers insisted upon the need to subsume the Irish in the body of the nation, the more anxious they became about the signs of Irish resistance—an anomaly that some of them came to think could only be effaced by a more or less genocidal eradication of the native Irish. For these propagandists Irish difference was something that simply *ought not to exist*—an unnatural aberration that the English were morally bound to extirpate. The most extreme form of this contradiction can be found in the writings of Spenser, who is at once among the more sympathetic and well-informed English observers of Irish culture and also among the most extreme advocates of its destruction by "the sword."

Difference of a sort had been the steady theme of medieval accounts of Ireland with their stress upon the country's estranging distance from the normative "centre."[9] From Giraldus Cambrensis to Caxton this "last of all the islands in the West" had been alternately stigmatized as barbarous and marveled at as a site of Mandevillean wonders; it was both a land of saints and miracles, a snake-free demiparadise filled with "great abundance of honey, milk, wine and vineyards," and a topsy-turvy "land of Ire." But as medieval fables were displaced by a ruthlessly imperialist ethnography, the tropes of difference were tellingly reinflected. Whereas Caxton had imagined Ireland as a quaint *mundus inversus* where, for example, "many men pass water sitting down, and many women do it standing up," sixteenth- and seventeenth-century writers, faced with the realities of Irish cultural difference, discovered in it a perverse determination to do everything by opposites only to spite the English.[10] Fynes Moryson declared that he had

heard twenty absurd things practised by them only because they would be contrary to us. . . . Our women, riding on horseback behind men, sit with their faces towards the left arm of the man, but the Irish women sit on the contrary side, with their faces to the right arm. Our horses draw carts and like things with traces of ropes or leather, but they fasten them by a withe to the tails of their horses, and to the rumps when the tails be pulled off, which hath been forbidden by laws, yet could never be altered. We live in cleanly houses, they in cabins or smoky cottages. Or chief husbandry is in tillage; they despise the plough, and where they are forced to use it for necessity, do all things contrary to us. To conclude they abhor from all things that agree with English civility.[11]

Similarly, for Spenser, Irish adherence to Catholicism amounts to nothing more than an obstinate assertion of difference: "Most of the Irish are so far from understanding of the popish religion as they are of the protestants' profession, and yet do they hate it, though unknown, even for the very hatred which they have of the English and their government."[12]

Where Medieval commentators had superstitiously recorded the ability

16. Sphaera Civitatis *(1588), reprinted by permission of the
Folger Shakespeare Library.*

of Irish "beldams. . . . to transform themselves into the likenesses of hares, in
order to milk their neighbours' cattle and steal their milk," in later texts such
as John Derricke's *Image of Ireland* (1581) the literally subhuman nature of
the Irish is figured in metaphors of bestial metamorphosis, recalling the
vicious transformations of Spenser's Malengin. They are "beasts," "swine,"
"foxes," "boars," "bears," "toads," "crocodiles," "ravening hungry dogs,"

"wolves," and "monsters," creatures whom Captain Josias Bodley (1603) describes as "a most vile race of men—if it be at all allowable to call them 'men' who live upon grass, and are foxes in their disposition and wolves in their actions."[13] Indeed the very faculty of speech, which distinguishes men from beasts and allows them to associate in political communities, they are allowed (like all barbarians) to possess only equivocally. Their language is such that "if no such tongue were in the world, I think it would never be missed either for pleasure or necessity."[14] Their most characteristic mode of expression is in shrieks and cries, sounds "which savour greatly of Scythian . . . barbarism, as their Lamentations at their burials, with despairful outcries, and immoderate wailings," or in the Babylonical confusion known as the Irish hubbub or hubbuboo—Spenser's "terrible yell and hubbub, as if heaven and earth would have gone together which is the very image of the Irish hubbub."[15] Characteristically, where the civilized world is imagined as called into being by the Apollonian power of language, Irish bards are the conjurers of chaos, alluring their hearers "not to love of religion and civil manners, but to outrages, robberies, living as outlaws, and contempt of the magistrates and the King's laws. Alas! how unlike unto Orpheus, who, with his sweet harp and wholesome precepts of poetry, laboured to reduce the rude and barbarous people from living in woods to dwell civilly in towns and cities, and from wild riot to civil conversation."[16]

By the very fact of their dwelling beyond the so-called pale (the area of traditional English control centered upon Dublin) and especially in the bogs, woods, and mountains to which the English drove them, the Irish confirmed their essential inhumanity. In Aristotelian terms they were not members of the *polis* and were barbarians therefore—denizens of the wild, falling short of the fully human. Accordingly they were presented as fundamentally uncivil, incurably "prone to tumults and commotions," and effectively lawless, having only the Brehon Law—a code that to English eyes appeared hopelessly irregular, Fynes Moryson remarking that although "in some things [it] had a smack of equity, [yet] in some others it was clean contrary to all divine and human laws."[17] Under this code, according to Davies, they lived "little better than *Cannibals*, who do hunt one another; and he that hath most strength and swiftness, doth eat and devour all his fellows." They inhabited, it seemed, something resembling a Hobbesian state of nature; for unless men are "contained in duty with fear of law," Spenser believed, they are reduced to a condition in which "no man should enjoy any thing, every man's hand would be against another." In contradistinction to this restless and hopelessly fluid condition "laws ought to be like to stony tables, plain steadfast and immoveable." The role of the English was thus to do for the Irish what the Romans and the Normans had done for their own wild ancestors, to draw them inside the immoveable sphere of law and civility (see fig. 16).[18]

The Irish, however, seemed stubbornly resistant to such fixing and containment; even worse, in an unnatural reversal of the project of civilizing incorporation, they repeatedly seduced unwary colonists into degenerate imitation of their own barbarous ways. "Degeneration" (like "going native" in a later period) was the great nightmare of early modern colonial policy, obsessively brooded over in the writing of the period. The adoption of Irish manners, costume, and speech by the descendants of the original Norman invaders, the so-called Old English, was construed as profoundly threatening to the deeply entrenched notions of "native [inherent] virtue" on which the idea of the nation in large part depended. To the sixteenth-century colonists (the so-called New English) and their supporters in England, it had rendered the degenerates "barbarous and bastardlike," in Spenser's words—"much more lawless and licentious than the very wild Irish [themselves]." What was especially disturbing was the speed with which such metamorphoses could occur. According to Sir John Davies the Old English settlers had been so rapidly Irished that "within less time than the age of a man, they had no marks or differences left amongst them of that noble nation, from which they were descended. For . . . they did not only forget the English language, and scorn the use thereof, but grew to be ashamed of their very English names . . . and took Irish surnames and nicknames" becoming "mere Irish in their language, names, apparel." Thus Ireland, whose people, according to John Derricke, were "sprung from MacSwyne, a barbarous offspring, which may be perceived by their hoggish fashion," comes to be figured as Circe's island, where men are transformed to the basest of animals. Here, in the words of the Old English chronicler Richard Stanihurst, "the very English of birth, [through being] conversant with the savage sort of that people, become degenerate, and, as though they had tasted of Circe's poisoned cup, are quite altered." To Davies similarly the Old English appear "degenerate and metamorphosed . . . like those who had drunk of *Circe's* Cup."[19] And Derricke warns the new settlers against the seductions of Irish nymphs who are capable of transforming "[sometime . . . honest men] from boars to bears":

> We know by good experience
> it is a dangerous thing,
> For one into his naked bed
> a poisoning toad to bring

Or else a deadly crocodile,
whenas he goeth to rest,
To lead with him and as his mate,
to place next to his breast.[20]

While commentators were occasionally tempted to attribute such transformations to some malign influence of the soil—Moryson noting how
"horses, cows, and sheep transported out of England into Ireland do each
race and breeding decline worse and worse"—the generally accepted explanation had much more disturbing implications, suggesting a human kinship
in corruption against which culture provided only the frailest of protections.
As Spenser put it, degeneration occurs not because "[it] is the nature of the
country to alter a man's manners" but because the English, like all fallen mor-
tals, are fatally susceptible to the lure of license and disorder. The great threat
of Irish "manners and customs," according to Moryson, is that they "give
great liberty to all men's lives, and absolute power to great men over the inferiors, both which men naturally affect." In Spenser's account, since "it is the
nature of all men to love liberty," as soon as the English settlers are removed
from the "restraints" and "sharp penalties" that keep them "under a straight
rule of duty and obedience" at home, "they become flat libertines and fall to
flat licentiousness." The Irish, that is to say, figure in the English imagination
(rather like the Africans of Conrad's *Heart of Darkness*) as incarnations of
"the wild man within," sinisterly seductive embodiments of the barbaric,
uncultivated state to which all men will instinctively return, given the chance.
As a result, a text such as *The Faerie Queene* can regard the extirpation of the
natives as a moral duty exactly congruent with the other great moral quests
of the poem.[21]

ENGLISH GARDEN, IRISH WILDERNESS:
STAGING NATIONAL DIFFERENCE

If the material I have so far cited belongs overwhelmingly to the realm of
polemic, this is because the English enterprise in Ireland seems, at first sight

anyway, to have had remarkably little impact upon imaginative literature—
the only notable exception being Spenser's "cloudily enwrapped" allegory
The Faerie Queene, which gave a sort of fantastical existence to the Irish wars
in the wild landscapes of book 5 and the antic transformations of the elusive
Malengin. In the theater Shirley's *St. Patrick for Ireland* (1639) carefully confined itself to the mythical past, and only in a few scenes of *The Famous
History of Captain Thomas Stukely* (1605) were the Irish wars actually
brought onto the stage—though they transparently underlie the courtly fantasies of Jonson's *Irish Masque at Court*.[22] Given the amount of political, military, and intellectual energy it absorbed, and the moneys it consumed,
Ireland can seem to constitute (along with, significantly, the New World) one
of the great and unexplained lacunae in the drama of the period. But as Joel
Altman, David Baker and Christopher Highley have shown, it is possible, by
practicing a variety of what Edward Said calls "contrapuntal analysis," to
give voice to an Ireland that is "silent or [only] marginally present" in this
writing.[23] Predictably, this shadowy presence is most strongly registered in
works such as history plays, which contemporaries like Nashe and Heywood
identified as playing a key role in the articulation and activation of patriotic
sentiment. And I argue that in Shakespeare's history plays Ireland functions
as a recurrent point of reference—the crucial implied term in an unstable
dialectic of national self-definition.

Thus, to take a well-known example, the garden scenes of *1* and *2 Henry
VI* and *Richard II* are inadequately explained simply as figurations of the
conventional political trope that represents England as the idealized Garden
of Plenty, Gaunt's Edenic demiparadise. A contrapuntal approach would
seek to read them (together with the plays' insistent horticultural imagery)
against the discourse of "plantation" that licenses Richard II's Irish war as it
licensed Elizabeth's.[24] Similarly in *Henry V*, a play full of conscious allusion
to the Irish wars, Burgundy's lament for France as the "best garden of the
world"—which has become "Corrupt[ed] in it own fertility" and so choked
with "hateful docks, rough thistles, kecksies, burs" that it turns to "wildness,"
savagery, "And everything that seems unnatural" (5.2.36–62)—echoes
numerous descriptions of Ireland as a fertile earthly paradise turned to
wilderness by the barbarity of its own inhabitants; and Henry's function as
the correcting "scythe" (l. 50) or "the coulter . . . That should deracinate such
savagery" (ll. 46–7), mirrors the civilizing mission attributed to Elizabeth's
generals by contemporary propagandists.[25]

The expropriation of Irish land (like that of Virginian "Indians"), the displanting of native weeds, and the planting of good English stock was expressly justified on the grounds that the Irish, as a wandering, pastoral people, unaccustomed to proper notions of ownership and inheritance, failed to cultivate the territory they inhabited. In the propaganda of Beacon, Spenser, Davies, and others, they are represented as an idle and essentially masterless crew, owning allegiance only to the loose networks of the sept and the unstable succession of tanistic chieftains—victims of a dysfunctional system "which makes all their possessions uncertain, and brings confusion, barbarism, and incivility."[26] Seen as equally lacking any fixed center of authority, any fixed abode, or any fixed means of support, they are imagined as fundamentally unsettled and disorderly—a mere "heap of Irish nations" in Spenser's words, "which there lie huddled together, without any to overrule them or keep them in duty." Of necessity, therefore, the Irish landscape is typed as the very opposite of the English garden-state, Ireland's wildness embodying the barbarous and chaotic nature of its inhabitants and their society. Gardening may be a metaphor for policy but horticulture also stands for culture, and for Davies Irish indifference to horticulture is the very sign of their rootless mode of existence. "Although the Irish be a nation of great antiquity," he observes, "yet (which is strange to be related) they did never build any houses of brick or stone. . . . Neither did any of them, in all this time, plant any gardens or orchards, enclose or improve their lands, live together in settled villages or towns, nor made any provision for posterity; which, being against all common sense and reason, must needs be imputed to those unreasonable customs which made their estates so uncertain and transitory in their possessions."[27]

The energetic English insistence on surveying, mapping, and shiring and on reducing wilderness to the ordered topography of gardens, orchards, parks, ploughlands, and townlands had its obvious practical value, but it functioned equally powerfully as a symbolic translation of the colonized landscape—an Englishing of Ireland, whose meaning the Irish understood so well that in the rebellion of 1641 (according to the commentator Gerald Boate) they sought to "extinguish the memory of [the New English] and of all civility and good things by them introduced amongst that wild nation" by venting particular rage against houses, gardens, enclosures, orchards, and hedges.[28] In this context it can be no accident that in *2 Henry VI* the scene of Cade's foray into Alexander Iden's tranquil garden is immediately followed by the invasion of "York and his army of Irish" (4.10—5.1), for Cade's own subversiveness has been systematically associated with his escapades as a soldier in Ireland, where (as York recalls) he even assumed the barbaric guise of the natives: "Full often, like a shag-hair'd crafty kern, / Hath he conversed with the enemy, / And undiscovered come to me again" (3.1.371). It is similarly telling that the crisis of order in *Richard II*'s "sea-wall'd garden" should be precipitated by the king's absence in Ireland, in those wild lands that lie beyond what the Gardener's Man pregnantly describes as "the compass of a *pale*" (3.4.40).[29]

The nationalist trope of England as a fortified *hortus conclusus* recurs in *Cymbeline*, where the queen speaks of Britain as "Neptune's park, ribb'd and *pal'd* / With [rocks] unscalable and roaring waters" (3.1.20–1) and is punningly elaborated in *King John* when Austria undertakes to force submission upon "that *pale*, that white-fac'd shore, / Whose foot spurns back the ocean's roaring tides / And coops from other lands her islanders" (2.1.23–5). A counterpointed reading would inevitably be attentive to the recurrence of "pale," with its inescapable Irish resonance and its double sense of an exclusive limit and a defensive barrier. No term better encapsulates the anxious bifurcation of Tudor propaganda with its simultaneous stress on defiant separateness and besieged vulnerability; and the ambivalence of "pale" is matched by that of the sea for which it often stands. The other face of Gaunt's "silver sea, / Which serves [his island] in the office of a wall" (*Richard II*, 2.1.46–7) is the "sea of blood" by which the Talbots are overwhelmed in *1 Henry VI* (4.7.14); for if Gaunt's England is protectively "bound in with the triumphant sea," the nature of that triumph is always ambiguous since the defensive moat is all too easily reconfigured as the very engine of "the envious siege / Of wat'ry Neptune," a sign of the aggressive "envy of less happier lands" (*Richard II*, 2.1.62–3, 49). Yet at a deeper level the destructive and preservative seas are one and the same, since the English are never more triumphantly themselves than when threatened with dissolution in a scene of hostile otherness, like *Henry V*'s "poor condemned English" at Agincourt (4.chor., l. 22), or Talbot's doomed army at Bordeaux:

> How are we park'd and bounded in a *pale*,
> A little herd of England's timorous deer
> Maz'd with a yelping kennel of French curs!
> 1 HENRY VI, 4.2.45–7

It is as if the Dublin pale, with its precariously floating boundaries, always under pressure from the surrounding Irish wild, were imagined as an epitome of the besieged English nation. England is always discovered elsewhere, defined by the encounter with the Other.

It might be argued, however, that the deliberate blurring of aggression and defense in *1 Henry VI*, which represents a war of foreign subjugation as an attack upon a small and vulnerable island, is ironically undercut by the detail in the action that shows the besieging English as suddenly themselves besieged. By the same token, in *Richard II*, Gaunt's cartographic lyricism can be seen to expose other contradictions in the construction of English nationhood. Even as it maps his country as a little world unto itself, his troping of the favorite Virgilian tag, *divisos ab orbe Britannos*, is confused by the fact that it is not "Britain" but "England" that is the subject of his panegyric. On the margins of the play (and of Richard's realm) are barbarous speakers of foreign tongues, unreliable Welsh and treacherous Irish, who do not properly belong to the English nation and whose anomalous nature highlights the difference between the haphazardly inclusive medieval "kingdom," its boundaries defined by feudal allegiance, and the culturally exclusive "nation." However much the emerging nation-state may have liked to appropriate the legendary past of "Britain," the remnants of its Celtic world posed extraordinary problems of classification. These peoples might be imagined either as a more or less recalcitrant part of the nation, like Richard's Irish "rebels" inviting the chastisement of their natural lord (1.4.38) or as an invading enemy, wild intruders in the garden state whom it is the king's duty to "supplant" (2.1.156). Or like the dangerously incorporated Goths of *Titus Andronicus*, they could even serve to stand for all those inner forces that threatened to tempt a "civil" people back into a condition of wild and licentious barbarity. Their speech was among the most characteristic signs of their intractability.[30]

"NATIVE BREATH": LANGUAGE AND NATIONAL IDENTITY

Benedict Anderson is no doubt right to insist that language has rarely (if ever) been accepted as a sufficient defining condition of nationality, but its exceptional capacity for mobilizing the sense of extended community on which the new nation-state would come to depend was first properly understood in the sixteenth century. At the dawn of the new age in 1492, the Spanish grammarian Antonio de Nebrija offered his pioneering *Gramatica Castellana* to Queen Isabella in terms that were to be echoed a century later by English successors—dictionary-makers like Robert Cawdrey and even theater-propagandists like Thomas Heywood.[31] For Nebrija, language, which in a famous phrase he called "the mate of Empire," was *the* essential instrument of political unity. The Castilian tongue had already served to "[gather and join] the scattered bits and pieces of Spain . . . into one single kingdom." His own work would further "enhance our Nation" by fixing and consolidating the language so as to ensure the founding myth of the Reconquest would remain accessible to all succeeding generations, binding the nation together through time as well as across space: "Unless the like of this be done in our language," he warned, "in vain your Majesty's chroniclers and historians shall . . . praise the memory of your undyingly praiseworthy deeds. . . . Either the remembrance of your feats will fade with the language, or it will roam abroad among aliens, unable to settle, lacking a home."[32]

Language, then, constituted a kind of home and, at the same time, an essential instrument of *settlement*. But as his metaphors suggest, Nebrija's idea of settlement involved something more than mere stabilization. For him, rather than serving to define a preexisting national home, language, as it "followed our soldiers whom we sent to rule abroad," became the very agent by which the boundaries of the nation were renegotiated: "After your Majesty shall have placed her yoke [upon] many barbarians who speak outlandish tongues, by your victory these shall stand in need not only of laws that always victors give the vanquished, but also of our language."[33]

The complex anachronisms of a play such as *Richard II* are especially eloquent about how far the notion of language as a kind of "home" had taken root in late sixteenth-century England. What it means to be "a true-born Englishman" (1.3.309) is defined in ways that can scarcely have been available to the actual personages represented in the play. If Gaunt's patriotic oratory is ultimately dependent on developments in sixteenth-century mapmaking, and if the legalist arguments of York and Bolingbroke are unthinkable without the burgeoning of Tudor constitutional theory and debate, then the linguistic romanticism of Mowbray is equally an expression of the Elizabethan preoccupation with what the poet Spenser called "the kingdom of our own language."[34] For Mowbray the pain of banishment is most acutely imagined as expulsion from a community of English speakers, an enforced geographical translation that will render him infantile and speechless *(infans):*

> The language I have learnt these forty years,
> My native English, now I must forgo,
> And now my tongue's use is to me no more
> Than an unstringed viol or a harp,
> Or like a cunning instrument cas'd up,
> Or being open, put into his hands
> That knows no touch to tune the harmony. . . .
> I am too old to fawn upon a nurse,
> Too far in years to be a pupil now.
> What is thy sentence [then] but speechless death,
> Which robs my tongue from breathing native breath?
> 1.3.159–73

Mowbray's English is "native" in a double sense: it is both that into which he is born and that which defines (and is defined by) the "nation" to which he belongs. By the same token, for the rhetorician George Puttenham, a tongue is only fit to be dignified with the name "language" when it becomes the recognized domain of a nation: "After a speech is fully fashioned to the common understanding, *and accepted by consent of a whole country and nation*, it is called a language." For the Tudor and Stuart inventors of the "English nation," however, it was precisely in that "consent of a whole country" that the most intractable difficulties lay. For what precisely constituted the "whole country" was by no means clear.[35]

In this context the role of Glendower in *1 Henry IV* nicely illustrates the ambivalent status of all the marginal Celtic peoples, as well as the anxieties aroused by their refractory speech. The Welsh leader is first described by Westmorland in the opening scene as an external menace to the nation, an "irregular and wild" barbarian whose "rude hands" are held responsible for the "beastly shameless transformation" performed upon the corpses of Mortimer's English troops by the unnatural Welshwomen (1.1.40–6). But when he appears in person it is as a kind of troublesome insider, the ally and father-in-law of Mortimer, conspiring to divide the kingdom with his English co-mates in rebellion. In this very capacity, however, he incarnates the threat of a more insidious kind of "transformation," such as the "degenerate" Old English in Ireland were supposed to have undergone. Like the most execrated of Elizabeth's Irish enemies, Hugh O'Neill, Earl of Tyrone, reputedly raised in the household of the Sidneys, Glendower can boast to Hotspur: "I can speak English, lord, as well as you, / For I was train'd up in the English court" (3.1.119–20). But the language of his own court is Welsh, a tongue that Hotspur invites the audience to hear as barbarian gabble ("I think there's no man speaks better *Welsh*. . . . I had rather hear Lady, my brach, howl in *Irish* [than the lady sing in Welsh]," 3.1.49, 236). We should notice that this interlude in Glendower's court, where Mortimer's bride sings and then talks to him in Welsh, is the only scene in Shakespeare where a character is made to utter words that are as entirely inaccessible to the audience as to most of the characters on stage, and for all the affecting pathos of her singing, Elizabethan audiences must have felt an unnerving cultural undertow in the spectacle of the warlike Mortimer yielding to a foreign enchantress.[36] The lady "[charms his] blood with pleasing heaviness" (l. 215), in what he himself tellingly figures as an act of linguistic submission:

> But I will never be a *truant*, love,
> Till I have learn'd thy language; for thy tongue
> Makes Welsh as sweet as ditties highly penn'd,
> Sung by a fair queen in a summer's bow'r,
> With ravishing division, to her lute.
>   3.1.204–8

Repeating in eroticized form the castration implied in the Welsh women's "beastly . . . transformation" of the English corpses, the spectacle significantly resembles that of the disarmed Verdant lying in the lap of the enchantress Acrasia in Spenser's Bower of Bliss. In the bower, as on Circe's island, men are transformed into beasts, simultaneously stripped of humanity and of phallic power. In Glendower's court, Mortimer surrenders both his Englishness and his martial masculinity in a scene of degeneration that renders inevitable his effacement from the subsequent action of the play.[37]

Degeneration typically manifested itself in this way as linguistic corruption. Observing, like Nebrija, that "communion or difference of language hath always been observed a special motive to unite or alienate the mind of all nations," Fynes Moryson lamented the failure of the English to follow the example of "the wise Romans, [who] as they enlarged their conquests, so did they spread their language"; instead, those whom he called the "English-Irish" had fallen into a perverse "community of language" with the "mere

Irish." Since such unnatural community involved a falling away from the laws of kind, its processes were often explained (as in the Circe trope) in significantly gendered terms.[38] Degeneration was repeatedly said to result from intermarrying and fostering with the "mere Irish" and from the linguistic contagion that such intimate contact with their women must entail. To Spenser it seemed flatly "unnatural that any people should love another's language more than their own . . . for it hath been ever the use of the conqueror to despise the language of the conquered, and to force him by all means to learn his." To behave otherwise could only betray a "devilish dislike of their own natural country, as that they would be ashamed of her name, and bite of her dug from which they sucked life." All this, however (mother-tongue being, almost literally, a kind of mother's milk) was the inevitable consequence of a mingling with the Irish, since children bred out of Irish mothers or fostered by Irish nurses must "draw into themselves together with their suck even the nature and disposition of their nurses; for the mind followeth much the temperature of the body, and also the words are the image of the mind, so as they proceeding from the mind, the mind must needs be affected with the words—so that *the speech being Irish, the heart must needs be Irish.* . . . how can such matching but bring forth an evil race?"[39]

If one solution (that notoriously most often favored by Spenser) amounted to genocide, an alternative was to find means of drawing the Irish instead within the colonizers' linguistic pale. "Since Ireland is full of her own nation," declares Spenser's Irenius in a moment of uncharacteristic mildness, "that may not be rooted out, and somewhat stored with English already (and more to be), I think it best, by an union of manners and conformity of minds, to bring them to be one people, and to put away the dislikeful concept both of the one and the other . . . by translating of them, and scattering them in small numbers amongst the English . . . to bring them by daily conversation unto better liking of each other." This indeed was the policy Sir John Davies would later claim was so successfully pursued in Ulster, where "his Majesty did not utterly exclude the natives out of this plantation with a purpose to root them out—as the Irish were excluded out of the first English colonies—but made a mixed plantation of British and Irish, that they might grow up together in one nation. Only, the Irish were in some places transplanted from the woods and mountains into the plains and open countries, that being removed (like wild fruit trees) they might grow the milder and bear the better and sweeter fruit."[40]

Not the least radical consequence of such a physical translation, Davies believed, was that it would induce the Irish to "send their children to schools, especially to learn the English language; so as we may conceive an hope that the next generation will in tongue and heart, and every way else, become English; so as there will be no difference or distinction but the Irish Sea betwixt us . . . [and] Ireland (which heretofore might properly be called the Land of Ire . . .) will from henceforth prove a Land of Peace and Concord." In this seemingly benign (but one-sided) "mingling" of peoples a double alienation was involved—one requiring that the native Irish be translated first out of their own lands to become tenants of the English settlers and then out of their own language to become denizens of the invaders' tongue. But what was already beginning to result, Davies believed, was a miraculous harmony, replacing the disordered hubbub of Irish division: "The strings of this Irish harp, which the civil magistrate doth finger, are all in tune . . . and make a good harmony in this commonweal."[41]

— ❊ —

TRANSLATING THE IRISH: THE TONGUES OF *HENRY V*

Just such a harmony is figured in the Shakespeare play where the perplexities of language, nationhood, and translation are most uneasily foregrounded, *Henry V*. Here, Exeter's Ciceronian commonplace of "government" as a system of orchestration in which "high, and low, and lower, / Put into parts, doth keep consent, / Congreeing in a full and natural close, / Like music" (1.2.180–3) is given a striking linguistic twist in the final scene where Henry professes to hear in Katherine's "broken English" a "broken music" that echoes the harmonious part-song of his kingdom (5.2.243–4).[42] Played by a "broken consort," made up of instruments from different "families," broken music seems an especially apt metaphor for the national voice that Henry, with the aid of the play's patriotic rhetoric, seeks to "corroborate" from its babel of "fracted" tongues.

In this sense Henry's enterprise replicates the triumphant role that Thomas Heywood was to ascribe to the theater itself. Not only did its staging of historical dramas serve to weld the nation together by "[instructing] such as cannot read in the discovery of all our English chronicles," but theater had a crucial unifying function in helping to reform the inchoate babble of a bastard tongue into a true national language, so that "our English tongue, which hath been the most harsh, uneven, and broken language of the world, part Dutch, part Irish, Saxon, Scotch, Welsh, and indeed a gallimaufry of many, but perfect in none, is now by this secondary means of playing, continually refined . . . so that in process, from the most rude and unpolished tongue, it is grown to a most perfect and composed language, and many excellent works and elaborate poems writ in the same, that many Nations grow enamoured of our tongue (before despised)." The soldiers whom Henry, harping on their recollection of English chronicles (3.1.17–23), urges to prove their national legitimacy by "clos[ing] the wall up with . . . *English dead*" (l. 2), turn out when we meet them to be just such a bastard "gallimaufry of many," a volatile mixture of English, Irish, Welsh, and Scots, whose desire to cut throats is as likely to be vented on one another as upon the French. The most dangerous of them, predictably, is the irascible Captain Macmorris, an "Irishman" whose hybrid surname (a Gallicized version of Fitzmaurice) and savage temper reveal him as an exemplar of that "bastard-like" degeneracy to which English conquerors were prone in the "Land of Ire," and whose broken English preeminently figures the disorder into which a nation made up of what Nebrija had called "scattered bits and pieces" may fall. Small wonder that the very mention of the word "nation" is enough to send Macmorris spiraling off into a frenzy of incoherence: "my nation? What ish my nation? Ish a villain, and a bastard and a knave, and a rascal? What ish my nation? Who talks of my nation?" (3.2.122–4).[43]

The Gaels, after all, as Caxton had insisted, were a heteroclite people whose language was devised by their eponymous ancestor Gaitelus "who could speak many languages after the diversification of languages at the Tower of [Babel]" and who invented their tongue, calling it " 'Gaitelaf,' signifying a language assembled from all languages and tongues."[44] There are more breaches than one at Harfleur into which those bodies whom death honors with English "brotherhood" must be thrown. And though Macmorris and Fluellen both nominally speak English, their propensity to "mistake each other" (3.3.134–5) is as great as if each were confined to the kingdom of his own language. The fate of the wild Macmorris, who has driven his mine so deep under the walls of Englishness that it indeed threatens to "blow up the town," is to be extirpated from the play—a fate that should not surprise us in a work whose fifth chorus compares Henry's French conquests to Essex's expected triumph in Ireland.[45] But the alternative strategy of translation and incorporation is exemplified in the case of his fellow pioneer, Fluellen, who is received into full membership of the English nation (rather as Henry's common soldiers are allegedly to be "gentled" by their presence at Agincourt, 4.3.63). This is accomplished first by the king's graceful acknowledgment of his own natal Welshness (4.7.105) and then by the purgative chastisement of Pistol in a fashion that asserts that the "native garb" of Welsh-English is after all no more than the cover for an Englishness paradoxically more essential than Pistol's "counterfeit" chauvinism:

✤

GOWER:
You thought, because he could not speak English in the native garb, he could not therefore handle an English cudgel. You find it otherwise, and henceforth let a Welsh correction teach you a good English condition.
5.1.75–9

✤

To be Welsh or Scots (or perhaps even Irish) is to be a subspecies of English, and to speak a dialect of English is to reveal an English heart (in a play where, as Henry insists, "a good heart . . . is the sun and the moon," 5.2.162–3). What is being passed off through this act of translation—in the guise of a national *generosity* that expands the idea of genus (or *gens*) to put away Spenser's "dislikeful concept . . . of the one and the other"—is an act of aggressive assimilation that the subsequent course of Empire would make only too familiar. Through a typically dishonest paradox, Englishness is shown as characterized by a relaxed inclusiveness that operates equally in the realms of rank and culture, while Frenchness (the truly not-English) is defined by its arrogant insistence upon *difference*, its loathing of inappropriate mixture, and disdain for the English as a "barbarous people . . . but bastard Normans, Norman bastards" (3.5.4–10).[46]

Yet the play struggles to suggest how even Frenchness might be subsumed in the English imperium—figuring Katherine's "broken English" not as the broken-hearted and confused speech of the country Henry threatened to "break . . . all to pieces" (1.2.225) but as the "broken music" of a French heart that may soon be Englished: "if you will love me soundly with your French heart, I will be glad to hear you confess it brokenly with your English tongue. . . . Therefore . . . break thy mind to me in broken English" (5.2.104–6; 244–6). "The husbandman must first break the land, before it be made capable of good seed," wrote Sir John Davies, "so a barbarous country must be first broken by a war, before it will be capable of good government." Henry's wooing offers itself as just such an exhibition of good husbandry, and language is the field on which it is displayed.[47]

Given that theatrical convention normally dictated that the speech of foreigners (even when comically "broken") be transparent to English ears, it is remarkable that Shakespeare should have placed at the very center of *Henry V* a scene of translation that foregrounds for the first time the fact that these "two mighty monarchies, / Whose high, upreared, and abutting fronts / The perilous narrow ocean parts asunder" (1.chor., ll. 20–22) as if in naturally ordained enmity, actually *speak different languages*. In act 3, scene 4, which immediately follows the surrender of Harfleur and the opening of her gates to the invader, the French princess begins the process of Englishing her own body, beginning with the hand (a metonymy for marriage) and ending (by an accident of translation—metaphorically if not properly) in the middle region with "le foot [fout] et le count [gown]." What Katherine's blazoned body stands for in this "litany of dismemberment" will have been perfectly apparent to an audience accustomed to think of conquest in gendered metaphor—we may recall Raleigh's now-infamous description of Guiana as "a country that hath yet her maidenhead."[48] But here, as in Elizabeth's projection of her own virgin body as a figure for the inviolate kingdom, the metaphoric translation is reversed. The effect of such a literalization, arguably, is to draw attention to the work of nation-building and empire upon actual women's bodies—the way in which, from the sack of Troy to the rape of Bosnia, the completeness of conquest has habitually been expressed in acts of sexual possession:

> What is't to me, when you yourselves are cause,
> If your pure maidens fall into the hand
> Of hot and forcing violation? . . .
> . . . in a moment look to see
> The blind and bloody soldier with foul hand
> Defile the locks of your shrill-shrieking daughters.
>   3.3.19–35

The point is reiterated in a ruthless final scene—a scene of national "spousal" (5.2.362) whose sly appropriation of comic convention is fittingly mediated by its recollections of Petruchio's violent conquest of another Kate.

The language of this final scene troubled Dr. Johnson, who expressed his incomprehension that "Shakespeare now gives the King nearly such a character as he made him formerly ridicule in Hotspur." But (as Katherine's remark about "the tongues of men being full of deceits" suggests) all Henry's "speaking . . . plain soldier" is by no means as plain as he pretends. As much "false French" as it is "true English" (to use his own terms), more bluff than genuine bluffness, his transformation into blunt "King Harry" is another consciously contrived linguistic performance to add to the archbishop's admiring list (1.1.38 ff.)—one whose calculated naïveté allows him ("most truly-falsely") to translate Katherine to his own purposes, converting her to "the better Englishwoman" in the process. Though it is customarily played for its superficial charm, this scene (with its echoes of Pistol's humiliation) is quite explicitly a scene of enforcement—one where, as Altman puts it, "rape is sanctioned . . . civilly, ceremoniously."[49] In it the conquering wooer deploys his "will and shall" as peremptorily as any Tamburlaine:

❀

KATHERINE:
Dat is as it shall please de roi mon pere.
K. HENRY:
Nay it will please him well, Kate. It shall please him.
5.2.247–9

❀

"My royal cousin," asks Burgundy, "teach you our princess English?" And Henry's reply is perfectly nuanced: "I *would have her learn,* my fair cousin, how perfectly I love her, and *that is good English*" (ll. 281–4). The bawdy transports of the conqueror's wooing make entirely plain what is at stake in the "possession" of this princess, what it means to "move [her] in French" (5.2.181,186)—or rather to translate Katherine into English "Kate":

I love France so well that I will not part with a village of it. I will have it all mine; and Kate, when France is mine . . . you are mine. . . . So the maid that stood in the way for my wish shall show me the way to my will.
5.2.173–76, 327–8

— ❀ —

"NO TONGUE, ALL EYES, BE SILENT"

The hybrid nation, ruled over by "a boy, half-French, half-English," that Henry means to found through an "incorporate league" in which "English may as French, French Englishmen, / Receive each other" (5.2.207–8, 366–8) is only the mask for an incorporation that means to be as violent and absolute as that which "the General of our Gracious Empress" (5.chor., l. 30) was about to initiate in Ireland. There, in Sir John Davies's fond expectation, "the next generation [would] in tongue and heart, and every way else, become English; so as there [would] be no difference or distinction but the Irish Sea betwixt us." Thus broken, "the Land of Ire" would "prove a Land of Peace and Concord," sounding its broken music in consort with the civil magistrate's sympathetically appropriated Irish harp. Yet details of Shakespeare's play notoriously resist the carefully orchestrated nuptial harmony of its ending. The hesitant, elliptical syntax of the fifth chorus's prophecy of Irish conquest (ll. 29–35) and the epilogue's world-weary confession of the imminent disintegration of Henry's hybrid empire are reminders that the voice of official history can no more answer Macmorris's ire than it can stamp out the subversive dialect of Eastcheap. Indeed the arbitrary suppression of Macmorris only serves to draw attention to the uneasy marginal presence of Ireland as that which both defines and calls into question the idea of England.[50]

Nor are the tongues of Macmorris and of Pistol's crew the only ones to be silenced in the play; after the one-sided linguistic duel that claims to break the French princess to the discipline of "broken English," Katherine's mouth too is conclusively "stopped" by the kiss of possession that signals the end of her speaking part (5.2.272–9), and she is conspicuously denied any part in the political maneuvering that ties up the conditions of her marriage. Moreover, just as the princess is finally rendered speechless by Henry's victorious speech, so she is rendered sightless by his conquering optic. For the blindness playfully associated with the king's "love" is symbolically transferred to Katherine's "naked seeing self" (defenseless and stripped of disguises) by the "perspective" that renders her body no more than a cipher for the "maiden cities" on which his desire is fixed (ll. 293–324). To recognize the power of the colonizer's "perspective" to transform and possess the body of a conquered territory we have only to think of Luke Gernon's unashamed erotic blazoning of the map of Ireland (ca. 1620):

> It was my chance once . . . to see a map of Europe, and it was described in the lineaments of a naked woman. . . . I dare not set down how every country was placed, lest I should misplace them, but one was in her forehead, another on her right breast, another on her left, others in her arms, others on her thighs, and France with a pope was in her placket. In such a form will I represent our Ireland.
>
> This Nymph of Ireland is at all points like a young wench that hath the green-sickness for want of occupying. She is very fair of visage, and hath a smooth skin of tender grass. . . . Her flesh is of a soft and delicate mould of earth, and her blue veins trailing through every part of her like rivulets. She hath one master vein called the Shannon, which passeth quite through her. . . . .She hath three other veins called the sisters, the Sewer, the Noyer [Nore], and the Barrow, which, rising at one spring, trail through her middle parts and join together in their going out. Her bones are of polished marble. . . . Her breasts are round hillocks of milk-yielding grass, and that so fertile that they contend with the valleys. And betwixt her legs (for Ireland is full of havens), she hath an open harbour, but not much frequented. She hath had goodly tresses of hair, *arboribusque comae*, but the iron mills, like a sharp toothed comb, have knotted and polled her much; and in her champion parts she hath not so much as she will cover her nakedness. . . . It is now since she was drawn out of the womb of rebellion about sixteen years— by'rlady, nineteen—and yet she wants a husband, she is not embraced, she is not hedged and ditched, there is no quickset put into her.[51]

The necessity of hedging, ditching, and quicksetting by the royal husbandman is a theme already familiar from Davies, but even more important in Gernon's salacious cartography is the idea of stripping naked the prostrate body of Ireland and laying her open to the conqueror's gaze. The nymph figured here in such anatomic detail is apparently without eyes, but unseen eyes are fixed upon every part of her. While the language of this passage has much in common with (say) Raleigh's excited vision of Guiana, the full suggestiveness of its penetrative stare becomes apparent only in the context of anxieties about the tricksy invisibility of the Irish that were fundamental to the English way of construing their resistance to English authority. The Irish were credited with a perfidious talent for concealment that was associated with the irregularity of native attire on the one hand and with the topographical peculiarities of their wilderness habitation on the other. To bring the wild Irish into the orbit of English power, Sir John Davies insisted, it was first necessary to bring them into view.

Indeed if Ireland figures in the staging of English history as marginal but insistent, just out of sight but rarely out of mind, always present but never quite apprehensible, this is perhaps not merely because Irish policy was regarded as dangerously contentious matter, for it corresponds to an obsessive preoccupation with the "crafty . . . shifts" and elusiveness of the Irish—their frustrating ability to evade the controlling optic of English law and military power.[52] This obsession makes comprehensible what might otherwise seem a disproportionate concentration on the subversive potential of the notorious garment known as the "Irish mantle" (or "rug") and the shaggy forelock called "glib" (see fig. 17)—fashions that are together punningly identified with innate barbarity in Richard II's description of the Irish as "rough, rug-headed kerns." Of course the persistence of traditional attire constituted both a defiant assertion of national difference and an implicit affront to the conventions of dress by which early modern society exhibited its hierarchy of place—what Keith Thomas has called the "vestimentary system." For these reasons, mantles and glibs were read as powerful statements of a wandering people's disorderly resistance to placement. But this effect was enormously and sinisterly enhanced by the way in which they seemed to grant their wearers the invisibility of an almost impenetrable disguise.[53]

According to Fynes Moryson, for example, "the nourishing of long hair (vulgarly called glibs) which hangs down to the shoulders, hiding the face" ensured that "a malefactor may easily escape with his face covered therewith," while the all-enveloping mantle could serve "as a cabin for an outlaw in the woods, a bed for a rebel, and a cloak for a thief."[54] Under this garment, according to Spenser,

[the wild Irishman] covereth himself from the wrath of heaven, from the offence of the earth, and from the sight of men. . . . Likewise for a rebel it is serviceable, for in his war that he maketh (if at least it deserve the name of war) when he still flieth from his foe and lurketh in the thick woods and strait passages, waiting for advantages, it is his bed, yea and

17. Rory Og O More in a wood; pl. 11 of John Derricke's Discoverie of Woodkerne *(1581). Reprinted, with permission, from the original (Shelfmark De.3.76) in the Drummond Collection of the Edinburgh University Library.*

almost all his household stuff. For the wood is his house against all weathers, and his mantle is his cave to sleep in. . . . Under it he can cleanly convey any fit pillage . . . and when he goeth abroad in the night on freebooting, it is his best and surest friend. . . . And, when all is done, he can in his mantle pass through any town or company, being close-hooded over his head as he useth, from knowledge of any to whom he is endangered, armed without suspicion of any.[55]

Spenser's desire to "forbid all mantles" and glibs had been anticipated by (among others) the legislators of 1537 and by Sir William Herbert who proposed to enforce the statute against mantles on the grounds that "the mantle serving unto the Irish as to a hedgehog his skin, or to a snail her shell, for a garment by day and a house by night, it maketh them, with the continual use of it, more apt and able to live and lie out in the bogs and woods, where this mantle serveth them for a mattress and a bush for a bed stead; and thereby they are less addicted to a loyal, dutiful, and civil life."[56]

It is this same "uncouth vestiment" that enables the foul Irish enchanter Malengin to perform his baffling metamorphoses (including transformation "into a hedgehog") in Spenser's allegorized account of the "slights, juggling feats, legerdemain, mysteries . . . guile, malice . . . [and] feigned semblance" that characterized guerrilla tactics in Munster. Typically associated with a landscape whose caves, bogs, bushes, thick woods, and strait passages are themselves dangerously concealing, mantles become at once the instrument and symbol of evasive native resistance to the organizing "view" of the colonizer. "So soon as they [are] out of sight," Spenser insists, the Irish invariably "shake off their bridles and begin to colt it licentiously . . . for the Irishman . . . fears the government no longer than he is within sight or reach." The Irish, as Moryson suspiciously remarks, are "a crafty and subtle nation," and hostility to the mantle reflects not merely the practical frustrations of a regular military force faced with an enemy that constantly melts into the hostile wilderness, but even more profound anxieties about the inscrutable otherness of subject peoples.[57]

The dis-covering, laying open, and display of what has been treacherously disguised or concealed, the penetrative power of surveillance, the organizing power of eyesight, epitomized in the topographic regulation of surveying and mapping—these are among the master-tropes of the process by which the colonizers will endeavor to relocate Ireland within the body of the English nation.[58] In Spenser's significantly named *View*, the map with its power of envisaging the landscape becomes a vital adjunct of military conquest, while the subsequent maintenance of control over the wayward natives will equally depend on ocular power, through reinstitution of the system of neighborly espionage by which King Alfred had contrived to place the once barbarous English "within the compass of duty and obedience": "no one bad person could stir, but that he was straight taken hold of by those of his own tithing and their borough-holder, who, being his neighbours or next kinsman, was privy to all his ways and looked narrowly unto his life."[59]

In book 5 of the *Faerie Queene* Talus is described as "that same iron man which could reveal / All hidden crimes" reminding us that he represents not merely the ruthless force on which the maintenance of civil order depends but the power of justice to thresh out hidden falsehood and to unfold the truth.[60] In Davies's *Discovery* the project of bringing the Irish within the pale of the law is once again represented as dependent upon ocular control. According to his analysis, the failure of Norman "plantation" resulted from a fundamental topographic miscalculation that allowed the Irish to slip out of view, while exposing the conquerors themselves to the malign gaze of their adversaries:

> They sat down, and erected their castles and habitations in the plains and open countries, where they found most fruitful and profitable lands, and turned the Irish into the woods and mountains—which, as they were proper places for outlaws and thieves, so were they their natural castles and fortifications; thither they drove their preys and stealths; there they lurked, and lay in wait to do mischief. These fast places they kept unknown by making the ways and entries thereunto impassable; there they kept their creaghts or herds of cattle, living by the milk of the cow, without husbandry or tillage; there they increased and multiplied unto infinite numbers by promiscuous generation among themselves; there they made their assemblies and conspiracies without discovery. But they discovered the weakness of the English dwelling in the open plains, and thereupon made their sallies and retreats with great advantage. Whereas . . . if the English had builded their castles and towns in those places of fastness, and had driven the Irish into the plains and open countries, where they might have had an eye and observation upon them, the Irish had been easily kept in order, and in short time reclaimed from their wildness; there they would have used tillage, dwelt together in townships, learned mechanical arts and sciences. . . . And the ways and passages throughout Ireland, would have been as clear and open as they are in England at this day.[61]

The great triumph of Mountjoy's policy, as Davies saw it, was to have opened "a passage" for "the law and her ministers . . . among them" so that

> all their places of fastness have been discovered and laid open; all their paces cleared; and notice taken of every person that is able to do either good or hurt . . . not only how they live and what they do, but it is foreseen what they purpose or intend to do. Insomuch as Tyrone hath been heard to complain that he had so many eyes watching over him as he could not drink a full carouse of sack but the state was advertised thereof within a few hours after. . . . For the under-sheriffs and bailiffs errant are better guides and spies in time of peace than any were found in the time of war.[62]

This process of bringing the Irish under the purview of the English justice has duly "reclaimed [them] from their wildness, caused them to cut off their glibs and long hair; to convert their mantles into cloaks; to conform themselves to the manner of England in all their behaviour and outward forms . . . as we may conceive an hope that the next generation will, in tongue and heart and every way else, become English, so as there will be no difference or distinction but the Irish Sea betwixt us."[63]

The translation that Davies imagined was duly enacted for the edification of the English court in Ben Jonson's *Irish Masque* (1613–4), where the Englishing of the king's Irish subjects is figured (through a properly tamed version of Tamburlaine's unshepherding) as a stripping away of the refractory marks of wildness, exposing the masquers to the penetrating and recuperative eye of the royal sun. In Jonson's program the wild Irish dancers (already rendered half-civil by their role as loyal "footmen" of the king) and their rough bagpipe music are made to give way to a group of Irish "Gentlemen" who dance to "a solemn music of harps"; the Gentlemen's dance in turn is interrupted by "a civil Gentleman of the nation," ushering in a reformed bard whose song, performed "to two harps" exactly mimics the music of Davies's civil magistrate, except that here the broken music of part-song is converted to unison. As he sings, the Gentlemen let fall their mantles to reveal the "masquing apparel" of English courtiers, a metamorphosis that is expressly effected by the power of the royal gaze:[64]

> Bow both your heads at once, and hearts;
> Obedience doth not well in parts.
> It is but standing in his eye,
> You'll feel your selves chang'd by and by. . . .
> 'Tis done by this; your slough let fall,
> And come forth new-born creatures all.
> So breaks the sun earth's *rugged* chains,
> Wherein rude winter bound her veins. . . .
> So naked trees get crisped heads,
> And coloured coats the *roughest* meads,
> And all get vigour, youth, and spright,
> That are but look'd on by his light.[65]

As a performance of national incorporation Jonson's masque leaves a little to be desired, and the element of wish-fulfillment in his fantasy of effort-

18. The Rainbow Portrait *of Queen Elizabeth I (ca. 1600), reprinted by permission of the Marquess of Salisbury from the original at Hatfield House, Hertfordshire.*

less royal power is especially difficult to ignore in the light of the circumstances that produced it—the presence in London of a delegation of discontented Old English Catholics who, having opposed the installation of Sir John Davies as speaker of the Irish Parliament, now wished to effect a change in James's Irish policies.[66] But we can find a much more potent and menacing demonstration of the same ideas in a work that dates from the very end of Elizabeth's reign. The "Rainbow Portrait," the last of a series of great royal icons in which the queen identified the idea of the nation with the display of her own royal body, is a frightening assertion of a royal power so absolute that it can absorb the very signs of barbarism into its scheme of civilizing control (see fig. 18). The emblematic reversal it performs exactly corresponds to that envisaged by Davies when he asserted that whereas "heretofore the neglect of the law made the English degenerate and become Irish . . . now, on the other side, the execution of the law, doth make the Irish grow civil and become English." Here, in a portrait whose program, Roy Strong has suggested (on the basis of its marked resemblances to the *Hymns to Astraea*), might "actually [have been] drawn up for the painter by Davies" himself, Elizabeth is shown in what the historian of her wardrobe has identified as a particularly luxurious version of the notorious Irish mantle, worked in rich stuff and elaborately painted with images of eyes and ears.[67] In a move that boldly appropriates the most threatening of all images of degeneration, it is now the queen who assumes the Irish cloak of inscrutability, here emblazoned, however, with the signs of her all-seeing power—the familiar iconography of *Ragione di Stato* as Ripa had described her:[68] "She is represented in a garment . . . woven with eyes and ears to symbolise her jealous hold over her dominion, and her desire to have the eyes and ears of spies, the better to judge her own plans and those of others."[69]

On Elizabeth's sleeve is a great jewel in the form of a serpent, symbolizing Wisdom, or that Machiavellian Providence whose powers of discovery are embodied in the "provision" of Prospero's art (*Tempest*, 1.2.28) and celebrated by Ulysses in *Troilus and Cressida* as a justification for his spying on Achilles: "The providence that's in a watchful state . . . Finds bottom in th' uncomprehensive depth, / Keeps place with thought, and almost, like the gods, / Do thoughts unveil in their dumb cradles" (3.3.196–200). On one level, then, the queen resembles a stylized version of Shakespeare's Henry V, shrouded in Erpingham's cloak to spy on his own subjects, or the provident monarch who sits in traitors' bosoms and by "interception" makes "discovery" of "all that they intend" (*Henry V*, 2.2.6–7, 162); on another, Elizabeth's elaborate coiffure establishes a correspondence with Henry's climactic wedding to the double kingdom of "French Englishmen." Copied from the "Sponsa Thessaloniciensis" in Boissard's *Habitus variarum orbis gentium* (1581), her bridal locks present her as the spouse of her kingdom.[70] And the punning motto displayed above the rainbow of peace in her right hand identifies her symbolic nuptials quite specifically with the conquest of Ireland: *Non sine sole Iris*—"there is no Rainbow without the Sun" but also (since *Iris* was one of the ancient names for Ireland that Camden had discovered in Diodorus Siculus), "there is no Ireland without her Queen."[71] It is the illuminating beams of Elizabeth's royal power and providence, that is to say, that have burst through the "fogs and mists" in which Ireland was notoriously shrouded, to dispel the clouds of war and convert the Land of Ire into the Garden of Hope and Peace whose flowers decorate her elaborately embroidered jacket.[72]

The Rainbow painting, which Roy Strong has conjecturally linked to the last great spectacle of Elizabeth's reign, her visit to Robert Cecil at Hatfield in December 1602, needs to be recognized as an occasional work with a political agenda no less particular than that of other great royal portraits—such as the Armada portrait of fourteen years earlier or *Henry V* itself, in which Annabel Patterson has discovered "yet another symbolic portrait of [Elizabeth]." Anticipating Mountjoy's imminent defeat of the most powerful and obstinate of the Irish rebels, Hugh O'Neill, Earl of Tyrone, and hence the final subjugation of Ireland, the painting's appropriation of one of the great symbols of cultural difference to symbolize the incorporation of a conquered people into the body of the English nation-state is a chilling reminder of what it meant to be subjected to the inquisitorial "perspective" of monarchical power—what Claudius calls the "cheer and comfort" of his eye (*Hamlet*, 1.2.116).[73]

Stephen Greenblatt has argued that *Henry V* exhibits a form of royal power that depends above all "upon its privileged visibility"; in the absence of a highly developed bureaucracy and police, he maintains, such power cannot yet "dream . . . of a panopticon in which the most intimate secrets are open to the view of an invisible authority." Yet it was something closely resembling this fantasy of panoptic control that Davies dreamed of establishing in Ireland, and the Elizabeth of the Rainbow portrait, Argus-eyed and mantled in symbolic invisibility, seems perfectly designed to install his fantasy in the minds of potentially dissident subjects. It is the same fantasy we can see played out in the effortless exposure of Cambridge and his fellow conspirators in act 2 of *Henry V* ("Their faults are open," 2.2.142), and again in act 4's reminders of "what watch the King keeps to maintain the peace" (4.1.283), where Henry's "liberal eye" with its "largess universal, like the sun" (4.chor., ll. 43–4) comically dispels the clouds of popular "treason" (4.8.21). Shakespeare, however, suggests the limits of solar omnipotence through Williams's surly refusal of the king's gold ("I will none of your money," l. 67), and in the quarrel between this recalcitrant English soldier, with his oddly Welsh-sounding name, and the loyal Welsh-Englishman Fluellen, the play comes close to restaging the crisis of nationality provoked by Macmorris.[74]

Like Henry V's achievement of "the world's best garden," Elizabeth's plantation of the Irish wilderness and her creation of a nation of "Irish Englishmen" was an equivocal success—in a way that makes Shakespeare's ambiguous endorsement of Irish-French adventure in his epilogue seem oddly prophetic. Not even Mountjoy's careful manipulation of the truth could altogether suppress the irony of the queen's death on the very eve of O'Neill's submission, and that irony may stand for another, even more far-reaching. For the very actions that had been designed to redefine and stabilize the uncertain boundaries of the English nation had only succeeded in generating an idea of nationhood among the warring Irish septs that three hundred years of colonial occupation would utterly fail to eradicate. Skeptical historians may be quite correct in supposing that O'Neill's patriotic appeals to the sanctity of "native soil" and his denunciations of a state in which "we Irishmen are exiled and made bond-slaves to a strange and foreign prince" were as much a tactical contrivance as the more systematic nationalism fostered by the Tudor monarchy across the Irish sea.[75] But especially in the hands of his contemporary and chronicler, Peter Lombard, Catholic Archbishop of Armagh, they helped (like the dangerously free-floating rhetoric of Englishness in Shakespeare's own histories) to create a myth of nationhood whose consequences would prove incalculable: "I call God to witness," declares Lombard's Earl to the English negotiators at Dungannon

> that neither was it ambition, nor any other unlawful desire, as you would persuade and palm off upon the world, but . . . the intolerable oppression and servitude of the whole of my country *[patria]*. A passionate desire to liberate it was the first stimulus which urged me to make this war. . . . And [I] now confirm with an oath before you, that the sword which I have drawn for the liberty of my native land I shall never sheath until all heresy and schism has been expelled from every corner of Ireland.[76]

14

"The Exact Map or Discovery of Human Affairs": Shakespeare and the Plotting of History

—— ❁ ——

In *1 Henry IV* the dying Hotspur, contemplating his own end, imagines Time ("Time that takes survey of all the world," *1 Henry IV*, 5.4.82) as a practitioner of the newly important art of surveying—the art by which, with the assistance of the sister arts of cartography and chorography, space was being reconfigured in the interests of nation and empire. The purpose of this chapter is to unpack some implications of his metaphor. Underlying Hotspur's speech, of course, is a concern for something much more traditional—the preservation of his own fame—a concern articulated again and again in the course of Shakespeare's death scenes: in Hamlet's anxiety, for example, that Horatio should salve his friend's "wounded name" by remaining alive to "tell his story." The reflexive nature of such moments is perfectly exemplified in the ending of *Antony and Cleopatra*, where Caesar's oration over the dead Cleopatra ("She shall be buried by her Antony— / No grave upon the earth shall clip in it / A pair so famous" 5.2.358–60) draws solemn attention to the self-consciousness with which Shakespeare set about the representation of history. The monument in which Cleopatra dies is a figure for the monumentalizing authority of the play itself, for the heroic "story" in which Enobarbus longed to earn his "place." But Enobarbus himself is also the

play's principal mouthpiece for a more skeptical version of that narrative—
one that, if it does not exactly correspond to the official "truths" of Roman
historiography with which Caesar means to enclose Cleopatra's fame, is
sometimes uneasily reminiscent of the "monumental mockery" to which
heroic legend is exposed in *Troilus and Cressida*.[1] The counterpointing of
Enobarbus's and Caesar's perspectives against the protagonists' erotic tri-
umphalism might be read as a reminder of the arbitrary determination of
what gets remembered as "history"; so that if one were to search the canon
for a suitable figuration of the Shakespearean sense of history, the opening of
2 Henry IV might seem quite as appropriate as the ending of *Antony and
Cleopatra*. The prologue who ushers in the action of this most skeptical of
English chronicles, with his emblematic costume, painted like that of Virgil's
Fama "full of tongues," actually represents—fittingly enough for a sequel
that cynically doubles the action of its first part—the untrustworthy double
of Fame known as "Rumour." Deriving his name from the Latin *rumor*
("noise, din"), this chorus presents himself not simply as the presiding spirit
of a narrative whose outcome is repeatedly determined by false report and
misprision but as the arch-patron of a theater whose audience is sardonically
hailed as his own "household," a "blunt monster with uncounted heads, /
The still-discordant wavering multitude" (induction, ll. 18–22). And from a
Thersitean perspective, the loud-tongued chorus of *Henry V*, who hectors
and cajoles the audience into sharing his patriotic vision of the past, might be
taken as another, more chauvinistic incarnation of this False Fame—especially since the drama he struggles to mold to his own purposes is as self-conscious about the dubious process of "making history" as Brian Friel's recent
play of that name.[2] Not only does the action repeatedly make us aware of the
glaring discrepancies between the chorus's heroic intoxication and the brutal
actualities of warfare; it also exhibits a pervasive skepticism about the way in
which the characters fashion history to their own political purposes—one
that inevitably reflects on the "bending author's" own manipulation of the
past. Henry constantly looks forward to a time when "our history shall with
full mouth / Speak freely of our acts" (1.2.230–1), but in the context of his
callous execution of Bardolph and shameless butchery of the French prisoners, it is possible to see the glorious remembrance of Agincourt that the king
projects onto the screen of English history ("This story shall the good man
teach his son . . . From this day to the ending of the world," 4.3.56–8) as no
less distortively interested than the politic construction of French dynastic
history with which the archbishop launched the war—or as no less corruptly

partial than the swaggering falsehoods with which Pistol will dress his syphilitic scars (5.1.79–80). History, even the chorus's last, surprisingly lame intervention seems to confess, is what you make of it.

It is easy to see how these two ways of troping history (as transcendent monument or propagandist fiction), however superficially opposed, both derive naturally from a historiographical tradition that viewed the study of the past as essentially instrumental. "On, on, you noblest English, / Whose blood is fet from fathers of war-proof, / Fathers that like so many Alexanders / Have in these parts from morn till even fought. Be *copy* now to men of grosser blood, / And *teach* them how to war" (*Henry V*, 3.1.17–25). Henry V's exhortation at the siege of Harfleur exemplifies not merely the method by which he welds his heterogeneous soldiery into a disciplined army united by common purpose and identity but the practice by which the theater itself, according to apologists like Nashe and Heywood, contributed to the project of national self-invention. In the theater the prime function of historical representation was one of incorporation, summoning the spectators to become participants in the drama of nationality through the spirit of virtuous emulation roused by the spectacle of "our forefathers' valiant acts, that have lain long in rusty brass and worm-eaten books . . . [now] raised from the grave of oblivion."[3] Englishness is realized through a genealogy of heroic imitation in which Alexander serves as "copy" for those warlike ancestors after whom Henry's troops must fashion themselves, if they in turn are to serve as a "*model* [of] greatness" (2.chor., l. 16) for those "men of grosser blood" who now behold this image of their fame. For Shakespeare and his contemporaries this was perhaps the most compelling aspect of a dominant historiographic tradition in which the aims of moral education or political suasion took precedence over any commitment to the "truth" of events—the tradition expounded at great length by the author from whom I have taken my title. In "Observation 5" of his popular conduct book *The English Gentleman* (1630) Richard Brathwait discourses at length upon those "recreations" best calculated to improve "the inward man," among which he gives pride of place to history. So important did he consider this study that he dedicated a second *Nursery for Gentry* entirely to its practices: this work, *A Survey of History*, expands the discussion of history in *The English Gentleman* to provide a convenient, if somewhat verbose, summary of early modern historiographical thinking.[4]

Most of what Brathwait has to say is thoroughly predictable: history is a "storehouse or treasury" of morality and of "memorable examples," at once a "theater of noble actions begetting a laudable envy, a glorious emulation," and a "sable theater of human vanity" stamping its audience with "*impressive motives of worldly contempt.*"[5] It is a textbook of political instruction, which by exhibiting "the revolution of the times, [and] the mutation of states" enables one to "judge of things present and discreetly to foresee what is to come" by pointing to "the infallible character of succeeding events."[6] And it is an instrument of moral and patriotic edification, inspiring pride in the deeds of ancestors and "a desire of imitation," while showing the reader "how his country was first planted; how by degrees it became peopled; how to civility reduced; how by wholesome laws restrained; and how by the providence of the *Almighty*, in so calm and peaceable manner established."[7] In such passages history is imagined as an established and familiar text, an authoritative body of received knowledge waiting to be quarried by the diligent enquirer for narratives whose functions are essentially didactic and rhetorical. At other times, however, Brathwait appears to imagine the discipline in terms that are at once more objective and more dynamic (we might say "modern"): such a history must free itself from the falsifications of "partiality," which Brathwait denounces as the grand corrupter of historical verity, it being "the highest honour of an historian to be accounted *sincere.*" Though it may still serve to "beget a manly spirit" of virtuous imitation, the essential function of such "sincere" history is to lay bare the hidden truths of the past and to produce what Brathwait calls "the exact map or discovery of human affairs."[8] Such an approach is arguably implicit in the very title of the *Survey*, drawing as it does on the new technology of cartographic delineation and display, and it is wittily glanced at in the frontispiece portrait of the author, mounted on a tomb, and "discovered" behind the parted curtains that symbolized resurrection (see fig. 19).

Of course this notion of history as a mode of discovery was hardly Brathwait's invention. It is announced, for example, in the title of Sir John Davies's history of Irish colonization, *A Discovery of the True Causes Why Ireland Was Never Entirely Subdued* (1612). And something similar is implicit in a key episode from Spenser's *Faerie Queene*—a poem whose "general end," like that of Brathwait's *Survey*, was "to fashion a gentleman, or noble person in virtuous and gentle discipline."[9] In cantos 9–10 of book 2, Guyon's quest for the perfection of Temperance, that supreme imperial virtue, is temporarily suspended while he and Arthur visit the House of Alma. There, "removed farre behind" in the very depths of the castle they discover a chamber "ruinous and old," presided over by the patriarch Eumnestes (Good

19. Frontispiece to Richard Brathwait, A Survey of History *(1638),
reprinted by permission of the Folger Shakespeare Library.*

Memory), the "decrepit" condition of whose ancient "corse" is only matched
by the extraordinary vigor of his mind. With the help of his youthful assis-
tant Anamnestes (the Reminder) he introduces them to the "antique
Registers" of their history, in the form of two "auncient booke[s]" entitled

Antiquitie of Faerie lond and *Briton moniments*" (2.9.55–60). The style of chorographic history suggested by these titles is realized in canto 10, most of which is devoted to Arthur's perusal of *Briton moniments*. Here, as though leafing through the pages of some Camden or Speed, the prince discovers not only a chronicle of his own dynastic and national history but a chorography of the physical memorials in which that past is registered on the landscape— including a description of his forefather Lud's construction of "that gate, which of his name is hight, / By which he lyes entombed solemnly" (46) and of the "doleful moniments" of Stonehenge, where those who "list to rew" may "vew"—as Jacobean readers would soon be able to do in Speed's *Theater of the Empire of Great Britaine*—"Th' eternall markes of treason" in the graves of slaughtered British nobility (66). Guyon meanwhile is rapt in the history of Faerie lond, with its corresponding "moniments"—Elfinan's "golden wall" that bounds the city of Cleopolis (London), Elfant's "Christall" Palace of Panthea (Windsor Castle? Westminster Abbey?), and Elfinor's "bridge of brass" that spans the "glassy See" of a mythic Thames (72–4). The effect of scanning these volumes is to summon patriotic enthusiasm by introducing the two knights to their own place inside a glorious national chronology that fills them with a "naturall desire of countreys state" (77): "Deare countrey, O how dearely deare / Ought thy remembraunce, and perpetual band / Be to thy foster Childe, that from thy hand / Did commun breath and nourriture receave? / How brutish is it not to vnderstand, / How much to her we owe, that all us gave" (69).

But this is also a moment of discovery or revelation that restores a buried past. If the wanderings of Spenser's heroes constitute a mythologized Gothic version of those elaborate itineraries by which early modern chorographers mapped the geographic surface of Britain, this conning of antiquity represents the complementary process of establishing the historical coordinates of the nation. There could be no more vivid illustration of the way in which the antiquarian "rediscovery of British antiquity" contributed to the early modern project of national invention that Richard Helgerson has so wonderfully explored.[10] The knights' penetration of that deep interior space in which Eumnestes tends his chronicles registers, among other things, a new sense of the past as something with a physical depth and presence, like Prospero's "dark backward and abyss of time" (*Tempest*, 1.2.50), a space that you can imaginatively enter and descry—as Raphael and Giovanni da Udine were famously lowered into the subterranean ruins of the Roman past to explore the painted witness of its glory, or as Stow in his *Survey of London* imaginatively descends into the foundations of London to "discover" the astonishing "depth" of local history.[11] And it is possible to suggest, I think, that it was just this newly spatialized sense of the past that helped to make history the powerful ideological weapon it was to become. In the case of *The Faerie Queene* this was linked to the poem's role as a kind of British *Aeneid*, providing a foundational myth of empire—one that nourished a dream of discovery extending beyond the boundaries of the familiar to the "delight of novelties" that their histories produce in Arthur and Guyon. *Antiquitie of Faerie lond*, in particular, turns out to offer not merely an account of the past, but the pattern of a still-to-be-attained future of "puissant kings, which all the world warrayed, / And to themselves all nations did subdue . . . [whom] all *India* obeyed, / And all that now *America* men call" (72). It is as if imagining the past not simply as a familiar storehouse of instructive exempla but as a kind of obscure territory awaiting discovery and the ordering power of the cartographic gaze makes it possible to envisage the future in a similar way—as it is imagined, for example, in that extraordinary figure of apocalyptic prophecy conjured up by Queen Elizabeth in *Richard III*: "I see, *as in a map*, the end of all"(2.4.53; emphasis added).

The simultaneous popularization of national history and chorography enabled, as Helgerson has shown, the projection of England as a concrete, physically imagined entity, with a body and a history separable from those of the monarch—a "model to [its own] inward greatness / Like little body with a mighty heart" (*Henry V*, 2.chor., ll. 16–17). The classic expression of that vision in the drama is John of Gaunt's evocation of England as a "blessed plot" inscribed with the legendary "deeds" of heroic ancestors (*Richard II*, 2.1.40–66), a "map of honour" to rival that which the queen discovers in the body of Richard himself (*Richard II*, 5.1.12).[12] "Plot" is a key term in Gaunt's speech since it encompasses, in a single rhetorical gesture, the "sea-walled garden" of England itself (l. 50), the cartographic "plot" (otherwise "plat" or "platform") on which the lyric mapping of this patriotic blazon depends, the providential "plot" or design of national history, and the "plat" or stage of the global theater onto which these plots are projected. The English theater, after all, was a space of discovery—a place in which, as Thomas Platter observed, a predominantly stay-at-home people could imaginatively range the world.[13] It is no accident that Gaunt's ecphrasis strongly resembles the chorographic enthusiasms of men like Camden and Speed, for it is a virtuoso expression of the cartographic and historical imagination, an act of lyrical mapping whose temporal and spatial coordinates invite all members of the audience to plot their own relation to the emerging nation-state (as Arthur and Guyon plot theirs) through the providential history that has shaped its vivid geographical presence.[14]

But history and chorography were more than simply complementary activities. The development of historical cartography proceeded hand in hand with the mapping of new worlds. Leo X commissioned Raphael to produce an archaeological map of ancient Rome in which, according to one contemporary, "as Ptolemy set up the world" so he would set out "the antique buildings of Rome, showing so clearly their proportions, forms and ornament that, having seen it, one would *seem to have seen Ancient Rome.*"[15] Geography, declared the great atlas maker Ortelius, was "the eye of history," which is perhaps why, in Vermeer's *Art of Painting*, Clio, the muse of history, stands with her eyes almost closed, while behind her hangs the magnificently illuminated map that supplies her deficient vision. The work of Ortelius's English disciple John Speed insists in a more literal fashion on the power of cartography to render the past visible. Here history is quite literally mapped onto the countryside, revealed as a kind of script legible to the attentive surveyor. Speed's sense of the intimate relation between chorography and history was indicated by the two-part design of his patriotic masterwork—his celebrated national atlas *The Theater of the Empire of Great Britain* (1611) being followed by a consecutively paginated volume of *History* that made use of the same monumental frontispiece: a triumphal arch adorned with figures representing the ancestral peoples who had contributed to the British "nation," Briton, Saxon, Dane, and Norman (see fig. 20). Moreover the historical dimension of Speed's chorographic theater is emphasized from the outset, not only by this frontispiece but also by an introductory series of maps and gazettes illustrating the sequence of national history from the Roman occupation through "the Saxon Heptarchy" and "the time of the *Normans*" to the present.[16]

Even more striking, perhaps, is the way historical materials are incorporated in the detail of his regional maps, which repeatedly illustrate Speed's protoarchaeological sense of history as something visibly inscribed on the land. Speed carefully plotted historical information onto his local "platforms"—the multiple "stages" of his *Theater*—first by emblazoning on the borders of each county map the arms of its earls, hieroglyphs of its feudal history, and then by marking the territory itself with illustrations of its "places of great battles" (B2v), its ancient buildings and antiquities. The significance of these "monuments" he explained in the accompanying gazettes

20. *Frontispiece to John Speed*, The Theatre of the Empire of Great Britaine *(1611), reprinted by permission of the Folger Shakespeare Library.*

21. Map of Cumberland in John Speed, The Theatre of the Empire of Great Britaine *(1611), reprinted by permission of the Folger Shakespeare Library*

and even in passages of text conspicuously imposed on the surface of the maps. The "plots" of Cumberland and Northumberland, for example, give particular attention to "The Picts Wall," describing its erection under Hadrian as a barrier against the barbarians of the north and enlarging its historical presence with marginal illustrations of surviving "monuments and Altars, [erected by Roman soldiers] with inscriptions to their idol Gods, for the prosperity of their Emperors and selves" (see figs. 21 and 22).[17] The map of Wiltshire is ornamented with an image of Stonehenge (see fig. 23), which is identified as a burial monument erected by Aurelius, King of the Britons, in memory of his nobility, slaughtered by the treacherous Vortigern. Herefordshire is flanked by an elaborate illustration of the battle of Ludlow with a description of the episode (famously dramatized in Shakespeare's *3 Henry VI*, 2.1) "Wherein before the battle was struck, appeared visibly in the firmament three suns which after a while joined all together" (see fig. 24). The map of Leicestershire gives great prominence to the battle of Bosworth, recording how "the corpse of the dead king being tugged and despitefully torn was laid all naked upon a horse and trussed like an hog behind a pursuivant at arms and as homely buried in the Gray Fr[iars] within Leicester, which being ruinated, his grave rests as obscure overgrown with nettles and weeds" (see fig. 25)—to which the gazette sardonically adds that "only the stone-chest wherein he was laid (a drinking trough now for horses in a common inn) retaineth the memory of that great monarch's funeral" (p. 61). In this way Speed discovers in the land itself a kind of historical "plot" whose story can be deciphered in all those visible characters of the past —the memorials or "monuments" (in the largest sense of that once comprehensive term) that antiquaries like John Weever were busy recording and preserving.[18]

Just as Speed claimed to be moved by "ardent affection and love to my *native country*," so Weever's frontispiece and title page for *Ancient Fvnerall Monvuments* (1631) stressed the commitment of his "Travels and Study" to "reviving the dead memory" of the "Royal Progeny, the Nobility, and

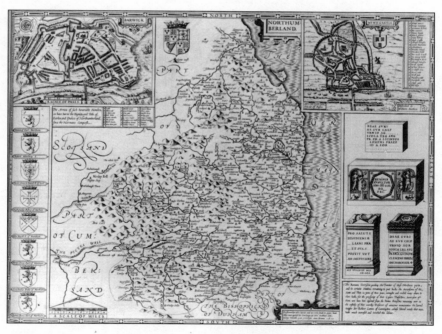

22. *Map of Northumberland in John Speed,* The Theatre of the Empire of Great Britaine *(1611), reprinted by permission of the Folger Shakespeare Library.*

23. *Map of Wiltshire in John Speed,* The Theatre of the Empire of Great Britaine *(1611), reprinted by permission of the Folger Shakespeare Library.*

Communality" of "the united Monarchy of Great Britain, Ireland, and the islands adjacent" (see fig. 26).[19] In this project Weever, like Speed, was consciously inspired by "that honourable Gentleman *Sir Robert Cotton*" the doyen of antiquaries, whom he describes in his prefatory epistle as "this worthy repairer of eating-times ruins, this *Philadelphus*, in preserving old monuments, and ancient records: this magazine, this treasury, this store-house of antiquities." He conceived of his work as combining elements of chorography and chronicle in the fashion pioneered by Camden's *Britannia* (sig. A-A2). The conceit of Weever's frontispiece, with its studied imitation of an elaborate neoclassical tomb, is wholly in keeping with his theme. The title is captured on a central tombstone-shaped tablet, flanked by supporters representing the Old and New Adam, and symbolizing the same triumph over mortality to which the memorializing power of history itself aspires. The Second Adam, armed with a cross and a banner of Saint George, triumphs over the serpent of death and sin, while the first is presented as a Vesalian skeleton, leaning on a spade and contemplating the fatal apple that accounts for his decayed condition. Viewed, however, from the perspective suggested by the adjacent portrait of Weever holding a skull with the same hand in which the skeleton grasps the apple, we might take this equivocal figure as a cadaverous type of the author himself, an antiquarian excavator inspecting the fruit of his mortal studies—a reading that helps complicate the meaning of the graveyard landscape in the oval superimposed on the tomb-chest at the base of the engraving (see fig. 27). This landscape is dotted with graves and sumptuous funeral monuments, some open (graves ready to receive new dead or ruinous witnesses to the depredations of time?), whose double message of mortality and transcendence the book itself is dedicated to preserving. The dominating tomb facade evokes the monumental splendors of a triumphal arch. And with its frontal platform ("tarras") and gabled pediment supported on twin pillars it bears a marked resemblance to an Elizabethan stage, so that Weever's text, like Speed's, can be imagined as a species of the-

24. *Map of Herefordshire in John Speed,* The Theatre of the Empire of Great Britaine *(1611), reprinted by permission of the Folger Shakespeare Library.*

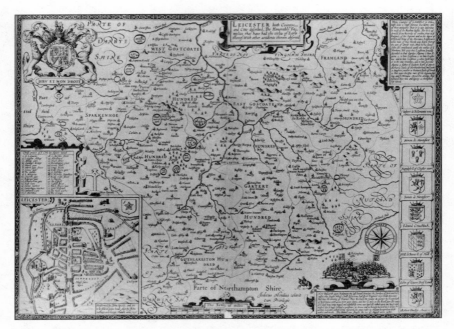

25. *Map of Leicestershire in John Speed,* The Theatre of the Empire of Great Britaine *(1611), reprinted by permission of the Folger Shakespeare Library*

ater whose monuments stand revealed in a kind of "discovery space," framed by the twin performers who mark the limits of human history.

Nowhere is this innovatory sense of history-as-discovery more eloquently displayed than in the work of one of the few contemporary historians cited by Brathwait, Sir Walter Raleigh.[20] The magnificent frontispiece for Raleigh's *History of the World*, shows History, flanked by Experience and Truth, trampling on Death and Oblivion, while supporting a globe displaying the New World and Terra Australis alongside Europe and Africa, flanked by the figures of Good and Ill Fame, and surmounted by the all-seeing Eye of Providence (see fig. 28). The verses printed opposite elucidate "The Mind of *The Front*" in orthodox monumental terms: "From *Death* and dark *Oblivion* (near the same), / The *Mistress of Man's life*, grave History, / Raising the *World* to good, or *Evil* fame, / Doth vindicate it to Eternity *Time's witness, Herald of Antiquity, / The light of Truth, and life of Memory*." But Raleigh's preface glosses "the light of Truth" in a way that explicitly illuminates the relationship between history and the frontispiece's symbols of geographical discovery: "History triumpheth over all human knowledge . . . for it hath carried our knowledge over the vast and devouring space of so many thousands of years, and given so fair and piercing eyes to our mind; that we plainly behold living now, as if we had lived then, that great World *the wise work of a great GOD.*"[21]

History, like a species of navigation "over the vast and devouring space"

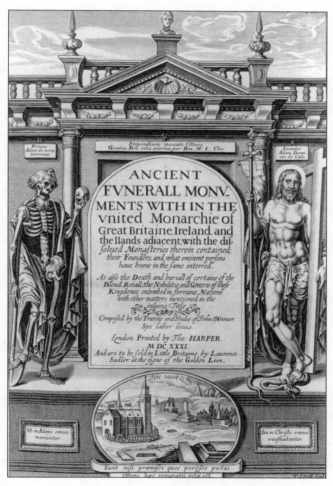

26. *Frontispiece to John Weever,* Ancient Fvnerall Monvments *(1631), reprinted by permission of the Folger Shakespeare Library.*

of the temporal ocean, gives us back the world—an idea that achieves a kind
of realization in the frontispiece to Samuel Purchas's *Hakluytus Posthumus*,
with its iconic genealogy of navigation and its offer of "a History of the
World, in Sea voyages, & lande-Trauells, by Englishmen & others" (see fig.
15). In Purchas's elaborate iconographic scheme, the monuments of English
providential history at the top of the page (including the double portrait that
identifies James and Charles with the body of the land) are balanced by the
symbols of discovery at the bottom—the twin globes inscribed with images

27. *Frontispiece portrait of John Weever in John Weever,* Ancient
Fvnerall Monvments *(1631), reprinted by permission of the Folger
Shakespeare Library.*

28. Frontispiece to Sir Walter Raleigh, The History of the World *(1614), reprinted by permission of the Folger Shakespeare Library.*

29. Ribaut's marker-column from Theodore de Bry, America, *pt. 1 (1591), reprinted by permission of the Folger Shakespeare Library.*

of the triumphant circumnavigations of Drake and Candish, which announce the God-like (or Ortelian) illumination of the world by "soldiers and merchants[,] the world's two eyes to see it self." It is as if these agents of terrestrial revelation have become proxies for the eye of providence itself. But the eyes that gaze out at us from between these discovered hemispheres are those of the historian, Purchas himself, the man whose learning enables him to take survey of all the world from his study—the Prospero of this scene, whose book (like the ending of Shakespeare's play) is inscribed with the legend of *vanitas*.

The Tempest itself, we have become accustomed to thinking, is Shakespeare's discovery play: a work spun out of the pages of voyaging literature that becomes an elaborate prophetic fantasy on colonial encounter and its imperial aftermath. As it happens, it is also a play that contains one of the folio's rare explicit directions for a "discovery scene"—"Here Prospero discovers Ferdinand and Miranda playing at chess" (5.1.173 SD)—a last "vision of the island" in which the Neapolitans are to recognize an emblem of the "providence divine" or artful "provision" that has brought them to this moment of renewal (1.2.160, 28). In the light of the elaborate system of symmetries that governs the play, however, it is tempting to suppose that this revelation, far from being unique, was meant to balance another at the beginning of the play's main action, symbolically displacing the figures of father and daughter in Prospero's cell with those of the daughter and her new spouse. Whether this was literally the case, it is clear that "discovery" is a key motif in both scenes. And just as the revelations of act 5, scene 1 are ushered in by Prospero's decision to "discase me, and myself present / As I was sometime Milan" (ll. 85–6), so in act 1, scene 2 his request to "pluck my magic garment from me" (l. 24) introduces the narrative discasing of his ducal identity to Miranda. That first gestural "discovery" unveiled, of course, not a new world but an old one—in a scene that notoriously becomes the longest history lesson ever staged. And the final scene returns to that same *chronicle of day by day*" (l. 165; emphasis added) immediately before its discovery of the lovers' ritual combat. The striking thing about Prospero's "uninhabited Island" (as the folio calls it) is that, by the time the audience reaches its shores, it is already drenched in history. From one point of view, Prospero's excavation of the "dark backward and abyss of time" (1.2.50) might be read as an allegory of colonial displacement and nostalgia. A restoration of the past is found necessary to the full discovery and possession of a "brave new world"—rather as the recent PBS series *Long Journey Home* could locate "the Irish in America" only by a return to the history of the Potato Famine that occupied nearly a quarter of its running time. But Shakespeare's play contemplates, I think, another kind of intimacy between discovery, colonization, and history that invites a less sentimental construction.

No sooner has Gonzalo recognized the providential *felix culpa* that has brought them all to rediscovery of themselves in this "bare isle" than he announces the imminent monumentalization of their history: "and set it down / With gold on lasting pillars " (5.1.210–11). These pillars have a recognizable theatrical ancestry: in act 3, scene 2 of *2 Tamburlaine*, the hero and his sons erect a monument to the dead Zenocrate against the prospect of a burning town, the latest of his imperial conquests:

❧

CALYPHAS:
This pillar placed in memory of her,
Where in Arabian, Hebrew, Greek is writ:
This town, being burnt by Tamburlaine the Great
Forbids the world to build it up again.

AMYRAS:
And here this mournful streamer shall be placed,
Wrought with the Persian and Egyptian arms,
To signify she was a princess born,
And wife unto the monarch of the East.

CELEBINUS:
And here this table as a register
Of all her virtues and perfections.

TAMBURLAINE:
And here the picture of Zenocrate
To show her beauty which the world admired;
That, hanging here, will draw the gods from heaven,
And cause the stars fixed in the southern arc. . . .
As pilgrims travel to our hemisphere,
Only to gaze upon Zenocrate.
    3.2.15–33

❀

With its heraldic attachments and multilingual record of conquest, Tamburlaine's "pillar" is the Scythian counterpart of those columns with which European discoverers and colonists, in conscious imitation of Roman practice, announced their claims on the territory of foreign peoples (see fig. 29). Ostensibly, of course, it is a funeral monument to his dead queen. But since Zenocrate—rather like the entombed Elizabeth on Purchas's title page—functions as a kind of muse to his martial art, it also doubles as a sign of possession, a mark of the imperial authority announced in its principal inscription. The memorial pillars envisaged by the pacific Gonzago are less aggressively inscribed, but their function is essentially the same: to write a history of possession on the land. Just as Caliban, who "did not know [his] own meaning," was allowed to *make sense* only by and in the language of his master, so his "poor island" is presented as "desert"—a historyless *terra nullius*—until Prospero undertakes to discover its past and to fill its emptiness with narrative, thereby enabling it to fulfil its meaning as the place of European self-recovery.

Yet, of course, *The Tempest* is no more programmatic than *Henry V* in its attitude to history and remains remarkably open-eyed about the collusion between colonial "discovery" and the fabrication of the past. The first act displays the process by which Prospero's illumination of time's "dark backward" systematically obscures the rival narratives of his enemies, those who in his judgment "made sinner[s] of [their] memory" (1.2.101). What results is an insecure historical palimpsest, uncannily resembling that which Antonio produced when he "new created / The creatures that were mine" (1.2.81–2); or that which Gonzalo discovers in the chorography of the western Mediterranean: "This Tunis, sir, was Carthage" (2.1.82); or that which Caliban reveals when he announces, "This island's mine, by Sycorax my mother, / Which thou tookst from me" (1.2.334–5). Like Tamburlaine's monumental column, Gonzalo's "lasting pillars" may be imaginatively bodied forth in the ornate columns that supported the gabled heavens of Shakespeare's globe. But then Prospero's melancholy prophecy has already anticipated the disintegration of that "baseless fabric," with all its vain imperial architecture of "cloud-capped towers gorgeous palaces [and] solemn temples" (4.1.151–3), so that Shakespeare's play contains within itself the seeds of the counternarrative that will become Aimé Césaire's reclamation of Calibanic history, *Une Tempête*. In case this should seem suspiciously like a postcolonial recuperation of the universal genius whose uncanny foreknowledge wrote the script of English history, it may be worth recording that Shakespeare's way of lifting the corner of his imperial palimpsest has a striking cartographic counterpart in a series of maps made to celebrate Lord Mountjoy's conquest of another "salvage and deformed monster" who had profited from the master's education only to learn how to curse—Hugh O'Neill, the Earl of Tyrone.[22]

The work of one Richard Bartlett, a military surveyor and cartographer with Mountjoy's army, these remarkable maps are nevertheless more illustrative than practical. They employ a hybrid convention, halfway between landscape painting and cartography, and four of the twelve make use of an extraordinary visual conceit whereby additional bird's-eye views appear overlaid on the principal scene, giving the strange impression that enormous maps are being unscrolled over the surface of the Ulster landscape and pinned to the conquered soil itself. So in map 9, a view of the new English fort at Monaghan with its elaborately geometrical design and broad approach-roads (representing the latest in European military architecture) has been laid across a wild Irish landscape of mountains, narrow forest paths, ruins, rough cabins and primitive *crannogs*—or lake-forts (see fig. 30). Placed on the scroll are an oversized scale and pair of compasses, which appear to function less as a practical adjunct to map reading than as a triumphant symbol of the technology whose contribution to the making of the map and to the building of the fort itself made it as much an instrument as a

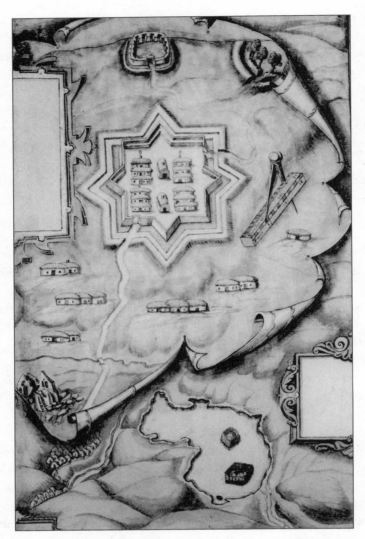

30. *"Monaghan Fort" by Richard Bartlett, reprinted by permission of the National Library of Ireland.*

witness of Mountjoy's conquest. Perhaps the most interesting of these maps
is the deeply ambivalent number 5. This shows Tyrone's slighted castle at
Dungannon, in a landscape overlaid with scrolls illustrating the siege of a
strategic *crannog* and the English army encamped before the O'Neill crown-
ing-stone at Tullaghogue (see fig. 31). The latter was the most important

political site in Ulster, carefully located in all the most important contemporary maps of the province, including an anonymous map of 1598 that marks
it with the inscription "O'Neill his stone," those of Francis Jobson that variously identify "the stone where they make the O'Neills" and "the stone
where O'Neill is made," and other maps by Bartlett himself, such as that of

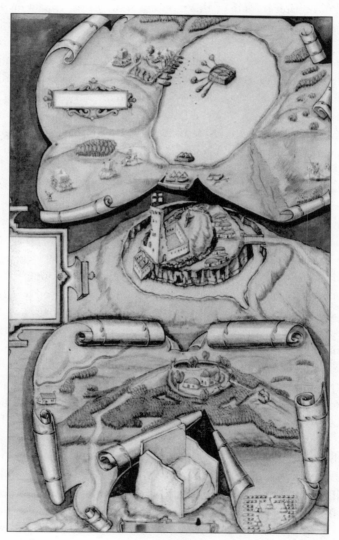

31. "Dungannon and Tullaghogue" *by Richard Bartlett,*
reprinted by permission of the National Library of Ireland.

1602 with its legend "Tullaghogue[:] on this hill the Irish create their O'Neill."[23]

Mountjoy's destruction of the stone in late 1602 was a well-calculated attempt to *un*make O'Neill, on the clear recognition that it was his clan title rather than the earldom conferred by Elizabeth that secured his power and prestige among the Irish. Yet even after its destruction, Bartlett felt constrained to register the site of this monument on his provincial map of 1603 ("Tullaghogue[:] on this hill were 4 stones in the manner of a chair, wherein the O'Neills this many years have been made"), and its presence remained visible for many years (along with those of the "fifty-six castles and forts" with which the province had been "secured") in the successive editions of John Speed's *Theater of the Empire of Great Britain* (1611) as "the stone where O'Neill is chosen." In the Dungannon picture-map the stone is displayed high on a wooded hillside in front of the small *rath* belonging to its O'Hagan guardians; camped below is Mountjoy's army with its disciplined array of pavilions and cabins, preparing to break down the throne that the cartographer's eye has already "captured." But a strange thing has happened at the bottom of the map, where an enlarged version of the chair has erupted through the fabric of this "view," so that the ragged chart seems about to split and roll back over the English camp.

Whatever Bartlett may have intended by this pictorial device, it is impossible, with hindsight, not to read it as a prophetic anticipation of the violent persistence of the very history that Bartlett's mapping aimed to efface. And within a short time, it seems, of his making this powerful image (whose ornamental cartouches, designed to frame the narrative conquest, remain so disconcertingly blank), Bartlett was given cause to understand its prescience; for, as Sir John Davies informed the Earl of Salisbury, "one Barkeley [i.e., Bartlett] being appointed by the late Earl of Devonshire to draw a true and perfect map of the north parts of Ulster (the old maps being false and defective), when he came into Tyrconnell the inhabitants took off his head, because they would not have their country discovered."[24] We might remember Caliban: "Batter his skull, or paunch him with a stake, / Or cut his wezand with thy knife," says Shakespeare's "salvage," laying out the "plot" that will undo his own discoverer, "But remember / First to possess his books; for without them / He's but a sot nor hath not / One spirit to command" (*Tempest*, 3.2.88–92). In any case Bartlett's way of "discovering" the landscape as a cartographic text densely inscribed with the signs of the conqueror's history, would ultimately prove a two-edged weapon. For beginning in the late eighteenth century, Irish antiquarians, following the course charted by English chorographers, would learn to decipher in the monuments of antiquity the legends of a very different past—one from which they could fabricate a "national" history of their own.

The World Beyond: Shakespeare and the Tropes of Translation

At the heart of every imperial fiction (its heart of darkness) there is a fiction of translation.
—Eric Cheyfitz, *The Poetics of Imperialism*

Having been borne across the world, we are translated men. It is normally supposed that something always gets lost in translation; I cling, obstinately, to the notion that something can also be gained.
—Salman Rushdie, "Imaginary Homelands"

Late in 1993 news reports were filed about the latest casualty of the Bosnian war. The Old Bridge in Mostar, from which this city straddling the Neretva River took its name, had finally been destroyed. Compared with the routine slaughter of civilians in this vicious intercommunal conflict, the destruction of a mere bridge, however ancient or beautiful, might have seemed a matter of small consequence. But it was clear that for Bosnians the event had a symbolic significance that went far beyond the bridge's historic and aesthetic value—or even its strategic importance as the last remaining link between the Croat and Muslim-dominated enclaves into which the city had become divided. A few months earlier its fate had been predicted by a Bosnian judge. For him the bridge stood for the possibility of coexistence; it was a symbol of the state's multicultural heritage, but, he confessed, "The people from the countryside don't believe in it. So they want to destroy it. The bridge is a metaphor—to them it must be finished."[1] There is a terrible poignancy to this story, not just because of what it says about the intensity of human investment in symbols but for what it reveals about the dangerous power of metaphor. This bridge, after all, is not just any metaphor, but a metaphor for metaphor itself or (to use a closely related and perhaps more evocative term) for translation. For "metaphor" and "translation," deriving as they do from the Greek and Latin words for "bear across" (μεταφερειν and *transfero*) are, at the most fundamental level, terms of bridging. More, it is clear, than the mere accidents of demography and military strategy determined the selection of Mostar as one of the most fiercely contested sites of the Bosnian war of partition. "I'm fighting for the bridge," one of its martyrs, a Croat in the predominantly Muslim government forces, is quoted as having said. "If the bridge falls, Mostar falls with it. It's our heart." In Serbo-Croat his words must have comprised a painfully tautological pun: "If the bridge disappears, there will be no [Place of the] Bridge." Mostar and its bridge stood for bridging, for metaphor, for translation, for the possibility of crossing over to the other side. In the minds of its enemies, on the other hand, the bridge stood for betrayal, for improper mixture; Turkish built, it was less an emblem of cultural exchange than a metaphor of conquest—a bridgehead of Islamic culture on the edge of Christian Europe. Like the imaginary bridge built "through the moving air" to "join . . . the Afric shore / And make that country continent to Spain" with which Marlowe's Faustus crowns his vision of universal empire (*Doctor Faustus*, 3.107–10), the bridge was a deeply ambivalent symbol—a site of profoundly ambivalent translations.

This chapter, it will be apparent by now, is only incidentally concerned with "translation" in its narrowly linguistic application. Even in this now-predominant sense, however, it is important to recognize that translation (as George Steiner's *After Babel* long ago demonstrated) is never a mechanical or even a purely linguistic process—a simple matter of replacing as accurately as possible one set of words with their nearest "equivalents" in another tongue. It is also (as its Latin root might suggest) a matter of trading between cultures, between different ways of imagining the world, involving both diachronic shifts and delicate synchronic adjustments. Linguistic translation is thus connected at a fundamental level with other forms of "bearing across," with the whole epistemologically vexed business of negotiating cultural boundaries. As the Latin equivalent for the Greek μεταφορα, *translatio* was the rhetorical device that transformed one thing into another—the figure by means of which, more than any other, language sought to cope with the experience of the new, the unfamiliar, the Other.[2]

❀ ❀ ❀

"There is a world elsewhere," declares Coriolanus as he turns his back on Rome (*Coriolanus* 3.1.135). For seventeenth-century audiences, tuned to the images of New World discovery, his line, like Antony's "Then must thou needs find out new heaven, new earth" (*Antony and Cleopatra*, 1.1.17), must have had a potent anachronistic resonance. Coriolanus, however, is constitutionally incapable of imagining, let alone inhabiting, a world that is anything more than a poor mirror of the one he has left behind. He crosses into the domain of the Volsces, but the translation is purely physical, and the fantasy of "a world elsewhere" serves only to express the pathos of an impossible transformation. It is a small detail, but its effect is symptomatic; for while Shakespeare's writing can often seem almost perversely indifferent to the geographic excitements of his age, it betrays at its margins, like so much literature of the period, a haunting awareness of worlds elsewhere. Only one of his plays makes significant use of discovery literature—and even then the approach to New World encounters is puzzlingly oblique; yet the experience of crossing over into the space of the Other is figured in play after play.

Shakespeare's fascination with such crossings was necessarily bound up with the role of his own theater as a place of miraculous translations—advertised, in the case of the Globe, by a name and sign that proclaimed its capacity to carry the audience to any quarter of the newly discovered world. The English, one foreign visitor observed, while generally not much given to actual travel, flocked to the theater as an imaginative surrogate for its excitements. It was precisely to this desire for vicarious transport that Marlowe vauntingly appealed in the manifesto-like prologue that promised to "lead" the *Tamburlaine* audience to the hero's "stately tent of war," and the same intoxicated sense of the theater's translative capacity informs the high rhetoric and mock disclaimers of Shakespeare's *Henry V* choruses. Unlike the medieval theater of communal self-realization, "this scene," in Peter Womack's words, "is not part of any community, but takes you *out of it* . . . as if the price of admission bought a ticket to Asia Minor," to France, to the Caribbean, to the very Antipodes.[3]

"Translation" seems a particularly convenient term for such crossings because of its broad range of meanings. Its Elizabethan connotations include forced transportation and theft at one extreme, and rapture at another. It has as much to do with changing places as with shifting speech, with the crossing of seas as with the crossing of linguistic frontiers, and with the bridging of cultural divisions as with the interpretation of unfamiliar tongues. It embraces the negotiation of all sorts of boundaries—physical, linguistic, and cultural. It is also a standard term for metaphor—Puttenham's "figure of transport"—the figure by which the proper is "translated" into the improper, the strange into the familiar. Something of the rich ambivalence of its processes can be illustrated from an essay of Montaigne's that was to provide the essential pretext for the greatest of all Shakespearean dramas of crossing and translation, *The Tempest*.[4]

"Of the Cannibals" anecdotalizes the same paradoxes of cultural relativity that Montaigne famously articulated in a wry pun on his own name: "What truth is that which these Mountains bound, and is a lie in the World beyond them?" It was a question to which Shakespeare and his contemporaries would return again and again. Whether that "world beyond" is called America, Illyria, Egypt, Mauritania, "a wood near Athens," or simply "the island," it is always conceived as a kind of epistemological or moral antipodes, in which the supposed absolutes of European civilization are exposed as mere accidents of language and location. In "Of the Cannibals" Montaigne makes a partial crossing into one such world, that of the Tupinamba people of northeastern Brazil. A double translation is involved in this encounter. Like so many other inhabitants of the New World, the Tupinamba whom Montaigne interrogates have themselves been subjected to violent translation from the South American rain forest to the streets of Rouen. Montaigne, offering himself as a species of go-between, will complete that process of appropriation by rendering them comprehensible— translating them—to his European readers. To bring this about he must negotiate the "wondrous distance between their form and ours," and through this attempt at imaginative self-translation, he discovers a perspective from which the mores of his own culture emerge as more barbarous and unnatural than anthropophagy itself. As it turns out, however, Montaigne's investigations grant him only fragmentary and unreliable glimpses of this other mentality, for his cultural translation is itself ironically dependent upon the mediation of an incompetent interpreter, "who through his foolishness was so troubled to conceive my imaginations, that I could draw no great matter from him." Given the radically unsettling potential of his discoveries, this is perhaps fortunate, and it is possible to sense a certain relief behind the abruptness with which the essay is cut short ("but what of that? They wear no kind of breeches nor hosen"), for however it may mock the complacencies of the essay's implied reader, this odd, ironic shrug also has the convenient effect of returning the Indians to the symbolic indecipherability of the naked condition in which they were first encountered.[5]

Translation, Montaigne's essay suggests, is always a two-edged sword. It is both an instrument of power, mastery, and expropriation, and a vehicle of self-transformation, entailing disorientation and even the threat of self-loss. In its aggressive mode, translation is the process described by Eric Cheyfitz that brings together the various forms of discursive and physical violence on which the creation of empire depends. "The imperialist mission," he writes, "is [essentially] one of translation: the translation of the 'other' into the terms of empire." Significantly enough "translation" became a term of art in the discourse of colonization, with men like Richard Beacon and Edmund Spenser arguing that the problems of Ireland could be resolved by the "translating of colonies" on the one hand and the "translating" of the native Irish out of their lands and language on the other. Yet the recurrent nightmare of "degeneration" that permeates such texts serves as a reminder that the appropriative drive of translation was always liable to unaccountable reversal, producing what their authors saw as a dangerous kind of alienation—an "unnatural" transformation in which the civil self was drawn into the orbit of the barbarous Other.[6]

❀ ❀ ❀

The aggressive face of translation, as I have argued elsewhere, is most obviously displayed in Shakespeare's history cycles. The negotiation of linguistic boundaries plays an especially crucial role in these plays, where imperial aggrandizement and the fashioning of national identity are seen as two sides of a single coin. In *1 Henry VI* the straightforward Talbot is confronted by the treacherous stratagems of a French witch, Joan La Pucelle, whose name punningly translates as "puzzel/puzzle," and whose magically persuasive speech is marked by all the duplicity supposedly native to her tongue. It is entirely characteristic that the only line of actual French spoken by Pucelle in the play should occur at the point when she and her soldiers gain entry to Rouen disguised as simple country folk coming to market ("Paysans, la pauvre gens de France," 3.2.14)—as if the language itself were the sign of national deceitfulness. Similarly in *Richard II*, to repudiate the ambiguous sleights of translation—as the Duchess of York does ("Speak 'pardon' as 'tis current in our land, / The chopping French we do not understand," 5.3.123–4)—is to claim community with the same fellowship of honest, plain-spoken souls who are assumed to make up the audience, the nation to whose sympathy Mowbray appeals when he laments his exile from the linguistic home of "native English." To yield to the siren music of alterity, as Mortimer surrenders to the untranslated Welsh song of Glendower's daughter in *1 Henry IV*, on the other hand, is to degenerate from kind in a way that compromises one's nationality and masculinity together.[7]

In *Henry V*, which presciently anticipates James I's creation of the "Empire of Great Britain" by insisting that the possession of a common speech is what, more than anything else, defines a nation, language and translation become all-important. But here, as in Spenser's Ireland, it is the conquered Other who is subjected to forcible translation. Englishness is consistently imagined as the not-French, and no play is more insistent upon the physical barrier that symbolically divides "two mighty monarchies, / Whose high, upreared, and abutting fronts / The perilous narrow ocean parts asunder" (prologue, ll. 20–2). Elsewhere the channel may be invoked as a symbol of separateness and defensive strength, but only in *Henry V* does crossing it seem to constitute a real difficulty. The audience are summoned to vicarious participation in Henry's enterprise by the rhetorical transports of the chorus, and all the force of their straining imaginations together with the fierce insistence of three choric orations is required simply to "transport the scene," "convey" the spectators, and "carry" Henry to France for the first time, while the fifth chorus, which has to get the king over the channel twice (and "our general" across the Irish Sea for good measure), wryly attempts to overcome the improbability of this triplicated translation with a punning appeal to the viewers' indulgence: "Then brook *abridgement*, and your eyes advance, / After your thoughts, straight back again to France" (5.chor., ll. 44–5; emphasis added).

Once conveyed to France, the hero himself becomes a "conveyor" in the sense used by Richard II (4.1.317), dispossessing the French of their lands in a process that is represented not merely in scenes of military violence but through metaphors of linguistic translation. Not for nothing is Henry presented as a master of all discourses (1.1.38–52), with a gift for histrionic self-translation carried over from his Eastcheap past. Not for nothing does he turn these very attributes into the instruments of imperial expropriation. In a scene (3.4) that immediately follows Henry's first victory on French soil, the French princess is shown preparing herself for an occupation that, like the entering of Harfleur's "maiden walls" (5.2.322), is also a defloration. She enacts her surrender by systematically Englishing her body, translating it into the conqueror's tongue, as Henry himself will convey the body of the land into his own power—an equation that is made perfectly explicit in the scene of linguistic enforcement that ends the play where "le possession de France" translates as the possession of its princess, and where French Katherine is translated to English "Kate." Behind the playful bullying of this thinly masked rape, with its talk of tongues and hearts, lies the assumption brutally articulated by Spenser in his *View of the Present State of Ireland*, that identity and loyalty are substantially determined by linguistic allegiance—the speech being English, Henry assumes, the heart must needs be English too.[8]

Yet, although the patriotic stage history of *Henry V* is enough to show how profoundly Shakespeare's writing was implicated in the Empire-building translations it describes, the play is far from simply endorsing the imperial propaganda on which it draws, and its reservations are nicely epitomized in the scene of comic mistranslation that parodies Henry's victory at Agincourt. Pistol's capture of Monsieur le Fer stands in much the same relation to the king's heroics as Katherine's self-blazoning to the surrender of Harfleur. It also asks to be read as a parodic prolepsis of Henry's wooing, for if Katherine submits to Henry as "mon puissant seigneur" (5.2.256), Le Fer (almost certainly with the same gesture of handkissing) capitulates to Pistol as "le plus brave, vaillant, et tres distingue seigneur d'Angleterre" (4.4.56–7). And if Katherine's dowry is the promise of a crown, Le Fer's ransom is the promise of two hundred crowns, while Pistol's mercenary concession ("Tell him my fury shall abate, and I / The crowns will take" (4.4.47–8) accurately parodies Henry's show of conquering magnanimity—just as his broken French, in the quarto version of act 4, scene 6, brutally translates Henry's order to kill the prisoners: "Couple gorge." These scenes remind us that if the king is master of several languages, so too is the play, and the burlesque idiom of the Pistol scenes repeatedly demonstrates how different Henry's patriotic rhetoric or the imaginative transports of the chorus can sound when translated into Eastcheap dialect:

> Then forth, dear countrymen! . . .
> Cheerly to sea! The signs of war advance!
> No king of England, if not king of France! . . .

Yoke-fellows in arms,
Let us to France, like horseleeches, my boys,
To suck, to suck, the very blood to suck.
     2.2.189–93; 2.3.54–6

The function of such restless switches of dialect is to expose the audience themselves to unexpected forms of translation, bearing them across from one point of view to another. It is just this translative capacity, it might be argued, that renders Shakespeare's plays so resistant to univocal reading, and it is something upon which they themselves repeatedly reflect.

❀ ❀ ❀

If *Henry V* plays off the discourse of colonization in which translation figures as a one-sided agent of imperial incorporation, other plays reach back to the discourse of wonder generated by the earliest encounters with the "world elsewhere"—to its moments of weird disorientation and to the experience of rapture that (as Stephen Greenblatt has argued) precedes the rape of possession.[9]

A marvelous illustration of the disorienting potential of such encounters is to be found in a contemporary text from the New World—Pedro de Quiroga's *Coloquios de la verdad* (1555). The principal figure in these "colloquies of truth" is a penitent conquistador and defender of the Peruvian natives named Barchilon. In the first dialogue he accosts a newly arrived soldier of fortune, Justino, whom he rouses from an exemplary colonial dream in which he has become "the most powerful and the richest man of the world." Having instructed his friend in the symbolic truth of this fantasy ("That for certain will be the dream of the wealth of this land, and of this century, all of which is a dream and a mockery"), Barchilon goes on to warn him against a land where "everything is the reverse of what it is in Castile" and where apparent resemblance is only a temptation to misrecognition: "Have nothing to do with the things of this land until you understand them, because they are different matters, and another language." Far from urging Justino to master this other language, however, Barchilon warns him that to understand it will involve him in a self-confounding cultural translation from which there can be no return: "Do not learn the language of this land. Nor even listen to it, for I tell you that if you do, one of two ends will befall you, for it will either drive you mad or you will wander restlessly for the rest of your life."[10]

The fear of derangement that attends such encounters with a "world beyond" is refracted in the confusion, halfway between "wonder" and "madness," that settles on Sebastian and Viola in Illyria (*Twelfth Night*, 4.3.1–4), or in the self-estrangement that renders the transported Syracusans of *The Comedy of Errors* "transformed . . . both in mind and . . . shape," as if "disguised" from themselves (2.2.195–214), or in the bizarre psychic metamorphoses that afflict the Athenians of *A Midsummer Night's Dream* when they cross so carelessly into Oberon's domain—a "wood" whose very name, the play punningly suggests, is madness (2.1.192). The type of all these metamorphoses is supplied by Bottom whose appearance in an ass's head fills his fellow performers with the panic always threatened by the Wild, but whose own experience of translation anticipates the sense of mysterious transfiguration felt by the play's awakened lovers—a benign lunacy in which Hippolita discerns the lineaments of wonder ("but howsoever strange and admirable," 5.1.27).[11]

"Bless thee, Bottom! Bless thee! thou art translated!" (3.1.118–19). Peter Quince's cry of alarm responds only to the weaver's grotesque physical appearance, but this bestial transformation turns out to be the sign of a much more radical translation—one that exemplifies the pattern of a comedy whose whole plot turns on the "bearing across" of characters from one world to another. The play begins, after all, with the spectacle of Theseus and the conquered queen whom he has forcibly brought to Athens to become his bride. And the violent translation of Hippolyta from the Amazonian wild to the civil world of Athens is matched by the equally abrupt translation of the young Athenian lovers from the city to a "desert place" (2.1.218), the estranging wilderness that renders them "wood within this wood" (2.1.192). Theseus's wooing of his captive Amazon is paralleled in Titania's dalliance with "a lovely boy stolen from an Indian king" (2.1.22)—the "changeling" whom Oberon in turn plans to carry off. And all these rapes are parodically replayed in Bottom's abduction by the fairy queen.

If the world into which Bottom is translated nostalgically reinvents the realm of "faery," onto which medieval fantasies of nature's wild otherness were projected, it belongs also with the play's dreamlike variations upon much more contemporary notions of alterity. Linked to a remote, unspecified Indies, not simply through their competing desire for the changeling child but through a shared familiarity with "the farthest steep of India" and its "spiced Indian air" (2.1.69, 124), the fairy king and queen share with Oberon's "buskin'd mistress" an association with barbaric exoticism. Thus the action of the play not only resonates, as Margo Hendricks has demonstrated, with the mercantile exoticism of East and West Indian voyaging but recalls the radically unsettling transpositions that would put a John Smith at the mercy of a Powhatan, bring a Pocahontas (in the guise of a Stuart courtier) to the court of King James, or reduce a Cabeza de Vaca to the "naked" condition of the Florida Indians among whom he was cast away.[12]

Of all the translated characters in *A Midsummer Night's Dream*, it is Bottom whose experience of being borne across into another world is most absolute and defamiliarizing. It is as if the playful self-translation of theatrical performance is made disconcertingly real by Puck's ironic whimsy: "I led them on in this distracted fear, / And left sweet Pyramus translated there" (3.2.31–2). Like one of those heroes of sixteenth-century bourgeois romance who are picked out to become the lovers of foreign princesses—figures whose narratives refract the self-transforming ambitions typically associated with voyaging enterprise—the weaver undergoes a translation that allows him miraculously to escape the confines of birth and rank. Shakespeare mocks such fantasies: for the same transformation that renders Bottom "gentle" in Titania's eyes (3.1.137, 164), bemonsters him in the eyes of his compatriots (in a fashion that recalls not merely the Mandevillean freaks of discovery literature, but the bestial "degeneration" thought to await those who surrender to the seductions of the Wild). Yet Bottom rises above such easy satire to the extent that he alone, of all the characters in the play, fully enters the alien world of the wood and is privileged to hear and understand its speech. And it is essential to the play's effect that he should not appear simply as a comic victim, for he is also a kind of explorer—one who crosses to the other side and returns—however confused the language in which his experience is conveyed.

Bottom, like many a returned traveler, faces the problem of authorizing an inconceivable narrative, whose truth will not readily translate back to the world from which he came. Anthony Pagden has shown how, if the chronicler of such a crossing into the unfamiliar wished to be believed, he could only fall back upon the appeal to "autopsy" (the incontrovertible witness of the I/eye who has seen)—the one thing that might distinguish his traveler's tale from the improbable romances that it otherwise so embarrassingly resembled. Since such self-sufficient authority emulates that of Scripture, it is perhaps not surprising that Bottom's stumbling attempt to articulate his dream should paraphrase a celebrated passage from 1 Corinthians (2.9): "the eye of man hath not heard, the ear of man hath not seen, man's hand is not able to taste, his tongue to conceive, nor his heart to report what my dream was" (4.1.209–12).

The biblical passage refers to the "hidden wisdom" of "the *deep* things of God" whose "mystery" is apprehensible only through spiritual revelation, and Bottom, whose dream "hath *no bottom*," conceives it as a secular epiphany. He has, as Starveling sagely remarks, been "transported" (4.2.3–4), and the effect produced by his sublimated rape (or rapture) is strikingly close to that sense of "wonder" and "ravishment" that Stephen Greenblatt finds expressed in the more ecstatic moments of discovery.[13] The problem with such rapturous transports however is that they typically involve a crossing into the inexpressible. "I am to discourse of wonders: but ask me not what," warns Bottom, faced with interpreting his experience, "for if I tell you, I am no true Athenian" (4.2.29–31). To tell the truth would render him untrue to the experience of his auditors, would make him something Other than true Athenian and would require another language: "I have had a most rare vision. I have had a dream, past the wit of man to say what dream it was. Man is but an ass, if he go about t' expound this dream. Methought I was—there is no man can tell what. Methought I was—and methought I had—but man is but a patched fool if he will offer to say what methought I had" (*Midsummer Night's Dream*, 4.1.204–11).

Like Enobarbus struggling to evoke an Oriental exoticism that "beggar'd all description" (*Antony and Cleopatra*, 2.2.198), or like Columbus driven to his sterile repetitions of the phrase "that it was a wonder," the weaver is baffled by the sheer intractability of language to descriptions of the unfamiliar. What he faces, then, is exactly the recurrent crisis of "incommensurability" described by Pagden, a crisis produced by a place "filled with things for which there was no adequate classification, no known terms"—in short, an untranslatable world. Bottom plans a ballad of his dream, a traveler's tale to amuse the duke, but the performance never comes to pass because he, like Barchilon, knows only too well that in the last analysis "it is incommensurability itself which is ultimately the *only* certainty, the only possible context in which America [or Fairyland] can be made at all intelligible" and that "in a world where no translation is possible, silence is the necessary condition of speech."[14]

✿ ✿ ✿

In its mixture of the poignant and the grotesque, the rapture of ass-headed Bottom is a neat emblematic reminder of how close the marvelous stands to the monstrous. And as the woeful history of discovery from Columbus onward repeatedly illustrates, it is an equally short step from the wonder of discovery's primal moment to the expropriative brutality of colonization. Thus, as Peter Hulme and others have shown, the paradigmatic move of colonizing discourse is to redefine the naked innocents of first encounter as monstrous cannibals. If Montaigne seeks to reverse this move through a translative maneuver of his own that makes the ethics of cannibalism themselves an occasion for admiration, Shakespeare's *Tempest* reasserts the colonial paradigm but does so in full consciousness of the discursive violence on which its translations depend. The ideal community of the Tupinamba has here been reduced to a mere flourish of Gonzalo's fancy (2.1.144–169), as remote from possibility as the "imagnary commonwealth" of Plato, whereas Montaigne's noble cannibals are metamorphosed into the "salvage and deformed" Caliban, a creature whose incorrigibly "bastard" condition is the reverse of their "original naturality." On Prospero's island, moreover, the wonder that in "Of the Cannibals" and *A Midsummer Night's Dream* is the defining attribute of the "world elsewhere" has become an effect of the colonizer's power. The only marvels that Bottom's clownish counterparts dream of carrying back to their city are monsters and dead Indians—the loot of fairgrounds and *wunderkammern*, objects to be possessed and translated at will.[15]

If the physical transportation of island exotics appears a quite unproblematic prospect to these voyagers, the same goes for the more sophisticated translations to which the island and its denizens are subjected by Prospero. Under his aegis this other world, in contrast to the almost impenetrable strangeness of Barchilon's Peru, is made to seem so filled with lucid meanings that even the billows, wind, and thunder appear to "speak" to Alonzo (3.3.96–9), whereas the "people of the island," when they do not simply communicate with the courtiers in mysteriously perspicuous speech, have recourse to "a kind / Of excellent dumb discourse" (3.3.38–9) exhibiting the universal eloquence attributed to the human body by so many early explorers.[16] Before the arrival of Prospero and Miranda, however, the island is said to have been languageless. Like those Arawaks who, Columbus proclaimed, must "learn to speak" under Spanish tutelage, Caliban, whose brutish gabble supposedly barred him even from knowledge of his own meaning has been "made to speak" by Miranda. It is as if he needed the intervention of his enslavers to translate him to himself; as if, miraculously, it is not they who are out of place, but he; not they who have been "carried across" to this strange world, but Caliban who has needed rescue from the isolation of his primitive self-estrangement.

The obverse of Bottom's delicious vertigo, the feeling that the new is beyond naming, untranslatable, is this belief that it only requires the transforming touch of the colonizer's language to spring into meaning. "This isle is mute without me," as Prospero disdainfully puts it in Aimé Césaire's satiric postcolonial reworking of *The Tempest*. The physical translation that brings the Italian courtiers (like their colonizing counterparts in the Virginia pamphlets) to this still unbraved new world necessarily entails a further translation through which the "salvage" Caliban (like Columbus's Indians) is salvaged—brought into the civil fold of Prospero's language, learning "how / To name the bigger light, and how the less, / That burn by night and day" (1.2.334–6). In the process the very topography of the island is transformed; for, no less than the obscure "purposes" of Caliban's inner world, "the fresh springs, brine pits, barren place and fertile" of his supposedly preverbal habitat have been "endow'd . . . with words that made them known" (1.2.338, 357–8).[17]

If language is the play's principal instrument of cultural translation, clothing is another. Indeed the two are closely related, for as denizens of a culture in which dress was organized by codes of signification, Europeans, as Cheyfitz observes, "typically . . . equated . . . nakedness with either absence of or a deficiency in language." Thus, as the troping of nakedness in *King Lear* persistently suggests, to be bare of clothes was to be relegated to the unintelligible chaos of nature, so that it is more than simply a figurative association that links the nakedness of "poor Tom" with his gibberish, and both with the wildness of the heath. In the same way the routine denigration of the so-called wild Irish as a "naked" people (even while so much attention was given to their "improper" mode of dress) was entirely of a piece with the denigration of their language as barbarous nonspeech. One reason why peoples of the New World and sub–Saharan Africa proved so difficult to assimilate into the mental universe of early modern Europe (and why, in consequence, their bodies could be treated with such savagery) was that they too were perceived as "naked peoples," located not merely by virtue of their barbarous speech but by fundamental bodily habit outside the domain of culture and therefore of meaning.[18]

So it is that on Prospero's island costume is what effectively determines the legibility, the visibility, in effect the *reality*, of bodies. As surely as

Prospero's "magic garment" renders him invisible, it is Antonio's stolen costume that makes visible his ducal person ("look how well my garments sit upon me, / Much feater than before," ll. 272–3). Antonio is translated into the role he usurps precisely as costume translated the actor. So too Prospero's reassumption of the "hat and rapier" of "sometime Milan" (5.1.84–6) not only renders him visible to the enchanted Neapolitans but also allows a wonder-filled Caliban to perceive his "actual" princely identity for the first time ("How fine my master is!" 5.1.262). Similarly the awakening of the Boatswain and crew from their deathlike sleep is experienced as a mysterious self-restoration figured in the recovery of "all our trim" (5.1.236), the proper attire of their seamen's calling. If bodies are formed only from "such stuff as dreams are made on," it is "stuff" (the material of costume), the play keeps insisting, that bodies forth those dreams and makes them appear substantial. Thus it is not merely Antonio's usurpation but also Prospero's restoration that is parodied in the entry of Stephano and Trinculo, tricked out in the glistering apparel filched from Prospero's line.

By contrast the natives of what Prospero will call "this *bare* island" (epilogue, l. 8) are understood as being in one way or another naked, with bodies that in consequence are either illegible or invisible. Caliban's virtual nakedness, like his disdain for the costumes of fake authority, is a part of his "salvage" condition—the bodily equivalent of the languageless state in which Prospero supposedly found him. The only clothing attributed to him is the shapeless "gaberdine" that renders his body virtually indecipherable to his clownish discoverers, who read onto him the predictable signs of Mandevillean monstrosity (2.2.27–34, 57–70), Trinculo discovering fins even where he plainly sees arms. Thus Caliban's much-stressed but curiously ill-defined "deformity" seems to be as much an effect of undress as of any actual physical malformation—just as Ferdinand's "brave form" and "goodly person," or the beauty that Miranda discovers in the "goodly creatures" of her "brave new world," like the "fine" appearance of the restored Prospero (1.2.412, 417; 5.1.181–4, 262), are essentially sartorial phenomena.

If Caliban's virtual nakedness appears to unform his body, laying it open to the autoptic invention of old and new masters, the other inhabitants of the island are presented as essentially bodiless—invisible except when dressed by Prospero's magic in the guises that allow them to appear as harpies, goddesses, nymphs, and "REAPERS, properly habited" (4.1.138) or as those "strange SHAPES," whose "living drollery" seems to confirm the wildest inventions of travelers—unicorns, phoenixes, "mountaineers, / Dewlapp'd, like bulls. . . . [and] men / Whose heads stood in their breasts" (3.3.22–47). Just as Caliban must be taught to "know his own meaning," so it is only after Prospero brings culture to this bare island, it would seem, that its denizens, under his colonizing gaze, acquire bodies and become capable of meaning—though these bodies and meanings (like those of the actors who perform their parts) will never be "properly" their own.

The insistent analogy between these corporeal transformations and the translations wrought by the theater itself is foregrounded not only by the histrionics of the masque but also by the witty reflexivity of an epilogue that makes Prospero's crossing back to Italy a figure for the actor's return from his "translated" condition—as well as (traditionally) a metaphor for the dramatist's own retreat to the bourgeois solidities of his Stratford life. In a different context such analogies might appear subversive, and there are certainly moments in Shakespeare—Henry V's "ceremony" speech, for example, or Lear's discovery that "robes and furr'd gowns hide all"—where the translative power of costume and personation suggests the hollow fictiveness of all social identity. But such moments can be staged perhaps only because of the more powerful persistence of a belief in the metamorphic efficacy of translation, including the conviction that at some very deep level clothes really do make the man—ironically the same belief that inspired many of the most ferocious denunciations of theatrical pretence. Caliban's "How fine my master *is*" (where he might have said "looks") registers the substantive nature of Prospero's change: what he acknowledges is not so much a shifting of shape as a secular epiphany.

The translations experienced by those who are really "borne across" to the island—as opposed to those who, like Antonio, Sebastian, Stephano, and Trinculo, have in effect never left home—are real transformations, experiences from which they emerge, even as they cross back to their former selves, changed. For all of them (as for Bottom) something is gained in the translation ("in one voyage / Did Claribel a husband find at Tunis, / And Ferdinand, her brother, found a wife / Where he himself was lost; Prospero his dukedom / In a poor isle, and all of us, ourselves / When no man was his own," 5.1.208–13). But these transformations are no longer conceived as produced by the shock of an unmediated encounter with the Other; for the "world elsewhere" is now recognized as always-already reformed/deformed by the colonizer's translative vision.

Greenblatt has made much of the possibility that a single, apparently untranslatable word—"scamel"—stubbornly survives from Caliban's pristine tongue. But the truth of this nostalgic supposition is probably irrelevant; for once Caliban has been translated, all he can do is repeat the history of his transformation, either in the key of farce—as when Stephano offers to "give language to him" and he responds exactly as he had to his first master ("I'll show thee every fertile inch o' th' island; and I will kiss thy foot; I prithee, be my god. . . . Thou wondrous man," 2.2.148–64)—or in the key of abject pathos—as in his resubmission to Prospero ("I will be wise hereafter, / And seek for grace," 5.1.295–6). By Prospero's act of naming, Caliban's island has been changed as surely and irremediably as the newly mapped Irish landscape of Brian Friel's play *Translations* is altered (rendered Other) by the surveyor's Name-Book. Even when his oppressor is gone Caliban will have to live in a translated world, like Friel's Hugh Mor O'Donnell: "We must learn those new names. . . . We must learn where we live. We must learn to make them our own. We must *make* them our new home."[19]

But how far the victims of translation can learn to truly inhabit the new tongue, as Friel insists is necessary, remains highly questionable, and what is arguably missing from Shakespeare's play is anything resembling Friel's defiant sense that cultural translation might, after all, become a creative two-way process of the kind that the anthropologist Marshall Sahlins celebrates in his studies of early Pacific contact—any hint that for Caliban the trappings of Prospero's culture could ever amount to more than the borrowed frippery, the "glistering apparel" that hangs seductively on Prospero's "line." Everything depends, perhaps, on what you make of the speech with which the dramatist endowed Caliban, that powerfully individualized dialect of cursing and lyrical ecstasy that so impressed the play's earliest recorded critics, moving them to marvel that "Shakespear had not only found out a new character in his Caliban but had also devised and adapted a new manner of Language for that character."[20]

Yet over and above the play's apparent confirmation of the interpretative authority asserted by the European gaze, there are hints that the island itself remains, in the last analysis, as resistant to real translation as Barchilon's Peru or Bottom's Fairyland. These arise partly from the recurrent demonstrations of the arbitrariness of the intruders' translative moves; for the most basic physical realities of the island seem absurdly dependent on the interpretative impulses of those who observe it, rendering it alternately a desert filled with the "confused noise" that signs its unredeemed condition and a verdant landscape infused with the mysterious transcendental harmonies that mark it as an earthly paradise. By the same token, the "monstrous shape" of

Ariel's companions inspires dread in the king's party, even while Gonzalo hails them as *"people* of the island . . . more *gentle, kind,* than of / *Our human generation* you shall find" (3.3.31–3; emphasis added)—thus opening to question the whole matter of "kind" and "likeness" upon which the last scene lays so much emotional stress. In much the same way, Caliban is simultaneously repudiated as a deformed and bestial monster, "a freckled whelp, hag-born," and acknowledged as a "man" with "a human shape" (1.2.283–4, 446). From one perspective (established in the play by his pairing with Ferdinand, as log-bearer, suitor, and potential rapist of Miranda) he is a man exactly like the Neapolitans; from another he seems so unimaginably different from them as to be almost beyond satisfactory description.

Nor is even Prospero's power sufficient to effect a lasting translation of this wild place, with its resistance to containing definition, into the civil domain of European empire. Indeed the very fact that Prospero's own mastery of the island's "strangeness" is dependent upon the arcana of "magic" is a sign of how much this place belongs to the realm of the inexpressible, the untranslatable. It is true that the books that are the reputed source of his control have come from Italy, but in Milan they were merely the source of bookish impotence, the occasion of his downfall. The power they confer is an island thing, something Prospero must bury or drown before, like the other Italians, he can be "himself" again, retranslate himself from the estrangement of exile to the familiar world of Milan. For Prospero, as for Barchilon, the crossing over into another world exacts its price, and its very incompleteness means that in Milan, where "every third thought shall be my grave," he will be haunted by an even bleaker version of the Spaniard's displacement, a sense of fretful imperfection that only death can assuage. In this playing out of the colonizer's self-defeating dream of triumphant return, as in so many other ways, *The Tempest* seems prophetic. No wonder that the epilogue gives us a Prospero still pleading for release from the "bare island" to which Shakespeare's uncharacteristic refusal of the theater's translative magic has kept him confined.

✺ ✺ ✺

It is perhaps *The Tempest*'s very hesitancies about the ultimate possibilities of translation that require that its dream of empire be in the end surrendered—even if it can never be forgotten. In this, like Fletcher's parasitic *Sea-Voyage,* where the island colony is once again gratefully abandoned, Shakespeare's play no doubt reflected the uncertain fluctuations of English colonizing ambition in the New World. But the dream of theater remains intact. When Miranda speaks her distress at the destructive spectacle of the tempest ("I have suffered with those that I saw suffer") she is made to describe an experience of emotional translation that Shakespeare seems to have seen theater as uniquely equipped to produce—an experience that she has in fact just shared with the theater audience. Translation now becomes another name for the power to move and to be moved; it occurs at the point where the stillness of patience (the lonely virtue of the Stoic wise man, calm on his storm-beaten rock) gives way to the motion of compassion and its claim of human community. The even more intense challenge Lear issues in another tempest— "Expose thyself to feel what wretches feel"—is to just such a displacing of the self, which the audience is at that very moment being forced to experience. Such translation is itself a kind of exploration and (in a way that perfectly accords with the Renaissance rewriting of Aristotle that made "wonder" an essential component of theatrical experience) it is always, even in its most forlorn moments, infused with a sense of the marvelous, for it creates the illusion (which the discovery literature of the period never manages to supply) that it may after all be possible to cross over into the space of the Other, whether its name is Caliban, or Shylock, or Othello, or even La Pucelle.

It is partly because Shakespeare more than any other writer of his period is capable of glimpsing how it might feel to inhabit the other side of Montaigne's mountains that he himself seems worth the labor of translation—the unending task of carrying him across to the present. But to make such a claim is emphatically not to place his work outside history, to smuggle in a new version of the universal Shakespeare through the back door. Indeed it is not because he stands above history but because he was so intensely embroiled in it that Shakespeare still translates. If his plays continue to survive and to challenge us—in spite of all that postcolonial and feminist criticism have disclosed about their role as cultural bridgeheads—it is in part because of their extraordinary capacity to reflect on the very translative processes in which they were from the very beginning implicated.

Translation, the tragedy of Mostar reminds us, is always an ambiguous process. It can be either active or passive, empathic or aggressive, an instrument of conquest, a vehicle of trade, or a passport to wonder. A translator (one who bears across) is, according to the punning Italian proverb, always a traitor—*traduttore vuol dire traditore*—and can also be, as Ben Jonson recognized, a kind of "conveyor," or thief.[21] But beyond that translation is the process by which (as Bottom discovers in the Athenian woods) one may become, in Salman Rushdie's phrase, "a translated person"—one who is, whether willingly or inadvertently, borne across into the "world beyond," the experience of the Other. In this sense, the archetypal translator is Malintzin/Dona Marina, Cortés's Indian interpreter and mistress, at once execrated as the betrayer of her people and celebrated as the founding mother of mestizo culture, a bridge between worlds. Translation is never innocent, and its motives are usually mixed, but only through its uncertain operations, Shakespeare suggests, can human beings stretch their fragile pontoons into the unknown.

Notes

INTRODUCTION

1. Paul Yachnin, "The Powerless Theater," *English Literary Renaissance* 21 (1991): 49–74 (67); see also Leah S. Marcus, *Local Reading and Its Discontents* (Berkeley: University of California Press, 1988), pp. 29–30.
2. Ben Jonson, *Volpone*, ed. David Cook (London: Methuen, 1962), p. 56; Yachnin, p. 57.
3. Marcus, p. 215.
4. On the contingent nature of dramatic meaning, see the provocative arguments of Terence Hawkes in *Meaning by Shakespeare* (London: Routledge, 1992).
5. For a trenchant critique of New Historicist and Cultural Materialist criticism, see Graham Bradshaw, *Misrepresentations: Shakespeare and the Materialists* (Ithaca, N.Y.: Cornell University Press).
6. John Wilmot, Earl of Rochester, "A Satyr [against Reason and Mankind]," l. 81, cited from *The Poems*, ed. Keith Walker (Oxford: Blackwell, 1984), p. 93.
7. Lawrence Stone, *The Family, Sex, and Marriage in England, 1500–1800* (London: Weidenfeld and Nicholson, 1977).

I · SERVANT OBEDIENCE AND MASTER SINS

1. On the homoerotics of master-servant relationships, see Mario DiGangi, *The Homoerotics of Early Modern Drama* (Cambridge: Cambridge University Press, 1997), esp. chap. 3, pp. 64–99. Lisa Jardine, *Reading Shakespeare Historically* (London: Routledge, 1996), p. 70.
2. Andrew Gurr, *The Shakespearean Stage, 1574–1642*, 2d ed. (Cambridge: Cambridge University Press, 1980), pp. 78–80; *Ratseis Ghost* (London, n.d. [1605?]), A3v.
3. William Harrison, *The Description of England*, ed. George Edelen (Ithaca: Cornell University Press for the Folger Shakespeare Library, 1968), p. 119. A. L. Beier, *Masterless Men: The Vagrancy Problem in England, 1560–1640* (London: Methuen, 1985), cites compelling statistics for the numbers of servants in the

vagrant population: "They made up nearly half of those arrested who had trades listed in Essex from 1564 to 1596; 56% of those taken to Bridewell from 1597–1608; and in Norwich a third between 1564 and 1610, rising to two thirds from 1626 to 1635" (p. 24); *The Life and Death of Gamaliell Ratsey* (London, 1605), sig. A2; emphasis added. The quotation from the Act of 1572 is cited in Gurr, *Shakespearean Stage*, p. 28; emphasis added. On actors and vagrancy, see Beier, pp. 96–9. On vagrancy among former soldiers, see Beier, pp. 93–5

4. Thus in *The Tempest*, the rebellious servant Caliban announces his submission at the point when he is overwhelmed by the spectacle of Prospero dressed in his ducal robes and attended by a train of courtly followers: "How fine my master is" (5.1.262).

5. Harrison, p. 117; cf. the debate in the anonymous *English Courtier, and the Countrey Gentleman* (1586) in *Inedited Tracts*, ([London]: Roxburghe Library, 1868), pp. 35–43.

6. Little evidence survives as to how often, if at all, they were even summoned to perform for their nominal masters—at least until the London companies were reorganized under royal patronage by James I. See Andrew Gurr, *The Shakespearian Playing Companies* (Oxford: Clarendon Press, 1996), p. 34.

7. Ibid.

8. See for instance, David Starkey et al., *The English Court: From the Wars of the Roses to the Civil War* (London: Longman, 1987); Starkey's "Intimacy and Innovation" (pp. 71–118) gives an excellent account of the rise of the Privy Chamber and the key office of Groom of the Stool during the reigns of Henry VII and Henry VIII. See also Neil Cuddy, "The Revival of the Entourage: The Bedchamber of James I, 1603–1625," in Starkey (pp. 173–225), for an account of James's substitution of the bedchamber as the new center of intimacy and influence.

9. George Gifford, *A Dialogue Concerning Witches* (London: 1603), sig. B3; emphasis added. Gifford's treatise was first published in 1593 and its terminology may represent a direct response to Marlowe's play. For further discussion of the motif of service in *Doctor Faustus*, see Judith Weil, "Full Possession: Service and Slavery in *Doctor Faustus*," in Paul Whitfield White, ed., *Marlowe, History, and Sexuality: New Critical Essays on Christopher Marlowe* (New York, AMS Press, 1998), pp. 143–54. Unfortunately Weil's essay did not become available to me until after I had completed this essay.

10. John Donne, *Letters to Severall Persons of Honour* (1651), intro. M. Thomas Hester (New York: Scholars Facsimiles and Reprints, 1977), p. 51. So much was a servant "part" of his master's social body that an affront to or assault upon the servant might be deemed an assault upon the master's honor, as we can see from the opening scene of *Romeo and Juliet* or from the disguised Tranio's impertinent challenge to his real master in *Taming of the Shrew*: "Sir, what are you that offer

to beat my servant?" (5.1.63–4). Hence Lear's outrage at Kent's "shameful lodging" in the stocks: "What's he that hath so much thy place mistook / To set thee here ... 'tis worse than murder / To do upon respect such violent outrage" (*Lear*, 2.4.12–24). William Gouge, *Of Domesticall Dvties Eight Treatises* (1622), p. 160.

On the decline in numbers of retainers in the late Elizabethan period and the progressive alienation of the gentry from domestic service, see Felicity Heal, *Hospitality in Early Modern England* (Clarendon Press: Oxford, 1990), pp. 164–70. By the 1620s, according to Heal, it had become significantly more common for the sons of gentry and nobility "to receive formal classical education than to undertake a period of service" (p. 165)—in the way that, say, Young Allworth, becomes the page of Lord Lovell in Philip Massinger's nostalgic social comedy *A New Way to Pay Old Debts* (ca. 1623).

11. See Alice T. Friedman, *House and Household in Elizabethan England: Wollaton Hall and the Willoughby Family* (Chicago: University of Chicago Press, 1989), pp. 43–5. At Wollaton most household members "were tied to the Willoughby family through long-standing bonds of service" (p. 43), and the principal officers "were in most cases cousins or distant relations of the Willoughby family" (p. 44). The sheer numbers of servants employed in early modern households can now seem astonishing: the average number for a noble household at the end of the medieval period seems to have been about 150, and for a gentry household about 65 (see Heal, p. 47).

12. Robert J. Steinfeld, *The Invention of Free Labor: The Employment Relation in English and American Law and Culture, 1350–1870* (University of North Carolina Press: Chapel Hill, 1991), p. 18; Richard C. Barnett, *Place, Profit, and Power: A Study of the Servants of William Cecil, Elizabethan Statesman* (Chapel Hill: University of North Carolina Press, 1969), p. 12.

13. Gloria Anzilotti, ed., *An English Prince: Newcastle's Machiavellian Political Guide to Charles II* (Pisa: Giardini, 1988), p. 145. Newcastle regarded such ceremonious exhibitions of the ladder of service as an essential instrument for the preservation of social order. Richard Brathwait, *The English Gentleman* (London, 1630), p. 115.

14. For further discussion of the vicarious nature of servant identity, see chap. 3.

15. Seymour's motto cited in Starkey, p. 110. For an account of the peculiar role assigned to female servants, see Mark Thornton Burnett, *Masters and Servants in English Renaissance Culture* (Basingstoke: Macmillan, 1997), chap. 4. Gouge, p. 604.

16. Steinfeld, pp. 70–1.

17. Gouge, p. 664. He goes on: "Some [caring only for profit] will sell them ... when they have them beyond sea to Turks and Infidels; some to Papists; some to profane persons; some to cruel inhuman beasts; some to men of unlawful trades; some to men of no trades" (p. 665). The statutes governing service did however

establish clear limits to a master's power, as Grumio reminds us when he claims
to discover in Petruchio's violence "a lawful cause for me to leave his service"
(*Taming of the Shrew*, 1.2.29–30).

18. Steffano Guazzo, *La civile conversatione* (1574), cited in Dennis Romano,
Housecraft and Statecraft: Domestic Service in Renaissance Venice, 1400–1600
(Baltimore: Johns Hopkins University Press, 1996), p. 20; John Dod and Robert
Cleaver, *A Godly Forme of Household Gouernment* (London, 1630), sig. Aa3. The
latter passage is worth citing at greater length: "Good and faithful servants, liking and affecting their masters, understand them at a beck, and obey them at a
wink of an eye or bent of the brow, not as a water-spaniel, but as the hand is
stirred to obey the mind."

The original sense of *livery* was "the dispensing of food, provisions or
clothing" to servants or retainers (*OED* n. 1a).

The Puritans Dod and Cleaver, however, exhibit a certain unease with the
theological implications of their organic simile: "For as the hand is said to be the
instrument of instruments . . . so is the servant said to be an instrument of instruments, because he keepeth all the instruments of the household occupied. . . .
[But] he differeth from all other instruments. For where they are things without
soul, he is divinely enriched with a soul: and herein he differeth from the hand,
for that the hand is fastened and united to the body, but he is separate and disjoined from his master" (Aa3). The paradoxical image of a hand that is at once
faithfully instrumental and yet disjoined nicely suggests the contradictions of the
servant's role during the early modern transformation of household government. It is rather as if "the great toe of this assembly" (*Coriolanus*, 1.1 142) were
to announce itself "separate and disjoined" from Menenius's body politic.

19. The urban context of *The City Madam* complicates its thematization of service
by the inclusion of a pair of errant apprentices (Goldwire and Tradewell) whom
Luke incites to rebellion. The relationship between apprentices and their masters
constituted a form of "service" that was often difficult to distinguish from
domestic employment, and the conduct of apprentices was governed by many of
the same laws that regulated the lives of household servants. But apprenticeship,
because it constituted a form of training designed to lead to full membership in a
guild, differed in crucial ways from domestic service, and its treatment in drama
therefore deserves separate study. For a detailed social history of apprenticeship
in the period, see Paul Griffiths, *Youth and Authority: Formative Experiences in
England, 1560–1640* (Oxford: Clarendon Press, 1996). The literature of apprenticeship, crafts, and trades is extensively dealt with in Burnett, chaps. 1–2 (pp.
14–78).

20. "An Homily against Disobedience and Willful Rebellion," in Ronald B. Bond,
ed., *Certain Sermons or Homilies* (Toronto: University of Toronto Press, 1987), p.
209. See for, example, Gouge, p. 167, citing 1 Cor. 7.22.

21. In Middleton's *Chaste Maid in Cheapside*, by contrast, Allwit's complaisant cuck-oldry strips him of mastery in the eyes of his servants, who scornfully dismiss him as "but our mistress's husband . . . but one pip above a serving-man" (1.2.65–70).

22. Jonas A. Barish and Marshall Waingrow, " 'Service" in *King Lear*," *SQ* 9 (1958): 347–55. See also Richard Strier, "Faithful Servants: Shakespeare's Praise of Disobedience," in Heather Dubrow and Richard Strier, eds., *The Historical Renaissance: New Essays on Tudor and Stuart Literature and Culture* (Chicago: University of Chicago Press, 1988), pp. 104–33; Frank Whigham, *Seizures of the Will in Early Modern English Drama* (Cambridge: Cambridge University Press, 1996), pp. 216–7; and Burnett, pp. 83–6. For a historian's account of early mod-ern service that argues that "the ideal community bound together by ties of patronage and deference did exist outside the world of theory," while conceding that "the power of masters" was open to significant abuse, see Susan Dwyer Amussen, *An Ordered Society: Gender and Class in Early Modern England* (Oxford: Blackwell, 1988), 159–61.

23. The idea of an individual's "train" of servants as constituting a kind of "dress" for his social body is also implicit in *The Taming of the Shrew*, where Christopher Sly's dream-identity as a lord is constituted by "sweet clothes" and "brave atten-dants" (Induction, 1.34–7; and cf. the remarks of Biondello and Grumio on the dress of Petruchio's servants, 3.2.65–71; 4.1.47–51, 90–4).

24. For Kent's debt to the classical trickster-servant, see Burnett, pp. 83–4. For a through account of "feudal" elements in the play—a topic first opened up by John Danby in *Shakespeare's Doctrine of Nature* (London: Faber, 1951) and much debated since—see Richard Halpern, *The Poetics of Primitive Accumulation: English Renaissance Culture and the Genealogy of Capital* (Ithaca: Cornell University Press, 1991), chap. 6, pp. 215–69. Cf. the services required of the Groom of the Stool—an office occupied under James I by his captain of the guard, Sir Thomas Erskine, who in addition to his "lavatorial tasks" was required "to sleep . . . on a pallet at the foot of the royal bed; [and] to put on the king's under-shirt" (Cuddy, p. 186).

25. Cf. Peter Laslett's assertion in *The World We Have Lost—Further Explored*, 3d ed. (London: Methuen, 1983) that inside the patriarchal household "every rela-tionship could be seen as a love-relationship" (p. 5).

26. The fullest account of the mechanisms of patronage in the period is Linda Levy Peck's magisterial *Court Patronage and Corruption in Early Stuart England* (Boston: Unwin Hyman, 1990).

27. Burnett, p. 1. In a domestic context "officer" could even have a contemptuous edge; see *Taming of the Shrew*, 5.2.37: "Spoke like an officer." *English Courtier*, p. 28; emphasis added.

28. See Beier, p. 23. In the country as a whole the percentage of persons in live-in

domestic service fell from 20 percent of the population in 1520 to less than 10 percent in 1700, while the numbers of apprentices fell from 15 percent in 1600 to 4–5 percent in 1700 (pp. 23–4).

29. *English Courtier*, pp. 35, 43.

30. Ibid., pp. 33–4, 39–41.

31. "I.M.," *A Health to the Gentlemanly Profession of Seruingmen: or, The Seruingmans Comfort* (London, 1598) in *Inedited Tracts*, pp. 114–5. The hypocritical Luke Frugal appeals to this same ideal of service in *The City Madam* when he says of his apprentices "What's mine is theirs. They are my friends, not servants" (4.1.38). For an extended treatment of hospitality and its decline see Heal.

The Marston quotations are from H. Harvey Wood, ed., *The Plays of John Marston*, 3 vols. (Edinburgh: Oliver and Boyd, 1939), vol. 3. In Chapman's *Gentleman Usher* (ca. 1602–3) the degraded condition of the servants retained by the upstart "minion" Medice/Mendice is attributed to simple want of aristocratic magnanimity. Not only does Medice himself "go . . . like / A prince's footman, in old-fashioned silks" but he is "So miserable [miserly] that his own few men / Do beg by virtue of his livery; / For he gives none, for any service done him / Or any honor, any least reward" (1.1.113–9). Medice's meanness is contrasted with the generosity of the true nobleman, Lasso, toward his gentleman usher, Bassiolo: " He has been my good lord, for I can spend / Some fifteen hundred crowns in lands a year, / Which I have gotten since I serv'd him first . . . so much as makes me live, my lord, / Like a poor gentleman"; cited from the Regents edition, ed. John Hazel Smith (Lincoln: University of Nebraska Press, 1970).

32. "I.M.," pp. 165–6; cf. also p. 117, and Richard Brathwait, *Rules and Orders for the Government of the House of an Earle*, in *Miscellanea Antiqua Anglicana* (London: Robert Triphook, 1816), pp. 32–3.

33. See Burnett, pp. 16–28. Although most of the texts Burnett discusses concern the worsening relations between masters and prentices, it seems reasonable to assume that this period of falling incomes and shortages must also have put additional strains upon households and given an additional spur to the changes in domestic organization that so worried conservative social critics. Richard Brathwait, *The English Gentleman* (London, 1630), pp. 158–9. For a good account of the importance of "gratitude" in the Senecan doctrine of "benefits" that underpinned sixteenth-century ideas of generosity and housekeeping, see John M. Wallace, "*Timon of Athens* and the Three Graces: Shakespeare's Senecan Study," *Modern Philology* 83 (1986): 349–63; and Peck, pp. 12–14, 28–9.

34. It is symptomatic of the lack of felt distinction between military and other forms of service that the word was immediately extended to the domestic realm—so in *Histrio-mastix* (1599) the young lords are described as having "cashiered their trains" of servants (3:370).

35. See Michael Neill, *Issues of Death: Mortality and Identity in English Renaissance*

Tragedy (Oxford: Clarendon Press, 1997), p. 334.

36. *The Communist Manifesto*, quoted in Laslett, p. 16; "I.M.," pp. 158, 147.

It was not, of course, that "I.M." undervalued the material rewards of service but rather that the reliance on wages as the sole form of reward seemed to him a niggardly and mechanical substitute for the exhibitions of bounty on which serving-men had once relied: "'Why do I give you wages, but in regard of your service,'" he imagines a master snarling at his superannuated servant, who has expected "the lease of a farm . . . or some other preferment" in exchange for his "long and dutiful" career. " 'If you like not me or my wages, you may provide for yourself when you will, I will not be your hinderance'; not weighing and considering that his wages is not able to find his man necessities from the middle down: but I dare not speak what I think, neither what might be spoken, concerning wages in these days" (p. 160). On wages as a defining condition of the servant role, see Burnett, pp. 2–3, Gouge, p. 685.

37. Cf. Henry Fitzgeoffrey's 1617 satire cited by Burnett (p. 98): "What bred a *scholar*, born a *gentleman*. . . . And shall I basely now turn *serving-creature?*"

38. Tommaso Garzoni, *Piazza universale di tutti le professionii del mondo* (1586), cited in Romano, p. 25; "I.M.," pp. 106–7, 112, 113, 146, 157, 116; Friedman, pp. 44–45.

39. On extravagance of dress as a symptom of ambition and social irreverence among servants, see Gouge pp. 602–3:

> The apparel also which servants wear must be so fashioned and ordered, as it may declare them to be servants, and under their masters, and so it will argue a reverend respect of their masters. One end of apparel is to show a difference betwixt superiors and inferiors, persons in authority and under subjection. . . . Exceeding great is the fault of servants in their excess apparel. No distinction ordinarily betwixt a man's children and servants: and none betwixt masters and their men, mistresses and their maids. It may be while men and maids are at their masters' and mistresses' finding, difference may be made: though even then also, if they can any way get it, they will do whatever they can to be as brave as they can. . . . New fashions are as soon got up by servants as by masters and mistresses. What is the end of this but to be thought as good as master or mistress? If the Queen of *Sheba* were now living, she would as much wonder at the disorder of servants in these days, as then she wondered at the comely order of Solomon's servants.

For further evidence of the decline of the gentleman-servant, see Burnett, pp. 176–8.

40. See Steinfeld, pp. 79–98. For the Virginia pioneer Captain John Smith, the new colony was a place where "every man may be master and owner of his own labour and land"; cited in Eric Foner, "The Rallying Cry" *Humanities* 19, no. 2

(1998): 18. Harrison, p. 118.

41. Platter quotation is from Beier, pp. 24–5. James M. Osborn, ed., *The Autobiography of Thomas Whythorne* (London: Oxford University Press, 1962), pp. 10, 28, 34. Whythorne's ambiguous position casts an interesting light on the role-playing in *The Taming of the Shrew* where the servant Tranio plays the role of master, while Lucentio and Hortensio adopt the evidently servile roles of Latin and music masters.

42. Whythorne's words are worth quoting in full: "I do think that the teachers thereof [i.e., music] may esteem so much of themselves as to be free and not bound, much less to be made slave-like" (p. 46). The idea of "being one's *own man*" meant literally, of course, that one was bound to serve only oneself.

Overton quoted in the edition by Andrew Sharp in his *English Levellers*, Cambridge Texts in the History of Political Thought (Cambridge: Cambridge University Press, 1998), p. 55. Overton's opening paragraphs are worth quoting more extensively, especially for his emphasis on selfhood as a species of inalienable and indivisible property:

> To every individual in nature is given an individual property not to be invaded or usurped by any. For every one, as he is himself, so he has a self-propriety, else he could not *be* himself; and of this no second may presume to deprive any of without manifest violation and affront to the very principles of nature and the rules of equity and justice between man and man.... No man has power over my rights and liberties, and I over no man's. I may be but an individual, enjoy myself and my self-propriety and may right myself no more than my self, or presume any further; if I do I am an encroacher and an invader upon another man's right—to which I have no right. For by natural birth all men are equally and alike born to like propriety, liberty and freedom; and as we are delivered of God by the hand of nature into this world, every one with a natural, innate freedom and propriety—as it were writ in the table of every man's heart, never to be obliterated—even so we are to live, every one equally and alike to enjoy his birthright and privilege; even all whereof God by nature has made him free.
>
> And this by nature everyone's desire aims at and requires; for no man naturally would be befooled of his liberty by his neighbour's craft or enslaved by his neighbour's might ... every man by nature being a king, priest and prophet in his own natural circuit and compass.

With this, compare Marrall's sense that his service to the tyrannical Overreach has reduced him to "a property." See pp. 92–3 of this volume.

43. Gouge, pp. 591–4.
44. Ibid., pp. 599–600.
45. Ironically once installed in his new role as bourgeois tyrant Luke complains that

"The masters never prosper'd since gentlemen's sons grew prentices" (5.2.47–8).

46. It is characteristic of the remarkably dense linguistic texture of this collaborative play that the same romantic language is deployed by the courtly Alsemero in his offer to fight with Piracquo for Beatrice's hand (2.2.22–6) and by the disguised courtier, Antonio, in his attempted seduction of Isabella (3.3.127).

For extended analysis of the play's quibbling on service, see Christopher Ricks, "The Moral and Poetic Structure of *The Changeling*," *Essays in Criticism* 10 (1960): 296–9; and Anthony B. Dawson, "Giving the Finger: Puns and Transgression in *The Changeling*," in A. L. Magnusson and C. E. McGee, eds., *The Elizabethan Theatre* (Toronto: P. D. Meany, 1993), 12:93–112 (pp. 100–2). Cf. also Lucio's bawdy compliment to the duke in *Measure for Measure*: "he had some feeling of the sport; he knew the *service*" (3.2.115–6).

47. Gouge, p. 604.

48. Burnett similarly concludes, though on rather different grounds, that although "De Flores might be a subversive . . . he is equally a force for the restoration of order" (p. 109).

49. See Michael Neill, " 'Hidden Malady': Death, Discovery, and Indistinction in *The Changeling*," *Renaissance Drama* n.s. 22 (1992): 95–121; reprinted as chap. 4 of Neill, *Issues of Death*.

50. Dod and Cleaver, sig. Aa2v, Aa5; Harrison, p. 119.

51. Wentworth quoted in Friedman, p. 60. Gouge, p. 616. Cf. also p. 650: "After that masters have chosen good servants, their duty is well to use them: which by reason of the difference betwixt masters and servants cannot be well done, except masters wisely maintain their authority. A master therefore must be able *well to rule his own house*. . . . Not one servant of a thousand, that is not kept under authority, will do good service . . . [so] that masters [must] keep their servants in awe and fear. Children must be *kept in subjection*: much more servants."

52. Romano, p. 220, 40; Fabio Glissenti, *Discorsi morali contra il dispiacer del morire* (1596), cited in Romano, p. 38; Tommaso Garzoni, *Piazza universale di tutti le professionii del mondo* (1586), cited in Romano, p. 25;Cissie Fairchilds, *Domestic Enemies: Servants and Their Masters in Old Regime France* (Baltimore: Johns Hopkins University Press, 1984), pp. 156, 131.

53. Quoted in Fairchilds, pp. 137, 100.

54. For the idea of servants as treacherous spies see Baptista's suspicion in *Taming of the Shrew*: "Pitchers have ears and I have many servants" (4.4.52).

55. Frances E. Dolan, *Dangerous Familiars: Representations of Domestic Crime in England, 1550–1700* (Ithaca: Cornell University Press, 1994), p. 41. Burnett pays particular attention in chapter 3 to the way in which the trickster-servant of classical comedy was adapted as an instrument for exploring "a perceived crisis in service" (p. 79).

56. Some more recent historians, such as Susan Amussen, have been less embarrassed

about using the word "class." For Amussen "class" seems to be little more than a synonym for "rank" and "refers to the socio-economic hierarchy and the social relations imposed by it" (pp. 3–4).

57. For a useful discussion of the erotics of service in the play's romantic plot, see Jardine, pp. 67–77. *The English Courtier* lists fools among "subserving-men"; this lowly category includes "bakers, brewers, chamberlains, wardrobers, faulconers, hunters, horsekeepers, lackeys; and (for the most part) a natural fool or jester to make us sport: also a cook, with a scullion or two, launderers, hinds and hog-herds, with some silly slaves, as I know not how to name them" (p. 39).

58. Fairchilds, p. 100; Gouge, pp. 593, 165. On eye-service, see also Brathwait, *English Gentleman*, p. 159. An exemplar of such service is Bassiolo, the foolishly ambitious title character of Chapman's *Gentleman Usher* whose meticulous "show" of "order" and "fit attendance" among the underservants of Lasso's household (3.2.4–21) masks "two inward-swallowing properties . . . servile avarice / And overweening thought of his own worth" (1.2.169–71). Bassiolo, however, is a more ambiguous figure than most servants of his kind—a gentle-man-servant who, unlike the placeless former mendicant Medice/Mendice, can be recuperated at the end of the play.

59. Gouge, pp. 165, 617; Whythorne, pp. 29–34.

60. See Lionel Trilling, *Sincerity and Authenticity* (London: Oxford University Press, 1972), pp. 27–34. For Rameau's nephew, life is constituted as an elaborate dance whose aesthetic is governed by the desire for place; believing that "there is only one man in the whole kingdom who walks, and that is the sovereign. Everybody else takes up positions," he insists "I am myself, and I remain myself, but I speak and act as occasion demands"; cited from Denis Diderot, *Rameau's Nephew and D'Alembert's Dream* (Harmondsworth: Penguin, 1966), pp. 121, 82.

61. Camille Wells Slights, "Slaves and Subjects in *Othello*," *Shakespeare Quarterly* 48 (1997): 377–90.

62. Heal, p. 167. Heal also detects "a widening gulf between employers and employed" as a result of which "servants became more definitively part of the lower household" (p. 166). For another valuable account of conditions of service in eighteenth-century English households, see J. Jean Hecht, *The Domestic Servant Class in Eighteenth-Century England* (London: Routledge and Kegan Paul, 1956). Hecht stresses the importance in this period of the increasingly "independent attitude of the servant" in the progressive elimination of what remained of a "system based upon fixed status" and its replacement by "one that [was] almost entirely contractual" and based on "the purest self-interest" (p. 71).

Heal notes that the household of the Archbishop of Canterbury, for exam-ple, remained "overwhelmingly male" until at least the 1630s, whereas "after the Restoration . . . about a third of the smaller establishment was female" (p. 167).

2 · "THIS GENTLE GENTLEMAN"

1. Catherine Belsey, "Alice Arden's Crime," *Renaissance Drama*, n.s. 13 (1982): 83–102. A revised version (from which I quote here) appeared in Belsey's *Subject of Tragedy* (London: Methuen, 1985), pp. 129–48 (p. 147).

2. All citations from *Arden* are to the New Mermaid edition, ed. Martin White (London: Ernest Benn, 1982). Lena Cowen Orlin, *Private Matters and Public Culture in Post-Reformation England* (Ithaca: Cornell University Press, 1994), p. 76.

3. Orlin, p. 93. The suggestion of domestic regicide is underlined in the woodcut printed as a frontispiece to the 1633 quarto by the crownlike appearance of Arden's bonnet. For a reading that is particularly sensitive to the close analogies between different types of domestic rebellion in the play (those involving wives and servants) see Frances E. Dolan, *Dangerous Familiars: Representations of Domestic Crime in England, 1550–1700* (Ithaca: Cornell University Press, 1994), pp. 48–58, 71–9.

4. Garrett A. Sullivan Jr., " 'Arden Lay Murdered in That Plot of Ground': Surveying, Land, and *Arden of Faversham*," *ELH* 61 (1994): 231–52 (pp. 234–5, 244).

5. Frank Whigham, *Seizures of the Will* (New York: Cambridge University Press, 1996), chap. 2 pp. 63–120 (pp. 63, 77).

6. Cited from the appendix to White's edition, p. 109.

7. Whigham, p. 118: "In my mind's eye she shatters, smashes, defaces, demolishes her constricting bond to Arden, that so hatefully authorised his control of her."

8. On the consciously phallic significance of the sword in early modern culture, see my introduction to *Anthony and Cleopatra* (Oxford: Oxford University Press, 1994), pp. 114–20. Whigham too recognizes this gesture, together with Arden's ensuing threat to make Mosby "crawl on stumps [instead of legs]," as mixing "castration . . . and social debasement" (p. 76). For indications of the generally feminized role ascribed to tailors, see the jokes at the expense of the timorous Starveling in *A Midsummer Night's Dream* and the satiric treatment of Feeble the woman's tailor in *2 Henry IV*. On the play's tendency to collapse into the idiom of low comedy, see Dolan, pp. 77–8.

9. White, appendix, pp. 110, 112.

10. Ibid., p. 104.

11. Whigham (p. 64) calls in question the reliability of the aspersions Arden casts on Mosby's rank; it is significant, however, that (unlike Arden's boasted gentility) Mosby's base origins go unchallenged in the play and are acknowledged even by Alice. This in no way compromises, of course, the parallels between Arden's and Mosby's social ambition, which Whigham rightly emphasizes (pp. 70, 75).

12. Sir Philip Sidney, *An Apology for Poetry*, in Edmund D. Jones, ed., *English Critical*

Essays (Sixteenth, Seventeenth and Eighteenth Centuries) (London: Oxford University Press, 1947), p. 26.

13. John Donne, "An Anatomie of the World. The First Anniversary," l. 215, cited from *Poetical Works*, ed. Herbert Grierson (London: Oxford University Press, 1933); Philip Stubbes, *The Anatomie of Abuses* (London, 1595), epistle dedicatory.

14. Peter Laslett, *The World We Have Lost* (London: Methuen, 1965), pp. 26–7.

15. Philip Massinger, *A New Way to Pay Old Debts*, ed. T. W. Craik, New Mermaid edition (London: Ernest Benn, 1963), 1.1.39, 70–1; emphasis added. See the discussion in chap. 3.

16. Orlin, pp. 63–4; Laslett, p. 35; Frances Dolan, by implication at least, also appears to accept Arden's claims.

    The significance of the name as a marker of social status is discussed by White (pp. xxii–xxiii), who appears, however, not to notice its implications for Arden's uncertain rank—even though he acknowledges Arden's "desire for land and status" as one of "the driving forces behind the play" (p. xxix).

17. Historically, Alice was the stepdaughter of Sir Edward North (subsequently Lord North of Kirtling), Thomas Ardern's former master at the Office of Augmentations, which was responsible for the dispersal of Abbey lands; see M. L. Wine, ed., *Arden of Faversham*, Revels Plays (London: Methuen, 1973), p. lxv. But the playwright occludes this fact—perhaps to avoid offending the influential North family, perhaps because he wished to involve Alice in the general uncertainty about rank. Nevertheless, although we only have Alice's and Greene's (flattering) word for her superior origins, there is something about the way Arden constantly soothes her with "*gentle* Alice" that bespeaks a certain abject regard on his part.

    Following the suggestion in Martin White's commentary (p. 12), Whigham interprets Alice as referring to the children she will have with Mosby (p. 83), but the sarcastic tone of the passage makes it more likely that Alice is referring dismissively to the role she is expected to play in securing Arden's bourgeois lineage.

18. Whigham astutely notes how Greene here "responds as one traditionalist gentle to another" (p. 70).

19. On the semantics of power and solidarity, see Roger Brown and Albert Gilman, "The Pronouns of Power and Solidarity," in Thomas A. Sebeok, ed., *Style in Language* (Cambridge, Mass.: MIT Press, 1960), pp. 253–76; Angus McIntosh, " 'As You Like It': A Grammatical Clue to Character," in McIntosh and M. A. K. Halliday, *Patterns of Language* (Bloomington: Indiana University Press, 1967), pp. 70–82; and Neill, *Anthony and Cleopatra*, appendix C, pp. 368–9.

    The shifting of pronoun usage in order to express shifts of mood and tone (or "transient attitudes") appears to have been particularly common in English;

see Brown and Gilman, pp. 274–5, and McIntosh, p. 71.

20. Clarke, who is seeking Mosby's and Alice's patronage as a route to Susan Mosby's hand, and hence to his own social advancement, is equally careful to flatter Alice for her "noble mind" (l. 269).

21. For this pun see *Othello*, 2.1.317–8: "the lusty Moor / Hath leaped into my seat."

22. Sara Youngblood, "Theme and Imagery in *Arden of Faversham*," *Studies in English Literature* 3 (1963): 207–18.

23. The "part" concerned is, of course, the same "part" that Alice threatens to "consume" by damming the fire of lust in her breast (viii.48).

24. Dolan (p. 54) argues that "Alice is not generally presented as seeking *self*-government; she seeks, rather, the liberty to *elect* her governor," but this is to miss the point of Alice's self-contradictions and to misunderstand the difficulty of imagining how, in that society, female self-government might be achieved.

25. Whigham (p. 102) also notes the erotic suggestiveness of Will's phrase.

3 · MASSINGER'S PATRIARCHY

1. Philip Massinger, *A New Way to Pay Old Debts*, ed. T. W. Craik, New Mermaid edition (London: Ernest Benn, 1963), pp. xii–xiii. All citations from *A New Way* are to this edition.

2. See L. C. Knights, *Drama and Society in the Age of Jonson* (Hammondsworth: Penguin, 1962), pp. 228–9. See also Patricia Thomson, "The Old Way and the New Way in Dekker and Massinger," *MLR* 51 (1956): 168–78; Massinger, p. xiii.

3. *Merchant of Venice*, 1.3.11–15.

4. Cf. Knights, p. 233, and Thomson, p. 170.

5. *Merchant of Venice*, 3.2.57; 4.1.103, 142.

6. See for instance 3.1.83, 3.2.120–2, 4.1.149–57. He is not only Mammon but also in effect the true "spirit of lies" who has entered Marall (3.2.248). Cf. Knights, p. 232: "I do not think it is too much to say that he represents Avarice—one of the Seven Deadly Sins."

7. For detailed accounts of seventeenth-century patriarchal thinking, see Gordon J. Schochet, *Patriarchalism in Political Thought* (New York: Basic Books, 1975), and Schochet, "Patriarchalism, Politics, and Mass Attitudes in Stuart England," *Historical Journal* 12 (1969): 413–41. Peter Laslett, *The World We Have Lost* (London: Methuen, 1965).

8. Thomson, pp. 172–6; for further discussion of ideas of "service" in this play and in early modern culture generally, see above chap. 1.

9. Knights, p. 229n. 2

10. *The Communist Manifesto*, cited from Laslett., pp. 16–17.

11. Schochet, *Patriarchalism*, pp. 1, 55, 92–6. A classic statement of this position can be found in Richard Hooker, *Of the Laws of Ecclesiastical Polity*, 1.10.4.

12. Schochet, *Patriarchalism*, p. 15, and "Patriarchalism," pp. 413–15. See also W. H. Greenleaf, *Order, Empiricism, and Politics* (London: University of Hull, 1964), pp. 88–9.

13. Schochet, *Patriarchalism*, pp. 73–81.

14. The *Exposition* went through eighteen printings by 1632, *Household Gouernment* at least seven by 1630.

15. Bartholomew Batty, *The Christian Mans Closet*, trans. William Lowth (London, 1581), Q3v-R1v; John Dod and Robert Cleaver, *A Godly Forme of Household Gouernment* (London, 1630), Y4: Dod and Cleaver, *A Plaine and Familiar Exposition of the Ten Commandements* (London, 1618), p. 185.

16. Dod and Cleaver, *Household Gouernment*, A8, V5–6, Z5–6. Cf. also Jean Bodin's description of the family as "the true image of a commonweal," cited in Greenleaf, p. 128. Schochet, *Patriarchalism*, p. 66.

17. Schochet, *Patriarchalism*, p. 26.

18. Laslett, p. 21. "One Out of Many," the second section of V. S. Naipaul's novel *In a Free State* (Hammondsworth: Penguin, 1973) gives an illuminating account of the trauma suffered by a man suddenly transferred from the anonymity of a communal culture to a contemporary individualist society. Santosh, the displaced Indian servant, recalls his master as "the man who adventured in the world for me.... I experienced the world through him.... I was content to be a small part of his presence" (p. 37). For further discussion of the servant's role as part of his master's "countenance," see chap. 1.

19. Cf. Cicero, *De Officiis*, 3.6–7:

> For a man to take something from his neighbour and to profit by his neighbour's loss is more contrary to Nature than ... anything else that can affect either our person or our property. For, in the first place, injustice is fatal to social life and fellowship between man and man. For, if we are so disposed that each, to gain some personal profit, will defraud or injure his neighbour, then those bonds of human society, which are most in accord with Nature's laws, must of necessity be broken.... That is an absurd position which is taken by some people, who say that they will not rob a parent or a brother ... but that their relation to the rest of their fellow-citizens is quite another thing. Such people contend in essence that they are bound to their fellow-citizens by no mutual obligations, social ties, or common interests. This attitude demolishes the whole structure of civil society.
>
> QUOTED FROM THE LOEB EDITION, TRANS. WALTER MILLER (LONDON: HEINEMANN, 1961), PP. 289–95.

20. Michael Walzer, *The Revolution of the Saints: A Study in the Origins of Radical Politics* (Cambridge, Mass.: Harvard University Press, 1966), pp. 186, 190.

21. Cf. Ben Jonson, *Volpone*, 1.1.30–3:

> I glory
> More in the cunning purchase of my wealth,
> Than in the glad possession, since I gain
> No common way.

22. Laslett, pp. 26–7.

23. In effect Overreach and Tapwell propound a secularized version of that Puritan attitude to the past so pithily expressed by Rev. John Stockwood in a Paul's Cross sermon in 1578, when he urged men with "earnest minds" not to be "blinded with those vain shadows of fathers, times and customs" (quoted in Walzer, p. 187). The families to which they are committed are significantly narrow, conjugal families of the type whose emergence Walzer connects with Puritan mores. Where a child of the true patriarchal family was tied to the past by the bonds of "the old kinship system, [and] committed in advance to the family allies and followers" (p. 189), the members of the conjugal family are bound by no such absolute allegiances.

24. Dod and Cleaver, *Household Gouernment*, F_2, quoting Proverbs 22.7. Cf. the autocratic leveling of the God imagined by Puritan "covenant theology": "Through the covenant men became the 'bondsmen' of God—not the children—and the image implied the voluntary recognition of an existing debt, a legal or commercial obligation. *God was the creditor of all men*" (Walzer, p. 168; emphasis added). Overreach once again resembles a secular caricature of Puritan doctrine, the legal bonds by which he attempts to build a society of creditors constituting a kind of blasphemous social covenant.

25. Cf. Dod and Cleaver, *Exposition*, p. 218: "The master therefore (that the house may be well ordered) must let everyone know his place and calling. . . . The house might be enriched, everything might be done in good order, and would fall out in their just and due compass, where every one were diligent in his place."

26. Cf. Dekker's injunction in *The Seven Deadly Sins of London:* "Remember, O you rich men, that your servants are your adopted children; they are naturalized into your blood, and if you hurt theirs, you are guilty of letting your own" (quoted in Walzer, p. 189).

27. Once again the contrast recalls the Puritan attack on traditional political thought: Overreach's tyranny with its indifference to "fitting difference" resembles the leveling despotism of the Calvinist God (Walzer, pp. 151–2), while Lovell asserts the Anglican doctrine of hierarchy, in which "men of different degrees in the body politic related to one another in terms not of command and obedience, but rather of authority and reverence. Hierarchy depended on mutual recognition of personal place" (Walzer, p. 159). General slavery is also the condition to which Luke, the pious "hypocrite" of *The City Madam*, seeks to reduce his enemies,

while the virtuous Lord Lacie and Sir John Frugal combine to restore a sense of fitting "distance 'twixt the city and the court" and to reinstate the proper ordering of Frugal's patriarchal family (5.3.156). Both orders have been undermined by the tyrannical ambition of Lady Frugal and her daughters.

28. In his claim to the power of life and death over his child, Overreach has the authority not only of Puritan divines like Perkins but of the Anglican convocation of 1606 (Walzer, pp. 185–91). Margaret, on the other hand, might appeal to the more liberal ethic of Seneca's *De Beneficiis* (2.29), which sharply contests the view that mere begetting is a benefit that no child can ever adequately repay.

29. Cf. the conclusion to which Luke is ironically brought in *The City Madam:* "I care not where I go; what's done with words / Cannot be undone" (5.3.147–8).

30. Dod and Cleaver, *Household Gouernment*, E_3-E_3 v, quoting Proverbs 21.6, 13.

31. Here once again Overreach's individualism turns him into a kind of monstrous inversion of the alienated Puritan saint as Walzer describes him—the wanderer, cut off from family and kin, a self-chosen "masterless man" turning his back on the cries of his wife and children in his remorseless quest for salvation.

32. Ironically, he makes the same foolish confusion as is fostered by Lady Frugal. Milliscent flatters her mistress's pride with the hope "to see / A country knight's son and heir walk bare before you / When you are a countess," while she herself expects to "take the upper hand of a squire's wife, through justice" *(City Madam,* 1.1.71–7). Luke Frugal similarly promises to revive "the memory / Of the Roman matrons who kept captive queens / To be their handmaids" *(City Madam,* 3.2.162–4). Massinger's revolutionaries (like the Commonwealth leaders after them) can still conceive of social change only within the framework of what Andrew Sharp has called "heraldic definition" (see Sharp, "Edward Waterhouse's View of Social Change in Seventeenth-Century England," *Past and Present*, 62 (1974): 27–46).

33. Cf. Greedy's marvelous comical iconoclasm when Lovell offers his hand: "This is a lord, and some think this a favour; / But I had rather have my hand in a dumpling" (3.2.165–6).

34. Dod and Cleaver, *Household Gouernment*, V_5 v-V_7. Walzer (pp. 193–6) notes the way in which the Puritans' insistence on voluntary marriage tended to "subtly . . . undermine" the authority of parents that they ostensibly maintained.

35. Dod and Cleaver, *Household Gouernment*, Y_4-Z_1. Batty, S_4 v,Bb_4. Cf. George Wither's *Fidelia*, in which the poet inveighs against parental tyranny:

> For though the will of our Creator binds
> Each child to learn and know his parents' minds,
> Yet sure am I so just a deity
> Commandeth nothing against piety.
> QUOTED IN WALZER, P. 194.

For a thoroughgoing patriarchalist like Filmer on the other hand, no such qualification of authority is possible. Filmer maintained:

1. That there is no form of government, but monarchy only.
2. That there is no monarchy but paternal.
3. That there is no paternal monarchy, but absolute, or arbitrary.
4. That there is no such thing as an aristocracy or democracy.
5. That there is no such form of government as a tyranny.
6. That the people are not born free by nature.

QUOTED IN SCHOCHET, *Patriarchalism*, P. 115.

36. Batty, S_{3v}-S_{4v}.
37. Coleridge quoted in John Danby, *Elizabethan and Jacobean Poets* (London: Faber, 1965), p. 184. On the king's displeasure, see Andrew Gurr, *The Shakespearean Stage, 1574–1642*, 2d ed. (Cambridge: Cambridge University Press, 1980), pp. 75–6.
38. Seneca, *De Beneficiis*, 3.2–5; Thomas Otway, *Venice Preserved*, ed. Malcolm Kelsall, Regents Renaissance Drama Series (Lincoln: University of Nebraska Press, 1969), 1.1.201–11.

4 · "THE TONGUES OF ANGELS"

1. Philip Massinger, *The Plays and Poems of Philip Massinger*, ed. Philip Edwards and Colin Gibson, vol. 4 (Oxford: Clarendon Press, 1976), 4.3.46–7. All citations from *The City Madam* are to this edition. All biblical quotations (except where otherwise indicated) are from the Authorized (King James) Version.

It is worth noting, in view of its preoccupation with charity, that *The City Madam* was first licensed on 25 May 1632 and may therefore have been intended for performance in the week of 11 June, the feast of Saint Barnabas. Saint Barnabas, who in Acts 4.36–7 sells his property in order to distribute the proceeds among the poor, has a particular connection with charity; the Gospel for the day is John 15.12 ("This is my commandment, That ye love one another"). Performance on Saint Barnabas's Day would give a special intensity to Frugal's final proclamation of mercy: "This day is sacred to it" (5.3.126). The feast was omitted from the 1552 Calendar, but the service was retained and in 1636 Bishop Wren issued an order that "ministers forget not to read the collect, epistles, and gospels appointed for 'Saint Barnaby's Day' "; see J. H. Blunt, *The Annotated Book of Common Prayer* (London: Longmans, Green, 1893).

2. Cf. Mary's sneer at those who think "the happiness of man's life consists / In a mighty shoulder of mutton" (1.1.153–4).
3. Psalm 58.4; cited from the 1660 Prayer Book version.
4. In the light of the play's satiric denigration of inspiration in favor of charity, it

may be worth noting that Saint Paul's encomium on charity seems to exalt this virtue above the pentecostal gifts: "Though I speak with the tongues of men and of angels . . . / And though I have the gift of prophecy, and understand all mysteries, and all knowledge; and though I have all faith, . . . and have not charity, I am nothing" (1 Cor. 13.1—2).

5. Cf. chap. 3.

6. Cf. also 1.3.118; 2.2.68 SD; 3.2.94; 4.3.3; and perhaps 4.2.103; 4.4.140–1.

7. W. K. Jordan, *Philanthropy in England, 1480—1660: A Study of the Changing Pattern of English Social Aspiration* (London: Allen and Unwin, 1959), pp. 146, 77, 18–19, and chap. 6. For a detailed discussion of the process by which charity became progressively institutionalized, see Gareth Jones, *History of the Law of Charity* (Cambridge: Cambridge University Press, 1969), chaps. 1–5.

8. *Three sermons or homelies to moove compassion towards the poore* (1596); Henry Smith, *Sermons* (1599), quoted in Jordan, pp. 168—9.

9. Thomas Gataker, *A sparke toward the kindling of sorrow for Sion* (1621), quoted in Jordan, p.186. William Perkins, *Works* (1605), quoted in Jordan, p. 152; cf. also the sermon by William Whately, *Sinne no more* (1628), quoted on p. 184: "Bountiful and merciful actions are the best bargains, and the best purchases."

10. See Whately, in Jordan p. 184: "Let your abundance supply their wants, whom God therefore hath called to want, that he might give you occasion of declaring the abundance of your charity"; cf. also Edward Dering's argument that "men are made rich for no other reason than they may give to the poor" (p. 153).

11. See for instance Jordan's account of Thomas Lever's teaching (pp. 163–4).

12. Adams quoted in Jordan, p. 192.

13. Ibid, p. 193; Richardson quoted in Jordan, p. 192.

14. Massinger, *Plays and Poems*, vol. 2. All citations from *A New Way to Pay Old Debts* are to this edition.

15. For a reading that emphasizes the new city alignment of Massinger's later comedy, see Martin Butler, "Massinger's *The City Madam* and the Caroline Audience," *Renaissance Drama*, n.s. 13 (1982): 157–87.

16. Cf. Luke's "Madam-punk" (2.1.102) and Hippolita's contemptuous phrase in Ford's *'Tis Pity She's a Whore* "your goodly Madam Merchant" (2.2.49); cited from Derek Roper's Revels edition (London: Methuen, 1975). "Madam" had the double sense of "a lady of rank" and "affected fine lady" (*OED*, n.3a,c); Massinger plays with both meanings.

17. Butler (p. 166) points out that the provisos take the appropriately City form of a mock indenture.

18. *A New Way*, 2.2.78–89; cf. also Anne's ambition to have "some decay'd lady for my parasite, / To flatter me, and rail at other madams" *(City Madam*, 2.2.123–4).

19. Cf. A. G. Gross, "Social Change and Philip Massinger," *Studies in English Literature* 7 (1967), 329–42. Gross declares, "I think it is possible to advance,

though it is not possible adequately to support, an hypothesis that in the decade that passed between writing these two plays Massinger's social views matured decidedly" (p. 341n. 9; emphasis added); I take issue with his qualification.

20. Cf. Tapwell's boast to Welborne:

> poor Tim Tapwell with a little stock,
> Some forty pounds or so, bought a small cottage,
> Humbled myself to marriage with my Froth here;
> Gave entertainment . . . [to whores and canters,
> Clubbers by night]. . . .
> The poor income
> I glean'd from them hath made me in my parish
> Thought worthy to be Scavenger, and in time
> May rise to be Overseer of the Poor;
> Which if I do, on your petition Welborne
> I may allow you thirteen pence a quarter,
> And you shall thank my worship.
>
> *A New Way to Pay Old Debts,* 1.1.59–63, 75–81

21. The parallel entry of "SHERIFF, MARSHALL, *and Officers*" to Goldwire, Tradewell, and their accomplices at 4.2.72 only reinforces this point.

22. See my discussion of *The Tempest* in "Remembrance and Revenge: *Hamlet, Macbeth,* and *The Tempest,*" in Ian Donaldson, ed., *Jonson and Shakespeare* (London and Canberra: Macmillan/Humanities Research Centre, 1983), pp. 35–56. Butler (p. 185) speaks of the conclusion of the play as "an epiphany" fulfilling "a sacramental pattern."

23. Despite Massinger's long apprenticeship with Fletcher, Jonson was his principal mentor in comedy; it is interesting to note that—as Anne Barton argues in *Ben Jonson, Dramatist* (Cambridge: Cambridge University Press, 1984), pp. 259, 279–81)—the master was engaged in his own reassessment and reworking of Shakespeare's romances at about the same time.

24. See n. 6 this chapter.

25. See Goldwire's use of the term "pagan," 2.1.110.

26. Since Luke vainly imagines it a key to heaven, it may be worth recalling, as a source of additional irony, the key to the bottomless pit given to the fifth angel in Revelation 9.1.

27. On this point see Gary B. Nash, "The Image of the Indian in the Southern Colonial Mind," in Edward Dudley and Maxmilian E. Novak, eds., *The Wild Man Within* (Pittsburgh: University of Pittsburgh Press, 1972), pp. 55–86; Benjamin Keen, "The Vision of America in the Writings of Urbain Chauveton"; Haydn White, "The Noble Savage Theme as Fetish"; and Arthur J. Slavin, "The American Principal from More to Locke," all in Fredi Chapelli et al., eds., *First*

Images of America: The Impact of the New World on the Old, 2 vols. (Berkeley, Los Angeles, and London: University of California Press, 1976), 1:107–20, 121–35, 139–64; and A. L. Rowse, *The Elizabethans and America* (London: Macmillan, 1959), pp. 27, 199–200. Naturally the Indians' supposedly communalist societies and their alleged indifference to pelf were most emphasized by primitivists like Montaigne ("Of the Cannibals") who wished to present them as possessing the felicities of the golden age, denied to Europeans by the doubtful gift of civilization. But even those with a clearer commercial vision, like the Virginia Council, rejoiced in the innocence of a people from whom the English "do buy . . . the pearls of the earth, and sell to them the pearls of heaven" (Nash, p. 57). More hostile later commentators tended to denigrate their material carelessness as "improvidence," but even Captain John Smith, who found them "Generally covetous of copper, Beads, and suchlike trash" did not credit them with any proper sense of value—*Works*, ed. Edward Arber (Birmingham: English Scholar's Library, 1884), p. 361. Smith's observations echo the astonishment of John de Verrazano (1524) who found that the Florida Indians esteemed copper above gold, which because of its indifferent color "is counted the basest" (see Richard Hakluyt, *The Principal Navigations, Voyages, Traffiques, and Discoveries of the English Nation*, 12 vols. [1598–1600; rpt. Glasgow: J. MacLehose, 1903–5], 8:433). The popular image of the Indian attitude to wealth in Massinger's day is probably still best represented by the feckless negligence of Othello's "base Indian" throwing away a pearl "richer than all his tribe."

Butler (pp. 177–85) emphasizes the Indians' reputation for Devil-worship and argues that this makes them "a visual sign" of Luke's damnability—but the Devil they adore speaks good English.

28. For charity as a way of ensuring posthumous fame, see Jordan, pp. 143–239, 215–28.

5 · "IN EVERYTHING ILLEGITIMATE"

1. Among Wilder's intermediate ancestors is the fratricidal (and apparently matricidal) "monster," Robert Wringhim, the hero of James Hogg's *Private Memoirs and Confessions of a Justified Sinner*, whose alleged bastardy is an important factor in his complex psychological motivation. For the identification of the "natural child" with unredeemed nature and the suggestion that it may have derived from the practice of abandoning bastard children in the wilderness to survive, see Alison Findlay, *Illegitimate Power: Bastards in Renaissance Drama* (Manchester; Manchester University Press, 1994). Arthur Conan Doyle, *The Complete Sherlock Holmes* (New York: Doubleday, n.d.), p. 558.

2. The persistence of the type may even have something to do with the peculiar invective connotations of "bastard" in modern English, where (in contrast to

other European languages) the term is used to impugn the moral character of a man rather than to slight the honor of his family; more significantly, it can be also be used to express a grudging admiration of exactly the sort invited by Elizabethan stage bastards.

Peter Laslett, Karla Oosterveen, and Richard M. Smith, eds., *Bastardy and Its Comparative History* (Cambridge: Harvard University Press, 1980), pp. 4–5.

The most comprehensive treatment of the topic is Findlay's book (see n. 1 this chap.), which in turn acknowledges a debt to Leah Scragg's master's thesis, "The Bastard in Elizabethan and Jacobean Drama," University of Liverpool, 1964. In addition a number of so-far unpublished papers were contributed to the seminar on Shakespeare's bastards chaired by Mary Ann McGrail at the 1988 Shakespeare Association of America meeting in Vancouver.

3. Cf. 3.4.40–4: "Such an act / That . . . takes off the rose / From the fair forehead of an innocent love / And sets a blister there."

4. Ruth Nevo, "Mousetrap and Rat Man: An Uncanny Resemblance," in Tetsuo Kishi, Roger Pringle, and Stanley Wells, eds., *Shakespeare and the Cultural Traditions* (Newark: University of Delaware Press, 1994), pp. 350–63, also draws attention to Hamlet's inevitable uncertainty about his paternity.

5. In a brilliantly suggestive article, "*Henry IV* and the Death of Old Double," *Essays in Criticism* 40 (1990): 14–53, John Kerrigan explores the theatrical and verbal play on the "bastard" and "legitimate" in the *Henry IV* plays and notices their intimate association with ideas of counterfeiting (pp. 41–4).

6. John F. Danby, *Shakespeare's Doctrine of Nature*, (London: Faber, 1961), p. 44; Kingsley Davis, "Illegitimacy and the Social Structure," in William J. Goode, ed., *Readings on the Family and Society* (Englewood Cliffs, N.J.: Prentice-Hall, 1964), pp. 21–32 (p. 21).

7. See Chris Given-Wilson and Alice Curteis, *The Royal Bastards of Medieval England* (London: Routledge and Kegan Paul, 1984), pp. 43, 51–3; I. Pinchbeck, "Social Attitudes to the Problem of Illegitimacy," *British Journal of Sociology* 5 (1954): 309–23 (pp. 314–5); Alan Macfarlane, "Illegitimacy and Illegitimates in English History," in Laslett, Oosterveen, and Smith, pp. 75–6.

8. Thus the section in the 1576 Poor Law "Concerning bastards begotten and born out of lawful matrimony (an offence against God's and Man's laws)" objects to their "great burden of the . . . Parish, and . . . defrauding of the relief of the impotent and aged true poor of the same parish, [as well as to] the evil example and the encouragement of lewd life" constituted by their mere existence. The parents of such offspring are not only to provide for their maintenance but to be treated as criminals and punished with whippings and imprisonment; see Pinchbeck, pp. 315–6; and cf. Given-Wilson and Curteis, p. 54; Martin Ingram, *Church, Courts, Sex, and Marriage in England, 1570–1640* (Cambridge: Cambridge University Press, 1987), pp. 151–8. For a suggestion that changing attitudes to bastardy reflect

a more general shift toward a tighter regulation of sexual relations as part of the "civilizing" process of the early modern period, see Norbert Elias, *The Civilising Process: The History of Manners*, trans. Edmund Jephcott (Oxford: Basil Blackwell, 1978), pp. 183–4.

Peter Laslett, "Long-term Trends in Bastardy in England," in Laslett, ed., *Family Life and Illicit Love in Earlier Generations* (Cambridge: Cambridge University Press, 1977), esp. pp. 113–5; Macfarlane, p. 82.

9. By Findlay's reckoning (p. 5) there are more than one hundred plays from the period in which bastardy figures as a major subject, including fifty-seven featuring adult bastards (real or supposed).

10. See Ralph A. Houlbrooke, *The English Family, 1450–1750* (London: Longman, 1984), p. 117; Pinchbeck, p. 316; and Given-Wilson and Curteis, p. 54.

11. On Don John's ambitions, see J. H. Elliott, *Imperial Spain, 1469–1716* (London: Penguin, 1970), p. 265. As the hero of Lepanto, Don John also contributed to the paradoxical tradition of the Virtuous Bastard—and it is thus that he appears in Webster's *Devil's Law-Case* (4.2.358–9), for example; cited from the New Mermaid edition, ed. Elizabeth M. Brennan (London: Benn, 1975).

The Tudor claim to the throne had been derived in the first instance from Henry VII's great-grandfather John Beaufort, a bastard son of John of Gaunt, and it was dubiously bolstered by his grandfather Owen Tudor's marriage to the widow of Henry V—a secret marriage of disparagement in which the clerk of the household's "presumption in mixing his blood with that of the noble race of kings" caused much scandal. Elizabeth's personal claim was further clouded by Henry VIII's Second and Third Acts of Succession, in which he had successively bastardized and then legitimated Mary and Elizabeth, the daughters of his first two marriages. Catholic propagandists, such as Cardinal Allen (*Admonition to the Nobility and People of England and Ireland*, 1588), were to use Elizabeth's alleged illegitimacy to argue the illegality of her succession. The princesses were bastardized to clear the way for the remarried king's expected male heirs, but when subsequent marriages produced only the sickly Edward, it seemed expedient to re-legitimate his daughters (see Given-Wilson and Curteis, pp. 47, 51–3). Later, Elizabeth herself was to decline marriage to Mary's widower, Philip of Spain, partly on the grounds of an embarrassing parallel with Henry's marriage to his deceased brother's wife, Catherine of Aragon: "If she approved the marriage of one man and two sisters, then she sanctioned the union of one woman to two brothers. And 'if that were a good Marriage, then she must be illegitimate'" (Jack Goody, *The Development of the Family and Marriage in Europe* [Cambridge: Cambridge University Press, 1983]). Possible connections between Elizabeth's "bastardy" and theatrical interest in bastard figures were pursued by contributors to the 1988 SAA seminar on Shakespeare's bastards. James's situation was less complicated, but the Stuarts themselves traced their succession from a bastard line, and the circumstances of Jame's birth were muddied both by his mother's rumored affair with David Rizzio and by her notorious involvement with the Earl of Bothwell, the assassin. Thus the king's own warnings in *Basilikon Doron* (Scolar Facsimile, pp. 96–7) against the propensities of bastards to "unnatural" usurpation may be tinged with complex ambivalence. For further comment on anxieties surrounding Elizabeth's and James's births and the question of inheritance, see Stephen Orgel's introduction to *The Tempest* (Oxford: Oxford University Press, 1987), pp. 37–40.

12. There may indeed be a sense, as Janet Adelman suggests, in which daughters are always in some sense "illegitimate," simply by virtue of their capacity to "disrupt the patriarchal ideal, both insofar as they disrupt the transmission of property from father to son and insofar as they disrupt the paternal fantasy of perfect self-replication. Even more clearly than the mother's son, the daughter is but 'the shadow of the male,' carrying within her the disruptive sign of the mother's presence"; see Adelman, *Suffocating Mothers: Fantasies of Maternal Origin in Shakespeare's Plays, "Hamlet" to "The Tempest"* (New York and London: Routledge, 1992), p. 108.

   According to the "logic of illegitimacy," which Adelman traces in *King Lear*, "the female sexual place is necessarily the place of corruption, the 'sulphurous pit' . . . that is Lear's equivalent to Edgar's 'dark and vicious place'; present only as a site of illegitimacy, the mother . . . transmits her faults to her issue, the children whose corrupt sexuality records their origin" (p. 108).

13. John Donne, *Paradoxes and Problems*, ed. Helen Peters (Oxford: Clarendon Press, 1980), p. 31. For further evidence of the natural energy and vivacity attributed to bastards, see Findlay, pp. 129–36.

14. Donne, p.32. On virtuous bastards, see Findlay, chap. 5; and Margaret Loftus Ranald, "The British Bastard as England's Savior," a paper from the Vancouver Shakespeare's Bastards Seminar. I am indebted to the organizer, Mary Ann McGrail, for giving me access to several papers from this seminar.

15. It is significant, in this context, that *The Misfortunes of Arthur* (1588), which presents Arthur as a type of virtuous bastardy, is nevertheless at pains to emphasize that he is destroyed by Mordred, the bastard issue of his own incestuous adultery, whose usurping ambitions extend to the seduction of his stepmother, Gueneuora. Likewise, the otherwise heroic Spurio in Nabbes's *Unfortunate Mother* (1639) is brought down by his incestuous passion for his own mother, meeting his end in a duel with the similarly ambiguous bastard Notho—where each kills the other, as if in enactment of the self-canceling energy of bastard appetite.

16. Fuller wrote of Henry Fitzroy, natural son to Henry VIII, that he confuted this etymology "and verified their deduction, deriving it from *besteard*, that is, the 'best disposition' "; see Thomas Fuller, *The History of the Worthies of England*, 3 vols., ed. P. A. Nuttall (London: Thomas Tegg, 1840), p. 499.

John Fortescue, *A Learned Commendation of the Politique Lawes of England* (London, 1567; facsimile ed., Amsterdam and New York: Theatrum Orbis Terrarum, 1969), fo. 95v-97v. G. E. Aylmer, ed., *The Diary of William Lawrence* (1961), p. 6, cited by Macfarlane, pp. 71–85 (p. 76).

17. In support of the civil law's discrimination, Fortescue noted that the church judged bastards "unworthy to be received into holy orders and rejecteth them from all prelacy" (fo. 95v). The same superstitious restrictions may help to account for the bastard's exclusion from membership of guilds and societies (see Findlay, pp. 31–2). Practically speaking, bastards could, of course, be ordained on payment of a substantial fee of dispensation—as the presence of the Bishop of Winchester (a member of the illegitimate Beaufort clan) in *1 Henry VI* reminds us.

   Macfarlane, pp. 78–9. It was perhaps for this very reason that Sir George Buck found it necessary to cite scripture when urging that it should be thought "[no] disparagement for a noble family to be descended from natural issue, considering that there . . . are infinite number of noble and princely families which are derived and propagated from bastards." In addition to the Beauforts and the royal Stuarts, he cited "this one example . . . above all, to wit, that Jesus Christ, the greatest and most noble king, was content to descend from Phares, a bastard"; cited in Given-Wilson and Curteis, p. 53. Buck's other examples included the genealogies of Aeneas, Romulus, Theseus, Themistocles, Hercules, and William the Conqueror.

   The text of Shaw's sermon is also cited by Fortescue, fo. 95v.

18. On the "unnatural" character of the bastard, see Findlay, chap. 3. Mary Douglas, *Purity and Danger: An Analysis of Concepts of Pollution and Taboo* (Praeger: New York and Washington, 1966).

19. Douglas, p. 36.

20. Joseph A. Candido, "Blots, Stains, and Adulteries: The Impurities in *King John*," in Deborah Curren-Aquino, ed., *King John: New Perspectives* (Newark: University of Delaware Press, 1989), pp. 114–25, notices how the language used to describe John's death makes it seem an expression of his polluted blood (pp. 118–9). Findlay (p. 100) cites Alonzo's rebuke to the ambitious Gaspar in the anonymous *Bastard* (pub. 1652): "thy tainted blood / Thinks to pollute mine" (sig. B2v).

21. Presumably we are to take this as a sign of the true-bred instinct of a child who has been cast out as the bastard offspring of her mother's adultery with Leontes. The misogynist pamphlet *Hic Mulier: Or, The Man-Woman* (London, 1620), obsessed as it is by what the pamphleteer perceives as threats to the proper differentiation of gender, turning women to "stranger things than ever Noah's Ark unladed, or Nile engendered," extends this notion of the bastard to the illegitimate mixtures in dress, the "monstrousness of deformity in apparel," which

includes "the false armoury of yellow Starch (for to wear yellow on white, or white upon yellow, is by the rules of heraldry baseness, bastardy, and indignity)," sig.A3v-A4.

22. Edmund Spenser, *A View of the Present State of Ireland*, ed. W. L. Renwick (London: Eric Partridge, 1934), p. 58. Likewise, Sir John Davies's *Discoverie of the True Causes why Ireland Was neuer entirely Subdued* (London, 1612) attributes Irish factiousness and want of civil government partly to the "mischief" bred by "that Irish custom of gavelkind," which allowed all sons to inherit "as well bastard as legitimate" (p. 172).

23. By this description of "native," I mean to exclude Ariel and the other spirit creatures (as Caliban himself does in remembering his lonely rule)—ultimately, of course, the island has no "true" natives, only spirits and colonists, and no true inheritors either since, like any bastard, Caliban can claim only through the female line.

24. Spenser, pp. 84–6.

25. The quasi-allegorical scheme I outline will not of course encompass all the play's notorious ambivalencies. Caliban's lyrical response to the beauties of the island—together with Gonzalo's observation that the "people of the island . . . though they are of monstrous shape . . . Their manners are more gentle, kind, than of / Our human generation you shall find / Many, nay, almost any" (3.3.30–4)—significantly complicates the meanings that attach to his seemingly "monstrous" and "unnatural" character, and hence to the whole issue of inheritance in the play. In this context it is worth observing the existence of a number of postcolonial texts in which bastards are figured as inheritors (or potential inheritors) of a recuperative hybridity—notably Brian Friel's plays *Translations* and *Making History*, and Salman Rushdie's novels *Midnight's Children* and *Shame*. Since *Midnight's Children* itself asks to be read as (among other things) a reply to Forster's *Passage to India*, one might view its narrator, Saleem (a racial and cultural "bastard" as well as a literal illegitimate), as embodying exactly the hybrid possibilities that Forster (who had made a bastard child the emblem of one kind of hybridizing "connection" in his novel of class, *Howard's End*) balked at in his novel of empire.

26. Thus for Coriolanus to adopt the hypocritically subservient role toward the plebeians required by his mother will be to "dissemble with [his] nature" and use "words that are . . . but *bastards* and syllables / Of no allowance to your bosom's truth" (*Coriolanus*, 3.2.62, 55–7; emphasis added).

27. Among the apparent coinages listed in *OED* are "adulterate, *v*. (1531); adulterate, *ppl.a* (1590); adulterated *p.ppl.a* (1607); adulterately, *adv*. (1619); adulterating, *vbl.sb*. (1610); adulteration, *sb* (1606); adulterator, *sb*. (1632); adultered, *ppl.a* (1624); adulterine, *a* and *sb* (1542); adultering, *ppl.a* (1599); adulterously, *adv*. (1599)." *Hic Mulier*'s tirade against the blurring of gender distinctions in dress

similarly discovers in current fashions not merely bastard deformity but a species of adulterate counterfeiting, "Mimic and apish incivility." Its followers are "but rags of gentry, torn from better pieces for their foul stains . . . adulterate branches of rich stocks, that taking too much sap from the root, are cut away, and employed in base uses. . . . It is exorbitant from Nature, and an *Antithesis* to kind. . . . What can be more barbarous, than with the gloss of mumming art to disguise the beauty of their creations? To mould their bodies to every deformed fashion. . . . To have their gestures as piebald, and as motley-various as their disguises. . . . They turn maskers, mummers, nay monsters in their disguises . . . [through] this miscellany or mixture of deformities" (sig. A3v, B1-B1v, C2, C3v).

28. Cited from Giorgio Melchiori, ed., *The Reign of King Edward III* (Cambridge: Cambridge University Press, 1998).

29. Cited from Eric Sams, ed., *Shakespeare's Lost Play, Edmund Ironside* (New York: St Martin's Press, 1985). Cf. the bastard Fallacy's travesty of Edmund in Richard Zouche's *Sophister* (1631): "Sacred Deceit, to thee be consecrate / My temples; aid thou goddess mine attempt" (A4); and see Findlay's discussion of this play (pp. 121–4).

30. An important detail in this complex system of ironic equivalences is Mosca's suggestion that coinage, in the form of gold, is the sovereign medicine that "transforms / The most deformed, and restores them lovely" (5.1.117–8). It is also worth noting that the principal domestic function of Volpone's bastard brood is apparently theatrical counterfeiting, the "pleasing imitation / Of greater men's actions, in ridiculous fashion" (3.1.13–14) and that their first performance concerns the systematic debasement of the soul of Pythagoras. This deformed counterfeiting supplies an ironic mirror for "the too much licence" of contemporary dramatic practice by which, according to Jonson's epistle dedicatory, the poetasters of his day have "much deformed their mistress . . . adulterated her form."

31. Compare the antipatriarchal stratagems of the aptly named bastard Antipater in Markham and Sampson's *Herod and Antipater* (1622), whose viciousness similarly stems from his having been "begot when sin was revelling" (2.1.57); cited from the edition by Gordon Nicholas Ross (New York: Garland, 1979).

32. In John Florio's dictionary *Queen Anna's World of Words, Spurio* is glossed as "a bastard, a baseborn. Also adulterate or counterfeit." Findlay, who also notices the virtual anonymity of the bastard, cites William Clerke's *Triall of Bastardie* (1594) (sig. E1v), to the effect that *spurius* was the technical Latin term for the son of a concubine and *nothus* for the son of an adulteress (p. 20).

33. Candido (p. 117) observes how counterfeiting extends even to the king himself, whose sense of "being tainted by a corrupt, debased, or illegitimate stock . . . manifests itself . . . in an almost compulsive strategy of concealment and deception."

34. James Calderwood, *The Properties of Othello* (Amherst: University of Massachusetts Press, 1989), p. 10. In *3 Henry VI* (5.5.115) Richard of Gloucester and his brothers are denounced by Queen Margaret as "the bastard boys of York" in a context where York's patronage of the usurper Cade (a counterfeit Plantagenet) and appearance at the head of an Irish army associates the Yorkist faction with illegitimacy of all kinds.

35. Pinchbeck, p. 315. The alternative description was *filius populus* as Fortescue, citing a popular rhyme, points out: "Your natural or bastard son is the son of the people. . . . To whom the people father is, to him is father none and all. To whom the people father is, well fatherless we may him call" (fo. 93v).

36. Barnabe Barnes, *The Divils Charter* (4.2.1980); cited from the edition by R. B. McKerrow, *Materialen zur Kunde des älteren Englischen Dramas*, vol. 60 (Louvain: A. Uystpruyst, 1904). Compare Antipater's "None or alone" in *Herod and Antipater* (1.3.407).

The bastard-figure's propensity for "willing of identity" is also noticed, from a rather different perspective, by Bruce Young in "The Bastard as Self and Other: Levinas, Renaissance Attitudes, and Shakespeare's Bastards," a paper from the Vancouver Shakespeare's Bastards Seminar.

Thomas Hyde, "Boccaccio: the Genealogies of Myth," *PMLA* 100 (1985): 744, cited in Phyllis Rackin, *Stages of History: Shakespeare's English Chronicles* (Ithaca: Cornell University Press, 1990), p. 159. Gaspar, the hero of the anonymous *Bastard* (1652), seems to make his bastard condition similarly representative: "The world so swarms with bastards now, that I / Need no despair for want of company; / I'm in among the throng" (A4v), cited in Findlay, p. 213.

37. Danby, p. 44. Arguably even Caliban's invention of a history of usurpation in which he once figured as "mine own king" fits this general pattern of egotistical self-sufficiency. On the blasphemous character of the bastard, see Findlay, chap. 2. Findlay, (esp. pp. 62–72), also traces some of the bastard's generalized viciousness to his descent from the Medieval Vice.

38. The ironic symmetries in the scene with the dying duke are reinforced by the way in which the imagery of eating links Spurio's erotic banquet with the poison that gnaws the duke's lips ("Those that did eat are eaten," l. 159)—it is as if Spurio *were* a devouring poison compounded of the duke's own blood/lust.

39. Cited from J. W. Cunliffe, ed., *Early English Tragedies* (Oxford: Clarendon Press, 1912).

40. In her paper *"Filius Nullius:* Bastards, Younger Sons, and Daughters in *King Lear,"* delivered to the Vancouver Shakespeare's Bastards Seminar, Kathy Howlett observes how accusations of bastardy abound in the play, embracing Regan, Edgar, and Oswald ("whoreson . . . son and heir of a mongrel bitch," 16–20), as well as Edmund, Cordelia, and Goneril.

41. The logic of this fantasy is beautifully traced in Janet Adelman's psychoanalytic account of the meaning of illegitimacy in *King Lear* (*Suffocating Mothers*, pp. 105–9). Adelman writes that "maternal origin and illegitimacy are synonymous in the Gloucester plot—and throughout *Lear*—because sexuality *per se* is illegitimate and illegitimizes its children; whether or not the son is biologically his father's, the mother's dark place inevitably contaminates him, compromising his father's presence in him" (p. 107).

42. OED *bastard,sb.* and *a*, B4, B2, A3.

43. Pinchbeck, p. 315. Kathy Howlett's *"Filius Nullius"* argues that in *Lear* Edmund's bastardy associates him with a whole range of characters whose nature "Cannot be bordered certain in itself" (4.2.33) and who thus represent a threat to the categories and boundaries of "an enclosed system."

44. Cited from Fredson Bowers, ed., *The Dramatic Works in the Beaumont and Fletcher Canon*, 10 vols. (Cambridge: Cambridge University Press, 1966–96).

45. Francis Bacon, *Essays* (London: Dent, 1906), p. 25. Deuteronomy (23.1–2) similarly links eunuchs and bastards in its list of those forbidden to enter the congregation of the Lord (cf. also Lev. 21.18–20). Canon law accordingly excluded eunuchs as well as bastards from the priesthood—indicating that both groups were seen as polluted by their failure to conform fully to the category "man."

   Significantly, in *Volpone* Corbaccio's bastardizing of Bonario is mockingly announced by Mosca as a "monstrous" wrong (3.1.91). The bastard's monstrosity is compounded by the fact that through his very existence he proves his mother a whore, thus demonstrating her own monstrosity, since, as Nicholas Breton declared: "A whore is no perfect woman; for every woman is either a maid, a wife, or a widow; and being neither of these, she must needs be a monster, and so an imperfect woman"(*Diverse Newes Out of Divers Countries* in *Complete Works*, 2:8). Edmund is a "whoreson [who] must be acknowledged"— but ironically that very acknowledgment, as his lowering presence reminds us, publicly brands his mother as a whore.

46. Findlay (pp. 53–8) notes that Caliban's deformity, like that of his kinsman Suckabus, bastard child of the witch Calib in *Seven Champions of Christendom*, is also a reflection of his allegedly diabolic paternity. However she cites other examples of the association of the bastard with the monstrous and deformed (pp. 49–59, 107–8, 148–51).

47. Phyllis Rackin, *Stages of History: Shakespeare's English Chronicles* (Ithaca: Cornell University Press, 1990), p. 184.

48. Rackin, p. 186. For Joseph Candido, the bastard's "personal defilement" represents the impossibility of untainted action in "an adulterate world." Candido (p. 114) discovers in the play "a Hamletesque obsession with sullied purity and . . .

adultery."

49. Candido, p. 123. For some discussion of the bastard's association with carnivalesque topsy-turveydom, see Findlay, pp. 146–65. Although Faulconbridge's discovery of an unambiguously heroic-patriotic language at the end of the play signals a kind of legitimation, arguably "the four voices of the bastard" defined by Michael Manheim in Deborah Curren-Aquino, ed., *King John: New Perspectives* (Newark: University of Delaware Press), pp. 126–35, are themselves an illustration of his mixed nature.

50. See Homer, *Iliad*, book 2; Erasmus *Adages*, "Thersitae Facies."

51. Heinrich Heine, *Shakespeare's Girls and Women*, trans. C. G. Leland (1839; 1891); A. C. Swinburne, *A Study of Shakespeare* (1880) both in Priscilla Martin, ed., *Troilus and Cressida: A Casebook* (London: Macmillan, 1976), pp. 45, 55.

Elsewhere Ajax appears as a kind of Plinian monster "who wears his wit in his belly and his guts in his head" (2.1.73–4); and if Ajax is a monster, so too, is that horned beast Menelaus, for example, "both ass and ox" in Thersites's estimate and rhetorically tainted too with the qualities of "a dog, a mule, a cat, a fitchook, a toad, a lizard, an owl, a puttock . . . a herring without a roe . . . [and] the louse of a lazar" (5.1.59–65).

Sir Philip Sidney, *An Apology for Poetry*, in Edmund D. Jones, ed., *English Critical Essays (Sixteenth, Seventeenth, and Eighteenth Centuries)* (London: Oxford University Press, 1947), p. 46; Giambattista Guarini, "The Compendium of Tragicomic Poetry," in Allan H. Gilbert, ed., *Literary Criticism, Plato to Dryden* (Detroit: Wayne State University Press, 1962), pp. 507, 513.

52. See René Girard, "The Plague in Literature and Myth," in his *To Double Business Bound* (Baltimore: Johns Hopkins University Press, 1978). In *King John* too, adultery and bastardy are figured as symptoms of moral plague, through Constance's tirade against Elinor's alleged adultery and John's consequent illegitimacy: "God hath made her sin and her the plague / On this removed issue, plagued for her, / And with her plague, her sin. . . . A plague upon her!" (2.1.185–90).

53. At this point Shakespeare, like the author of *The Revenger's Tragedy* in the celebrated "bony lady" scene, seems to produce a grotesquely literal version of Sidney's apocalyptic ideal of tragedy as "show[ing] forth the ulcers that are covered with tissue" (p. 28). The figure must of course recall the prologue, "suited in like condition as our *argument*," who so pompously ushers in a play where "all the *argument* is a whore and a cuckold."

54. For a wonderfully supple exploration of the play as "monumental mockery," see Rosalie L. Colie, *Shakespeare's Living Art* (Princeton: Princeton University Press, 1974), chap. 8.

55. Douglas, p. 161.

6 · BASTARDY, COUNTERFEITING, AND MISOGYNY

1. For useful treatments of the authorship question see Roger Holdsworth, *Three Jacobean Revenge Tragedies* (London: Macmillan, 1990), pp. 11–13, 79–105; concerning the play submitted to Keysar, see Holdsworth, p. 106.

2. See chap. 5.

3. Phyllis Rackin's essay "Patriarchal History and Female Subversion" in her *Stages of History: Shakespeare's English Chronicles* (Ithaca: Cornell University Press, 1990), pp. 146–200, analyzes bastardy as a motif that discloses "the repressed knowledge of women's subversive power" (p. 188) and its threat to patriarchal fictions of lineage. An abbreviated version of the same essay, concentrating on the Bastard Faulconbridge in *King John* is printed in Deborah Curren-Aquino, ed., *King John: New Perspectives* (Newark: University of Delaware Press, 1989), pp. 76–90.

4. See chap. 5.

5. For discussion of how the circumstances of conception were thought to affect the nature of the child see Gail Kern Paster, *The Body Embarrassed: Drama and the Disciplines of Shame in Early Modern England* (Ithaca: Cornell University Press, 1993), chap. 4, pp. 162–214. John Fortescue, *A Learned Commendation of the Politique Lawes of England* (London, 1567; facsimile ed., Amsterdam and New York: Theatrum Orbis Terrarum, 1969), fo. 95v–97v. Alison Findlay, "The World So Swarms with Bastards Now: The Bastard in Elizabethan, Jacobean, and Caroline Drama," Ph.D. diss., University of Birmingham, 1988, cites the proverb "Bastards by chance are good, by nature bad" (p. 33).

6. See chap. 5.

7. Rice Vaughan, *A Discourse of Coin and Coinage* (London, 1675; New York: Johnson Reprint, 1975), pp. 45, 53; cited from G. C. Moore Smith, ed., *The Reign of King Edward III* (London, 1897). Vaughan went on to advise the king against the "dishonour" of importing foreign coin on the grounds that he would thereby "communicate a principal point of sovereignty unto a stranger, and . . . pay a tribute to a foreign prince out of your own country, and you shall never have any material coin to be coined in your own mint" (pp. 83–4). For his sire, the bastard resembled such coin, dishonorably stamped in another's mint.

8. See Stephen X. Mead, " 'Thou art chang'd': Public Value and Personal Identity in *Troilus and Cressida" Journal of Medieval and Renaissance Studies* 22 (1992): 237–59. Mead stresses the way in which the development of credit, the use of bills of exchange, and regular manipulations of exchange rates undermined notions of the absolute value of money, threatening to make value seem as arbitrary and mutable a matter as reputation—"What's aught, but as 'tis valued?" as Troilus puts it. Ironically enough the repeated attempts of monarchs "to bring money

back to some ancient, absolute value" only served to emphasize "the chimerical nature of intrinsic worth" (p. 240).

9. Vindice's own gathering sense of self-alienation is registered in a series of asides—"All this is I!" (4.2.130); "Oh, I'm in doubt / Whether I'm myself or no" (4.4.24–5); "I think man's happiest when he forgets himself" (4.4.85)—climaxing in his wry confession to Antonio at the end: " 'Tis time to die when we are ourselves our foes" (5.3.110).

10. Jonson cited from "An Expostulation with Inigo Jones," l. 52; epigram 64, ll. 1–2, in *Complete Poems*, ed. George Parfitt (Harmondsworth: Penguin, 1975).

11. Mead, p. 242.

12. At the same time, Lussurioso's bribing of Piato is figured both as a diabolical sexual coupling, in which gold coin is transformed to seed, and as an especially corrupt form of usurious investment:

❊

LUSSURIOSO:
So, thou'rt confirmed in me
And thus I enter thee.
[Gives him money]

VINDICE:
This Indian devil
Will quickly enter any man: but a usurer,
He prevents that by entering the devil first!
  1.3.85–8

❊

13. John Florio, *Queen Anna's New World of Words* (1611), s.v. "spurio." In this sense the discourse of bastardy merely reflected larger habits of thought that, as Gail Paster (p. 78) has pointed out, did not yet properly "distinguish between the ethical and physical domains."

14. Thomas Laqueur, *Making Sex: Body and Gender from the Greeks to Freud* (Cambridge: Harvard University Press, 1992), p. 56, quoting Isidore, *Etymologiarum*, 9.6.4 ("Semen") and 4.5.4 ("Blood")—emphasis added.

15. For a discussion of the concept of *filius nullius*, see chap. 5.

16. Paster, pp. 23–63.

17. See Peter Stallybrass, "Reading the Body: *The Revenger's Tragedy* and the Jacobean Theater of Consumption," *Renaissance Drama* n.s. 18 (1987): 121–48, and "Patriarchal Territories: The Body Enclosed," in Susan Snyder, ed., *Othello: Critical Essays* (New York and London: Garland Publishing, 1988), pp. 251–74; Frank Whigham, "Reading Social Conflict in the Alimentary Tract: More on the

Body in Renaissance Drama," *ELH* 55 (1988): pp. 333–5; and Michael Neill, " 'Hidden Malady': Death, Discovery, and Indistinction in *The Changeling*," in Neill, *Issues of Death: Mortality and Identity in English Renaissance Tragedy* (Oxford: Clarendon Press, 1997), pp. 168–97.

18. See chap. 5.

19. "Outlaw feminine" is the term coined by Marilyn French, *Shakespeare's Division of Experience* (London: Jonathan Cape, 1982).

20. Note the curious chime between the duchess's "had he cut thee a right diamond, / Thou hadst been next set in the dukedom's ring" (1.2.148–9) and Vindice's evocation of Gloriana's eyes as "heaven-pointed diamonds . . . set / In those unsightly rings" (1.1.19–20).

21. The duchess's three sons clearly owe something to the three seemingly fatherless sons of Tamora, the barbarous Queen of the Goths in *Titus Andronicus*. Although (unlike the child she bears to Aaron the Moor) they are not explicitly illegitimate, Chiron and Demetrius, like Ambitioso and Supervacuo, are mother's sons who seek to profit from their mother's marriage by improperly inserting themselves into a line of royal succession.

22. I am assuming that the quarto stage direction "her son" is not a mistaken description of Lussurioso but a misprint for "her sons," since although their place in the procession is not highlighted by Vindice, their exclusion from this emblematic display of deformed patriarchal order seems unlikely.

23. For the question of James's possible illegitimacy see chap. 5, n. 11, and Stephen Orgel's introduction to his edition of *The Tempest* (Oxford: Oxford University Press, 1987), pp. 37–40.

7 · "AMPHITHEATERS IN THE BODY"

1. *Merchant of Venice*, 3.1.59; Frank McGuinness, *Observe the Sons of Ulster Marching towards the Somme* (London: Faber, 1986) p. 37. The ambivalence of Pyper's gesture is underscored by the fact that it is his left hand he mutilates, while the heraldic device displays a bloody right hand.

2. Sigmund Freud "The Uncanny" in S. Freud, *Art and Literature*, trans. James Strachey et. al., ed. Albert Dickinson, Pelican Freud Library (Harmondsworth: Penguin, 1985), 14:366: "Dismembered limbs, a severed head, a hand cut off at the wrist, as in a fairy tale of Hauff's ["The Story of the Severed Hand"], feet which dance by themselves . . . all these have something peculiarly uncanny about them" (p. 366).

3. Ibid. However his placing of the discussion in the general context of animism, magic, sorcery, and madness as uncanny phenomena suggests other parameters (pp. 365–6). Earlier he relates feelings of the uncanny to the "intellectual uncertainty as to whether an object is alive or not" (p. 354). Elias Canetti, *Crowds and*

Power, trans. Carol Stewart (Harmondsworth: Penguin, 1973), suggests that the symbolic power of the hand has much to do with its "faculty of independent life" (p. 256).

4. Robert Hertz, *Death and the Right Hand*, trans. Rodney Needham and Claudia Needham (Aberdeen: Cohen and West, 1960), notes the difficulty of resolving whether "We are right handed because we are left brained" or vice versa (p. 90).

See also Hertz, pp. 89–106: "To the right hand go honours, flattering designations, prerogatives: it acts, orders, and *takes*. The left hand, on the contrary, is despised and reduced to the role of a humble auxiliary: by itself it can do nothing; it helps, it supports, it *holds*. The right hand is the symbol and model of all aristocracy, the left hand of all common people. . . . The former is used to express ideas of physical strength and 'dexterity,' of intellectual 'rectitude and good judgement,' of 'uprightness' and moral integrity, of good fortune and beauty, or juridical norm; while the word 'left' evokes most of the ['sinister'] opposites of these. . . . The right is the 'side of life' (and of strength) while the left is the 'side of death' (and of weakness). . . . [As in the iconography of the Last Judgment] the right represents what is high, the upper world, the sky; while the left is connected with the underworld and the earth. . . . The right is the *inside*, the finite, assured well-being, and peace; the left is the *outside*, the infinite, hostile, and the perpetual menace of evil. . . . The right hand stands for *me*, the left for *not-me, others*. . . . The left hand is the hand of perjury, treachery, & fraud."

5. Important contributions to the process of reimagining this early modern body include, Norbert Elias, *The History of Manners* (1939), vol. 1 of *The Civilizing Process*, trans. Edmund Jephcott (New York: Pantheon, 1978); Thomas Laqueur, *Making Sex: Body and Gender from the Greeks to Freud* (Cambridge: Harvard University Press, 1990); Gail Kern Paster, *The Body Embarrassed: Drama and the Disciplines of Shame in Early Modern England* (Ithaca: Cornell University Press, 1993); Peter Stallybrass, "Patriarchal Territories: The Body Englosed," in *Othello: Critical Essays*, ed. Susan Snyder (New York: Garland, 1988), pp. 251–74; Stallybrass, "Reading the Body: *The Revenger's Tragedy* and the Jacobean Theater of Consumption," *Renaissance Drama* n.s. 18 (1987): 121–48; and Nancy Vickers, " 'The Blazon of Sweet Beauty's Best': Shakespeare's *Lucrece*," in Patricia Parker and Geoffrey Hartman, eds., *Shakespeare and the Question of Theory* (New York and London: Methuen, 1985), pp. 95–115.

6. For an exceptionally thorough analysis of Rembrandt's anatomy scene, see William S. Heckscher, *Rembrandt's Anatomy of Dr. Nicholaas Tulp* (New York: New York University Press, 1958).

On the hand as the most characteristically human part of the whole body, see Heckscher, p. 73; and Jonathan Goldberg, *Writing Matter: From the Hands of the English Renaissance* (Stanford, Calif.: Stanford University Press, 1990), pp. 84–6. On anatomy as a discipline of self-knowledge, see, e.g., Helkiah Crooke,

Mikrocosmographia. A Description of the Body of Man (London, 1618), chap. 5; and Caspar Barlaeus cited in Heckscher, p. 14.

7. "Good pilgrim you do wrong your hand too much. . . . For saints have hands that pilgrims' hands do touch, / And palm to palm is holy palmers' kiss" (*Romeo and Juliet*, 1.5.97–100). Ernest Schanzer, "Marriage-Contracts," *Shakespeare Survey* (1960): 81–9. On the *fede*, see Dale J. Randall, "The Rank and Earthy Background of Certain Physical Symbols in *The Duchess of Malfi*," *Renaissance Drama*, n.s. 18 (1987): 171–203, esp. pp. 172–9.

8. The blasphemous effrontery of Marlowe's *Tamburlaine* is thus perfectly expressed in the power of the "hand" with which he claims to "turn fortune's wheel about" (*1 Tamburlaine*, 1.2.175). Citations from Marlowe are to J. B. Steane, ed., *The Complete Plays* (Harmondsworth: Penguin, 1969).

9. Johan Rothmann, *Cheiromantia: or, The Art of Divining by The Lines and Signatures Engraven in the Hand of Man, By the Hand of Nature . . . Wherein you have the Secret Concordance, and Harmony betwixt It, and Astrology*, trans. George Wharton (London: 1642), pp. 175–6. Here, as in all other quotations in this chapter (unless otherwise indicated), the capitals and italics follow those of the original.

10. Sir Thomas Browne, *Religio Medici* in *Religio Medici and Other Writings* (London: Dent, 1965), pp. 68–9.

11. On the wider symbolism of the *Malfi* hand, see Randall, sect. 1, "The Dead Man's Hand," pp. 172–9. Randall describes the hand as "a horrid, mixed hand-in-hand image that is part sadistic trick, part erotic gesture, part *memento mori*, part perversion of the traditional *fede*, and part reminder of the Duchess's own marriage scene" (pp. 178–9). Middleton and Rowley rework this episode in *The Changeling*, where an amputated finger and a mutilated hand become the visible signs both of Beatrice's violated bond with Piracquo and of the new bond his murder has established with de Flores (3.4.37–8, 88; 4.1.0.9–10). Rothmann, p. 183.

12. See n. 6 this chap.

13. On the manuscript hand as a sign of privacy, inwardness, and the secrets of the heart see Bruce R. Smith, *Homosexual Desire in Shakespeare's England* (Chicago: University of Chicago Press, 1991), pp. 235–45. Citations from *The Changeling* are to the New Mermaid edition by Joost Daalder (London: A. and C. Black, 1990).

14. Cf. also *Twelfth Night* where Malvolio's excited identification of Olivia's "sweet Roman hand" becomes tantamount to possession of her "sweet heart": "this is my lady's hand. . . . 'Tis my lady" (2.5.86–93; 3.4.28–31).

15. In line 10 of the sonnet a quibble associates the "foot" of time with the metrical feet whose mastery by the poet's writing hand will enable him to keep time—the hand's struggle to hold back the foot of time being imaged in the extra stressing

of this heavily spondaic line. This complex of wordplay also includes line 4's "action," which because of its legal-oratorical context must involve gestural *actio* as well as "action" in the sense of "legal case."

Benedick's conceit wryly undoes the familiar hand-on-heart gesture that expresses the ideal integration of inner and outer selves.

16. Constantia Munda, *The Worming of a Mad Dog*, in Katherine Usher Henderson and Barbara F. McManus, eds., *Half Humankind: Contexts and Texts of Controversy about Women in England, 1550–1640* (Chicago: University of Chicago Press, 1985); John Bulwer, *Chirologia: or, the Natural Language of the Hand and Chironomia: or, The Art of Manual Rhetoric* (London, 1644): *Chirologia*, p. 82; *Chironomia*, 146.

17. Bulwer, *Chirologia*, p. 95, and "Dactylogia, or Dialects of the Fingers" in *Chirologia*, p. 157. Bulwer attributes the symbol to the Stoics.

18. Ibid., pp. 2, 86, 110, 111.

19. Bulwer, *Chironomia*, p. 2; *Chirologia*, p. 8.

20. Bulwer, *Chirologia*, p. 6.

21. Thomas Diconson in Bulwer, *Chirologia*, A2v.

22. Bulwer, *Chironomia*, p. 2; *Chirologia*, p. 114.

23. Bulwer, *Chironomia*, p. 1. Without any apparent sense of contradiction Bulwer also cites Galen's opinion "that because Man was the wisest of all creatures, therefore he had *Hands* given him" (p. 1).

24. "As a man watched his hands at work, the changing shapes they fashioned must gradually have impressed themselves on his mind. Without this we should probably never have learnt to form symbols for things, nor, therefore to speak" (Canetti, p. 254). The peculiar (and supposedly proper) articulacy of the right hand stressed by rhetoricians from classical times onward, may indeed be related to the fact it is controlled by the same hemisphere of the brain that contains the centre for articulate speech (Hertz, p. 90).

25. William Diconson, commendatory verses on *Chirologia*, A1v. This alliance is one of the things that Claudius has in mind when he insists that the "hand is . . . instrumental to the mouth" (*Hamlet*, 1.2.48)

26. Bulwer, *Chirologia*, pp. 7, 2.

27. John Florio, trans., *Montaigne's Essays*, ed. L. C. Harmer, 3. vols. (London: Dent, 1965), 2:xii, "An Apology of *Raymond Sebond*," pp. 144–5. The passage is worth quoting in greater detail. Arguing that human beings might "argue and tell histories by signs," Montaigne emphasizes the infinitely expressive capacity of the hand: "Do we not sue and entreat, promise and perform, call men unto us and discharge them, bid them farewell and be gone, threaten, pray, beseech, deny, refuse, demand, admire, number, confess, repent, fear, be ashamed, doubt, instruct, command, incite, encourage, swear, witness, accuse, condemn, absolve, injure, despise, defy, despise, flatter, applaud, bless, humble, mock, reconcile,

recommend, exalt, show gladness, rejoice, complain, wail, sorrow, discomfort, despair, cry out, forbid, declare silence and astonishment . . . with so great variation, and amplifying, as if they would contend with the tongue" (p. 144).

Giovanni Bonifacio, *L'arte de'cenni* (Vicenza, 1616), pp. 11–12, cited in Dilwyn Knox, "Ideas on Gesture and Universal Languages, c. 1550–1650," in John Henry and Sarah Hutton, eds., *New Perspectives on Renaissance Thought* (London: Duckworth, 1989), pp. 101–36 (p. 129).

28. In passages cited in successive editions of Omer Talon's *Rhetorica* (Paris, 1552; Frankfurt, 1581), Cicero (*De Oratore*, 3, 59, 223) observed that "a certain power is bestowed by nature on everything pertaining to gesture. For this reason it has a great effect even on the uneducated, the common people and indeed savages"; and Quintilian (*De Institutione Oratoria* 11, 3, 87) went so far as to suggest that "gesture . . . seems a language common to mankind"(quoted from Knox, pp. 121–2). But no classical rhetorician theorized this conjecture as Bulwer was to do.

Knox, pp. 130–3. Knox describes a significant shift from the precepts of the medieval world in which "gesture var[ied] from one profession or vocation to another," forming a "Babel of vernaculars" that could be learned only through "observation and practice," to the late sixteenth-century belief that gesture is "amenable to theory" because it belongs (despite local variations) to a universal human language; in response to this shift, rhetorical manuals from the middle of the sixteenth century begin to discuss delivery and gesture in much greater detail (pp. 102–4).

29. Bulwer's interest in New World cultures is amply illustrated in his treatise on bodily adornment *Anthrometamorphosis; Man Transform'd* (London, 1653).

30. Bulwer, *Chirologia*, pp. 3–4.

31. See the verses on *Chirologia* by Thomas Diconson and Jo. Harmanus, pp. A2v-A4. On the belief of early explorers in the universal accessibility of gesture, see Tzvetan Todorov, *The Conquest of America: The Question of the Other* (New York: Harper and Row, 1984), p. 30; Stephen Greenblatt, "Learning to Curse," in *Learning to Curse: Essays in Early Modern Culture* (New York: Routledge, 1990), pp. 16–39; and Eric Cheyfitz, *The Poetics of Imperialism* (New York: Oxford University Press, 1991), p. 109.

32. See Andrew Gurr, *The Shakespearean Stage, 1574–1642*, 2d ed. (Cambridge: Cambridge University Press, 1980), p. 97.

33. Bulwer, *Chironomia*, pp. 103–4, 17. Bulwer instances "The trembling *Hand*" and "strik[ing] the Breast with the *Hand*" as "Scenicall" affectations. Bulwer explains the significance of these figures on p. 17.

34. See Gurr, pp. 99–100.

35. Arguably one may see this reflected in the concern for gestural precision apparent in Hamlet's advice to the players. If the "Tragedians of the City" are in some sense to be identified as a touring London company (as their unlucky experiences

with boy-players and the "late innovation" half suggest) it is easy to see why they might wish to preface their performance with a dumb show that exactly summarizes the subsequent action—a use of mime otherwise unparalleled in English theater.

36. Fynes Moryson, *Itinerary*, cited from G. Blakemore Evans, ed., *Elizabethan and Jacobean Drama* (London: A. and C. Black, 1989), p. 50; emphasis added. A complete account of the place of hands in the theater would need to consider the important role played by the audience's hands; for at the end of a performance convention allowed the actors to reach out and claim the gestural acknowledgment of a special bond:

Give me your hands, if we be friends,
And Robin shall restore amends.
    Midsummer Night's Dream, 5.1.437–8

Ours be your patience then, and yours our parts;
Your gentle hands lend us, and take our hearts.
    All's Well That Ends Well, EPILOGUE, LL. 5–6

But release me from my bands
With the help of your good hands.
    Tempest, EPILOGUE, LL. 9–10

Through such characteristically English variations on the ancient Latin *plaudite*, it is possible to glimpse how in this theater even applause had a subtly different meaning from the mechanical expression of pleasure with which we are familiar; for it was expressly located as the crowning gesture in a carefully orchestrated rhetorical sequence—one that completed a graceful circle of mutual "benefits" in a metaphorical "giving" and "joining" of hands.

37. Citations from *The Spanish Tragedy* are to Andrew S. Cairncross's Regents Renaissance Drama edition (London: Edward Arnold, 1967). The gestural significance of this scene is briefly glanced at from the perspective of stage history by Robert Hapgood in "Speak Hands for Me: Gesture As Language in *Julius Caesar*" *Drama Survey* 5 (1966): 162–70.

38. Bulwer, *Chirologia*, p. 2.

39. That hands were to be bathed "up to the elbows," seems to register the fact that Roman *manus* (hand) included the forearm.

40. Conceivably both were suggested by the brief passage in Plutarch that records the wounding and bloodying of Brutus's hand in the melee around Caesar's body. The conspirators' gesture of waving their bloodied hands also seems to resonate uncannily with Casca's description of the slave who "Held up his left hand, which did flame and burn . . . and yet . . . remain'd unscorch'd" (1.3.16–18).

The singling out of the ill-omened left hand is a Shakespearean addition to Plutarch's anecdote. Interestingly, John Bulwer also seems to have been sensitive to the suggestive resonances of hands in Plutarch. Discussing the significance of handclasping, he is reminded of a serendipitous quibble in Sir Thomas North's version of the *Life of Brutus*, where Caius Ligarius, taking the hero *by the right hand* inquires if has "any great enterprise in *Hand*," *Chirologia*, p. 95.

41. See also *Richard III*, 1.4.172, where the Second Murderer laments: "How fain, like Pilate, would I wash my hands"; and 4.1.67, where Anne recalls Richard's wooing "When scarce the blood was well wash'd from his hands"; and *Hamlet*, 3.3.43–4 where, in an even more obvious anticipation of *Macbeth*, Claudius broods over his "cursed hand . . . thicker than itself with brother's blood." Bulwer, *Chirologia*, Gestus 11, p. 40

42. The context makes it plain that Antony's handshakings combine aspects of three closely allied gestures described by Bulwer:

Gestus 56 *Data fide promitto:* TO STRIKE ANOTHER'S PALM . . . the habit and expression of those who plight their troth, give pledge of faith and fidelity, promise, offer truce, confirm a league . . . warrant and assure.

Gestus 57 *Reconcilio:* TO SHAKE THE GIVEN HAND . . . an expression usual in friendship, peaceful love, benevolence . . . reconciliation, and well-wishing. . . . An expression usual between those who desire to incorporate, commix, or grow into one, and make a perfect joint.

Gestus 58 *Injurias remitto:* TO PRESS HARD AND WRING ANOTHER'S HAND . . . a natural insinuation of love, duty, remembrance, supplication, peace, and of forgiveness of all injuries.

Chirologia, PP. 93, 109, 116.

43. Herman Roodenburg, "The 'Hand of Friendship': Shaking Hands and Other Gestures in the Dutch Republic," in Jan Bremner and Herman Roodenburg, eds., *A Cultural History of Gesture* (Ithaca, N.Y.: Cornell University Press, 1992), pp. 152–89. Perhaps the most graphic illustration of the symbolic power invested in the early modern handclasp is in the parodic stage business of *King John*, 3.1.226–321, where the frenetic making and breaking of royal treaties is expressed in the successive grasping and dropping of hands.

44. Bulwer, *Chirologia*, pp. 101, 116–7, 110–11. For the heart as symbolic double of the hand see, e.g., *Richard II*, 5.1.82, "Hand from hand my love, and heart from heart" or Bassanio's "forfeit of my hands, my head, my heart" (*Merchant of Venice*, 4.1.212). In Webster's *Duchess of Malfi* Ferdinand's sinister practical joke, in which he gives his sister a dead man's hand (supposedly cut from her husband's body) to kiss in lieu of his own, depends upon the same conceit: "here's a hand. . . . bury the print of it in your heart. / I will leave this ring with you, for a love token; / And the hand, as sure as the ring: and do not doubt / But you shall

have the heart too" (4.1.43–9); cited from the New Mermaid edition, ed. Elizabeth M. Brennan (London: A. and C. Black, 1983). The conceit had a physiological basis, for the heart was supposed to be directly linked to the ring finger by a so-called master vein; see, for example, Middleton, *A Chaste Maid in Cheapside*, 3.1.20–2: "Place that ring upon her finger; / This the finger plays the part / Whose master vein shoots from the heart."

45. Bulwer, *Chirologia*, pp. 110–11.

46. The New Cambridge edition plausibly adds a direction that Philip and John should enter "hand in hand" at l. 74; presumably the newly married Dauphin and Blanche should use the same gesture; see L. R. Beaurline, ed., *King John* (Cambridge: Cambridge University Press, 1990).

47. Beaurline once again supplies the necessary direction at 3.1.320.

48. Bulwer, *Chirologia*, p. 101. Compare also Hubert's insistence upon the correspondence between his "maiden . . . innocent hand" and the purity of his "thought" and "mind" (*King John*, 4.2.251–9).

49. Plutarch, "The Life of Marcus Tullius Cicero," trans. Sir Thomas North, cited from Geoffrey Bullough, ed., *Narrative and Dramatic Sources of Shakespeare*, 5 vols. (London: Routledge and Kegan Paul, 1964), 5:140; Plutarch, "The Life of Marcus Antonius," in Bullough, 5:269; Bulwer, *Chironomia*, p. 17. Like Shakespeare, Bulwer was probably familiar with Sir Thomas North's translation of Plutarch's "Life of Marcus Tullius Cicero."

50. On the first Andronicus see J. C. Maxwell's introduction to his Arden edition (London: Methuen, 1953), p. xxx. For an extensive discussion of the significance of hands and manual dismemberment in *Titus*, see Katherine A. Rowe, "Dismembering and Forgetting in *Titus Andronicus*," *Shakespeare Quarterly* 45 (1994): 279–303. Rowe's essay has affinities with my own, and I regret that it did not appear in time for me to make full use of its arguments.

The second Andronicus is actually cited in *Chirologia* (pp. 99–100) as a rare instance of manual hypocrisy: "Thus *Andronicus* coming to *Onias* who had fled to the sanctuary at *Daphne*, hard by Antiochia, counselled him craftily, GIVING HIM HIS RIGHT HAND with an oath, by that fair show of peace persuaded him to come out: whom incontinently without any regard of righteousness, he slew according to *Menelaus*' instigation." This episode is grotesquely reworked in act 3, scene 1 of Shakespeare's play, where Titus instructs Aaron to "give his majesty my [amputated] hand" as a prelude to his treacherous revenge.

On the proverbial eloquence of Cicero's hand, see Goldsmith's commendatory verses in Bulwer and cf. Bartolomé de Las Casas, *Historia de Las Indias*, ed. Augustin Millares Carlo, 3 vols. (Mexico, 1951), 2:27: "To give substance *(encarnecer)* to the greatness of the Indies one would need all the eloquence of Demosthenes and the hand of Cicero"; cited in Anthony Pagden, *European Encounters with the New World: From Renaissance to Romanticism* (New Haven:

Yale University Press, 1993), p. 61. The mutilation of Cicero seems also to be remembered in Marlowe's *Massacre at Paris* when Anjou triumphs over the murdered Admiral: "Cut off his head and hands, / And send them for a present to the Pope" (scene 6, ll. 43–4).

51. See Maxwell, p. xxx. Gaius Mucius Scaevola's name appears to be echoed in that of Andronicus's son, Mutius. The episode was well enough known to be cited in John Foxe, *The Acts and Monuments [The Book of Martyrs]*, ed. Josiah Pratt, 8 vols., 4th ed. (London: Religious Tract Society, n.d.). Foxe describes the burning of Rose Allin's hand by the papist Edmund Tyrell (1557) and of a blind harper's hand by the Marian Bishop Bonner (8:385–6), comparing both episodes to the voluntary mutilation of Scaevola and adding, "But thus to burn the hands of poor men and women which never meant any harm unto them . . . we find no example of such barbarous tyranny, neither in Titus Livius, nor in any other story amongst the heathen" (p. 386).

52. Scevola's hand resonates with the "*Iovial* hand" that Brutus makes a synecdoche for Jupiter and the "purple hands of death and ruin" that stand for the Tarquins (ll. 2616–20). Citations from Heywood's *Rape of Lucrece* are to the edition edited by Alan Holaday (Urbana: University of Illinois Press, 1950).

53. Foxe, 8:86–90.

54. John Stubbs, letter to Sir Christopher Hatton, cited from Lloyd E. Berry, *John Stubbs's* Gaping Gulf *with Letters and Other Relevant Documents* (Charlottesville: University of Virginia Press for the Folger Shakespeare Library, 1968), p. 111. In later life Stubbs, who became a polemicist for the government, took to signing his letters "John Stubbe, Scaeva [left-handed]," thereby proudly associating his sacrifice with that of the patriotic Scaevola. See Ilona Bell, "Elizabeth, Stubbs, and the *Gaping Gulf*," in Julia M. Walker, ed., *Dissing Elizabeth: Negative Representations of Gloriana* (Durham, N.C.: Duke University Press, 1998), p. 117n. 30.

55. See Michel Foucault's now classic account of the language of public mutilation in *Discipline and Punish* (New York: Vintage, 1977).

56. Letter of Mendoza to Philip, 13 January 1580, *Calendar of State Papers Spanish, 1580–1586*, pp. 1–2, cited in Berry, pp. xxxviii–ix.

57. Michel Ragon, *The Space of Death*, trans. Alan Sheridan (Charlottesville: University of Virginia Press, 1991), p. 85.

58. Foxe, 8:88. Cranmer's hand is on conspicuous display throughout this part of the narrative. On his way to the fire Cranmer self-consciously shakes the hands of sympathetic bystanders but is rebuffed by a priest named Ely who "drew back his hand, and refused, saying it was not lawful to salute heretics, and specially such a one as falsely returned unto the opinions that he had foresworn . . . and chid those sergeants and citizens which had given him their hands" (p. 89).

59. Cited from Berry, pp. xxxv, xxxviii.

60. The idea of the hand as a second self is what underpins Stephano's favorite oath "by this hand" (*Tempest*, 3.2.49, 69; 4.1.227)

61. Similarly in *Antony and Cleopatra* the gendered oppositions of the play can be traced through an elaborate pattern of contrasts between the erotic power associated with the "flower-soft hands" of Cleopatra's court ("a hand that kings / Have lipp'd, and trembled kissing," 2.5.29–30) and the violent hand of power associated with the Roman world ("that self hand / Which writ his honour in the acts it did," 5.1.21–2)—the masculinized hand to which Cleopatra finally trusts herself (4.16.51).

62. I prefer the folio reading here to the first quarto's "give['t] that accord" printed in Riverside.

63. For the Virginia story as a Roman foundation myth, see Patricia Kleindienst Joplin, "Ritual Work on Human Flesh: Livy's Lucretia and the Rape of the Body Politic," *Helios* 17 (1990): 51–70.

64. The two are collapsed together in the monstrous pageant of act 3, scene 1 where Lavinia's mouth appears to devour her father's severed hand as if grotesquely literalizing Lear's paradigm of filial ingratitude: "Is it not as this mouth should tear this hand / For lifting food to it" (3.4.15–16).

65. See A. C. Hamilton, "*Titus Andronicus:* The Form of Shakespearean Tragedy," *Shakespeare Quarterly* 14 (1963): 201–13; M. C. Bradbrook, *Shakespeare and Elizabethan Poetry* (Harmondsworth: Penguin, 1964), pp. 96–101.

66. Folger Ms. V.b.142, f.54v, quoted in Berry, pp. xxxv–vi.

67. See Berry, pp. 108, 111. The persecuted Rose Allin, recalling Tyrell's burning of her hand, quibblingly remarked that she might have struck him in the face with the pot in her left hand, "for no man held my hand to stay me therefrom" (Foxe, 8:386).

68. Bulwer, *Chirologia*, A5. Cf. also pp. A1–A1v; A2; A3v; A4: "We may know Alcides by his foot, and a lion by his claw; / I rejoice that you can be known by your hand"; "I joy (dear friend) to see thy *Palm* display / A new *Chirosophy*, which hidden lay / In Nature's Hieroglyphic grasp'd"; "We all desirous are to limn [limb] Thee forth: / But blushing, must confess, none can command / A pencil worthy Thee, but Thy own *Hand*"; "See here appears a *Hand*, one limb alone, / Born to the World, a perfect *sunalon* [companion] / And mark how well 'tis muscled, how it speaks / Fresh from the Press's womb. . . . By *Chiromancy's* leave I must divine: / He need not fear bold *Atropos* her knife, / For in his *Hand* each line's a line of life."

69. But see Warwick's defiant asseveration in *3 Henry VI*. Rather than submit to York, he maintains, "I had rather chop this hand off at a blow / And with the other fling it at thy face" (5.1.50–1); and Bassanio's hyperbolic "Why I were best to cut my left hand off, / And swear I lost the ring defending it" (*Merchant of Venice*, 5.1.178).

70. James's remark is cited by Bacon in *The Advancement of Learning*: "Your Majesty saith most aptly and elegantly, *As the tongue speaketh to the ear, so the gesture speaketh to the eye*," quoted from the edition by G. W. Kitchin (London: Dent, 1915), p. 107; later in the *Advancement* Bacon discusses the use of gesture "in the commerce of barbarous people, that understand one another's meaning" (p. 137). The first Bacon passage is cited in Bulwer's dedication to *Chirologia*, A5v. Cf. also Bulwer's dedication to *Philocophus, or, The Deafe and Dumbe Mans Friend* (London, 1648), where he promises to teach the deaf to "hear with your eye" in "a happy *metempsychosis* or *transmigration* of your senses" (A6-A6v); and Thomas Diconson's verses on the same treatise, which declare that through it "The Deaf and Dumb get Hearing Eyes, which break / Their Bar of Silence, and thence learn to speak / Words may be seen or heard: W'are at our choice / For to give Ear, or Eye unto a Voice" (A8).
71. In the complex wordplay of this passage "that great bond / Which keeps me *pale*" refers not simply to the bond of moral law that has kept Macbeth fenced in but to the bond of common humanity that has not only made him tender-hearted but kept him in the world of light.
72. Cf. also Gloucester's apparent inability to respond to Edgar's request for blessing (5.3.196–10).
73. J. M. Coetzee, *The Master of Petersburg* (London: Secker and Warburg, 1994), p. 10: "The innocence of hands, ever renewed. A memory comes back to him: the touch of a hand, intimate in the dark. But whose hand? Hands emerging like animals, without shame, without memory, into the flight of day." McGuinness, p. 54.

8 · CHANGING PLACES IN *OTHELLO*

1. For an argument that the marriage is never properly consummated, see T. G. A. Nelson and Charles Haines, "Othello's Unconsummated Marriage," *Essays in Criticism* 23 (1983): 1–18.
2. All citations from *Othello* are to Kenneth Muir's Penguin edition (Harmondsworth: Penguin, 1968).
3. For further comment on the significance of commercial imagery in the play, see Edward A. Snow, "Sexual Anxiety and the Male Order of Things in *Othello*," *English Literary Renaissance* 10 (1980): 384–412.
4. Emrys Jones, " 'Othello,' 'Lepanto,' and the Cyprus Wars," *Shakespeare Survey* 21 (1968): 47–52.
5. Northrop Frye, *Fools of Time* (Toronto and London: University of Toronto Press, 1967), p. 102.
6. See M. R. Ridley, ed., *Othello*, the Arden Shakespeare, paperback edition (1965), app. 1, p. 238.
7. Since this essay was first published some of its arguments have been amplified by

Julia Genster's "Lieutenancy, Standing In, and *Othello*," *ELH* 57 (1990): 785–805.

8. See the introduction to Muir's New Penguin edition, pp. 20, 15.

9. John Florio, *Queen Anna's World of Words* (London, 1611), p. 82, glosses *capo di squadra* as "a ring-leader or chief " and *squadra* as "a part of a company of soldiers of twenty or five and twenty whose chief is a corporal." In English parlance, however, *corporal* could refer, to a relatively junior noncommissioned officer (much as it does now) or to a high-ranking military officer known as the "corporal of the field," and this may help to account for Cassio's elevated position in the play. For more detailed discussion of the various ranks in the play, see Henry J. Webb, "The Military Background in *Othello*," *Philological Quarterly* 30 (1951): 40–52; and Paul A. Jorgenson, *Shakespeare's Military World* (Berkeley: University of California Press, 1956), pp. 100–18.

   It is just possible the pun was emphasized by Shakespeare's preferred pronunciation of the word, since the alternative spelling "lieftenant," which is thought to represent the usual seventeenth-century pronunciation, occurs only once in the canon (in the quarto text of *Henry IV*, 5.5.95). That Shakespeare was thinking of his titles of rank in this way is given some independent confirmation by the apparent play on Iago's rank (ancient/ensign) at 1.1.57–8: "I must show out a flag and sign of love, / Which is indeed but sign."

10. The idea of jealousy as a kind of "monstrous birth" seems to have been a potent one for Shakespeare. It lies behind Othello's "strong conception / That I do groan withal" (5.2.55–6) and is built into the structure of *The Winter's Tale*, where a clear parallel is developed between the corrupted "issue" of Leontes's suspicious mind and the supposedly corrupt "issue" of Hermione's womb. The self-generating nature of jealousy is noted by Freud in "Some Neurotic Mechanisms in Jealousy, Paranoia, and Homosexuality" (*The Complete Psychoanalytic Works of Sigmund Freud*, ed. James Strachey et al., 22 vols. [London: Hogarth Press, 1955–64], 18:223) and is discussed by the American psychologist Leslie H. Farber in "On Jealousy," in *Lying, Despair, Jealousy, Envy, Sex, Suicide, Drugs, and the Good Life* (New York: Basic Books, 1976), pp. 188, 193–9. For Farber jealousy is the expression of a personality that has taken refuge from its own felt inadequacy in an excessive dependence on the love and esteem of another—in this sense "the crucial source of [the jealous person's] pain *is* his corruption" (p. 196); jealousy therefore "is self-confirming: it breeds itself " (p. 188).

11. For an account of resentment that makes it seem a much more exact description of Iago's ruling passion than the traditional "envy," see Robert C. Solomon, *The Passions: The Myth and Nature of Human Emotion* (New York: Anchor/Doubleday, 1976), pp. 350–5.

12. See Freud, pp. 223–4; and Farber, pp. 190–1. The same pornographic excitement can be sensed in the excesses of Othello's imagination—"I had been happy if the

general camp, / Pioners and all, had tasted her sweet body" (3.3.342–3), and he attempts to give these fantasies a hideous reality in the brothel scene (4.2).

13. Cf. Iago's description of jealousy as "mock[ing] The meat it feeds on" (3.3.165–6), where "meat" includes *both* the psyche on which the monster battens and (at a further remove) the object of sexual appetite itself.

14. A wound in the thigh is, of course, a traditional euphemism for gelding, and the emphasis on the place of the wound seems to gather a special significance from the obscene imagery of Iago's dream-fantasy ("then laid his leg / Over my thigh, and sighed and kissed," 3.3.421–2).

15. W. H. Auden, "The Joker in the Pack," in *The Dyer's Hand* (London: Faber, 1937).

16. For the bawdy meanings of the italicized words in this and the previous quotation, see the relevant entries in Eric Partridge, *Shakespeare's Bawdy* (London: Routledge, 1968). Nelson and Haines (pp. 15–16) also notice the importance of bitter sexual punning as a sign of Othello's gathering dementia.

17. For an equivalent use of "government," see for instance, Middleton's *Women Beware Women*, 1.3.43 (New Mermaid edition, ed. W. C. Carroll [London: A. and C. Black, 1994]).

18. *The Winter's Tale*, 1.2.187–90. For a discussion of wordplay in *The Winter's Tale* see Molly Mahood's brilliant essay in *Shakespeare's Wordplay* (London: Methuen, 1957).

19. See Curt A. Zimansky, ed., *The Critical Works of Thomas Rymer* (New Haven: Yale University Press, 1956), p. 163.

20. For the hand as a repository of meaning, see chap. 7. For the suggestion that the handkerchief with its strawberry spots constitutes a kind of visual pun on the wedding sheets, see Snow, pp. 390–2; Nelson and Haines, pp. 8–10; and Lynda E. Boose, "Othello's Handkerchief: 'The Recognizance and Pledge of Love,' " *English Literary Renaissance* 5 (1975): 360–74. In the Nelson and Haines reading the pun becomes especially cruel because Othello's wedding sheets remain unstained with virgin blood until the murder.

21. See Michael Neill, "Horned Beasts and China Oranges: Reading the Signs in *The Country Wife*," in Jocelyn Harris, ed., *Studies in the Eighteenth Century* no. 7, in *Eighteenth-Century Life* 12 (1988): 3–17.

22. "Siege" (throne, seat) also carries, as the *OED* shows, the standard metaphoric senses of "class" and "place of [rule]."

23. See chap. 10, for a more detailed investigation of this paradox.

24. For a sensitive account of this aspect of the play, see Jane Adamson, *"Othello" As Tragedy: Some Problems of Judgement and Feeling* (Cambridge: Cambridge University Press, 1980).

25. John Bayley, *Shakespeare and Tragedy* (London: Routledge, 1981), pp. 213–4. The pun emphasizes an underlying symmetry in the power relationships of the

play: Desdemona is to Othello and Iago as Cyprus is to the Venetians and the Turks. The analogy is not, I believe, a casual one.

26. For "hell" as a cant term for the female pudendum, see Partridge (p. 120), who cites Sonnet 144 ("I guess one angel in another's hell"). For an account of a production that emphasized the sexual significance of the "place" imagined in these speeches, see Robert Cushman's review of the 1971 Mermaid and Stratford *Othellos* in *Plays and Players* 19, no. 2 (November 1971): 32–6. Cushman attributed to Bruce Purchase's Moor (at the Mermaid) "one glory: Othello delivers the speech beginning 'Had it pleased heaven to try me with affliction' looking Desdemona straight in the crotch which makes unusual sense of the lines about 'The fountain from the which my current runs' and particularly of the instruction 'Turn thy complexion there.' "

27. The grammatical oddity is the more striking because of its distortion of a familiar text, "Whom the Lord loveth He chasteneth" (Heb. 12.6).

28. For an analysis of act 3, scene 3 as a "seduction scene" systematically perverting the language of love, see Robert Heilmann, *Magic in the Web: Action and Language in "Othello"* (Lexington: University of Kentucky Press, 1956), pp. 176–9.

29. One might add that this is a consummation that leads to its own obscene kind of pregnancy. The "monstrous birth" dreamed up by Iago in act 1 and echoed in Emilia's idea of jealousy as a "monster / Begot upon itself born on itself," is finally brought to life in a murder that Othello describes as "the strong conception / That I do groan withal" (5.2.55–6)—where "conception" puns on the archaic sense of "baby" or "fetus."

30. F. R. Leavis, "Diabolic Intellect and the Noble Hero," in *The Common Pursuit* (London: Chatto and Windus, 1952).

9 · "UNPROPER BEDS"

1. Quoted in James R. Siemon, " 'Nay, that's not next': *Othello*, V.ii in Performance, 1760–1900," *Shakespeare Quarterly* 37 (1986): 38–51 (p. 39).

2. See Balz Engler, "Othello's Great Heart," *English Studies* 68 (1987): 129–36. All *Othello* quotations are from the New Penguin edition, ed. Kenneth Muir (Harmondsworth: Penguin, 1968).

3. The exceptional nature of this ending is also noted by Helen Gardner, "The Noble Moor," in Anne Ridler, ed., *Shakespeare Criticism, 1935–1960* (Oxford: Oxford University Press, 1963), pp. 348–70 (p. 366).

4. The Variorum *Othello*, ed. H. H. Furness (Philadelphia: J. B. Lippincott, 1886), p. 300; quoted in Siemon, p. 39.

5. Sensationalized bedchamber scenes that seem indebted to *Othello* include Lussurioso's murderous eruption into his father's bedchamber in *The Revenger's*

Tragedy (ca. 1606); Evadne's heavily eroticized murder of the king in *The Maid's Tragedy* (ca. 1610); and the climactic bedroom scene that forms part of Ford's extensive reworking of *Othello* in *Love's Sacrifice* (ca. 1632). Shakespeare himself appears to play on recollections of his own *coup de théatre* in the bedroom scene of *Cymbeline* (ca. 1609), and it is treated to a parodic reversal in Fletcher's *Monsieur Thomas* (ca. 1615), where the humiliation of the comic protagonist is accomplished by means of "A bed discovered with a [female] black moor in it" (5.5.2 SD), provoking his Emilia-like cry, "Roar again, devil, roar again" (1.41).

Jackson and Kemble quoted in Julie Hankey, ed., *Othello*, Plays in Performance Series (Bristol: Bristol Classical Press, 1987), pp. 18, 315; emphasis added.

6. See Norman Sanders, ed., *Othello*, New Cambridge edition (Cambridge: Cambridge University Press 1984), p. 48.

7. The art file at the Folger Shakespeare Library, for example, contains 109 illustrations of individual scenes in the play, no fewer than 40 of which show act 5, scene 2; the bed is invariably the center of attention and often occupies the entire pictorial space. For further discussion, see Paul H. D. Kaplan, "The Earliest Images of Othello," *Shakespeare Quarterly* 39 (1988): 171–86.

8. The process of cutting can be traced in Hankey. Already by 1773 Bell's edition had removed the exchange between Iago and Othello at 4.1.3–8 about Desdemona's being "naked with her friend in bed"; while in 1829 Cumberland's acting edition found it necessary to take out Desdemona's instructions to Emilia, "Lay on my bed my wedding sheets" (4.2.104). Macready followed the Cumberland text in finding any reference to the physical reality of the wedding night as indelicate as the word "whore" itself. Thus at 2.3.26 his Iago could no more be allowed to wish "happiness to their sheets!" than to envisage that happiness in "he hath not yet made wanton the night with her" (2.3.15–16). Predictably, most versions from Bell onward cut the more lurid details of Iago's fantasy of lying with Cassio and its strange sexual displacements (3.3.418–23); more surprisingly, not one Desdemona from Macready's time until the early part of this century was permitted to greet Othello in the murder scene with "Will you come to bed, my lord?" (5.2.24). Even her promise to Cassio that Othello's "bed shall seem a school" was thought too strong meat for eighteenth-century Dublin playgoers and for English audiences after John Philip Kemble's production of 1785.

9. For an account of the Orientalizing process that culminated in Beerbohm Tree's confident pronouncement that "Othello was an Oriental, not a negro: a stately Arab of the best caste," see Hankey, pp. 65–7 (p. 67). Westland Marston, *Our Recent Actors*, quoted in Hankey, pp. 64, 317; William Archer and Robert Lowe, eds., *Dramatic Essays by John Forster and George Henry Lewes*, quoted in Hankey, p. 64.

10. Quoted in Hankey, p. 317. This critic's reaction was echoed in the murmurs of

dissatisfaction with which the audience greeted Rossi's 1881 London performance, where the Italian actor strangled his Desdemona in full view of the audience (see Siemon, p. 478).

11. To some observers Macready's restrained, gentlemanly, and dignified Moor seemed "almost English" (Hankey, p. 66), but the startling color contrast of this scene seems to have acted as a disturbing reminder of Othello's blackness and therefore (to the Victorian mind) of his savage sexuality.

12. Both directors introduced the bed early, making it into the centerpiece of the brothel scene, and Miles, whose production notoriously highlighted the sexual suggestiveness of the murder with a naked Desdemona, emphasized the perverse excitements of the earlier scene by leaving Iago and Roderigo at the end "to argue amongst the discarded bedclothes and around the bed itself . . . [while Roderigo handled] the sheets in rapture." Eyre transposed this piece of stage business to his Othello at the beginning of the scene; Donald Sinden was directed to pull the sheets from Desdemona's laundry basket, throw them about the stage, and then at the line "This is a subtle whore" (l. 20) press the soiled linen to his face—"sniffing [at it] like a hound," according to one reviewer. See Hankey, pp. 291, 281.

13. N. S. Sodkhanskaya ("N. Kokhanovskaya") in a letter to the Slavophile newspaper *Dyen* (1863), quoted in Herbert Marshall and Mildred Stock, *Ira Aldridge: The Negro Tragedian* (London: Rockliff, 1958), pp. 265–6. See also Siemon, p. 45, for English reactions to the scene "that [mimic] the language and strategies of pornography."

14. Thomas Rymer, *A Short View of Tragedy* (1693), quoted in Brian Vickers, ed., *Shakespeare: The Critical Heritage*, 6 vols. (London and Boston: Routledge and Kegan Paul, 1974), 2:27; F. R. Leavis, "Diabolic Intellect and the Noble Hero," in *The Common Pursuit* (London: Chatto and Windus, 1952), pp. 136–59. For acute analyses of the racial assumptions underlying Leavis's approach, see Hankey, pp. 109–16, and Martin Orkin. "Othello and the 'Plain Face' of Racism," *Shakespeare Quarterly* 38 (1987): 166–88, (183–6), now incorporated in his *Shakespeare against Apartheid* (Craighall, South Africa: Ad. Donker, 1987). Both show how much Leavis's interpretation contributed to Olivier's version of the tragedy.

15. A. C. Bradley, *Shakespearean Tragedy* (1904; rpt. New York: St. Martin's Press, 1985), p. 165n.; Lamb quoted in Hankey, pp. 65–6; Edward Snow, "Sexual Anxiety and the Male Order of Things in *Othello*," *English Literary Renaissance* 10 (1980): 384–412 (387, 400).

16. See M. R. Ridley, ed., *Othello*, Arden edition (London: Methuen, 1958) p. li.

The geographical referent of Olivier's mimicry significantly varies in different accounts of the production. Hankey, for example, refers to his "extraordinary transformation into a black African" (p. 111); Sanders praises "his careful imitation of West Indian gait and gesture" (p. 47); while Richard David speaks of "Olivier's . . . 'modern negro,' out of Harlem rather than Barbary" (*Shakespeare in the Theatre* [Cambridge: Cambridge University Press, 1978], p. 46). The embarrassing conclusion must be that Olivier's much-praised fidelity to detail was simply fidelity to a generalized stereotype of "blackness."

Sanders, p. 47; emphasis added. Sanders almost exactly paraphrases Laurence Lerner's account of the way in which "the primitive breaks out again in Othello," which Orkin uses to exemplify how even liberal South African critics of the play find themselves reacting to it in terms of the paradigms of apartheid (pp. 184–5). Olivier himself declared that Othello "is a savage man," adding hurriedly, "not on account of his colour, I don't mean that" (Hankey, p. 109), but it is a little difficult to know quite what else he could have meant—especially in the light of reviewers' reactions to his mimicry of negritude, which concluded "that Othello's brutality was either of the jungle and essentially his own, or that, as one of Nature's innocents, he had taken the infection from a trivial and mean white society" (Hankey, p. 111). Whatever the case, the choice is simply between noble and ignoble savagery. For a good account of the ideas behind the Olivier production and critical reactions to it, see Hankey, pp. 109–13.

17. Orkin, 188. The word "racism" itself dates from only 1936, and "racialism" from 1907 *(OED)*. Hankey, p. 15.

18. Here I include my own essay "Changing Places in *Othello*," *Shakespeare Survey* 37 (1984): 115–31, and chap. 8; I ought to have noticed more clearly the way in which racial identity is constructed as one of the most fiercely contested "places" in the play. Honorable exceptions include Eldred Jones, *Othello's Countrymen: The African in English Renaissance Drama* (London: Oxford University Press, 1965); G. K. Hunter's celebrated lecture "Othello and Colour Prejudice," *Proceedings of the British Academy* 53 (1967): 139–57; Doris Adler, "The Rhetoric of *Black* and *White* in *Othello*," *Shakespeare Quarterly* 25 (1974): 248–57; G. M. Matthews, "*Othello* and the Dignity of Man," in Arnold Kettle, ed., *Shakespeare in a Changing World* (London: Lawrence and Wishart, 1964), pp. 123–45; and Karen Newman, " 'And Wash the Ethiop White': Femininity and the Monstrous in *Othello*," in Jean E. Howard and Marion F. O'Connor, eds., *Shakespeare Reproduced: The Text in History and Ideology* (New York: Methuen, 1987), pp. 143–62.

19. For more recent theoretical accounts of the evolution of a discourse of "Englishness" and "otherness" as an enabling adjunct of colonial conquest, see Stephen Greenblatt, *Renaissance Self-Fashioning: From More to Shakespeare* (Chicago and London: University of Chicago Press, 1980), pp. 179–92; David Cairns and Shaun Richards, *Writing Ireland: Colonialism, Nationalism, and Culture* (Manchester: Manchester University Press, 1988), chap. 1, pp. 1–21; and Anne Laurence, "The Cradle to the Grave: English Observation of Irish Social

Customs in the Seventeenth Century," *Seventeenth Century* 3 (1988): 63–84.

20. The wordplay, which may well reflect a folk-etymology, occurs elsewhere in Shakespeare; see, for example, *Twelfth Night*, 4.2.31 ("hideous darkness"), and *King John*, 5.4.22 ("hideous death").

21. The proper derivation is from *caenum* (dirt), but the imagery of Carlisle's speech in *Richard II* clearly seems to imply the folk-etymology from *scaenum* (stage): "*show* so heinous, *black, obscene* a deed" (4.2.122); see also *Love's Labor's Lost*, 1.1.235–9.

22. Snow, p. 385.

23. Rymer, quoted in Vickers, 2:43.

24. T. G. A. Nelson and Charles Haines, "Othello's Unconsummated Marriage," *Essays in Criticism* 33 (1983): 1–18. Their arguments were partially anticipated in a little-noticed article by Pierre Janton, "Othello's Weak Function," *Cahiers Élis-abéthains* 7 (1975): 43–50, and are paralleled in William Whallon, *Inconsistencies* (Totowa, N.J.: Biblio, 1983). I regard my own willingness to take these arguments seriously (see chap. 8, n. 1) as further evidence for the point I am making.

25. Norman Nathan, "Othello's Marriage Is Consummated," *Cahiers Élisabéthains* 34 (1988): 79–82 (p. 81).

26. This aspect of the play is recognized by Stanley Cavell in *Disowning Knowledge in Six Plays of Shakespeare* (Cambridge: Cambridge University Press, 1987): "My guiding hypothesis about the structure of the play is that the thing *denied our sight* throughout the opening scene—the thing, the scene, that Iago takes Othello back to again and again, retouching it for Othello's enchafed imagination—is what we are shown in the final scene, of murder" (p. 132). See also James L. Calderwood, *The Properties of "Othello"* (Amherst: University of Massachusetts Press, 1989), p. 125.

27. Nelson and Haines, for example, use her lines as prime evidence for the noncon-summation of the marriage on its first night (p. 13).

28. Among the grounds cited for such exhibitions of popular censure were "a great disparity in age between bride and groom . . . or the fact that the husband was regarded as a 'stranger.' . . . Charivaris thus stigmatized marriages in which bride and groom . . . failed to maintain a 'proper distance' "; see Daniel Fabre, "Families: Privacy versus Custom" in Philippe Ariès and Georges Duby, gen. eds., *A History of Private Life*, trans. Arthur Goldhammer, 3 vols. (Cambridge: Harvard University Press, Belknap Press, 1987), 3:533. For English forms of the charivari, see David Underdown, *Revel, Riot, and Rebellion: Popular Politics and Culture in England, 1603–1660* (Oxford: Clarendon Press, 1985), pp. 99–103. The grotesque animal imagery of Iago's speeches outside Brabantio's house echoes the horned masks and animal heads of the wild procession paraded at the offender's windows (see Underdown, p. 101).

29. For a full discussion of the charivari-like aspects of this scene, see Nelson and

Haines, pp. 5–7.

30. "Topped" here is simply a variant of "tupped," a verbal form deriving from the dialectal "tup" = ram *(OED)*.

31. For the adulterous character of the temptation scene see chap. 8.

32. For the handkerchief as "the public surrogate of secrecy," see Kenneth Burke's suggestive "*Othello:* An Essay to Illustrate a Method," in Susan Snyder, ed., "*Othello*": *Critical Essays* (New York and London: Garland, 1988), pp. 127–68 (p. 160).

33. See Snow, and Lynda E. Boose, "Othello's Handkerchief: 'The Recognizance and Pledge of Love,' " *English Literary Renaissance* 5 (1975): 360–74. See also Nelson and Haines, pp. 8–10. Peter Stallybrass, "Patriarchal Territories: The Body Enclosed," in Snyder, pp. 251–74, esp. pp. 254, 269, identifies the handkerchief as a social symbol connected to the policing and purification of bodily orifices. Some useful historical perspectives on its significance are suggested by Newman, pp. 155–6.

34. See Clare Gittings, *Death, Burial, and the Individual in Early Modern England* (London: Croom Helm, 1984), pp. 111–12.

35. I give the stage direction in its folio form, with the necessary addition (in square brackets) of the first quarto's torch. It is not clear whether the bed is merely to be displayed inside a discovery space or to be thrust forward onto the main stage. Economy of design favors the former alternative; theatrical effectiveness, the latter, which is supported by Richard Hosley in "The Staging of Desdemona's Bed," *Shakespeare Quarterly* 14 (1963): 57–65. Hosley further suggests that Lodovico's final order may have been a signal for the bed to be "drawn in" again, making his gesture of effacement even more absolute.

36. The relation between names and identity in the play is sensitively analyzed by Calderwood, pp. 40–5, 50–2.

37. For a suggestive discussion of ideas of propriety and property in the play, see Calderwood, pp. 9–15.

38. Siemon, p. 50.

39. Henry Morley, *The Journal of a London Playgoer*, quoted in Hankey, p. 307. Fechter was the first to remove the bed from its traditionally central position to the side of the stage, where he placed it with its back to the audience. If this was intended to diminish the threat of the scene, it apparently had the reverse effect, as Sir Theodore Martin complained, "bringing it so far forward that every detail is thrust painfully on our senses" (quoted in Siemon, p. 40).

40. The sense of this connection clearly persisted into the Restoration theater. Rowe's illustration for *Antony and Cleopatra* (1709) shows the dead Cleopatra in her monument lying on what is evidently a bed but in a posture recalling tomb-sculpture. It was not for nothing that the marriage bed became a favorite model for so many Elizabethan and Jacobean dynastic tombs, where the figures of man

and wife, frequently surrounded on the base of the tomb by their numerous off-spring, signify the power of biological continuance, the authority of lineage—see my *Issues of Death: Mortality and Identity in English Renaissance Tragedy* (Oxford: Clarendon Press, 1997), chaps. 1 (pp. 38–42), 9, 10.

41. Susan Snyder, *The Comic Matrix of Shakespeare's Tragedies* (Princeton: Princeton University Press, 1979), pp. 70–4; see also Cavell, p. 132.

42. Rymer, quoted in Vickers, pp. 54, 51, 47, 37, 42. Jonson seems to anticipate Rymer's mockery in the jealousy plot of *Volpone* (1606) when Corvino denounces his wife: "to seek and entertain a parley / With a known knave, before a multitude! You were an actor with your handkerchief" (2.3.38–40). In a paper exploring the relations between *Othello* and the myth of Hercules, "Othello *Furens*," delivered at the Folger Shakespeare Library on 17 February 1989, Robert S. Miola has suggested that the handkerchief is a version of the robe of Nessus; such ludicrous shrinkages are characteristic of comic jealousy plots—as, for example, in the transformation of Pinchwife's heroically flourished sword to a penknife in Wycherley's *Country Wife*. Certain objects become grotesquely enlarged to the jealous imagination or absurdly diminished in the eyes of the audience—it is on such disproportion that the comedy of jealousy depends.

The misalliance of youth and age in the play is treated by Janet Stavropoulos, "Love and Age in *Othello*," *Shakespeare Studies* 19 (1987): 125–41.

43. Coleridge quoted in T. M. Raysor, ed., *Shakespearean Criticism* 2 vols. (London: J. M. Dent, 1960), 1:42; emphasis added; Hunter, p. 163; emphasis added.

44. For an account of the social basis of these contradictions, see Stallybrass, pp. 265–7.

45. For the opposite view of Venice, described by the traveler Thomas Coryat in *Coryat's Crudities* as "that most glorious, renowned and Virgin City of Venice," see Stallybrass, p. 265.

46. A curious sidelight is cast on nineteenth-century attempts to contain the scandal of the play's ending by the habit of having Othello finish off Desdemona with his dagger on "I would not have thee linger in thy pain"—a piece of stage business that must have heightened the sado-erotic suggestiveness of the scene (see Siemon, pp. 46–7).

47. Kenneth Burke beautifully observes the power of inarticulate suggestion in the play: "There is whispering. There is something vaguely feared and hated. In itself it is hard to locate, being woven into the very nature of 'consciousness'; but by the artifice of Iago it is made local. The tinge of malice vaguely diffused through the texture of events and relationships can here be condensed into a single principle, a devil, giving the audience as it were flesh to sink their claw-thoughts in" (p. 131).

48. Matthews, p. 145.

49. Significantly, eighteenth- and nineteenth-century promptbooks reveal that

Emilia's request was invariably denied.

50. Greenblatt, p. 233 and p. 248, quoting Saint Jerome. Compare Tamyra's prevarication before her amorous husband (whom she is busy cuckolding with Bussy) in Chapman's *Bussy D'Ambois:* "Your holy friar says / All couplings in the day that touch the bed / Adulterous are, even in the married" (3.1.91–3).

51. In addition to their usual technical sense, "adulterous" and "adulterate" came at about this time to carry the meaning "corrupted by base intermixture"; while by extension "adulterate" also came, like "bastard," to mean "spurious" and "counterfeit" (*OED, adulterate, ppl. a,* 2; *adulterous* 3; *bastard, sb.* and *a* 4. See also *adulterate, v,* 3; *adulterine* 3). Thus Ford's Penthea, who imagines her forced marriage to Bassanes as a species of adultery, finds her blood "seasoned by the forfeit / Of noble shame with *mixtures of pollution*" (*The Broken Heart,* 4.2.149–50; emphasis added).

   By one of those strange linguistic contradictions that expose cultural double-think, an illegitimate son could be at once "spurious" and "unnatural" and a "natural son." When the bastard Spurio, in a play that performs innumerable variations on the theme of the counterfeit and the natural, declares that "Adultery is my nature" (*The Revenger's Tragedy,* 1.3.177), he is simultaneously quibbling on the idea of himself as a "natural son" and elaborating a vicious paradox, according to which—by virtue of his adulterate birth *(natura)*—he is naturally unnatural, essentially counterfeit, and purely adulterous. A very similar series of quibbling associations underlies the counterfeiting Edmund's paean to the tutelary of bastards in *King Lear:* "Thou, Nature, art my goddess" (1.2.1 ff.). See chaps. 5–6.

52. When Ford's Hippolita curses her betrayer, Soranzo, for what she regards as his adulterous marriage to Annabella, she envisages adultery's monstrous offspring as constituting its own punishment—"mayst thou live / To father bastards, may her womb bring forth / Monsters" (*'Tis Pity She's a Whore,* 4.1.99–101)—a curse that seems likely to be fulfilled when Soranzo discovers the existence of the "gallimaufry" (heterogeneous mixture) that is already "stuffed in [his bride's] corrupted bastard-bearing womb" (4.3.13–14).

53. *OED, adultery,* 1b. It scarcely matters that Othello's contempt for the "circumcisèd dog" he killed in Aleppo shows that he sees himself as a Christian, since "Moor" was a virtual synonym for Muslim or pagan, and it is as a "pagan" that Brabantio identifies him (1.2.119).

54. In seventeenth-century English the word "bastard" was habitually applied to all products of generic mixture. Thus mongrel dogs, mules, and leopards (supposedly half lion and half panther) were all, impartially, bastard creatures, and this is the sense that Perdita employs when she dismisses streaked gillyvors as "Nature's bastards" (*The Winter's Tale,* 4.4.83). In Jonson's *Volpone* the bastard nature of Volpone's "true . . . family" is redoubled by their having been "begot

on . . . Gypsies, and Jews, and black-moors" (1.1.506–7). Jonson's location of this adulterate mingle-mangle in Venice may even suggest some general anxiety about the vulnerability of racial boundaries in a city so conspicuously on the European margin—something apparent also in *The Merchant of Venice*.

55. John Block Friedman, *The Monstrous Races in Medieval Art and Thought* (Cambridge: Harvard University Press, 1981), pp. 16–17. Calderwood notes the resonance of Othello's lodging at the Saggitary—or Centaur (1.3.115)—stressing the monster's ancient significance as a symbol of lust, barbarism, and (through the centaurs' assault on Lapith women) the violation of kind (Calderwood, pp. 22–5, 36).

56. On Elizabethan views about black people, see Newman, pp. 145–53; Elliot H. Tokson, *The Popular Image of the Black Man in English Drama, 1550–1688* (Boston: G. K. Hall, 1982), pp. 80–1; Friedman, pp. 101–2; and Calderwood, p. 7.

   Flouting his father's taboo upon copulation in the Ark, Cham (Ham), in the hope of producing an heir to all the dominions of the earth, "used company with his wife . . . for the which wicked and detestable fact, as an example for contempt of Almighty God, and disobedience of parents, God would a son should be born whose name was Chus, who not only itself, but all his posterity after him should be so black and loathsome, that it might remain a spectacle of disobedience to all the world. And of this black and cursed Chus came all these black Moors which are in Africa," George Best, "Experiences and reasons of the Sphere . . ." in Richard Hakluyt, *The Principal Navigations, Voyages, Traffiques, and Discoveries of the English Nation*, 12 vols. (1598–1600; rpt. Glasgow: J. MacLehose, 1903–5), 7:264.

57. The association of blackness with adultery is also encouraged by a well-known passage in Jeremiah, where the indelible blackness of the Moor's skin is analogized to the ingrained (but hidden) vices of the Jews: "Can the black Moor change his skin? Or the leopard his spots. . . . I have seen thine adulteries, and thy neighings, the filthiness of thy whoredom" (Jer. 13.23–7, Geneva Bible). In the context of *Othello*, the passage's rhetorical emphasis on discovery is suggestive, as is the Geneva version's marginal note: "Thy cloak of hypocrisy shall be pulled off and thy shame seen." A second marginal note observes that the prophet "compareth idolaters to horses inflamed after mares," a comparison that may be echoed in Iago's obscene vision of Othello as a "Barbary horse" (1.1.112). I am grateful to my colleague Kenneth Larsen for drawing this passage to my attention.

58. See Newman; and Greenblatt, pp. 239–54.

59. Whether or not one accepts Foucault's notion of the sixteenth century as the site of a major cultural shift in which a "pre-classical *episteme*" based on the recognition of similarity was replaced by a "classical *episteme*" based on the recognition of difference, it seems clear that the definition of racial "difference" or otherness

was an important adjunct to the development of national consciousness in the period of early colonial expansion. See the works by Cairns and Richards, Laurence, and Greenblatt (cited in n. 19 this chap.)

60. See Danielle Régnier-Bohler, "Imagining the Self," in Ariès and Duby, 2:311–93, esp. pp. 327–30.

61. See Dominique Barthélemy and Philippe Contamine, "The Use of Private Space," in Ariès and Duby, 2:395–505, esp. p. 500.

62. See Lawrence Stone, *The Family, Sex, and Marriage in England, 1500–1800* (New York: Harper and Row, 1977), p. 334; and Georges Duby and Philippe Braunstein, "The Emergence of the Individual," in Ariès and Duby, 2:507–630, esp. p. 589.

63. Régnier-Bohler, p. 329.

64. The archaic spells that form part of the convention of epithalamia and wedding masques testify to a continuing sense (albeit overlaid with a show of sophisticated playfulness) of the marriage bed as a dangerously liminal space in the marital rite of passage.

65. Othello is made up of such paradoxical mixtures—at once the governing representative of rational order and the embodiment of ungovernable passion, cruel and merciful, general and "enfettered" subordinate, "honourable murderer"— he is an entire anomaly. See Newman (p. 153): "Othello is both hero and outsider because he embodies not only the norms of male power and privilege . . . but also the threatening power of the alien: Othello is a monster in the Renaissance sense of the word, a deformed creature like the hermaphrodites and other strange spectacles which so fascinated the early modern period."

66. For discussion of the "satisfaction" that the final scene grants an audience, see Calderwood, pp. 125–6.

10 · "MULATTOS," "BLACKS," AND "INDIAN MOORS"

1. Vaughan, *Othello: A Contextual History* (Cambridge: Cambridge University Press, 1994), p. 70.

2. See, for example, Kim Hall, *Things of Darkness: Economies of Race and Gender in Early Modern England* (Ithaca: Cornell University Press, 1995); Margo Hendricks, "Civility, Barbarism, and Aphra Behn's *The Widow Ranter*," and Linda Boose " 'The Getting of a Lawful Race': Racial Discourse in Early Modern England and the Unrepresentable Black Woman," both in Hendricks and Patricia Parker, eds., *Women, "Race," and Writing in the Early Modern Period* (London: Routledge, 1994), pp. 225–39, 35–54. The literature on the treatment of race in *Othello* has become so extensive as to make full citation impossible, but a convenient summary will be found in Vaughan's invaluable *Othello*, chap. 3, pp. 51–70.

3. Emily C. Bartels, "*Othello* and Africa: Postcolonialism Reconsidered," *William and Mary Quarterly* 3d series, 54 (1997): 45–64 (61–2); emphasis added.

4. See, e.g., Patricia Coughlan, ed., *Spenser and Ireland: An Interdisciplinary Perspective* (Cork: University of Cork Press, 1989); Willy Maley, *Salvaging Spenser: Colonialism, Culture, and Identity* (New York: St. Martin's Press, 1997); Christopher Highley, *Shakespeare, Spenser, and the Crisis in Ireland* (Cambridge: Cambridge University Press, 1997); and chap. 13.

5. In his first book, for example, Leo breaks off his description of the vices to which "they" are subject in order to acknowledge his own implication in the world of these Others as one whose life resembles that of the strange fish-bird he calls "Amphibia": "Neither am I ignorant, how much mine own credit is impeached, when I myself write so homely of Africa, unto which country I stand indebted both for my birth, and also for the best part of my education. . . . For mine own part, when I hear the Africans evil spoken of, I will affirm myself to be one of Granada: and when I perceive the nation of Granada to be discommended, then will I profess myself to be an African" (pp. 41–3). For a more extended treatment of Leo's ambivalence about his identity, see Emily C. Bartels, "Making More of the Moor: Aaron, Othello, and Renaissance Refashionings of Race," *Shakespeare Quarterly* 41 (1990): 433–54 (436–8).

6. Citations from *Othello* are to the Arden edition, ed. E. A. J. Honigmann (London: Thomas Nelson, 1997). The significance of the subtitle is indicated by the remarkable consistency with which (in contrast to the generally fluid treatment of nomenclature in the period) it is repeated from the Stationers' Register entry to the quarto and folio and the other early texts deriving from them.

7. The same point is made by Peter Swaab in his program notes for the Royal National Theatre production of *Othello:* "Shakespeare's title has the force of a paradox. How far can 'the Moor' really be 'of' Venice? Like Marlowe's Jew of Malta, Othello is a resident who remains in important ways alien; like Shakespeare's Timon of Athens, his downfall involves too much trusting that a culture can give him an identity; and as with a historical figure such as Lawrence of Arabia, the word 'of' conceals a vulnerable fantasy of power in distant lands. 'The Moor of Venice' is a mixed marriage of a phrase"; cited from the program for the season at the Brooklyn Academy of Music, 8–11 April 1998; this production was first staged at the Salzburg Festival on 22 August 1997 and subsequently at the Lyttelton Theatre in London.

8. "There's . . . *Obed* in *Bairseth*,*Nones* in *Portugal*, / Myself in *Malta*, some in *Italy*, / Many in *France*, and wealthy every one" (1.1.124–7); citations from Marlowe are to *The Complete Works*, ed. Fredson Bowers, 2d ed. (Cambridge: Cambridge University Press, 1981).

9. For an outstanding account of the cultural fantasies surrounding Jews in early modern culture see James S. Shapiro, *Shakespeare and the Jews* (New York:

Columbia University Press, 1996), esp. chap. 6. See also Avram Oz, " 'Which Is the Merchant Here? And Which the Jew': Riddles of Identity," in *The Yoke of Love: Prophetic Riddles in "The Merchant of Venice"* (Newark: University of Delaware Press), pp. 93–133, esp. pp. 100–3.

10. For the resemblances between Moor and Jew as figures of alterity, see Leslie A. Fiedler, *The Stranger in Shakespeare* (New York: Stein and Day, 1972), pp. 103–6, 195–6; and cf. Shapiro, pp. 171–2 on Jewish "blackness." For Best's story, see "George Best's Discourse" in Richard Hakluyt, *The Principal Navigations, Voyages, Traffiques, and Discoveries of the English Nation* (1598–1600; rpt. Glasgow: J. MacLehose, 1903–5), 7:262–3.

The Geneva Bible gives particular prominence to the figure by printing "The black Moor" as a title at the head of the column. On the history of this motif in literature and the visual arts, see Jean Michel Massing, "From Greek Proverb to Soap Advert: Washing the Ethiopian," *Journal of the Warburg and Courtault Institutes* 58 (1995): 180–201; and Karen Newman, " 'And Wash the Ethiop White': Femininity and the Monstrous in *Othello*," in Jean Howard and Marion F. O'Connor, eds., *Shakespeare Reproduced: The Text in History and Ideology* (London: Methuen, 1987), pp. 143–62.

11. On the forcible conversion of the Spanish Moors and the suspicion to which it paradoxically rendered them vulnerable, thereby exposing them to the malice of the Inquisition, see Henry Charles Lea, *The Moriscos of Spain: Their Conversion and Expulsion* (New York: Greenwood Press, 1968). The near paranoia that inspired the official campaign for *limpieʒa de sangre* (purity of blood) in Spain issued directly from this fear of the hidden stranger masquerading as one of the familiar.

12. See also Bartels, "Making More of the Moor," 434.

13. Marlowe, *Faustus*, 1.1.122; the phrase is common to both A and B texts.

14. For a useful account of the significance of "turning Turk" in this period, see Daniel J. Vitkus, "Turning Turk in *Othello:* The Conversion and Damnation of the Moor," *Shakespeare Quarterly* 48 (1997): 145–76.

15. See, e.g., William Cornelison Schouten of Horne (Voyage of 1615–7) in Samuel Purchas, *Hakluytus Posthumus or Purchas his Pilgrimes* (1625), 20 vols. (Glasgow: James MacLehose and Sons, 1905), 2:280.

16. Cf. Shapiro (pp. 170–2) on the ambiguities surrounding "what happened to racial otherness when [Jews] converted."

17. For a useful account of the complex entanglement of color and religion in early Iberian racism, see James H. Sweet, "The Iberian Roots of American Racist Thought," *William and Mary Quarterly* 3d series, 54 (1997): 143–66; see also Robin Blackburn's essay in the same issue, "The Old World Background to European Colonial Slavery," 65–102 (77–8). On the uncertain denotation of "Moor" in the play, see Vitkus (p. 160): "Othello, the noble Moor of Venice, is

... not to be identified with a specific, historically accurate racial category; rather he is a hybrid who might be associated, in the minds of Shakespeare's *Moor, Turk, Ottomite, Saracen, Mahometan, Egyptian, Judean, Indian*—all constructed and positioned in opposition to Christian faith and virtue." The opposition, however, is never *simply* religious or even cultural.

18. Karen Ordahl Kupperman, "Presentment of Civility: English Reading of American Self-Presentation in the Early Years of Colonization," *William and Mary Quarterly* 3d series, 54 (1997): 193–228 (193). On English attitudes toward the Irish, see chap. 13.

19. Purchas, *Hakluytus Posthumus*, p. 546. Benjamin Braude's richly informative "Sons of Noah and the Construction of Ethnic and Geographical Identities in the Medieval and Early Modern Periods," *William and Mary Quarterly* 3d series, 54 (1997): 103–42, discerns an analogous shift in the treatment of African peoples between 1589 and 1625, as the biblical curse of Ham was increasingly interpreted as an explanation of both color and moral character: "slavery," he argues, "had started to make it credible" (p. 138).

20. John Huighen Van Linschoten, *Iohn Hvighen Van Linschoten his Discours of Voyages into ye Easte & West Indies* (London, 1598), pp. 14, 28, 29, 40, 37.

21. George Best, *A True Discourse of the late voyages of discouerie, for the finding of a passage to Cathaya, by the Northwest* (London, 1578) p. 28, cited in Alden T. Vaughan and Virginia Vaughan, "Before *Othello:* Elizabethan Representations of Sub-Saharan Africans," *William and Mary Quarterly* 3d series, 54 (1997): 19–44 (27); cf. also Kupperman, 207–8, 226–7. Thomas Candish, in Purchase, *Hakluytus Posthumus*, p. 181.

22. For American examples, see Kupperman, 207.

23. Cited from the edition edited by Fredson Bowers in *The Dramatic Works in the Beaumont and Fletcher Canon*, 10 vols. (Cambridge: Cambridge University Press, 1966–96), vol. 5.

24. In a deliberate confusion of reality, the Islamic allegiance of the actual Moluccans is assimilated in the play with idolatry through the disguise adopted by the villainous Governor of Ternata who is at once a (presumably Mahometan) "Moore Priest" (4.1.0) and the false prophet of "the Sun and Moon" (4.5.70). For more detailed discussion of this play as an instrument of mercantile colonialism, see Shankar Raman, "Imaginary Islands: Staging the East," *Renaissance Drama* n.s. 26 (1995 [1997]): 131–61, and chap. 12.

25. See Sweet, esp. pp. 146–7, 149, 155–6, 166.

26. See, for example Purchas, *Hakluytus Posthumus*, vol. 5, chap. 9, "The Journall of Master Nathaniel Courthop," p. 109; cf. also the continuation of Courthop's journal by Robert Hayes, 5:126, 135; and "An Answere to the Hollanders Declaration, ..." 5:155–74, esp. p. 170.

27. Boose, p.38. Quotation from *The City Madam*, cited from the edition by Cyrus

Hoy, Regents Renaissance Drama (Lincoln: University of Nebraska Press, 1964). In this episode Luke Frugal salutes the supposed "Indians" of the play (in fact a group of disguised Londoners led by his own brother) for their worship of Plutus, god of riches. Samuel Purchas, *Purchas his Pilgrimage or Relations of the World and the Religions Observed in All Age* (London, 1613), p. 546. On Purchas's shift toward an increasingly moralized construction of blackness in his later writing, see Braude, 135–7.

28. The different MS origins of the two versions are suggested by numerous minor variants. Purchas, while he acknowledges making significant cuts, also includes a number of short passages missing from the pamphlet, which enhance its vilification of the Dutch. At one point, it is true, he claims to have "mollified the author's style, and left out some harsher censures" of the Hollanders (marginal gloss, p. 483), but this defensive tactic (like others in the collection) only serves to further blacken these rivals by implying that there are even worse things to be said.

29. See chap. 4.

30. 1606 version, sig. C2v.

31. Edmund Scott, *An Exact Discourse of the Subtilties, Fashions, Religion, and Ceremonies of the East Indians* (London: 1606), C2v. Unless otherwise indicated, citations are to this edition.

32. For Scott, the designation "mulatto" seems to describe any person of part-European ethnicity; although the term is nowadays considered offensive, I have felt bound to replicate Scott's usage, since the protagonist of his story is identified in no other way.

33. Marginal note, p. 461.

34. Dympna Callaghan, " 'Othello Was a White Man': Properties of Race on Shakespeare's Stage," in Terence Hawkes, ed., *Alternative Shakespeares 2* (London: Routledge, 1996), pp. 192–215.

35. "Dull Moor"—involving as it does acomplicated quibble that depends on the resemblances and etymological links (supposed or otherwise) between Medieval Latin *Morus* = Moor, Latin *morus* (from Greek μογρρασ) = dull, stupid, and *morum* = blackberry or mulberry (hence *morulus* = black, dark-colored)—can be construed as a contemptuous inversion of the oxymoronic "Moor of Venice."

11 · PUTTING HISTORY TO THE QUESTION

1. The very want of a firm theoretical base means that it is in many ways misleading to think of New Historicism as a "school" in any strict sense. Indeed some of the most powerful criticisms of the Greenblattian approach have been made by other so-called New Historicists. See, for example, Louis Montrose, "New Historicisms" in Stephen Greenblatt and Giles Gunn, eds., *Redrawing the*

Boundaries: The Transformation of English and American Studies (New York: MLA, 1992), pp. 392–418. Montrose traces what he sees as a want of theoretical rigor to Geertz's own practice (pp. 399–400) and argues that its synchronic approach to the study of culture results in a criticism whose preoccupation with cohesive and closed systems often seems more formalist than truly historicist in that "it makes no theoretical space for change or contestation. Such a position might be said to reinstate the Elizabethan world picture but now transposed into the ironic mode" (p. 403). A similar critique of Geertzian cultural analysis is offered by the historian Ronald G. Walters: "The tendency of thick description and semiotics is to reinforce the impulse to burrow in and not to try to connect the dots. That occurs because what is an analytical strength—Geertz's attention to particularity and his orientation toward the actor's perspective—is a weakness for synthesis. Thick description leads to brilliant readings of individual situations, rituals, and institutions. It does not require saying how 'cultural texts' relate to each other or to general processes of social and economic change." ("Signs of the Times: Clifford Geertz and Historians," *Social Research* 47 (1980): 551–2, cited in Aletta Biersack, "Local Knowledge, Local History: Geertz and Beyond," in Lynn Hunt, ed., *The New Cultural History* [Berkeley: University of California Press, 1989], pp. 72–96 [p. 79]). For a hard-hitting analysis of the political implications of Geertz's approach to culture, see also Vincent P. Pecora, "The Limits of Local Knowledge," in H. Aram Veeser, ed., *The New Historicism* (New York: Routledge, 1989), pp. 243–76. Frank Lentricchia's "Foucault's Legacy: A New Historicism?" in the same collection (pp. 231–42), though directed mainly at the residual humanism of Foucault, makes some sharp jabs at Greenblatt's anecdotal method.

2. Stephen Greenblatt, *Learning to Curse: Essays in Early Modern Culture* (New York, Routledge: 1990), p. 5. Subsequent citations to this work are given in the text.

3. Joel Fineman, "The History of the Anecdote: Fact and Fiction," in Veeser, *The New Historicism*, pp. 49–76, cited in Greenblatt, p. 5; emphasis added.

4. Greenblatt is by no means alone in such waywardness, of course. New Historicist contextualizing can be remarkably selective and sometimes seriously distortive. Karen Newman's justly admired (and several times reprinted) essay on race and gender in *Othello*, for example, cites a passage on slavery from Bodin (*The Six Bookes of a Commonweale*, trans. Richard Knolles (London, 1606), vol. 3, sect. 8, p. 387), which is said to display "the conventional prejudice about black sexuality": "There be in man's body some members, I may not call them filthy (for that nothing can so be which is natural) but yet so shameful, as that no man except he be past all shame, can without blushing reveal or discover the same: and do they [blacks] for that cease to be members of the whole body?" Bodin, she explains, "is so shamed by those members, *and by the Africans' custom of exposing them*, that he dresses his prose in a series of parentheses which effectively obscure its meaning" (Karen Newman, " 'And Wash the Ethiop White': Femininity and the Monstrous

in *Othello*," in Jean E. Howard and Marion F. O'Connor, eds., *Shakespeare Reproduced: The Text in History and Ideology* (London: Methuen, 1987), pp. 148–9; emphasis added). The passage does indeed read like a remarkable illustration of a familiar European racial neurosis, so that it comes as something of a shock to discover that Newman's glossing of "slaves" as "blacks" and her reference to African genital exposure have no warrant whatsoever in Bodin's text, which is discussing the classical institution of slavery in a context utterly removed from the sixteenth-century African slave trade. Bodin is engaged in a theoretical argument with Aristotle and other classical authors concerning "the orders and degrees of citizens," which at this point has only a marginal contemporary application; indeed he is particularly anxious to fend off any supposition that "I should desire slavery *long since taken away out of our Commonweal*, to be thereunto again restored" (p. 387; emphasis added). Admitting, however, that "the force and boldness of men is so far broken out, as that we see servitude and slavery by little and little to creep in, and return again," he hopes that his arguments may serve an ameliorative purpose. But race is *nowhere* at issue.

5. Edmund Scott, *An Exact Discourse of the Subtilties, Fashions, Religion and Ceremonies of the East Indians* (London: 1606). Subsequent citations to this work are given in the text.

6. Scott may well have hoped the pamphlet would improve his standing with the company. As an unpaid supernumerary who had to finance his own way to the Moluccas by taking up a two-hundred-pound share in the first voyage, he was in an uncertain position, despite his *de facto* succession to the agency. But the circumstances of its publication suggest that his pamphlet was written before the dispute broke out. It was dedicated to Sir William Romney, governor of the East India Company (1606–7), and printed for Walter Burre, a bookseller who was later to publish tracts associated with the Virginia company, as well as treatises on trade, surveying, and the cultivation of tobacco. Burre was brother-in-law to Sir Henry Middleton, general of the second voyage, and had issued the anonymous account of Middleton's expedition, *The Last East-Indian Voyage* (London, 1606), earlier in the same year. Burre entered *The Last East-Indian Voyage* on the Stationer's Register as early as 20 May 1606, a bare fortnight after the arrival of Middleton's small fleet, and since his epistle "To the Reader," vigorously advertises Scott's forthcoming pamphlet, the *Exact Discourse* must presumably have been written very soon after Scott's return. Samuel Purchas's decision to reprint it in *Hakluytus Posthumus* (1625) is almost certainly a sign of East India Company interest in the document since Purchas's compilation was produced under company patronage.

7. A trenchant attack on Greenblatt's failure to explore the psychological basis of Scott's frenzy is mounted by Anne Barton in her review of *Learning to Curse, New York Review of Books* 28 March 1991, pp. 52–3.

8. The Gunpowder Plot, which must have been the principal political talking point

for the East India Company returnees in the spring of 1606, was already being mobilized as a focus of national self-consciousness, and the bonfires and bells with which the besieged Protestant nation celebrated the defeat of treason would ultimately take the place of Elizabeth's Accession Day in the calendar of political festivals described by David Cressy in *Bonfires and Bells: National Memory and the Protestant Calendar in Elizabethan and Stuart England* (Berkeley and Los Angeles: University of California Press, 1989). The conspiracy against the English factory, its near blowing up, and the fiery torture of the plotters are given a similar symbolic centrality in Scott's narrative of the vulnerable "English nation at *Bantan*."

9. Greenblatt's use of the term "Javanese" is technically inaccurate since the people of Bantam were properly speaking Sundanese. Accordingly I have preferred the usefully imprecise contemporary term "Javan."

10. As outsiders, the English, like the Dutch, were required to establish their factory in the Chinese quarter, outside the city walls on the western side of the river that served as part of the town's defenses.

11. It is only at this point that Scott, as if alarmed by the disturbed and disturbing force of his own recollections, is at pains to insist to his employers that "I speak not this to that end I tendered my own private life so much, but for fear of the great loss and damage the adventurers and my country, should have sustained if we should have miscarried" and to reassure future employees that "the country is grown to much better civility" and is now much better disposed toward the English (C2).

12. Scott's anxieties about fire are supported by the instructions that Middleton left behind on his departure, which significantly begin by detailing the precautions to be taken to secure the factory against fire. See Sir William Foster, ed., *The Voyage of Sir Henry Middleton to the Moluccas, 1604–6* (London: Hakluyt Society, 1943), p. 195.

13. The "Protector" was the *Pangeran*, an uncle of the boy-king, who was acting as regent.

14. M. P. Tilley, *A Dictionary of Proverbs in the Sixteenth and Seventeenth Centuries* (Ann Arbor: University of Michigan Press, 1950), F277; and cf. *Coriolanus* 4.7.54, "one fire drives out one fire."

15. Compare the way in which fire is used to purge or "quench" the fire of Diaphanta's lust in *The Changeling* (5.1.31–116).

16. *Revenger's Tragedy*, 3.5.160. Of course, the same fastidiously vicious symmetry was often thought to characterize the operations of divine justice—see, for example, Thomas Beard's *Theatre of Gods Iudgements* (1597), where the atheistical Christopher Marlowe is made to stab himself in the eye: "Herein did the justice of God most notably appear, in that he compelled his own hand which had written those blasphemies to be the instrument to punish him," quoted in J. Leslie Hotson, *The Death of Christopher Marlowe* (London: Nonesuch Press, 1925), p. 13.

17. Specifically Scott represents the protector as being so shocked by the sight of the mine ("he said it was a most villainous piece of work") that "he bid us do justice on those we had when we would, and so soon as the rest could be found, we should have them, so that if we had no more care then he; we might have executed one that was not in fault" (F1).
18. See the account of Lancaster's voyage in Samuel Purchas, *Hakluytus Posthumus: Purchas His Pilgrimes*, as reprinted in Sir William Foster, ed., *The Voyages of Sir James Lancaster* (London: Hakluyt Society, 1940), p. 99. Purchas also records that Lancaster had been given specific "commission from the king [of Bantam] that whosoever he took about his house in the night, he should kill them" (p. 115).
19. See James Heath, *Torture and English Law* (London: Greenwood Press, 1982), 142–7; Edward Peters, *Torture* (Oxford: Blackwell, 1985), p. 59; Elizabeth Hanson, "Torture and Truth in Renaissance England," *Representations* 34 (1991): 53–84 (56–8). A significant exception was the Council of the Marches in Wales, which was specifically authorized to use torture in cases of murder, felony, and treason—a convenience of which Burghley was apparently happy to avail himself—since unlike the Star Chamber it was empowered to try such capital offenses. See G. R. Elton, *The Tudor Constitution* (Cambridge: Cambridge University Press, 1960), p. 199; and P. Williams, *The Council in the Marches of Wales under Elizabeth I* (Cardiff: University of Wales, 1958), p. 49.
20. At least one well-known dramatist, Thomas Kyd, was himself subjected to the rack during an investigation of a "libel that concerned the State"—a fate from which Marlowe was saved only by his assassination (see F. S. Boas, ed., *The Works of Thomas Kyd* [Oxford: Oxford University Press, 1901], p. lxiv)—while another, Thomas Norton, the amateur coauthor of *Gorboduc*, acted as a torturer for Burghley in the interrogation of Thomas Campion and other Catholic prisoners. Norton subsequently issued a pamphlet justifying the torture on the grounds that their offense was not religious dissent but treason (see n. 23 this chap.).
21. Heath, p. 110; and Hanson, pp. 53–84.
22. L. A. Parry, *The History of Torture in England* (London: Sampson Low, Marston, 1933), records the occasional use of torture in instances of robbery, murder, embezzling the queen's plate, and even failure to enforce regulations against stage players, but the overwhelming majority of instances involved treason (pp. 42, 54). See also Peters, pp. 79–80; Hanson, pp. 56–8, 62–8.
23. Significantly scripture and official doctrine tended to conflate the crimes of witchcraft and treason—"For rebellion is as the sin of witchcraft" (1 Sam. 15.23); see also Stuart Clark, "King James's *Daemonologie*: Witchcraft and Kingship," in Sydney Anglo, ed., *The Damned Art: Essays in the Literature of Witchcraft* (London: Routledge and Kegan Paul, 1977), pp. 156–81 (p. 176).
   Katharine Maus, *Inwardness and the Theater in the English Renaissance*

(Chicago: University of Chicago Press), pp. 34–5, quoting Fernando Pulton, *De Pace Regis et Regnis* (London, 1610), p. 108, and Francis Bacon, *A Declaration of the Practices and Treasons Attempted by Robert, Late Earl of Essex, and His Complices* (London, 1601), K2r. For an interesting discussion of treason and the early modern discourse of inwardness, see Karin S. Coddon, " 'Suche Strange Desygns': Madness, Subjectivity, and Treason in *Hamlet* and Elizabethan Culture," *Renaissance Drama* 20 (1989): 51–75. The legal redefinition of treason from a physical to a mental action was originally made in a statute of Edward III in 1352 (25 Edw. 3, St. 5, C2)—see Karen Cunningham, " 'A Spanish Heart in an English Body': The Ralegh Treason Trial and the Poetics of Proof," *Journal of Medieval and Renaissance Studies* 22 (1992): 327–51 (327–8).

24. See, e.g., the apologetic pamphlet *A Declaration of the fauourable dealing of her Maiesties Commissioners appointed for the Examination of certaine Traitours, and of tortures vniustly reported to be done vpon them for matters of religion* (London, 1583), produced for Burghley, but now reckoned to be the work of the playwright and torturer Thomas Norton. The whole thrust of Norton's text is to suggest that torture provides the only proper method of exposing the deceitful treachery of Campion and his associates, who not only "secretly wandered in . . . *England* in a disguised sort . . . to make special preparations of treasons" but contrived to hide their "curst heart" and "to keep themselves covert under pretence of temporary and permissive obedience to her Majesty," seeking to protect themselves during interrogation by never answering "plainly, but sophistically, deceitfully and traitorously" and by using "hypocritical and sophistical speech" (Aiiv– Aaiiiv).

25. Elaine Scarry, *The Body in Pain: The Making and Unmaking of the World* (New York: Oxford University Press, 1985), pp. 46, 53; Hanson, p. 53.

26. Kyd quoted in Charles Nicholl, *The Reckoning: The Murder of Christopher Marlowe* (New York: Harcourt, Brace, 1994), p. 43. Hanson, p. 66; and see Michael Neill, "What Strange Riddle's This: Deciphering *'Tis Pity She's a Whore*," in Neill, ed. *John Ford: Critical Re-Visions* (Cambridge: Cambridge University Press, 1988), pp. 153–79 (pp. 156–8). The problematics of proof in a context where treason is imagined as something hidden within the body are interestingly discussed by Cunningham (p. 345), who recognizes the symbolic importance of displaying the traitor's heart as a form of material proof.

27. Hanson, pp. 54–5; emphasis added.

28. Foster, *Voyages of Sir James Lancaster*, p. 161.

29. Purchas similarly avers that "the Javians be reckoned among the greatest pickers and thieves of the world" (ibid., p. 115).

30. On *peine forte et dure* as the legally prescribed response to a refusal to plead, see Parry, chap. 14; and Heath, pp. 248–9, n. 51.

31. For a similar episode involving an Eskimo who "for very choler and disdain . . .

bit his tongue in twain with his mouth," see George Best, *Three Voyages of Martin Frobisher*, ed. Richard Collinson (London: Hakluyt Society, 1867), p. 74.

32. Henslowe dispensed forty shillings to Jonson for additions to the play on 25 September 1601, which suggests it was revived in the latter part of that year. I know of no evidence concerning Scott's theater-going habits, but it is an interesting detail that his colleague in Java, Captain William Keeling, commander of the *Susan* in Sir Henry Middleton's relief fleet, has a small but significant place in theater history as the first known producer of an amateur production of *Hamlet*, during a subsequent voyage to the East Indies as commander of the *Dragon* (1607–8).

33. Fifteen years after the publication of Scott's pamphlet, the dramatist John Fletcher contrived a tellingly displaced version of its narrative in his tragicomedy *The Island Princess*, set in the Moluccas. Here undermining and "sudden fire" become the weapons of the heroic Portuguese Armusia in his struggle with the "subtleties" of the "unfaithful" and "barbarous" Governor of Ternata. Posing as a trader in "the merchants' house next joining" (2.3.43), he succeeds in firing the governor's castle in an action that the Ternatans regard as the "treason" of a villainous "neighbour" but that he himself successfully presents as a legitimate agent of "discovery" and the proper expression of his inflamed passion for the Princess of Tidore, whose brother the governor treacherously holds captive:

> The fire I brought here with me shall do something,
> Shall burst into material flames, and bright ones,
> That all the Island shall stand wondering at it. . . .
> An hour hence, my brave friends, look for the fury,
> The fire to light us to our honour'd purpose.
> Let it flame on, a comely light it gives up
> To our discovery.
>   2.2.38–46, 2.3.54–5

As a result of this action Armusia will win the hand of the princess and secure her conversion to the Christian faith, but not before he has been captured and threatened with fiery torture by the "firebrand" governor and himself rescued by "fire-spitting" cannons of the Portuguese (5.2–4). Although Fletcher's story is based on a Spanish history almost contemporary with Scott's, he clearly intends his audience to read the virtuous Portuguese as surrogates for the English; see chap. 12.

34. See n. 6 this chap.

35. See Foster, *Voyage of Sir Henry Middleton*, pp. xi–xvi, xxx.

36. Scott's language associates his pamphlet with a long line of company propaganda, beginning with the translation of *John Huighen Van Linschoten his*

Discours of Voyages into ye Easte and West Indies (London, 1598), which is offered by its printer, John Wolfe, to Julius Caesar, judge of the High Court of Admiralty, as a work "very commodious for our *English nation*" because its author brings "rare *intelligences* with him from foreign parts . . . [and] should be examined by such as are in place and Authority appointed for such purposes" (A1v). Wolfe goes on to persuade his readers "that this poor translation may work in our *English nation* a further desire and increase of honour over all *countries* of the *world*, and as it hath hitherto advanced the credit of the realm by defending the same with our *wooden walls* . . . so it would employ the same in foreign parts" (A4).

37. "Three times every week I used to search all the *Chineses* houses round about us, for fear of more undermining" (K1).

38. The Dutch factory was established by agreement with the ruler during the voyage of Cornelius Houtman, 1595–7. One possible explanation for the confusion is that Drake was favorably remembered in the Malayan archipelago and was invoked by the English themselves to demonstrate their prior right to trade—see Foster, *Voyage of Sir Henry Middleton*, pp. 26, 50. John Wolfe's address "To the Reader" of *Linschoten his . . . Voyages* emphasizes the priority of Drake and subsequent English voyagers, claiming that "the *people* of the *Low Countries* . . . fell to the like traffic into the *Indies*" only because they were "instructed by the diligent search and travel [travail?] of the *English nation*" (A3v).

39. See Cressy, pp. 50, 52. The best accounts of the popular festivities organized throughout the kingdom on Accession Day are in Cressy, pp. 50–9, and Roy Strong, *The Cult of Elizabeth: Elizabethan Portraiture and Pageantry* (London: Thames and Hudson, 1977), pp. 117–28.

40. The conduct of such musters, which were often organized as part of the May Day festivities, is elaborately parodied in act 5 of Francis Beaumont's *Knight of the Burning Pestle* (1607), where the apprentice Rafe and his company parade with drums, colors, and shot, and cast themselves in a crescent, among other "whimsical figures" popular with Elizabethan militia. For useful commentary on these maneuvers, see the introduction and notes to Herbert S. Merch's edition of the play, *Yale Studies in English* 33 (New York: Henry Holt, 1908), pp. cxi–cxiii, 249–61.

41. Strong, pp. 126–7; see also Cressy, pp. 52–4.

42. A similar view is attributed to the natives of Ternate in the anonymous pamphlet *The Last East-Indian Voyage* (1606), with its more openly hostile view of the Dutch: "The people of the country, understanding the Hollanders had procured our banishment, were much offended that the petty prince of Holland and his [people?] (whom they esteemed but debauched drunkards) should be esteemed before the mighty King of England and his subjects" (cited from Foster, *Voyage*

of Sir Henry Middleton, p. 57). The difficulties experienced with the Dutch contrasted with the company's expectations, as set out in Sir Henry Middleton's commission, which anticipated only "the malice of the Portingals towards our discovery of the trade to those parts" (*Voyage of Sir Henry Middleton*, p. 187).

43. The abbreviated version of the pamphlet printed in *Hakluytus Posthumus*, which apparently has an independent manuscript derivation, includes a passage in which Scott himself advances a quarrel over which party should march first in the processions celebrating the king's circumcision. The Dutch, Scott explains, "would by no means go behind our men; neither would our men go behind them: they were proud because they were many more in number: and our men were proud because they had much gayer apparel: for they were all in their silk suits, having scarves and hatbands of their country's colors which made a very fair show; and they [the Dutch] had on their tarred coats, greasy thrumbed caps, and those that had shirts on, they hung out between their legs" (K4v). In the Purchas version Scott adds that "the next time we saw their merchants . . . I asked one of them if he thought Holland were now able to wage war with England, that there should be such equality between their men and ours, to strive who should go foremost; and likewise we told them all that, if Englishmen had not once gone before, their nation might have gone behind all nations of Christendom long ago" (cited in Foster, *Voyage of Sir Henry Middleton*, p. 154). If such passages were deliberately cut from Burre's edition, the purpose must have been to mute Scott's attacks on England's Protestant allies, the Dutch, a motive that no longer applied to Purchas's publication in the immediate wake of the Amboyna massacre.

44. For a more detailed examination of this episode and discussion of its racial implications, see chap. 10.

45. Foster, *Voyages of Sir James Lancaster*, p. 133 n. 1; Foster,*Voyage of Sir Henry Middleton*, p. 98 n. 1. The Amboyna massacre seems to be foreshadowed in another of the passages absent from Burre's edition, where the violent brawl that erupted on the eve of the English departure is described in much greater detail. Here the English are warned "with weeping eyes" by fellow-countrymen among the Dutch crews not to come aboard their ships, "for strait order was given to kill as many Englishmen as they could, either aboard or on shore" (cited in Foster, *Voyage of Sir Henry Middleton*, pp. 165–6 n. 1).

46. Arthur Wilson, *The History of Great Britain* (1653), p. 281. I am indebted to Albert Braunmuller for drawing this passage to my attention.

47. Ibid.; emphasis added.

48. Ibid., pp. 281–2.

49. J. M. Coetzee, *Foe* (London: Secker and Warburg, 1986), pp. 141, 148. Subsequent citations to this work are given in the text.

12 · "MATERIAL FLAMES"

1. *OED,globe*, 1–3.

2. Thomas Platter, *Thomas Platter's Travels in England, 1599*, trans. Clare Williams (London: Jonathan Cape, 1937), p. 170.

3. The literature on nationalist and colonial discourse in Shakespeare is by now extensive, but among the more important contributions are Emily C. Bartels, *Spectacles of Strangeness: Imperialism, Alienation, and Marlowe* (Philadelphia: University of Pennsylvania Press, 1993); John Gillies, *Shakespeare and the Geography of Difference* (Cambridge: Cambridge University Press, 1994); Stephen Greenblatt, *Marvelous Possessions* (Oxford: Oxford University Press, 1991); Richard Helgerson, *Forms of Nationhood: The Elizabethan Writing of England* (Chicago: University of Chicago Press, 1992); Margo Hendricks and Patricia Parker, *Women, " 'Race," and Writing in the Early Modern Period* (London: Routledge, 1994); Peter Hulme, *Colonial Encounters: Europe and the Native Caribbean, 1492–1797* (London: Methuen, 1986); Clare McEachern, *The Poetics of English Nationhood* (Cambridge: Cambridge University Press, 1996); and Peter Womack, "Imagining Communities: Theatres and the English Nation in the Sixteenth Century," in David Aers, ed., *Culture and History, 1350–1600* (London: Harvester, 1992), pp. 91–145.

4. See, e.g., Louis Montrose, "The Work of Gender in the Discourse of Discovery," *Representations* 33 (winter 1991): 1–41; Jeffrey Knapp, "Distraction in *The Tempest*," in Knapp, *An Empire Nowhere: England, America, and Literature from "Utopia" to "The Tempest"* (Berkeley: University of California Press, 1992), pp. 220–42; and John Gillies, "Shakespeare's Virginian Masque," *ELH* 53 (1986): 673–707.

5. See Dryden's prefatory epistle for the Dryden-Davenant adaptation of *The Tempest*, in *The Dramatic Works of John Dryden*, ed. George Saintsbury, 8 vols. (Edinburgh: 1882), 3:106. All citations from Dryden are to this edition.

6. Gordon McMullan, *The Politics of Unease in the Plays of Beaumont and Fletcher* (Amherst: University of Massachusetts Press, 1994); Shankar Raman, "Imaginary Islands: Staging the East," *Renaissance Drama* n.s. 26 (1995 [1997]), 131–61.

7. Citations from Fletcher are to *The Dramatic Works in the Beaumont and Fletcher Canon*, ed. Fredson Bowers, 10 vols. (Cambridge: Cambridge University Press, 1966–96).

8. For further comment on the "otherworldliness" of both *The Tempest* and *The Sea-Voyage* see Knapp, pp. 241–2.

9. This was due in part to the continuing European anxiety about Islamic (and specifically Turkish) expansionism in the Mediterranean and in part to the much greater rewards anticipated from Eastern trade—which had, after all, provided the origi-

nal motivation for Atlantic voyaging. Although the formation of the English East India Company in 1600 postdated that of the Virginia Company, it had important predecessors in the Muscovy and Levant Companies (1555, 1581), which had pioneered overland caravans to the Middle East and India and had already sent feelers into the Moluccas by the end of the century.

10. Raman, 143, 139.
11. Bks. 3–5 deal almost exclusively with events up to January 1621 but include a translation of a Dutch propaganda pamphlet published in 1622 and two English replies to it (bk. 5, chap. 12). Purchas took care, however, to insert an account of subsequent events, leading up to Amboyna in a later section (pt. 1, bk. 10, chap. 16).
12. Purchas formally divided his text into two equal parts, dealing with the "Old" and "New" worlds—but since his "New World" includes China, Japan, and other formerly "unknown" parts of East Asia, the space devoted to America is relatively slight, amounting to about a quarter of the whole and consigned to the final section of the book.
13. James A. Boon, *Other Tribes, Other Scribes: Symbolic Anthropology in the Comparative Study of Cultures, Histories, Religions, and Texts* (Cambridge: Cambridge University Press, 1982), pp. 155–6.
14. McMullan also attributes a local orientation to *Hakluytus Posthumus* but (in line with the Atlantic bias of his approach to early modern expansionism) treats it as a work essentially concerned with New World plantation—a "lengthy commentary on the travels of the colonists" (p. 199).
15. Philip Lawson, *The East India Company: A History* (London: Longman, 1993), p. 30
16. Samuel Purchas, *Hakluytus Posthumus or Purchas his Pilgrimes*, 20 vols. (Glasgow: James MacLehose and Sons, 1905–7), vol. 1, pt. 1, bk. 1, chap. 1, sects. 1, 2, 3, and chap. 2, sect. 1.
17. Ibid., vol. 1, pt. 1, bk. 1, chap. 1, p. 10.
18. Ibid., vol. 2, pt. 1, bk. 3, chap. 1, p. 322; cf. also Samuel Purchas, *Purchas his Pilgrimage* (1617), p. 696.
19. It is true that in the final part of *Hakluytus Posthumus*, the angry response to the massacre of 1622 entitled "Virginia's Verger," Purchas offers a very different view of colonial expropriation, arguing that since "Virginia [has been] violently ravished by her own ruder natives," these "unnatural naturals" have forfeited their rights to her soil by their "disloyal treason." Nevertheless "King Salomons Navie," in arguing for the superior morality of trade, enjoys the rhetorical advantage of setting an argumentative context that treats the property rights of infidels as (albeit inferior to the rights of Christians) fundamentally inalienable (pp. 9–13, 38–45).
20. Purchas, *Hakluytus Posthumus*, "King Salomons Navie," p. 56.

21. Ibid., vol. 1, pt. 1, bk. 1, chap. 2–bk. 2, chap. 5.

22. The insistence on English priority is a recurrent theme of company propaganda and surfaces again in Dryden's *Amboyna* (1673), a lurid dramatization of the massacre designed to inflame public opinion in favor of the Second Dutch War. Here the Dutch merchant Van Herring is made to confess that the English "were first discoverers of this isle, first traded hither, and showed us the way" (1.1. p. 15).

Friction with the Portuguese continued but on a much smaller scale and mainly on the Indian subcontinent, so that Fletcher's romanticization of the period of Portuguese domination would not have seemed especially contentious—especially in court circles. For a lively and concise account of the struggle with the Dutch, see John Keay, *The Honourable Company: A History of the East India Company* (New York: Macmillan, 1991), chap. 2, pp. 24–51.

23. Purchas substituted, for example, a version of Edmund Scott's *Exact Discourse* that was much more fiercely hostile to the Dutch than the readily available pamphlet printed in 1606. Purchas's vision, in Boon's words is of "a royal British order, [excluding both] Catholics and Dutch Protestants alike, which tied exotic courts to the monarch, over and above any companies, parliaments, or other forces of interest" (p. 157)—though *Hakluytus Posthumus* characteristically strives to elide together the interests of monarch, nation, and company.

For annotations about the Dutch, see, e.g., vol. 2, pt. 1, bk. 3, chap. 1, p. 313; chap. 6, p. 535; vol. 3, pt. 1, bk. 3, chap. 9, pp. 93, 108, 109; bk. 4, chap. 1, p. 433; vol. 4, pt. 1, bk. 4, chap. 15, p. 303; bk. 5, chap. 3, pp. 510, 525, 527; vol. 5, pt. 1, bk. 5, chap. 7, p. 8; chap. 9, pp. 90, 97, 100; chap. 10, p. 135; vol. 6, pt. 1, bk. 5, chap. 12, p. 167; and chap. 15, pp. 210, 223.

The quotation is from vol. 5, pt. 1, bk. 5, chap. 9, p. 92.

24. Thomas Spurway for example recounts Dutch boasts after the conflict at Banda in 1617: "Also may it please your Worships to understand, that the Hollanders having been by some of our people, told of their vile abuses done unto us, and that it will lie heavy upon them at home, being known; the better sort of them have replied, that they can make as good friends in the Court of England as you (the Honourable Company our Employers) can" (cited in Purchas, *Hakluytus Posthumus*, vol. 4, pt. 1, bk. 5, chap. 3, p. 531).

25. See Lawson, pp. 20–3. This argument was pursued with particular vigor because the company, finding little demand for English goods in the East, had secured a special dispensation to export bullion. Cf. also *Calendar of State Papers (Colonial)*, entries for 14 June 1621, nos. 1022–5, esp. no. 1023: "Reasons to prove that the trade from England unto the East Indies doth not consume but rather increase the treasure of this kingdom."

26. In February 1615 the company persuaded the Archbishop of Canterbury to suppress the pamphlet; it then took advice from the attorney general, in whose opinion Kayll had come close to treason, and considered Star Chamber proceedings.

488 12 · "MATERIAL FLAMES"

Finally on 4 April, Kayll was summoned for questioning by the Privy Council and temporarily committed to the Fleet prison, from which he secured his release on 17 April. See John B. Hattendorf's introduction to Tobias Gentleman, *Englands Way to Win Wealth, and to Employ Ships and Marriners* (1614), with Robert Kayll, *The Trades Increase* (1615), and Edward Sharpe, *Britaine's Busse* (1615) (New York: Scholar's Facsimiles and Reprints, 1922), pp. 15–16.

Dudley Digges, *The Defence of Trade* (London, 1615), p. 1.

27. Purchas, *Hakluytus Posthumus*, vol. 5, pt. 1, bk. 5, chap. 17. In Purchas, Mun is introduced as "one of the Society" (i.e., a member of the East India Company). On the effective propaganda war conducted by Digges and Mun, see Lawson, pp. 35–7.

28. See *Calendar of State Papers (Colonial)*, entries for 14 June 1621, no. 1025: "Reasons against dissolving the East India Joint Stock and deserting that trade, showing the loss the king and kingdom would sustain in doing so."

29. Richard Hakluyt, *The Principal Navigations, Voyages, Traffiques, and Discoveries of the English Nation*, 12 vols. (1598–1600; rpt. Glasgow: J. MacLehose, 1903–5), 11:125.

30. In 1605 the king wrote to James I, recalling his predecessor's dispatch of a "token of remembrance" to Queen Elizabeth and feeling out the possibility of using the English as a counterbalance against the newly ascendant Dutch. In his letter the king accused the Dutch of having dishonestly persuaded him that the English "came not as peaceable Merchants, but to dispossess us of our kingdom" (Purchas, *Hakluytus Posthumus*, vol. 5, pt. 1, bk. 5, chap. 14, p. 191).

Purchas, *Hakluytus Posthumus*, vol. 5, pt. 1, bk. 5, chap. 9, p. 87; vol. 4, pt. 1, bk. 5, chap. 3, p. 511; vol. 5, pt. 1, bk. 5, chap. 15, p. 193; vol. 5, pt. 1, bk. 5, chap. 9, p. 106; chap. 12, pp. 147, 156–60; vol. 5, pt. 1, bk. 5, chap. 9, p. 109.

31. *A True Relation of the Vnivst, Crvell, and Barbarovs Proceedings against the English at Amboyna. . . . Also the copie of a Pamphlet, set forth first in Dutch . . . falsly entituled, A True Declaration of the Newes that came out of the East-Indies . . . which arrived at Texel in June, 1624. Together with an Answer to the same Pamphlet. By the English East-India Companie* (London, 1624), sig. A4v. The author of this pamphlet claims that its publication has been delayed out of a desire to preserve "the ancient amity and good correspondence held between this realm and the Netherlands" (A1), insisting that the company has at all times gone out of its way to respond peaceably to Dutch provocation. Both before and after the 1619 Treaty "the English Company from time to time contented themselves with informing His Majesty and his honourable Privy Council with their grievances privately in writing, to the end that necessary relief and reparation might be obtained, without publishing any thing to the world in print, thereby to stir up or breed ill blood between these nations which are otherwise tied in so many reciprocal obligations" (A2-A2v).

32. Purchas, *Hakluytus Posthumus*, vol. 5, pt. 1, bk. 5, chap. 10, p. 133.

33. *Calendar of State Papers (Colonial)*, no. 1180 for 1621.

34. Boon, p. 157.

35. Traces of Salama's assumption of the Tidorian throne remain in the governor's hints that Armusia seeks the princess's hand only because she is heir to the kingdom and in Pyniero's wish that the children of Quisara and Armusia's union will be "Kings at least" (4.1.63; 5.5.71).

36. See Patricia Parker, "Rhetorics of Property," in her *Literary Fat Ladies: Gender, Order, Rule* (London: Methuen, 1987), esp. pp. 139–54; and Montrose "The Work of Gender."

37. Boon, p. 176.

38. Purchas, *Hakluytus Posthumus*, vol. 19 , pt. 2, bk. 9, chap. 20, p. 229; vol. 5, pt. 1, bk. 5, chap. 15, p. 237.

39. Cited from Purchas, *Hakluytus Posthumus*, vol. 5, pt. 1, bk. 5, chap. 13. pp. 176–7, "A pithie Description of the chiefe Ilands of Banda and Moluccas, By Captaine Humphrey Fitz-herbert in a Letter to the Companie" (1621).

40. Dryden, *Amboyna*, 4.2–3. Ysabinda's rape is oddly prefigured in the episode that Towerson perceives as a "heavy omen to my nuptials" (3.3. p. 53) in which Captain Middleton brings on an Englishwoman "all pale and weakly, and in tattered garments" who has been barbarously mistreated by the Hollanders; the parallel appears to invite a construal of Ysabinda's rape as an act of national violation.

41. Purchas, *Hakluytus Posthumus*, vol. 5, pt. 1, bk. 5, chap. 13, p. 177. For a reading of the play that explores how "reproductive [hetero]sexuality sustains the ideology of masculine colonial domination," see Mario DiGangi, *The Homoerotics of Early Modern Drama* (Cambridge: Cambridge University Press, 1997), pp. 155–60 (p. 156).

42. On the trope of *opening, unfolding, discovering* (or "disclosing") see Parker, "Rhetorics of Property," pp. 140–6. The bawdy sense of *pride* as "sexual desire" is clearly involved here (*OED* n. 11). On the function of *enargeia/evidentia* as "a substitute for direct ocular experience for those who could not be present to see with their own eyes," see Parker, *Fat Ladies*, pp. 138–40; Parker associates the technique with the role of the *nuntius*, or messenger, but (as the choruses to *Henry V* repeatedly remind us) it is also the principal means by which the theater works on the imagination of the audience to transform the abstract space of the stage into a "local habitation" for the exotic.

43. "Here whole shires of fruitful grounds, lying now waste for want of people, do prostitute themselves unto us, like a fair and beautiful woman, in the pride and flower of desired years" (Lawrence Keymis, *A Relation of the Second Voyage*, in Hakluyt, *Principal Navigations*, p. 487; cited in Montrose, 18).

44. It is surely no coincidence that when Dryden revisited this struggle half a cen-

tury later in *Amboyna*, he did it with a partial reworking of Fletcher's story of the Indian bride.

45. Raman also notes the parallel between the "stranger" Armusia and belated English enterprise, but understands it in terms of Drake's intrusion into Portuguese colonial territory (pp. 137–9).

46. On company propaganda denigrating the Dutch, see, e.g., Thomas Spurway's letter of 1617 reporting English negotiations at Poolaroon, where they assure the Bandanese that "we desired not to usurp, and bring them in subjection, or bondage, as the Hollanders, and other nations have formerly," Purchas, *Hakluytus Posthumus*, vol. 4, pt. 1, bk. 5, chap. 3, p. 511.

47. This confusion is referred to in a succession of documents in Purchas, *Hakluytus Posthumus* documents—see, e.g., vol. 5, pt. 1, bk. 5, chap. 12, "An Answere to the Hollanders Declaration," where the company pamphleteer claims that "the Hollanders robbed and spoiled other nations under the English colours, pretending (to disgrace the English) that they were Englishmen, counterfeiting the Coin of other Nations, charging the English with the same" (p. 161). The issue is treated at length in Edmund Scott's pamphlet; see chap. 11.

48. Edmund Scott, *An Exact Discourse of the Subtleties, Fashions, Religion, and Ceremonies of the East Indians* (1606), H3.

49. "The Journall of Master Nathaniel Courthop" (1616–20) in Purchas, *Hakluytus Posthumus*, vol. 5, pt. 1, bk. 5, chap.9, p. 108.

50. *A True Relation of the Vnivst, Crvell, and Barbarovs Proceedings against the English at Amboyna* . . . sig. A3v-A4. Cf. also the claims of Thomas Spurway, quoted in nn. 24 and 46 this chap. In Purchas, *Hakluytus Posthumus*, material on "the Dutch Navigations to the East Indies" (vol. 5, pt. 1, bk. 5, chap. 15, p. 197) quotes the Portuguese warning to the rulers of Java and Bantam that the Dutch "were not merchants but pirates, and if they had access now in ten or twelve years they would return and subdue their country: and this spark, if now unquenched would set the whole East on fire."

51. Raman discusses the significance of Armusia's merchant guise in similar terms but relates it to tensions inside the East India Company between the dominant merchant faction and resentful gentry. In the interests of reconciling these groups, Armusia reveals that "the merchant is really a knight in disguise. . . . In so doing [he] redefines . . . the notion of nobility, which he presents as an interleaving of mercantile and military" (pp. 144–5).

52. Scott, I3v.

53. The governor's disguise may have been suggested by a historical detail (preserved in the 1617 edition of Purchas's *Pilgrimage*) from Achen in Sumatra where "they had one Prophet, disguised in his apparel, whom they much honoured" (p. 695). For the important but ambiguous role played by "toys" and "trifles" in the English discourse of trade, see Knapp, pp. 3, 76, 120–1. The governor's disdain

may also reflect the fact that (not surprisingly) the English experienced particular difficulty in the vending of their principal export, woolen cloth, in the tropical East Indies.

54. See also 4.2.155–9.

55. Dryden employs a similar device in *Amboyna*, where the suspicion that English motives are all too like those of the Dutch (whose "religion . . . is only made up of interest" [2.1. p. 38]) is disarmed by being put into the mouth of the villainous Harman Senior: "interest is their god as well as ours. To that almighty will they sacrifice a thousand English lives, and break a hundred thousand oaths" (1.1. p. 16).

56. Letter to James I, quoted by Fitzherbert in Purchas, *Hakluytus Posthumus*, vol. 5, pt. 1, bk. 5, chap. 14, p. 191.

57. See chap. 10.

58. Le Seigneur de Bellan, *L'Histoire de Ruis Dias, et de Quixaire, Princess des Moloques* (1615), p. 338. Cf. Thomas Candish [Cavendish] in Purchas, *Hakluytus Posthumus*, vol. 2, pt. 1, bk. 2, chap. 2, p. 181. For a searching examination of early modern ideas of "color," see Kim F. Hall, *Things of Darkness* (Ithaca: Cornell University Press, 1995).

59. Compare Ysabinda's fear that the pollution of her "black and fatal" rape will turn her into "A black adulteress" in Towerson's eyes (4.3. p. 65).

60. Purchas, *Hakluytus Posthumus*, vol. 1, pt. 1, bk. 1, chap. 1, p. 55. In *Amboyna*, Towerson dissociates himself from the "endless jars of trading nations" and implicitly identifies his nation with "those who can be pleased with moderate gain" (1.1. p. 22).

61. Boon, p. 158.

62. de Bellan, p. 339.

63. Writing of this episode, Gordon McMullan discovers a "scene of highly inflammable native houses succumbing to fire ignited by Europeans [that] rehearses familiar colonists' narratives" and cites the wanton burning of a West African village in one of Hakluyt's narratives (p. 231 and p. 309n. 64). But once again this is a detail that seems to invite a more local reading.

64. See chap. 11.

65. Scott, sig. E-F4v.

66. Compare Anthony Nixon's account of Robert Sherley's triumphal display of the heads of thirty captured Turkish captains "according to the custom of Persia," in which (as Anthony Parr writes) "the implication is not that Robert has 'turned Turk' in a savage land but that he has legitimized Persian custom by making it a tool of Christian retribution"; see Anthony Parr, "The Sherley Brothers and the 'Voyage of Persia,' " in Jean-Pierre Maquerlot and Michele Willems, eds., *Travel and Drama in Shakespeare's Time* (Cambridge: Cambridge University Press, 1996), pp. 14–31 (p. 25).

67. The Citizen's taste for huge quantities of drink and for smoked herrings sounds like a piece of incidental anti-Dutch satire, like the naming of Dryden's Dutch merchant, Van Herring.

68. The direction in *2 Tamburlaine* for a display of "The town burning" during Zenocrate's funeral at the beginning of act 3, scene 2 suggests that such displays were part of the theater's standard repertory of effects. As *Tamburlaine*'s Mermaid editor comments: "Perhaps fireworks were used to simulate flames or to produce realistic smoke (as they had been in medieval drama), perhaps a symbolic backdrop was hoisted up or fiery streamers hung from the tiring house wall, or perhaps, if it could be managed, an emblematic structure of some kind representing a city . . . was actually burned. Such spectacular effects were not unknown during the 16th and 17th centuries"; see Christopher Marlowe, *Tamburlaine, Parts One and Two*, ed. Anthony B. Dawson (London: A. and C. Black, 1996), p. 124.

69. On Scott's obsession with fire, see chap. 11.

70. See Boon, p. 177: "Whitehall rhetorically courted Indic realms as trading partners, all the while desiring commercial concubines."

13 · BROKEN ENGLISH AND BROKEN IRISH

1. The five epigraphs are quoted from the following sources: *Illustrations of Irish History and Topography, Mainly of the Seventeenth Century*, ed. C. Litton Falkiner (London: Longmans, Green, 1904), p. 272; G. Blakemore Evans, ed., *The Riverside Shakespeare* (Boston: Houghton Mifflin, 1974); Sir John Davies, *A Discovery of the True Causes why Ireland Was never entirely Subdued* (1612), pp. 4–5; and Peter Lombard, *The Irish War of Defense, 1598–1600*, ed. and trans. Matthew J. Byrne (Dublin: Cork University Press, 1930), pp. 15–17. Quotations of Fynes Moryson have all been drawn from Falkiner, who reprints three sections of Moryson's *Itinerary*: "The Description of Ireland," pp. 214–32; "The Commonwealth of Ireland," pp. 233–309; and "The Manners and Customs of Ireland," pp. 310–25. Only the first of these was included in the 1617 edition of Moryson's travelogue; the latter two did not appear in print until 1903. Citations elsewhere in this chapter are to these texts; the emphasis (unless otherwise indicated) is my own.

   Ngũgĩ wa Thiong'o, *Decolonising the Mind* (London: James Currey, 1986), p. 1.

2. For a scientifically well-informed and philosophically acute account of the biological vacuousness of "race" and racialist doctrine, see Anthony Appiah, "Illusions of Race," in Appiah, *In My Father's House* (New York: Oxford University Press, 1992), pp. 28–46.

   On the fictive character of the "nation," see Benedict Anderson, *Imagined Communities* (London: Verso, 1991). Anderson's is probably the best recent account of the genesis of the national idea, though by its insistence on nationalism as a post-Enlightenment phenomenon it seriously underestimates the development of nationalist ideology in early modern England.

For a useful discussion of protonationalist sentiment in late sixteenth- and early seventeenth-century Irish texts, see Bernadette Cunningham, "Native Culture and Political Change in Ireland, 1580–1640" in Ciaran Brady and Raymond Gillespie, eds., *Natives and Newcomers: Essays on the Making of Irish Colonial Society, 1534–1641* (Dublin: Irish Academic Press, 1986), pp. 148–70.

3. See, e.g., David Cairns and Shaun Richards, *Writing Ireland: Colonialism, Nationalism, and Culture* (Manchester: Manchester University Press, 1988), and the important symposium published by the Field Day Theatre Company, *Ireland's Field Day* (Dublin: Gill and Macmillan, 1985).

4. Four entries in the *OED* (occurring under *commonweal*, sb. 2, and *commonwealth*, sb. 2 and 3) suggest that a significant but fiercely contested shift in the meaning of the word *commonwealth* (or *commonweal*) was taking place in the sixteenth century. Lord Berners in 1534 can imagine it only as a name for the kind of state with which he is familiar—a polity "Of divers men, and one lord, is composed a commonwealth" (*OED commonwealth* sb. 2); by contrast Sir Thomas Elyot (in *The Boke named the Governour*, 1531) is at pains to distinguish the "commonweal" from the state proper: "There may appear like diversity to be in English between a public weal and a commonweal, as should be in Latin between *Res publica* and *Res plebeia*." By 1577 Sir Thomas Smith (*The common-welth of England*, pub. 1589) offers a definition that already begins to look forward to the political language of the English Revolution: "a society . . . of a multitude of free men, collected together and united by a common accord and covenants among themselves"; while for Raleigh (*Maxims of State*, 1616) it defines an unambiguously republican or democratic society: "A commonwealth is the swerving or depravation of a free, or popular state, or the government of the whole multitude of the base and poorer sort, without respect of the other orders."

5. On the supposed Spanish origins of the Irish, see, e.g., Edmund Spenser, *A View of the Present State of Ireland*, ed. W. L. Renwick (London: Eric Partridge, 1934), pp. 56–9; William Camden, *Britain, or A chorographicall description of England, Scotland, and Ireland* [i.e., Britannia] (London: 1610), p. 64.

6. See Nicholas Canny, "Ireland as *Terra Florida*" and "The Theory and Practice of Acculturation: Ireland in a Colonial Context," both in his *Kingdom and Colony: Ireland in the Atlantic World, 1560–1800* (Baltimore: Johns Hopkins University Press, 1988), pp. 1–29, 31–68; Canny, *The Elizabethan Conquest of Ireland: A Pattern Established* (New York: Barnes and Noble, 1976), pp. 122–33; and David Stannard, *American Holocaust: Columbus and the Conquest of the New World* (New York: Oxford University Press, 1992), pp. 98–99, 223–5.

7. Ann Rosalind Jones and Peter Stallybrass, "Dismantling Irena: The Sexualizing of Ireland in Early Modern England," in Andrew Parker et al., eds., *Nationalisms and Sexualities* (New York: Routledge, 1992), pp. 157–71 (p. 158).

8. Richard Beacon, *Solon his Folly, or A Politic Discourse, touching the Reformation of commonweals conquered, declined or corrupted* (Oxford, 1594), p. 94; Spenser, *View*, p. 197. On the distinction between "the King's Irish subjects" and "the King's Irish enemies," see, e.g., Davies, pp. 102–13.

   For a seventeenth-century discussion of the significance of the 1541 act, see Davies, pp. 242–7. See also Ciaran Brady, "Court, Castle, and Country: The Framework of Government in Tudor Ireland," in Brady and Gillespie, pp. 27–30; Canny, "Identity Formation in Ireland: The Emergence of the Anglo-Irish," in Nicholas Canny and Anthony Pagden, eds., *Colonial Identity in the Atlantic World* (Princeton, N.J.: Princeton University Press, 1987), pp. 161–2. Davies (pp. 211–4) cites the Statutes of Kilkenny and Statute 10 of Henry VII that classified mixed marriages and fostering as "high treason," arguing that "as long as these laws were put in [use] and execution, this land continued in prosperity and honour" (p. 214).

9. See, e.g., Caxton, *The Description of Britain: A Modern Rendering*, ed. Marie Collins (New York: Weidenfeld and Nicholson, 1988): "Note, what with all these and other marvels and wonders, that new ones often occur at the outermost limits of the world, as if Nature were amusing herself in private with greater license in the most distant regions, than in public near the centre of the world" (p. 162).

10. Caxton, pp. 151, 161. Cf. also Barnabe Rich, *A New Description of Ireland* (London, 1610), pp. 6, 25. For a discussion of the trope of Ireland as Earthly Paradise, see Jonathan Gil Harris, "Food beyond the Pale: Ireland, Forbidden Fruit, and the Ravenous Body Politic," in "The Incontinent Body Politic: Authority and the Boundaries of Organic Political Metaphor in the English Renaissance," Ph.D diss., University of Sussex, 1990, pp. 53–104.

11. Moryson, "Commonwealth," p.263; cf. Moryson, "Manners and Customs," p.322.

12. Spenser, *View*, p. 208.

13. Caxton, p. 161. John Derricke, *The Image of Irelande with a Discoverie of Woodkarne*, ed. D. B. Quinn (Dublin: Blackstaff Press, 1985), pp. 9, 11, 183, 188, 191, 192, 197, 200–3. Spenser cites Camden's view that stories of Irish werewolves merely demonstrate the prevalence of lycanthropy among the Irish, but at the same time avers that "some of the Irish do use to make the wolf their gossip" (p. 77).

   "An Account of a Journey of Captain Josias Bodley into Lecale, in Ulster, in the year 1602–3," in Falkiner, pp. 328–44 (p. 329).

14. Moryson, "Manners and Customs," p. 317.

15. Spenser, *View*, pp. 72, 70. Cf. also Barnabe Rich, p. 8. Apparently deriving from the Irish war cry *abu*, the term was subsequently applied to the incomprehensible shouts of both Africans and Amerindians (*OED hubbub*). The *OED* cites W. Watreman's *Fardle Facions* (1555): "[The Icthiophagi of Afrike] flocke together

to go drincke . . . shouting as they go with an yrishe whobub"; and Spelman's *Relation of Virginia* in John Smith's *Workes*, 1613) on an Indian "whopubb."

16. Moryson, "Commonwealth," pp. 247–8. Cf. also Spenser, *View*, p. 95. Ben Jonson's *Irish Masque at Court* offers a flattering variation on the trope of Irish bard-as-anarch, in the form of a reformed bard, loyal to James I, whose closing song literally reduces the wild Irish dancers to civility by conjuring away their barbarous mantles to "discover their [courtly] masquing apparel" (*Ben Jonson: The Complete Works*, ed. C. H. Herford, Percy Simpson, and Evelyn Simpson, 11 vols. [Clarendon Press: Oxford, 1925–52]), 7:404–5.

17. Moryson, "Commonwealth," pp. 223, 273.

18. Davies, p.168; Spenser, *View*, pp. 5, 44. Cf. the characterization of Talus, the agent of Justice, in bk. 5 of Spenser's *Faerie Queene*, as *"immoveable*, resistless, without end,"* bk. 5, canto 1, st. 12, l. 7 (*The Poetical Works of Edmund Spenser*, ed. J. C. Smith and E. de Selincourt [London: Oxford University Press, 1959]); and the well-known woodcut from John Case's *Sphaera Civitatis* (1588), which shows *Iustitia Immobilis* as the axletree of Elizabeth's concentric political universe (see fig. 16).

19. Spenser, *View*, pp. 86, 82; Davies, pp. 182, 212–3; Derricke, *Image*, p. 11. Indeed Derricke even argues that the Irish, whom he repeatedly calls "monsters," are worse than the wildest beasts since beasts at least can be tamed, whereas the Irish will invariably revert to their wildness: "Yea though they were in court trained up, / and years there lived ten, / Yet do they look to shaking bogs, / scarce proving honest men. / And whenas they have gained the bogs, / such virtue hath that ground, / That they are worse than wildest kern, / And more in sin abound" (p. 187). Richard Stanihurst, "The Description of Ireland" in Raphael Holinshed, *The Second Volume of Chronicles: containing the Description, Conquest, Inhabitation, and Troblesome Estate Of Ireland* (London: 1586), vol. 6, *Holinshed's Chronicles*, intro. Vernon Snow (New York: AMS, 1965), p. 69. The second volume was first published in the 1587 edition, though its own title page bears the date 1586.

20. Derricke, p. 183.

21. Moryson, "Manners and Customs," p. 310. Spenser's *View* similarly begins by addressing the possibility that the problems of Ireland "proceed from the very *Genius* of the soil . . . or that [God] reserveth her in this unquiet state still, for some secret scourge which shall by her come unto England" (p. 3); Lodowick Bryskett (1582) was of the opinion that "the secret judgement of God hangeth over this soil, that causeth all the best endeavours of those that labour the reformation thereof to come to naught" (cited in the commentary to *View*, p. 252).

Spenser, *View*, p. 196. Spenser is particularly offended by the Irish love of "liberty and natural freedom, which in their madness they affect" (p. 17). Fynes Moryson ("Commonwealth," pp. 260–2) lists five causes of the Old English "alienation from us and application to the mere Irish":

1. Roman Religion ("the grand cause")
2. Profit from the "barbarous laws and customs of the Irish, by tyrannical oppression of the poor people under them" (described as a "predominant [cause] though in lower degree")
3. Marriage and fostering with the Irish
4. "Community of apparel"
5. "Community of language"

Moryson is especially concerned to stress "the [well-known] power of these three last causes to corrupt the manners and faith of any nation. . . . These outward signs being the touchstones of inward affection" ("Commonwealth," pp. 260–2).

22. The author (or authors) of this anonymous work seems to have had some Irish experience since a number of the Irish scenes are written in brogue interlaced with reasonably accurate Gaelic. But the representation of the Irish as "savage slaves" and "naked savages" is unremittingly propagandist. A familiar sign of their barbarity is their appetite for decapitating their enemies—though this was of course routinely practiced by the English, not least in Ireland. Indeed the only heads actually displayed in the play prove to be those of the Irish rebel Shane O'Neill and his secretary, but responsibility for this English barbarism is characteristically displaced onto the Irish auxiliaries Alexander Oge and Mack Gilliam Busk. For a disturbing account of English practice see Thomas Churchyard, *Churchyarde's Choice, a General Rehearsal of Wars* (London, 1579), cited in Canny, *The Elizabethan Conquest of Ireland*, p. 122. Churchyard describes how Sir Humphrey Gilbert used to line up "the heads of all those . . . which were killed in the day [to create] a lane of heads which he used *ad terrorem*, the dead feeling nothing the more pains thereby; and yet did it bring great terror to the people when they saw the heads of their dead fathers, brothers, children, kinsfolk and friends lie on the ground before their faces, as they came to speak with the said colonel." Yet Moryson denounces the Irish for "mangling the bodies of their dead enemies, but never believing them to be fully dead till they have cut off their heads" ("Commonwealth," p. 288).

23. On the money expended, see Joel B. Altman, " 'Vile Participation': The Amplification of Violence in the Theater of *Henry V*," *Shakespeare Quarterly* 42 (1991): 1–32 (8–13); Altman (p. 8) cites figures that show Elizabeth expending nearly 2 million pounds on her ten-year campaign against Tyrone (1593–1603)— more than she spent on nearly twenty years of fighting in France and the Low Countries (1585–1603).

Edward Said, *Culture and Imperialism* (New York: Alfred A. Knopf, 1993), p. 66; Altman, passim; David J. Baker, " 'Wildehirissheman': Colonialist Representation in Shakespeare's *Henry V*," *English Literary Renaissance* 22

(1992): 37–61; Christopher Highley, "Wales, Ireland, and *1 Henry IV*," *Ren.D.* n.s. 21 (1990): 91–114.

24. Compare the sardonic punning of Antonio and Sebastian on Gonzalo's projected "plantation of this isle" in *The Tempest*: "He'd sow't with nettle-seed . . . Or docks, or mallows" (2.1.144–5).

25. For a list of the many details that reveal Shakespeare's "preoccupation with Irish affairs" in *Henry V*, see Gary Taylor, ed., *Henry V* (Oxford: Oxford University Press, 1984), p. 8. For further useful discussion of the play's bearing on Irish affairs, see Philip Edwards, *Threshold of a Nation* (Cambridge: Cambridge University Press, 1979), pp. 75–8; and Jonathan Dollimore and Alan Sinfield, "History and Ideology: The Instance of *Henry V*," in John Drakakis, ed., *Alternative Shakespeares* (Methuen: London, 1985), pp. 206–27.

Burgundy's description of the unkempt French hedgerows resembling "prisoners wildly overgrown with hair" (l. 43) may even deliberately recall contemporary illustrations of "wild Irish" captives with their notoriously shaggy forelocks (or "glibs"), discussed in more detail later in this chapter.

26. On the wandering, uncentered life of the Irish, see Spenser, *View*, pp. 67–9, 206, and Davies, pp. 117–8, 160–1, 170–1; Moryson, "Description," pp. 222, 231; and Holinshed, "The Description of Ireland," p. 68. Beacon argues the desirability of instituting in Ireland a law such as that imposed by the Romans on the conquered Macedonians, prescribing capital punishment for "such as should wander and travel from province to province, or should change their habitation, or contract affinities, or use merchandise with those of other provinces." (pp. 95–6). For discussion of the Elizabethan association of Irish placelessness with the notorious wandering habits of "masterless men" thought to be so destabilizing to the English Commonweal, see D. B. Quinn, *The Elizabethans and the Irish* (Ithaca: Cornell University Press, 1966), pp. 32, 126, and Mihoko Suzuki, "Gender, Class, and the Social Order in Late Elizabethan Drama," *Theatre Journal* 44 (1992): 31–45 (33 n. 7).

The quotation is from Davies, p. 120. Davies seems to have believed, following the teachings of Machiavelli, that confirmation of individual property rights by the English law would distract the Irish people from rebellious notions—a view that had been even more bluntly articulated by another lawyer, Richard Beacon, in *Solon his Folly* (1594), for whom the best way of suppressing the Irish "desire [of their] former liberty" was to satisfy their wish "to possess that which is their own freely and securely; so as, enjoying the same, they have attained the end of their desires, and rest for the most part contented with the government" (p. 79). For the influence of Machiavelli on Irish policy, see Tony Grafton and Lisa Jardine, " 'Studied for Action': How Gabriel Harvey Read his Livy," *Past and Present* 129 (1990): 30–78.

27. Spenser, *View*, p. 171; Davies, pp. 169–70.

28. On the English penchant for reducing wilderness, see, e.g., Spenser, *View*, p.166–7; Davies, pp. 122–3, 163–5, 170–1. Gerald Boate, *Ireland's Natural History* (London, 1652), pp. 89–98, cited in Canny, "Identity Formation in Ireland," p. 195.

29. It is conceivable that the play's Irish dimension may have been one of the things that commended it to the Essex plotters in 1601. Given Essex's conviction that his failure in Ireland was due to the parsimony of the queen's support, a play that featured the deposition of a monarch after a mistaken venture in Ireland may have seemed especially germane to their cause.

30. Degeneration, Spenser argues, reveals the "bad minds of them who having been brought up at home under a strait rule of duty and obedience . . . so soon as they come thither, where they see law so slackly tended . . . they grow more loose and careless of their duty, *as it is the nature of all men to love liberty*, so they become flat libertines and fall to flat licentiousness" (p. 196); once outside the pale of culture, it is plain, anyone may discover himself a wood-kern under the skin.

31. See Thomas Heywood's *Apology for Actors* (London, 1612); and Robert Cawdrey's epistle "To the Reader" of his pioneering English dictionary, *A Table Alphabetical* (London, 1604), which urges the need to avoid "outlandish English" and "foreign apparel" and to "use altogether one manner of language" in the interests of national unity.

32. From the dedicatoria to Elio Antonio de Nebrija, *Gramatica Castellana* (Salamanca, 1492); I am grateful to Ivan Illich for generously supplying me with a copy of his MS translation.

33. Ibid. On the role of language in colonization see Stephen Greenblatt, "Learning to Curse: Aspects of Linguistic Colonialism in the Sixteenth Century," in *Learning to Curse: Essays in Early Modern Culture* (New York: Routledge, 1990), pp. 16–39.

34. For a rich account of the role of cartography and chorography in shaping the national identity of early modern England, see Richard Helgerson, *Forms of Nationhood: The Elizabethan Writing of England* (Chicago and London: University of Chicago Press, 1992), chap. 3. Spenser's phrase appears in a 1580 letter to Gabriel Harvey and is quoted here from Helgerson. Helgerson's book also gives extensive attention to the promotion of vernacular literature and to theorizing of the Common Law as agencies of national self-consciousness; see his introduction pp. 1–18; chap. 1, pp. 19–62; and chap. 2, pp. 63–104.

35. George Puttenham, *The Arte of English Poesie*, ed. Gladys Doidge Willcock and Alice Walker (Cambridge: Cambridge University Press, 1936), p. 144.

36. For an argument that persuasively associates Tyrone and Glendower and gives evidence of suspected Welsh support for Tyrone's rising at the time the play was first performed, see Highley.

37. The symbolic parallel is explored by Highley, pp. 104–5. Highley remarks that "since England's Celtic borderlands could be cognitively mapped along one axis

as symbolically continuous and interchangeable, it follows that in their wider provenance the castrating energies of . . . Shakespeare's Welshwomen evoke the dangers of Celtic women generally" (pp. 101–2)

38. See Jones and Stallybrass, in Parker, pp. 163–4.

39. Spenser, *View*, pp. 86, 84, 88–9.

40. Ibid., p. 197; Davies, p. 278.

41. Davies, pp. 281–2, 272.

42. Taylor, in the commentary to his edition of *Henry V* (p. 109), cites the relevant passage from Cicero's *De Republica* (2.43).

43. Heywood, *An Apology for Actors* (London, 1612), F3. Henry's metadramatic anticipation of a "history" that "with full mouth [shall] / Speak freely of our acts," overwhelming the "tongueless mouth" of oblivion, emphasizes how closely the project of nation-building, for Shakespeare, as for Nebrija and Heywood, is entwined with that of forging a language.

It seems likely, as Hiram Morgan has pointed out to me, that the hybrid character of Macmorris was suggested by that of the Norman invader Maurice Fitzgerald, whose oration during the siege of Dublin, as recorded by Giraldus Cambrensis, contains the angry reflection that "as we be odious and hateful to the Irishmen, even so we now are reputed: for Irishmen are become hateful to our own nation [ut sic ut Hibernicis Angli, sic et Anglis Hbernici sumus], and so are we odious both to the one and to the other" (John Hooker's translation in Holinshed, *Second Volume of Chronicles*, p. 152). The name had been brought into prominence again through the activities of James Fitzmaurice Fitzgerald, leader of the second Desmond rebellion, who returned to Ireland in 1579, armed with a papal bull of indulgence, to declare a holy war against Elizabeth; see Hiram Morgan, "Hugh O'Neill and the Nine Years War in Ireland," *Historical Journal* 36 (1993): 21–37 (23).

Philip Edwards has argued that far from objecting to an imagined slur on the Irish nation (as is usually supposed), Macmorris resents the imputation that he is a member of a separate Irish nation at all. It seems to me virtually impossible to determine exactly *what* he means and that his inarticulateness on the topic of nationality is precisely Shakespeare's point.

44. Caxton, p. 154.

45. See the essays by Altman and Baker. Altman even speaks of England's antagonists in the play as "French-cum-Irish" (p. 19). For an argument that the choruses were an addition to the play (made after the publication of the quarto text from which they are missing) and that Mountjoy, rather than Essex, is the subject of Shakespeare's encomium, see Warren D. Smith, "The *Henry V* Choruses in the First Folio," *JEGP* 53 (1954): 38–57. If Smith is right. then the prominence given to the French herald Montjoy must have developed an unexpected complimentary resonance in the revised version.

46. The French preoccupation with difference is equally apparent in the Dauphin's

anxiety that Frenchwomen "will give / Their bodies to the lust of English youth, / To new store France with bastard warriors" (3.5.29–31), in the extreme concern for hierarchy apparent in Montjoy's anxiety about the indifference of death, and his insistence on the need

> To sort our nobles from our common men—
> For many of our princes, woe the while,
> Lie drowned and soaked in mercenary blood,
> So do our vulgar drench their peasant limbs
> In blood of princes.
>
> 4.7.69–73

Even the Black Prince's conquests are punningly figured as a defacement of the proper "patterns" of Frenchness, derived from "God and . . . French fathers," by the "seed" of that "mountant sire" Edward III (2.4.57–61).

47. Davies, pp. 8–9.

48. The phrase "litany of dismemberment" is Altman's: he further notes how this episode "however charmingly presented as a language lesson, lingers in the imagination to foster ever-expanding fantasies of vulnerability and savage projection" (p. 18).

For a dazzling analysis of the ideological functioning of the virginity trope, see Louis A. Montrose, "The Work of Gender in the Discourse of Discovery," *Representations* 33 (winter 1991): 1–41.

49. Johnson cited from Arthur Sherbo, ed., *Johnson on Shakespeare*, Yale Edition of the Works of Samuel Johnson, 16 vols. (New Haven: Yale University Press, 1958–90), 8:565; Altman, 31.

50. Davies, p. 269. Writing two decades later, the Old English pamphleteer (and follower of Davies) John Cusacke spoke as though Davies's ideal were already an accomplished fact, urging Charles I to confirm its practice, so that "all the natives of Ireland may from their form of subjection to English government be by your Majesty declared to be Englishmen by their national appellation and Irishmen by their legal denomination as perfect members of the English colony in Ireland, and free denizens of England" (Folger MS G.A. 10, fol. 174). Cusacke's was, however, an eccentric and marginal voice. I am grateful to Linda Levy Peck for drawing this passage to my attention.

51. Luke Gernon, *A Discourse of Ireland*, in Falkiner, pp. 348–62 (pp. 348–9). For a parodic version of the woman's body as map, in which Ireland is revealingly associated with the hidden parts, see *The Comedy of Errors* (3.2.114–18) where Dromio describes Nell the kitchen maid as "spherical, like a globe; I could find out countries in her. . . . Ireland . . . sir, in her buttocks, I found it out by the bogs."

52. Davies, p. 177. Like Davies, Moryson associated the Irish with the tricksy slaves of Roman New Comedy, writing of them as "subtle temporisers" whose "shifting devices" recall "crafty Davus in the comedy" ("Manners and Customs," pp.

315–6). Davies's perception that such behavior was a direct consequence of their conquered state provides an interesting gloss not only on the Irishman-as-Davus but on the equivalent modern stereotype of the comic but fundamentally untrustworthy "paddy": "This oppression did of force and necessity make the Irish a crafty people; for such as are oppressed and live in slavery are ever put to their shifts. . . . And therefore in the old comedies of Plautus and Terence, the Bondslave doth always act the cunning and crafty part" (p. 177).

53. On Irish "slipperiness" and the "ability to disappear" associated with native costume, see Jones and Stallybrass, in Parker, pp. 165–6. "Rug-headed" is usually glossed as referring to the unkempt locks of the Irish, but "rug" (etymologically connected to "rough") is the usual English synonym for "mantle"—as, for example, in Jonson's *Irish Masque* (l. 146). See also Janet Arnold, "Jane Lambard's Mantle," *Costume* 14 (1986): 58–9.

54. Moryson, "Commonwealth," p. 261. Moryson is partly dependent on a passage in Spenser's *View*: "[The mantle] is a fit house for an outlaw, a meet bed for a rebel, and [an] apt cloak for a thief, [who] wandering in waste places far from the danger of law maketh his mantle his house" (p. 67). The closeness of his paraphrase makes it plain that he had read Spenser's tract (which was denied publication until 1633) in manuscript.

55. Spenser, *View*, pp. 66–8. This passage has been dismissed by the historian Ciaran Brady as "some curious, but I suspect not altogether serious remarks concerning the pernicious effects of native dress and hair-style"; see Ciaran Brady, "Spenser's Irish Crisis: Humanism and Experience in the 1590s," *Past and Present* 111 (1983): 17–49 (28), but the seriousness of such complaints is vouched for by repeated administrative attempts to suppress native costume. The surprising indifference of historians to such cultural material is indicated by the fact that mantles are not even indexed in the authoritative *New History of Ireland*, ed. T. W. Moody, F. X. Martin, and F. I. Byrne (Oxford: Clarendon Press, 1993).

56. Spenser, *View*, 69–70; entry in *Calendar of State Papers Ireland* (1589, 144.57.ii): "A note of such reasons as moved Sir W. Herbert to put the statute in execution against Irish habits."

57. Spenser, *Faerie Queene*, bk. 5, canto 9, st. 18, l. 5; Spenser, *View*, pp. 9, 171. The preoccupation with the optics of power apparent in Spenser and Davies is equally evident in the illustrative program of John Derricke's suggestively titled *A Notable Discouery . . . of the Wilde men in Ireland,properly called Woodkarne*, appended to his *Image of Ireland*. Woodcuts 1–5, showing the "actions . . . exercises . . . [and rebellion]" of the kern, and 11, showing the plight of the defeated Rory Og O'Moore, are executed in a rough, primitive style appropriate to their subject, while 6–10 and 12, celebrating the triumph of Sir Henry Sidney over the barbarians, make use of a much more sophisticated Renaissance idiom, the conspicuous symmetry and regularity of whose designs embody the reforming power of the colonizers' vision. Moryson, "Commonwealth," p. 237.

58. See also the striking anatomical metaphor that describes the method of Richard Beacon's *Solon his Follie*: "You have made a perfect anatomy of this word reformation, and not only with the cunning painter you have described the outward shows and lineaments, but, with the wise physician, you have well known, and laid open the inward parts thereof; but now disclose unto us, the secrets which lie hidden under the words subsequent, . . . namely of a declined commonweal" (p. 65).

59. On the practical and ideological significance of mapping in Irish conquest and colonization, see Bruce Avery, "Mapping the Irish Other: Spenser's *A View of the Present State of Ireland*," *ELH* 57 (1990): 263–79; and Mercedes Maroto Camino's trenchant critique of his arguments in "Methinks I See an Evil Lurking Unespied," *Spenser Studies* 12 (1998): 169–96; Spenser, *View*, p. 186.

60. Spenser, *Faerie Queene*, bk. 5, canto 12, st. 26, ll. 5–6; see also canto 1, st. 12, l. 9.

61. Davies, p. 163.

62. Ibid., p. 268.

63. Ibid., pp. 268–9.

64. David Lindley, "Embarrassing Ben: The Masques for Frances Howard," *English Literary Renaissance* 16 (1986): 343–59, suggests that this detail may even have been inspired by Davies's vision in *Discovery* (1612) of a civilized Irish nation "convert[ing] their mantles into cloaks"(p. 353). For further comment on the absurdity of this masque's "comfortable colonial optimism," see Lisa Jardine, " 'Mastering the Uncouth': Gabriel Harvey, Edmund Spenser, and the English Experience in Ireland," in J. Henry and S. Sutton, eds., *New Perspectives on Renaissance Thought: Essays in the History of Science, Education, and Philosophy in Memory of C. B. Schmitt* (London: Duckworth, 1990), pp. 68–82 (pp. 68–72).

65. Jonson, *Irish Masque*, pp. 404–5. The stage direction requiring the Gentlemen to "let fall their mantles" during this song points up the puns on "rough" and "rugged," while Jonson's reference to earth as bound in "rude winter" plays on Camden's claim that "Some derive *Hibernia* from *Hiberno tempore*, that is, from the Winter season"; see William Camden, *Britain* (London, 1610), p. 61.

66. See Lindley, 351–3. Ironically, even as the masque was performed, one of their number, Sir William Talbot, lay in the Fleet, awaiting his Star Chamber trial for refusing to declare for the king rather than the Pope (p. 352).

67. Davies, p. 269; Roy Strong, *The Cult of Elizabeth: Elizabethan Portraiture and Pageantry* (London: Thames and Hudson, 1977), p. 50; Janet Arnold, *Queen Elizabeth's Wardrobe Unlock'd* (Leeds: Maney, 1988), p. 81.

68. Arnold, *Queen Elizabeth's Wardrobe*, p. 81; see also Strong, p. 52. Frances Yates's otherwise useful iconographic analysis of the painting mistakenly interprets folds on the garment as mouths and accordingly misreads its "ears, eyes, and tongues" as symbols of Fame (Frances A. Yates, *Astraea: The Imperial Theme in the Sixteenth Century* [London: Routledge, 1975], p. 217.)

69. Cesare Ripa, *Iconologia*, cited in Arnold, *Queen Elizabeth's Wardrobe*, p. 81.

70. Arnold, *Queen Elizabeth's Wardrobe*, p. 82.

71. William Camden, *Britannia* (London, 1586), p. 490. Cf. Camden's 1610 translation: "This isle by Orpheus, Aristotle, and Claudian is named IERNA; by Juvenal and Mela IUVERNA; by Diodorus Siculus IRIS" (p. 61). The identification of Iris with an idealized Ireland is worth meditating in the context of her appearance in the marriage masque of *The Tempest*—especially since Paul Brown has noted analogies between Ireland and Prospero's island, highlighting resemblances between Caliban and the Wild Irish, in " 'This Thing of Darkness I Acknowledge Mine': *The Tempest* and the Discourse of Colonialism," in J. Dollimore and A. Sinfield, eds., *Political Shakespeare: New Essays in Cultural Materialism* (1985), pp. 48–71.

72. On the fogs and mists of Ireland, see, e.g., Barnabe Rich: "*Ireland* is wonderfully inclined to fogs & mists, & given to very much rain" (p.5); and Moryson, "Description": "The land of Ireland is . . . open to winds and floods of rain, and so fenny it hath bogs on the very tops of the mountains. . . . Our mariners observe the sailing into Ireland to be more dangerous, not only because many tides meeting make the sea apt to swell upon any storm, but especially because they ever find the coast of Ireland covered with mists, whereas the coast of England is commonly clear to be seen far off " (p. 220).

73. For a discussion comparing the quarto *Henry V* to the Rainbow painting, see Annabel Patterson, "Back by Popular Demand: The Two Versions of *Henry V*," *Ren.D.* n.s. 19 (1988): 29–62 (46–7). In the late summer of 1602 Mountjoy had fought a triumphant campaign in Ulster that achieved a symbolic climax in his destruction of the O'Neill coronation stone at Tullaghogue. Elizabeth's anticipation of final success is indicated by a letter written to the lord lieutenant in her own hand on 2 September, expressing her joy "that so good event hath followed so troublesome endeavours, laborious cares, and heedful travels" (cited from John Nichols, *The Progresses and Public Processions of Queen Elizabeth*, 4 vols. (London: John Nichols, 1823), 3:596.

74. Stephen Greenblatt, "Invisible Bullets: Renaissance Authority and Its Subversion, *Henry IV* and *Henry V*," in Dollimore and Sinfield, pp. 18–47 (p. 44).

75. Cited in Edwards, p. 79.

76. Lombard, pp. 40–1.

14 · "THE EXACT MAP OR DISCOVERY OF HUMAN AFFAIRS"

1. For a more extensive discussion of Enobarbus's role as a "choric fool," see my introduction to the Oxford edition (Oxford: Oxford University Press, 1994), pp. 89–94.

2. See Michael Neill, "*Henry V*: A Modern Perspective," in Barbara A. Mowat and

Paul Werstine, eds., *Henry V*, The Folger Shakespeare (New York: Washington Square Press, 1995), pp. 253–78.

3. Thomas Nashe, *Pierce Pennilesse, The Unfortunate Traveller, and Other Works*, ed. J. B. Steane (Harmondsworth: Penguin, 1972), p. 113; and cf. Thomas Heywood, *An Apology for Actors* (London: 1612), B4.

4. Richard Brathwait, *The English Gentleman* (London, 1630), p. 210; Richard Brathwait, *A Survey of History: Or, A Nursery for Gentry* (London, 1638), first published in 1614 as *The Schollers Medley*.

5. Brathwait, *Survey*, pp. 70, 390, 60; and cf. pp. 2–4, 19–20, 22, 102, 136–7, and Brathwait, *English Gentleman*, p. 210.

6. Brathwait, *Survey*, pp. 267, 56, 12; Brathwait, *English Gentleman*, p. 216.

7. Brathwait, *Survey*, p. 20; Brathwait, *English Gentleman*, p. 217.

8. Brathwait, *Survey*, pp. 76, 72, 19.

9. Spenser's letter to Raleigh in *The Poetical Works of Edmund Spenser*, ed. J. C. Smith and E. de Selincourt (London: Oxford University Press, 1959), p. 407. All citations from Spenser are to this edition; quotations from *The Faerie Queene* are not modernized since the antique patina of the poem's language is part of Spenser's own design.

10. R. D. Dunn, introduction to William Camden, *Remaines Concerning Britaine* (1605), ed. Dunn (Toronto: University of Toronto Press, 1984), p. xvi; Richard Helgerson, "The Land Speaks," in Helgerson, *Forms of Nationhood : The Elizabethan Writing of England* (Chicago and London: University of Chicago Press, 1992), p. 132.

11. See Giorgio Vasari, "Giovanni da Udine," in *The Lives of the Painters, Sculptors, and Architects*, ed. William Gaunt, 4 vols. (London: Dent, 1963), 4:9; John Stow, *A Survey of London* (1603). For Stow's strong sense of London as a "vertically" defined space and his emphasis on the depth of London's remains, see Crystal Bartolovich, "Inventing London," in Mike Hill and Warren Montag, eds., *Counter-Publics* (London: Verso, forthcoming).

12. Cf. also the king's description of the Duke of Gloucester in *2 Henry VI*: "uncle Humphrey in thy face I see / The map of honour, truth, and loyalty" (3.1.203).

13. For further discussion of the interpenetration of the narrative and cartographic senses of "plot" and their relation to "a geographical, antiquarian approach to Irish history," see Julia Reinhard Lupton, "Mapping Mutabilitie: Or, Spenser's Irish Plot," in Brendan Bradshaw, Andrew Hadfield, and Willy Maley, eds., *Representing Ireland: Literature and the Origins of Conflict, 1534–1660* (Cambridge: Cambridge University Press, 1993), pp. 93–115 (p. 93); and Bernard Klein, "The Lie of the Land: English Surveyors, Irish Rebels, and *The Faerie Queene*," *Irish University Review* 27 (1997): 207–25 (208).

      Thomas Platter, *Travels in England*, trans. Clare Williams (London: Jonathan Cape, 1937), p. 170.

14. In his *Remaines* Camden describes Britain as "well known to be the most flourishing and excellent, most renowned and famous Isle of the whole world: so rich
in commodities, so beautiful in situation, so resplendent in all glory, that if
the most Omnipotent had fashioned the world round like a ring, as he did like
a globe, it might have been most worthily the only gem therein. . . . For water,
it is walled and guarded with the Ocean most commodious for traffic to all
parts of the world, and watered with pleasant and navigable rivers, which
yield safe havens and roads that it may rightly be termed the *Lady of the sea*";
cited from William Camden, *Remaines Concerning Britain*, ed. R. D. Dunn
(Toronto: University of Toronto Press, 1984), p. 5; cf. also Speed's descriptions
of England as a "Paradise" in the prefatory epistles to *The Theatre of Great
Britaine* (1611), sig. B2-Bv; and Speed, *The History of Great Britaine* (1611), sig.
Mm2v.

15. Letter of Marcantonio Michiel, cited by Ferdinando Castagnoli, "Raphael and
Ancient Rome," in *The Complete Work of Raphael*, intro. Mario Salmi (New
York: Harrison House, 1969), p. 570.

16. Abraham Ortelius, prefatory epistle to *Theatrum Orbis Terrarum* (1570), facsimile edition, intro. R. A. Skelton (Amsterdam: N. Israel, 1964): "Geographiae
(quae merito à quibusdam historiae oculus apellata est)." John Speed, *The History
of Great Britaine Under the Conquests of ye Romans, Saxons, Danes and Normans.
Their Originals, Manners, Warres, Coines, and Seales: with ye Succesions, Lives,
acts and Issues of the English Monarchs from JULIUS CAESAR, to our most gracious Soueraigne King JAMES* (London, 1611). All citations from Speed's atlases
are to his *Prospect of the Most Famous Parts of the World* (London: 1631), which
incorporates the 1627 edition of *The Theatre of the Empire of Great Britaine*
(1611).

17. Speed is careful to stress the antiquarian credentials of the Cumberland illustrations, many of which, he emphasizes, "yet remaining in divers places, are [still]
to be seen" and which are shown "according to their true forms as they have
been, most carefully and exactly taken by men of worthy note and credit," while
those in the Northumberland map are said to be copies of antiquities now "in the
custody of that worthy preserver of ancient monuments, the learned knight Sir
Robert Cotton of Cunnington."

18. Similarly in *2 Henry VI* the king's marriage to Margaret is seen as erasing the
script of English history from French territory, "cancelling your fame, / Blotting
your names from books of memory / Razing the characters of your renown, /
Defacing monuments of conquered France, / Undoing all, as all had never been"
(1.1.95–9).

    Deriving from Latin *monere* = remind, and *mens* = mind, *monument* denoted
anything capable of bringing the past to mind. Thus Weever opens his treatise by
declaring that "a monument is a thing erected, made, or written, for a memorial

of some remarkable action, fit to be transferred to future posterities. And thus generally taken, all religious foundations, all sumptuous and magnificent structures, cities, towns, towers, castles, pillars, pyramids, crosses, obelisks. amphitheaters, statues, and the like, as well as tombs and sepulchres, are called monuments. Now above all remembrances (by which men have endeavoured, even in despite of death to give unto their fame's eternity) for worthiness and continuance, books, or writings, have ever had the preeminence" (p. 1).

19. Speed, *History*, sig. Mm2. *The Theatre of Great Britaine* similarly offered his book as a sacrifice "upon the altar of love to my country" (sig. C1), the very detail and fidelity of whose descriptions honors a correspondence between Britain and the original Promised Land (B2, B2v).

20. In the course of his attack on "partiality," Brathwait quotes Raleigh's canny appraisal of the dangers involved in writing "a modern history": "Whosoever shall follow Truth too near the heels, it may happily strike out his teeth" (pp. 71–2). The passage is from Raleigh's preface to *The History of the World* (London, 1614), sig. E4.

21. Speed, *History*, sig. A2.

22. For a reading of *The Tempest* that places it in an Irish context, see Paul Brown, " 'This Thing of Darkness I Acknowledge Mine': *The Tempest* and the Discourse of Colonialism," in Jonathan Dollimore and Alan Sinfield, eds., *Political Shakespeare: New Essays in Cultural Materialism* (Manchester: Manchester University Press, 1985), pp. 48–71.

23. See G. A. Hayes-McCoy, ed., *Ulster and Other Irish Maps* (Dublin: Stationery Office for the Irish Manuscripts Commission, 1964), p. 9. For further discussion of these unique maps, see Mercedes Maroto Camino, "Unfolding the Map of Early Modern Ireland: Spenser, Moryson, and Bartlett," *Cartographica* 34, no. 4 (1997): 1–17.

24. Hayes-McCoy, p. xii.

15 · THE WORLD BEYOND

1. Quoted from John Pomfret, "Bosnia's Bridge Too Far," *Guardian Weekly* (*Washington Post* section), 5 September 1993, p. 18.

2. George Puttenham, *The Arte of English Poesie*, ed. Gladys Doidge Willcock and Alice Walker (Cambridge: Cambridge University Press, 1936), p. 178. For a sharply informed discussion of "the historical relationship between translation and metaphor," see Eric Cheyfitz, *The Poetics of Imperialism: Translation and Colonization from The Tempest to Tarzan* (New York: Oxford University Press, 1991), pp. xvii-iii, 35–40.

3. Thomas Platter, *Travels in England*, trans. Clare Williams (London: Jonathan Cape, 1937), p. 170; Peter Womack, "Imagining Communities: Theatres and the

English Nation in the Sixteenth Century," in David Aers, ed., *Culture and History, 1350–1600: Essays on English Communities, Identities, and Writing* (Brighton: Harvester, 1992), pp. 91–145 (p. 108).

4. Patricia Parker, "*The Merry Wives of Windsor* and Shakespearean Translation," *MLQ* 52 (1991): 225–61; Puttenham, p. 178.
5. *Montaigne's Essays*, trans. John Florio, 3 vols. (London: J. M. Dent, 1965), vol. 2, chap. 12, p. 297; vol. 1, chap. 30, pp. 227, 229.
6. Cheyfitz, p. 15. See Richard Beacon, *Solon his Follie, or A Politique Discovrse, touching the Reformation of common-weales conquered, declined or corrupted* (Oxford, 1594), p. 110; and Edmund Spenser, *A View of the Present State of Ireland*, ed. W. L. Renwick (London, 1934), p. 197. Even Spenser, whose project of translation is sometimes disturbingly close to genocide, seems to have experienced the seductive pull of alterity through his efforts to have the poetry of Irish bards translated; and the disturbance that resulted from his discovery of "sweet wit . . . good grace and comeliness" directed (as it seemed) "to the gracing of wickedness and vice" (Spenser, *View*, pp. 97–8) is reflected in *The Faerie Queene*'s obsessive fascination with the Circe motif and its associated bouts of anti-aesthetic violence.
7. For a discussion of Shakespeare's history cycles, see chap. 13.
8. Spenser, *View*, p. 88.
9. Stephen Greenblatt, *Marvelous Possessions: The Wonder of the New World* (Chicago: University of Chicago Press, 1991), p. 16.
10. See Anthony Pagden, *European Encounters with the New World* (New Haven: Yale University Press, 1993), pp. 38–41. The Quiroga quotations are from this text.
11. For a marvelously agile exploration of translation tropes in this play, whose emphases are very different from my own, see James A. Calderwood, *A Midsummer Night's Dream* (Hemel Hempstead: Harvester Wheatsheaf, 1992), pp. 96–116.
12. Margo Hendricks, "Obscured by Dreams: Race, Empire, and Shakespeare's *A Midsummer Night's Dream*," *Shakespeare Quarterly* 47 (1996): 37–60.
13. Greenblatt, *Marvelous Possessions*, p.16.
14. Pagden, p. 41.
15. Peter Hulme, *Colonial Encounters: Europe and the Native Caribbean, 1492–1797* (London: J. M. Dent, 1986); *Montaigne's Essays*, vol. 1, sect. 30, pp. 227, 220.
16. For further discussion of this universal eloquence, see chap. 7.
17. Aimé Césaire, *Une Tempête* [A tempest], trans. Richard Miller (New York: Ubu Repertory Theater Publications, 1985), p. 73.
18. Cheyfitz, p. 120. Cf. Stephen Greenblatt, *Learning to Curse: Essays in Early Modern Culture* (New York: Routledge, 1990), for Robert Fabian's reaction to the Indians he encountered at Westminster Palace, who seemed to him to have been transformed by clothing from inarticulate brute beasts to people whom "I could not discern from Englishmen, till I learned what they were" (p. 18).

On Irish "nakedness" see, e.g., *The Famous History of Captain Thomas Stukely* (1605; Oxford: Oxford University Press, 1975), ll. 1179–80.

19. Greenblatt, *Learning to Curse*, p. 31; see also, Cheyfitz, pp. 107–8. Brian Friel, *Translations* (London: Faber, 1981), p. 66.

20. Marshall Sahlins, "Goodbye to Tristes Tropes: The Anthropology of History in Polynesia," Robb Lectures (sound recording), University of Auckland, 1992. The critics' quotation is from a conversation between Lucius Cary, John Hales of Eton, Chief Justice Henry Vaughan, and others, reported by Nicholas Rowe, cited in Alden T. Vaughan and Virginia Mason Vaughan, *Shakespeare's Caliban: A Cultural History* (Cambridge: Cambridge University Press, 1991), pp. 95–6.

21. The saying plays on the Latin root of *traditore: traditor*—literally "one who hands over." For a witty exploration of Shakespeare's own play with the idea of translation as theft, see Patricia Parker, "The Merry Wives of Windsor and Shakespearean Translation," *MLQ* 52 (1991): 225–61, esp. pp. 253–6; Parker cites Jonson's *Poetaster*, 5.3: "I could tell you, he were a translator, / I know the authors from whence he has stolen" (p. 253).

Index

Abbott, Morris, 321

Accession Day, celebration of, 278, 301, 302, 303, 309, 479, 483

Aceh (Achen), 318, 418

acting, as gesture, 180–181

Adams, Thomas, 103

Adamson, Jane, 462

Adelman, Janet, 441, 445, 446

Adler, Doris, 466

adultery and adulteration, in *Othello*, 263–264

Aers, David, 485, 507

Aldridge, Ira, 245, 465

Alençon, Duke of, 188

Allen, Cardinal, 440

Allin, Rose, 458, 459

Altman, Joel, 349, 361, 496, 499, 500

Amboyna, Massacre of, 305, 306, 315, 321, 324, 327, 484, 486, 487, 488, 489, 490, 491

America. *See* New World; Virginia

Amussen, Susan Dwyer, 423, 427, 428

Anaxagoras, 175

Anderson, Benedict, 340, 352, 492

Andronicus, stage-player, 180, 186, 187

Andronicus Commenus, 186

Anglo, Sydney, 480

Antipodes, 401, 402

Anzilotti, Gloria, 421

Appiah, Anthony, 492

Arafat, Yasser, 184

Arawaks, 410

Arber, Edward, 438

Archer, William, 464

Arden of Faversham, 3, 22, 34, 38, 49–72, 107, 247, 429, 430, 431

Ardern, Thomas, 50, 53, 58, 430

Ariès, Philippe, 467, 472

Aristotle, 77, 170, 175, 191, 416, 478, 503

Arnold, Janet, 501, 502, 503

Auden, W.H., 222, 462

Avery, Bruce, 502

Aylmer, G.E., 442

Bacon, Francis, 142, 207, 222, 295, 446, 460, 481

Baker, David J., 349, 496

Banda, 319, 320, 323, 324, 487, 489

Bantam (Java), 278, 279, 281, 282, 283, 285, 287, 289, 290–306, 320, 326, 479, 480, 490

Barish, Jonas, 24, 423

Barlaeus, Caspar, 452

Barnes, Barnabe, 445

Barnett, Richard C., 421

Bartels, Emily, 270, 283, 473, 474, 485

Barthélemy, Dominique, 472

Bartlett, Richard, 393, 394, 395, 396, 506
Bartolovich, Crystal, 504
Barton, Anne, 437, 478
bastard: as counterfeit, 70, 128, 129, 136, 137, 138, 140, 141, 144, 149–165, 251, 264, 265, 439, 444, 445, 470; as deformed, 135, 138, 141, 142; as dirt, 134, 139, 140, 147; as *filius nullius*, 130, 138, 139, 141, 158, 160, 449; as monster, 129, 130; as mother's son, 138,150, 158, 160, 163; as natural/unnatural, 140, 141, 151, 160, 470; as self-made, 139; as usurper, 129, 131, 136, 137, 142, 143, 150; deformity of, 142, 143, 144, 152; property, propriety and, 138; unholiness of, 133, 134; vigour of, 151
Bastard, The, 442
bastardy, 127–147, 149–165, 264, 265, 358, 359, 410, 438, 439, 440, 441, 442, 443, 444, 445, 446, 447, 448, 470, 500; and gender, 131–132; and indistinction, 146–147; and race, 264; and undifferentiation, 152; as monstrous, 135, 138, 139, 141, 144–145, 146, 152; generic, 144–145, 147, 152; stain of, 132, 151
Batty, Bartholomew, 77, 78, 94, 432, 434, 435
Bayley, John, 228, 462
Beacon, Richard, 342, 350, 403, 493, 497, 502, 507
Beard, Thomas, 189, 479
Beaufort, John, 440
Beaumont, Francis, 446, 475, 485; *Knight of the Burning Pestle, The*, 483
Beaurline, L.R., 457

Beck, Cave, 179
Becon, Thomas, 133
bed: in *Antony and Cleopatra*, 468; in *Othello*, 130, 133, 137, 157, 163, 212, 220, 223, 229, 230, 234, 237–268, 464, 465, 468; bed of state, resemblance of tombs to, 260
Behaim, Martin, 311
Behn, Aphra, 472
Beier, A.L., 419, 420, 423, 426
Bell, Ilona, 458
Belsey, Catherine, 49, 50, 53, 72, 429
Berry, Lloyd E., 458, 459
Best, George, 272, 276, 471, 474, 475, 482
Biersack, Aletta, 477
Blackburn, Robin, 474
Blackfriars Playhouse, 2
blackness, and adultery, 265, 471; as monstrous, 265; as sign of evil and death, 265; as sign of sexual transgression, 265. *See also* colour)
Blunt, J.H., 435
Bodin, Jean, 432, 477, 478
Bodley, Captain Josias, 346, 494
body: early modern, 169; body politic, 137, 143, 160, 186, 188, 198, 341, 343, 422, 433
Boitard, Francois, 239
Bond, Ronald B., 422
Bonifacio, Giovanni, 178, 454
Bonner, Bishop, 458
Boon, James, 322, 323, 486, 487, 489, 491, 492
Boose, Lynda A., 256, 277, 462, 468, 472, 475
Bothwell, James Hepburn, 4th Earl of, 441
Bowers, Fredson, 446, 473, 475, 485
Boydell, Josiah, 243, 244

Bradbrook, M.C., 4, 459
Bradley, A.C., 246, 465
Bradshaw, Brendan, 62, 66, 504
Bradshaw, Graham, 419
Brady, Ciaran, 493, 494, 501
Brathwait, Richard, 22, 31, 375–376,
    386, 421, 424, 428, 504, 506;
    Survey of History, A, 375–376,
    504; *The English Gentleman*, 31,
    375, 421, 424, 504
Braude, Benjamin, 475, 476
Braunstein, Philippe, 472
Bremner, Jan, 456
Brennan, Elizabeth M., 440, 457
Breton, Nicholas, 446
Brome, Richard, 274
Brown, Paul, 503, 506
Brown, Roger, 430, 431
Browne, Sir Thomas, 172, 452
Bryskett, Lodowick, 495
Buck, Sir George, 442
Buckingham, Villiers, George, Duke of,
    76
Bulwer, John, 174–187, 194, 199, 453,
    454, 455, 456, 457, 459, 460
Burbage, Richard, 15
Burghley, William Cecil, Lord, 22, 480,
    481
Burke, Kenneth, 468, 469
Burnett, Mark Thornton, 27, 41, 48,
    421, 422, 423, 424, 425, 427
Burre, Walter, 300, 478, 484
Butler, Martin, 436, 438
Byrne, F.I., 501
Byrne, Matthew J., 492

Cabeza de Vaca, 408
Caernarvon, Dormer, Robert, Earl of,
    43, 75
Cairncross, Andrew S., 455
Cairns, David, 466, 472, 493

Calderwood, James, 138, 444, 467, 468,
    471, 472, 507
Callaghan, Dympna, 282, 476
Calvinism, 433
Camden, William, 28, 371, 378–379,
    384, 493, 494, 502, 503, 504, 505
Campion, Jane, 168
Campion, Thomas, 480
Candido, Joseph A., 144, 442, 444, 446
Candish, Thomas, 276, 390, 475, 491
Canetti, Elias, 167, 176, 450, 453
cannibalism, 346, 402, 410
Canny, Nicholas, 493, 494, 496, 498
cartography. *See* mapping and survey-
    ing
Cary, Lucius, 508
Case, John, 495
Casserio, Giulio, 170
Castagnoli, Ferdinando, 505
Castiglione, Baldassare, 29
Catherine of Aragon, 440
Cavell, Stanley, 467, 469
Cavendish, Thomas. *See* Candish,
    Thomas
Cawdrey, Robert, 353, 498
Caxton, William, 344, 358, 494, 499
Cecil, Sir Robert, 371
Césaire, Aimé, 393, 411, 507
Cham (son of Noah), and blackness,
    265, 471
Chapelli, Fred, 437
Chapman, George, 237; *Bussy
    D'Ambois*, 237, 470; *Gentleman
    Usher, The*, 424, 428
charity, 99–125, 435, 436, 438
charivari, 467; in *Othello*, 252, 254, 467
Charles I, 97, 316, 333, 388, 500
Chen Kaige, 168
Cheyfitz, Eric, 399, 403, 411, 454, 506,
    507, 508
Chinese: compared with Jews, 296;

English rivalry and suspicion, 276, 281, 282, 287, 288, 290, 291, 292, 296, 297, 303, 305, 336
chiromancy, 172
chorography, 378, 379, 380, 384, 393, 397, 498. *See also* mapping and surveying
Churchyard, Thomas, 496
Chus (grandson of Noah), cursed with blackness, 471
Cicero, Marcus Tullius, 83, 180, 186, 187, 188, 190, 357, 432, 454, 457, 458, 499
city. *See* merchant class
Clark, Stuart, 480
Clarke, John, torture of, 307
Claudian, 503
Cleaver, Robert, and Dod, John, 23, 35, 39, 73, 77, 78, 79, 85, 90, 94, 422, 427, 432, 433, 434
Clerke, William, 444
clothes, social meanings of, 274, 411–413. *See also* livery; nakedness
Coddon, Karin S., 481
Coetzee, J.M., 203, 285, 307, 308, 460, 484
coining. *See* bastard, as counterfeit
Coleridge, Samuel Taylor, 97, 218, 246–247, 261, 435, 469
Colie, Rosalie L., 447
Collins, Marie, 494
color: as marker of alterity, 275, 277, 281, 282, 283, 304; as marker of racial difference, 331–332. *See also* race
Columbus, Christopher, 170, 409, 410, 411, 493
comedy of manners, 56
Condell, Henry, 173
Congreve, William, 41, 43, 93; *Double Dealer, The*, 43, 47; *Love for Love*, 97; *The Double Dealer*, 43, 47, 93
Conrad, Joseph, 289, 311
Constantia Munda, 174, 453
Contamine, Philippe, 472
Coryat, Thomas, 469
Cotton, Sir Robert, 384, 505
Coughlan, Patricia, 473
Courthop, Nathaniel, 475, 490
Craik, T.W., 430, 431
Cranmer, Thomas, 188, 189, 458
Cressy, David, 479, 483
Crooke, Helkiah, 451
Cuddy, Neil, 420, 423
Cultural Materialism, 4, 503, 506
culture, as marker of alterity, 275
Cunliffe, J.W., 445
Cunningham, Bernadette, 493
Cunningham, Karen, 481
Curren-Aquino, Deborah, 442, 447, 448
Curteis, Alice, 439, 440, 442
Cusacke, John, 500
Cushman, Robert, 463
Cyprus, in *Othello*, 211–212

Daalder, Joost, 452
Danby, John, 130, 139, 423, 435, 439, 445
Daniel, Samuel, 314; anticolonialism of, 314–315
Davenant, Sir William, 485
David, Richard, 466
Davies, Sir John, 339, 346, 347, 350, 356–357, 360, 362–364, 366–369, 370–371, 376, 396, 443, 492, 494, 495, 497, 498, 499, 500, 501, 502
Davis, John, 318
Davis, Kingsley, 130, 439
Dawson, Anthony B., 427, 492
de Argensola, Bartolome Leonando, 321

de Bellan, Seigneur, 321, 322, 325, 328, 330–331, 334, 491
de Bry, Theodore, 390
de Loutherbourg, Philippe Jacques, 241
Defoe, Daniel; *Robinson Crusoe*, 308
degeneration, trope of, 135, 272, 330–331, 332, 342, 347–348, 354–356, 358, 370, 403–404, 408, 498
Dekker, Thomas, 431, 433; *The Witch of Edmonton*, 130
Demosthenes (orator), 180, 187, 457
Dering, Edward, 436
Derricke, John, 345, 347, 494, 495, 501
Dickinson, Albert, 450
Diconson, Thomas, 454, 460
Diconson, William, 453
Diderot, Denis, 45, 428
DiGangi, Mario, 419, 489
Digges, Sir Dudley, 319, 321, 488
Diodorus Siculus, 371, 503
discovery, 169, 293, 295, 299, 312, 316, 330, 337, 366, 367, 379, 387, 388, 390–392, 401, 408–409, 410, 416, 471, 482; and torture, 295; history as, 373–397; in *Changeling*, 39; in *Othello*, 258
discovery scenes, 379, 386, 390, 391, 468
Dod, John. *See* Cleaver, Robert
Dolan, Frances E., 38, 41, 427, 429, 430, 431
Dollimore, Jonathan, 497, 503, 506
Don John of Austria, 131
Donaldson, Ian, 437
Donne, John, 21, 46, 132, 312, 420, 430, 441
Douglas, Mary, 133–134, 147, 442
Doyle, Arthur Conan, 127, 438
Drakakis, John, 497
Drake, Sir Francis, 315, 318, 320, 390, 483, 490
Droeshout, Martin, 173

Dryden, John, 312, 321, 324, 447, 485, 487, 489, 491, 492; *Amboyna*, 324; *Aureng-Zebe*, 97
Dubrow, Heather, 423
Duby, Georges, 467, 472
Dudley, Edward, 437
Dungannon, 372, 394, 395, 396
Dunn, R.D., 504, 505
Dutch, English relations with, 2, 132, 273, 275, 278–279, 280–281, 283, 290, 292, 294, 296, 299, 300–303, 305–306, 313, 315, 318, 319–322, 323–327, 330, 338, 358, 456, 475, 476, 483, 484, 486, 487, 488, 489, 490, 491

East India Company, Dutch, 2, 313, 315, 327
East India Company, English, 2, 273, 278–279, 287, 300, 313, 315, 316, 319, 324, 327, 478, 479, 486, 487, 488, 490
East Indians, alleged treachery of, 296
East Indies, 2, 269, 273, 275–279, 281, 285–309, 310–338, 476, 478, 479, 482, 486, 487, 488, 490, 491
Edmond Ironside, 136
Edward III, 136, 153, 444, 448, 481, 500
Edward the Confessor, 198
Edward VI, 440
Edwards, Philip, 435, 497, 499
Elias, Norbert, 167, 176, 440, 450, 451
Elizabeth I, 131, 165, 188, 194, 301, 349, 360, 392, 396, 440, 441, 479, 488, 496, 503; Armada Portrait of, 371; Rainbow Portrait of, 369–371, 503
Elton, G.R., 480
Elyot, Sir Thomas, 493
empire, ideology of, 4, 134, 135, 309, 311–338, 360, 362, 373, 379, 400, 403, 415, 443

Engler, Balz, 463
English Courtier, and the Country Gentleman, The, 27, 29, 428
Englishness, discourse of, 279, 280, 293, 294–295, 299, 301, 303, 305, 341, 353–357, 358–359, 372, 375, 379, 404, 466
equivocation, 1, 2, 3
Erasmus, Desiderius, 447
Erskine, Sir Thomas, 423
Essex, Devereux, Robert, Earl of, 2, 16, 358, 420, 481, 498, 499
European, defined by color, 277
Evans, G. Blakemore, 455, 492
Eyre, Ronald, 243

Fabian, Robert, 507
Fabre, Daniel, 467
Fairchilds, Cissie, 40, 44, 427, 428
Falkiner, C. Litton, 492, 494, 500
Falstaff, 16
family, early modern ideas of, 9; Puritan idea of, 433. *See also* household government
Famous History of Captain Thomas Stukely, The, 349, 508
Farber, Leslie H., 461
Farquahar, George, 47, 48; *Beaux' Stratagem, The*, 47–48
Fechter, Charles, 260, 468
fede, 170, 452
felix culpa, 391
Fiedler, Leslie A., 474
Fiennes, Celia, 46
Filmer, Sir Robert, 75, 77, 435
Findlay, Alison, 438, 439, 440, 441, 442, 444, 445, 446, 448
Fineman, Joel, 286, 477
fire, troping of in East Indian narratives, 290–293, 294–299, 334–338
Fitzgeoffrey, Henry, 425
Fitzgerald, James Fitzmaurice, 499

Fitzgerald, Maurice, 499
Fitzherbert, Humphrey, 323, 324, 489, 491
Fitzroy, Henry, 441
Fletcher, John, 73, 311, 312, 482; *Island Princess*, 2, 276–277, 311–338, 482; *Maid's Tragedy, The*, 464; *Monsieur Thomas*, 464; *Sea-Voyage, The*, 312, 313–315, 485; *Woman's Prize, The*, 142, 312
Florio, John, 157, 444, 449, 453, 461, 507
Ford, John, 134, 141, 436, 464, 470; *Broken Heart, The*, 134, 470; *Lover's Melancholy, The*, 211; *Love's Sacrifice*, 130, 464; *'Tis Pity She's a Whore*, 141, 436, 470, 481
Foreman, Simon, 198
Forster, E.M., 443
Forster, John, 240, 464
Fortescue, Sir John, 132, 151, 441, 442, 445, 448
Foster, Sir William, 479, 480, 481, 482, 484
Foucault, Michel, 5, 286, 458, 471, 477
Foxe, John, 188, 458, 459
French, Marilyn, 450
Freud, Sigmund, 168, 169, 449, 450, 451, 461
Friedman, Alice T., 421, 425, 427, 471
Friedman, John Block, 471
Friel, Brian, 374, 414, 443, 508; *Translations*, 414
Frye, Northrop, 212, 460
Fuller, Thomas, 132, 441
Furness, Horace, Howard, 238, 463

Ganges, 323
gardens, as emblem of civil order, 348–349, 350, 351, 352, 356
Gardner, Helen, 463
Garrick, David, 238
Garzoni, Tommaso, 33, 40, 425, 427

Gataker, Thomas, 436
Geertz, Clifford, 285, 477
Genster, Julia, 461
Gentleman, Tobias, 488
Gernon, Luke, 363, 500
Gibson, Colin, 435
Gifford, George, 21, 420
Gilbert, Allan, H., 447
Gilbert, Sir Humphrey, 496
Gillespie, Raymond, 493, 494
Gillies, John, 4, 485
Gilman, Albert, 430, 431
Giovanni da Udine, 378, 504
Giraldi Cinthio, 215, 216
Giraldus, Cambrensis, 344, 499
Girard, René, 447
Gittings, Clare, 468
Given-Wilson, Chris, 439, 440, 442
Glissenti, Fabio, 40, 44, 427
Globe Playhouse, 2, 311, 312, 401
Goldberg, Jonathan, 173, 451
Golden Fleece, legend of, 317–318
Goode, William J., 439
Goody, Jack, 440
Gouge, William, 13, 20, 21, 22, 23, 24,
    33, 35, 36, 38, 40, 44, 421, 422, 425,
    426, 427, 428
Graces, Three, 199, 424
Grafton, Tony, 497
Graham, J., 244
Greenblatt, Stephen, 4, 5, 264, 285–291,
    293, 299, 306–309, 371, 406, 409,
    413, 454, 466, 470, 471, 472, 476,
    477, 478, 479, 485, 498, 503, 507,
    508; on anecdote, 286; on wonder,
    286, 287, 307, 309
Greenleaf, W.H., 432
Gresham, Sir Thomas, 121
Grierson, Herbert, 430
Griffiths, Paul, 422
Gross, A.G., 436
Guarini, Giambattista, 145, 447

Guazzo, Steffano, 23, 422
Guiana, 324, 332, 360, 363
Gunn, Giles, 476
Gunpowder Plot, 289, 478
Gurr, Andrew, 15, 181, 419, 420, 435,
    454

Hadfield, Andrew, 504
Haines, Charles, 249, 250, 460, 462, 467,
    468
Hakluyt, Richard, 178, 265, 275, 276,
    315, 438, 471, 474, 479, 480, 482,
    488, 489, 491
Hales, John (of Eton), 508
Hall, Kim F., 127, 421, 439, 471, 472,
    491
Halliday, M.A.K., 430
Halpern, Richard, 423
Ham. *See* Cham
hand, 167–203; actor's, 174, 180;
    Adamic eloquence of, 178; and
    eye, 200, 201; and head, 175, 200;
    and heart, 185, 200, 224; and writ-
    ing, 172; as emblem of service,
    422; as instrument of blessing,
    202; as mark of human presence,
    169; as second self, 174, 189, 459;
    as site of meaning, 23, 170,
    171,177, 180, 190, 192, 193, 195,
    200, 201; as symbol of power, 169;
    bicameral brain and, 169; bloody,
    183, 190, 195–201, 202; clasping,
    170, 183, 199, 201; gendered, 191;
    hidden virtue of, 184; in anatomy,
    170; in witchcraft, 172; left and
    right, meanings of, 451; modern,
    desanctified, 202, 203; of Fatima,
    169; of God, 169, 170, 172, 178,
    195, 199; of power, 194, 195, 196;
    Red Hand (of Liberty, Ulster),
    167,169; royal, 195, 197, 198; sev-
    ered, 185, 186, 188, 189, 191, 195,

196, 197, 450, 459; signatures of, 172; speaking, 175, 182, 186, 191; sympathy with the will, 184; universal language of, 178, 191; washing, 183, 196–198; writer's, 173, 174

handfasting, 170, 173

handkerchief, in *Othello*, 185, 223–224, 256, 257, 260

Hankey, Julie, 247, 248, 464, 465, 466, 468

Hanson, Elizabeth, 294, 295, 480, 481

Harris, Jocelyn, 462

Harris, Jonathan Gil, 494

Harrison, William, 13, 15, 16, 34, 35, 419, 420, 426, 427, 505

Harvey, Gabriel, 497, 498, 502

Hattendorf, John B., 488

Hatton, Sir Christopher, 458

Hawkes, Terence, 419, 476

Hayes-McCoy, G.A., 506

Heal, Felicity, 421, 424, 428

Heath, James, 480, 481

Hecht, J. Jean, 428

Heckscher, William S., 451, 452

Heidegger, Martin, 167

Heilmann, Robert, 463

Heine, Heinrich, 145, 447

Helgerson, Richard, 4, 378, 379, 485, 498, 504

Heminge, John, 173

Henderson, Katherine Usher, 453

Hendricks, Margo, 408, 472, 485, 507

Henry VII, 420, 440, 494

Henry VIII, 343, 420, 440, 441

Henry, John, 454, 502

Henson, Father Josiah, 39

Herbert, Sir William, 365, 501

Hermes Trismegistus. *See* Hermetic magic

Hermetic magic, 114, 115

Hertz, Robert, 451, 453

Hester, M. Thomas, 420

Heywood, Thomas, 188, 312, 349, 353, 357, 375, 458, 498, 499, 504; *Fair Maid of the West, The*, 312; *Rape of Lucrece, The*, 188, 193

Hic Mulier, 442, 443

hierarchy. *See* place

Highley, Christopher, 349, 473, 496, 498

Hinting (Chinese goldsmith), arrest and torture of, 5, 291–293, 295, 297–299, 304, 305, 306, 309, 336

historicist criticism, 1–9, 41, 49, 50, 72, 164, 247, 285–287, 307, 312, 419, 476, 477

history: early modern ideas of, 373–397

history plays, function of, 357–358, 375

Hogg, James, 438

Holaday, Alan, 458

Holdsworth, Roger, 448

Holinshed, Raphael, 49, 50, 53, 54, 55, 495, 497, 499

Holland, Hugh, 173, 174

Hollanders. See Dutch

Homer, 144, 447

homoeroticism, in *Othello*, 255

Honigmann, E.A.J., 473

honorifics, 14, 57, 63–66, 82, 83, 86, 89, 105, 110–112, 123, 213

Hooker, John, 499

Hooker, Richard, 431

Hosley, Richard, 468

hospitality. *See* housekeeping

Hotson, Leslie, 479

Houlbrooke, Ralph A., 440

household government, 13–47, 50, 57, 59, 73, 76–79, 82, 83, 85, 86, 87, 92, 93, 100, 101, 104, 105, 119, 421, 422, 423, 428

housekeeping, 28, 29, 30, 84, 85, 87, 89, 103, 104, 108, 120, 123, 424

Houtman, Cornelius, 483
Howard, Jean E., 466, 474, 478
Howlett, Kathy, 445, 446
Hulme, Peter, 4, 410, 485, 507
Hunter, G.K., 261, 466
Hutton, Sarah, 454
Hyde, Thomas, 445

I.M.,
Iago: displacement of, 214–215; motivation of, 213, 218–221; racial attitudes of, 249; Spanish name of, 213; temptation of Othello as wooing, 232–233; use of wordplay by, 222
A Health to the Gentlemanly profession of Seruingmen, 30, 424, 425
images, power of, 153
Indians, New World, 112, 116–118, 121, 122, 124–125. *See also* East Indians
Ingram, Martin, 439
inwardness, early modern discourse of, 481
Ireland, 16, 135, 168, 270, 309, 339–372, 376, 384, 403, 404, 440, 443, 466, 473, 492, 493, 494, 495, 496, 497, 498, 499, 500, 501, 502, 503, 504, 506; as Circe's island, 347, 355, 356, 507; as conquered female, 363; as England's first colony, 342; as province of England, 342; as wilderness, 348, 352, 364, 366, 393; Brehon Law of, 346; idea of nationhood in, 341, 372; *mundus inversus*, 344; "Old English" in 135, 270, 347, 354, 369, 495, 500
Irish, 135, 136, 168, 270, 274, 323, 339–372, 376, 391, 396–397, 403, 404, 411, 414, 443, 445, 466, 475, 492, 493, 494, 495, 496, 497, 498, 499,

500, 501, 502, 503, 504, 506, 507, 508; animality and monstrosity of, 345–348; as cannibals, 346; as naked people, 411, 496; bards, 346; Catholicism, 341, 344, 496; craftiness and elusiveness, 364–366, 500–501; incorporation and assimilation of, 343, 362, 368, 371; language, 342, 346, 356, 358; lawlessness, 341; liberty and license, 348, 498; mantles and glibs, 364–366, 368, 370, 495, 497, 501, 502; Spanish origins of, 341, 493; surveillance of, 363–364, 366–368, 371; wandering and vagrancy, 341, 350, 364, 497; wildness and barbarity, 341, 343–344, 346–347, 349, 350, 352, 358, 360, 364, 367, 496
Isabella I, of Spain, 353

Jackson, Henry, 238, 248
James I, 77, 131, 165, 200, 321, 333, 368, 369, 388, 404, 408, 420, 423, 435, 440, 460, 480, 488, 491, 495; *Basilikon Doron*, 77, 441
Janton, Pierre, 467
Jardine, Lisa, 14, 419, 428, 497, 502
Java, English contact with, 278, 279, 282, 285, 287, 290, 292, 294, 296, 298, 302, 304, 305, 335, 479, 482
Javans, 276, 278, 282, 290, 291, 296, 303, 304, 305, 327
jealousy, and desire, in *Othello*, 262
Jeremiah, Book of, 471
Jews: Chinese compared with, 296; and secret difference, 272; stereotypes of, 272
Jobson, Francis, 395
John of Gaunt, 379, 440
Johnson, Dr Samuel, 237, 238
Johnson, Dr. Samuel, 361

Jones, Ann Rosalind, 342, 493
Jones, Edmund D., 429, 447
Jones, Eldred, 466
Jones, Emrys, 211, 460
Jones, Gareth, 436
Jones, Inigo, 449
Jonson, Ben, 2, 56, 73, 80, 93, 97, 114,
    137, 145, 154, 156, 173, 210, 274,
    298, 349, 368–369, 416, 419, 431,
    433, 437, 444, 449, 469, 470, 471,
    482, 495, 501, 502, 508; *Irish
    Masque at Court*, 349, 368–369,
    495; *Masque of Blackness*, 274;
    Volpone, 2, 43, 80, 137, 142, 154,
    155, 210, 262, 264, 419, 433, 444,
    446, 469, 470
Joplin, Patricia Kleindienst, 149, 459
Jordan, W.K., 101, 436, 438
Joseph, B.L., 180
Juvenal, 503

Kaplan, Paul H.D., 464
Kayll, Robert, 319, 487, 488
Keay, John, 487
Keeling, Captain William, 482
Keen, Benjamin, 437
Kelsall, Malcolm, 435
Kemble, Fanny, 238
Kemble, John Philip, 464
Kerrigan, John, 439
Kettle, Arnold, 466
Keymis, Lawrence, 489
Keysar, Robert, 150, 448
Kilkenny, Statutes of, 494
King's Men, The, 238, 312
Kishi, Tetsuo, 439
Kitchin, G.W., 460
Klein, Bernard, 504
Knapp, Jeffrey, 485, 490
Knights, L.C., 4, 76, 431
Knox, Dilwyn, 178, 454

Kupperman, Karen Ordahl, 274, 475
Kyd, Thomas, 181, 295, 298, 299, 480,
    481; *Spanish Tragedy, The*, 150,
    181, 298, 455

Lamb, Charles, 246
Lancaster, Sir James, 290, 294, 296, 300,
    480, 481, 484
land: as commodity, 58; as female body,
    323–324, 363, 405; as marker of
    status, 51–53, 58, 104, 107, 325,
    330; commodification of, 51–52
language, and national identity, 342,
    352–354, 356, 358, 403; and defini-
    tion of human, 191. *See also* hands
Lantore (Lonthor), 321
Laqueur, Thomas, 158, 449, 451
Las Casas, Bartolomé de, 457
Laslett, Peter, 4, 21, 41, 56, 57, 58, 75,
    82, 128, 423, 425, 430–433, 439,
    440
Laurence, Anne, 466, 472
Lawson, Philip, 486, 488
Lea, Henry Charles, 474
Leavis, F.R., 236, 246, 247, 463, 465
Lentricchia, Frank, 477
Leo Africanus, John, 265, 270, 473
Leo X, Pope, 380
Lerner, Laurence, 466
Levant Company, 486
Lever, Thomas, 436
Lewes, George Henry, 464
lieutenancy, 234; in *Othello*, 214,
    216–217, 220–222, 229, 230,
    234–235, 254, 503
Lindley, David, 502
livery, 16–19, 22, 23, 25–28, 30, 31, 32,
    45–48, 121, 276, 331, 422, 424
Lloyd E. Berry, 458
Lombard, Peter, 340, 372, 492, 503
Lord Chamberlain's Men, 311

Lowth, William, 77, 432
Ludlow, battle of, 382
Lupton, Julia Reinhard, 504

Macfarlane, Alan, 133, 439, 440, 442
Machiavelli, Niccolo, 80, 271, 497
Macready, W.C., 240, 241, 244, 245
Macready, William, 464, 465
Magellan, 318
Magnusson, A.L., 427
Mahood, Molly, 462
Maley, Willy, 473, 504
Mandeville, Sir John, 318
mapping and surveying, 311, 352, 363,
    366, 373, 376, 379, 380, 382,
    393–396, 500, 504, 505, 506; ideol-
    ogy of, 169, 350, 366, 379, 396, 502
Maquerlot, Jean-Pierre, 491
Marana, Jean Paul (Giovanni Paolo), 40
Marcus, Leah S., 2, 419
Markham, and Sampson, *Herod and
    Antipater*, 444
Marlowe, Christopher, 20, 26, 189, 231,
    247, 270, 271, 273, 312, 400, 401,
    420, 452, 458, 473, 474, 479, 480,
    481, 485, 492; *Doctor Faustus*,
    20–21, 231, 235, 400, 420, 474;
    Edward II, 26; *Jew of Malta, The*,
    222, 270, 271, 272; *Massacre at
    Paris, The*, 458; *Tamburlaine*, 79,
    81, 312, 361, 368, 391, 392, 393,
    401, 452, 492
Maroto Camino, Mercedes, 502, 506
marriage, as trope of conquest, 360–361
marriage bed, in early modern culture,
    266
Marshall, Herbert, 465
Marston, John, 30, 31, 424, 447, 480;
    Histrio-mastix, 30, 424
Marston, Westland, 240, 464
Martin, F.X., 501

Martin, Priscilla, 447
Martin, Sir Theodore, 468
Marx, Karl, 33, 76, 77
Mary I, 188, 189, 440
Mary Queen of Scots, 131
Massing, Jean Michel, 474
Massinger, Philip, 3, 24, 27, 36, 41–43,
    43, 57, 73–97 99–125, 277, 312,
    421, 430, 431, 434, 435, 436, 437,
    438; *A New Way to Pay Old Debts*,
    23, 24, 42–43, 57, 73–97, 103, 105,
    107, 109, 119, 124, 421, 426, 430,
    431, 433, 434, 436, 437; *City
    Madam, The*, 23, 36, 99–125, 277,
    422, 424, 433, 434, 435, 436, 475,
    476; *The Roman Actor*, 93
masterless men, 3, 15–16, 18, 19, 21, 25,
    57, 61, 89, 350, 419, 434, 497
masters, 3, 13–48, 56, 71, 90, 93, 96, 103,
    214, 232, 412, 420, 422, 423, 424,
    425, 426, 427. *See also* servants
Matthews, G.M., 263, 466, 469
Maus, Katherine, 481
McEachern, Clare, 485
McGee, C.E., 427
McGrail, Mary Ann, 439, 441
McGuinness, Frank, *Observe the Sons of
    Ulster*, 167–168, 203, 450, 460
McIntosh, Angus, 430, 431
McKerrow, R.B., 445
McManus, Barbara F., 453
McMullan, Gordon, 313–314, 315, 323,
    485, 486, 491
Mead, Stephen X., 448, 449
Meany, P.D., 427
Melbourne, *Argus*, 240
Melchiori, Giorgio, 444
mercantilism: and nationalism, 299, 309,
    313; and imperialism, 313–338;
    and romance, 338; as instrument
    of providence, 318; versus

planatation, 313, 316

Merch, Herbert S., 483

merchant class, 99, 100, 102, 104, 105, 107, 108, 109, 111, 115, 116, 117, 118, 119, 123, 302, 316, 328, 330, 337, 390

metamorphosis, 110–114, 116, 118, 154, 156, 225, 267, 274, 331, 342, 345, 368, 413

metaphor. *See* translation

Metz, Conrad Martin, 242

Michiel, Marcantonio, 505

Middleton, Sir Henry, 319, 478, 479, 482, 483, 484

Middleton, Thomas:*Chaste Maid in Cheapside*, 130, 423, 457; *Game at Chess, A*, 321; *Women Beware Women*, 207, 462

Middleton, Thomas and Rowley, William, *Changeling, The*, 3, 36–39, 43, 45–46, 71, 173, 427, 450, 452, 479

Miles, Bernard, 243, 465

Miller, Walter, 432

Miola, Robert S., 469

Misfortunes of Arthur, The, 140, 441

Moluccas, 313, 315, 320, 321, 323, 324, 326, 327, 475, 478, 479, 482, 486, 489. *See also* Temaka, Tidore

Mompesson, Sir Giles, 73, 76

Monaghan, 393, 394

Monasteries, Dissolution of, 52

monsters, 415

monstrosity: and Africa, 264; in *Othello*, 209, 212, 254, 260–265, 267–268, 283

Montaigne, Michel de, 178, 402, 403, 410, 416, 438, 453, 507; "Of the Cannibals," 402, 410, 438

Montrose, Louis, 4, 323, 476, 477, 485, 489, 500

Moody, T.W., 501

"Moor," indeterminacy of, 271, 272–274

Moore Smith, G.C., 448

Morality Drama, 94

Morgan, Hiram, 499

Morley, Henry, 468

Moryson, Fynes, 181, 339, 344, 346, 348, 355, 364, 366, 455, 492, 494, 495, 496, 497, 500, 501, 503, 506

Mostar (Bosnia), 399, 400, 416

Mountjoy, Charles Blount, Lord, 367, 371, 372, 393, 394, 396, 499, 503

Muir, Kenneth, 215, 216, 460, 461, 463

Mun, Thomas, 319, 488

Muscovy, 50

Muscovy Company, 486

Nabbes, Thomas, *Unfortunate Mother, The*, 441

Naipaul, V.S., 432

nakedness, troping of, 411–412. *See also* clothes, social meanings of; Irish, as naked people

Nash, Gary B., 437

Nashe, Thomas, 349, 375, 504

Nathan, Norman, 250, 467

nation, ideology of, 4, 135, 194, 271, 275, 278, 281, 283, 296, 299–306, 309, 316, 319, 320, 329, 338, 340–343, 347, 350, 352–354, 356–360, 362, 366, 368, 370–373, 378–380, 404, 473, 479, 483, 484, 487, 491, 492, 496, 499, 502. *See also* Englishness

national identity: discourse of, 379; theatre as instrument of, 375. *See also* Englishness

Nebrija, Antonio de, 353, 355, 358, 498, 499

Nelson, T.G.A., 249–250, 460, 467, 468

Netherlanders. *See* Dutch

Nevo, Ruth, 439

New Criticism, 49

New World, 178, 195, 273, 314–315, 318, 323, 343, 349, 386, 401, 402, 406, 411, 416, 438, 449, 454, 457, 486, 493, 507

Newcastle, Cavendish, William, Marquis of, 22, 48, 421

Newman, Karen, 466, 471, 472, 474, 477

Ngugi wa Thiong'o, 340, 492

Nicholl, Charles, 481

Nichols, John, 503

Nixon, Anthony, 491

Noble, George, 243

North, Sir Edward, 430

North, Sir Thomas, 456, 457

Norton, Thomas, 480, 481

Novak, Maximilian E., 437

Nuremberg, 311

O'Connor, Marion F., 466, 474, 478

Olivier, Sir Laurence, 247, 465, 466

office. See place

O'Neill, Hugh. See Tyrone, Earl of

O'Neill, Shane, 496

Oosterveen, Karla, 439

Ophir, Solomon's voyage to, 318, 330; as type of merchant-voyaging, 317–318

Orange Order, 168

Orgel, Stephen, 441, 450

Orkin, Martin, 247, 465, 466

Orlin, Lena Cowen, 50–51, 58, 72, 429, 430

Orpheus, 100, 112, 113, 346, 503

Ortelius, Abraham, 380, 390, 505

Osborn, James M., 426

Othello: paradoxes of character, 267; placelessness of, 226, 227, 228, 230, 236; self-annihilation of, 259; suicide as repetition of Desdemona's murder, 258; wordplay and jealousy in, 222, 224–225, 228, 248, 252

Otway, Thomas, 97, 210, 262, 435; Venice Preserved, 97, 210, 262, 435

Overton, Richard, 35, 426

Oz, Avram, 474

Pagden, Anthony, 408, 409, 457, 494, 507

Page, William, 188

Paget, William, Lord, 46

pale, 346; Irish, 343, 351, 352

parables: Dives and Lazarus, 96, 125; Prodgial Son, the, 95; Prodigal Son, 17; Unjust Debtor, 100; Unjust Steward, the, 96

Parfitt, George, 449

Parker, Andrew, 493

Parker, Patricia, 5, 323, 451, 472, 485, 489, 507, 508

Parr, Anthony, 491

Parry, L.A., 480, 481

Partridge, Eric, 443, 462, 463, 493

Paster, Gail Kern, 4, 159, 448, 449, 451

patriarchy, and inheritance, 158, 160, 161–163, 164; order and theory, 38, 40, 50, 51, 65, 71,73, 76–79, 85, 87, 89, 91–95, 97, 104, 107, 120, 127, 130, 131, 137, 143, 144, 150, 152–154, 158, 159–161, 163, 234, 251, 266, 376, 423, 431, 433–435 441, 448, 450

Patterson, Annabel, 371, 503

Peck, Linda Levy, 48, 423, 424, 500

Pecora, Vincent P., 477

Pembroke, Herbert, Henry, Earl of, 76

Pentecost, 100, 118

Perkins, William, 102, 436

Peters, Edward, 480

Peters, Helen, 441

petty treason, 38, 50

Philip II, King of Spain, 131, 440

Philologus, 188

Phoenix playhouse, 73, 93

Pilate, Pontius, 183, 197, 456

Pinchbeck, Ian, 439, 440, 445, 446

place (office, rank, status), 3, 16, 21, 22, 27, 32, 34, 35, 41, 51, 52, 54–62, 64, 66, 68, 69, 71, 77, 82, 83, 84, 86, 97, 103, 104, 105, 106, 108–111, 116, 120, 135, 158, 213, 215–217, 220, 223, 225, 226, 230, 251, 280, 281, 287, 300, 354, 423, 428, 430, 461; and "occupation," 228; and displacement, 218, 219, 221, 223, 235; Desdemona as Othello's, 227, 230, 231; domestic, 225; exchange of, 225, 228, 234; Iago as usurper of Desdemona's, 231, 232, 235; Iago as usurper of Othello's, 235; marriage as, 227; Othello as besieged place, 213; physical, 207, 208; sexual, 220, 221, 222, 229, 230

plantation, discourse of, 312–314, 316, 323, 342, 349, 350, 356, 367, 372, 486, 497; methods in Ireland and Virginia, 342

Platter, Thomas, 34, 312, 379, 426, 485, 505, 506

Plautus, 44, 145, 501

players, as servants, 15, 17

Plutarch, 158, 181, 186, 188, 455, 456, 457

Pocahontas, 323, 408

Pomfret, John, 506

Poolaroon. See Pula Run

Pooloway. See Pulo Ai

Poor Law, 101, 130, 439

Portuguese, in East Indies, English attitudes to, 273, 276, 290, 313, 314, 315, 318, 321, 322, 325–326, 329, 334, 484, 487

Powhatan, 408

Pratt, Josiah, 458

primogeniture, 158

Pringle, Roger, 439

pronouns, personal, early modern usage, 6–9, 63–64

property, and propriety, 160, 256

prostitution, as usury of the flesh, 156; Venice as capital of, 210

proviso scenes, 105, 106

Pula Run, 320, 321, 323

Pulo Ai, 320

Pulton, Fernando, 481

Purchas, Samuel, 178, 277, 278, 280, 281, 315–320, 322–324, 330–333, 335, 337, 388, 390, 392, 474, 475, 476, 478, 480, 481, 484, 486, 487, 488, 489, 490, 491

Purchase, Bruce, 463, 475

Puttenham, George, 354, 402, 498, 506, 507

Quinn, D.B., 494, 497

Quintilian, 454

Quiroga, Pedro de, 406, 409, 410, 414, 415, 507

Rabin, Yitzhak, 184

race, 289, 304, 306; and adultery/bastardy, 264; and religion, 331; early modern ideas of, 134, 208, 244–249, 253, 254, 260, 261, 264, 265, 269, 272–274, 277, 279, 282, 283, 304, 309, 331, 341, 342, 443, 465, 466, 471, 474, 475, 478, 484; in Othello, 244–250, 253, 264–268, 269–284. See also color

Rackin, Phyllis, 134, 142, 445, 446, 448

Ragon, Michel, 458

Raleigh, Sir Walter, 324, 332, 360, 363, 386, 493, 504, 506; History of the World, The, 316, 386, 388, 389,

506

Raman, Shankar, 313, 315, 338, 475, 485, 486, 490

Ranald, Margaret Loftus, 441

Randall, Dale J., 452

rank. *See* place

Raphael, 378, 380, 505

Ratsey, Gamaliell, 14–18, 44, 47, 420

Raysor, T.M., 469

Régnier-Bohler, Danielle, 472

religion, as marker of alterity, 275

Rembrandt, 170, 451

Renwick, W.L., 443, 493, 507

Revenger's Tragedy, The, 127, 130,132 134, 137, 138, 140–142, 144, 149, 150–152, 154–165, 264, 441, 444, 445, 447, 449, 451, 463, 470, 479

Rich, Barnabe, 494, 503

Richard III, 133, 383

Richards, Shaun, 466, 472, 493

Richardson, Charles, 103

Ricks, Christopher, 427

Ridler, Anne, 463

Ridley, M.R., 247, 460, 465

Ripa, Cesare, 370, 503

Rizzio, David, 441

Rochester, Wilmot, John, Earl of, 5, 419

Rolfe, John, 323

Romano, Dennis, 40, 422, 425, 427

Romney, Sir Edward, 478

Roodenburg, Herman, 456

Roper, Derek, 436

Roscius (stage-player), 180, 187

Rothmann, Johann, 172, 452

Rouen, Brazilian Indians in, 402

rough music, *see* charivari

Rowe, Nicholas, 238, 457, 468, 508

Rowse, A.L., 438

Rushdie, Salman, 399, 417, 443

Rymer, Thomas, 223, 246, 249, 260, 261, 462, 465, 467, 469

Sahlins, Marshall, 414, 508

Said, Edward, 349, 496

Saint Luke, 119

Saint Paul, 44, 99, 101, 102–103, 116

Saint Peter, 117, 229

Salisbury, Earl of. *See* Cecil, Sir Robert

Sams, Eric, 444

Sanders, Norman, 247, 464, 466

Scaevola, Gaius Mucius, 188, 189, 190, 458

Scarry, Elaine, 295, 481

Schanzer, Ernest, 452

Schochet, Gordon, 77, 78, 431, 432, 435

Schouten, William Cornelison, 273, 318, 474

Scott, Edmund, 4, 278–283, 287–305, 308, 309, 326, 327, 335, 336, 337, 476, 478, 479, 480, 482, 484, 487, 490, 491, 492

Scragg, Leah, 439

Sebeok, Thomas A., 430

Seneca, L.A., 97, 424, 434, 435

servants, 3, 13–48, 63, 64, 78, 79–80, 85, 87, 90, 91, 92, 95, 96, 103, 333, 419, 421, 422, 423, 424, 425, 427, 428, 429, 433; as domestic enemies, 39, 40, 41, 42, 43, 44, 45, 46, 47, 48, 427; service (early modern ideas of), 3, 5, 13–48, 55, 59, 61, 65–67, 69, 74–76, 78–79, 83, 85–89, 95–97, 100, 110, 118, 184, 191, 193, 214, 226, 230, 234, 279, 309, 323, 419, 420, 421, 422, 423, 424, 425, 426, 427, 428, 431, 432, 435; Anabaptist attitudes to, 35, 38; anglican doctrine of, 24; courtly love as, 24, 37

sexuality, and status, 68, 70–71

Seymour, Jane, 22, 421

Shakespeare, William, 1, 5, 6, 9, 13–14, 19, 21, 48, 67, 74, 90, 112, 113, 114,

131, 133, 135, 142, 144, 152, 167,
168, 170, 173–174, 180–188, 190,
195, 197, 198, 207–236, 237–267,
269–271, 280, 282, 286, 312, 314,
328, 332, 339, 349, 355, 357, 360–
362, 370, 372, 373–375, 382, 390,
391, 393, 396, 399, 401–403, 405,
406, 408, 410, 413–417, 419, 420,
423, 424, 428, 435, 437, 439, 440,
441, 444, 445, 446, 447, 448, 450,
451, 452, 454, 456, 457, 458, 459,
460, 461, 462, 463, 464, 465, 466,
467, 468, 469, 473, 474, 475, 476,
478, 485, 491, 492, 496, 497, 499,
500, 503, 504, 506, 507, 508; *All's
Well That Ends Well*, 455; *Antony
and Cleopatra*, 27–28, 71, 172,
207–208, 239, 332, 373–374, 401,
409, 429, 430, 459, 468, 503; *As
You Like It*, 30, 430; *Comedy of
Errors, The*, 180, 407, 500; *Coriolanus*, 181, 186, 401, 422, 443, 479;
Cymbeline, 149, 312; *Hamlet*, 2, 15,
45, 128–129, 150, 161, 165, 173,
181, 207, 239, 288, 311, 371, 373,
437, 439, 441, 453, 454, 456, 481,
482; *1 Henry IV*, 354–355, 361,
373, 404, 496; *2 Henry IV*, 129,
374, 429; *Henry V*, 57, 135, 302,
339–340, 349, 351, 357–359, 361–
362, 370–372, 374–375, 379, 392,
401, 404–406, 413, 440, 489, 496,
497, 499, 503, 504; *1 Henry VI*,
131, 134, 135, 302, 349, 351–352,
403, 416, 442; *2 Henry VI*, 350–
351, 504, 505; *3 Henry VI*, 382,
445, 459; *Julius Caesar*, 153–154,
181–183, 185–188, 455, 456, 458;
King John, 132, 136, 138–139, 142,
144, 146, 152, 184–185, 351, 442,
446, 447, 448, 456, 457, 467; *King

Lear*, 3, 5–9, 21, 23, 24–26, 28, 29,
30, 33, 39, 45–46, 60, 127, 132,
138–139, 140–141, 144, 151, 173,
202–203, 207, 229–230, 411, 413,
416, 421, 423, 441, 445, 446, 459,
470; *Love's Labor's Lost*, 467;
Macbeth, 1, 68, 172, 183, 195, 197–
202, 207, 437, 456, 460; *Merchant
of Venice, The*, 74–75, 79, 84, 89–
90, 96, 123, 167, 208–209, 271–
272, 312, 328, 416, 431, 450, 456,
459, 471, 474; *Midsummer Night's
Dream, A*, 260, 407–410, 429, 455,
507; *Much Ado About Nothing*, 131,
139, 142, 174; *Othello*, 26, 27, 28,
31–32, 37, 39, 40, 43–45, 46, 134,
185, 207–236, 237–268, 269–284,
312, 416, 428, 431, 438, 444, 449,
451, 460, 461, 462, 463, 464, 465,
466, 467, 468, 469, 470, 471, 472,
473, 474, 475, 476, 477, 478; *Rape
of Lucrece, The* 133, 138, 451, 458;
Richard II, 2, 183, 195–198, 349,
351–353, 364, 379, 403–404, 456,
467; *Richard III*, 90, 138, 195, 222,
379, 456; *Romeo and Juliet*, 28,
170, 207, 261, 263, 420, 452;
Sonnets, 174, 231; *Taming of the
Shrew, The*, 19, 29, 313, 420, 422,
423, 426, 427; *Tempest, The*, 21,
23, 24, 25, 47, 71, 112–114, 135–
136, 139, 142, 160, 180, 209, 280,
287, 312–313, 314, 370, 378, 390–
393, 396, 402, 410–416, 420, 437,
441, 443, 445, 446, 450, 455, 459,
485, 497, 503, 506, 508; *Timon of
Athens*, 271, 424, 473; *Titus
Andronicus*, 168, 186, 188, 190–
192, 272, 352, 450, 457, 459;
Troilus and Cressida, 67, 129,
136–137, 139, 144–147, 152, 154,

370, 374, 447, 448; *Twelfth Night*, 24, 41–42, 63, 407, 452, 467; *Two Gentleman of Verona, The*, 271; *Winter's Tale, The* 112–114, 125, 134, 208, 223, 461, 462, 470
Shapiro, James S., 473, 474
Sharp, Andrew, 426, 434
Sharpe, Edward, 488
Shaw, Dr Ralph, 133, 442
Sherbo, Arthur, 500
Sherley, Robert, 491
Shirley, James, 349; *St. Patrick for Ireland*, 349
Shorthose, Henry, 16
Siddons, Sarah, 238
Sidney, family, 355
Sidney, Sir Henry, 501
Sidney, Sir Philip, 55, 429, 447
Siemon, James R., 463, 465, 468, 469
Sighelm, Bishop, 318
Sinden, Donald, 465
Sinfield, Alan, 497, 503, 506
Skelton, R.A., 505
Slavin, Arthur J., 437
Slights, Camille Wells, 46, 428
Smith, Bruce R., 452
Smith, Captain John, 408, 425, 438, 495
Smith, Henry, 102, 436
Smith, John Hazel, 424
Smith, Richard M., 439
Smith, Sir Thomas, 493
Smith, Warren D., 499
Snell, George, 16, 17
Snow, Edward, 246, 248, 256, 460, 462, 465, 467, 468
Snyder, Susan, 260, 449, 451, 468, 469
social mobility, 3, 42, 52, 57, 67
Sodhkanskaya, N.S., 245, 465
Solomon, Robert C., 461
Spain and the Spanish, English attitudes to, 50, 54, 135, 195, 213, 273, 299,

304, 318, 326, 332, 353, 410, 458, 474, 481
Speed, John, 378, 379, 380, 381–386, 396, 505, 506
Spenser, Edmund, 135, 270, 342–348, 353, 355, 356, 359, 364, 365, 366, 376, 378, 403, 404, 405, 443, 473, 493, 494, 495, 497, 498, 499, 501, 502, 504, 506, 507; *Faerie Queene, The*, 348–349, 355, 366, 376–380, 495, 501, 502, 504, 507; *View of the Present State of Ireland, A*, 135, 342–348, 356, 365–366, 403, 405, 443, 493, 502, 507
Spice Islands, 2, 318, 319, 321, 324, 335
Spurway, Thomas, 487, 490
Stallybrass, Peter, 4, 342, 343, 449, 451, 468, 469, 493, 499, 501
Stannard, David, 493
Starkey, David, 420, 421
status. *See* place
Stavropoulos, Janet, 469
Steane, J.B., 452, 504
Steiner, George, 400
Steinfeld, Robert J., 421, 425
Stock, Mildred, 465
Stockwood, Rev. John, 433
Stone, Laurence, 9, 419, 472
Stonehenge, 378, 382
Stow, John, *Survey of London*, 378, 504
Strachey, James, 450, 461
Strier, Richard, 423
Strong, Sir Roy, 370, 371, 483, 502
Stubbes, Philip, 56, 430
Stubbs, John, 188–190, 194, 458
Sullivan, Garrett A., 51, 52, 429
Sumatra, 318, 490
sumptuary laws, 55
surveying. *See* mapping
Sutton, S., 502
Suzuki, Mihoko, 497

Swaab, Peter, 473
Sweet, James H., 474
Swinburne, A.C., 145, 152, 447

Talbot, William, 502
Talon, Omer, 454
Taylor, Gary, 497, 499
temperance, as imperial virtue, 332–334, 336
Terence, 44
Ternata, 313, 320, 322, 325, 329, 330, 334, 336, 337, 475, 482, 483
Theatre, The (playhouse), 311
Thomas, Keith, 364
Thomson, Patricia, 76, 431
Tidore, Temaka, 273, 313, 320, 322, 324, 325, 326, 328, 329, 330, 334, 337, 482
Tillyard, E.M.W., 4
titles. See honorifics
Todorov, Tzvetan, 454
Tonson, Jacob, 239
torch, symbolism of, 251
torture, English attitudes to, 294–295, 297, 298, 299, 306
Tourneur, Cyril, The Atheist's Tragedy, 95
Towerson, Gabriel, 281, 291, 305, 306, 324, 489, 491
translation, 399–417; and imperialism, 403–406, 414; and metamorphosis, 407; and metaphor, 400; as betrayal, 416; as theft, 417; cultural, 399, 400, 402, 406, 408, 411, 417; historical, 416; imaginative, 406–409, 411, 414, 416, 417; linguistic, 357, 359, 361, 368, 399, 400, 401, 402, 404, 405, 409, 411, 414; physical, 356, 361, 368, 399, 401, 405, 407, 410; theatrical, 413, 415, 416; vestimentary, 412–413
treason, as secret crime, 295–296

Tregear's Black Jokes, 245, 246
Trilling, Lionel, 428
Troublesome Raigne of King John, The, 136, 142
Tudde, Thomas, 291
Tudor, Owen, 440
Tullaghogue, 394–396, 503
Tupinamba (Brazilian Indians) , 402, 410
Tyrell, Edmund, 458
Tyrone, Hugh O'Neill, Earl of, 16, 355, 367, 371–372, 393–396, 496, 498

Ulster, 167–168, 356, 393, 395–396, 450, 494, 503, 506
Underdown, David, 467

vagrancy. See masterless men
Van Linschoten, John Huighen, 275, 277, 475, 483
Vasari, Giorgio, 504
Vaughan, Alden T., 475, 508
Vaughan, Henry (Chief Justice), 508
Vaughan, Rice, 153, 448
Vaughan, Virginia Mason, 269, 283, 472, 508
Veeser, H. Aram, 477
Venice, as city of prostitution, 266; in Othello, 208–211
Vereenigde Oostindische Compagnie. See East India Company, Dutch
Vermeer, Jan, 380
Vesalius, Andreas, 170, 171, 384
vestimentary system, 16, 169, 364
Vickers, Brian, 465, 467, 469
Vickers, Nancy, 451
Viper and Her Brood, The. See Revenger's Tragedy, The
Virgil, 352
Virginia, 43, 100, 101, 106, 115–117, 314, 323, 342, 411, 425, 438, 458, 459, 475, 478, 486, 495

Virginia Company, 314
Vitkus, Daniel J., 474
voyaging, 178, 277–278, 295, 313–316, 319, 329, 390, 408, 486

Waingrow, Marshall, 24, 423
Walker, Alice, 498, 506
Walker, Julia M., 458
Walker, Keith, 419
Wallace, John M., 424
Walzer, Michael, 79, 432, 433, 434
Webb, Henry J., 461
Webster, John, 32, 33, 72, 440, 456; *Duchess of Malfi, The* 32–33, 172, 452, 456; *White Devil, The,* 33, 103
wedding sheets, as shrouds, 257–258
Weever, John, 383–386, 387, 388, 505
Weil, Judith, 420
Wells, Stanley, 439
Welsh: barbarity, 354; language, 355
Wentworth, William, 39, 427
Whallon, William, 467
Whately, William, 436
Whigham, Frank, 41, 52, 53, 61, 72, 423, 429, 430, 431, 449
White, Hayden, 437

White, Martin, 53, 429, 430
Whythorne, Thomas, 34–36, 44–45, 426, 428
Willcock, Gladys Doidge, 498, 506
Willems, Michele, 491
Williams, P., 480
Wilson, Arthur, 305, 484
Wine, M.L., 430
Wither, George, 434
Wolfe, John, 483
Womack, Peter, 401, 485, 507
women: and property, 158–159; as leaky vessels, 164; as property, 209
Wood, H.Harvey, 424
Wren, Bishop, 435
wunderkammern, 410
Wycherley, William *Country Wife, The,* 224, 469

Yachnin, Paul, 1, 2, 419
Yates, Frances A., 502
Young, Bruce, 445
Youngblood, Sara, 431
Yugoslavia, 309

Zimansky, Curt A., 462
Zouche, Richard, *Sophister, The,* 1, 444